The Respectable Career of Fritz K.

Studies in German History
Published in Association with the German Historical Institute, Washington, D.C.

General Editors:
Hartmut Berghoff, Director of the German Historical Institute, Washington, D.C.
Uwe Spiekermann, Deputy Director of the German Historical Institute, Washington, D.C.

Volume 1
Nature in German History
Edited by Christof Mauch

Volume 2
Coping with the Nazi Past: West German Debates on Nazism and Generational Conflict, 1955–1975
Edited by Philipp Gassert and Alan E. Steinweis

Volume 3
Adolf Cluss, Architect: From Germany to America
Edited by Alan Lessoff and Christof Mauch

Volume 4
Two Lives in Uncertain Times: Facing the Challenges of the 20th Century as Scholars and Citizens
Wilma Iggers and Georg Iggers

Volume 5
Driving Germany: The Landscape of the German Autobahn, 1930–1970
Thomas Zeller

Volume 6
The Pleasure of a Surplus Income: Part-Time Work, Gender Politics, and Social Change in West Germany, 1955–1969
Christine von Oertzen

Volume 7
Between Mass Death and Individual Loss: The Place of the Dead in Twentieth-Century Germany
Edited by Alon Confino, Paul Betts and Dirk Schumann

Volume 8
Nature of the Miracle Years: Conservation in West Germany, 1945–1975
Sandra Chaney

Volume 9
Biography between Structure and Agency: Central European Lives in International Historiography
Edited by Volker R. Berghahn and Simone Lässig

Volume 10
Political Violence in the Weimar Republic, 1918–1933: Battle for the Streets and Fears of Civil War
Dirk Schumann

Volume 11
The East German State and the Catholic Church, 1945–1989
Bernd Schaefer

Volume 12
Raising Citizens in the "Century of the Child": The United States and German Central Europe in Comparative Perspective
Edited by Dirk Schumann

Volume 13
The Plans that Failed: An Economic History of the GDR
André Steiner

Volume 14
Max Liebermann and International Modernism: An Artist's Career from Empire to Third Reich
Edited by Marion Deshmukh, Françoise Forster-Hahn and Barbara Gaehtgens

Volume 15
Germany and the Black Diaspora: Points of Contact, 1250–1914
Edited by Mischa Honeck, Martin Klimke, and Anne Kuhlmann

Volume 16
Crime and Criminal Justice in Modern Germany
Edited by Richard F. Wetzell

Volume 17
Encounters with Modernity: The Catholic Church in West Germany, 1945–1975
Benjamin Ziemann

Volume 18
The Respectable Career of Fritz K.: The Making and Remaking of a Provincial Nazi Leader
Hartmut Berghoff and Cornelia Rauh
Translated by Casey Butterfield

THE RESPECTABLE CAREER OF FRITZ K.

The Making and Remaking of a Provincial Nazi Leader

Hartmut Berghoff and Cornelia Rauh

Translated by Casey Butterfield

First published by
Berghahn Books
www.berghahnbooks.com

English-language edition
©2015, 2020 Berghahn Books
First paperback edition published in 2020

German-language edition
©2000 Deutsche Verlags-Anstalt
Fritz K.: Ein deutsches Leben im zwanzigsten Jahrhundert

All rights reserved. Except for the quotation of short passages for the purposes of criticism and review, no part of this book may be reproduced in any form or by any means, electronic or mechanical, including photocopying, recording, or any information storage and retrieval system now known or to be invented, without written permission of the publisher.

Library of Congress Cataloging-in-Publication Data
Berghoff, Hartmut.
 [Fritz K. English]
 The respectable career of Fritz K.: the making and remaking of a provincial Nazi leader / Hartmut Berghoff and Cornelia Rauh; translated by Casey Butterfield. -- First edition.
  pages cm. -- (Studies in German history; 18)
 Includes bibliographical references and index.
 ISBN 978-1-78238-593-6 (hardback: alk. paper) -- ISBN 978-1-78238-594-3 (ebook)
 1. Kiehn, Fritz, 1885-1980. 2. Nazis--Germany--Trossingen--Biography. 3. Trossingen (Germany)--Biography. 4. Industrialists--Germany--Trossingen--Biography. 5. National socialism--Germany--Württemberg. 6. Denazification. I. Rauh, Cornelia, 1957- II. Butterfield, Casey, translator. III. Title.
 DD247.K525B4713 2015
 324.243'0238092--dc23
 [B]
                                                                                                2015006167

British Library Cataloguing in Publication Data
A catalogue record for this book is available from the British Library

ISBN: 978-1-78238-593-6 hardback
ISBN: 978-1-78920-846-7 paperback
ISBN: 978-1-78238-594-3 ebook

Contents

List of Figures and Tables	vii
Preface	ix
List of Abbreviations	xii
Introduction	1
1. Kiehn's Rise to the Middle Class: A Traveling Salesman Becomes a Factory Owner	11
2. Rapid Ascent through the Nazi Ranks: From Local Party Leader to Reichstag Delegate	28
3. Between *Gleichschaltung* and the Party Purge of 1934: Fritz Kiehn Becomes "Leader of the Württemberg Economy"	45
4. Riding Nazi Party Coattails: Kiehn's Industrial Ambitions	73
5. Between Corruption and Camaraderie: The National Socialist Campaign to Curb Abuses	87
6. Kiehn and Gustav Schickedanz in the Race for Aryanization	102
7. Wartime Deals and "Marriage Politics"	131
8. "The King of Trossingen": Fritz Kiehn as a Local Grandee in the Third Reich	144
9. From "War Criminal No. 1" to Sought-After Employer	187
10. "Scot-Free, by the Skin of Their Teeth": Denazification and Compensation	202

11. "Ripe for Satire": Entering the Social Market Economy with Public Loans — 228

12. "Kiehn Left No One Behind"? The "Factory Community" as a Network of "Old Comrades" — 257

13. Honored Citizen Again: Kiehn and the "Economic Miracle" — 273

14. The Twilight Years of an Honored West German — 289

15. Coming to Terms with the Past in the Twenty-First Century — 312

Conclusion: The (A)Typical Life of an Industrialist? — 323

Bibliography — 339

Index — 357

Figures and Tables

Fig. 1: Fritz Kiehn in 1900 — 12
Fig. 2: Gasthof Rose, the Neipp family's inn — 12
Fig. 3: A good match (1911) — 13
Fig. 4: Notice of Kiehn's takeover (1912) and Kiehn's first business on Rosenstraße (1912) — 14
Fig. 5: Kiehn (seated) as a war volunteer — 15
Fig. 6: Efka label — 16
Fig. 7: At a distance to old Trossingen: Kiehn's villa in Deibhalde — 16
Fig. 8: Rehearsing upper-class prestige: the study in Deibhalde — 17
Fig. 9: A family on the way up: Fritz, Herbert, Gretl, and Berta Kiehn — 21
Fig. 10: A closed society: the Trossingen "ladies' circle" (*Damenkränzchen*) before Berta Kiehn's inclusion, circa 1929 — 22
Fig. 11: Efka factory with swastika banner (ca. 1931–1932) — 33
Fig. 12: Friends in more than politics: Fritz Kiehn and Gregor Straßer in Deibhalde — 39
Fig. 13: President Fritz Kiehn, MdR (Reichstag delegate), 1937 — 46
Fig. 14: Self-dramatization: Kiehn's New Year's card from 1938–1939 — 51
Fig. 15: "Happy hunter" Prützmann (second from left) and Kiehn — 65
Fig. 16: Kiehn in his SS uniform with honorary dagger — 66
Fig. 17: Small-scale production facilities at the Efka factory (1930s) — 74
Fig. 18: Automotive exhibition in 1936: Kiehn, next to his son (from left), stands with the Führer — 77
Fig. 19: Pride of title and ownership in Kiehn's letterhead — 139
Fig. 20: Souvenirs of the "wartime acquisitions" in the family album from the 1970s. Okriftel is on the bottom — 140
Fig. 21: The Hohner accordion orchestra with *Reichsstatthalter* Wilhelm Murr (1933) — 145
Fig. 22: "May Queen" Gretl Kiehn on National Workers' Day — 147
Fig. 23: Silver wedding anniversary (1936): the private element — 149
Fig. 24: Silver wedding anniversary (1936): the National Socialist element—portrait of a trio — 149
Fig. 25: The trappings of self-aggrandizement (1936) — 150
Fig. 26: Kiehn and Hitler — 152
Fig. 27: Trossingen in a sea of swastikas — 161

Fig. 28: Kiehn's Mercedes, with SS pennant — 164
Fig. 29: Invitation to Efka factory anniversary, bearing the new company coat of arms, 1937 — 166
Fig. 30: Efka factory with political propaganda — 168
Fig. 31: No industrialist mansion: the Ermingen homestead — 197
Fig. 32: Kiehn, "not fully his old self," with his wife and daughter after his release from internment — 205
Fig. 33: The Chiron factory celebrates: "The President's 65th Birthday" (1950) — 240
Fig. 34: Trippel and the Kiehns at a social evening at Chiron (ca. 1950) — 241
Fig. 35: Portrait with the new star of the family, from the left: Fritz and Gretl Wieshofer, as well as Herbert E., Berta, and Fritz Kiehn — 263
Fig. 36: Baldur von Schirach wishes Gretl Wieshofer-Kiehn a happy fiftieth birthday (1968) — 265
Fig. 37: The park behind the new house in Deibhalde — 275
Fig. 38: Mayor Maschke congratulates the old and new honorary citizen of Trossingen on his seventieth birthday — 277
Fig. 39: New Efka building (1958) — 283
Fig. 40: A symbolic handshake: Ernst Hohner and Fritz Kiehn (1957) — 285
Fig. 41: Academic honors at the University of Innsbruck in the 1960s — 293
Fig. 42: Bruno Heck arranges a meeting between the Kiehns and Chancellor Adenauer — 298
Fig. 43: The Kiehns and the Walters in Deibhalde — 301
Fig. 44: Kiehn, the big-game hunter, in Africa — 303

Table 1: Reichstag election results in Trossingen and in Germany, 1930–1933 (in percentages) — 35
Table 2: Kiehn's donations to Nazi organizations, 1935–1944 (in RM) — 60
Table 3: Kiehn's donations to SS offices, 1935–1944 — 61
Table 4: Efka's profits and sales, 1928–1948 — 132
Table 5: Staff and sales at Efka, 1957–1973 — 269

Preface

Some research projects begin with great expectations but fail to reach their set targets because of adversity or a lack of material. We encountered the opposite case when writing this biography. For a good decade and a half—while we were both in Tübingen, Germany, albeit in very different professional contexts—we continued to come across the character of Fritz Kiehn, a middle-class business owner and Nazi functionary, in our research. We first planned to write an article dealing with the political biography of this colorful personality, who through years of radical political change always managed to succeed in his social and professional life. The project grew into a book, practically on its own, and was published in German in 2000. We were constantly coming across new sources and informants, such that a multifaceted picture developed of the day-to-day political and social life of this remarkable person and his small-town world, with a depth of field that is rarely possible.

The sources did not dry up after the book's publication. The Internet continued to provide us with new information about the political networks that Kiehn belonged to during the upheavals of 1933 and 1945 and the attempts to remember the injustice and its victims, for which Kiehn had been partly responsible. Recent studies and newly accessible archival materials made it possible to shed more light on the darkest chapter of Kiehn's professional life—the plundering of Jewish-owned businesses—and to put it into context. The debates that our book stimulated in Kiehn's hometown, on its Nazi past and Kiehn's prominent fellow citizens, ended up giving us material for a new chapter (chapter 15) in this revised second edition.

Our study covers more than just Fritz Kiehn's path through life. It examines nearly a century of German history that stretches from the German Empire to the present. Kiehn's biography reflects not only everyday life in the Nazi regime and in the postwar era up to the 1960s, but also the prologue to Nazi rule and the often-difficult attempt to come to terms with this history that continues into the present. The subtitle of the German edition, *A German Life in the Twentieth Century*, points to the fact that as eventful and unique as Kiehn's biography was, his life had many representative features. Key problems of German twentieth-century history figured in his life and in later work on him. This remains true for the response to this book in the place that was once Kiehn's home, where we saw how difficult it still is to come to terms with the Nazi past.

This English edition of our book would have been very difficult to accomplish without the communication possibilities of the Internet, since during the revision phase each author was on a different continent, with one at the German Historical Institute in Washington DC and the other at the Leibniz Universität Hannover. Just as with the German edition, this book could only be realized through the support of numerous friends and colleagues. We are grateful once again to Trossingen archivist and museum director Martin Häffner. The staff of numerous other archives also deserve our thanks. For especially involved inquiries we thank the archivists in Ludwigsburg, Nuremberg, and Sigmaringen, and we are also grateful to the staff of the Department Central State Archives of Stuttgart, the Landesarchiv Berlin, the Federal Archives in Berlin, Potsdam, and Koblenz, the Wirtschaftsarchiv Baden-Württemberg, and the Archives de l'Occupation française en Allemagne et en Autriche in Colmar.

Philipp Heldmann reviewed the appointment calendar of Heinrich Himmler for us at the State Archives in Berlin; Nils Fehlhaber carried out research at the Staatsarchiv Ludwigsburg and the Landesarchiv Berlin. We thank Peter Zinke for his assistance in searching for files at the Bavarian State Archives in Nuremberg. Heather Hester and Vivianne Lüer worked on the notes and the bibliography, and the former also graciously compiled the index.

We became acquainted with Herbert E. Kiehn through our research. Klaus von Schirach and Toni Pierenkemper helped us to establish this valuable contact, a grandson of Fritz Kiehn's born in 1937. He passed on important sources to us and was repeatedly willing to participate in multiday interviews and provide detailed written information. In this way, he allowed us to relive his memories of his own grandfather and adoptive father, Fritz Kiehn, and his family, as well as the history of the Efka factory in Trossingen that he himself experienced. Herbert E. Kiehn confronted his own family history with precise recall, intellectual distance, and exceptional candidness. His unreserved willingness to provide information was of great help to us. We very much regret that our book set off turbulence in his family, and we were sorry to hear the news of his death in 2007. We as the authors take sole responsibility for all interpretations and possible errors in the book today, just as we did when the German edition was published.

Finally, we are grateful to Marion Berghahn for accepting our book as part of Berghahn Books' publishing program, and to the German Historical Institute for accepting the book for the GHI Studies in German History series and for financing the translation of our manuscript. Uwe Spiekermann and David Lazar were involved during various stages in the new publication, but the principal in-house work was completed by Patricia C. Sutcliffe. She shepherded the manuscript throughout the translation process and expertly reviewed, copy-edited, and proofread every line. The volume would certainly not have been possible without her outstanding efforts. Casey Butterfield took on the difficult task of translating the manuscript into English and of creating an eminently readable English-language manuscript despite a multitude of specialized terms and sometimes old-fashioned quotes from sources. Caitlin Mahon copy-edited the text with great care and diligence. We are enormously grateful for all the help we have received.

Hartmut Berghoff and Cornelia Rauh
Washington DC/Hanover, December 2014

Abbreviations

ADGB	Allgemeiner Deutscher Gewerkschaftsbund (umbrella association of German unions)
ASD	Archiv der sozialen Demokratie der Friedrich-Ebert-Stiftung, Bonn / Archive of Social Democracy
AVT	*Allgemeine Volkszeitung Trossingen*
BA	Bundesarchiv / German Federal Archives
BdM	Bund Deutscher Mädel / League of German Girls
BHE	Bund der Heimatlosen und Entrechteten / Alliance of the Expellees and Rights-Deprived
Bü	Büschel (badge)
C	Caisse / box
CDU	Christliche Demokratische Union / Christian Democratic Union
d	Dossier
DAF	Deutsche Arbeitsfront / German Labor Front
DC	Document Center
DDP	Deutsche Demokratische Partei / German Democratic Party
DGB	Deutscher Gewerkschaftsbund / Confederation of German Trade Unions
DHHV	Deutscher Handharmonika Verband / German Accordion Association
DINTA	Deutsches Institut für technische Arbeitsschulung / German Institute for Technical Labor Training
DM	Deutschmark(s)
DNVP	Deutschnationale Volkspartei / German National People's Party
DRA	*Deutscher Reichsanzeiger und Preußischer Staatsanzeiger*
DVP	Demokratische Volkspartei / Democratic People's Party

FAZ	*Frankfurter Allgemeine Zeitung*
FDP	Freie Demokratische Partei / Free Democratic Party
FWV	Freie Wählervereinigung / Free Voters' Association
GEG	Großeinkaufs-Gesellschaft Deutscher Consumvereine / Wholesale Purchasing Company of German Consumer Cooperatives
GLT	Gauamtsleiter für Technik / NSDAP district leader for technology
GRP	Gemeinderatsprotokoll / town council minutes
GWB	Gauwirtschaftsberater / NSDAP Gau district economic adviser
HHStA	Hessisches Hauptstaatsarchiv Wiesbaden / Hesse Main State Archives
HMT	Harmonikamuseum Trossingen / Trossingen Harmonica Museum
HStAS	Hauptstaatsarchiv Stuttgart / Central State Archives of Stuttgart
IfZ	Institut für Zeitgeschichte, Munich / Institute of Contemporary History
IHK	Industrie- und Handelskammer / Chamber of Industry and Commerce
KAT	Kreisarchiv Tuttlingen / District Archives for Tuttlingen
KdF	Kraft durch Freude / Strength through Joy (Nazi organization)
KHD	Klöckner-Humboldt-Deutz AG
KPD	Kommunistische Partei Deutschlands / Communist Party of Germany
KRUA	Kreisuntersuchungsausschuß / district review committee
KWB	Kreiswirtschaftsberater / district economic adviser of the NSDAP
LAB	Landesarchiv Berlin / Berlin State Archives
LKAS	Landeskirchliches Archiv Stuttgart / Archive of the regional Protestant Church, Stuttgart
MAE Colmar	Ministère des Affaires Étrangères, Archives de l'Occupation française en Allemagne et en Autriche, Colmar / French Foreign Office, Archives of the French Occupation in Germany and Austria

MdL	Mitglied des Landtags / Member of State Parliament.
MdR	Mitglied des Reichstags / Reichstag member
NL	Nachlass / estate
NS	National Socialism (Nazism) / National Socialist
NSDAP	Nationalsozialistische Deutsche Arbeiterpartei / National Socialist German Workers' Party (Nazi Party)
NSF	Nationalsozialistische Frauenschaft / National Socialist Women's League
NSV	Nationalsozialistische Volkswohlfahrt / National Socialist People's Welfare Organization
OPG	Oberstes Parteigericht der NSDAP / Party Supreme Court of the NSDAP
PCO	Property Control Office
PUA	Parlamentarischer Untersuchungsausschuß / parliamentary review committee
RAD	Reichsarbeitsdienst / Reich Labor Service
RF-SS	Reichsführer-SS (Heinrich Himmler, 1929–1945)
RGBl	*Reichsgesetzblatt*
RKF	Reichskommissar für die Festigung des deutschen Volkstums / Reich Commissioner for the Consolidation of the Ethnic German Nation
RLM	Reichsluftfahrtministerium / Reich Aviation Ministry
RM	Reichsmark(s)
RMK	Reichsmusikkammer / Reich Chamber of Music
RSHA	Reichssicherheitshauptamt / Reich Security Main Office
RStDI	Reichsstand der Deutschen Industrie / Reich Estate of German Industry
RuSHA	Rasse- und Siedlungshauptamt / Race and Settlement Main Office
RWM	Reichswirtschaftsministerium / Reich Economics Ministry
RWWA	Rheinisch Westfälisches Wirtschaftsarchiv zu Köln / Regional Economic Archives for Rhineland and Westphalia, Cologne
SA	Sturmabteilung / Storm Division
SAJ	Sozialistische Arbeiterjugend / Socialist Workers Youth

SD	Sicherheitsdienst / Secret Service of the SS
SHAEF	Supreme Headquarters, Allied Expeditionary Force
SK	Staatskommissar für die politische Säuberung / State Commissioner for Political Cleansing
SPD	Sozialdemokratische Partei Deutschlands / German Social Democratic Party
SS	Schutzstaffel / Protection Squadron
StAL	Staatsarchiv Ludwigsburg / State Archives in Ludwigsburg
StAN	Staatsarchiv Nürnberg / State Archives in Nuremberg
StAS	Staatsarchiv Sigmaringen / State Archives in Sigmaringen
StAT	Stadtarchiv Trossingen / Municipal Archives in Trossingen
TZ	*Trossinger Zeitung*
Uschla	Untersuchungs- und Schlichtungsausschuß / NSDAP Committee for Investigation and Settlement
UWZ	Umwandererzentrale / Central Office for Resettlement
WABW	Wirtschaftarchiv Baden-Württemberg / Regional Economic Archives for Baden-Württemberg, Stuttgart-Hohenheim
WHW	Winterhilfswerk / Winter Relief Agency
WVT	Württembergische Verwaltungs- und Treuhandgesellschaft / Württemberg Administrative and Audit Corporation

Introduction

When the Allied troops occupied Germany in 1945, Nazi symbols were abolished throughout the former Third Reich. The almost ubiquitous Hitler Streets (Hitler-Straßen) were given new names. Wherever the symbolic break with the Third Reich did not take hold in the local population, the occupation forces were there to step in.[1] In the small, French-occupied manufacturing town of Trossingen, Württemberg (located between the Black Forest and the Swabian Alps), the street names were changed on 1 May 1945. But here, along with Adolf Hitler Street, Fritz Kiehn Street had to go as well. The former Karl Street had been given its new name in October 1933 to commemorate the great service that Fritz Kiehn, the owner of the Efka factory, had rendered to the NSDAP, or German Nazi Party, during the *Kampfzeit,* or time of struggle, i.e. before 1933. After the Nazis had seized power in January 1933, Kiehn became "one of the most active members" of the National Socialist German Workers' Party (NSDAP), who to contemporaries such as the postwar Minister-President of Baden-Württemburg Gebhard Müller was "potentially deeply convinced" of Nazi ideology.[2] Through money, relationships, and no small amount of his time, Kiehn had supported National Socialism in the region prior to 1933 and had received positions and symbolic capital from the regime in return. He was celebrated as a "leader of the Württemberg economy," and his fellow citizens saw Kiehn as the "king of Trossingen" who was happy to hold court. Anyone would do well to be in his good graces. In 1935, the city of Trossingen made Kiehn an honored citizen (*Ehrenbürger*), a distinction that he shared with the Führer as well as his Gauleiter Wilhelm Murr, who was Württemberg's highest party leader.

This distinction too became obsolete in 1945, long before Kiehn, who had enriched himself at the expense of various Jewish businesses, became the last prisoner of the French occupation zone of Württemberg to be freed from detention and declared a "Lesser Offender" (*Minderbelasteter*) by the denazification court (*Spruchkammer*). Although his denazification proceedings and other court proceedings had laid bare Kiehn's deep involvement in Nazi injustices,

---

Notes from this chapter begin on page 8.

he rehabilitated himself in stealthy fashion. The further that the shock of losing the war and the collapse of the Nazi regime lay behind them, the more clearly the manufacturer mutated for many of his fellow citizens into a rescuer of the regional economy, one who had faced ostensibly wrongful political persecution and who deserved their loyal support against the criticism from outside the local milieu. His visible position during the Third Reich meant as little to Fritz Kiehn as it did to most of the Nazi offenders. Those who came from the middle class in particular emerged largely unscathed, retained their social capital, and in most cases were able to continue their professional trajectories. Kiehn's career in business was far from over in 1949, when he resumed management of his company at sixty-three, especially since the industrialist continued to prove himself a generous employer and sponsor. By 1955, the Trossingen local council had informally allowed Kiehn's honorary citizenship to be revived, and in 1957 they named a large sports hall after him. In 1960, a street was named after Kiehn once again, when a centrally located square in the city was dedicated to him in honor of his seventy-fifth birthday. In the 1960s and 1970s, he could thus take pleasure and satisfaction in looking back on his life's work. Even if Trossingen was known for manufacturing musical instruments and the social fabric of the city was completely dominated by the long-established Hohner manufacturing family,[3] Kiehn too had been given honorary titles and distinctions as a patron of sports, music, and science. His birthdays began to be marked by public ceremony again, with visits from federal and regional political representatives. The speakers on such occasions would acknowledge Kiehn as one of the "most outstanding industrialists in the land." He was celebrated as a man with a "golden heart" who never failed to "let the people around him take part in his ascent as well."[4]

The speakers would gloss over the fact that Kiehn's ascent to his place of honor in the Federal Republic had not been the smoothest. But the Efka factory owner himself made no secret of this, as a Festschrift Kiehn commissioned in 1958 gravely puts it: "Once, in 1945, he seemed to face complete ruin." Yet this look back, which fashions the political upheaval of 1945 into a fateful natural phenomenon, leads contentedly into the declaration that, "when after the war the inevitable loomed ... Fritz Kiehn, despite all resistance, found his way back to the pinnacle he deserved. He strode through the muddle, upright and unbroken."[5]

Kiehn had come from very modest beginnings, growing up in a Protestant civil servant's household where there was not enough money for the numerous children to go on to higher education. His business career — shaped in equal measure by his social ambitions, appetite for risk, luck, and hard work — began when he married up into a well-to-do Trossingen family. He arrived in 1908 as an "elegant nobody,"[6] a simple traveling salesman in fine patent-leather shoes who carried a small trunk and had to tramp through the rainy, manure-covered streets of the village to find the local inn where he was staying. Fifteen years later, to general astonishment, he was moving his young family into one of the largest villas in the area and acquiring expensive hobbies.

It was obvious to everyone that Kiehn's lavish lifestyle fed his symbolic conflict with the more established small-town industrialists. But these notables, who had grown up in the Pietist tradition, had already disqualified the social climber for his pretentious manner. The brusque rejection Kiehn experienced at the hands of the leading society figures was another factor in his receptiveness to the early 1930s trend toward radicalization, despite his economic successes.

Kiehn quickly rose to the helm of the local Trossingen NSDAP group, and soon thereafter to Tuttlingen district leader, even becoming part of the Nazi faction in the Reichstag in 1932 and thus compensating for the social recognition he had missed out on before. The high point of Kiehn's career was doubtless during the "Thousand-Year Reich" of the Nazis, during which he not only attained influential positions in the region but also acquired important-sounding titles such as Wehrwirtschaftsführer (military industrial leader) and access to Himmler's personal staff as well as to the Freundeskreis Reichsführer-SS (Circle of Friends of the Reichsführer-SS). There he enjoyed the company of high-ranking SS (Schutzstaffel) functionaries and some of the most important industrialists and bankers in the Third Reich. As a card-carrying Nazi industrialist and unscrupulous Aryanizer who was willing to take risks, the Kiehn of the Third Reich appeared to have managed the transition to the big leagues.

His politically grounded position as "province leader" and regional economic functionary gave the middle-class executive wholly new opportunities for pointed self-expression after 1933,[7] when the Führer cult around Adolf Hitler and the invocation of the "national community" (*Volksgemeinschaft*) fit right into the staging of patriarchal "industrial leader" Kiehn, his "model Nazi family," and the "factory community" (*Betriebsgemeinschaft*). The propaganda methods typical of the regime, the constant emphasis on social harmony that accompanied these in the local context, and the "beautiful façade of the Third Reich"[8] manifested in the seas of banners and marching columns became the ideal means for Kiehn's social self-affirmation.[9] The new political culture accommodated both his personal leanings and the prevailing style of small-town society. The provincial town flourished as a *Volksgemeinschaft* at the same time that it basked in the glory of its ostensibly distinguished *Wirtschaftsführer* (economic leader).

A characteristic feature of Fritz Kiehn's life was the constant intertwining of local and "high" politics, of personal business interests and economic principles of the regime, of family matters and social calculations. This multifacetedness is just one of the reasons it is worthwhile to examine his biography. Beyond the purely biographical interest in him as a character, engaging with the life of this middle-class industrialist, local political leader, and Nazi "business leader" yields complex insights into the internal system of Nazi leadership and Nazi daily life in the province, a subject that few ambitious analytical microstudies have addressed.[10]

Kiehn's biography is the story of a social climber who managed to defend his hard-won position in the bourgeoisie through all of the political caesuras of the twentieth century. The common thread of his story is a struggle for social recognition independent of political systems. In other words, it describes the way that one businessman who grew up in the German Empire spent his entire life wrestling to improve his reputation in the patriarchally structured small-town cosmos of Württemberg. Our microhistorical approach not only allows us to portray Kiehn's contradictory path through life; it also helps us to answer general questions about continuities and breaches in twentieth-century German history. Kiehn's biography only becomes understandable within the context of his local realm of impact and experience. Yet its importance goes beyond local history. For example, his career clarifies the link between "the social motivation and Führer bond in National Socialism" that Martin Broszat pointed out decades ago and gives insight into the functioning, contradictions, and long-term effects of the Nazi *Volksgemeinschaft*.[11]

As a local political leader, Kiehn belonged to a group that served as a hinge between political leadership and the *Volksgemeinschaft* and was among the most important supports of the Nazi state after 1933.[12] These "province leaders" had a substantial influence on the functioning of the Nazi regime, yet few biographical or sociohistorical studies of them exist.[13] Kiehn's life as a Nazi functionary traces the political ups and downs of an "old fighter" (*alter Kämpfer*) beyond his term in office. He built himself a career as a representative of the *Mittelstand* industry of small and midsized companies, using the politically realigned structure of Nazi chambers of industry and trade, as well as professional associations, to make it to the top as a regional business leader. We know relatively little about the regional political elites in general, and even less about the role of economic elites in the various associations of the Third Reich. Scholarly studies of the behavior of *Mittelstand* businessmen within the polycratic jungle of the Nazi regime have only been carried out for a few firms and sectors.[14]

Until now, research has practically overlooked this group, which is not insignificant in size, and concentrated on big business on the one hand and the old *Mittelstand* of independent artisans, retailers, and peasants on the other. These groups not only exhibit extreme differences from one another, they also possess few commonalities with the industrial middle class, which still represents the majority of German business owners today and continues to have a particularly strong presence in southwest Germany.

Owners of small companies who offered their services as economic functionaries to the regime after 1933 in the same way as Kiehn and his colleagues Hans Kehrl, Paul Pleiger, and Wilhelm Keppler (whom Paul Erker has described as "card-carrying [Nazi] industrialists" for their intent to bypass the established economic elites with the help of the Nazi economic system) occupied a special position in the *Mittelstand* economy.[15] Their role in economic policy has also been reasonably well studied. Young, ambitious members of the *Mittelstand* (such as mechanical engineering entrepreneur Paul Pleiger [1899–1985] and textile manufacturer Hans Kehrl [1900–1984]), who, as regional economic functionaries, had put themselves forward for higher commissions, were tremendously important to the Nazi state: they combined ideological dependability, unscrupulous striving, and an expert understanding of economic and technological issues with antipathy toward the traditional bourgeoisie. As head of the Reichswerke Hermann Göring, Pleiger managed the largest industrial group in Europe during the war and on repeated occasions would emphatically defy the interests of Ruhrarea industry. The motto of Kehrl, himself the son of an industrialist, was "throw the old bums out";[16] Kehrl ruthlessly pursued the use of synthetic materials in the textile industry and rose to become the leading organizer of the German war economy under Albert Speer in 1943. Wilhelm Keppler (1882–1960) is another prominent but significantly older member of the *Mittelstand* within the Office of the Four-Year Plan worth mentioning. Keppler was a partner in a small chemical factory who had already been declared a "Special Representative of the Führer on Economic Issues" by 1933 and a "Special Commissioner for German Raw and Processed Materials" by 1934.[17] Kiehn did possess contacts to Keppler and Kehrl, but unlike them he did not push his way to the higher echelons of the regime. His arena remained the regional level. In other regions as well numerous small business owners functioned as political leaders alongside other groups. We still know almost nothing of the work and lives of these functionaries.

Despite his regional focus as a business owner and Nazi functionary, Kiehn repeatedly came into contact with "high politics." He moved in circles that included top Nazi leaders: his social and political ambitions had made him a generous donor who successfully deployed his financial resources to establish connections to important party and SS representatives. Kiehn's network of high-ranking contacts changed as a result of internal party disputes that the manufacturer became caught up in several times beginning in 1933. Invariably, however, he was able to secure backing from one or another influential clique within the Hitler state.

Kiehn's biography illustrates the polycratic clash of jurisdictions between rival groups and institutions that was particularly pronounced in Württemberg. It also sheds light on the background of the murder of Hermann Mattheiß, who in Württemberg in 1934 became the sole victim of the purge carried out by the SS and party leaders against the SA (Sturmabteilung). What's more, Kiehn's life story provides new insight into the run-up to the alleged suicide of his political ally, Gregor Straßer.

Kiehn's ascent after 1933 also shows the extent to which corruption, party loyalty, and nepotism were fundamental structural characteristics of the *Führerstaat*, not least when it came to eliminating Jews from the economy. Here the tightening of legal norms went hand in hand with radicalization, because regional forces diligently "worked toward the Führer."[18] Newly accessible sources have made the nature of the special interest-driven "bureaucratic execution" of the Nazi "race project" even more apparent than when the German edition of this book was published, as well as to what degree largely indifferent actors were complicit in the running of the regime. The case of Kiehn and his competitor, Gustav Schickedanz, who owned a mail-order firm and a brewing concern, underlines this phenomenon and highlights the terrible practice of Aryanization: apart from both being "old fighters," the two of them did not behave like radical anti-Semites aiming to exterminate the Jews, yet nonetheless (and to the great detriment of Jewish victims) they engaged in a ruthless contest to Aryanize the economy.[19]

Exploring this theme through biography provides a focus on the victims—as well as the perpetrators, long neglected in the literature. Individuals materialize behind the abstract term of "Aryanization": on one side, Jewish business owners who saw the basis of their livelihoods brutally destroyed, and on the other, their adversaries, who with a mixture of "initiative," profit-driven greed, and pseudo-legal formalism made resolute use of the opportunities to enrich themselves that the Nazi regime offered. In Kiehn's case, the business and political dimensions, the social and the everyday intermingled in an inextricable tangle. This mélange is characteristic of Kiehn's career as well as of the mechanics of the Nazi regime. This is why Kiehn's biography must not be reduced to his economic and political impact. The social and cultural-historical aspects of his resume are essential to understanding the complexity of his life.

Because the systemic transformation in the political system in 1945 changed Kiehn's life decisively, his biography not least contributes to our knowledge of how Germans have come to terms legally and morally with *individual* involvement in Nazi injustices. This addresses a problem of perception that can only be adequately grasped if we look at it in the context of contemporary society's examination of its Nazi past. For a long time, the experience of the political upheaval of 1945 went unnoticed. Postwar Germany may have been "researched in all facets of its domestic and foreign policy, but there was scarce psychological reckoning of the … 'Volksgemeinschaft,' which had been discharged from its Nazi usage but absolutely still existed in people's minds."[20]

Biographies are particularly well suited to getting closer to the mentality of the society of the early Federal Republic. Life histories of individual protagonists of the SS policy of terror and annihilation[21] — and more recently of some of the members of the economic elite — have expanded our level of knowledge considerably.[22] Fritz Kiehn's biography falls within this research context, but it is also a contribution to the social history of the province and the history of mentalities within it. The microhistorical approach transcends political caesuras, thus illuminating the relationship of continuity and discontinuity in the sociopolitical views and cultural preferences not only of Fritz Kiehn as a person, but also of his provincial surroundings. His career in the Third Reich, just like his comeback in the postwar era, inevitably became a part of Trossingen's recent past, and, in the end, a problem of the political culture of the small German state of Südwürttemberg-Hohenzollern. Continuing to associate with the previously exposed Nazi as a regionally significant business owner plunged the government of the small state into a serious crisis in the early 1950s.

In the 1960s, when Kiehn became involved in the newly founded Lions Club of Tuttlingen, the county seat, there began a juxtaposition between tradition and new beginnings that was typical of post-1945 German history. This organization, founded in the United States and first gaining traction in Germany in the 1950s, embodies a piece of sociocultural Americanization. The Lions Club combines voluntary, private philanthropy with international cooperation and civilian conviviality.[23] The contrasts of the Adenauer era come into painful focus when we note that Fritz Kiehn, of all people — the former NSDAP district leader and important Nazi agitator in the region — helped to anchor this institution where he lived. This is the era when West Germany came to the Western community of values and began to transform itself into a liberal civil society, even as it failed to make a strong break with its Nazi past. Both paths were possible: one of social continuity encouraged through "communicative silence" (Hermann Lübbe), and one of cultural and political reorientation that was largely an external push, that is, from the Western allies. Fritz Kiehn's postwar career reflects both these paths. He defended his economic and social position throughout the systemic changes of 1945, and in the process transformed himself from an "old fighter," Nazi functionary, and admirer of Hitler into a prosperous and honored citizen of the Federal Republic, who stood firmly on constitutional ground and sincerely admired the Federal Republic chancellor Konrad Adenauer, a former enemy of his party. At the same time, Kiehn made his enterprise into a refuge for ex-Nazis. The brown-shirted past of the patriarchs continued to shape Kiehn's operations and family life until the end of the 1960s. He took in former Third Reich youth leader Baldur von Schirach after his release from Spandau Prison; Schirach's son and also his former aide-de-camp had married into Kiehn's family some years before.

After 1949 Kiehn returned to a secure middle-class existence in both his business and private life. But still, for a time, he polarized the people who knew him. To many Trossingers in the early postwar era, he served as a scapegoat for the military defeat, for the shattered illusion of the Third Reich, for Nazi crimes, or for their own personal misery. One competitor accused him of being an unscrupulous profiteer "they had forgotten [to hang] in Nuremburg."[24] Others, however, demonstrated their loyalty as his staff, neighbors, and fellow club members. Some of his business colleagues from other industries offered Kiehn moral support. And so from the mid-1950s onward, a silence fell about the political past of this executive who had remained in business through it all. This is how, in the year of the manufacturer's death in Trossingen, he was perceived not only as an honored citizen, but also as a sort of "brown-shirted Samaritan." The obituary in the local newspaper in 1980 stated that in 1933–1945 Kiehn had "done much for those persecuted at the time. ... Both his human and entrepreneurial qualities shaped the history of the city of Trossingen: they ensure him an enduring place and an honored memory there."[25]

By then, those who had suffered much under Kiehn two decades earlier had been banished from the collective memory of the small city. Not until after the year 2000 would this gradually change, as the pressures of the general transformation in dealing with Germany's historical legacy and above all a concentration on the fate of the victims of the regime came to bear on it. The publication of the German edition of this book in 2000 — which had doubtless already been historiographically influenced by that paradigm shift in the culture of memory — brought this transformation into the Trossingen discourse but has not yet put an end to it. Despite all the hostility from some of the locals about our book and the press reports about forced labor in Trossingen, these confrontations with their own history actually touched off a serious debate for the first time about the city's relationship to its prominent "honorary citizens" and to its own past, sixty-five years after the end of the Nazi regime. This book describes the connection between history that is experienced and history that is remembered, between small-town life and individual biography, between business history and "high politics," through three changes in the political system — four if we count the cultural shift engendered by the collapse of the East German state in 1989–1990. It explores the economic and political roles Kiehn played before, during, and after the Nazi dictatorship. It analyzes how the end of the German Empire in 1918, Hitler's seizure of power, the dissolution of the Nazi regime, the French occupational policy, and the denazification of German society each affected Kiehn personally. We study Kiehn's experience of his environment (with its associated political upheavals), his motivations for his actions, and his perception of himself, but we always come back to the resonance his career had among his contemporaries and their descendants. To describe the life of Fritz Kiehn is to bring almost a century of German social, economic, political, and cultural history into vivid reach, including the real-world consequences of radical political changes that would otherwise be difficult to grasp.

Notes

1. See Werner, *Adolf-Hitler-Platz*, 30.
2. Universitätsarchiv Innsbruck, Akte Fritz Kiehn, letter from Müller to the rector, 12 Apr. 1962.
3. See Berghoff, *Kleinstadt*.
4. TZ, 18 Oct. 1965 and 3 Sept. 1980.

5. Anon., *Fritz Kiehn*, 10.
6. Fallada, *Kleiner Mann*, 162. In original: "talmideleganter [from *Talmi-Gold*, or imitation gold] Garnichts."
7. There continues to be little study of the regional Nazi elites; see Kißener and Scholtyseck, *Führer*.
8. Title of the German-language book by Peter Reichel, *Der schöne Schein des Dritten Reiches*.
9. On the recent debate over the nationalist power of such stagings, see Bajohr and Wildt, *Volksgemeinschaft*; Frei, "Zeitgeschichte"; Gelatelly, *Hingeschaut*; Reichel, *Schein*; Schmiechen-Ackermann, "Einführung"; Selle, "Sinnlichkeit"; Stöver, *Volksgemeinschaft*; Thamer and Erpel, *Hitler*.
10. But see Berghoff, *Kleinstadt*; Rauh-Kühne, *Milieu*.
11. Broszat, "Motivation"; Kater, *Nazi Party*; Frei, "Volksgemeinschaft."
12. Kettenacker, "Aspekte"; Kershaw, *Hitler-Myth*.
13. Arbogast, *Herrschaftsinstanzen*; Fait, "Kreisleiter"; John, Möller, and Schaarschmidt, *NS-Gaue*; Kißener and Scholtyseck, *Führer*; Reibel, *Fundament*; Roth, *Parteikreis*.
14. Berghoff, *Kleinstadt*; Bräutigam, *Unternehmer*; Gehrig, *Rüstungspolitik*; Köster, *Hugo Boss*; Rauh-Kühne and Ruck, *Eliten*.
15. See Erker, *Industrie-Eliten*, 27.
16. "Die alten Säcke müssen weg." Cited in Müller, *Manager*, 9.
17. Müller, *Manager*, and Riedel, *Eisen*, offer details on the occupations of Keppler, Pleiger, and Kehrl, but the biographical dimension has been given short shrift thus far.
18. Kershaw, *Hitler, 1889–1936*, 527–531.
19. Dean, *Robbing the Jews*.
20. Frei, *Eliten*, 303. For a long time, research focused on legislative changes and their continuity effects on the careers of civil servants. See Frei, *Vergangenheitspolitik*; Frei, *Eliten*; Rauh-Kühne, "Entnazifizierung"; Berghoff, "Verdrängung."
21. See Herbert, *Best*; Hachmeister, *Gegnerforscher*; Wildt, *Generation*.
22. On the experience of economic elites in the early days of the Federal Republic who enjoyed largely continuous careers, see Erker and Pierenkemper, *Deutsche Unternehmer*; Plato, "'Wirtschaftskapitäne'"; Berghahn, Unger, and Ziegler, *Wirtschaftselite*; Priemel, *Flick*; Scholtyseck, *Aufstieg*; Hayes, *Degussa*.
23. Biedermann, *Logen*; Gradinger, *Service Clubs*.
24. ASD, NL Erler, Box 85, letter to Erler of 25 Oct. 1950.
25. TZ, 3 Sept. 1980.

Chapter 1

KIEHN'S RISE TO THE MIDDLE CLASS
A Traveling Salesman Becomes a Factory Owner

Fritz Kiehn was born in Burgsteinfurt, Westphalia, on 15 October 1885, the tenth of twelve children born to a policeman and his wife, a hatmaker's daughter. His childhood was shaped by modest circumstances and a strict Prussian Protestant upbringing within the Catholic environment of the Münsterland. After his father's early death in 1896, Kiehn grew up in Lemgo, in the Lippe district. He attended middle school at the Realschule and completed a commercial apprenticeship from 1901 to 1903 at a cardboard box factory in Hanover (fig. 1). He then eked out a living as a traveling salesman for a succession of employers. In 1908, he found a permanent sales position at the Birk-Koch cardboard box company through an ad in a newspaper. The company was located in Trossingen, Württemberg, an isolated small town between the Black Forest and the Swabian Alps. He shared a room at the Bären inn with one other boarder. Three years later, he married Berta Neipp, the daughter of the innkeeper at the Gasthof Rose, another local inn (figs. 2 and 3). The newlyweds moved into the neighboring "Rosenvilla," built by Berta's mother. Marrying into an old Trossingen family allowed Kiehn to get rid of some of the stigma of being a newcomer, a fact that had very real significance in a small town of 5,146 inhabitants (in 1910). The wedding also paved the way for his economic independence, since his in-laws were quite well off. The married couple took a six-week honeymoon in Switzerland, Italy, and Egypt, after which Kiehn took over a bookstore and bookbindery in 1912 that they acquired with funds from Berta's impressive dowry (fig. 4). The Kiehns moved into the residence above the bookstore, where their children were born: their son, Herbert, in 1913 and their daughter, Gretl, in 1918.

Kiehn fought in World War I as a volunteer and emerged wounded and decorated (fig. 5). He expanded his business before and after the war, adding stationery

---

Notes from this chapter begin on page 26.

Fig. 1: Fritz Kiehn in 1900. (Private collection of the Kiehn family)

Fig. 2: Gasthof Rose, the Neipp family's inn. (Private collection of the Kiehn family)

and tobacco supplies, safes, and more books, as well as business machines and office furniture. This diversification points to Kiehn's pronounced desire for advancement. He intended to leave the hardships of his youth behind, to be more than just a shopkeeper or lowly employee. Increasingly, he would leave the sales counter in the care of his wife and have a go at success as a traveling salesman or, soon afterward, as a small-scale manufacturer. In 1919, the family began using a back room in the shop as a small cardboard production facility. In 1920, Kiehn started a mail-order cigarette paper company when he temporarily took over the business of a man who had been sentenced to prison. Unlike Kiehn's other business ventures, this one flourished tremendously. Because loose tobacco was taxed at a considerably lower rate than finished cigarettes, many people resorted to rolling their own during the poverty-stricken postwar years. Orders poured in, and the profits on these were high. Thus, the economic potential of cigarette papers could not be overlooked, and Kiehn did not hesitate to seize the opportunity. Within a few months, he went from being a temporary middleman to an independent manufacturer. He had the first machine installed in the back room of the shop in the fall of 1920. By 1921, Kiehn had acquired a total of thirty-six machines. In a flash, the former mail-order company developed into a factory with some seventy employees, such that Kiehn was able to give up the shop altogether.

A variety of factors contributed to this success. Kiehn's ability to manufacture a brand-name product that would take hold because of its high quality was crucial. What's more, Kiehn gave the products and the company a catchy name derived from the phonetic spelling of his first and last initials, the four-letter "Efka" brand. The little packs of gummed papers, sold at a fixed price, had an attractive and unmistakable design: Kiehn had chosen the emblem of an Egyptian pyramid to commemorate his honeymoon (fig. 6). The idea was said to have occurred to him as he leafed through his photo albums, when a picture of his wife riding a

Fig. 3: **A good match (1911)**. (Private collection of the Kiehn family)

Fig. 4: (a) **Notice of Kiehn's takeover (1912)** (*Allgemeine Volkszeitung Trossingen*, July 1, 1912) and (b) **Kiehn's first business on Rosenstraße (1912)** (Private collection of the Kiehn family)

camel caught his eye.[1] The symbol was easy to remember and became a proven trademark, recognized by millions. Efka became a household name, alongside the thirty-three other German cigarette paper manufacturers.

In addition to the quality and image of his product, Kiehn's willingness to act fast boosted his success. He dared to put all his eggs in one basket, pounced on an unfamiliar line of business, and took on substantial debt to finance the machines. Had it failed, he would have been ruined. Kiehn ruthlessly assailed the competition and quickly developed a reputation as an aggressive outsider who would not adhere to cartel agreements and ignored the boycott urged by shopkeepers' associations against consumer cooperatives aligned with the labor movement. It also appears that Kiehn first introduced giveaways to encourage sales in the cigarette paper industry. In 1935 these gifts were banned by the Nazi government. His

Fig. 5: Kiehn (seated) as a war volunteer. (Private collection of the Kiehn family)

competitors saw him as flouting traditional business practices without hesitation; they considered this "newcomer" to be a "danger to our entire industry."[2]

Two more factors favored Kiehn's rise and were particular to the time. Kiehn was quite literally an "inflation profiteer," since poverty had made rolling one's own cigarettes into a mass-market phenomenon. Furthermore, he took out loans when inflation began and used the high profits from devaluation to minimize that debt in 1923. Kiehn went so far as to drive about five hours to a paper factory in Gernsbach to benefit from the hyperinflation. This allowed him to buy the most important raw material at low real prices. He would go there in the morning in person, buy paper, and pay for it in cash at the previous day's price. He saw the inflation mechanism for what it was and transferred money into tangible assets on a grand scale, purchasing investments and raw materials. Within three years, the former shopkeeper had become the owner of a midsized factory. He immediately acquired the external trappings of this success, moving with his wife Berta and their two children into a prestigious villa in Deibhalde, Trossingen (figs. 7 and 8), in 1924. The villa had been built according to his specifications on a large estate on the outskirts of the city. The monumental property dwarfed all the other upper-class houses in the small town.[3]

The purchase in Deibhalde — Kiehn's main residence until his death — was characteristic of him in many respects. First, this transaction confirmed his skill

Fig. 6: Efka label. (Private collection of the Kiehn family)

at profiting from the currency devaluation, since he paid for all of the building materials in one fell swoop during hyperinflation and before construction began. Second, the sheer size and imposing architecture of the property impressively testified to the former salesman and shop owner's social ambitions and drive for self-expression.[4] Both of these qualities constitute a recurrent theme in Kiehn's biography. Some of their root causes can be found in the experiences of his childhood: the early death of his father and Kiehn's depressing circumstances as a half orphan thereafter.

Fig. 7: At a distance to old Trossingen: Kiehn's villa in Deibhalde. (Private collection of the Kiehn family)

Fig. 8: Rehearsing upper-class prestige: the study in Deibhalde. (Private collection of the Kiehn family)

Kiehn's struggle for social advancement reflects experiences typical of many middle-class members of his generation, whose "social motivation" and authoritarian bent helped to destroy the Weimar Republic.[5] But what set Kiehn apart from the average employee or shopkeeper was his constant search for new economic opportunities, his willingness to temporarily take on extremely high risks to go after them, and his tendency to be anything but timid when choosing his means.

In many things, Kiehn tried to emulate grand bourgeois role models. He strived for recognition, often naïvely, and in as unambiguous a way as possible. The purpose of the villa was nothing less than to provide the status he craved. No one could pass by the property without being impressed: the place spoke for itself and its owner.[6]

Kiehn's rapid rise from renting half a room in an inn to owning the most impressive villa in the small town irritated more established prominent locals. Foremost among them were the owners of the large harmonica factories that dominated industrial life in Trossingen and constituted the leading international production center for the small industry. The first businesses were founded in the 1850s; by 1914, they had grown from their modest beginnings into musical instrument manufacturers with strong exports and global reach. As of 1924, they employed 6,450 factory staff, shop clerks, and home workers, including 4,368 for Matth. Hohner AG alone. Andr. Koch AG had 1,372 employees, and Ch. Weiss AG had 710.[7] In light of Trossingen's mere 5,698 inhabitants in 1925 and its sparsely settled surrounding area with few modes of public transport, the labor market was decidedly tight. Besides the harmonica factories, there were only a few small paper goods businesses, most of which produced cardboard boxes for the instrument factories. As early as 1911, the shortage of local labor and the overwhelming supremacy of the harmonica dynasties had forced the emerging cardboard box company of Mich. Birk (1,200 employees by 1927) to transfer the headquarters of its export-oriented business from Trossingen to Tuttlingen, the county seat.

The industrialization of the small rural town completely reordered the conventional social fabric. Peasants and artisans became workers. The factory owners, who also came from this level of society, encountered great resistance from the traditional upper classes at the start. By the late nineteenth century, large-scale peasant farmers, in particular, had risen to the top of local society, as had artisans, owners of carriage businesses, and some innkeepers. They experienced a relative decline around 1900, falling back to a second tier behind the new wealth of the harmonica manufacturers and facing ever more frequent challenges to their social rankings and municipal political power.

We can see an example of this upheaval in the Neipp family of innkeepers that Kiehn married into. A profitable inn, a similarly lucrative carriage company, and considerable land holdings had made the Neipps part of Trossingen's preindustrial elite. They were still very well off after the turn of the century, as the size of the dowry for their three daughters (thirty thousand marks each) shows. In 1901, two of the Neipps paid some of the highest taxes in the region.[8] But the harmonica manufacturers were grossing millions every year, across the globe. The Neipps were only a few steps below them statistically, but the two families were worlds apart in terms of actual taxes paid. The multimillionaire Hohners led the list of the region's wealthiest by a comfortable margin. From a precarious starting position, and an uncertain place on the mid-to-lower rungs of the tax hierarchy, they had catapulted themselves to the top of local society in only a few decades and left the Neipps far behind them. This fall from grace had burrowed deeply into the collective memory of the family. And their newest member, Kiehn, made their grudge against the harmonica kings his own. This rivalry was constantly present in the 1920s and 1930s, so that within Berta and Fritz Kiehn's marriage, the resentments of industrialization's small-business losers intermingled with the ambitions of a lower-middle-class social climber. This shaped not only their political philosophy but also their relationship to the local economic elite.

In the closed-off world of Trossingen, where the Hohners' economic supremacy had gone unchallenged since the beginning of the century, Fritz Kiehn initially found himself in a position of direct dependence on the harmonica kings:

specifically, in 1908 Hohner AG purchased Kiehn's new employer, the Birk-Koch cardboard box factory. Even after Kiehn took over the paper goods shop, he still relied on the Hohners — the large company was his most important customer. He supplied them with paper goods and typewriters. Moreover, he profited from municipal orders that would have been endangered without the goodwill of the most important manufacturing family in town, a family with strong representation on the local council. The Hohners gave Kiehn letters of credit, even loans. As the wealthiest family in the small town, they extended credit to many residents, supporting a paternalistic claim on the region that extended far beyond their own factory staff. The Hohners ultimately even made a small investment in the Efka factory.

With Kiehn's company on the way up, his relationship with the Hohners began to sour. Traditionally, the harmonica makers had kept an eye on the scarce labor in Trossingen, so that no new manufacturers would be able to settle in the town. They controlled the property market and the local council as an effective means to this end. The first conflicts arrived with the swift, inflation-fueled expansion of Efka, when Kiehn needed to enlarge his modest workshop. The period from 1922 to 1923 brought a clash of interests that threw a distinctive light on local Trossingen politics and on how the municipal government treated the owners of smaller businesses. A piece of municipal land was for sale, which Hohner immediately tried to secure for the Birk-Koch corporation he had bought earlier. The harmonica makers frequently snapped up properties in order to keep them out of the hands of others, even if they had no specific purpose for them in mind. But now Kiehn applied for the land alongside Hohner. In line with local custom, the Trossingen mayor immediately reported Kiehn's involvement to the Hohner board of directors, whereupon Kiehn received a letter from board member Dr. Will Hohner, who wished to caution him "against emerging as a competitor ... I believe I need not remind you of a[n existing] consideration vis-à-vis Birk-Koch, my company, and me, resp[ectively]. ... Would you therefore be so kind as to send me a straight and unequivocal answer."[9]

Kiehn replied immediately, in exactly the manner that the local hierarchy required: it had all been a misunderstanding. He had never imagined "buying the property ... out from under the nose of your firm" or "appearing as a price gouger or competitor. ... This was obviously the furthest thing from my mind, and the very idea would be inconceivable." Besides, Kiehn wrote, there was no danger, since the municipal administration was watching out for the "natural order" of things: "Mr. Mayor also said that the town obviously will not carry out the sale without first having offered the Hohner AG company the opportunity to buy ... for which reason I can only assume that [you] were not in full possession of the facts. I am glad, however, that the question was directed to me, so that I had the opportunity to clear things up. ... With very best regards, and highest esteem, I remain, Papierhaus Fritz Kiehn."[10]

This correspondence illuminates the political practices of a town dominated by a large corporation and underlines the social distance between the harmonica kings and other business owners. Confidential agreements, as were made in comparable situations with the large corporate competitors in Trossingen, were out of the question with "someone like Kiehn." None of the individual Hohners would allow Kiehn so much as a brief meeting, even though the devoted tone of Kiehn's letter shows his efforts to fit in with the circumstances and accept the rules of the game.

The paper goods manufacturer broke through these rules for the first time over the course of 1923, and his previous obsequiousness completely disappeared. In early 1923, Will Hohner ended up squabbling with Kiehn over Hohner's participation in the Efka factory; Kiehn refused to give him access to business documentation. The rise in Efka's fortunes had accelerated during the last year of inflation. As sales increased, Kiehn's confidence grew, and plans for expansion progressed. The property issue escalated. In the end, Kiehn was able to acquire a site on which to build, but only on undeveloped land. As a result, the town planned to build a road that would divide the plot into two triangles, such that Kiehn could not move forward with his building plans. The planned road went against the layout suggested by the Planning Advisory Board in Stuttgart, Württemberg's capital, and had been suggested by one of the urban planning officers who was employed part-time by both the municipality and Hohner. Kiehn interpreted the situation as conscious obstruction, since he had already failed to purchase appropriate property despite the presence of large, undeveloped parcels of land at the site. In 1924, he resolved to enter into a desperate battle. He broadcast his anger in the local press through multipage advertisements and letters to the editor and leveled severe accusations against the mayor and the town council. Kiehn did not explicitly accuse Hohner, even though every Trossingen inhabitant knew the actual lines of battle. This public confrontation culminated in fierce reciprocal allegations and a grandiose threat from Kiehn to move his business to the neighboring town of Rottweil. The attempt at extortion came to nothing — his firm had too little economic weight — but in later years Kiehn would use this same tactic repeatedly, with greater success. The stabilization crisis after the end of hyperinflation dramatically worsened Efka's business situation in late 1924, so Kiehn did not make good on his threat to relocate, suffering an embarrassing defeat on all counts.[11]

In the years that followed, Kiehn made no appearances in politics or in public. Trossingen celebrated its elevation from town to city in 1927, an accomplishment led largely by the Hohners. The official Festschrift, dedicated to Will Hohner, did not mention the existence of the Efka factory in its detailed chapter on "local industry." Amid the rush of the celebration and the several large donations from the Hohners, Kiehn's cautious attempt to join the ranks of local philanthropists by donating a bandstand was practically invisible.[12]

Efka's business lagged until 1925: smokers were increasingly buying finished cigarettes as a result of the general economic upswing, and retailers had already stocked up heavily during hyperinflation. Most cigarette paper manufacturers collapsed. Business began to pick up again in late 1925. In 1926, Efka was on a tear, employing 120 people and acquiring a workshop and property in Trossingen. Kiehn expanded his product range, adding cardboard boxes of all types and a small printing shop. But the overly ambitious, publicly announced plans for expansion did not have a chance. The contrast between Kiehn's goal of becoming a large-scale manufacturer with more than one thousand employees and his modest reality as a small business owner could not have been more glaring.

The economic difficulties — and more so the conflicts with Trossingen manufacturers — ensured that by the mid-1920s Kiehn was still excluded from the local elite. This fact grieved Berta Kiehn as well, who was no less desperate for admiration. The daughter of the prosperous innkeeper may have wished even more fervently than her husband to rise through the ranks of society, which would have reestablished the old town hierarchy at the same time (fig. 9). There is no mistaking her energetic support for Kiehn's firm. As was typical of business families on the rise, her help shifted from direct involvement to advice and representation. She probably continued to play a large part in her husband's business success even after her withdrawal from direct participation in the working world. Such involvement was typical of many family-led companies but was disavowed publicly, in consideration of the middle-class family ideal. Berta Kiehn would later play a similarly important role in her husband's political career.

Fig. 9: **A family on the way up: Fritz, Herbert, Gretl, and Berta Kiehn.** (Private collection of the Kiehn family)

Fig. 10: A closed society: the Trossingen "ladies' circle" (*Damenkränzchen*) before Berta Kiehn's inclusion, circa 1929. (Martin Häffner et al. *Trossingen. Vom Alemannendorf zur Musikstadt*. Trossingen, 1997)

She was not admitted to the Trossingen "ladies' circle" (*Damenkränzchen*) until the late 1920s, a group in which practically all the academic and corporate wives participated (fig. 10). This exclusion was inconsistent with her husband's economic position: while Efka was not the slightest bit comparable to the three big harmonica firms, the factory was larger than many other *Mittelstand* companies in the region. Its owners comprised part of the local elite in the same way that the few academics in town did. These elites not only ignored Kiehn but also profoundly despised him. His rapid success and lavish lifestyle ran afoul of the Pietist professional ethics of the town's more established residents, whose worldview had been shaped by perseverance, diligence, and thrift.

When Will Hohner was asked for confidential information about Kiehn in 1925, he described him as an unreliable blowhard who had submitted "splendid plans" to Hohner in 1921 when requesting a loan. As Hohner smugly noted,

> he did not enjoy great trust at this time. ... But I deigned to support him nonetheless, just as I have given a leg up to so many others. I first assisted him with M[ark] 10,000, at a time when no one in all of Germany would have offered a loan. He could not give me any collateral because his house was mortgaged at the time. His

business developed very slowly, and he always knew how to get me to advance him more money.

Since Kiehn did not pay back the loans, he made Will Hohner a partner with a 50 percent stake in the business. Hohner continues:

> Naturally, as time went on, I wanted information about the course of business. ... But I could never find out anything. So I called in the debt at the beginning of 1923, but he did not react for months, pretending to be poor and claiming that the business was bad and unprofitable. Yet he was happily driving an automobile as well. I finally had to use a competent attorney for help, but he also struggled with him [Kiehn] for months. In the end I got him ... to the point where he paid back the ... amount in ... installments, some of it in cash and some in typewriters. ... I had scarcely been bought out when the business got going quite splendidly. He spent lavishly, building a grand villa and purchasing a large automobile. Anyone would wonder how the little newcomer came into such means so quickly ... construction plans were drawn up for a factory where he intended to employ 3[00]–400 workers. His needless ostentation got him into squabbles with the municipal administration. ... He also expanded his villa and played at being a great man, to general indignation at his manner and conduct. Because he had help from me at the right time, he was able to take full advantage of the economic situation.[13]

The Hohners considered Kiehn a parvenu who ignored the regional social hierarchy. To them, his lifestyle was a provocation, since he had reached the level of demonstrative personal consumption and blurred its ability to establish distinction. A "little newcomer," with a firm that the Hohner establishment had long disparaged as a "small shop" (*Lädle*),[14] had no business turning the local spending customs upside down with impunity.

In 1929, however, Kiehn succeeded in erecting a new building directly next to the parcel he had acquired in 1926. During the construction work, Efka was affected by the increase in the cigarette paper taxes adopted by the federal government under Sozialdemokratische Partei Deutschlands (German Social Democratic Party, or SPD) chancellor Hermann Müller. Taxes rose by more than 300 percent on 1 January 1930, which canceled out the price advantage of "roll-your-own" cigarettes over finished ones, attracted smuggled foreign goods, and jeopardized the existence of the company. For several months, the firm teetered on the brink of ruin. The rash tax increase, which by 1 August 1930 had already been reduced to 67 percent, was the impetus for Kiehn (who according to some sources had been a Nazi sympathizer since 1926) to join the NSDAP and found a local party group. In Kiehn's worldview, the hard-hitting "insane" tax had been "created ... by that Galician Jew Hilferding to take jobs away from the workers."[15]

There were obviously various reasons for Kiehn's swing to the right. For want of personal testimony from the late 1920s, however, we cannot precisely determine the weight of the individual causes. Certainly, preformed ideological convictions specific to his class and generation would have played a role. The experiences of World War I (where Kiehn had been slightly wounded and awarded a Military Merit Cross with Swords), the disappointment about Germany's defeat, and the Treaty of Versailles gave Kiehn and many of his contemporaries a receptiveness to far-right, nationalist thinking.

The parliamentarianism of the Weimar Republic disgusted Kiehn. He found the quarreling and fragmentation of the parties an abomination, a sign of weakness and decadence. For this Prussian policeman's son, raised by his father to blindly obey, the only good state was a strong, authoritarian one. Kiehn had a fondness for troop marches and torchlight processions, as well as for rituals and uniforms of all kinds. The plain, sober Weimar Republic had little to offer in this regard, whereas National Socialism bet not only on terrorist violence, but also on the "aestheticization of politics," "beautiful worlds of make-believe," and the aura of sacred cults.[16] This peculiar mix of brutal violence and emotional fascination and of politics and religion appealed to Fritz Kiehn.

He was also receptive to the anti-Semitism of the Nazis, since he harbored both vague and popular prejudices against "international Jewry." One feature of Kiehn's anti-Semitism was that he saw no contradiction in keeping company with his Jewish business colleagues at the same time. He also lacked a narrowly nationalist perspective: for all the emphasis on German national pride, Kiehn seldom held devotedly to anti-Western prejudices. On the contrary, he was very interested in the technical advances in the United States; like many German engineers and entrepreneurs, he visited the country in 1930. In addition — and despite all the outrage about the Treaty of Versailles — he had a soft spot for France and an unlikely respect for Weimar democratic politicians Friedrich Ebert and Gustav Stresemann.[17] He shared this enthusiasm for the United States and technology with his fellow *Mittelstand* entrepreneur Hans Kehrl, who would later become Albert Speer's chief of planning in the Armaments Ministry.[18] The attraction of the Nazi Party's spirit of optimism, its premonition of "future greatness," and the speculation about the career opportunities that could arise from a "national revolution" were likely also significant in both men's political development. Economic reasons played a large role in Kiehn's path to the NSDAP as well. The *Mittelstand* agitation by the party appealed to a man who had only just exchanged his shop for a factory office and who, in the late 1920s, suddenly felt his rise to be under threat. Add to this the fact that Weimar financial policy had actually endangered his business in particular, since the enterprise could only flourish on the basis of a pronounced tax differential between loose tobacco and finished cigarettes.[19]

We can see another parallel to Kehrl in Kiehn's social mind-set and his campaign against the established entrepreneurial middle class. His overriding concern for the "little guy" (a worry of Cottbus textile manufacturer Kehrl as well) came from middle-class paternalism, which saw personal enterprise as a model for politics. It is no surprise that both business owners sympathized with

Gregor Straßer, who as an exponent of the left-wing element of the Nazi Party emphasized the sociopolitical mission of National Socialism.[20] The popular term *Volksgemeinschaft* thus also became highly attractive to the employer faction.[21] Kiehn shared the anticapitalism that had spread through the Nazi Party to a certain degree, since he distrusted banks and large corporations. He opposed joint-stock companies. One of his many maxims was "Compagnie ist Lumperie," meaning that a corporation led by managers is synonymous with dirty tricks. His model was the *Mittelstand* family business in which the owner had personal responsibility and was "good to his people."[22]

There is no evidence that reading the extensive variety of ideological tracts competing with one another in the first third of the twentieth century influenced Kiehn's political worldview. Even if the former book and paper goods seller constructed a handsome library in his villa as a demonstration of his upper-class ambitions, he found little joy in reading as a pastime. Kiehn, who professed to work "20 hours a day,"[23] found the sports section more interesting "than any book." As his grandson recalled: "He did *not* read. … Books did not influence his politics, but rather tradition, the zeitgeist, the political structures of the Weimar Republic, anti-Marxism and the 'decline in moral standards' [*Verlotterung der Sitten*]. Along with tradition there was also the press, his *Stammtisch* [friends Kiehn drank with regularly] … and his circle of acquaintances."[24]

Finally, Kiehn's everyday life in Trossingen included ample opportunity for his political radicalization. The ambitious striver viewed himself in opposition to a hermetically sealed group of notables who treated him with condescension. These old-style liberals who followed the Hohners embodied for Kiehn the "system" and the "democrats" he so detested and who had attacked him personally. The members of the Hohner family who were active in local politics belonged to either the Deutsche Demokratische Partei (German Democratic Party, or DDP) or the Bürgerliche Vereinigung, a citizens' movement organized on the municipal level. Taken together, these two factions had enjoyed an absolute majority on the town council since 1922. As the third political force, the SPD had been losing significance since then. Kiehn could no more consider becoming a Social Democrat than joining the liberals: his disputes with the Trossingen trade unions, which since 1923 had been only minor figures, were just as heated as those with the mayor. Assuming the tone of a patriarch, he had insisted in the press that outsiders had no business inquiring into the circumstances inside his company. He also made use of a tactic that he would later use frequently: he sent his employees in his stead — as the presumably authentic "voice of the people" — who would then put Kiehn's opponents in their place, in this case the trade union officials. In a full-page public letter in 1923, the "workers of Fritz Kiehn's firm" affirmed "that never before have we had occasion to request a raise in our salaries from the owner of our company." Even violations of working hours had been gladly accepted in the interest of higher wages, they said. "Above all, why is it any of the trade union secretary's business anyway?"[25]

As a member of the middle class who was a pretender to the higher ranks, Kiehn saw the labor movement as his "natural" enemy. In the local two-party system, however, the more established notables who held him in contempt already occupied the liberal spectrum. Regional groups of conservative nationalists and *völkisch* movements did not exist in the 1920s. Kiehn's only chance to make a name for himself politically was, therefore, to occupy the vacancy on the right. When he joined the NSDAP in April 1930, he could see that the Nazis had just shrugged off their status as a sectarian splinter party. The emotionally charged right-wing campaign against the Young Plan in 1929 had brought the Nazis out of isolation. An increased share of the votes in the state and municipal parliamentary elections, the spectacular electoral victories in some of the rural regions and at the universities, the Nazi participation in the government of Thuringia, and a wave of new party members constituted a clear upward trend. With the Reichstag election of September 1930, when the NSDAP suddenly increased from 2.6 to 18.3 percent of the vote, the party of Hitler had established itself as a political force to be reckoned with.

Notes

1. StAT, A 938, FS n.d.
2. ASD, NL Erler, Box 85, letters from paper goods companies to Erler of 21 Sept. and 25 Oct. 1950. Both letters concern Kiehn's practices in the 1920s. See also ibid., letter from Großeinkaufsgesellschaft Deutscher Konsumgenossenschaften (the central purchasing organization of the German cooperative societies) to Erler of 4 Jan. 1951.
3. StAT, A 938; BA DC, Akte Kiehn; Kiehn, *Unsere Deibhalde*. On the stock character of the inflation profiteer, see Geyer, "*Verkehrte Welt,*" 244–45.
4. On the much-derided mimicry of the petite bourgeoisie, the "pursuit of respectability," and a typical "excessive concern for order and decorum," see Crossick and Haupt, *Petite Bourgeoisie,* 11; Schilling, *Kleinbürger,* 28; Wehler, "Geburtsstunde." For the twentieth century, see Bourdieu, *Distinction,* 394–395.
5. See Broszat, "Motivation"; Crossick and Haupt, *Petite Bourgeoisie,* 178–180.
6. On the search for prestige that manifested in bourgeois home décor culture at the turn of the century, see Meyer, *Theater,* 22–46; Crossick and Haupt, *Petite Bourgeoisie,* 262. On the "petit bourgeois habitus" as a sign of one's origin and social differentiation, see Bourdieu, *Distinction,* 143, 330–331.
7. WABW, B 35 (Bestand Hohner) II (temporary call numbers), Bü 400, 1 Apr. 1924. More generally, see Berghoff, *Kleinstadt*; Berghoff, *Marketing Diversity*.
8. Berghoff, *Kleinstadt,* 42–43, 95–104, 222.
9. WABW B 35 II, Bü 394a, letter from Will Hohner to Kiehn of 6 Feb. 1923.

10. WABW B 35 II, Bü 394a, letter from Kiehn to Will Hohner of 9 Feb. 1923. After Kiehn had withdrawn his interest, Hohner made an offer that the town rejected as being too low. The sale was therefore aborted. See StAT, B 68, GRP of 28 Feb. 1923.
11. See AVT, 15, 17, and 19 Mar. 1924; StAT, B 69, GRP, 29 Feb. 1924.
12. See Berghoff, *Kleinstadt*, 348–352.
13. WABW B 35 II, Bü 400, letter from Will Hohner to customs asst. Aden of 15 Oct. 1925.
14. Interview by Hartmut Berghoff of 3 Dec. 1994.
15. AVT, 26 Aug. 1930. Rudolf Hilferding, former SPD minister of finance, had long since resigned when the tax increase took effect, but he was influential in its preparation. See Winkler, *Schein*, 738–759.
16. Benjamin, *Kunstwerk*, 49; Vondung, *Magie*; Reichel, *Schein*, 11–45 (quotations on pp. 30 and 35).
17. Ebert was the Social Democratic president of the Weimar Republic from 1919 until his death in 1925. Stresemann, a member of the liberal Deutsche Volkspartei (DVP), was chancellor from August 1923 to November 1923 and foreign minister from 1923 until his death in 1929. Both were much hated by the NSDAP.
18. Kehrl had struggled through two years working in the United States, where he completed a correspondence course in "Scientific Management." Müller, *Manager*, 18, 26; Müller, "Hans Kehrl."
19. Brustein, *Logic*, shows that a sober calculation of interests often drove middle-class elements into the party.
20. Recent work on Straßer includes Kershaw, *Nazi Dictatorship*, 81; Stachura, *Gregor Strasser*; Lilla, Döring, and Schulz, *Statisten*, 133f.
21. Müller, *Manager*, 23–25. See also Rauh-Kühne, "Sozialpartnerschaft"; Berghahn and Friedrich, *Otto A. Friedrich*, 86–87.
22. Interview with Herbert E. Kiehn of 15–16 June 1999.
23. StAS, Wü 1, Bü 100a, PUA, 8th public meeting, p. 47.
24. Herbert E. Kiehn, in letter to the authors of 15 Sept. 1998. All the same, Fritz Kiehn possessed an often astoundingly precise knowledge of modern and recent history because of his newspaper reading, personal experience, and good memory. On the lack of book learning among many of the petite bourgeoisie, and on the bourgeois symbolism of the library, see Crossick and Haupt, *Petite Bourgeoisie*, 273.
25. AVT, 2 June 1923.

Chapter 2

RAPID ASCENT THROUGH THE NAZI RANKS
From Local Party Leader to Reichstag Delegate

On 26 May 1930, just weeks after joining the NSDAP, Kiehn founded an NSDAP Ortsgruppe, or local branch of the party, in Trossingen. Only eighteen months later, in 1931, he won the local council elections as the top candidate on the Nazi slate, beating the new top man at Hohner AG. At 3,021 votes, he banished Ernst Hohner to third place, with 2,262 votes: Trossingen snubbed the harmonica kings, and the Nazis swept the election in a political landslide. Winning 31.1 percent of the vote right off the bat, the NSDAP became the strongest party, while all the other groups lost ground. Hohner's Bürgerliche Vereinigung party dropped from 42.4 percent to 18.5 percent; the DDP dropped from 31.9 to 25.6 percent. The left proved relatively stable in contrast, since the SPD's decline from 25.7 to 23.5 percent could be attributed solely to the votes lost to the Kommunistische Partei Deutschlands (Communist Party of Germany, or KPD), which had run for the first time in Trossingen and won 1.3 percent of the vote. Municipal elections law in Württemberg specified that only half of the local council seats were up for election every three years, so the NSDAP at first occupied just three of eighteen seats, despite the party's electoral success. Five seats belonged to the Bürgerliche Vereinigung, four to the DDP, and six to the SPD. The National Socialists acquired considerable voter potential in Trossingen substantially earlier than in Württemberg overall, as the Reichstag elections show. In 1928, the NSDAP in Trossingen won 0.8 percent of the vote, still clearly below its state and Reich averages. But in 1930, two months after the founding of the Ortsgruppe, the Nazis in Trossingen achieved 19.1 percent of the vote, a number that was more than double their state result and slightly exceeded their sensational result in Germany overall.[1]

Notes from this chapter begin on page 42.

Why was NSDAP agitation so effective in the small town, when the region had not been particularly hard-hit by the global economic crisis and the unemployment rate was only 14 percent at its highest? Reduced working hours and the establishment of a rotation system had allowed Hohner to safeguard most of its workers from losing their jobs or their unemployment benefits, which were granted only for a limited time; in January 1933, only thirty-three people in Trossingen were living on *Wohlfahrtsunterstützung* (public alms). Yet the global economic crisis impacted the political decision-making process nonetheless. Even if the town was not a picture of mass misery and social disintegration, the standard of living continued to drop, and its effects were becoming more widespread. Hardly a working family was spared from salary cuts or reduced hours. Many of them had more than a passing acquaintance with malnutrition. State benefits dropped in Trossingen just as they did elsewhere. Reports in the media and skillful agitation by the NSDAP made the frightening scenes in the larger cities a constant presence: "The island … in the sea of German poverty … is becoming increasingly eroded … and it is only the briefest matter of time before this island is dragged into the maelstrom."[2] This perception became the basis for political radicalization that benefited the NSDAP almost exclusively. This was a marked contrast to the more urban areas, where the proletarian unemployed voted KPD. In other words, workers in Trossingen were more concerned with keeping their own homes and their own property, and this gave them a more petit bourgeois perspective. They therefore had only one alternative to the parties of the Weimar Republic. Research into voting patterns confirms that the NSDAP appealed to the middle class in particular, which in Trossingen included a large chunk of the workforce.[3]

Local and transregional factors reinforced each other to perpetuate the erosion of democratic parties across Germany. This process was accelerated in Trossingen because of the striking shift in the fabric of the local upper class, a shift that transfixed the region in the late 1920s. Weiss and Koch, the most important other harmonica manufacturers, encountered difficulties and were absorbed by Hohner in 1928 and 1929, respectively. Since then, there had been only one large employer in the region — Hohner. Economic dependence on the family now reached its peak. The precarious situation gave the workers practically no alternative in the region; the town pastor reported that the mergers had provoked "manifold excitement, indeed dismay and indignation. … The deepening of the gulf between employers and employees is palpable. The latter worry about where they would find a job if they needed one, since there is no more alternative industry or competition present."[4] In the eyes of the workers, the city of harmonicas had become the city of the Hohners.

Tellingly, the Trossingen offices of the metalworkers' and woodworkers' unions were shuttered at almost the same time that Weiss and Koch closed down. The unions had first set up shop in 1918–1919, and during the inflation boom they had temporarily challenged the paternalistic rule of the factory owners. But they were not influential after 1924. The political arm of the workers' movement was also less and less able to effectively represent the interests of its voters. In the early years of the Weimar Republic, the SPD had controlled half the seats in the Trossingen council and occasionally managed to prevent the implementation of the manufacturers' interests, but the party had been in the minority since 1922 and continued to lose influence. To make matters worse, the mayor, who had at least sometimes been critical of Hohner, was replaced by Walter Bärlin in 1929, a young and "Hohner-friendly" successor. In sum, the latter half of the 1920s saw one counterweight to the Hohner family after another drop out. The harmonica dynasty's power in Trossingen hit its peak in 1930.[5]

Many Trossingers were deeply worried by this situation. Local disquiet with the apparently "all-powerful" Hohners coincided with the general loss in credibility of liberal principles, whose primary local representatives came from this very family. Fritz Kiehn reaped two different benefits from this situation: for one thing, he was absolutely the only person in the region who vociferously presented himself as an alternative to the prevailing rule by the local dignitaries. For another, the coincidence of the economic and political crisis of the Weimar Republic gave a lift to Kiehn and his party, so that he was soon able to pass himself off as a local political bigwig.

German liberalism was hamstrung by the erosion of its political constituency, which progressed with breathtaking swiftness during the Great Depression. The failure to recognize the danger imminent in this situation and to take effective countermeasures was reflected by the Hohner family's behavior in an almost archetypal way. The harmonica family members' overwhelmingly local perspective, centered on their own firm, led them to misjudge the growing threat. They did not take the "little newcomer" Kiehn seriously, considering him "a notorious troublemaker" instead. The Bürgerliche Vereinigung shut out reality, preferring to obstinately cling to its character as an ostensibly apolitical club of local dignitaries. Its defining concepts were "prudence" and "thrift": the group conscientiously refused to address any ideological conflicts, relying instead on the prestige of its leading members. The Bürgerliche Vereinigung did not pursue "party politics," counting instead on "such an expert industrialist as [our] Director Ernst Hohner." Like all members of his family, however, Hohner had no time for high politics and little time for municipal power mongering because of his constant concern for his firm and the large private losses he had incurred in the stock market crash of 1929. During the 1930 election campaign, the *Schwenningen Volksstimme* accused him of having supported the Stahlhelm, the paramilitary arm of the right-wing conservative Deutschnationale Volkspartei (German National People's Party, or DNVP). An aggrieved Hohner angrily repudiated the charge in the local press, citing his neutrality: "We have better and more important things to do in these grave times." With an attitude like that, Ernst Hohner was often absent from the local council, which made him vulnerable. He arrogantly dismissed criticism in the press concerning these absences: "I ascribe no particular significance to … politically biased reports in the newspapers."[6]

The NSDAP, on the other hand, pressed every demagoguery button in the book and had a knack for piggybacking its agenda onto national and local themes so as to "prove" its slogans on the ground. For example, the Nazis seized on the people's displeasure with municipal administrative measures and their prejudices against city officials, caricaturing public servants as representing a cabal of democratic "fat cats" (*Bonzentum*). Their propaganda portrayed the local council as enriching itself at the people's expense, and the mayor as drawing a salary more appropriate to a cabinet minister abroad; excessive electricity rates and high-priced train tickets, "senseless spending sprees," and "tax Bolshevism" would reduce every Trossinger to penury. The NSDAP criticized some of the smaller apartment buildings that were obviously out of place in town as expressions of the "uncivilized" (*kulturwidrig*) construction style of the Weimar Republic. Moreover, the Nazis presented themselves as a party that was friendly to labor and seized on the long-standing local issue of the commons. With Trossingen's population rising, there were now 350 claimants waiting for the parcels of communal land to which they were entitled. So the NSDAP borrowed a proposal originally made by the DDP: to convert forest into arable land and slightly reduce the size of all existing claims. Once this proposal had been accepted, the Nazis could convincingly sell it as proof of the party's pragmatic social policy: the new method for apportioning the land would primarily benefit new residents (that is, those who had previously been dependable SPD voters) and young families.[7]

The NSDAP successes created more intense political disputes than the small town had ever seen, on a spectrum ranging from verbal spats to brutal violence. On 28 May 1930, one day after their Ortsgruppe in Trossingen had been established, the Nazis held their first rally. Eight hundred supporters attended, most of them from out of town. The strong labor movement in neighboring Schwenningen considered this a provocation and an attempt to establish a Nazi base of operations in their own backyard, so four hundred members of the KPD and SPD (tellingly, in separate buses) descended on Trossingen. Truncheons and steel rods featured in the resulting brawl. History threatened to repeat itself in August: the police report details how well over a thousand National Socialists assembled in a beer hall, allegedly peacefully, as Communists in front of the venue "blocked traffic" and "disturbed the peace," their ringleaders getting arrested for "impudent and provocative behavior. … A great number of looky-loos from Trossingen" followed the proceedings with a mixture of horror and vicarious excitement. More mass demonstrations followed as the year went on, events of huge scale for a town of a scant six thousand inhabitants. That winter, two thousand people took part in a demonstration against the NSDAP that was organized largely by Social Democratic paramilitary groups (*Reichsbannerverbände*) from Schwenningen, Villingen, and Tuttlingen. At the same time, new Ortsgruppen of the Socialist

Workers Youth (Sozialistische Arbeiterjugend, SAJ), the Reichsbanner, and the National Socialist SA sprang up.[8]

Many Trossinger citizens were worried about how deeply politics had penetrated into their community and had transformed it into a place where military marches and brawls among outsider organizations regularly occurred. The NSDAP, playing up its role as upholding order even as the party promoted its destruction, had the most to gain from residents' concerns. Kiehn benefited, acting as the "defender of the homeland," leading hundreds of SA marchers, and working closely with the police. Riots of this type decreased after 1930, allowing the Nazis to reap the benefits of the violence they themselves had sown and profit from the deeply rooted local hostility toward their red neighbors.

In his factory, where the staff had been reduced from 120 in 1926 to 70 in 1932, Kiehn designed an alternative model to the Hohners' paternalism. A few days before the local council elections in 1931, he announced to his workers that in the future they would directly benefit from profit sharing. He celebrated the move in a fake letter to the editor: "We should recognize the actions of manufacturer Mr. Fritz Kiehn as a beautiful example of brotherly love. In spite of these difficult times, Mr. Kiehn … has taken in his employees and workers as associates, even giving them a share … of the profits." In the words of the writer, Kiehn's actions corresponded to "authentic German socialism." Other signs of Kiehn's personal politics, stylized as "National Socialist entrepreneurship," included treating workers and employees equally, renouncing piecework, and paying higher wages than the Hohners. Another sideswipe at Hohner AG, and an outright lie besides, was a reference to the supposed complete avoidance of "reduced hours or dismissal."[9] A swastika banner fluttered over the Efka factory even before 1933, still a highly unusual sight for a German factory in this era (fig. 11).

Kiehn's political statements showed him to be a staunch propagandist of the *Gemeinschaft* ideology. Again and again he emphasized the ostensibly egalitarian structure of the party, drawing an analogy to his Efka factory: "In the National Socialist German Workers' Party there are only party comrades, only members! Class has no meaning for us! Everyone is equal within our ranks. In my business I see only colleagues, only workers; I am one of them," gushed Kiehn in the local paper. "The brown uniform of honor makes everything equal … it guarantees a feeling of community across all classes."[10]

His statements about economic policy strongly diverged from the party line, if such a thing even existed during the internal power struggles from 1930 to 1932. Hohner AG, the largest employer in the region in 1929, did 84 percent of its sales abroad, so the NSDAP's efforts to isolate the economy in line with the imperatives of a war economy and Germany's withdrawal from world trade were difficult for Kiehn, given that the livelihood of most of his local constituents depended on unhindered access to western European and US markets. The DDP and especially the SPD were particularly fond of drawing attention to this

Fig. 11: Efka factory with swastika banner (ca. 1931–1932). (Private collection of the Kiehn family)

massive contrast to local economic interests, alleging that workers would never be able to overcome the crisis without the earnings from exports. This argument put Kiehn in a difficult position and led him to declare wholeheartedly that the "Third Reich" would "do its best to support" export-dependent businesses. His party only talked about the domestic market so much, reasoned Kiehn, because there was no other way out of the crisis given the international situation. The concentration on stimulating demand at home was an emergency measure that would only be temporary. In short, Kiehn summarily denied those parts of the party platform that proved unappealing at the local level.[11]

The campaign for the 1932 state elections marked Kiehn's first explicit attack on a representative of the established dignitaries in Württemberg. He detailed the contrast between National Socialist and democratic entrepreneurship. He criticized the behavior of Fritz Mauthe, a DDP representative in the Württemberg parliament and the owner of a watch factory in Schwenningen (whom Kiehn ran against without success), as thoughtless and antisocial. He accused Mauthe of establishing branch factories outside Germany, "to save on customs duty, systematically nurturing the competition for our domestic export industry. The victims were the workers. ... The antithesis: Fritz Kiehn in Trossingen! From the humblest beginnings, he fostered and grew a completely new kind of industry in Germany. ... In the process, he fed and employed German workers and saved the German economy millions of marks each year on foreign imports." This "National Socialist act by Fritz Kiehn" qualified him for a seat in the state parliament, he asserted. Alluding to Mauthe's large lead over him in voter confidence (his opponent was a member of an old Schwenningen family that was even related to the Hohners), Kiehn concluded his advertisement with an appeal: "Free yourselves from false, small-minded local patriotism." His assertions combined his personal need for admiration with the smear tactics of his party. Kiehn, who boasted of the service he had given to the nation as a "benefactor" of the balance of trade and the German workforce, employed about seventy people in 1932, while Mauthe's staff numbered around a thousand. The latter's branches abroad were simply sales offices. To top it all off, Kiehn's portrayal of himself as a pioneer in the German paper goods industry was completely bogus.[12]

At his company Kiehn kept an eye on the political "reliability" of his employees and had the works committee write letters to the editors during the election to testify to "our boss's fine way of thinking."[13] Kiehn really was popular with his workers, and he understood how to establish a community of "co-conspirators" against the overly powerful harmonica factory. Without attacking Hohner directly, he cleverly gave the impression that the region needed an economic and political counterweight. In sum, the NSDAP manifested a considerable adaptability to local conditions and represented itself as the dynamic party of the little people and of social progress.

During election campaigns Kiehn made himself out to be a self-made businessman with heart who had never forgotten his modest origins. This set him apart from the older business community, which he described as having become bourgeois, self-satisfied, and lethargic. Their members, he argued, had nothing more to offer.[14] In December 1932, he published an open letter in the *Nationalsozialistische Volkszeitung* addressed to the local DDP committee: "Enough, you liars! I will stress it once again: democracy is synonymous with unprincipled politics!"[15] Kiehn's aggressive dissociation from the social group that he was actually keen to ascend to can be interpreted as a reactive psychological response to the obstacles put in his path by the town's more established locals. But this group's reservations about Kiehn also came from the anticapitalist and antibourgeois slogans of the NSDAP that dominated the party's agitation prior to 1933 and disgusted many business people. As a factory owner, then, Fritz Kiehn found himself in a strange position that can only be understood within the context of his local environment and the social climber's experiences with the established business class.

Open support for the NSDAP from a middle-class business owner was rather exceptional at that time in Württemberg. This changed following Hitler's appointment to the chancellorship. Although he had numerous rivals within the party, Kiehn had received repeated praise for his outstanding merits before 1933. His early and outstanding dedication when he had been an *alter Kämpfer* repeatedly worked to his benefit when he was caught up in party court proceedings. Five years after the Nazi "seizure of power," Kiehn was esteemed in the Württemberg NSDAP as "nearly ... the only 'man of industry'" in Württemberg that the party had been able to depend on during the years of its arduous climb to the top. Whereas the large firms in neighboring Tuttlingen and Hohner AG in Trossingen "had no time at all for the movement," Kiehn had "repeatedly donated resources from his business, which at that time was relatively small" to the party.[16] Analysis of other Württemberg business owners has shown that they generally kept their distance from the NSDAP prior to 1933. Württemberg represents an emphatic rejection of Turner's thesis that the owners of large corporations were the only ones to remain aloof from National Socialism, while smaller and midsized entrepreneurs were disproportionately likely to be early supporters of the NSDAP.[17]

Kiehn's work allowed the NSDAP to gain new ground in Trossingen,[18] as shown in table 1. In 1930, the SPD was still the strongest party in town, with 39.3 percent (German average 23.8 percent), ahead of the NSDAP's total of 19.1 percent (9.4 in Germany) andthe DDP/Deutsche Staatspartei's[19] (which earned a bump as the "party of the Hohners" in the city of harmonicas) total of 13.9 percent (9.9 in Germany). On 31 July 1932, the SPD lost its status as the strongest party to the NSDAP. The DDP/Deutsche Staatspartei achieved an impressive result in Trossingen that was many times higher than its percentages in the state

Table 1: Reichstag election results in Trossingen (and in Germany), 1930–1933 (in percentages of voters)

	NSDAP	DNVP	DDP	SPD	Center Party	KPD
14 Sept. 1930	19.1 (18.3)	4.9 (7.0)	13.9 (3.8)	39.3 (24.5)	4.3 (11.8)	2.4 (13.1)
31 Jul. 1932	32.2 (37.2)	2.5 (5.9)	19.3 (1.0)	27.8 (21.6)	4.3 (12.5)	4.2 (14.3)
6 Nov. 1932	32.9 (33.0)	3.8 (8.3)	19.3 (1.0)	24.2 (20.4)	4.4 (11.9)	6.0 (16.9)
5 Mar. 1933	35.1 (43.9)	* (8.0)	17.3 (0.9)	25.9 (18.3)	4.7 (11.2)	3.8 (12.3)

* Party did not run in this local election
Sources: *Gränzbote,* 1 Aug. and 7 Nov. 1932; AVT, 11 Aug. 1932; Häffner, Ruff, and Schrumpf, *Trossingen,* 502; Dederke, *Reich und Republik,* 284f.

and the country. The SPD suffered some losses in Trossingen in the Reichstag election of 6 November 1932, while the NSDAP slightly increased its result even with the declining trend in the state of Württemberg and in Germany as a whole. The DDP drew slightly less than one-fifth of the votes relatively consistently. In the Reichstag election of 5 March 1933 (which was overshadowed by violent attacks on left-wing parties across Germany, including in Trossingen), the NSDAP achieved no more than a solid third of the votes, whereas the SPD slightly improved and the DDP lost a bit. These numbers reflect the relative uniformity of the Social Democrat milieu in the small town, as well as the effect of the special Hohner factor. A substantial part of the large company's permanent staff traditionally copied the management's politics and thus delivered an unusually high share of the votes to the DDP. The NSDAP enjoyed a solid voter bloc of about a third of Trossingen residents but had little possibility of expanding it. The clear margin they had achieved in 1930 over the statewide average was gone. In 1932 at the latest, one could no longer speak of a "National Socialist stronghold" in Trossingen. Nevertheless, Kiehn continued using this "honorary title" to refer to his adopted hometown in order to highlight his own service to the "movement."

The actual core group of National Socialist followers was small. Before 1933, the Ortsgruppe in Trossingen comprised a few dozen members, most of them Efka employees. Even outside of his company, Kiehn encouraged those who were dependent on him to join the party and make donations. For example, Efka patronized a machinery company threatened by the Great Depression whose owner had become a member of the NSDAP in 1930. A doctor, a notary, a teacher, a building commissioner (*Baurat*), and various small business owners were also part of the Ortsgruppe. Management of the group was practically a family affair: Kiehn acted as Ortsgruppenleiter, or head of the local branch, until 1933 and was also Kreisleiter, or district leader, until 1932. The most important female activist after Berta Kiehn was Toni Hunger, who worked closely with Kiehn at Efka and had power of attorney. Kiehn's brother-in-law Christian Messner, a sawmill owner, continued to belong to the Bürgerliche Vereinigung until the local council elections of 1931, when he joined the NSDAP. Messner swiftly penetrated the close-knit leadership circle and served as Ortsgruppenleiter from 1934 to 1940. The covered hall at the Gasthof Rose (the inn belonging to Berta Kiehn's family) became a regional base for the Württemberg NSDAP. The party held countless meetings there for audiences numbering over a thousand.[20]

We can assume that Kiehn and his relatives also benefited economically from Trossingen's new function as a center of Nazi agitation. The Hitler supporters who came from miles around likely generated considerable income for the Gasthof Rose. Efka also took over the large-scale production of Nazi propaganda. It is probably no coincidence that Kiehn established his own printing shop in 1930, the very same year that he entered the party.[21] When the Baden

Gauleitung, the administration of the neighboring NSDAP regional district of Baden, fell behind on payments for printed materials in late 1931, Kiehn called in NSDAP Reichsorganisationsleiter (head of the party administration) Gregor Straßer and informed him that "I considered this … purely a case of meeting a need, and I certainly see no reason why I should forgo the money. So be so good, dear Gregor, as to tell the … gentlemen that they will need to pay within a few days."[22] The Württemberg Gauleitung in Stuttgart, however, received most prints free of charge. Later accounts from Kiehn claimed that during the Reichstag election campaign of 1930 he printed "all of the propaganda pamphlets for the Württemberg Gau (over 1.6 million pamphlets)" in his shop "on day and night shifts … without billing or making a pfennig for it." He allegedly also took on sending the pamphlets "to hundreds of addresses" free of charge. In an eight-page letter to Hitler's "Deputy Führer, Mr. Rudolf Heß," written in the summer of 1933, Kiehn catalogued his services and reminded the Munich party leadership of the "sacrifice" he had made, which he estimated at RM 150,000. To the *NS Kurier* alone (a Nazi propaganda newspaper published by the Gauleitung in Stuttgart), he noted that he had consistently given interest-free loans ranging from RM 20,000 to occasionally more than RM 40,000.[23]

Kiehn's own account from 1936 claims that he "made direct and indirect financial and material sacrifices during the *Kampfzeit* and after the seizure of power as well … that no one else in Württemberg has even come close to doing." He had practically "not set foot in" his business during the *Kampfjahre* (years of struggle) and had "seen almost as little" of his family during that time.[24] Between 1930 and 1935, Kiehn bragged, he had spoken at more than one thousand assemblies and founded more than fifty Ortsgruppen. He began publishing a regionally distributed National Socialist weekly in 1931, organized the election campaigns in southern Württemberg, and supplied the NSDAP with numerous donations and new members.[25]

Some of these assertions may nevertheless have been exaggerated. What we know for certain is that the Württemberg NSDAP had found in this Trossingen business owner an unusually enthusiastic activist before 1933. During election campaigns he would give three to four speeches daily. Kiehn's son, Herbert Kiehn, who was due to begin college in 1933, reported to a confidant that once the news arrived about the dissolution of the Reichstag, he had known "from the start" that "my father would not give me permission to travel, since in this case [of political opportunity] my place was with him." Herbert was initially assigned to lead propaganda in three districts and ended up as an aide-de-camp to his father, who acted "in the capacity of a higher SS Führer." Kiehn was now "giving 3–4 speeches a day." His son, whose internship in a factory now took second place to his father's campaign obligations, described the strain of these activities: "We never got home before 3 a.m., since we were going all around Württemberg and Baden."[26]

The intensified time and financial commitment could not have happened without the significant sales gains at the Efka factory prompted by the opportunities of the Great Depression. The cigarette paper sector was again flourishing. Business was going so well that Kiehn added a large new swimming pool to his villa in 1930 and contacted the leading manufacturer of special machines for the cigarette paper industry, a "Jewish company" in Vienna called Lerner, to purchase the entire two-year production run of a new type of machine. With this risk-laden move, Kiehn managed to temporarily cut off his entire competition from the latest technology and to satisfy the rapidly expanding demand. The orders piling up would cover the high purchase cost of the machinery, and Efka ended up as the market leader. Plans for expansion into the US market were dropped after a fact-finding trip to the United States. Nonetheless, during the Great Depression Kiehn came a good deal closer to his ultimate goal: becoming a large-scale industrialist.[27] All of this points to Kiehn's massive support of the NSDAP as being rooted not only in ideological but also in business concerns.

Despite Kiehn's regional successes, the Württemberg NSDAP was still last among all the party Gau organizations as of September 1930.[28] But his efforts paid off two years later when the Reichstag was again dissolved prematurely and the breakthrough to a mass movement took hold in Württemberg as well. The Nazi Gauleitung in Stuttgart nominated its supporter and creditor Kiehn as one of the most promising Württemberg candidates for a Reichstag seat.[29] The contacts that Kiehn cultivated with men at the head of the party inside and outside Württemberg proved helpful in facilitating his entrance into national politics. His acquaintance with candidate selection administrator (Reichswahlleiter) Wilhelm Frick[30] — whom Kiehn had hosted at his villa on occasion and who served as Minister of the Interior from 1933 until 1943 — and his friendship with Reichsorganisationsleiter Gregor Straßer were now becoming especially useful. These two Nazi functionaries were the ones who "filled the safe slots" on the candidate list "based purely on consideration of usefulness." There were many reasons to nominate Kiehn in the Württemberg Gau (where the NSDAP continued to be poorly organized): the crucial factors that garnered him a fourth-place slot on the state list were likely his business connections, his popularity in the region, his gift for public speaking, and his service, as well as the financial relief he had repeatedly given the heavily indebted party.[31]

Kiehn was a confidant of Gregor Straßer, and this was no coincidence. The NSDAP functionary, who had risen from a small-town pharmacist to the organizer of a mass movement party, shared some biographical features with Kiehn. Straßer was seven years younger than Kiehn but had volunteered for World War I and, just like Kiehn (and many other NSDAP *alte Kämpfer*), had been wounded and returned home full of formative experiences and militaristic ideals. But Straßer, who had finished college before the war, became an officer, whereas Kiehn had to carry out his military service as only a private. Straßer, like Kiehn, had a feel for staging propaganda, and shared with him and many other members of the lower middle class a "fondness for a mass culture of appearances and the confirmation of a nonexistent social identity"³² that was characteristic of National Socialism. This explains why Straßer declared 9 November a day of mourning to commemorate the "fallen" in the Hitler Putsch of 1923.³³ Kiehn was just as receptive to such ideas, so the two felt a kinship. In 1931 Straßer was also "the only high-ranking National Socialist" who commanded "a certain measure of respect" among large-scale industrialists.³⁴ Straßer remained a dilettante in the economic sphere, however, and in his function as the Reichsorganisationsleiter of the NSDAP he found himself constantly looking for appropriate staff and advisors, primarily for the party's economic policy functionaries. After the Reichstag election of September 1930, he became one of a select group of Nazi officials who were regularly given large sums of money by Ruhr industrialists, a practice that financed his lavish lifestyle.³⁵

The Straßers were family friends of the Kiehns (fig. 12). Both men shared a love of expensive cars. The cigarette paper manufacturer would invite his friend in the party to visit him in Deibhalde, where Kiehn and his wife would offer Gregor and Else Straßer "Rehkeule [leg of venison] und Spätzle." A swim in their outdoor pool would follow, as well as "a swell game of cards [*Skat*]."³⁶ Political observers of the era considered Gregor Straßer to be "perhaps the most famous Nazi personality,"³⁷ so Kiehn's friendship with the Reichsorganisationsleiter and prominent politician amounted to valuable political capital. He therefore did his utmost to keep up the relationship and did not shy away from using it for his

Fig. 12: Friends in more than politics: Fritz Kiehn and Gregor Straßer in Deibhalde. (Private collection of the Kiehn family)

own purposes. The same went for his political ambitions in Trossingen. During the municipal election campaign of 1931, Kiehn encouraged Straßer to respond to an article by the DDP/Deutsche Staatspartei Ortsgruppe in the Trossingen local newspaper. "The cursed society must be put down," Kiehn reasoned, "so hurry up and do what you can to stick it to society."[38] Shortly thereafter, a reply credited to Straßer actually appeared in the local newspaper, offering the local society impressive proof of Kiehn's political connections.

Kiehn's letters to Straßer were full of obsequious attempts to curry favor. Exhibiting the discourse style made popular by the Führer ideology even before 1933,[39] the correspondence between the two documents the effect of the Hitler myth even then — even on Straßer, whom researchers had long wrongly depicted as engaged in an intraparty rivalry with Hitler for the leadership of the Nazi Party.[40] For example, Kiehn told Straßer in 1932 of an 85-year-old aunt who was "one of those Hitler admirers of the kind that you could turn into ten more perfectly good Hitler fans." The aunt, who at that point possessed only a Hitler poster, positively "idolized" it and kept it safe "with a touching sort of care." She had "only one wish," Kiehn went on, to receive "an autographed picture of the Führer." "You ought to meet the good old lady sometime," Kiehn wrote to Straßer, attaching a few photographs of Hitler and enclosing return postage, "I ... would ask you on this one occasion to pass them [the photos] on to the Führer and request that he send the old woman ... a picture with his signature."[41]

On 12 May 1932, Straßer gave a keynote speech in the Reichstag on economic policy that for the first time in years contained a statement of the NSDAP platform and could be understood as signaling a certain willingness to cooperate with the right-wing middle-class parties and even with the SPD-affiliated umbrella association of German unions, the Allgemeiner Deutscher Gewerkschaftsbund (ADGB). In the speech, which Hitler had somewhat reluctantly agreed to, Straßer suggested the cultivation of swamps and wastelands and the construction of housing projects and roads as a means to combat unemployment. Many voters, in particular those from the middle class, were very receptive to these proposals. "Work creates capital!" and not the reverse, went Straßer's slogan, bringing him closer to a more demand-oriented model of managing the economic cycle. The speech received unprecedented media attention across the political spectrum.[42] The NSDAP published Straßer's statements, entitled "Emergency Economic Program" (*Wirtschaftliches Sofortprogramm*), as talking points for speeches in the campaign for the Reichstag elections of 31 July 1932. The lead paragraph described the program as a "unifying guiding principle for NSDAP speakers as well as for publications in the press. Any comments by party members that deviate from this material or contradict it shall be regarded as mere personal opinion."[43]

Fritz Kiehn also contributed to the popularity of Straßer's speech and sympathized with its content. Efka printed and mailed two thousand copies of the

Sofortprogramm at the factory's own expense. Naturally, Kiehn did not fail to pass on the details of this to Straßer; a brawl between the National Socialists and Communists in the Prussian parliament provided a welcome opportunity to send him a cheerful letter in which Kiehn enthused about the fray that had injured many of the members of parliament: "The cleanup of the Prussian parliament was marvelous. What a shame that I could not be there. — I hope to be there [when it happens] in the Reichstag. — I'd like to get right into [the fray] to my heart's content." Nor did Kiehn forget to invite his friend in the party, now a popular and important man, to come to Trossingen again: "Our garden is so beautiful right now, and so restful to visit. This would be a nice change for the two of you again and especially for you, dear Gregor; a couple of days of relaxation with us would not do you any harm." Kiehn added on a portentous conclusion: "In general, I feel as if we will soon be finished with the others and able to come to power! ... Please do come, so that we can speak freely once again."[44]

A few days later, a notice appeared in the *Trossinger Zeitung* on the occasion of Straßer's fortieth birthday, ostensibly from a reader, that powerfully recalled Straßer's political significance, describing him as "one of the most outstanding leaders" of the Nazi Party. The anonymous author, most likely Kiehn, predicted that "Straßer — one can say this already today — is ... destined to take a leading position in the 'Third Reich.'" Without question, wrote the author, he was "a natural leader in the truest sense of the word: full of vigor, calm deliberation, [and] the most selfless of action."[45]

Kiehn's impressive connections to representatives in national politics gave him a degree of political capital in his small town that is difficult to overestimate. Many Trossingen residents saw him as possessing a trump card that the much richer and more deeply rooted Hohner family did not. Never before had anyone in the secluded little town taken such a prominent political stance beyond the boundaries of the region. No Trossinger had ever served in the state parliament, much less in the Reichstag. So when Kiehn took up a seat in the Reichstag after the election of 31 July 1932, when the NSDAP had achieved such overwhelming success, he became a local sensation.

Kiehn was also admired because he had managed to bring prominent Nazi speakers to Trossingen. In the news reports of the Trossingen election campaigns and party rallies between 1930 and 1933, we do indeed find an unusual concentration of prominent Nazi speakers compared to other regions of its size. The local council election campaign of 1931, for example, included the speakers Wilhelm Frick, Gottfried Feder, and the Gauleiter of Westphalia and Hesse. As Kiehn noted, such "speakers are generally only deployed in large cities, and this is a special privilege for Trossingen." Compared with the usual sleepy election campaigns, conducted in line with the catchphrase that "politics does not belong in the town hall," the events then taking place with more than a thousand attendees exceeded any known dimensions. The sparse and weakly attended rallies of the other parties and their scattered advertisements, flyers, and newspaper articles looked markedly poor in contrast. None of the comparable activities they put on generated nearly half as many press reports and letters to the editor, nor did they present a single speaker whose fame transcended the region. The NSDAP knowingly politicized the local council election campaign with its unmistakable knack for effecting the voting public. Fritz Kiehn had a particular feel for it, whereas Ernst Hohner's Bürgerliche Vereinigung had the following pallid motto: "Far be it from us to tread in the realm of high politics. There will be no world history written in Trossingen."[46]

Kiehn's high-ranking connections brought Trossingen a touch of that very "world history" that the old guard so blatantly disregarded. "The presence of Dr. Goebbels is a special event for all voters, from the left to the right," was how the local newspaper announced the appearance of the well-known demagogue in 1932, who caused a downright sensation.[47] The effect of this event could only be outdone by the appearance of Adolf Hitler himself in nearby Schwenningen, again due solely to Kiehn's efforts. Hitler spoke to an audience of thirty-two thousand at a rally led by Fritz Kiehn, who had organized the party event and helped finance it.[48] "World history," as many of his contemporaries viewed it, had encroached on this province in southwest Germany. Fritz Kiehn, so it seemed, had connected the provincial town with high politics.

Notes

1. AVT, 27 May, 28 May, 31 May 1930, and 10 Dec. 1931; *Gränzbote*, 15 Sept. 1930; Schnabel, *Machtergreifung*, 312; Schnabel, "NSDAP."
2. StAT, B 78, GRP of 8 July 1932.
3. On voting patterns research, see Falter, *Hitlers Wähler*, 288, 303–314; Winkler, *Weimar*, 388–389; Brustein, *Logic*, 63–119. On local attempts to fight the crisis, see Berghoff, *Kleinstadt*, 420–431.
4. LKAS, Pfarrbericht (parish report) Trossingen 1929, pp. 5, 22. See also interview by Berghoff of 10 May 1993.
5. See Berghoff, *Kleinstadt*, 318–330, 345–352.
6. All citations in this paragraph are from AVT, 5 Dec. 1931 and 27 Sept. 1930; StAT, B 78, GRP of 3 Mar. 1932.
7. See StAT, B 78, GRP of 12 July and 22 Sept. 1932. All citations in this paragraph are from StAT, A 1238, pamphlet of the NSDAP Ortsgruppe; AVT, 23 Aug. 1930 and 23 Apr. and 29 July 1932.
8. See AVT, 27 May, 28 May, 31 May, 29 Nov., and 5 May 1930; Conradt-Mach, "*Arbeit*", 262, 272–277; StAS, Wü 65/37 Vol. 3 Bü 502, Police report for district of Tuttlingen (cit.).
9. AVT, 4 Dec. 1931.
10. AVT, 3 June and 25 Aug. 1930. On *Volksgemeinschaft* ideology, see Schoenbaum, *Revolution*, 76–107; for criticism, see Kershaw, *Opinion*, Part I, 373–375; Kershaw, *Hitler Myth*; Mallmann and Paul, *Herrschaft*, 114–163.

11. AVT, 29 July 1932.
12. See AVT, 23 Apr. 1932 (cit.); Schnabel, *Württemberg*, 110–122; Conradt-Mach, *Arbeit*, 16, 253–258; Schmidt-Bachem, *Papier*.
13. AVT, 22 Apr. 1932.
14. AVT, 23 Apr. 1932.
15. *Nationalsozialistische Volkszeitung*, 3 Dec. 1932.
16. BA DC, Akte Kiehn, Report on Kiehn from 14 Dec. 1938.
17. Turner, *Big Business*, 191–203, developed his thesis on the basis of the ironware industry in the Berg and Mark region. See also Broszat, "Struktur," 57. On Württemberg in detail, see Rauh-Kühne, "Die Unternehmer," 320–22; Rauh-Kühne, "Mittelständische Unternehmer"; Bräutigam, *Unternehmer*, 389.
18. A good graphical representation of election results can be found at http://de.wikipedia.org/wiki/Reichstagswahl_1930 (accessed 30 Jan. 2013).
19. In 1930 the two former liberal parties DDP and DVP merged and became the Deutsche Staatspartei.
20. See StAT, A 480, MS "Trossingens Kampf um die nat. soz. Idee" (1935); StAS, Wü 13, Akz. no. 6/0/1013, no. 2253 (G. Koch denazification records); *Gränzbote*, 1 Aug. 1934.
21. The print shop also manufactured boxes for cigarette papers. Interview with Herbert E. Kiehn of 19–20 May 1998.
22. BA NS, 22/1077, letter from Kiehn to G. Straßer of 24 Nov. 1931.
23. BA NS, 46/7, letter from Kiehn to Heß of 12 Sept. 1933. After the Nazis had seized power, Kiehn did make demands based on his earlier service to the party. His assertions in the summer of 1933 are credible because he had to know that the veracity of his statements to the party chancellery could be checked at any time. On the precarious financial situation before 1933 of the *NS Kurier* published by the Gauleitung in Stuttgart, see Schnabel, *Württemberg*, 352–354; Sauer, "Württemberg".
24. BA DC, Akte Kiehn, minutes from 7 Apr. 1936 of Kiehn's interrogation as part of the SS inquest opened against him.
25. BA DC, Akte Kiehn; letters from Kiehn to Heß of 12 Sept. and 29 Nov. 1933.
26. Letter from Herbert Kiehn of 15 Dec. 1933, courtesy of the Kiehn family.
27. Interview with Herbert E. Kiehn of 19–20 May 1998; letter from Herbert E. Kiehn to the authors of 15 June 1998.
28. Orlow, *History*, 269; Schnabel, Württemberg, 81–83.
29. For more on the Gauleitung nominations process, see Kiehn's statements at the SS hearing of 7 Apr. 1936 in Stuttgart, BA DC, Akte Kiehn.
30. On Frick, see Neliba, *Wilhelm Frick*; Schulz, "Wilhelm Frick"; Lilla, Döring, and Schulz, *Statisten*, 160–161.
31. Horn, *Führerideologie*, 359, 417 (cit.); Orlow, *History*, 266–67.
32. Selle, "Sinnlichkeit," 92. See Reichel, *Schein*.
33. Heiden, *Geschichte*, 226.
34. Berlin agent of the Gute Hoffnungshütte company, cited in Turner, *Großunternehmer*, 240.
35. Kissenkoetter, *Gregor Straßer*, 13–16, 100; Turner, *Großunternehmer*, 185–189, 317.
36. BA NS, 22/1077, letter from Kiehn to Straßer of 28 May 1932.
37. According to Konrad Heiden in 1932, who emphasized the impressive appearance of this "massive guardsman with the voice of a lion and the strength of a bear." Next to Straßer, wrote Heiden, "Hitler is a bundle of nerves." Quoted in Kissenkoetter, *Gregor Straßer*, 120. See also Stachura, *Gregor Strasser*, 84–106. See also Stachura, *Fall*, 88.
38. BA NS, 22/1077, letter from Kiehn to Straßer of 11 Nov. 1931.
39. For examples, see Kißener and Scholtyseck, *Führer*, as well as Heiber, *Reichsführer!*; Kershaw, *Hitler, 1889–1936*, 431–32; Kissenkoetter, *Gregor Straßer*, 192–94.
40. See Kissenkoetter, *Gregor Straßer*, 164–165; Kershaw, *Hitler*, 500.

41. BA NS, 22/1077, letter from Kiehn to Straßer of 28 May 1932. On the Hitler myth's effect on Straßer even after his resignation from politics in December 1932, see Orlow, *History,* 291. Kissenkoetter, *Gregor Straßer,* 176, writes of Straßer having a "paladin complex" about Hitler, following Karl Paetel.
42. Verhandlungen des Reichstags, 5th Wahlperiode 1930, Bd. 446, pp. 2510–2521. All Reichstag minutes can be found online at http://www.reichstagsprotokolle.de/index.html. See also Kissenkoetter, *Gregor Straßer,* 118–20.; Wörtz, "Programmatik," 172–182.
43. Quoted in Kissenkoetter, *Gregor Straßer,* 119.
44. BA NS, 22/1077, letter from Kiehn to Straßer of 28 May 1932. On the brawl in the state parliament, see Figge, "Opposition," 163–164.
45. AVT, 31 May 1932.
46. AVT, 2 Dec. and 28 Nov. 1931.
47. On Goebbels, see Longerich, *Goebbels*; Thacker, *Joseph Goebbels*.
48. AVT, 21 Oct. 1932. On Hitler in Schwenningen, see BA DC, Akte Kiehn, and diary entry of 23 Oct. 1932; Goebbels, *Tagebücher,* part 1, *Aufzeichnungen 1923–1941,* vol. 2/3, 42–43; "Nationalsozialismus, Holocaust, Widerstand und Exil 1933–1945," online database, De Gruyter, document ID: TJG-2331.

Chapter 3

Between *Gleichschaltung* and the Party Purge of 1934
Fritz Kiehn Becomes "Leader of the Württemberg Economy"

Once the National Socialists had taken control of the government, Kiehn's dedication to the Hitler movement paid off quickly. Even though he had no experience with industrial associations and was somewhat of an unknown quantity to most Württemberg industrialists, he soon had plenty of positions at his command and could present himself to the public as the "leader of the entire southern German economy." Berta Kiehn was appointed Tuttlingen district leader of the Nationalsozialistische Frauenschaft (National Socialist Women's League, or NSF) in 1934, and it is obvious that she too gleaned social benefits from the turn in the political tide.

As a Nazi representative in the Reichstag, Fritz Kiehn was made Kreisinspektor (district inspector) in early May of 1933 as part of the *Gleichschaltung* process, the effort to bring society and the nation into line with National Socialist policy. He was responsible for ensuring that no "politically unreliable" civil servants or municipal officials were allowed into the party and that those with undesirable politics were excluded from public service.[1] Just fourteen days later, on orders from Reich commissioner for the economy Otto Wagener and Deutsche Arbeitsfront (German Labor Front, or DAF) leader Robert Ley, Kiehn was promoted to Bezirksleiter der Wirtschaft (district leader for the economy) for the territory covered by the southwest German labor exchange.[2] There were thirteen district economic leaders in total, who were to take sole charge of "economic peace and development" in their territories, set tariffs, avoid labor unrest, and supervise workplace safety as well as labor law. As the *Nationalsozialistische Volkszeitung* put it, Kiehn's responsibility as "our party colleague" was to "prevent economic sabotage by any means necessary."[3] Shortly thereafter, Kiehn also became president of the Industrie- und Handelskammer (Chamber of Industry

---

Notes from this chapter begin on page 67.

and Commerce, or IHK) of Rottweil and took over the chair of the Verband Württembergischer Industrieller (Association of Württemberg Industrialists), the latter of which was soon incorporated into the Reichsstand der Deutschen Industrie (Reich Estate of German Industry, or RStDI). In the spring of 1934, Kiehn was finally "summoned to Stuttgart," as he put it, to take over the presidency of both the important Stuttgart Chamber of Industry and Commerce and the Württembergischer Industrie- und Handelstag (WIHT) and bring each into line with the Nazi *Führerprinzip*, or "leader principle." Kiehn, who continued to chair the Rottweil IHK as well, owed this accumulation of offices to his good contacts in the party administration in Stuttgart, especially to Reichsstatthalter and Gauleiter Wilhelm Murr.[4] Kiehn took over his new position in Stuttgart from Dr. Gustav Kilpper, CEO of the Deutsche Verlags-Anstalt publishing house, who was highly regarded in industrial circles. Kilpper, a staunch Democrat, was considered a political undesirable in the Nazi state.[5] To top it all off, in 1934 Kiehn was made director of the Württemberg-Hohenzollern Economic Chamber (Wirtschaftskammer für Württemberg-Hohenzollern), which began work in 1936. This institution was to control the economy and was managed by the Stuttgart IHK. The IHK president therefore automatically also became chair of the Economic Chamber, although by this time Kiehn had become a controversial figure even in the NSDAP.[6] Finally, Kiehn also belonged to the International Chamber of Commerce (Internationale Handelskammer) from 1936 to 1943, a position that often took him to France.[7]

Fig. 13: "President" Fritz Kiehn, MdR (**Reichstag delegate**), 1937. (Archiv der sozialen Demokratie der Friedrich-Ebert-Stiftung, Bonn, Erler Papers)

In a few years of National Socialist rule, the small-town manufacturer had risen to become the "leader of the Württemberg economy," a title he proudly had others spread in celebration of his fiftieth birthday.[8] The NSDAP ascent to power had partially revolutionized Württemberg society, as the cases of other Nazi functionaries in Württemberg also make clear.[9] The Württemberg *Ehrbarkeit*, described by Michael Ruck as a "highly interconnected class from whose ranks most civil servants, pastors, teachers, doctors, and professionals and businessmen of the duchy had been recruited for centuries," was extraordinarily homogeneous by tradition. When newly created, prestigious offices were filled by men from the radicalized lower middle class in 1933, it shook the *Ehrbarkeit* system more deeply than had previously been recognized. The pronounced continuity of the traditional civil service had long overshadowed the phenomenon of social ascent achieved through the National Socialist "revolution."[10]

In Kiehn's own subjective view, his rapid political ascent had admittedly been anything but smooth, and his position — overshadowed by various scandals — would always remain precarious. Even after his election to the Reichstag in the fall of 1932, it seemed as if his foray into high politics would be very brief. The new Reichstag had scarcely been constituted when it was dissolved again on 12 September, with new elections imminent on 6 November 1932. The outcome did not bode well for the NSDAP: ever since Reich president Paul von Hindenburg had turned down Hitler's request on 13 August to be appointed chancellor, morale among NSDAP members had been "greatly depressed" — particularly in the Reichstag faction, where increasing numbers of delegates feared losing their parliamentary expense accounts and therefore questioned Hitler's strategy of all-or-nothing politics. Relying instead on a takeover by stealth, they intended for the NSDAP to take part in a coalition government created by former chancellor Heinrich Brüning or military representative General Kurt von Schleicher. Once again it was Gregor Straßer, the NSDAP Reichsorganisationsleiter, contemplating innovative methods; he aired the plan publicly and sought to attract Hitler to a change in strategy. At that time, in the fall of 1932, the average NSDAP member considered Straßer a man "of practical politics who carried out the tough everyday work, whereas legendary Führer Adolf Hitler pointed out the grand goals and means of the German national revival."[11]

As Straßer and others had feared, the NSDAP lost a good two million votes in the Reichstag election of 6 November 1932 as compared to the previous election in July of that same year. It was patently clear that the Reichsorganisationsleiter's original strategy to compromise with other political powers had been the right one. What's more, the party's financial worries were growing ever larger after the electoral defeat. The number of NSDAP members in the Reichstag had fallen from 230 to 196, and the Nazi delegates from Württemberg, where losses had been well above the average, now numbered five rather than seven, including Fritz Kiehn.[12] During this time of internal crisis in the NSDAP, he allegedly spoke out to say that "now was the time ... to prepare the ground for a Straßer chancellorship." Hitler was "out of the question" for "such an important office," since "he was ... only good for drumming up propaganda."[13] Although the authenticity of this statement is far from clear, Kiehn — like many of his NSDAP colleagues in the Reichstag — would likely have advocated Straßer's coalition strategy. "Many party comrades wanted to finally be able to work actively, too; they wanted state-level posts with influence, high standing, and security. Why else would they have worked in the party for years and years!" Estimates from contemporaries indicate that of the 196 Nazi delegates, 60 to 100 were prepared to go over to Straßer in the case of an overt split. His followers and confidants included precisely those prominent politicians whom Kiehn had brought to Trossingen. Foremost among them was Wilhelm Frick, the NSDAP party whip in the Reichstag; he too had used his influence until the bitter end to encourage Hitler to come around on the coalition strategy.[14]

If Kiehn and his fellow party members, like some sections of the public, had hoped that Straßer would engage in a public power struggle with Hitler and that the Reichsorganisationsleiter would be determined to take all of the power for himself, they were in for a disappointment: "Gregor Straßer did not wish to give any sign of a power struggle within the NSDAP, nor to establish any anti-Hitler opposition." When Hitler held fast to his intransigent policy in late 1932, despite the internal party crisis and numerous regional electoral defeats, Straßer resigned. On 8 December, he wrote a letter of resignation to Hitler in which he declared that he would withdraw "without personal resentment toward the ranks of ordinary party comrades." He had always been a National Socialist, he wrote, and would always remain one.[15] Straßer and his family then repaired to South Tyrol on vacation, while Hitler assembled the NSDAP faction in the Reichstag around him that very night to counter the trend toward a split in the party. "After Frick had cleared himself of the suspicion that 'he and other members of the faction had denied allegiance to the Führer' by vowing 'unwavering loyalty to the Führer and creator of the movement,'" Hitler settled the score with Straßer in a speech, following which "each individual member of the faction" then needed "to swear an oath of loyalty ... to the Führer personally."[16]

It can no longer be established whether Kiehn witnessed this event. At any rate, he initially saw no reason to turn his back on his friend Straßer, who stayed with Kiehn in Trossingen, as he so often did, on his return journey from Italy to Berlin. From there, he presumably went on to Freudenstadt in the Black Forest to meet with one of his earlier negotiating partners, former German chancellor and chair of the Center Party (Zentrum) Heinrich Brüning, to discuss politics.[17] If a report submitted to Reichsführer-SS Heinrich Himmler in 1940 is to be believed, Gauleiter Murr was behind Straßer's conspiratorial meetings in Trossingen.[18] Whatever Murr's role may have been in the Straßer affair, what we know for certain is that the NSDAP was seething with the knowledge that Straßer's followers and other unsatisfied party members throughout the Reich were forming so-called *Notgemeinschaften* (emergency associations) and that offshoots of this unrest had evidently stretched as far as Württemberg. Reports from the left-wing press about an NSDAP Kreisleiter conference in Stuttgart in mid-December 1932 described a "great rift in the Nazi camp."[19] It also appears as if Trossingen was not the only place where tensions between various party organizations overlapped with personal rivalries and the conflict over whether Straßer or Hitler would lead. This likely contributed to the abiding friction between the SA — with Minister-President Christian Mergenthaler as its honorary leader — and the SS — the honorary leader of which was Mergenthaler's archrival, Gauleiter Murr.[20]

In the meantime, the NSDAP national leadership had managed to halt the series of electoral defeats by unleashing an enormous propaganda contingent for the election on 16 January 1933 in the small state of Lippe. This stabilized Hitler's position within the party for the moment, and he was able to purge the party of the remaining Straßer supporters. Hitler's appointment as chancellor on 30 January 1933 (a complete surprise to the party base) wholly undermined any intraparty opposition. Even though Straßer, at the center of the unrest, reaffirmed his intent to stay out of politics, the struggle against real and supposed dissidents typical of totalitarian movements intensified, fostered by the rivalries among the various party organizations and associations.[21]

Fritz Kiehn was caught up in this purge too, which threatened to push him into a political no-man's-land at precisely the moment that his years of commitment to the NSDAP promised to pay off. On 10 January 1933, the differences of opinion between the Trossingen party management and the local SA leadership were enough to subject Kiehn to an investigation of his performance as NSDAP Ortsgruppenleiter before the Untersuchungs- und Schlichtungsausschuß (Committee for Investigation and Settlement, or Uschla), an internal NSDAP tribunal system. He was accused of "damaging the party" by "attempting to create a Straßer group."[22] As Kiehn later recalled, a party judge spent eight to fourteen days on discovery proceedings in Trossingen, calling between forty and fifty witnesses. Kiehn was also forced to resign his post as Ortsgruppenleiter until the investigation was called off in August 1933. Although the highest level of the Uschla system ordered "all SA leaders involved ... to henceforth cease all hostilities against Pg. [*Parteigenosse,* party comrade] Kiehn," Kiehn found that his ambitions continued to be stymied by harassment from party headquarters in Munich and around Trossingen.

Having forfeited important contacts to party leaders as a result of Straßer's unforeseeable departure, Kiehn tried to glom on to his old friend Frick, now Reich minister of the interior. Frick, who himself had warmed to Straßer's rapprochement strategy the previous year, received a letter from Kiehn thanking him for his "most decent conduct toward me always." Kiehn now beseeched Frick, much in the style of his earlier entreaties to his friend Straßer, to give him permission to put the minister's portrait, immortalized on a postcard, in "a place of honor in the SS action squad office in Trossingen, as well as in my office and my home." With the "utmost politeness and courtesy," Kiehn requested that Frick send him "three cards with your signature" in "the enclosed stamped envelope." A few weeks later, Kiehn sent Frick a cheerful thank-you note: "You could not have given me any greater pleasure than by sending back your picture; the nicest of you, by the way, that I have ever set eyes on." At another time, he conveyed to the Reich interior minister his "concerns about the leadership of the German economy in the National Socialist sense" — concerns he shared with "infinitely many good, old National Socialists." In a very subservient manner, using highly stilted language, he assured Frick that "if I send these few lines to you in unconditional faith and confidence, then I do it out of a sense of duty to the Führer and our movement, for Germany's sake."[23]

Kiehn turned to Frick yet again to prevent further misinterpretations of his position within the party. Otto Wagener, who was already head of the economic policy division under Straßer, had withstood the initial staff turnover in the party administration unscathed — probably because alternative, economically literate candidates were hard to come by. On 15 April 1933, he was appointed commissar of the Reichsverband der Deutschen Industrie (Federation of German Industry) by the Reich economics minister. A few weeks later, he had made arrangements to implement his own policy, which was shaped by ideas of the corporative state (*Ständestaat*). To this end, he appointed five Reich commissars for the economy, including Fritz Kiehn for the state of Württemberg. Kiehn consequently informed Frick that he had "taken up the office that had landed in my lap as a matter of course, in order to prevent anything worse from happening." The idea of again being tied to a former Straßer confidant must have made Kiehn highly uneasy. So he immediately distanced himself from the "strange figure of comrade Dr. Wagener," warning that "the Führer is certain to fail with this man, and the German economy will ... be maneuvered into a chaotic condition by a fantasist, which, in the end, must cause our entire movement to collapse."[24]

But despite these reassurances at the expense of erstwhile Straßer followers and the abandonment of the party tribunal proceedings against him, Kiehn nonetheless had to contend with people in the party chancellery taking a negative view of his business and political ambitions. A visit to the Reich interior minister confirmed Kiehn's suspicions that he continued to be regarded in Hitler's milieu as a "suspected Straßerite." "The most dreadful thing to me is that even the Führer takes this view," Kiehn complained to Frick. Eager to take over printing the Trossingen newspaper, he lamented, "I do not ... deserve this."

Hence, it was extremely doubtful that Kiehn would again be nominated as a candidate for the Reichstag on the NSDAP one-party list in the national referendum of 12 November 1933. He vented his feelings in various letters to Frick "in confidence and in the full knowledge that you, honorable minister, that you are the only person in the world who can make the Führer hear my voice." Kiehn reaffirmed "the wrong that has been done to me," asking Frick whether the Führer would really want "old, deserving party comrades, who never got anything out of the movement and indeed have only ever contributed to it, to be knowingly thrown under the bus?" "Re: my candidacy," Kiehn informed the minister that "this question allows me no rest, because my loss of face here, throughout Württemberg and beyond, among all my party comrades and in the entire professional world, would be unbearable."[25]

Such an overestimation of both his reputation and his economic importance was typical of how Kiehn perceived himself. Like a political celebrity he enjoyed having his photograph taken to demonstrate his social aspirations and would distribute copies of his likeness afterward in great numbers. His New Year's cards included a photo of him adopting the upper-class habitus, posed at his desk with cigar, fountain pen, and spectacles in hand, his impassioned motto printed in black letters behind him: "Stand tall or crumble!" (fig. 14). The saying seemed grand. It referred to Ernst Jünger's "struggle as inner experience" and advocated the heroism of the will.[26] The pictured open folio signaled important activity. Kiehn sent out so many of these cards that he was unable to sign all of them

Fig. 14: Self-dramatization: Kiehn's New Year's card from 1938–1939. (Bundesarchiv Berlin)

himself. He delegated some of the work to his brothers, who effortlessly imitated his handwriting.

Despite Kiehn's overestimation of his own importance, the smug, obsequious, occasionally maudlin, and often even scheming tone he took when dealing with heads of the new state did achieve the goal he sought. Frick apparently decided in 1933 that Kiehn's complaints were justified and seems to have secured him the audience with Hitler that Kiehn had been hoping for. At any rate, Kiehn asserted as much in the SS investigational proceedings against him in 1936, when another attempt was made to invoke his Straßer connection: "Back then ... I was summoned one Sunday afternoon in Weimar to personally appear before the Führer, and at that time — after the Führer had read several letters from me in my presence and had personally interrogated me, and I had been made to reaffirm with a handshake that I had been and would always be loyal to him — he cleared my name and put me back on the list of his [Reichstag] delegates." Kiehn in fact kept his Reichstag seat until 1945, even though he was caught up in several other controversies and intraparty disputes in the interim and frequently had cause to give further self-justifications and vows of loyalty.[27]

Kiehn seems not to have met with Gregor Straßer privately again after the end of 1932, although his adversaries and antagonists within the party would return to the old accusations again and again to turn party or government authorities against him. As Straßer's correspondence with the party chancellery shows, he was completely cast out by party leadership and placed under tight surveillance after he returned to the Reich capital. Spring 1934 brought the arrest of one of his former confidants, "one of the few people he still had some private contact with." Straßer then appealed to Rudolf Heß on 18 June 1934 in the form of a five-page letter. The pathos of this communication resembles Kiehn's correspondence: Straßer affirmed that he had not returned to politics since he had withdrawn from the party leadership and that he did not wish to in the future. He submissively begged the "deputy Führer" to give him information about "what, in the party's view, I should do to make my fully implemented abstinence from politics abundantly clear to the outside world, as provided in my various statements." Straßer recalled his ten years of "selfless and committed work in building the party" and begged Heß for "support" to help him "disappear from any debates and above all to remove the feeling — indescribably hurtful and humiliating to me — that [I have] a hostile attitude toward the party." The letter ended with a request for "understanding of my situation, which I can hardly bear any longer."[28] Written a few days before Straßer was murdered on Hitler's orders, his despairing letter illuminates the psychologically destructive forms of contact that the Nazi leadership cultivated toward supposed party apostates once Adolf Hitler was in power as Führer and chancellor of the Reich. In a situation that was critical for the party and its leader, Straßer had sown doubt about Hitler's political infallibility, a sin for which there was no absolution.

Kiehn had grasped this even before Straßer was killed. In October 1933, he pledged to Frick that he had only met once with Straßer since 5 March 1933, the date of the last election in which Kiehn had won a Reichstag seat. Kiehn declared that he had met with Straßer, who was then chair of the Verband der Heilmittelindustrie (Healthcare Industry Association), only once since December 1932 in Tuttlingen "in my official capacity as regional president of the Reichsstand der deutschen Industrie" in the presence of three of the industrialists concerned and in the interest of the troubled Tuttlingen surgical instruments industry. The negotiations lasted fifteen minutes; Kiehn attested that he had witnesses "to every word." Reaffirming his "unwavering loyalty to the Führer," he distanced himself from his former party colleague: "In closing, I ask you to please stop suspecting me of being a Straßerite. — I have faced enough unjust punishment for Straßer's stop at my home on his way back from Italy after resigning his office. — Had I known what consequences could arise from this for me, I would have asked him to take his leave."[29]

When Kiehn was again confronted with the old accusation two years after Gregor Straßer's alleged suicide, however, he was more open about acknowledging his murdered comrade: "There was a time," he explained, "when I was genuinely envied for my friendships with Gregor Straßer and many other men who are leaders today. Gregor Straßer and his family were very close friends of my family and myself." He added with regret that "after Straßer's unfortunate falling-out with the Führer and the movement," Kiehn had "obviously separated" himself from Straßer "as any serious, reputable soldier of the Führer would have done."[30]

This confession was directed to an SS officer at the district headquarters in Stuttgart. Kiehn may have been relying on the Württemberg SS (some of whom had supported Straßer in those days) to muster up some understanding for his past. Yet perhaps he had also found out through Else Straßer that those close to the head of the SS believed their former comradeship with Straßer obligated them to his surviving family members. Since spring 1936 Else, Straßer's widow, had been given a monthly allowance of RM 500 from Himmler's funds for her own maintenance and that of her two underage sons.[31]

Kiehn also enjoyed the support of Himmler's elitist protection squad, the SS. He had joined the General SS (Allgemeine SS, the noncombat branch) in spring 1933, when the Uschla investigation made it appear that his conflicts with the local SA leadership could erode his position in Trossingen. During the initial months of National Socialist rule, the SS's expansion from a small paramilitary unit that served as Hitler's personal protection squad into a major Nazi organization generated "constant friction" in many parts of the Reich, especially with the SA. Trossingen was not excepted from these internal conflicts. Pastors in Trossingen declared after 1945 that "even before 1933 and again then, a deep division arose between the SA and the SS. Fritz Kiehn himself took to the SS."[32]

SA accusations against Kiehn in his capacity as NSDAP Ortsgruppenleiter of Trossingen may have played a role in this. The SS in this era was already regarded as an instrument of Hitler's absolute will as Führer. As a politically beleaguered factory owner, Kiehn may have calculated that joining its ranks could be considered a further declaration of loyalty to Hitler. The fact that an SS troop of one hundred men was about to be posted to Trossingen could also have played a role. Kiehn needed to attain influence and high standing in a timely fashion; after all, his business interests were at stake. Kiehn's commitment to the SS involved an astounding level of activism. He reported that by the time the war began, he had spoken at "every [instructional] course at the SS Führerschule in Dachau." The "cult of performance" within the SS, and the group's image as an elitist order, certainly suited Kiehn's identity as a self-made man.[33]

Whatever his individual motives for joining the SS may have been, by the fall of 1933 Kiehn was a senior SS leader (analogous to a captain in the military) with an aide-de-camp of his own.[34] By the summer of 1934, the "leader of the Württemberg economy" was likely to have considered his connections to the SS (which by then were well established) as a valuable life insurance policy against the then-escalating fear of an SA coup.

SA group leader (Gruppenführer) Hermann Mattheiß was the second of Kiehn's acquaintances, after Straßer, to fall victim to the crazed purges within the party. The circuit judge, who had come from lower-middle-class origins, had become the first local leader of the Nazi Party in the small town of Oberndorf, not far from Trossingen. The seizure of power had allowed him to rise from his temporary position, as junior commissioner (Unterkommissar) in various administrative units in Südwürttemberg, to SA-Sonderkommissar zur besonderen Verwendung (SA special commissioner for special assignments) in the Württemberg Ministry of the Interior, and finally to president of the state political police. Spurred on by his zeal for persecution, Mattheiß had made sure "that Württemberg had the highest number of paid auxiliary policemen in the Reich and, comparatively, the highest number of [prisoners in so-called protective custody], even though, as Finance Minister Dehlinger complained, there was really no bastion of Marxists in the 'little state.'"[35] The brutal SA leader had repeatedly expressed his concern "that the power of National Socialism was under threat of being watered down." No small amount of his hate was directed toward the conservative elites, against whom he repeatedly organized sensational attacks. One particularly scandalous incident during the election of 12 November 1933 is likely to have identified Mattheiß to Nazi higher-ups as part of an SA problem that was already worrying those around Hitler at the time and would ultimately lead the SS to appear on the scene: Mattheiß orchestrated an SA mob in Stuttgart against Duke Philipp Albrecht[36] (who had stayed away from the elections) and ultimately took the aristocrat into "protective custody."[37] Secret surveillance of SA activities started in January 1934 on Hitler's orders, which would have put

Mattheiß right in the crosshairs of investigations by the Gestapo, the SS, and the SS's secret service, the SD (Sicherheitsdienst).[38]

In the months that followed, numerous complaints piled up about Mattheiß's high-handed actions disregarding the state's bureaucratic authority, not to mention the SS and the SD. Consequently, the dossier on him in the Württemberg Ministry of the Interior grew to a considerable size. In early May 1934, Reichsstatthalter Murr finally suspended Mattheiß from his position as head of the political police in Württemberg. An arrest warrant for Mattheiß, on the other hand, was kept under lock and key and "resolved" when Mattheiß was killed.[39] Mattheiß's suspension had previously puzzled scholars. It was also unclear who had ordered his execution. Various parties alleged after 1945 that the kill order had come from Reinhard Heydrich or from Himmler, but these suspicions could not be proven.[40] According to one statement from Mattheiß's widow filed as part of Berta Kiehn's denazification proceedings, Hermann Mattheiß had "grave differences with Reichsführer-SS Himmler … about the exercise of his [Mattheiß's] office," a conflict that is reflected in the ministerial records as well and seems to have induced Mattheiß to resign from the SS.[41] The new finding, however, is that Mattheiß appears to have challenged the Reichsführer-SS "to a duel because of the offense done to him," a challenge that, according to his widow's description, entailed his immediate suspension from office.[42]

While Mattheiß then took an involuntary vacation at Lake Constance, SD and Gestapo forces in the Reich worked "at full speed to circulate alarming news about the supposed threat of an SA revolt." The regional SD administrative bodies worked on naming the people who were to be eliminated given the right opportunity. By all appearances, it was Heydrich's deputy, Werner Best, who put Mattheiß on the kill list at the SD Southwest Regional Headquarters (Oberabschnitt Südwest).[43] The rumors of an ostensibly imminent SA coup spread quickly, reaching Württemberg by late June 1934. An SA march in Stuttgart on 30 June that had been scheduled for months was apparently perceived as the start of the anticipated SA revolt. A warrant of arrest was issued for the highest SA leader in Württemberg, Oberführer Hermann Berchtold. The SS mobilized in and around Trossingen to fend off a supposedly imminent SA attack on the Mauser building, a weapons factory in Oberndorf.[44] Finally, Mattheiß too was arrested on some pretext at his parents' house in Überlingen on the evening of 30 June 1934, by orders of the head of the SS Southwest Regional Headquarters. Among his persecutors was Otto Glück, the head of the Württemberg SD. According to statements his mother later made, Mattheiß considered Glück his "greatest enemy" and felt extremely threatened as soon as he realized that Glück was one of the SS leaders.[45] After his arrest, Mattheiß was taken to the SS barracks in Ellwangen. He was executed by firing squad that same Night of the Long Knives; many of those he persecuted must have breathed a sigh of relief. One such victim was Reinhold Maier, the minister-president of Württemberg-Baden after

1945. Mattheiß had gone after him with spiteful perseverance for political disagreements. In his memoirs, Maier describes how he found out about Mattheiß's death: at the start of the week following 30 June, a taxi driver called on him in his chancellery "in the strictest confidence" and said: "They burned your enemy this morning, at 4 a.m., in the crematorium at the Pragfriedhof [Prague Cemetery]. I drove the corpse to Stuttgart in my car last night."[46]

Very likely it was Himmler himself who gave the order for Mattheiß's execution. He had been in charge of the Württemberg political police since December 1933, and therefore would have wished to get the insubordinate police president out of his way.[47] Hitler had personally sanctioned this "liquidation" as "state defense" by including Mattheiß on the "quasi-official list of those who perished from 30 June to 2 July 1934."[48]

Allegations that Mattheiß's execution was somehow related to him supposedly being a former Straßerite are baseless. In the postwar era, Mattheiß's widow portrayed her husband, who had been largely responsible for terrorizing and persecuting political enemies of the NSDAP in Württemberg, as a "victim of National Socialism." This depiction has been rightly characterized as "deriding" those who fell victim to Mattheiß's zeal for persecution in the early period of Nazi rule.[49] Since Lolo Mattheiß must have had difficulty proving the oppositional stance to the party she imputed to her husband, she likely found his acquaintance to Fritz Kiehn — the "Straßerite" — very advantageous after the collapse of the Third Reich. In any case, she was willing to make the following sworn statement at Berta Kiehn's denazification proceedings: "My husband, like Mr. and Mrs. Kiehn, supported Gregor Straßer's direction for the party, and as such was completely opposed to Himmler's dictatorship and system of violence." With this sort of "exoneration testimony," Straßer's widow was able to take advantage of the Kiehns and burnish her own image as a "victim" of fascism at the same time, although she therefore did not contribute to clarifying the circumstances of Hermann Mattheiß's violent end. Neither did Mattheiß's supposedly close friend Fritz Kiehn, who at his own trial in 1948 likewise alleged that Mattheiß died for his allegiance to Straßer.

Kiehn's role in Mattheiß's capture, and the purge in which the Nazi regime executed more than one hundred people for political reasons,[50] was anything but unambiguous; it is difficult to shed light on his involvement because the surviving records are incomplete. Kiehn himself later alleged — consistent with statements from Mattheiß's widow — that he had "hidden" the couple in his home in Nußdorf for fourteen days.[51] Kiehn also claimed to have had a telephone conversation on 29 June 1934 with "Dr. Mattheiß, with whom he had grown very friendly, in which [Kiehn] encouraged him to flee." Kiehn alleged that he went on the run himself on 29 June 1934, hiding in the woods until the morning of 1 July 1934. By his account, Kiehn too would have been "arrested and probably shot" on 30 June 1934, had he not managed to avoid arrest by going on the run.[52] Kiehn called his gamekeeper as a witness, who swore under oath that the industrialist had taken refuge with him in the Tuningen forest during the time in question.[53] Various interviews with Kiehn's contemporaries in later decades have confirmed either this version or one in which the Trossingen manufacturer narrowly escaped the danger that threatened him "as a left-wing party official" during that time in 1934. It has been reported in Trossingen that Kiehn's name appeared on a list in the run-up to the wave of killings, but that he hid for "eight to fourteen days" and had "already been given amnesty" by the time he resurfaced.[54]

But Kiehn's portrayal of himself, as the thwarted rescuer of his allegedly close friend and as a potential victim of political assassination, was contested from the beginning. Most notably, Mattheiß's parents did not view Kiehn after the fact as a sworn supporter of their son but as complicit in his violent death. After the war, they initiated preliminary judicial proceedings against Kiehn as an accessory to murder. Mattheiß's mother testified in court that her son in June 1934 had been in Überlingen at his parents' house before his arrest and categorically had not stayed in Nußdorf. According to her, he had intended to abscond to Switzerland on 30 June 1934 after learning that a warrant had been issued for the arrest of SA senior leader Berchtold. There were also apparently already rumors by 30 June that the SS was demolishing SA facilities. But a call from Kiehn then dissuaded Mattheiß from his plan to flee, playing right into the hands of his SS pursuers.[55] Even if this accusation seems fabricated as well, it is supported by a string of witness statements.

In 1948, the SS leader from the SS Southwest Regional Headquarters who had been assigned to arrest Mattheiß stated that he and the SS men who accompanied him had headed to Nußdorf first, on orders from his superiors. He described how they had gone to the villa of presumed "head party official" (Parteiamtsleiter) Kiehn and asked for Mattheiß on orders from Hans-Adolf Prützmann, leader of the SS Southwest Regional Headquarters. When they were told by an occupant of the house (Otto Kiehn, whom they initially mistook for his brother Fritz) that Mattheiß was staying in Überlingen, they left him alone. The SS leaders made no move to search the house or make an arrest: "We had no orders to do so, and what's more, we trusted Kiehn in his capacity as party leader," one of the participants later explained.[56]

This accords with the recollections of a former member of the SS Motor brigade (Motorsturm) in Trossingen, who in 1993 reported on a "commando company" that his SS superiors had transferred to him during the Night of the Long Knives. He was assigned to take Kiehn's SS uniform to Stuttgart in the sidecar of his motorcycle. Kiehn put on the uniform and then briefly went into hiding.[57] There is also a report from Kiehn's grandson that his grandfather harbored no great affection for "'old fighters' who had rendered outstanding service in aiding the National Socialist seizure of power" and that many of his remarks later in life indicate that he was embarrassed by the "hooliganism" that the SA personified during the "time of struggle."[58]

These statements raise doubts about Kiehn's almost-victimhood and ostensibly protective role concerning his "friend," and the strict denazification proceedings that the French military government brought against Kiehn in 1949 produced more witnesses who called his version into question. Right away, two witnesses — including Kiehn's brother-in-law Christian Messner — indicated that the morning after the "Röhm purge,"[59] Fritz Kiehn had been on the phone both with the Gestapo in Oberndorf and party offices in Stuttgart. Messner testified that Otto Kiehn, whom he had visited in Nußdorf with his wife on Sunday, 1 July, had spoken with Fritz Kiehn by telephone at the insistence of Mattheiß's anxious father, who knew his son had been arrested the night before and wanted to know what had happened to him. Fritz Kiehn called Otto back only forty-five minutes later with the news that Hermann Mattheiß was dead.[60]

The unavoidable (though unprovable) conclusion was stated in 1949 by a former SA leader in Trossingen, who himself had ended up in the crosshairs of the Gestapo in connection with the politically motivated mass murder of 30 June 1934. He declared to the French military government: "I had the feeling that Fritz Kiehn was the SS informer in the Röhm purge affair and that he turned in his SA comrades, because otherwise Kiehn would never have survived. It appeared that they looked for Kiehn but didn't find him, and once Röhm's SA leaders and supporters had been murdered, Kiehn popped up again scot-free, and he even became an SS Sturmführer." However, this witness stated his relationship to Kiehn as having "never been on good terms, since he [Kiehn] was closer to the SS than the SA. On his orders, I was temporarily arrested in Oberndorf in 1934 [on the Night of the Long Knives] by Gestapo officers S. and F., and would surely have been shot had I not spoken with Fritz Kiehn by telephone in the presence of the Gestapo officials." The witness, a forester, had just evaded arrest again; ultimately, he was prosecuted for illegal weapons possession and sentenced to prison. He was excluded from the Nazi Party and the SA as part of the first large-scale purge of the giant paramilitary organization, whose membership numbers exceeded those of the party organization by 1934. The reprimanded forester was also forced to give up his career.[61]

Kiehn the industrialist faced no such repercussions when he put an end to his forest sojourn on the afternoon of 1 July. This, coupled with the abrupt sacrifice of his hiding place at a time when the true targets of the purge were not "out of the woods" in any sense of the word,[62] supports the idea that Kiehn's precautionary measures pertained to a different scenario than the one he wanted others to believe after 1945. If he really had felt that he was in danger during those summer days in 1934, and because of this had withdrawn to his hunting grounds dressed in his SS uniform, it was likely because he had heard rumors of a planned revolt by the SA. After all, we know from Kiehn himself that he was an SS leader and that he knew of the deep division between the SA and the SS. The attacks that the Uschla investigation had exposed him to the previous year had also come from the SA. An SA coup, then, would have represented a highly worrisome prospect for Kiehn.

He left his hiding place as soon as it became apparent that the Gauleitung, backed by the Gestapo and the SS, was in control. It must have been an unpleasant surprise for Kiehn that Gregor Straßer, once his close political ally, was among the dead in this orgy of killing. Yet after 1945 it proved to be a stroke of luck. There is no way to know whether Kiehn grieved over Mattheiß, whether their friendship was already well in the past, or whether it ever existed at all.[63] Nor can we determine the extent of Kiehn's personal involvement, if any, in the arrests of Mattheiß and other local SA leaders. The idea that he deliberately intended to deliver Mattheiß to his death would presuppose that Kiehn was in on the murderous plans of the party administration and SS leadership. But this seems unlikely; he was of minor rank in the SS, and his position in the party was too insignificant. Yet his top-tier connections could still have ensured that he heard the news — circulating in the capital since 25 June — that an SA revolt was supposedly imminent. Kiehn himself repeatedly declared later that he had been informed of the looming trouble while in Berlin — perhaps by his hunting companion SS leader Kurt Daluege, who was on familiar terms with Himmler and played a key role in the Night of the Long Knives.[64] But Kiehn could hardly have been given specifics about the planned SS "counteraction" and its designated victims. Thus, the public prosecutor in Ellwangen also came to the conclusion after the war that there was no way to prove Kiehn had been involved in Mattheiß's murder at all, and he abandoned the proceedings at the end of 1950. In court and in public, Kiehn's reputation as a former Straßer supporter worked to his advantage, creating instant credence for his role as almost-victim — all the more so when Kiehn was able to plausibly claim that Mattheiß had been a Straßerite as well.[65]

Four days after he resurfaced in Trossingen, Kiehn approached the local newspaper with a public "Warning to Rumormongers" that was a posthumous stab in the back to his supposed friends. The notice warned against dragging "particular leading National Socialists" through the mud as if they stood "on the same low level as those 'Also-Nazis' who did not escape their rightful punishment from the Führer." In the propaganda campaign that preceded the vote on 19 August 1934 to unite the offices of chancellor and president of the Reich, Kiehn took on the task of describing "the motivations and the sequence of events" of the "Röhm revolt" that had "led our people and our fatherland to the brink of an all-consuming abyss." Months later, he was still expressing his approval for the wave of killings, which most of the German public had welcomed as an overdue act of liberating the government.[66] Kiehn wrote to a Tuttlingen businessman in December 1934 that "our brave SS men and leaders are the absolute backbone of the movement and therefore the backbone of the [German] state. Our Führer Adolf Hitler was able to rely on his SS one hundred percent on 30 June of this year, on the occasion of the Röhm revolt, and the Führer also knew, with clear foresight, why he had created exactly those SS units."⁶⁷ We can no longer ascertain whether Kiehn was expressing a consensus opinion here or whether sheer opportunism motivated his statement.

It also bears mentioning that Kiehn had an uncommonly good connection to one of the main actors in Mattheiß's murder, group leader Hans-Adolf Prützmann, director of the SS Southwest Regional Headquarters. Prützmann, who regarded Mattheiß as a personal enemy,⁶⁸ had been one of Kiehn's colleagues in the NSDAP Reichstag faction since July 1932, and his SS unit reaped no small benefit from Kiehn's generous donations. In February 1936, Prützmann was forced by Himmler's Reichsführer-SS court to give the reasons he had delayed the SS investigational proceedings opened against Kiehn. Having "taken on" the "Kiehn matter," Prützmann wrote to Munich that he took the blame for Kiehn's case not going forward.⁶⁹ The complaint against Kiehn being brought to Reichsführer-SS Himmler stemmed not least from Kiehn's penchant for talking big and his high-handed leadership style as president of the Stuttgart Chamber of Industry and Commerce. One of his denouncers, a "longtime staff member" of the chamber with certified "comprehensive expert knowledge," attested that the impression Kiehn gave was "less the impression of a hard-working, experienced, and solid businessman than that of a crafty racketeer," one who could afford to use "three or four cars ... at the same time (with an SS-uniformed chauffeur)." In the words of this informer, Kiehn was "either a naïve, hesitant sort," who was "not exactly brainy ... but at the same time [had] an extremely strong and unbridled need for recognition, or [he was] a very crafty profiteer."

Table 2: Kiehn's donations to Nazi organizations, 1935–1944 (in RM)

SS	SA	NSDAP	Hitler Youth	NSF	Misc.	Total
232,709	2,833	27,771	12,400	16,468	643,464	935,645

Source: MAE Colmar, WH C 3541 d 11, Affaire Kiehn.

Such accusations, however, evidently could not undermine Kiehn's reputation with the SS.⁷⁰ After Prützmann, as the SS Southwest Regional Headquarters director, finally interrogated Kiehn in April 1936, he recommended that the top-level Reichsführer-SS court "refrain from further investigation of the matter and call off ... proceedings." The surprising opinion indicated that the accusations brought against the industrialist would not stand up to any form of scrutiny.⁷¹ Prützmann's conduct was tantamount to siding with Kiehn, who at that time was involved in serious conflicts with the Economics Ministry and the National Socialist district economic adviser over Kiehn's speculative trades in the Magirus company in Ulm. These political battles had "raised a lot of dust" in Württemberg, according to Prützmann, since "almost the entire party and organizational leadership had been dragged into this dispute." But the dust settled quickly once Kiehn handed out several hundred thousand Reichsmarks in donations to political agencies that would chiefly benefit the SS.[72]

The details of why Prützmann shielded Kiehn from attacks, at least some of which were well warranted, must remain a mystery. Perhaps the two men's shared passion for hunting played a role. In an internal staff report from 1938, Prützmann described Kiehn as a "very good comrade" and praised him as an "outstanding businessman ... open and honest, fair and decent" — attributes that glaringly contradicted Kiehn's reputation in Württemberg at the time.[73] As the list of donations (compiled by the French military government after 1945) in table 2 makes clear, Kiehn's good connections came at no small cost. Along with the Reichsführer-SS office in Munich, the SS regional headquarters in Stuttgart repeatedly received very handsome donations.[74]

Table 3: Kiehn's donations to SS offices, 1935–1944.

SS office	Total in Reichsmarks
Reichsführer-SS	71,157
SS Main Riding School, Munich	66,200
SS Southwest Regional Headquarters	33,239
SS District Headquarters, Konstanz	19,820
SS Standarte, Reutlingen	ca. 12,000
SS Regional Headquarters, Munich	7,999
SS Battalion, Trossingen/Donations for SS members	4,200
SS Riders' Association, Schwenningen	4,181
SS "Ihle" Standarte	3,000
Total	220,971

Source: MAE Colmar, WH C 3541 d 11, Affaire Kiehn.

Kiehn enriched SS coffers considerably, whereas the SA and the NSDAP party administration had to settle for smaller amounts. In the early years of his membership in the SS, the Württemberg industrialist was particularly generous to the offices and units that he or his son, Herbert, were involved with personally. In later years, he concentrated his donations on the SS Main Riding School in Munich, which the SS Southwest Regional Headquarters had founded in 1937. Promoting horseback riding, an upper-class sport, added to the halo of elitism around the SS and offered Kiehn a very welcome direct line to the head of the riding school, SS colonel (Standartenführer) Hermann Fegelein, and to the Reichsführer-SS's personal staff. The careerist colonel was part of Himmler's entourage; in the latter half of the war he became involved in serious war crimes and was an SS liaison officer in Hitler's headquarters and brother-in-law to Eva Braun. His membership in Hitler's inner circle, however, did not prevent Hitler from having him summarily shot for defeatism in 1945.[75]

Fritz Kiehn also ensured that other entrepreneurs would be open-handed with the SS. The factory owner's aggressive fund-raising methods often ostracized his industrialist peers. For example, Kiehn had only just been appointed president of the Economic Chamber when he used his new title to send "strictly confidential" letters to his business colleagues soliciting donations. In December 1934, he wrote to the chair of the association of shoe manufacturers in Tuttlingen with a reminder "that our SS units are almost entirely on their own with respect to their finances," for which reason Kiehn was striving "to seek out helping hands" anywhere he could. He asked him to endeavor to get "any company owners from whom I have had the opportunity to commission orders" to "make shoes and boots available to the Württemberg SS brigade" equivalent to those they had already delivered to the armed forces administration. Kiehn's own donations to various SS offices are listed in table 3. The donations were to constitute "between ½, but if at all possible 1%, of the shoe and boot orders carried out" and were supposed to be ready in time for the holidays "so that those brave boys of ours can have an unexpected Christmas gift." "Naturally" the matter was to remain confidential, with Kiehn's disingenuous assurance that it was "just a suggestion."[76]

The initiative Kiehn showed in his service to the SS[77] helped the "leader of the entire southern German economy" rise quickly in the ranks of Himmler's unit as well. In June 1938, he was admitted to the Reichsführer-SS's personal staff.[78] As a member of the Circle of Friends (Freundeskreis) of the Reichsführer-SS, Kiehn had pushed his way into an illustrious group "in which from time to time three dozen of the most influential industry and money managers" would meet. The primary purpose of the circle was to encourage these rich men to donate to the SS. Founded by *Mittelstand* businessman Wilhelm Keppler, the Freundeskreis had been led by his similarly business-inclined nephew Fritz Kranefuß since 1933. The group included important industrialists such as Friedrich Flick, Albert Vögler (Vereinigte Stahlwerke), Heinrich Bütefisch (IG-Farben), Rudolf Bingel (Siemens-Schuckert), Emil Helfferich (HAPAG and Deutsch-Amerikanische Petroleum-Gesellschaft / ESSO), Karl Lindemann (Norddeutsche Lloyd), and Württemberg local Hans Walz, CEO of Bosch.[79] The banking sector was represented by Karl Rasche (Dresdner Bank), Friedrich Reinhart (Commerzbank), and Hitler's old patron, Baron Kurt von Schröder. The association counted the following prominent party administration and SS officials as members in 1943: Fritz Kranefuß, executive director of the Freundeskreis and part of Himmler's personal staff; Wilhelm Keppler (Hitler's economic policy adviser); Hans Kehrl (head of the Main Department of Industry in the Reich Economics Ministry since 1942 and influential director of the Raw Materials Office in Speer's ministry since 1943); Oswald Pohl (head of the Main Administrative and Economic Office of the SS); Franz Hayler (director of the Reich Group for Commerce and Trade); Otto Ohlendorf (CEO of the Reich Group for Commerce and Trade and head of department in the Reich Economics Ministry); Professor Walther Wüst (president of Ahnenerbe e.V., the SS "ancestral heritage" think tank); and Werner Naumann (state undersecretary in Goebbels's ministry).[80] Neither Kiehn's party rank nor his industrial significance were sufficient to admit him to this lofty group; his membership seems probably to have been due to both his generous donations and his connection to an old friend, Gottlob Berger. Berger had been a senior SA leader (Oberführer) and special commissioner in Württemberg during the "time of struggle," but soon had fallen out with the Stuttgart Gauleitung. After conflicts with several NSDAP functioners of the Gau level the same happened to Kiehn.[81] Unlike Kiehn, Berger had transferred his loyalty to the SS as soon as conflicts with the Württemberg SA had arisen.[82]

Beginning in 1939, Berger ran the SS Head Office in Berlin and became one of the masterminds behind the eventual creation of the Waffen-SS. In the SS ranks he was known as one of Himmler's "Twelve Apostles" and was nicknamed "Almighty Gottlob."[83] What is certain is that Berger was also the man pulling the strings in the years that followed, when the scandal around Kiehn threatened to undermine his relation to the Reichsführer-SS's personal staff.[84] The Freundeskreis met monthly — although the number of attendees obviously fluctuated. The Reichsführer-SS rarely took part in meetings after the war in the east began, and the irregular attendance of some members frequently moved his representative, Kranefuß, to complain. But Fritz Kiehn was not mentioned as one of the gentlemen who stood out for this. He was evidently glad to use the opportunity provided by the Freundeskreis to rub shoulders with the economic and politically prominent. He evidently regarded the lectures on subjects such as "The Norman Conquest of England, as Reflected in the Bayeux Tapestry" as worth the trip to the Reich capital, even if the actual goal of the trip was less a hunger for culture than an eagerness to maintain contact with Himmler's circle.[85] After all, Kiehn's admission to the association gave him more than the increase in prestige that he demonstrated through a special uniform and an SS emblem on his car; he also gained invaluable political connections.[86]

Kiehn had "earned" these honors too: he had purposefully initiated contact with the Reichsführer-SS and made a name for himself as a fund-raiser and generous donor. In 1937, Kiehn used his position as president of the Economic Chamber to compel "Württemberg industry" to give Hitler a portrait by Adolf Menzel (1815–1905), a painter Hitler revered, to celebrate the dictator's birthday. Kiehn was to present the gift in person, accompanied by other chamber representatives.[87] The RM 325,000 cost of the portrait was later deemed by the SD to be wildly overpriced, and exceeded the amount available for the purchase from private donations by more than three times. Internal party investigations accused Kiehn of "hunting down connections" and being willing to "shanghai" his business colleagues. Without even informing them of the planned gift in advance, Kiehn had asked the business owners to pay up after the fact, which was generally considered scandalous. "A string of influential industrialists" then refused to share in the costs.[88]

But Kiehn was not discouraged by a handful of "grumblers": a few years after the Menzel portrait affair had blown over, he decided to remind the Reichsführer-SS of his existence once again — likely also because of his ongoing "Aryanization matters" — by rendering outstanding service to the Führer's art collection. On this attempt, he intended to become a patron of the arts at the same time. He informed SS group leader Karl Wolff, the head of Himmler's personal staff, that he had met Professor Franz Kienmayer, "the famous painter," who was working on a monumental oil painting "that portrays the signing in the Reich chancellery of the alliance with Italy." The work would cost RM 15,000, Kiehn relayed, but "the money must first be procured." Kiehn imagined that he would carry out "the entire affair in such a way that I take care of the fund-raising — obviously without any fuss — the Herr Reichsführer-SS [would] take possession of the painting and have it at his disposal — entirely as he chose — and [would] present it to the Führer as a gift from the SS if at all possible." Kiehn also wished to "personally dedicate" a preliminary study by the painter to "Herr Reichsführer-SS." But his plans came to naught. Months went by before Kiehn received a note that Himmler wished to thank him for his well-meaning efforts to "selflessly volunteer himself once again." A viewing of the painter's preliminary study, however, had revealed that "the reproduction of the personages appearing in the painting ... is not at all acceptable."[89]

Another of Kiehn's "selfless" projects, about which Kiehn had personally approached Himmler several months before, appears to have been similarly unsuccessful. Misinterpreting an order from the Reichsführer-SS, Kiehn had wanted to apply right away for guardianship of three "children of good blood whose father was killed in action." "It would be a particular joy and honor for my wife, my daughter, and me if you could transfer each of us a guardianship. I await your further orders and instructions, Reichsführer, and wish you the best with all my heart at this great time. With my most obedient salute to the Führer, I remain your devoted Fritz Kiehn, SS-Hptstuf. [chief storm leader, equivalent to captain]." It became apparent, however, that Himmler was concerned with funding the Lebensborn (Fountain of Life) organization, an establishment that used the National Socialist ideology of "racial hygiene" and health to promote births of "Aryan" children and the adoption of those children from the occupied territories who were seen as racially "superior." Very often such children had been forcibly separated from their biological parents. Individual demonstrations of charity, as Kiehn had in mind, were unwelcome. Kiehn was consoled with the prospect of sponsoring a child through the Lebensborn project.[90]

Kiehn's propensity for staging events on a grand scale verging on the absurd is evident from a hunting invitation he allegedly issued to the Reichsführer-SS in 1937 and the resentment it generated. Like many entrepreneurs and most NS officials, Kiehn had a passion for hunting. Among his various hunting grounds was one he leased in Wildbad, a densely wooded health resort town in the northern

Black Forest, with an abundant population of red deer. SD statements indicate that the Reichsführer-SS allegedly was to bring down a royal stag in that area in the fall of 1937, and Fritz Kiehn had not left anything to chance, having taken precautions as early as six months before to ensure his high-ranking guest's success in the hunt. He purchased deer from the owner of a deer park on Sommerberg, a mountain near Wildbad, and released the thirteen tame animals (including Max, a royal 18-point stag) into the wild, where the herd did heavy damage to neighbors' gardens and fields. This continued until Max, who had been raised in captivity and allowed Sommerberg hikers to feed him, was finally hunted down at the end of October.[91] The lucky shooter was not Heinrich Himmler, of course — contrary to the information from the SD — but the head of the SS Southwest Regional Headquarters, group leader Hans-Adolf Prützmann, who has already come up several times in this chapter. Kiehn had photographic evidence taken of Max's downfall. An entire album was devoted to the adventure with Prützmann, who visibly relished his hunting success and likely earned his reputation for being "vain, lazy, and a braggart" through performances like the one in Wildbad, where he proudly posed for souvenir photographs with the stag and his trophy (fig. 15).[92]

Several months after the incident, Himmler warned the senior SS leaders under him about accepting hunting invitations, pointing out "that most people who invite us do not have selfless reasons for doing so." Kiehn's critics held the same view, and the farce with Max had reminded some of "court hunts in the Byzantine mold."[93]

Fig. 15: "Happy hunter" Prützmann (second from left) and Kiehn. (Private collection of the Kiehn family)

Fig. 16: **Kiehn in his SS uniform with honorary dagger.** (Stadtarchiv Trossingen)

Fritz Kiehn not only invested lots of time and money in hunting; he also pursued it with a genuine passion that had first been awakened in his youth. His formative memories of his time in Hanover included meeting regional nature poet Hermann Löns at the age of seventeen. Löns took Kiehn hunting with him from time to time after that. Kiehn left no one in the dark about his personal relationship to the "poet of the Lüneburg Heath," who had been killed in 1918 as a volunteer on the Western Front and became highly distinguished during the Third Reich. Kiehn invariably used hunting to maintain his political and business contacts — as his relationship to Prützmann vividly demonstrates — and to obtain social and cultural capital. For example, Kiehn was able to take part in multiple large hunting parties organized by leading representatives of the regime, most notably Hermann Göring.

Kiehn's great extravagance in ensuring the support of the SS seems to have paid off for him. Once he was admitted to the "RF-SS personal staff," he enjoyed a measure of protection in the following years that, despite dubious business deals and serious tensions with the Stuttgart Gauleitung, ensured his long-term political survival and, last but not least, a share in the proceeds from Aryanization. When his SS position ultimately became precarious as well, and people there started to see him as a "Janus-face" that one had to keep "one hell of an eye on … whether you're on the good or the bad side with him," Kiehn consolidated his good relations with the SS by marrying his 23-year-old daughter off to a member of the Reichsführer-SS's personal staff, Dr. Ernst Fähndrich.[94] Such personal dedication kept Kiehn's position on Himmler's team safe to the end. He was a paying member of the Lebensborn organization, and in 1942, at the suggestion of his old friend Gottlob Berger (who had since become director of the SS Head Office and a senior SS group leader), he was promoted to senior battalion (Sturmbann) leader and awarded the honorary dagger (*Ehrendolch*) and Yule lantern (*Julleuchter*) of the SS (fig. 16). The personal bonds of this controversial "leader of the Württemberg economy" and his family to the Reichsführer-SS and his inner circle proved to be stronger than the doubts that arose about Kiehn's National Socialist conduct. Such relationships were an important advantage in a polycratically organized regime in which personal relations counted more than rules and structures. Kiehn knew this and did not shy away from methods that bordered on the feudalistic in cultivating and maintaining relationships.[95]

Notes

1. *Nationalsozialistische Volkszeitung*, 2 May 1933; StAT, GRP of 22 May 1933; MAE Colmar, WH C 3541 d 11, Affaire Kiehn.
2. On Hitler's economic advisers see Turner, "Otto Wagener."
3. *Nationalsozialistische Volkszeitung*, 18 May 1933. The post of district leader for the economy lost its significance soon after 1933. See BA NS, 46/7, letter from Kiehn to Frick of 15 May 1933.
4. On Wilhelm Murr see Sauer, *Wilhelm Murr*; Scholtyseck, "Mann."
5. BA DC, Akte Kiehn, interrogation by the SS on 7 Apr. 1936 in Stuttgart; Schnabel, *Württemberg*, 205; Winkel, *Industrie- und Handelskammern*, 11.
6. Winkel, *Industrie- und Handelskammern*, 49–51.
7. MAE Colmar, WH C 3541 d 11, Affaire Kiehn.
8. *Württembergische Wirtschafts-Zeitschrift* 15, no. 41 (12 Oct. 1935).
9. Nazi Gauleiter Wilhelm Murr was the archetypal social striver: once a minor employee at the Maschinenfabrik Esslingen, he rose to Reichsstatthalter, the highest national office in Württemberg. Numerous Nazi officials in Württemberg followed a similar path, achieving high-level state and economic positions in the Third Reich. For more examples, see Berghoff and Rauh-Kühne, *Fritz K.*, 368n8.
10. Ruck, *Korpsgeist*, 30, has a summary: "the traditional cartel of elites ... has demonstrated its tremendous persistence through the Nazi era and into the present day." Ibid., 262.
11. Kissenkoetter, *Gregor Straßer*, 145–149, cit. 149; Kershaw, *Hitler, 1889–1936*, 380–404.
12. Schnabel, *Machtergreifung*, app. 4, p. 312; on the crisis within the Nazi Party, see Kissenkoetter, *Gregor Straßer*, 159–160; Joseph Goebbels's diary entries, 1–10 Dec. 1932, in Goebbels, *Tagebücher*, part 1, *Aufzeichnungen 1923–1941*, vol. 2/3, p. 70–80, digital edition in "Nationalsozialismus, Holocaust, Widerstand und Exil 1933–1945," online database, De Gruyter, document ID: TJG-2375, TJG-2376.
13. BA DC, Akte Kiehn. After Straßer had been removed from power and murdered, the comment was imputed to Kiehn in the SS investigational proceedings opened against him in 1936. It was paraphrased based on hearsay.

14. Kissenkoetter, *Gregor Straßer*, 164 (cit.), 170, 174; Wörtz, "Programmatik," 228.
15. Cited in Kissenkoetter, *Gregor Straßer*, 172, based on the surviving draft of Straßer's letter of resignation; on the situation in the Nazi Party, see Horn, *Führerideologie*, 367–368.
16. Wörtz, "Programmatik," 233.
17. Kissenkoetter, *Gregor Straßer*, 191.
18. Geheime Kommandosache — SS-Brigadeführer Berger an Himmler, 3 Dec. 1940, (NO-2249) In: "Nationalsozialismus, Holocaust, Widerstand und Exil 1933–1945." Online-Datenbank. http://db.saur.de.nationalsozialismusholocaustwiderstandundexil1933–45.shan01.han.tib.eu/DGO/basicFullCitationView.jsf?documentId=NO02111 Dokument-ID: NO02111.http://db.saur.de/DGO/basicFullCitationView.jsf?documentId=NO02111.
19. *Süddeutsche Arbeiter-Zeitung*, 19 Dec. 1932, in Schnabel, *Württemberg*, 160.
20. Before Gauleiter Murr was nominated to be president of Württemberg, there had been heated conflicts in March 1933 between his and Mergenthaler's supporters. Hitler ultimately decided these in Murr's favor; previously, the SA had championed Mergenthaler and the SS had supported Murr. Nothing seemed to have changed on this front in the months that followed. Schnabel, *Württemberg*, 382; Schnabel, "NSDAP," 73–74. Reichardt, *Kampfbünde*, 174, 181.
21. See Linz, "Typen," 551.
22. BA DC, Akte Kiehn, Uschla Reichsleitung decision of 11 Aug. 1933 to abandon investigational proceedings; for more examples of the party court system being utilized against presumed Straßer supporters long after the Nazi takeover, see Kissenkoetter, *Gregor Straßer*, 188–189; for general information on the practices of the party court system, see Block, *Parteigerichtsbarkeit*; McKale, *Courts*.
23. BA NS, 46/7, letters from Kiehn to Reich minister Frick of 30 May, 9 Aug., and 1 Oct. 1933.
24. BA NS, 46/7, letter from Kiehn to Reich minister Frick of 15 May 1933. On Wagener, see Kissenkoetter, *Gregor Straßer*, 101, 134; Bracher et al., *Machtergreifung*, 395–397, 639–640, 849–851.
25. BA NS, 46/7, two letters from Kiehn to Reich minister Frick, both from 18 Oct. 1933, as well as other notes from 20 Oct. and 6 Nov. 1933. Kiehn's intervention may also have been inspired by Walther Funk, a competitor of Wagener's within the party whom Kiehn knew well. For the background to Wagener's departure and Funk's plotting, see Turner, *Business*, 283–285.
26. Jünger, "Kampf"; Hannah Arendt observed that the lifelong cultivation of this sort of empty pathos as a method of linguistic expression was Adolf Eichmann's most striking feature. Once a shop clerk, Eichmann rose to become one of the administrators of the Final Solution. In her view, he was "genuinely incapable of uttering a single sentence that was not a cliché," and boasting and bragging had become his favorite habits early on. Arendt, *Eichmann* (English edition), 48. See also ibid, 36–55.
27. Frick's comments in the margin on Kiehn's petition seem to indicate that Frick supported Kiehn's request. BA DC, Akte Kiehn, interrogation by the SS on 7 Apr. 1936. On Kiehn's tenure in the Reichstag from 1932 to 1945, see Schumacher, MdR, no. 774, 772.
28. Cited in Kissenkoetter, *Gregor Straßer*, 193–194.
29. BA NS, 46/7, letter from Kiehn to Frick of 18 Oct. 1933. Kiehn distanced himself from Straßer publicly in Trossingen at a meeting of the Ortsgruppe. See AVT, 16 Oct. 1933.
30. BA DC, Akte Kiehn, Kiehn's interrogation of 7 Apr. 1936.
31. Kissenkoetter, *Gregor Straßer*, 195, indicates that Frick also advocated providing for Straßer's widow.
32. Letter from Trossingen town pastors of both denominations, 18 July 1945, in MAE Colmar WH C 3541 d 11, Affaire Kiehn; for general information, see Horn, *Führerideologie*, 400, 403; McNab, *SS*, 12–21.

33. For a contemporary deconstruction of the myth of SS elitism, see Hein, *Elite*; for confrontations between the SS and SA from 1930 to 1934, see ibid., 77–91. Kiehn's SS member number was 239,095; his date of membership is given in the SS Southwest Regional Headquarters examination minutes from 7 Apr. 1936 as 1934, whereas his SS files give the date as 15 Mar. 1933. BA DC, Akte Kiehn. The first date cannot be correct, because in a letter from his son from fall 1933, Fritz Kiehn is mentioned as a supposed SS captain ("höherer SS-Führer"). On the placement of a hundred-member SS troop in Trossingen, see StAT, B 79, GRP of 22 May 1933; letter from Herbert Kiehn of 15 Dec. 1933, private collection.
34. Kiehn's then twenty-year-old son filled this role, accompanying his father to propaganda speeches that fall. Letter from Herbert Kiehn of 15 Dec. 1933, private collection.
35. Schuhladen-Krämer, "Exekutoren," 411–412; Ruck, *Korpsgeist*, 102. Reinhold Maier, *Familie*, 21–30, recalls Mattheiß as a frightening persecutor. On SA activities in and around Trossingen, see StAT, A 480, MS "Trossingens Kampf um die nat. soz. Idee" (1935).
36. Fritz, "Haus Württemberg."
37. Schuhladen-Krämer, "Exekutoren," 411; on Hitler's confrontation with the nearly identical rhetoric of Chief of Staff Röhm and other SA leaders, see Kershaw, *Hitler, 1889–1936*, 500–512. See also Wilhelm, "Württembergische Polizei," 109–10.
38. Contrary to the supposition by Schuhladen-Krämer in "Exekutoren," 416, then, Mattheiß's execution was very likely related to "events at the highest level" on 30 June. See Evans, *Third Reich in Power*, 27–41; McNab, *SS*, 19–21; Wheeler-Bennett, *Nemesis*, 319–320.
39. Schuhladen-Krämer, "Exekutoren," 413, 416.
40. Ibid., 416.
41. StAL, EL 902/2, Bü 7590 (denazification proceedings records for Malsen-Ponickau and Prützmann). Reproduction of a note from Mattheiß to Minister of the Interior Jonathan Schmid, original document not preserved.
42. StAL, EL 902/22, Bü 1502, sworn statement by Lolo Mattheiß of 2 Dec. 1947. Even though Mattheiß's widow seems only partly credible, her explanation of her husband's sudden dismissal sounds plausible; it matches information indicating that Mattheiß opposed his subordination to Himmler's SD. See Herbert, *Best*, 138. Investigations undertaken by the French national police force on orders from the French military government in postwar Germany also point to Mattheiß having quarreled with the SS in 1934. MAE Colmar, WH C 3541 d 11, Affaire Kiehn.
43. Kershaw, *Hitler, 1889–1936*, 511; Herbert, *Best*, 143, 570n 29.
44. Schnabel, *Württemberg*, 380–381. On precautionary measures that the SS Standarte in Tuttlingen took against the supposed SA plan to attack the Mauser building, see the recollections of the "Röhmputsch" by a former member of this SS unit, StAT, Häffner interview collection.
45. StAL, EL 902/2, Bü 7590.
46. Maier, *Familie*, 29.
47. See Sauer, "Württemberg," 61–62. Several of Himmler's contemporaries suspected that he gave the order, and Schuhladen-Krämer also considers this possibility. This supposition becomes more plausible in view of the previously ignored fact that the order to arrest Mattheiß was issued by Prützmann, the SS group leader of the SS Southwest Regional Headquarters, in the presence of SS brigade leader Johannes Erasmus, Baron of Malsen-Ponickau, who was a member of Himmler's personal staff. Wilhelm, *Polizei*, 222; Grieser, *Himmlers Mann*, 38, 40; StAL, EL 902/2, Bü 7590.
48. Schuhladen-Krämer, "Exekutoren," 415; the official list of the dead from 30 June 1934 names a "Dr. Matheis" — spelled incorrectly — in thirty-ninth place. This puts his date of execution at 1 July, whereas Straßer's execution is listed as 30 June. Bennecke, *Reichswehr*, 87–88.
49. Schuhladen-Krämer, "Exekutoren," 416.

50. New studies estimate the number of arrests in the Night of the Long Knives at over eleven hundred, of whom "some 150 to 200 persons" were killed, more than half of them members of the SA. See Hein, *Elite*, 88.
51. StAS, Wü 13, T2 no. Bü 2775/001, letter from investigating magistrate to Ellwangen regional court of 20 Oct. 1950.
52. This is according to Kiehn's account, cited as "very credible" on the basis of judicial inquiries by the criminal division of the Ellwangen regional court in the decision to suspend proceedings as of 30 Dec. 1950, in StAL, EL 902/2, Bü 7589 (Spruchkammerakte Beck). Kiehn's reputation among his family and circle of friends also supports his role as a potential victim in the Night of the Long Knives. Information from Herbert E. Kiehn on 12 Dec. 1998 and 13 Jan. 1999.
53. StAS, Wü 13, T 2 no. 2775/001, http://www.landesarchiv-bw.de/plink/?f=6-1039573 (accessed 4 Sept. 2012), letter from investigating magistrate to Ellwangen regional court of 20 Oct. 1950.
54. StAT, Häffner interview collection; interview by Hartmut Berghoff of 10 May 1993.
55. STAS, Wü 13 T 2 no. 2775/001, http://www.landesarchiv-bw.de/plink/?f=6-1039573 (accessed 4 Sept. 2012); Schuhladen-Krämer, "Exekutoren," 414; Schnabel, *Württemberg*, 380–381.
56. StAL, EL 902/2, Bü 7590, statement by former SS leader Johann Beck of 21 Aug. 1948 in the criminal case against Fritz Kiehn, Johann Beck, and others.
57. StAT, Häffner interview collection.
58. Letter from Herbert E. Kiehn to the authors of 15 June 1998.
59. "Röhm-Putsch" was the official name for the purge of 30 June 1934, when Hitler ordered the SS killing of SA leader Ernst Röhm and more than a hundred other SA leaders and some politically suspect conservatives, for example, the former Reich chancellor Kurt von Streicher and his wife.
60. Statement by Christian Messner to the military government, MAE Colmar, WH C 3541 d 11, Affaire Kiehn.
61. MAE Colmar, WH C 3541 d 11, Affaire Kiehn.
62. Compare this to the case of SA senior leader Hermann Berchtold, who was not arrested until 2 July 1934; Schnabel, *Württemberg*, 380–381.
63. Unlike Straßer, Mattheiß was never mentioned in Kiehn family lore in the years that followed. Information from Herbert E. Kiehn of 6 Dec. 1998.
64. Daluege, who was then head of the Department for Police Matters in the Reich Interior Ministry, is said to have been the one who delivered the news to the army (Reichswehr) about the supposedly imminent SA purge. Bennecke, *Reichswehr*, 51. On Daluege's "significant involvement in the ... wave of killings against the SA," see Wilhelm, *Württembergische Polizei*, 145.
65. See chap. 10.
66. *Gränzbote*, 1 Aug. 1934 (cit.); of the same tenor, see *Gränzbote*, 18 Aug. 1934. For general information on how the Röhm purge resonated with the public, see Kershaw, *Hitler, 1889–1936*, 517–519.
67. *Gränzbote*, 5 July 1934; BA DC, Akte Kiehn, letter from Kiehn to manufacturer Jakob Henke of 12 Dec. 1934.
68. Schuhladen-Krämer, "Exekutoren," 416, indicates Mattheiß and Prützmann's disputes over their respective powers of authority frequently degenerated into insult contests.
69. BA DC, Akte Kiehn, letter from Prützmann to RF-SS, SS court of 19 Feb. 1936. Various biographical information and a photo of Hans-Adolf Prützmann (1901–1945, appointed senior SS and police leader in 1937) can be found in Schuhladen-Krämer, "Exekutoren," 414–416; Schumacher, M.d.R., no. 1171, 372; Krausnick and Wilhelm, *Truppe*, 641–42.

70. BA DC, Akte Kiehn, internal report (presumably from 1935).
71. BA DC, Akte Kiehn, letter from SS Southwest Regional Headquarters to RF-SS, SS court of 13 May 1936.
72. Ibid.; judgment by the Gau court of Württemberg-Hohenzollern in NSDAP vs. Kiehn of 28 Feb. 1939, digital edition in "Nationalsozialismus, Holocaust, Widerstand und Exil 1933–1945," online database, De Gruyter, document ID: APK-019245.
73. See chap. 4; on the utilitarian practice of SS disciplinary jurisdiction, see Hein, *Elite*, 200; Buchheim, "Befehl," 258; Longerich, *Heinrich Himmler*, 276–277.
74. MAE Colmar, WH C 3541 d 11, Affaire Kiehn. The information in tables 2 and 3 is based on a list of donations compiled by the French military government after the war that presumably was based on Kiehn's accounting records and bank statements.
75. For information in French military records on Kiehn's connections to Fegelein, see MAE Colmar, WH C 3541 d 11, Affaire Kiehn. On Fegelein and the SS Main Riding School, see Hein, *Elite*, 105. See also Kershaw, *Hitler, 1936–1945*, 816–819.
76. BA DC, Akte Kiehn, letter from Kiehn to manufacturer Jakob Henke of 12 Dec. 1934.
77. Table 3 includes only those recipients of donations in the amount of RM 1,000 or more. This explains the discrepancy in the total donations to the SS seen in table 2. The sequence of the entries clearly shows that for quite a while the SA got nothing, and never donations of RM 1,000 or more. It seems that after 1933, the NSDAP party organization was completely snubbed.
78. BA DC, Akte Kiehn.
79. Lang and Sibyll, *Adjutant*, 53–56; Vogelsang, *Freundeskreis*; for emphasis on the political role and goals of the Freundeskreis as part of pan-European plans, see Padfield, *Himmler*, 149, 207.
80. The names are mentioned in a letter that Kranefuß sent to Himmler on 21 Apr. 1943 in which Pohl, Hayler, Ohlendorf, Naumann, SS group leader Rösener, SS brigade leader Schieber, and SS battalion (Sturmbann) leader Schäfer are described as "nearly all the members" of the Freundeskreis who are "in the inner circle of the SS itself, as it were." BA DC, Akte Hans Walz. See also Bütow and Bindernagel, *KZ*, and *Der Spiegel* 42, Himmler-Kreis.
81. See chaps. 4 and 6.
82. Rempel, "Gottlob Berger"; Hoffmann, "Drang"; Scholtyseck: "'Schwabenherzog'"; Hein, *Elite*, 139.
83. Nichol and Rennell, *Last Escape*, 359; Weale, *Army*, 116–118, 246–255.
84. BA NS, 19/790, letter from Berger to the head of the RF-SS personal staff of 10 Oct. 1940.
85. BA DC, Akte Hans Walz, letter from Kranefuß to Himmler of 21 Apr. 1943.
86. Lang and Sibyll, *Adjutant*, 54; BA DC, Akte Kiehn, letter from Kiehn to Frick, the chair of the NSDAP faction in the Reichstag, of 19 Apr. 1939. In the letter, Kiehn informs Frick that "Herr Reichsführer-SS" (Himmler) had allowed him to wear the SS uniform again. On the SS chevron, see Zentrale Stelle der Landesjustizverwaltungen, Ludwigsburg, SS-Akte Kiehn; on the significance of the car as a means of distinguishing senior SS leaders, see Padfield, *Himmler*, 194.
87. It is not known whether this gift was "Friedrich der Große auf Reisen," the Menzel painting that hung in the study of the Führerbau in Munich. On Hitler's art collection, see Schwarz, *Geniewahn*; Schwarz, *Hitlers Museum*.
88. IfZ MA, 288, 9174–9176 (RF-SS Pers. Stab III), copy of Fritz Kiehn's resume; BA DC, Akte Kiehn, report from the SD subdivision for Württemberg-Hohenzollern of 10 Dec. 1937. Lang and Sibyll, *Adjutant*, reproduces a photo of Hitler (following p. 160, uncredited) receiving a Menzel painting *from Himmler* — presumably on his birthday in 1938. The caption reads: "1938: Paid for with donations from the Freundeskreis, the SS [*sic*] gives Hitler an original Menzel painting for his birthday." This date may be in error, and the photo may actually capture the presentation made affordable by Württemberg industrialists thanks to the fundraising

of Kiehn. Kiehn's admission to the Freundeskreis would then be a veritable quid pro quo for his service to the RF-SS, who thanks to Kiehn was able to favor Hitler with an original piece by his favorite painter. Kiehn's total personal contribution to the Menzel purchase was RM 16,317; MAE Colmar, WH C 3541 d 11, Affaire Kiehn. The amounts collected in Württemberg at Kiehn's prompting were held in an account at the Deutsche Bank in Stuttgart under the code word "RF-SS Foundation Raffael Menzel." This makes it likely that the Menzel painting was not the only work of art the money was spent on. IfZ, MA 288, 9174–80 (RF-SS Pers. Stab III), letter from head of personal staff to treasurer of RF-SS personal staff of 17 Dec. 1938.

89. IfZ, MA 288, 9174–80 (Pers. Stab RF-SS III), letter from Kiehn to group leader Wolff of 21 Mar. 1940, reply from Wolff of 4 Sept. 1940.
90. IfZ, MA 288, 9174–80 (Pers. Stab RF-SS III), letter from Kiehn to Himmler of 20 Nov. 1939, reply from RF-SS personal staff of 15 Oct. 1940; Clay and Leapman, *Master Race*; Ericsson and Simonsen, *Children*.
91. BA DC, Akte Kiehn, report from the political leader of the Neuenbürg branch to the SD subdivision for Württemberg-Hohenzollern of 26 Oct. 1937. On the spread of the hunting craze among high-ranking National Socialists, see Lang and Sibyll, *Adjutant,* 78.
92. Prützmann was said to have "proved himself" to be something of an "expert" at killing during the war. He became a wanted war criminal for the brutal crimes perpetrated under his leadership against the "partisans" in the Ukraine.; cit. ibid. in Trevor-Roper, *Tage,* 76; for Prützmann's responsibilities in the last days of the Third Reich see also Henke, *Besetzung,* 945–946.
93. Himmler's warning about heedlessly accepting hunting invitations can be found in a letter from RF-SS to SS group leader Sepp Dietrich of 27 Aug. 1938, in Heiber, *Reichsführer!,* p. 59, doc. no. 37; for criticism of Kiehn, see BA DC, Akte Kiehn, five-page unsigned report on Kiehn of 14 Dec. 1938, presumably from the SD subdivision for Württemberg-Hohenzollern.
94. On the dubious reputation that Kiehn eventually acquired in the SS as well, see BA NS, 19/790, letter from SS brigade leader Berger, Kiehn's friend in the "time of struggle," to SS group leader Wolff, 10 Oct. 1940.
95. On Kiehn's rank in the SS, see BA DC, Akte Kiehn; on his son-in-law, Fähndrich, see chap. 7.

Chapter 4

RIDING NAZI PARTY COATTAILS
Kiehn's Industrial Ambitions

As a Reichstag delegate and representative of the Württemberg economy, Kiehn could soon count himself as part of the Nazi state establishment. Although he assured Reich interior minister Frick in May 1933 that he had no desire to rise to "anything" in the movement or hold any sort of office, this social striver had not even begun to satisfy his ambition.[1] A political career within the party was not what Kiehn the industrialist had in mind, however. Nor did he wish to climb the ladder of the National Socialist economic apparatus as card-carrying *Mittelstand* industrialists Keppler, Pleiger, and Kehrl had done so successfully. In fact, Kiehn's long-term plans hewed closely to the small-town world of Trossingen, especially Deibhalde and "his" Efka factory (fig. 17). Shifting the center of his life to Stuttgart or even Berlin appealed to him as little as the positions arising in large numbers at the companies in the Office of the Four-Year Plan or its administrative arm.

Kiehn's focus was first and foremost his own company. With the help of the Nazi Party, he hoped to expand the business further and rise to the level of a universally respected captain of industry. As a *Mittelstand* "Trossingen manufacturer" in 1933, Kiehn was still playing economic second fiddle in his own neighborhood, a circumstance that he meant to put to rights at the earliest opportunity. To this end, after the Uschla investigation, when his reputation had been restored,[2] he finally stepped down from his position as Ortsgruppenleiter in 1933 (his brother-in-law assumed the office) and transferred management of routine business operations at the Efka factory to his brother Victor. This freed him up for "higher" tasks.

Kiehn's first project in the new Nazi state was a logical continuation of the diversification into the printing sector he had begun before 1933. The irregular,

---

Notes from this chapter begin on page 84.

Fig. 17: Small-scale production facilities at the Efka factory (1930s). (Private collection of the Kiehn family)

on-demand, and often barely profitable production of propaganda material for the NSDAP was now to be replaced by fixed, long-term, and above all lucrative orders, and the *Gleichschaltung* of the press provided an ideal opportunity for Kiehn to solicit some.

In the summer of 1933, Kiehn took out loans, purchased property to round out his factory site, and traveled to state authorities and party offices in Berlin and Munich to secure a contract with the Nazi press in Stuttgart owned by the Gauleitung for printing a National Socialist regional newspaper. Through Gauleiter Murr, his contact at the Interior Ministry, Kiehn acquired printing presses and other movable assets from Volksstimme GmbH, a Social Democratic newspaper publisher in the small town of Schwenningen that had been forced to cease operations, for RM 9,932. Since the purchase was made even before the publisher's assets had been officially seized, Kiehn paid less than 20 percent of the actual market value of the items.[3] Kiehn's figures put the investments and expenses incurred as part of his newspaper project at more than RM 130,000.

When the project was still in its early stages, however, Kiehn encountered opposition in his adopted hometown. Walter Scharr, the publisher of the Trossingen local newspaper, who had joined the Nazi Party in 1932, was pursuing similar plans. Before 1933, his newspaper had been politically independent and had given all parties access to its columns. At the same time, Scharr occasionally published a regional Nazi screed called the *Honbergwarte*. This meant that both Scharr and Kiehn were putting out feelers for commissions from the party in 1933. Given the proceeding Uschla investigation and the distrust of Kiehn that remained after his acquittal, things did not turn out the way he had planned. In the fall of 1933, he tried using his connections to party leaders to lock out his competition. He denounced Scharr directly to Heß and Frick as having been a "Democrat," having waged a "furious battle against us," and having spoken out against "the Führer" in the "basest" of ways. He alleged that in 1931, in the Trossingen "Democrat paper," Scharr had written after Kiehn's spectacular election victory that everyone had "lost their senses." Scharr had only joined the party in 1932, complained Kiehn, in order to acquire commissions for his own business. According to Kiehn, Scharr had besmirched Kiehn's name with the Reich leadership in 1933 by dredging up social resentment against the paper manufacturer:

> I have to sit by and let this young man — whose character and morals as a married man also offer ample cause for complaint — spread rumors about me publicly in the business world. [This is] Scharr, the same man who just a few days ago was calling me a bigwig and a kingpin in the local economy. In the pubs he frequents ... he gets tipsy and passes around the letters you [Heß, who wrote them] and he exchanged, giving them to the barmaids and other unworthy and unsavory types to read.[4]

Scharr, for his part, lodged complaints with the party leadership that accused Kiehn, among other things, of having enjoyed an unfair advantage thanks to his close personal relationship with Gauleiter Murr, the publisher of the *NS Kurier*. He spread the rumor that Murr's wife was staying with Kiehn, an allegation that at any rate implies he was familiar with Kiehn's methods of cultivating political contacts. Kiehn disputed such connections, but he had to realize that the party leadership continued to regard him with suspicion because of his former connection to Straßer.

Without evident success, Kiehn sent multipage letters to Rudolf Heß, the Führer's deputy, in which he enumerated his services in a manner as detailed as it was maudlin. He denied any close relationship with Reich governor Murr or with Straßer.[5] In his letters Kiehn contrasted the dark example of Scharr the opportunist with the model he himself had set: "I have sacrificed my fortune and my livelihood (I can and am entitled to claim this, and I can prove it) ... to the movement. ... I can prove that for four years, I have done nothing but stand at the service of the party and have sacrificed more than RM 150,000 ... besides the years sacrificed and the health sacrificed to the party struggle. My business, which back then was flourishing, is no longer recognizable. ... [A]t the personal level, I am as good as ruined."[6] Again and again, Kiehn turned to Frick and Heß, asking in vain for his letters to be forwarded to the Führer and to be allowed to speak to Hitler personally about the matter. But the party leadership decided to centralize the presses under its new press czar, Max Amann, who had been part of Hitler's most trusted inner circle since the earliest days in Munich. Kiehn's failure was initially very costly to his expansion-oriented company, even if he was able to quickly resell the printing machines he had acquired and at least partially recoup his costs.

After his plans to make a big splash in the Nazi publishing business went awry, Kiehn directed his full attention to the industrial sector. In 1934, just one year after Hitler came to power, Kiehn sat on the supervisory boards of two Württemberg automobile companies. Their prospects looked rosy at that time, as the Nazi "motorization" policy fostered increased use of automobiles. Only slightly later, however, Kiehn would profess to never having had anything to do with stock trading "in my whole life or in the practice of my business."[7] He joined these boards, one at NSU in Neckarsulm and the other at Magirus AG, as part of the bringing into line (*Gleichschaltung*) of the economy.[8] Kiehn saw his position on the supervisory body of the latter company, an important and long-established firm, as his chance to break into big business. Founded in 1864, C.D. Magirus AG was one of the numerous joint-stock companies in Württemberg that had started out as family businesses. The company had fallen under the dominating influence of the banks during the hyperinflation of the early 1920s and had been struggling to survive since the Great Depression. As a leading manufacturer of fire engines, Magirus AG had helped to shape early motor vehicle construction in Germany and had been the largest industrial employer in the city for decades. Originally specializing in military field kitchens and telescope devices for wireless telegraphy, during World War I Magirus began producing cargo trucks and train engines for heavy artillery and underwent a vast expansion. The number of employees rose during the war from eight hundred to some twenty-eight hundred. Thus, the end of the war was a "harsh blow for the factory," as an authorized officer of the company put it in the mid-1930s. With no more military orders coming in, the company pivoted to concentrate on motor vehicle manufacture. But strong competition, technological backwardness compared to the rest of the world market, and an economic policy that neglected the expansion of motorization put a strain on the development of automobile construction in Germany and ultimately threatened to put the respected Ulm company out of business.[9] The losses had accumulated to RM 2,235,000 by the end of 1932. Selling part of the company to the city of Ulm, reducing capital, and issuing new shares of company stock allowed the company to continue to exist. The reorganization put 75 percent of Magirus share capital into the hands of four large banks. The 1932–1933 fiscal year ended with another loss, on the order of RM 1.5 million, stoking fears that the company would eventually lose its independence, especially since the banks on Magirus's supervisory board were pushing for the company to be absorbed, and some of its board members were also on the board of Daimler-Benz, its competition in Stuttgart (fig. 18).[10]

Fig. 18: Automotive exhibition in 1936: Kiehn, next to his son (from left), stands with the Führer. Daimler-Benz board chair Wilhelm Kissel is in the center. (Private collection of the Kiehn family)

The chair of the company, director Karl Trefz, strongly opposed allowing the company to be absorbed by a larger firm. He believed that the National Socialist takeover would help him prevent it, since for years the Nazi Party had waged propaganda attacks against big capital becoming concentrated in ever fewer hands. Trefz figured that having a prominent National Socialist on the board, one with important economic administrative powers, would be advantageous for his firm. This is why Trefz, who did not join the Nazi Party until after the NSDAP takeover, turned to Fritz Kiehn in the spring of 1934. He offered Kiehn, now president of the Stuttgart Chamber of Industry and Commerce, the prospect of joining the Magirus supervisory board as part of a special election to be held in June 1934, and invited him to begin attending board meetings immediately as an unofficial member. Kiehn did not hesitate, and from that point on he had access to the company's monthly balance sheets. These gave him cause for the highest expectations: Magirus received a large order from the NSDAP in 1933–1934 for more than one hundred special field kitchen vehicles. Magirus also built the vehicles for the Reich's car-carrying train in 1934, a propaganda instrument on wheels. Production and employee numbers rose rapidly; the dry spell was over.[11]

Magirus stock was about to skyrocket as a result of this state of affairs; it was still a mere 15 percent of its par value in the spring of 1934. Using his insider knowledge, Kiehn hastily contracted an intermediary to acquire the majority of the shares through a private bank in Stuttgart. But Kiehn had no capital of his own to use as collateral, and Magirus AG's creditors were of course out of the question for the transaction. This engendered serious delays that forced him to resell the securities in 1935 and ultimately made him an object of scandal in the Württemberg economy and a persona non grata with the NSDAP Gauleitung.

A few days after Kiehn had officially been elected to the Magirus board for the sake of the firm's independence, he signed a debt-financed stock order prepared by his intermediary, a businessman friend from Tuttlingen named Otto Stäbler, to acquire securities with a par value of up to RM 1.5 million. The order was accepted by Pick & Cie, a bank in Stuttgart; Stäbler's fellow Freemason Heinrich Glaub served on the management team there. Edgar Pick, a Jew, was a limited partner and the bank's plenipotentiary.[12]

The size of the order corresponded to 75 percent of Magirus AG's share capital, the majority stake necessary to accomplish Kiehn's intended purpose: to convert Magirus AG from a public joint-stock company into a private partnership. The change in the legal structure would have made him an absolute dictator, no longer required to publish the company's accounts or hold annual shareholder meetings. Moreover, such conversion of joint-stock companies into private partnerships was directly in line with Nazi party goals. As early as 1933, the Nazis had prohibited the founding of new joint-stock companies and banned existing publicly held corporations from increasing their share capital. The Loan Stock Act of 1934 (Anleihestockgesetz) limited dividend payouts to a maximum of 6 percent of nominal stock capital in order to incentivize conversions to private partnerships.[13] Had Kiehn's attempted coup succeeded, his importance as a Württemberg industrialist would have soared. He also expected to receive gratitude from Magirus employees, the city of Ulm, and above all the Nazi Party. He copiously denied that his business was speculative in character, alleging that he wished to "set up an example of National Socialist economic leadership." Indeed, at first the Magirus executive board, the company "council of trust" (Vertrauensrat), and the NSDAP's district economic adviser (Kreiswirtschaftsberater) all supported Kiehn in his attempt to rescue Magirus from the clutches of the big banks and avert the supposedly imminent "foreign infiltration" of the company, even though there was early resistance from the Gauleitung and especially the Economics Ministry.[14]

But Kiehn's calculations did not add up, and his lack of experience with joint-stock companies came back to haunt him. Because the stocks were owned by various large shareholders, his purchase order had to come together piece by piece, as the Magirus stock price continued to shoot up in sync with the revitalized national economy.[15] By October 1934 its price had reached 90 percent of its par value, which amounted to six times what it had cost that past spring. And Kiehn, who had acquired a block of shares during this price peak from one of the creditor banks for a mere RM 185,000, wrote to the bank that he had "allocated the financing for the transaction using a substantially lower price than has now arisen," and requested a grace period for payment. Nevertheless, by 1934 he had acquired shares with par value of RM 828,000. His sources of capital included a loan from Magirus of more than RM 120,000, but none of his own capital. The average purchase price was 80 percent of the par value, more money than Kiehn would ever be able to raise: his credit from Pick & Cie was due to expire in the summer of 1935.

At the Magirus AG general meeting on 27 November 1934, Kiehn held the majority of the shareholder capital — since some of the shareholders had transferred their voting rights to him — and he used it to push through a radical transformation in the composition of the supervisory board. Its previous members, primarily representatives of the big banks, were advised to resign. Kiehn allowed himelf to be elected the new chair of the board. His stock purchase intermediary, Stäbler, the non-Nazi Freemason, became his deputy. The third spot on the board was given to Stäbler's fellow Freemason, Glaub, the banker from Pick & Cie. Only one representative from Ulm would serve on the board from that point on, a lawyer. Kiehn announced that he would maintain the absolute independence of Magirus AG and would make the company a model of National Socialist industry. Before delegations from the council of trust and the "followers," as the Nazis labeled employees, the new chairman of the board gave a speech in which he repudiated any form of "dividend economy" and offered assurances that helping staff keep their jobs would always be his first priority.[16]

In the months that followed, he continued his efforts to achieve a three-fourths majority of share capital. In June 1935, he managed to acquire an option from Daimler-Benz AG to purchase shares with a par value of RM 605,000 that were still owned by Deutsche Bank. Daimler-Benz, however, had managed to secure a right of first refusal for the shares in order to keep an undesirable competitor from taking over Magirus. Kiehn then tried to make sure that the "power struggle" that had since broken out on the Magirus executive board would end in his favor. First, he dismissed director Karl Trefz, the very man who had brought him onto the supervisory board the year before.

Trefz, who had since been appointed president of the Ulm Chamber of Industry and Commerce, enjoyed great prestige in Ulm Nazi Party circles and had rendered outstanding service to the local NSDAP. Even before Kiehn had successfully infiltrated the Magirus supervisory board, Ulm district leader and NSDAP Gau inspector for Südwürttemberg Eugen Maier[17] had remarked of Magirus, "the leadership and staff of the firm have already been extremely helpful in sticking by the [party] movement despite their own difficulties (social, bank-related). ... The leadership, staff, and workers of this firm represent an effective NS factory cell [*Betriebszellengemeinschaft*] as we understand it. ... The Ulm [NSDAP] movement will always [find] a sympathetic ear with the firm when jobs must be found for more comrades ... or the movement needs any other support." The files of the district party office document that the Magirus management was always ready to serve the party's interests and its organizations. It was reported to the Reichszeugmeisterei (National Materials Control Office) in Munich that "even before the seizure of power, Magirus was one of the few large firms to put all of its efforts into supporting our movement everywhere and always, and whenever possible to hire party comrades kicked out of other companies for their party membership." The reports also indicate that after the Nazis took over, Magirus once again managed to take in and hire "hundreds of workers," and the NSDAP district leadership had only the best to report about Magirus's social practices as well.[18]

It is no surprise, then, that the news of director Trefz's imminent dismissal horrified the National Socialist employees of Magirus, and the Ulm district leadership even more. District leader Maier sided with Trefz and asked Reichsstatthalter and Gauleiter Murr to intervene. But Kiehn explained to Murr that his plan to make Magirus a model National Socialist factory "such as Germany has never seen" would not work with Trefz at the helm, and Murr then granted Kiehn authorization to do "what he believes justifiable" in the Trefz case. This sealed Trefz's ouster as far as Kiehn was concerned. Kreisleiter Maier insisted on a further discussion with Murr, but their talk changed nothing. Neither did a heated argument between adversaries Kiehn and Maier that culminated in the district leader challenging Kiehn — Württemberg's "economic leader" — to a duel in the presence of Gauleiter Murr.[19]

A few days later, Murr received a despairing letter from a Magirus manager. "For reputation's sake, and in the interest of the party," the sender begged "Reichsstatthalter und Gauleiter of the NSDAP, comrade Murr" to utter "a redeeming word and bring together the squabbling parties, Kiehn and Trefz. This morning, these simple words were painted all over the walls of the Magirus factory: 'Für Trefz.' The city is talking about the case; you can feel it in the air in the factory itself, and everyone is wondering how it is possible that the authority of the party has not intervened. ... It shouldn't be this way, that three capitalists control the factory — the very Württ.[emberg] company that an upstanding, hard-working, and enterprising director got through the hardest of times." The Magirus employee demanded that Murr "call the gentlemen's attention to the National Socialist worldview," asking, "why does one give the capitalists, two of them Freemasons and whose interests are being financed, as far as I can tell, by Pick the Jew, of Pick bank, so much power to be able to do whatever they like to anyone?"[20]

In fact, the question of why the Gauleitung let Kiehn do as he liked and gave him free rein in Ulm came up frequently during this period, in both Württemberg industry circles and the party. It remains difficult to answer that question conclusively to this day, but it has become even more urgent that we do so, because up to now only the "more harmless" part of this Kiehn-instigated scandal has been described.[21] Until the dismissal of the supervisory board, and the dismissal of Magirus's executive board afterward, in August 1935, Kiehn was able to pass off the adroitly engineered coup that made him the majority shareholder and plenipotentiary as a rescue mission to save the company. By the time his dealings triggered investigations by both the Economics Ministry and the NSDAP economic adviser for the Gau (Gauwirtschaftsberater), Kiehn — using the same verbose and melodramatic clichés as always — had already floridly described in December 1934 how he had just averted the danger that the previous shareholders supposedly presented to the long-established company. In a thirteen-page letter directed to the Gauleitung and other political agencies, Kiehn accused Daimler-Benz management in particular of having been out to take over its smaller competitor in Ulm: "Should utterly everything be driven into the jaws of big banks' capital and purely capitalist big corporations? ... No, I will not rest until anyone can see that Magirus has regained its absolute independence." He announced that his "intervention" would create "an example of National Socialist economic leadership."

Kiehn signified his new identity (which fit the current circumstances) by asking the party authorities "whether in Prussia they would ask the same questions of [banker and Freundeskreis member] Pg. v[on]. Schröder, president of the Cologne Chamber of Industry and Commerce, or of [Deutsche Bank supervisory board member and chair of the supervisory boards of several other big companies, including Daimler-Benz] Pg. von Stauß, vice president of the German Reichstag, as to why they were buying and then selling back these stocks, or how they were making use of their assets and credits?" Kiehn did not find it worth even mentioning that he, like other National Socialist candidates for Reichstag seats in earlier years, had been compelled to sign a declaration promising not to occupy "any supervisory board posts in banks or other enterprises" and "not to take up any such posts for the duration of my tenure as delegate."[22] Of course, such rules came from the time of struggle, the *Kampfzeit*, and had swiftly been forgotten once the NSDAP had seized power. In contrast, Kiehn seems to have adopted his "Compagnie ist Lumperie" motto only later on. He vehemently denied that he had created a "speculative enterprise" according to the old system model and deplored the "lack of understanding of economic matters" among "many" of his fellow party members. "Envy and resentment" were also to blame, he said, calling the "intrigues" hatched against him the work of "grumblers" and "industrious Jewish-style wheeling and dealing" that he intended to confront with his head held high.[23]

The written pleading, sent by the "leader of the Württemberg economy" to various party authorities and offices in December 1934, also instructed his fellow party members on the nature of a speculative enterprise, which required stocks to be "acquired cheaply and sold off again as rapidly as possible at the highest profit, without concern for the needs of the joint-stock company affected." He stressed at the time that "only once I have sold off the acquired shares and one could demonstrate what I earned" would there be evidence of speculative intentions. This scenario became a reality less than a year later.

Even at the time that Kiehn had managed to dismiss the Magirus director, with Gauleiter Murr's help, he was negotiating the sale of his Magirus shares with a member of the executive board of Klöckner-Humboldt-Deutz AG (KHD) in Cologne. The engine manufacturing firm in Cologne had been eyeing the Ulm company since 1918 and was now expressing renewed interest.[24] Kiehn, who by then was in serious financial straits, saw his chance to get out of the failed project largely unscathed. By this point he would have been aware that he lacked the capital to cover the purchase option he had acquired from Daimler-Benz that would have given him a three-fourths majority of shares. His bank debts in the meantime had risen to almost RM 700,000 and had yielded him nothing but attacks and anger. An agreement with KHD reached two weeks after Kiehn's discussion with Murr provided for "Herr Präsident Kiehn" to sell "Deutz-Motoren-AG ca. 80% of the share capital of C.D. Magirus A.G. in Ulm, which corresponds to 1.6 million M[ar]ks at the shares' nominal value. ... Deutz-Motoren-A.G. is to pay a rate of 150%." The planned settlement date was 7 September 1935.

Thus, the contract also extended to the shares still held by Deutsche Bank that were essential to Kiehn achieving his three-fourths majority — and Daimler-Benz AG held a right of first refusal for these shares in case of a resale. Kiehn did have an option to purchase these shares at this point in time, but no money to do it. With the help of a loan provided to him by KHD along with the financial know-how of his adviser and business colleague Stäbler, however, Kiehn managed to remove these obstacles. First, he needed to exercise his purchase option: the credit from a subsidiary of KHD, the Klöckner-Eisen AG in Duisburg, allowed him to purchase the shares still owned by Deutsche Bank for their par value of RM 622,100 and secure ownership of a three-fourths majority of Magirus AG shares. The next step was to zero in on eliminating Daimler-Benz AG's right of first refusal, which prevented Kiehn from selling the shares he had just acquired to a third party. At a general meeting on 9 September, Kiehn had himself appointed CEO of Magirus AG and amended the company's articles of association to award himself sole power of representation. On the same day, he concluded a "community of interests" contract with KHD, including a clause that from then on, the chair of Magirus's board of directors would always be a KHD board member. In addition, KHD secured the right to supervise Magirus's trading and business operations. Magirus, in turn, was required to solicit permission from KHD on all important decisions.

The fear at Daimler-Benz that one of Magirus's big competitors would exert an influence on the Ulm firm became a reality, making moot its right of first refusal. The "community of interests" contract, a mere stage in Magirus's merger with KHD set for 31 March 1936, fulfilled the deliberate intention of inducing Daimler-Benz to relinquish their right of first refusal.

The NSDAP national treasurer later calculated that Kiehn pocketed RM 702,482.63 in profit from this transaction. After some hesitation, Kiehn donated a large part of his speculation profits to the SS, "not least under the pressure of the circumstances," as the Gau court later certified. He did so in the hope of greater influence and because, according to the party judges, he must have known that had he done otherwise, "his position in Württemberg would have been simply untenable."[25]

Throughout Germany, the Magirus transaction had "provoked the strongest displeasure in both the party and the public." Kiehn's gambit drove long-established Württemberg industrialists off the Magirus supervisory board.[26] "World-renowned" Magirus AG had ceased to exist after seventy-two years of business and had fallen into the hands of an outside corporation, whose management — in contrast to that of outmaneuvered Daimler-Benz AG — party authorities regarded as politically undependable. In the end, general public opinion was that the city of Ulm had "lost" an important local company in this matter, and the rapidly growing staff of the Magirus factory was soon complaining about the continually worsening work atmosphere.[27]

Just three months after the merger, the factory cell representative was complaining that the DAF had lost all control over operating conditions at Magirus. Soon afterward there was talk of "reckless instigating and oppression" in the factory, and the company doctor warned the Nazi district leadership that the management was "exploiting the strength of the workers in such a way that he [the doctor] could no longer be responsible from a health standpoint."[28] Kiehn certainly was not personally responsible for this deplorable state of affairs. The worsening in the work situation was a consequence of the forced armament that was part of the Four-Year Plan, and very likely not a consequence of measures specific to KHD.[29] Even so, the NSDAP Gauleitung in Stuttgart made accusations against Kiehn. Having heard "few pleasant things" about the social environment at Magirus, Gauamtsleiter for technology Rudolf Rohrbach pointed out in a letter to Kiehn conditions "that contrast considerably from the intentions you announced a year ago to make the works a model National Socialist factory."[30] In no time at all, Kiehn the respected National Socialist endeavoring to be the company savior had done "exactly the opposite," in every sense of the word, of "what he promised to do ... when he joined the supervisory board of C.D. Magirus AG."[31]

Other examples of "National Socialist economic leadership" looked like trifles compared to Kiehn's failed attempt to use party ties to become a titan of industry. His status as "leader of the Württemberg economy" gave Kiehn numerous opportunities to secure advantages for himself. The magnitude of his expense allowances aroused the Gauleitung's disapproval.[32] As the leader of the district clearinghouse for public commissions at the Württemberg-Hohenzollern Economic Chamber, Kiehn was in a key position to decide the fortunes of many companies in the region, and the lucrative orders from the state became more and more important in the Nazi armament boom. Anyone in Kiehn's chamber district applying for publicly funded commissions had to stay on good terms with him. There are multiple reports of how he used this position and his other offices to exert pressure on other industrialists to persuade them to donate to the NSDAP and SS, and to dispute the size of their raw materials quotas in the more and more centrally controlled economy.[33] One can only assume that he probably also used his official functions to acquire state commissions for himself. All the same, Kiehn bragged after 1945 that the only reason a paper factory had not been decommissioned during the war was because he had "Aryanized" it: thanks to his excellent connections, he had been able to take care of finding the commissions necessary for the continued survival of the business.[34]

"Envious" and "grumbling" third parties behind the curtain could criticize his mingling of political and personal/business matters all they liked; for the moment, there was no damage to Kiehn's boastful and self-satisfied image as the "leader of the Württemberg economy."

Notes

1. BA DC, Akte Kiehn, letter to Reichsminister Frick of 15 May 1933.
2. See chap. 2.
3. Judgment of the Restitution Chamber of the Rottweil regional court in the case of Schwäbische Tagwacht GmbH, Stuttgart, vs. Fritz Kiehn of 5 Apr. 1949. StAS, Wü 28/2, T6 no. 382 (138/50R).
4. BA NS, 46/7, letter from Kiehn to Heß of 12 Sept. 1933. Some of Kiehn's correspondence is available in the online database "Nationalsozialismus, Holocaust, Widerstand und Exil 1933–1945," online database, De Gruyter, document ID: APK-016990. A judgment by the Gau court in May 1934 banned Scharr from holding public office following complaints from Scharr about losing printing clients he had acquired prior to 1933. See StAS, WÜ 13 T2 no. 2671 (denazification records Walter Scharr).
5. BA NS, 46/7, letters from Kiehn to the deputy Führer of 12 Sept. and 29 Nov. 1933. On the dramatic circulation increases in NS print media in Württemberg in the first six months of 1933, see Schnabel, *Württemberg*, 353; on how Kiehn maintained contacts with Murr and other politically prominent figures, see chap. 3.
6. BA NS, 46/7, letter from Kiehn to Heß of 12 Sept. 1933.
7. BA DC, Akte Kiehn, report compiled by Kiehn for the Gauleitung of 4 Dec. 1934.
8. Except where otherwise noted, the following description of Kiehn's Magirus transaction is taken from the NSDAP Gau court judgment of 28 Feb. 1939, BA DC, Akte Kiehn, available in the online database "Nationalsozialismus, Holocaust, Widerstand und Exil 1933–1945," De Gruyter, document ID: APK-019245.

9. On the history of C.D. Magirus, see RWWA, 107 (Klöckner-Archiv) V 20; StAL, PL 502/32, Bü 19, letter of 11 Dec. 1934 from Konrad Dieterich, NSDAP district economic adviser and authorized officer of Magirus AG, to the Gau economic adviser in Stuttgart; see also G. Goldbeck, *Klöckner-Humboldt-Deutz AG: Geschichte des Werkes Magirus Ulm 1884–1964*, unpublished manuscript. On motorization in Germany in general, see Edelmann, *Luxusgut*; Gregor, *Stern*, 29–54.
10. RWWA, 107, Goldbeck, *Magirus*, 36; BA DC, Akte Kiehn, Party Supreme Court (OPG) decision to abandon proceedings against Kiehn on grounds of hearing of 27–28 June 1939.
11. RWWA, 107, Goldbeck, *Magirus*, 33.
12. On Pick & Cie and its limited partners, especially Stäbler, see StAS, Wü 29/2B, Bü 1019; StAS, Wü 13, Bü. 2250 (denazification file Stäbler).
13. See Falkenhausen, "Anleihestockgesetz"; Lurie, *Investment*; Berghoff, *Kleinstadt*, 399–400.
14. Quoted from a report by Kiehn for the Gauleitung of 1 Dec. 1934, BA DC, Akte Kiehn. Acceptance of Kiehn's course of action can be found in StAL, PL 502/32, Bü 19, letter of 11 Dec. 1934 from Konrad Dieterich, KWB and authorized officer of Magirus AG, to NSDAP GWB.
15. See Spoerer, "Automobilindustrie," 64, fig. 3, for the progress of automobile industry stocks (not yet including Magirus AG) that shot up rapidly starting midway through 1934 after years of stagnation.
16. Kiehn's report of 1 Dec. 1934 for the Gauleitung, BA DC, Akte Kiehn; see also the OPG decision to abandon proceedings against Kiehn on grounds of the hearing on 27–28 June 1939, BA DC, Akte Kiehn. For further details on the institution of National Socialist model factories, see Frese, *Betriebspolitik*, 421–433.
17. On the party position of Gau inspector, see Arbogast and Gall, "Aufgaben."
18. StAL, PL 502/32, Bü 19, letter from Kreisleiter Maier in Ulm to his counterpart in Riesa of February 1934 and note from NSDAP Kreisgeschäftsführung in Ulm to Reichszeugmeisterei of 16 Nov. 1934.
19. NSDAP Gau court judgment of 28 Feb. 1939, BA DC, Akte Kiehn; on the challenge to a duel, see statement from senior SS leader Tondock, member of "HA SS-Gericht, RF-SS," during the negotiation before the OPG, BA DC, Akte Kiehn; on Eugen Maier, see Arbogast and Gall, "Aufgaben," 153–155; Arbogast, *Herrschaftsinstanzen*, 170–172; Schmidt, "Hilfsarbeiter."
20. StAL, PL 502/32, Bü 19, letter from Magirus advertising manager to Reichsstatthalter of 23 Aug. 1935.
21. It remains unclear what induced Murr to support Kiehn against Kreisleiter Eugen Maier, whom he otherwise appreciated, and drop Trefz. Much evidence suggests that the intraparty power struggles in the Württemberg-Hohenzollern Gau paved the way for Kiehn's Magirus affair as well (see chap 3). Murr may have felt a personal obligation to Kiehn; whatever the case, the industrialist alleged at an SS hearing on 7 Apr. 1936 that "I have always enjoyed … the best comradely bond to my Gauleiter. In those days … I went to Munich in March or April 1933 with various other fellow party members to advocate personally before the Führer for the Gauleiter [and not his intraparty rival Mergenthaler] to become state president [Reichsstatthalter] of Württemberg." BA DC, Akte Kiehn. On the negotiations with Hitler in Munich about the formation of the government in Württemberg, see Schnabel, *Württemberg*, 183.
22. BA DC, Akte Robert Zeller, signed declaration of Reichstag election candidate Zeller of 2 June 1932.
23. BA DC, Akte Kiehn, legal document by Kiehn of 4 Dec. 1934; BA DC, Akte Kiehn, judgment by NSDAP Gau court of 28 Feb. 1939; on the life and importance of Emil Georg von Stauß, a member of the Deutsche Bank board of directors until 1932 and therefore an optimal bogeyman for Kiehn to use, see the brief biography in Lilla, Döring, and Schulz,

Statisten, 641–642, and Hamburger Stiftung für die Sozialgeschichte des 20. Jahrhunderts and Ebbinghaus, *Daimler-Benz Buch,* 771; on Schröder, whose role in handing over power to the National Socialists has been demonstrated many times, see Turner, *Großunternehmer,* 377–379.
24. On the inquiries made into Magirus in 1918 by KHD, see RWWA, 107 (Klöckner-Archiv) V 20.
25. BA DC, Akte Kiehn, Gau court judgment of 28 Feb. 1939.
26. ASD, NL Erler, Box 85, letter from Otto Magirus to Fritz Erler of 7 July 1950 indicating that not only was Adolf von Magirus compelled to give up his seat as chair of the supervisory board, but Otto Magirus, who had been of "great service" to the company, was "simply dismissed from the board at his advanced age," which was "tough" on the family.
27. On suspicions of the Klöckner corporation being "a big KA [Katholische Aktion] prop," see BA DC, Akte Kiehn, eight-page unsigned report of 28 Feb. 1938 drafted in Stuttgart and designated "military secret"; on Peter Klöckner's political links to the Center Party, see Weisbrod, *Schwerindustrie.*
28. StAL, PL 502, Bü 19 (Akten der Kreisleitung Ulm), letter from DAF Kreisbetriebsgemeinschaftswalter and Kreisamtleiter Dr. Schwarz of May 1937.
29. On how KHD corporate management sought to increase productivity, crush solidarity, and fragment the workers, see Rüther, "Sozialpolitik."
30. StAL, PL 502, Bü 204, letter from GLT Rudolf Rohrbach to Kiehn of 30 Nov. 1936.
31. BA DC, Akte Kiehn, Gau court judgment of 28 Feb. 1939.
32. BA DC, Akte Kiehn, undated internal report, presumably prepared by the SD, for the SS proceedings against Kiehn that were abandoned in 1936.
33. BA DC, Akte Kiehn, letter from Kiehn to manufacturer Jakob Henke of 12 Dec. 1934; ASD, NL Erler, Box 85, descriptions of Kiehn's business practices in letter of 25 Oct. 1950 from a competitor; letter from retired state secretary Paul Binder to Kiehn of 29 Mar. 1954, private collection.
34. On 7 July 1947, Kiehn stated in a hearing carried out during his time in custody that he made "constant efforts" to distribute commissions, "especially [those] from offices of the Reich." StAS, Wü 29/2B, Bü 1019.

Chapter 5

BETWEEN CORRUPTION AND CAMARADERIE
The National Socialist Campaign to Curb Abuses

Having risen so quickly to new ranks and lofty positions, Fritz Kiehn never missed an opportunity during his public appearances to demonstrate how he personified National Socialist values and acted "in service to the people" (*Dienst am Volke*).[1] But his meteoric rise and boastful manner soon brought Kiehn, like many other "old fighters," into opposition with the expectations of political renewal prevalent both inside and outside the NSDAP. As Kershaw has noted, "the striking loss of prestige by the Party in the first years of Nazi rule can … be related to the poor image of local functionaries."[2] What's more, the "unbridled business acumen" Kiehn exhibited in the Magirus case, his perpetually reappearing tendency to "hunt down" connections to higher-ups, and his unscrupulous violations of his party's ideological principles made him a target for many different forms of criticism lodged by an array of different authorities within the Nazi administration, although admittedly nothing was said in public.

How the party dealt internally with Kiehn's numerous incidents and scandals merits further detail: the conflicts over Kiehn that played out among the polycratic power centers of the Third Reich illuminate the offensive reality of many local and regional leaders' hunger for power and the regime's inability to remedy this.[3] Once Kiehn had left his troubled past as a Straßer ally behind and had risen to become the "leader of the Württemberg economy" in the spring of 1934, thanks to his Gauleiter's protection, it did not take long before party and SS members began registering complaints about him through official channels or in the form of denunciations. Kiehn's stock purchases occasioned the first investigations, carried out by the Economics Ministry and the Gau economic adviser. As the new chairman of the board and majority shareholder of Magirus AG, smeared (rightly) as a speculator, Kiehn once again conveniently blamed the

---

Notes from this chapter begin on page 98.

"big competition" (meaning Daimler-Benz AG in Stuttgart) as the source of the "intrigues" allegedly hatched against him. Barring that, it had to be "Communist agitators in disguise." Kiehn regarded the criticism of his actions as the work of "grumblers ... whose comeuppance cannot be harsh enough for the party's sake."[4]

It appears that Stuttgart followed his recommendation, even when it became clear beyond a shadow of a doubt — at least among the general public at the time — that grave damage was being done to the Gau's economic interests and those of the city of Ulm, as well as the working conditions of Magirus employees. The SS launched a complaint in early 1935 about the Johnny-come-lately transformation in Kiehn's lifestyle, his use of political positions for personal gain, and his incompetence as an economic leader, which trickled through the dense network of official NSDAP channels. Compelled to issue an opinion by the Reichsführer-SS court, the SS Southwest Regional Headquarters in Stuttgart finally reopened the Kiehn case in February 1936. Evidently no one was very eager to ascertain the validity of the accusations — some of them very detailed — leveled against Kiehn: once he was served a summons, the investigations were abandoned without further questioning. The Stuttgart headquarters suggested to the RFSS court that if similar "complaints" came up in the future, one should "return [these] to the complainant and entreat him to submit evidence for his accusations."[5]

By the end of 1935, the Technology Office of the Gauleitung had already looked over the one-sided agreements reached with KHD that had done irreparable harm to Magirus AG, and the Economics Ministry had received a report on how the Magirus affair had damaged the Württemberg economy as fact filled as it was comprehensive. Yet Kiehn sailed through unscathed. He moved back into the Reichstag in March 1936, when his reputation was still glowing from the position he had added to his resume in January of that same year: the presidency of the newly created Württemberg-Hohenzollern Economic Chamber.[6]

But the accusations and concerns swirling around "Herr Präsident Pg. Kiehn" would have consequences. The conflicts still smoldering behind the scenes at the Württemberg NSDAP aggravated the polycratic chaos of the National Socialist state, preventing pending problems from being solved and creating new tensions. For example, when the Heilbronn Chamber of Industry and Commerce was liquidated as part of administrative reform efforts in 1934, despite lively protests from regional industry, there were no coordinated interventions in Berlin. Instead, the Reich Economics Ministry saw rival negotiations, with the president of the Economic Chamber on one side and the Gau economic adviser on the other. This competition would have done little to help the issue, but all negotiations were for naught. Not until 1945 was the Heilbronn IHK reactivated.[7]

A conflict between the Gauleitung and the large Stuttgart electronics company Bosch would soon disclose these tensions — which also influenced Kiehn's relationship to Gauamtsleiter for technology Rudolf Rohrbach — in a way that would do great damage to the party's reputation in economic circles. Kiehn played a key role in this affair, which was triggered by Rohrbach. The confrontation with the Bosch directorate, which ultimately degenerated into a disgrace for the Nazi Gauleitung, could have easily been avoided had Rohrbach and Kiehn not had such an icy professional relationship that allowed misunderstandings to fester between them in their respective capacities as Gauamtsleiter for technology and head of the Economic Chamber.[8]

Rohrbach was a young, ambitious, and educated party functionary, full of moral rigor and a socially motivated ideological enthusiasm for education. Born in Heilbronn in 1902, he belonged to the *Kriegsjugendgeneration,* those who had been too young to fight in World War I but in most cases regretted this exclusion very much, as presumably the bulk of the "specifically National Socialist economic elite" did.[9] He studied engineering and at twenty-four years of age began his career as a road construction engineer without finishing his degree. He joined the NSDAP in 1931 and became "one of the most active National Socialists in Württemberg" in the years after 1933, according to testimony by state councilor and Württemberg Democrat Konrad Wittwer.[10]

Even though it was outside the scope of Rohrbach's duties, he repeatedly reminded Kiehn of his promises to the employees of the Magirus factory and confronted him with the sad reality of the postmerger Ulm company. Kiehn, in turn, unleashed a torrent of complaints on the party functionary, accusing him of providing inadequate information, incompetence, and dereliction of duty that he would never have imagined even of the "youngest apprentice" at his Efka works. "How could you," Kiehn asked Rohrbach, "disregard the most elementary rules of reason and decency?" Rohrbach was happy to shed light on his motives, which had come from "the need for purity in the interest of the party."[11]

Once open mutual contempt was thus ensured, they appear to have stopped speaking. They ignored each other as much as they could, and each avoided drawing the other into any problems that would have required their cooperation in order for business to carry on efficiently. The Bosch affair, which like the Magirus case had broader implications, made this emphatically clear.

An article Rohrbach printed anonymously in the September 1937 edition of *Die Technik,* a journal published by the Gau Technology Office, triggered the difficult conflict between the leadership of the largest Württemberg industrial firm and the Gauleitung. In it, Rohrbach described the battle that the Nazi state was waging against honorary academic titles: these were given less out of "honoris *causa,*" he wrote, than an expectation that monetary donations would follow. In an unmistakeable allusion to the Robert Bosch firm, Rohrbach concluded that the National Socialism-led "upheaval" in the attitude of the German people had yet to leave its mark on this particular company. "Otherwise, it would not have been possible for the honorary title of 'Dr. h.c.' to be requested for four directors at the same time, even if the prospect of a very handsome six-figure sum in support of the state college was offered as an honorarium for this service." Rohrbach based his account on the denunciation — unmentioned, of course — filed by the dean of the college in question, the Stuttgart Technical College. His article was written in the defamatory muckraking style typical of the brown "Kampf sheets" that were repeatedly used to denounce industrialists. The author closed with the threat that it was no longer tolerable for "the dignity of technology to be besmirched by the purchasing of honorary titles."[12]

The insulted Bosch board of directors rejected the portrayal in an open letter directed to the company's own engineers, describing it as "grave injury to the truth," "libel," and "published fraud." Rohrbach, following orders from other Gauleitung offices and likely also at the request of Reichsstatthalter Murr, conducted talks with the Bosch directors over the next few weeks. Bosch CEO Hans Walz demanded that he correct the objectionable article in *Die Technik*. In return, the Bosch leadership would be willing to make a clean break with the affair as soon as Walz had informed his technicians that Bosch considered the case closed; that is, once the Gauamtsleiter had "realized, after the actual facts of the matter have been explained, that the account his sources gave him is erroneous."

This was the latest Rohrbach would have been informed that it was Fritz Kiehn, president of the Economic Chamber, who had handled the negotiations with the dean of the college about awarding honorary doctorates in the run-up to the Bosch company's fiftieth anniversary. The management denied that Kiehn had been commissioned to negotiate on the company's behalf: in fact, Kiehn was alleged to have approached the Bosch directorate himself with these suggestions. Rather than questioning Kiehn about his role, Rohrbach settled for turning again to his informer, the president of the university. An "old fighter" for the NSDAP,[13] the dean reaffirmed his account that Kiehn had approached him to request that the Reich education minister grant an exception to the rule on honorary doctorates in favor of the Bosch directors. Kiehn had drawn his attention to the "120 million in foreign currency" that Bosch brought into the Reich every year and demanded a special arrangement. Over the course of further negotiations, the dean was ultimately presented with the prospect of considerable monetary donations from the firm. These never arrived, of course — not after the dean's attempt to persuade the education minister was unsuccessful, as expected. Indeed, the minister's offer to appoint the three sitting Bosch directors as honorary senators of Stuttgart Technical College as compensation was rejected by the firm's leaders; this was, after all, a far less prestigious distinction. The dean, who mistakenly assumed that Kiehn's visit took place with the knowledge of Bosch management and on the company's behalf, saw their rejection of the honorary senatorial title as "an insult to the college."[14]

The conversation with the dean, Wilhelm Stortz, strengthened Rohrbach's resolve. Instead of publishing the contrary account that was dangled as a possibility in the negotiations with Bosch, therefore, he had a sensational article, "The Honorary Doctors," published in the next issue of *Die Technik,* this time under the byline of "Gauamtsleiter Rohrbach." The article repeated all of the allegations and dismissed the Bosch directors' attempts to distance themselves from the controversy as bald-faced lies. Rohrbach then had to suffer the reproaches of Bosch director Hans Walz in a new "open letter" to the engineers at Bosch: the Gauamtsleiter had "added new false allegations to the untruths concerning honorary doctorates that he presented to readers in issue 9/1937 of the journal *Die Technik* ... that he published — at least no longer anonymously this time." The Bosch director fiercely took aim at the Third Reich's common practice of denunciation by stating that "of our firm much has been said, written, and misrepresented ... but unheard of and unique" among such acts was the way "gossip" had been used in this case by "persons unknown ... in so rash and malicious a fashion for completely unjust public attacks and libelous remarks." Hans Walz, who could lean on the influence and reputation of a large (albeit politically controversial) industrial corporation, had no intention of bowing to such practices. He openly went on the warpath, a position that few industrial leaders dared to take during this time, and produced a sworn declaration from "President Kiehn" in which the latter denied ever having spoken of monetary donations in connection with the negotiations over the conferring of honorary doctorates.

This allegation, which openly contradicted the account by Rohrbach's source, Dean Stortz, may have been false — like so many of Kiehn's explanations — or, as the NSDAP Gau court later intepreted it, a mistake. It is not possible to clarify this point. There is no doubt that one piece of information Stortz gave to the Bosch board was made up, however, and Hans Walz repeated it in his open letter. He recalled that all of the evidence for the allegations Rohrbach had put forward up to that point had come from Rohrbach himself and noted "that from the beginning, before the publication of his libelous remarks, Herr Rohrbach refused to acquaint himself with the true facts of the matter from the authority who knew them best, namely the dean's office at the Technical College." Next came the remarkable sentence: "The dean assured us when we inquired that Herr Rohrbach had not gathered any information from the dean's office before publication took place."

Driven into a corner by the Bosch director's unusual penchant for conflict, the Gauamtsleiter for technology promptly disclosed his informants. The scandal now spread to the college. In another open letter, this time directed to the college faculty, the Bosch company attacked the dean who had been exposed as an informant, rejected his account of the matter, and held him responsible for the unwarranted accusations, whereupon Dean Stortz called a faculty meeting on 2 February 1938 in which he characterized Kiehn's sworn declaration "as contradictory to the facts." At the same time, he strove to arrive at a morally defensible interpretation of his turn as an informant. Playing down his role, he stated: "In the course of my regular contact with the Gau Technology Office of the NSDAP, particular information about the course of negotiations was given to the Gau office. I expressly declare that I, as a National Socialist college dean, am fundamentally entitled and obligated … to have this affiliation."[15]

After the case had made so broad an impact in the meantime that the Reich governor wanted to take over the investigation, Rohrbach finally commissioned the SD on 11 February 1938 to ascertain Kiehn's role in the controversial matter. On 25 February 1938, Kiehn once again took part in a discussion with Reich governor Murr; Rohrbach and Dean Stortz were also present. If we are to believe an internal SD memo, the only object of negotiation was "the conduct of Pres. Kiehn." He had conducted negotiations with Bosch and the college in a way that could be misunderstood by both sides, giving him a dubious role in this affair but by no means the leading one. Despite the Reich governor's intervention, an agreement could not be reached between Stortz and Kiehn, each of whom persisted in his own interpretation of the facts. Thus, the Bosch case became an affair of honor between long-serving party comrades Kiehn and Stortz, one in which the NSDAP Gau court would have the last word. At the conclusion of the affair, the SD tersely reported that "the Bosch company was advised in writing by Inspector General Dr. Todt of the ridiculousness of its conduct." The "relationship to Bosch" was to be resolved at a later date.[16]

Kiehn's "outrageous conduct" was blamed for the public disgrace that the controversy had turned into for the Gauleitung because of Rohrbach's unfounded accusations.[17] With a spring in their step, party officials started inquiries into the "leader of the Württemberg economy," who owed his simultaneous tenure as "military economic leader" to his "friendship to Reich Economics Minister Funk." According to SD reports, this had triggered consternation in Württemberg party circles.[18]

The investigations carried out against Kiehn revealed a long list of transgressions. The SD came up with questionable reports about Max, the "tame" deer that the unsuspecting Reichsführer-SS personally brought down. As previously mentioned, the lucky shooter was actually SS Southwest Regional Headquarters director Prützmann. The extortionate gift of an overpriced Menzel painting paid for by the Württemberg industrialists for the Führer's birthday the year before came up as well. Kiehn was accused of "hunting down connections," and it was discovered — with the evidence of Kiehn's failed newspaper project from 1933 and the Magirus business transaction effected with the help of "Freemasons" and a "Jewish bank" — "that Kiehn showed a lack of consistent adherence to National Socialist principles in favor of personal advantages." Kiehn's tax files ultimately confirmed the impression of "smarmy business conduct," as it was described in an internal Gauleitung report.[19]

On 3 August 1938, the opening decision against Kiehn that was required to begin Gau court proceedings was issued at the behest of the Party Supreme Court.

The plaintiff was not Dean Stortz but the Gauleitung and, in the Magirus matter, the NSDAP Reich treasurer. A few weeks before, on 15 June, Kiehn had been formally admitted to the Freundeskreis (Circle of Friends) of the Reichsführer-SS, a position that would be of great use to him in the imminent court proceedings and that he had managed to attain — according to Gauleitung investigations — by having "transferred or loaned larger amounts to various SS leaders in order to rehabilitate their finances."[20]

Kiehn may have thought he was protected as a member of Himmler's Freundeskreis, but the Gau court proceedings could not have come at a more unfortunate time for him: competition had broken out right then over the deals to be had on "objects of Aryanization" — and a significant number of Gauleitung functionaries were taking part wholeheartedly. The selling off of "Jewish firms" was in full swing in late summer 1938, and Kiehn could only participate in this lucrative trade — he had been warned — if he emerged unscathed from the Gau court proceedings. This also precluded the tempting possibility of using the Führer's amnesty of 27 April 1938 to have the proceedings called off.

In December 1938, in consideration of the pending proceedings, Kiehn had to vacate his seat in the Reichstag temporarily. The main hearing, on no fewer than eight charges, finally took place in Stuttgart in January 1939. The last charge was the accusation from "College Dean Pg. Stortz," ultimately judged as unverifiable because of a false statement declared under oath. Other charges that were dropped concerned Kiehn's alleged failure to provide collateral when opening a loan, as well as the alleged employment of Jewish representatives by his Efka firm.[21]

Unlike the Gauleitung, the court also did not deign to recognize any proof of "low business morals" in the complaint brought against Kiehn by one of his competitors. The Efka factory owner had gone to Gau economic adviser Reihle to blacken the name of a Dresden cigarette paper manufacturer because the latter's products — admittedly since as early as 1910, as the investigations showed — had been sold using symbols of the global revolution and Freemasonry. After the court had gotten a look at the incriminating cigarette papers, it came to the conclusion that these had "without a doubt" had a "provocative" effect. The party judges, therefore, did not wish to exclude the possibility in this case that Kiehn "had wanted to induce ... the responsible party officials to intervene because of his feeling of National Socialist obligation."

And with that, the list of accusations — most of which had been dropped "for lack of proof" — was exhausted. SS colonel (Standartenführer) Tondock, who had been assigned as Kiehn's "legal adviser" by the head of Himmler's personal staff, sent a report to group leader Wolff in Berlin once the hearing had concluded: the Gauleiter's representative was requesting "a warning and the revocation of the ability to hold party offices for a period of three years," which, "according to current regulations," would also have to result in Kiehn's "resignation as SS leader."

In order to avoid such an outcome, the SS emissary sought to bring about "a personal meeting between the Reichsführer-SS and Gauleiter Murr on the K. issue," which — as he made clear to Wolff — "is generally assessed to be extraordinarily serious."[22]

Kiehn, who once again was convinced that others wished to do him wrong, exercised calculated optimism and explained to his "venerated SS comrade Tondock" that "the hearing ... ultimately can only turn out in my favor."[23] In the end his prognosis would be proved right, even if the judgment issued by the Gau court in late February 1939 turned out to be devastating for Kiehn in every respect. He was certified to have "grossly contravened party discipline in the whole of his conduct" and to have "done considerable harm to the reputation of the NSDAP in Württemberg." The court objected in detail to how Kiehn had "forgotten his obligations" both as an administrator of the assets that had been entrusted to his safekeeping and as a National Socialist in his dealings with Jews and Freemasons. As a legal lever for the latter accusation, which took on great significance during the Gau court proceedings, the court in the Magirus affair considered not only Kiehn's business relationships to Pick, the "Jewish bank," and Kiehn's adviser, Stäbler the Freemason, but also a telling letter from 1932. Kiehn had written it in support of a man who was in debt to a Jewish cattle dealer in Tuttlingen. The note, the letterhead of which identified the sender as an "M.d.R." (member of the German Reichstag), concluded with an intimately worded postscript: "My dear Julius! Please make further allowances for poor Sauter; I too will ensure that the debt is soon repaid. Yours with best regards, F. K." Kiehn declared on the record that the recipient was a former comrade from his regiment in World War I.

From today's standpoint, the fact that Kiehn was charged with having contacts to Jews could serve to diminish his moral guilt. Recall, however, that this entrepreneur did not shrink from using inflammatory anti-Semitic slogans in both his personal correspondence with party offices and his propaganda appearances, and that he had no scruples about making a great deal of money from the Aryanization of Jewish businesses, as will be shown in more detail. If his conduct toward Jews was nothing less than friendly, it was also an expression of his ruthless opportunism in this central question of his National Socialist worldview and politics.[24]

As for Kiehn's efforts to acquire Magirus AG, the Gau court fell in line with the findings of the Economics Ministry, where the sale of the firm had long been on record as "share price profiteering and speculation" that "would have been highly typical of the era before the seizure of power." The danger of Magirus being taken over by the "big competition," which Kiehn allegedly averted, had never existed in the first place, but had become a reality through Kiehn's machinations. The court had absolutely no desire to consider Kiehn's investment of his speculative profits into the SS and the party as mitigating circumstances, stating instead "that the donations were used not least in service of his own advantage." Specifically, the ambitious business owner was proved to have waited after reselling the shares before bringing out his bonanza: the great majority of Kiehn's donations did not begin flowing until later years, "when he faced an ever louder outcry." The city of Trossingen was the only party to receive a considerable amount of money (publicized by Kiehn and given in honor of his fiftieth birthday, 15 October 1935) the same year that the Magirus shares were resold — and proved its gratitude by making Kiehn an honored citizen of the town.

The distribution of the money was also seen as scandalous by his enemies since the only party offices Kiehn showed favor to were those "from which he expected any advantages, such as an improvement in his reputation, whereas he donated practically nothing to party charity organizations such as the NSV or the WHW, where he would not have appeared to be such a big donor or to have become well known; any other manufacturer with the same income as the accused," stated the Gau court, "donates more to the WHW than what the accused donated from his Magirus profit." Finally, Kiehn had to cope with accusations of attempted tax fraud because he had not paid taxes on these capital gains.[25]

Kiehn, who had informed his SS "legal adviser" that he would carry the fight for his "good name ... to the extreme," was also proved in the main Gau court hearing to have supplied false information about crucial points on which he had given his word of honor. In the end he was forced to respond to accusations about how he treated his supporters in Ulm party circles and the Magirus factory. The court made Kiehn take to heart that "decency and comradeship" would have demanded he inform these party comrades of his intentions. Kiehn, on the other hand, had "engaged in disloyal conduct that is especially unbecoming of a man of the position and posts held by the accused, as even the council of trust and followers of the (former) Magirus company feel betrayed by him."

After all of these facts had been established with a recognizable effort at objectivity, the Gau court (which had to rule on conduct harmful to the party, rather than criminal guilt) arrived at the conclusion that the accused had "incurred a considerable penalty" because of the "severity of his transgressions." The court gave Kiehn a warning and expressly stated that there was no possibility of using the Führer's amnesty to have the proceedings abandoned, since Kiehn "had requested that the proceedings be carried out after express instruction." The verdict refrained from stripping Kiehn of his posts, as the Gauleitung representative had requested in the hearing, "in consideration of the fact that the accused himself declared that he would resign his posts within six weeks of this decision being delivered."[26]

It can no longer be determined whether, after the oral hearing with Colonel Tondock, there were hearings at the highest level before the issuance of the party court's decision "on the K. case," as was the original plan. Nevertheless, the judgment against Kiehn — reached in collaboration with an SS committee member, in accordance with the rules of the organization — exhibits features of a last-minute compromise between the SS and the Gauleitung. Kiehn, who had asked for continued "comradely help" from his SS adviser even after the main hearing on 16 January 1939, reminding Tondock that he had to emerge unscathed from the proceedings in order to avoid being hindered by the Gauleitung "in my economic future" or deterred from Aryanizing the "non-Aryan Fleischer paper factory in Eislingen (Württ.)." In any case, he had no intention of resigning his posts.[27] Quite the contrary, it is very likely that when Kiehn promised to step down from his positions, he had long since resolved to appeal the decision by the party court. And he could be certain that the head of Himmler's personal staff, as a "responsible SS Führer," would align himself with this request for an appeal. SS group leader Karl Wolff would not have lacked sympathy for the embattled patron of the Freundeskreis; he likely stayed with Kiehn many a time on hunting trips. At the same time, Wolff had to defend himself before the Party Supreme Court against suspicions of playing favorites and exploiting his high SS office for personal advantage. The head of the Party Supreme Court, Walter Buch, had let Wolff know that the Führer's amnesty of 27 April 1938 was the only way that the court would abstain from carrying out proceedings.[28]

The final appeal hearing in the Kiehn case took place in June before the Party Supreme Court in Berlin. Representing the SS on the judging panel was senior SS leader Hinrich Lohse, an old colleague of Kiehn's: both had belonged to the NSDAP faction in the Reichstag since July 1932.[29] If the judgment of the Gau court had been visibly influenced by efforts to earnestly try the allegations raised against Kiehn, the proceedings before the Party Supreme Court — the highest NSDAP authority — obviously only served to rehabilitate him. This had already become clear in the run-up to the main hearing, when as early as April Himmler had "spontaneously" reversed Kiehn's previously announced leave of absence from the SS and allowed him to wear the uniform once again. In addition, the chair of the Reichstag faction, Reichminister Frick, had allowed Kiehn to begin participating in Reichstag meetings again.[30]

The strategy that the party judges ultimately used in Kiehn's defense was complex, but transparent nonetheless. The Gau court had explicitly found that Kiehn had knowingly deceived his Gauleiter in the Magirus affair. Such an infringement of party discipline could not be allowed to go unpunished, or to jeopardize the authority of Gauleiter Murr. At the same time, however, Kiehn had to be spared the stench of having damaged the party or even of having engaged in defamatory conduct. The higher court rejected the finding of the Gau court that Kiehn had "stated untruths under word of honor" in court, on the grounds that "the passionate assertion by the accused in the main hearing, invoking his word of honor (which had not been required of him), cannot be seen as being his word of honor in view of a number of fundamental considerations." The witnesses called by the prosecution, culled from Ulm party circles and the Magirus staff, had their reputations damaged on the stand in front of the Party Supreme Court.

To preserve the authority of the Gauleiter, who had been deceived by Kiehn, the Party Supreme Court came to the conclusion that the accused was to be punished with a warning, "due to his conduct in the sale of the Magirus shares, which did not sufficiently safeguard the reputation and interests of the party." Thus, Kiehn, who had been explicitly cleared of having engaged in defamatory conduct, was completely rehabilitated with the help of a clear procedural error in the same move. The proceedings were abandoned, citing the Führer's amnesty of 27 April 1938. The grounds given by the senior party judges for this decision, "although the accused has requested that the proceedings be carried out and therefore has renounced any use of the amnesty," were unsurpassed in their sophistry, paralleling the entire trial.

A member of the Reichsführer-SS's personal staff when he faced the bar of the highest Nazi Party court, Fritz Kiehn enjoyed that "tendency toward moderation in practice," or camaraderie, that Hans Buchheim demonstrated decades ago as being characteristic of dealings within the SS and complementary to its rigorous official identity as an elite force. "*Cameraderie* [sic; emphasis in the original] was what made it possible to live with the harshness of the system, a loophole of which the majority frequently and unconsciously availed themselves. ... In the name of *cameraderie* [sic] increasingly serious failings become acceptable, offences can be covered up."[31]

Expediency was often the deciding factor in who would benefit from such "moderation in practice" and who would be subject to stronger measures. Sheer arbitrariness also frequently played a role. One of the prosecution witnesses in the Kiehn case, an SS colonel named Pfannenschwarz from Ulm who was also vice president of the state parliament, had such an experience. The attorney, an "old fighter" like Kiehn, held a position of trust under Gauleiter Murr and had also held public office as the state huntsman (*Landesjägermeister*). In 1935, he had used his influence with the Gauleiter to personally intercede on Kiehn's behalf in the dispute between director Karl Trefz and Kiehn. Kiehn consequently gave Pfannenschwarz a five-figure sum, just as he had done with other SS members. Being from Ulm, the onetime advocate for the Trossingen factory owner must have felt disappointed and deceived by the sale of Magirus to KHD, and in return he testified against Kiehn before the Gau court. This would be his undoing in the SS: investigations into the "uncomradely" prosecution witness began immediately. The official reason given was that his excessive demands for attorney fees had brought discredit on Pfannenschwarz. But the "crimes" of the Ulm attorney looked exceptionally modest compared to Kiehn's wealth-grabbing methods, which had been backed by the Party Supreme Court and the SS. The true reason, then, that "the Reichsführer-SS intend[ed] ... to dismiss Dr. Karl Pfannenschwarz from the SS" was that, in addition, as group leader Wolff informed the SS Southwest Regional Headquarters on 15 September 1939, "Pfannenschwarz [had] also attracted attention in the most unpleasant way during the party court proceedings against SS Chief Storm Leader Fritz Kiehn."[32]

The investigations opened against Pfannenschwarz at the SS's urging were introduced in the bar association (Württembergische Anwaltskammer) and the NSDAP Gau court as well, and they served their purpose. No one anywhere near the Württemberg Gauleiter would ever again dare to challenge Fritz Kiehn, member of the Reichsführer-SS's personal staff, even though his reputation within the SS, which he had showered so generously with donations, had taken a beating in Württemberg itself. When the Reichssicherheitshauptamt (Reich Security Main Office, or RSHA) sent an inquiry to the senior SS and police leader in Stuttgart about the moral character of Bosch CEO Walz, in advance of the planned appointment of a new military industrial leader in 1942 by Himmler's official representative at the Gau level, SS group leader Kurt Kaul replied that Walz had taken pains in his business approach to hire National Socialist staff and was "not malicious, at any rate — much more harmless than Military Industrial Leader SS Stubaf. [storm leader] Kiehn."[33]

Kiehn retained his public posts until the large-scale administrative reform of the economic chambers in 1942, however, and was able to dedicate himself to another Aryanization unmolested, during which he repeatedly made use of the expertise of his authorized agent, Stäbler, and the financial support of Pick & Cie, which had since been "purified" of its Jewish staff and was now owned by Freemasons Glaub and Stäbler. The system was obviously incapable of eliminating these documented "abuses" on its own, abuses that the Third Reich public criticized as not being National Socialist in nature. This protectionism that degenerated into camaraderie, and the resulting incapability of the Nazi administration to resolve crises, caused "a lingering crisis of confidence in the Party and its representatives, particularly at local and regional level." It emerged in the early years of Hitler's rule and "lasted for the duration of the regime."[34]

Notes

The translator wishes to acknowledge the Europäisches Übersetzer-Kollegium in Straelen, Germany, whose library was invaluable for her work on chapters 5 and 6.

1. See Kiehn's speech at the opening of the newly constituted Economic Chamber on 5 Feb. 1935 in Winkel, *Industrie- und Handelskammern*, 65.
2. Kershaw, *Myth*, 100.
3. See Kershaw, *Myth*, 96–104; Angermund, "Korruption"; Bajohr, *Parvenüs*; Gruchmann, "Korruption"; Schnabel, *Württemberg*, 379–402. On corruption during Aryanization, see chap. 6.
4. BA DC, Akte Kiehn, written pleading by Kiehn of 4 Dec 1934. The quote "Communist agitators in disguise" is in a letter from Kiehn to Gauamtsleiter Rohrbach of 28 Jan. 1937, StAL, PL 502/32.

5. BA DC, Akte Kiehn, letter from group leader Prützmann, SS Southwest Regional Headquarters, to RF-SS, SS court, of 13 May 1936.
6. StAL, PL 502/32, Bü. 204, Gau court judgment of 28 Feb. 1939, available in the online database "Nationalsozialismus, Holocaust, Widerstand und Exil 1933–1945," De Gruyter, document ID: APK-019245. The "Stiller Report of the Interior Ministry" cited here as app. 7 presumably has not survived but was at least seventy pages long and was repeatedly used as evidence against Kiehn. On the creation of the Economic Chamber, see Winkel, *Industrie- und Handelskammern,* 48–50.
7. Winkel, *Industrie- und Handelskammern,* 72–79.
8. Unless otherwise noted, all sources quoted in the Bosch affair are from BA DC, Akte Kiehn. See also Schnabel, *Württemberg,* 253–255.
9. According to Bajohr, the characteristics common to this economic elite were "a date of birth after 1900, the experience of being a child or young person during the war, academic education, career ambition and ideological convictions." Bajohr, *"Aryanisation,"* 146.
10. StAS, Wü 13, Bü 2994 (denazification records Rudolf Rohrbach); HStAS, EA2/150, unindexed personnel file of district administrator Theodor Zeller with Wittwer's political judgment of Rohrbach of 15 Oct. 1945. We are grateful to Michael Ruck for this reference.
11. StAL, PL 502/32, Bü. 204, letter from Rohrbach to Kiehn of 30 Nov. 1936 and 9 Feb. 1937, Kiehn's reply of 28 Jan. 1937.
12. "Berufs- und Berufsehrenfragen," in *Die Technik* (Gau Württemberg-Hohenzollern), no. 9 (September 1937); rejoinder in an "Open Letter to the Engineers of Robert Bosch AG," 23 Nov. 1937, in BA DC, Akte Kiehn. On the firm's relationship to the Nazi regime, see Tooze, *Wages,* 99–134; Bähr and Erker, *Bosch,* 169–251. See the controversy between Buchheim and Scherner, "Corporate," and Hayes, "Corporate," both in *Bulletin of the German Historical Institute* 45 (2009): 29–42 and 43–50. On the attacks against business owners, see Rauh, "Wirtschaftsbürger"; Bluhm, "'Wirtschaft'"; Mallmann and Paul, *Herrschaft,* 151–153. On the antibourgeois background of these propaganda attacks, see Schoenbaum, *Revolution,* 100–101.
13. Prof. Dr. Ing. Wilhelm Stortz was an associate professor of bridge construction theory at the Stuttgart Technical College. He initiated the first recruitment of college teachers for the NSDAP in the Reichstag election of July 1932. See Pommerin, *Geschichte,* 164; Müller, *Stuttgart,* 109. The Stuttgart Technical College must have found out very early on that the Nazi state would strongly disapprove of awarding honorary doctorates, since Hitler turned down their offer in spring 1933 to bestow this honor upon him as the new Reich chancellor.
14. StAL, PL 502/32, Bü. 204, Betriebsführer Hans Walz, open letter to the GLT Rudolf Rohrbach of 23 Nov. 1937; Bosch directorate reply of 7 Dec. 1937; letter from Prof. Stortz, dean of the Stuttgart Technical College, to GLT Rohrbach of 10 Dec. 1937.
15. StAL, PL 502/32, Bü. 204, Statement by Dean Stortz of 1 Feb. 1938.
16. Reports from SD subdivision in Württemberg-Hohenzollern to its superior office in Stuttgart of 4 Feb. [date illegible] and 25 Feb. 1938. Fritz Todt, inspector general for German roadways, was brought onto the case by Stortz. According to information circulating in RF-SS circles in 1943 that originated with the director of the SS Head Office, group leader Gottlob Berger, the Gauleitung's targeted "solution to Bosch" would lead to the firm's expropriation: "The Gauleiter wanted to annex the Bosch factory and transform it into a firm belonging to the Gau. ... The case went all the way to the Führer, who thwarted all of these efforts by naming Bosch Sr. as a labor pioneer [*Pionier der Arbeit*]." BA DC, Akte Hans Walz, hearing of group leader Berger of 21 Apr. 1943 in an SS discovery proceeding against the Bosch CEO; see Scholty-Seck, *Bosch,* 161–62.
17. BA DC, Akte Kiehn, report of 14 Dec. 1938, "Betr.[Re]: Fritz Kiehn."
18. BA DC, Akte Kiehn, SD report of 4 Feb. 1938. On the title of "military industrial leader" (Wehrwirtschaftsführer), which was not connected to any political or economic functions —

comparable to the "commerce councilor" (Kommerzienrat) title no longer customary in the Third Reich — and was frequently also given to industrialists who were a moderate distance from the NSDAP, see Erker, *Industrie-Eliten*, 95–99.

19. BA DC, Akte Kiehn, reports of 4 Feb. 1938 and 28 Feb. 1938.
20. Ibid.; BA NS, 46/14. One member of the RF-SS's personal staff who benefited from such common personal "rehabilitation," based on funds from the "Freundeskreis RF-SS," was its director, group leader Karl Wolff. Wolff had built himself a luxurious house on the Tegernsee and had fallen into financial distress that threatened his reputation. He was therefore facing the Party Supreme Court as well — paralleling Kiehn's case — and only avoided having party court proceedings opened against him because of the Führer's amnesty of 27 April 1938. Lang and Sibyll, *Adjutant*, 56–58; Hein, *Elite*, 203–204.
21. Such business relationships with Jews were claimed by many business owners after 1945 as proof of their supposedly constant friendliness toward Jews and sympathy for the resistance. The punishable offense of "associating with Jews," however, was nonetheless a widespread phenomenon among party and SS members, regardless of their ideological convictions. But the fact that the *Stürmer* publisher himself, Gauleiter Julius Streicher, had a *Volljude* working for him for four years should caution us against drawing conclusions about the hiring of Jews and the persecution practices of the regime. On Streicher, see Genschel, *Verdrängung*, 245n137.
22. BA DC, Akte Kiehn, Württemberg-Hohenzollern Gau court judgment of 28 Feb. 1939, containing telegram from SS colonel Tondock to SS group leader Wolff of 16 Jan. 1939.
23. BA DC, Akte Kiehn, letter from Kiehn to SS colonel Tondock, RF-SS, of 16 Jan. 1939, spelled incorrectly as "Tondok."
24. A propaganda speech that Kiehn gave in Stuttgart on 1 May 1933 exposes his position on the "Jewish question." On International Workers' Day Kiehn loudly denounced the "alien, international Jewish elements." One year later he was writing a justification for the Gauleitung in which he endeavored to warn them of "Jewish capital," the danger of which still had to be averted. On the latter, see BA DC, Akte Kiehn, written pleading by Kiehn of 4 Dec. 1934; Kiehn's speech on 1 May 1933 is from *Schwäbischer Merkur*, no. 102 (3 May 1933), quoted in Scherer and Schaaf, *Geschichte*, 431–433, doc. no. 144.
25. Kiehn mentioned in 1960 that the profits should later have been taxed at RM 190,000. Kiehn, who had since donated the money, most of it to the SS Main Riding School, ultimately settled with the German tax office. See TZ, 7 Aug. 2012.
26. All quotes in this section are from the Gau court judgment of 28 Feb. 1939. An exception is Kiehn's letter to his SS legal adviser of 16 Jan. 1939, BA DC, Akte Kiehn.
27. BA DC, Akte Kiehn, letter from Kiehn to SS colonel Tondock of 16 Jan. 1939. Kiehn alleged in the letter: "When I emerge 'reformed' [sic] from these proceedings, it is the Herr Reichsführer-SS's point of view that there should be nothing to stand in the way of the Fleischer paper factory being transferred to me."
28. On Wolff, see Lang and Sibyll, *Adjutant*; Lingen, *SS*; Simms, "Karl Wolff." Numerous other examples of corruption and excessive expenditures to support the lifestyles of senior SS leaders can be found in Bajohr, *Parvenüs*; Hein, *Elite*, 200–212; Lang and Sibyll, *Adjutant*, 57–58; Padfield, *Himmler*, 193–195.
29. On the judgment of the Party Supreme Court (unless otherwise noted), see BA DC, Akte Kiehn, judgment on the basis of the hearing of 27–28 June 1939. On Lohse, the Gauleiter for Schleswig-Holstein from 1925 to 1945, Reichstag delegate from 1932 to 1945, and later Reich Commissioner for the East (1941–1945), see Hüttenberger, *Gauleiter*, 29 (cit.), 216; Lilla, Döring, and Schulz, *Statisten*, 652–654.
30. BA NS, 46/14, letter from Kiehn to Frick of 19 Apr. 1939, and letter of permission from the party faction director of 21 Apr. 1939.

31. Buchheim, "Befehl," 257–259. English translation in Buchheim, "Command," 343. Kühne has written of the problem of camaraderie addressed here, which spread far beyond the SS, as a powerful myth of the Nazi era. See Kühne, *Kameradschaft*.
32. BA NS, 19/1125, letter from head of RF-SS personal staff Wolff to SS Southwest Regional Headquarters director Kaul of 15 Sept. 1939; BA DC, Akte Pfannenschwarz.
33. BA DC, Akte Walz, investigations of 12 Nov. 1942; on Walz, see Scholtyseck, *Bosch,* 156–161 passim.
34. Kershaw, *Myth,* 102. On the limits of totalitarian power generally, see Buchheim, *Rule,* 103–109.

Chapter 6

KIEHN AND GUSTAV SCHICKEDANZ IN THE RACE FOR ARYANIZATION

The inescapable resale of the Magirus shares had dashed Kiehn's hopes of entering big business for the time being. But the Nazi "dejudaization" (*Entjudung*) of the economy, which advanced rapidly in late 1935, offered him new opportunities to fulfill his dream of having a "thousand-man business."[1] As an "old fighter," Kiehn theoretically had a good chance through Aryanization of getting a share of "one of the greatest changes in property ownership in modern German history," especially since, as president of an important Chamber of Industry and Commerce, he enjoyed an information advantage.[2] Consequently, the establishment of the Württemberg Consultation and Referral Center for Industry and Commerce (Württembergische Industrie- und Handelsberatungs- und Vermittlungszentrale) on the premises of the Stuttgart IHK in 1936 cannot have escaped his notice. The declared purpose of the institution, which was legally established as a corporation, was to facilitate "transitioning Jewish businesses into Aryan ownership."[3] Soon generally known as the "Aryanization office," it quickly expanded from three employees initially to a staff of some twenty in 1938. The partners in the new enterprise were the private accounting and auditing firm Schwäbische Treuhand (known as Schitag), which invested RM 24,000, and the Württemberg-Hohenzollern Economic Chamber,[4] which invested RM 26,000.[5] The two investors each supplied the office with one of its two managing directors. According to statements made postwar by a witness involved in the association, it was "the then-president of the Chamber of Industry and Commerce, Mr. Kiehn," who delegated Otto Lachenmaier, employed as a clerk at the IHK, to be managing director of the Referral Center.[6] The involvement of Schitag, a private firm established in 1919 that held a monopoly-like position on auditing the accounts of large corporations in Württemberg, may have provided the desired

---

Notes from this chapter begin on page 120.

transparency of the financial circumstances and profitability of various "Jew firms" from early on, long before the decree "against aiding in the camouflage of Jewish commercial operations" was enacted in April 1938.[7] Whereas the Gauleitung had not participated financially in establishing the Referral Center — in an attempt to maintain its appearance as a neutral referral agency that obeyed the laws of supply and demand — the NSDAP Gau economic adviser, the Stuttgart municipal administration, and the Württemberg Economics Ministry each had a representative member on the organization's supervisory board. What's more, Reihle, the economic adviser, installed one of his female relatives as a secretary at the Referral Center. This ensured that no "Aryanization deals" (*Arisierungsgeschäfte*) would materialize without the Gauleitung's knowledge and permission. This was presumably already practiced before the Decree on the Registration of Jewish Property was officially adopted on 26 April 1938 and a permit requirement was stipulated for Aryanized businesses.[8]

A former managing director of the Referral Center recalled that the Gau economic adviser, because of his powerful position in the party, was able to force the buyers of Jewish businesses "to come to us in the office." If their visits to the Aryanization office were successful and they managed to receive the Gauleitung's approval for their Aryanization projects, they had to show their appreciation by means of "payments directed to the Gauleiter." Requirements for approval were that the purchase price not be "too high" and that the interested buyer be politically "reliable."[9] The "donations" flowed into a "foundation" that Murr had created under the cynical title of Gratitude of the Württemberg Economy (Wirtschaftsdank Württemberg). A Württemberg denazification court described these donations as monies "paid in more or less 'voluntarily,' out of 'gratitude'" by "manufacturers who had been given Jewish businesses." Altogether, the Gauleitung likely "obtained" around RM 1 million from such methods. Most of this was put toward financing a cement factory in Dotternhausen; Rudolf Rohrbach, Gauamtleiter for technology and a close friend of Murr's, was made a partner in the venture and given personal responsibility for the factory.[10] These circumstances in Württemberg confirm Bajohr's findings that corruption and nepotism "determined the character of the 'Aryanisations.'" They resulted from the "cliqueishness and clientelism" that had been spreading through the Third Reich, including at the regional level, since 1933. "Corruption and nepotism were the instruments that the Gauleiters in particular used to secure the political loyalty of their party comrades through a system of privileges."[11] The unscrupulous methods of wealth-grabbing by certain party functionaries that went on in Wilhelm Murr's entourage stood in stark contrast to the still openly propagated ideal: "Gemeinnutz geht vor Eigennutz," or "Common interest before self-interest."[12] The abuse of power also prompted critics both within the party and in Württemberg industrial circles to make cynical remarks. Industrialists were soon saying, for example, that Aryanization had "its upside. ... The faster these people [the Gauleitung functionaries] become capitalists, the quicker industry can get some peace!"[13]

As an "old fighter," Kiehn had a good chance in theory to benefit personally from Aryanization activities. However, it must have proved an extraordinary obstacle for him that in his own local sphere, Murr's confidant Walter Reihle, the Gau economic advisor and ironically one of Kiehn's most determined intraparty adversaries, had become the driving force and de facto monitoring authority of the newly established Referral Center.[14] When the Decree on the Registration of Jewish Property in April 1938 fired the starting shot, as it were, in the race for "'reasonable' Aryanization projects," Kiehn too obviously believed that the time had come to act, and he turned his attention to specific properties. At this point the dejudaization of the Viennese economy was already in full swing, "a combination of outright pogrom and undirected self-enrichment for National Socialist party men," and it demonstrated again just what could be achieved by means of plunder and brutality.[15]

Considering his disturbed relationship with the Stuttgart Gauleitung, Kiehn first switched over to less hostile terrain outside Württemberg, and in 1938 he purchased a small cigarette case factory with a staff of twenty from a Jew in Berlin named Hugo Büttner. Büttner had already been compelled to sell his firm to another interested party, and even had a signed contract, but Kiehn, who obviously was well aware that private legal contracts on "Aryanization deals" had only limited value if they had not been officially approved and the property exchange recorded in the land register, made a higher offer. He paid RM 300,000 — of which the previous Jewish owner would not receive a single mark — and became the new owner of the Berlin company, transferring the production facilities and a portion of the staff to Trossingen in 1940. Büttner, the previous owner, was allegedly deported to Warsaw.[16]

In summer 1938 at the latest, Kiehn and Reihle entered into an open power struggle over a paper factory in Eislingen, Württemberg. In business circles, Gau economic adviser Reihle was considered "one of the most single-minded and fanatical functionaries … in Württemberg."[17] Like Rohrbach, his colleague in the Gau office, Reihle (along with a series of "card-carrying party industrialists") was part of an economic elite that was characterized by its ideological rigor. Like most midlevel Nazi leaders, Reihle came from petit bourgeois origins and was as ambitious as he was eager to move up the ladder. In contrast to various other Gau economic advisers, however, who we know had university backgrounds, Reihle had no academic training. He was born in 1896, making him older, when he became Gau economic advisor at age forty in 1936, than was typical.

Reihle, who also directed the Württemberg Office of the Four-Year Plan, was a fanatical anti-Semite and regarded "dejudaizing" the economy as his ideological duty, to be executed with bureaucratic perseverance and free of "inappropriate sympathy."[18] In Reihle's denazification proceedings, Jewish textile industrialists

Max and Willy D. Elsas, who had been deprived of their property and were ultimately driven to emigrate from Stuttgart, described his practice of Aryanization. He treated his Jewish victims with a technocratic lack of scruples and, apparently, particular severity in comparison to other regions. The methods they spoke of facilitate our understanding of the comparable events that occurred in connection with the Aryanization of the Fleischer paper factory, albeit with the additional complication of the Kiehn-Reihle feud. We describe them here lest readers falsely assume that the thoughtless treatment of the Jewish Fleischer family in Württemberg was an isolated case.[19]

The Elsases, who had owned the weaving mill Mechanische Weberei, Cannstatt, Gebr. Elsas KG, reported the following: "We were forced ... to sell our factory — the value of which was estimated by qualified experts at almost RM 1,000,000 — a whopping five or six times, for the simple reason that the buyer was either not Nazi enough or the obviously laughably low price was always found by 'dear Herr Reihle' to be much too high." Whereas the first interested buyer had at least offered RM 600,000, a series of aborted contract submissions caused a new purchase contract to be concluded around November 1938. At RM 300,000, this purchase price remained below the limit that the Gau economic adviser had set.[20] "But then too, Reihle refused to grant his authorization, since R. [the buyer] was supposedly not Nazi enough, but above all in those days a Herr W. was trying to become a contender, who didn't even have RM 10,000 to call his own and had never had the least bit to do with the textile industry. He had the merit, on the other hand — his only asset in those days — of having a low number in the party [i.e., he had entered the party early on]."[21] Once W. failed to raise the necessary RM 300,000, negotiations came to a "standstill" for more than six months. When W. finally found a financial backer, the Elsas brothers "again had to reduce the price by ca. RM 100,000 and, in the end, were happy to have found any ray of light at all for their final emigration."

"We have Reihle to thank for all of this," they summed up in 1951. Their characterization of the Gau economic adviser's responsibility was certainly accurate, but they did not know that each of the numerous Gau districts in the Nazi state had its own "Reihle." What set Reihle apart from many of his colleagues, and what may have contributed to his ultimately "falling out with every influential person in Württemberg,"[22] was his dogged refusal to enrich himself when given the opportunity. To be sure, Reihle, who had joined the NSDAP in 1931 as a lowly banker and was seen as hard-working and competent, benefited unquestionably from the change in the system, since the Nazi state helped him to rise rapidly in his career. In no time at all, the former branch manager of a provincial cooperative bank had become the director of the largest savings bank in the state, with headquarters in Stuttgart. In 1936, he rose from deputy Gau economic adviser to Gau economic adviser, and in 1938, while still working in his main job as director of a savings bank, he was promoted from his voluntary Gauamtsleiter position to president of the Württemberg Association of Savings Banks (Württemberg Sparkassen- und Giroverband). This professional advancement gave Reihle a multitude of extraordinarily lucrative ancillary positions. He not only chaired the executive board of the Association of Savings Banks and the clearinghouse (Girozentrale), but also the supervisory board of the Stuttgart Pension Institution, the Württembergische Finanz company in Stuttgart, and Milei GmbH in Stuttgart, including its numerous subsidiaries. What's more, he sat on the supervisory boards of two large banks, as well as those of an insurance company and three industrial firms; last but not least, he served on the loan committee of the German Clearinghouse (Deutsche Girozentrale) in Berlin. Nevertheless, Reihle was able to prove in his denazification proceedings that he had put all of the supervisory board compensation and profit shares he had received, as well as his salary payments (when these exceeded RM 1,000 monthly) into a "fixed-term deposit account in the name of Wilhelm Murr, Reichsstatthalter ... special account GWB [Gau economic adviser]" and left it untouched, such that by 1945, RM 101,752 had accumulated.

Both Reihle's own self-image and the testimony of his subordinates — whom he advised to exercise similar material restraint — described the Nazi functionary as a "de facto socialist" of a "taciturn and sinister nature" who "mostly had only enemies." Reihle, they maintained, was interested in the philosophy of German idealism, and especially in Johann Gottlieb Fichte, who the Gau economic advisor considered "the ideal figure of the unselfish businessman."[23] Reihle saw himself as a "bitter enemy of the big banks," and even in the postwar era he emphasized his relentless struggle against monopolistic tendencies in the economy. In his battle against the Jews, he believed that he was standing up for "cleanliness and honesty in the economy" and — in the words of his lawyers — that he was championing "the decartelization of business, the preservation of a *Mittelstand* economy, the provision of cheap money for home construction with all his energy."[24]

It cannot come as a surprise that cigarette paper manufacturer and IHK president Kiehn — boastful, uninhibited by ideological principles, and always thinking of his own economic advantage — made the Württemberg Gau economic adviser see red. This was especially true once Kiehn had "handed over" Magirus, a long-standing Swabian company that was part of the *Mittelstand* economy he pretended to be protecting, to a major corporation in the Rhineland. Furthermore, in spring 1937 a police search of the house of a Jew from Tuttlingen had brought Kiehn's ingratiating letter of 1932 to Fröhlich the cattle dealer to light, generating serious doubts about his ideological reliability among radical anti-Semites in the Reihle mold.[25] Referral Center director Otto Lachenmaier testified in court that Reihle "doubtlessly hated Kiehn ... the authorities were aware that very personal feuds were involved in this case."[26]

When in the summer of 1938 Kiehn expressed interest in the Fleischer paper factory, an important industrial firm in Filstal owned by the Jewish Fleischer family since 1892,[27] it stands to reason that Reihle must have been highly alarmed. His reservations about the political consequences for the middle class and opposition to new industrial interdependencies in the paper industry would have been obstacles enough to a Kiehn takeover, but first and foremost were Reihle's doubts about Kiehn himself. When it came to excluding his archenemy from the "Aryanization deals" that had been flourishing on a grand scale since early 1938, no effort was too great for the Gau economic adviser. In fact, it does seem as if Reihle's endeavors are the definitive reason that Kiehn was ultimately summoned to appear before the Gau court. When Kiehn sought help from his "superior, Herr Reichsführer-SS [Himmler],"[28] the Fleischer "Aryanization matter" inevitably occasioned further polycratic conflicts between competing cliques in the Stuttgart Gauleitung and Himmler's personal staff. For a long time, it remained unclear who would come out on top. The losers, however, were clear from the beginning: the Jewish owners of the Fleischer company in Eislingen, brothers Kuno and David M. Fleischer, David M. Fleischer's two sons, Dr. Hermann Fleischer and Walther Fleischer, and their immediate families.[29]

The Fleischers had been running their paper factory in the Fils valley for three generations. David M. Fleischer, the oldest member of the business, born in 1867, had put up the strongest and most lengthy resistance to giving up the enterprise and selling it; the enterprise, which had to be completely rebuilt after a major fire in 1926, was his life's work. He had been a well-respected man in his hometown before the advent of the Third Reich. In celebration of his sixtieth birthday, in 1927, he had been appointed an honorary citizen of Groß-Eislingen. It was difficult for the family, so deeply rooted in the culture and economy of their country, to get used to the idea of emigrating, even though they had established a subsidiary in London in 1930 and David M. Fleischer had been asked by the Eislingen mayor in May 1936 to give back the letter certifying his honorary citizen status. At first, this did not bring any further consequences.[30]

But as it became ever clearer that the Nazi state aimed to completely push Jews out of the economy, the Fleischers made an initial attempt in 1937 (when their "predicament" began) to contact "banks and various agencies" to arrange the sale of the company.[31] Moreover, the branded goods of their London company (Swan) had been selling well in international markets,[32] so the younger generation of the family did not lack for future prospects. Yet at the same time that they were searching for buyers among their old business associates and had even entered into sale negotiations with the Trick cellulose factory in Oberhamersbach, Baden, the repression of Jewish companies was intensifying throughout the Reich. This process went hand in hand with increased bureaucratic requirements that marked the beginning of the ultimate "dejudaization of the economy." The structural changes in the German economy wrought by rearmament and the policy of autarky facilitated official interventions and harassment that had become successively more radicalized since Hitler's announcement of the Four-Year Plan in the summer of 1936. A sprawling economic bureaucracy developed in order to manage the foreign currency, raw materials, and labor shortages that were now evident everywhere. Currencies and raw materials had to be applied for and individually allocated, and commissions from the state, or export connections subject to authorization, were increasingly required if one wished to stay in business.[33]

It is likely that many Jewish business owners focused on exports in view of their precarious domestic situation. When the monitoring of foreign exchange increased throughout Germany as a consequence of this, in the summer of 1936, many ended up in the crosshairs of foreign currency and customs inspectors. At first the work of these civil servants was intended only to bring the sorely needed foreign exchange holdings of their fellow citizens (*Volksgenossen*) into the fiscal grasp of the regime; it did not have any specifically racial aims. Yet in this process, it began to become clear in 1937 that the Foreign Exchange Control Offices — midlevel authorities under the Reichsbank — were also effective instruments for Aryanizing the economy and plundering the fortunes of would-be Jewish emigrants, because anyone seeking to leave the country needed authorization from the Foreign Exchange Control Offices.[34] Frank Bajohr's study on Aryanization in Hamburg has drawn attention to the concept of "foreign exchange control" functioning as a "pacemaker for the process of expropriation."[35] Using records from the Hamburg Foreign Exchange Control Office, he showed "how Hitler's vaguely expressed 'intent' was interpreted and turned into a reality by government and bureaucratic agencies which developed their own momentum."[36]

Württemberg participated in the radicalization of the normative state — and acted on that radicalization — as much as elsewhere,[37] even though a 1937 SD Southwest Regional Headquarters report suggests that the policy of persecuting Jews had its limits: "The majority of the Jews of Württemberg," it reads, "had always been assimilated, and only very slowly is a transition occurring to an absolute Jewish consciousness." The reasons for this were "without doubt the lengthy residency of many Jewish families and the firm financial footing corresponding to the favorable economic structure of [Württemberg], but not least the mentality of the Swabian people, who are easily inclined to perceive Jewish insinuations of 'unjust oppression.'"[38]

Radical and anti-Semitic tendencies, meanwhile, clearly started with the party and state authorities.[39] The later minister-president of Württemberg-Baden, liberal politician Reinhold Maier, had this insight, which presumably many persecuted people in the country shared: "One became aware that it [was] downright dangerous ... to live in Württemberg. Here the administration of every system [was] in top form." Maier was incorrect, however, in his assessment that the proverbial joke about legislation — conceived in Berlin, mocked in Munich, carried out in Stuttgart — held true during Nazism as well. Often enough, "Berlin" only did what had been thought up and tested out "down there" in the Gauen.[40]

This became apparent when the foreign exchange regulations were tightened throughout the Reich at the end of 1936, and the addition of Section 37a expanded the Law on Exchange Control of 4 February 1935. The new provision allowed the Foreign Exchange Control Offices to prohibit a person from disposing of their property when any suspicion of capital flight existed, to appoint a custodian for the assets, and to take "other protective arrangements" necessary "to prevent the intended trafficking in property."[41] Ernst Niemann, a 37-year-old Reichsbank councilor, was designated the director of the Stuttgart office in September 1937 and became the "dreaded specter of the tortured Jewish population." He was an ambitious social climber from the war youth generation (*Kriegsjugendgeneration*) who had been a member of the Nazi Party since 1930 and, being from Berlin, arrived in Stuttgart claiming that he wanted to clean up the administration. Of himself he said, "I always had a National-German bent, even as a child. I joined the NS because some unimpeachable people I knew were in it, and I believed that this party could improve Germany's destiny. I joined for purely idealistic reasons."[42] In 1951, the Stuttgart Higher Regional Court would adjudge Niemann to be a "a person who had little regard for anything at all." He had scarcely taken up his post when he exposed an official of the Foreign Exchange Control Office in Stuttgart who had been accepting bribes from Jewish emigrants in exchange for helping them leave the country. At Niemann's behest, the employee was brought before the court on corruption charges and sentenced to years in a concentration camp.[43] Niemann was an overbearing superior to the 120 civil servants in his office and contagiously anti-Semitic. He was said to belong to the SD or the SS, but he actually kept his distance from party organizations. He clashed with Gau economic adviser Reihle on a number of occasions. Niemann made it clear to those who frequented his office that, although he knew he was "the most hated man," he was proud to be, because he brought in the most foreign currency for the Reich. He exploited to the fullest the room to maneuver that his position gave him, imposed draconian fines on Jewish citizens, and even held family members accountable for foreign exchange infractions of Jewish relatives who had fled abroad. In Reinhold Maier's estimation, "there could have been no other office in Stuttgart at the time that went after the Jewish members of the population with the same ruthlessness." "With all of his security directives," wrote Jewish lawyer Benno Ostertag, the Stuttgart Foreign Exchange Control Office director went "far beyond the mandates of the Reich Economics Ministry." It can be "assumed that, in general, Berlin introduced many of Niemann's directives."[44]

By 1938 at the latest, all Jews were being lumped together as "potential smugglers of capital." "Jewish firms" faced up to seven account and foreign exchange audits every year, and any formal infraction of the rules threatened a company's existence. Section 37a developed into "a clause dealing with dispossession in general … almost completely incapacitating" the Jewish owners of companies.[45]

It struck the paper factory in Eislingen on 3 June 1938. The company's junior partner, Dr. Hermann Fleischer, had absconded to England a few days before after facing great personal intimidation, providing the desired pretext for a Section 37a security directive forcing him to surrender the proceeds from his export businesses to a foreign exchange bank.[46] The factory employed about five hundred workers at its two locations in Eislingen and London and exported goods to seventy-two countries. The authorities, therefore, had deemed the company a "foreign exchange earner" for the Reich and — as elder partner Kuno Fleischer recalled — did not bother its owners with prosecution until the summer of 1938.[47] When the security directive was declared, however, the tissue paper factory was "urged" to inform its foreign debtors of the order. In the factory manager's estimation, this was "doubtless sufficient" to "damage the Fleischer firm's reputation abroad, since the customers had to have guessed that the company would not be able to pay or to have assumed that the owners were guilty of something in Germany."[48] David M. Fleischer therefore visited the Foreign Exchange Control Office in Stuttgart personally, accompanied by factory manager Roth.

An unperturbed Niemann explained to the oldest partner in the family business that he must now "have finally recognized that you can no longer hold on to your operation." "Now indeed," the Eislingen factory owner retorted, shaken and in tears, "you never put it to me so clearly before."[49] On 14 June 1938, the Foreign Exchange Control Office banned the owners of the Fleischer paper factory from managing the business. At the same time, Otto Lachenmaier (a Stuttgart IHK employee and head of the Referral Center) was assigned to take over management of the Fleischer company as trustee, although, as Kuno Fleischer reported in 1947, "he knew nothing about paper manufacturing." Naturally, the trustee's generous salary was paid out of company funds.[50]

The surviving records do not indicate whether IHK president Kiehn had a hand in a Chamber of Commerce and Industry employee being appointed as trustee; Kiehn's middlemen had previously shown interest in the Eislingen factory. Lachenmaier later claimed that the actual reason for appointing a trustee had been the disputes between Gau economic adviser Reihle and IHK president Kiehn.[51] The records only partially reveal the details of what went on behind the scenes in the months between the first purchase negotiations by the Fleischer family in spring 1938 and the final sale of their company to Fritz Kiehn in 1940. Kiehn did not meet the "previous owner" of his new firm in Eislingen until 1945. He left the purchase negotiations up to his bank, Glaub & Cie (formerly Pick & Cie), the monetary institution that had long been regarded with suspicion in party circles whose managing partner, Freemason Otto Stäbler, had been Kiehn's friend for decades.[52]

Kiehn later claimed that Stäbler had intervened in the Jewish owners' ongoing negotiations with the Trick cellulose company[53] because Glaub had purportedly heard from the Referral Center that "a sale to Trick alone had no prospect of approval." The Referral Center had advised the bank, Kiehn said, "to at least procure a comrade from the party as cobuyer," probably because there were political misgivings about the CEO of Trick-Zellstoff GmbH — another former Freemason — as well as about the main Trick shareholder, retired Reich minister Dr. Hermann Dietrich, who had formerly been a member of the German Democratic Party. "The [potential for] formation of a trust (cellulose factories, paper factory) was also cited as an objection." "Owing to these circumstances," Glaub alleged after 1945, "I interested Herr Fritz Kiehn in the case." Conjointly and with support from the notary involved in sealing the deal, Glaub, Stäbler, and Kiehn affirmed that when they had arranged the sale of the paper factory, both Stäbler and Glaub had been acting on the orders and in the interest of the Fleischer family and not at all as Kiehn's middlemen. If and when external pressures accompanied the contract negotiations, they claimed, these had come from third parties, especially the Referral Center and the Gau economic adviser.[54]

The Fleischer family, their Jewish lawyer, and their auditor, as well as prospective buyer Hermann Dietrich, presented a completely different story of the proceedings after the war. According to their account, both Glaub and Stäbler had acted on Kiehn's behalf and had not hesitated to assert his interests and obtain a kickback, or to repeatedly threaten the use of violence if necessary.[55] They claimed that on 13 July 1938, on bank premises and in Stäbler's presence, "the negotiations between Trick and Fleischer were to be committed to paper," with a targeted sale price of RM 4–5 million. During the negotiations, Stäbler suddenly informed everyone that "he had just come from the Aryanization office ... and brought notice that the Trick company would not be getting the Fleischer company alone, that Kiehn the manufacturer had to be involved." David M. Fleischer resisted this move and had decisively rejected selling the company when Stäbler finally revealed that "the intended sale price of RM 4–5 million would not be approved; only a sale price of two million would be possible." When the oldest partner in the Fleischer family business did not budge from his position, Stäbler replied, "You get two million, and not a pfennig more. You should make up your mind and realize what this means." Thus intimidated, and likely resigned after the protracted negotiations, David and Kuno Fleischer finally signed a contract that turned over their company for the price of RM 2 million "to the firm to be founded by 1) Herr Präsident Fritz Kiehn, Trossingen manufacturer, 2) the Trick Zellstoff company in Kehl."

The negotiator for Trick, Hermann Dietrich, and the Fleischer family's lawyer, Ostertag, had withdrawn from the negotiations because they found "the environment of using pressure against the sellers" to be "undignified." One week later, on 21 July 1938, shortly before midnight, the contract was certified by a notary with business ties to Glaub's bank. Its validity, without the signatures of the Fleischer sons, was disputable. The Jewish sellers, by their own account in 1947, were "compelled to disappear somewhere with our families right away so we wouldn't be found!" Otto Stäbler, Fritz Kiehn's authorized representative, signed on his behalf. In order to enter into force, the contract had to be authorized by the Württemberg Economics Ministry, a feat that, considering Kiehn's damaged reputation, was more than just a formality.[56]

The Fleischers had already been coerced and intimidated into accepting an unfair price for their business property. But if they had hoped to escape personal ramifications and be left in peace to complete their preparations to leave the country, they were in for renewed disappointment. What the Fleischers had to go through, as one employee of the Foreign Exchange Control Office observed, resembled "an Aryanization novel." The owners had to sell their factory a total of "only four times," as Kuno Fleischer dryly reported in 1947.[57]

Kiehn's access to the Fleischer company immediately brought the Gau economic adviser onto the scene, who did his utmost to summon up a new buyer for the paper factory that he found suitable. Kiehn's middlemen, meanwhile, endeavored to stop the Fleischer family from negotiating a sale elsewhere and to procure the still-missing signatures of the Fleischer sons by engaging the services of Lachenmaier, the trustee. They pointedly warned the Fleischers not to return to their family home. In negotiations and telephone conversations, they created an atmosphere of fear and intimidation that — according to testimony by Eberhard Mayer, the Fleischers' auditor — extended to him and his family as well. All of this was unfolding when the mood in the country had already intensified because of the Sudeten crisis and the resulting widespread fear of impending war, when "campaigns against the Jewish population ... took on a pogrom-like aspect in some southern and southwestern parts of the Reich."[58] After Messrs. Fleischer had failed to do as Kiehn, Glaub & Co. would have liked, and after the transfer of Fleischer's shares of foreign subsidiaries [in England and Switzerland] failed to occur, public auditor Eberhard Mayer was "informed one day by Herr Stäbler that the Fleischer family was to be arrested by the Gestapo the next morning." To counter the threat, David M. Fleischer hid in a sanatorium in the Black Forest with his daughters-in-law, while Kuno Fleischer journeyed by night to the Birnau monastery on Lake Constance, where Eberhard Mayer and his wife accommodated him.[59]

If we are to believe the matching stories that Stäbler and Glaub spread about these events after the war, their warnings were intended as well-meaning, altruistic information and were not threats in any way.[60] Hermann Fleischer's interpretation, by contrast, probably came closer to the truth. He was convinced in retrospect that "this demand to disappear was only given by Stäbler and his lot because they wanted to prevent the factory from being sold under pressure ... to another interested Nazi." The younger Fleischer saw Stäbler as "Kiehn's instigator and accomplice for his own advantage," a "profiteer and extortionist, economic highwayman and vulture." His uncle, Kuno Fleischer, sent an inquiry to Eberhard Mayer from his new home in the United States on 25 August 1946: "What's happening with the Glaub company? Did the men not end up safe behind barbed wire? That's where they belong!"[61]

In the fall of 1938, however, Kiehn's chances of finally taking over the Eislingen paper factory appeared to be dwindling, despite all the contractual arrangements and machinations. Even though Lachenmaier, as trustee, refused to give the interested buyers sent over by the Gau economic adviser access to the factory (he viewed "this ongoing behavior on Reihle's part [as] a clear dig at President Kiehn"),[62] one faction of interested buyers kept turning up in association with Franconian Gustav Schickedanz, who was said to have ties to Gauleiter Julius Streicher in Nuremberg.[63] Kiehn got the message in black and white on 13 October 1938: the Württemberg Economics Ministry had refused to approve the contract concluded between him, the eldest Fleischer partners, and the Trick company "because the Gauleitung found a more desirable purchaser in the Schickedanz firm in Nuremberg." Kiehn appealed to the Reich Economics Ministry in response. At the same time, he initiated negotiations by Lachenmaier with the Fleischer sons on 31 October 1938, with the aim of inducing them to accede to his purchase contract. Stäbler arranged a meeting in Zurich for 2 November 1938 of all four partners in the Eislingen company; trustee Lachenmaier was also in attendance. The two oldest partners had been specially furnished with passports valid for only a limited time. All now signed the contract, "according to which the factory was sold — without acquisition of liabilities — to Kiehn for a price of RM 1.5 mill." The Fleischers, however, were to maintain "the representation for England and the leadership of the Swan Mill Paper Co. for 3 years" on the condition that the Fleischer family members who were still in Germany be "guaranteed an orderly emigration and the transfer of their remaining assets." This was because, as Hermann Fleischer put it, "they threatened to send all of our relatives to concentration camps if we failed to agree."[64]

Although these signatures formally satisfied the civil law requirements for a purchase agreement, the Reich Economics Ministry informed Kiehn on 7 November that it too disapproved of his "Aryanization proposal." Kiehn promptly set out for Berlin and wrote letters of complaint to Hitler's chancellery and the responsible department officials in the Economics Ministry. In these letters, he alluded to Schickedanz's patrons in the Stuttgart and Nuremberg Gauleitungen and showed that he was determined to prevent "the emergence of a 'party operation' in Eislingen and any unwholesome corporate development in favor of individual creatures of the party." At the same time, he gave notice that he felt "compelled, for the protection of my honor and my rights, to report the case to my superior, Herr Reichsführer-SS, and to the Reich Economic Ministry, and to request protection."[65] Group leader Wolff, the head of the Reichsführer-SS's personal staff, then sent word to the Reich Economic Chamber that the Reichsführer-SS had found the objections to the expansion of Kiehn's enterprise "inscrutable"; as for the rest, they would have to wait for the conclusion of the party court proceedings initiated against Kiehn to clarify "whether and which reproaches may be leveled at party comrade Kiehn." But at the time of this intervention, Gau economic adviser Reihle had already established the precedent, and the events of Kristallnacht played right into his hand. As part of the pogrom, Security Police head Reinhard Heydrich had given the order that "in all districts as many Jews, especially rich ones, are to be arrested as can be accommodated in the existing jails."[66] The point of this, as it was cynically put in a report from the SD subdivision for Württemberg-Hohenzollern, was to bring about "an emigration with the highest speed and fewest losses possible."[67] In the city of Göppingen, sixty-year-old Kuno Fleischer was imprisoned along with thirty-five other Jewish men and taken to the Dachau concentration camp. He described what happened next in 1947:

> On the strength of a telegraphed instruction, I was released from Dachau on 20 November 1938. I had to report to Berlin, where the third round of sale negotiations for the factory was already underway with my brother. This time it was the Schikedanz company [sic] from Fürth, Bavaria (Messrs. H. Schikedanz, Dr. Kissling, lawyer Linhardt, Reile [sic], and Bernlöhr) with which the third sale contract had to be drawn up, despite the two previous contracts. Purchase price this time RM 1,550,000.

After subtracting company liabilities, this meant that the net price Schickedanz was to pay can be estimated at approximately RM 850,000.[68]

Kiehn appeared to have been defeated in the free-for-all over the Fleischer paper factory and the power struggle with the Stuttgart Gauleitung and his archenemy, Reihle. On 29 November he sent a telegram from Trossingen to SS group leader Wolff, declaring that despite the Brinkmann Agreement (Brinkmann was the state secretary in the Reich Economics Ministry), "Fleischer Jew also signed purchase contract under pressure late last week with Nuremberg firm. Nuremberg Messrs. in paper factory now, have free rein there as if they were already owners. Please have Brinkmann prevent authorization of Nuremberg contracts. Kiehn."[69]

On 7 December 1938, following consultation with the Reichsstatthalter in Württemberg, Hauptabteilung III of the Reich Economics Ministry (the office for "dejudaization of the German economy") decided against Himmler's suggestion (as transmitted by Wolff) "to defer a final decision on the sale of this paper factory until receipt of the verdict from the Party Supreme Court." Instead, the ministry determined "that the Fleischer paper factory should not devolve to Herr Präsident Kiehn. ... In the interest of maintaining the firm, which is not insignificant for exports," the sale was to be wound up rapidly, in favor of the sole alternate bidder, Franconian merchant Gustav Schickedanz.[70] For reasons that cannot be determined from the records, however, things did not stop there. On the contrary, in April 1939 the Reich Economics Ministry finally authorized the sale of the Fleischer company to Kiehn, and for a 20 percent lower price at that:

"RM 765,000 and payment of RM 35,000 to the Reich."[71] Since the various authorities and party offices that had been occupied with solving the "Jewish question" had been trying to outdo each other in their anti-Semitic activism in the weeks since the Night of Broken Glass on 9–10 November, the Fleischers (who had already been "contractually robbed") finally received an injunction from the Reich economics minister on 7 December 1938, in accordance with the Decree on the Utilization of Jewish Property of 3 December 1938,[72] to dispose of the family's assets within fourteen days. But David M. Fleischer, together with his two daughters-in-law, managed to emigrate illegally from Germany on 15 January 1939, whereupon the émigrés' German citizenship was revoked and their considerable private assets were declared property of the Reich. Their escape had devastating consequences for their relatives Kuno Fleischer and his wife. The head of the Foreign Exchange Control Office remanded Kuno into protective custody immediately, and as a requirement for authorizing his and his wife's emigration demanded an additional US$20,000 as an ostensible foreign exchange penalty, to pay for the Reich Flight Tax (Reichsfluchtsteuer) and the Jewish Property Levy. The amount far surpassed the value of the Fleischers' English enterprise. Kuno Fleischer was also stripped of the power to dispose of his private assets in Germany.[73] His American relatives scraped up the $20,000 needed to buy the prisoner out of his miserable situation. Niemann demanded that the currency be delivered in cash; Fleischer's relatives insisted that the handover happen in Switzerland. Consequently, Kuno Fleischer, who had fallen seriously ill in prison, and his wife were driven toward the Swiss border in June 1939 in a chauffeured Eislingen company car. Two officials from the Foreign Exchange Control Office and the Gestapo sat in the back of the car and told the Fleischers that they would be shot if they tried to escape. After the money had been handed over, the two were released near Constance, Switzerland, with a stamp from the British consulate in their passports. They had left behind property worth at least RM 2 million; now the two were traveling on foot, with twenty Reichsmarks between them. As a last indignity, the customs office attempted to confiscate the fur coat of Fleischer's wife, but after a lengthy effort their lawyer finally won out.[74] The couple ultimately emigrated to the United States by way of England. There Kuno Fleischer took on mundane jobs to survive and pay off his debts to his relatives bit by bit.

While Kuno Fleischer had been sitting in prison, the Göppingen tax office had hit the Swan company headquarters with claims for overdue Reich Flight Tax (25 percent) and the Jewish Property Levy (20 percent) imposed after Kristallnacht. Both were calculated based on the assessed value of the firm, although the purchase price authorized by the Reich Economics Ministry remained far below this amount. As Hermann Fleischer summed it up, for the four partners this would have meant "that we … still owed the German government RM 250,000 per head as a result of handing over our German and English companies."[75] The claims appear to have been reduced following complaints to the tax office. At any rate, a notice appeared in the *Göppinger Zeitung* newspaper on 23 October 1939 mentioning the smaller tax debts and basically criminalizing the Fleischers, who had faced wanton extortion and been driven into exile. As the newspaper of their former hometown put it:

> The following persons are wanted for tax delinquency: Dr. Hermann Israel Fleischer, last residence in Göppingen, Gartenstraße 29, currently in London. Delinquent Reich Flight Tax of RM 122,365 due 31 August 1938, with late fees. Walter Israel Fleischer and his wife ... delinquent Reich Flight Tax of 110,900 M[ar]k due 15 January 1939, with late fees ... Grete Sara Fleischer, née Katzauer, wife of Dr. Hermann Fleischer ... Delinquent Reich [Flight] Tax of 16,250 M[ar]k due 15 January 1939, with late fees. ... The taxpayers listed, if found in the country, are to be taken into temporary custody and brought before the local judge immediately.[76]

The denaturalization of David M. Fleischer and his sons had been published long before this in the official Reich gazette, as had the confiscation of all of their German property.[77]

The persecution of the Fleischers, having since banished them to two different continents, reached its bureaucratic conclusion before the First Criminal Division of the Berlin Regional Court. On 27 May 1940, this court sentenced "David M. Israel Fleischer" in absentia to nine months imprisonment and a fine of RM 40,000 for tax evasion. The grounds for the judgment included the cynical remark that the sentencing had taken into consideration "that the tax authorities are largely satisfied on account of [having received] the Reich Flight Tax."[78]

Meanwhile, none of the contracts concerning the sale of the Fleischer paper factory that had been created had entered into force. The Trick company backed out, irritated by the conditions under which the Fleischer company was to be sold. The Reich Economics Ministry withheld approval of the RM 1.5 million contract signed in Zurich by Kiehn's representative, Stäbler. But Gustav Schickedanz, owner of an industrial corporation "built on beer and paper," could not manage to get possession of the paper factory in Eislingen either, even with his relevant "Aryanization experience" and sales turnover of RM 40 million in 1938.[79]

Once David M. Fleischer and his sons' unauthorized emigration had provided the German Reich with a pseudolegal pretext for confiscating all of their property, the state stepped in as the new owner. Now the value of the Eislingen paper factory that had been so expertly assessed the year before seemed completely inadequate to the authorities. A new expert assessment called for Fritz Kiehn to pay an amount that was more than double the previous sum.[80] Kiehn sent complaints and counterassessments to the authorities, after which they granted that "the circumstances of the time and the risks involved therein need to be taken into account." The Moabit tax office thus recommended that the Fleischer company be sold to Fritz Kiehn for the price of RM 1.07 million. After two years of struggle, and a trusteeship by IHK employee Otto Lachenmaier that had lasted almost as long, Kiehn had achieved his goal.[81] The purchase price he had to pay was one-fifth of the price that had been the original basis of the sale negotiations. Section 15 of the purchase contract contained the comment "that the social fund and social [welfare] benefits to be managed for the employees of the Fleischer paper factory ... and the risk of war should be taken into account when calculating the price."[82] The fact that Kiehn used company assets to pay a substantial part of the sale price indicates that this risk cannot have been very large.[83] Again, the business partner of the Glaub & Cie bank, who acted as notary, as well as the shareholders Stäbler and Glaub also benefited from the deal with the Fleischers' stolen property, because the purchase agreement stipulated a broker's fee of RM 45,000, 4.2 percent of the purchase price, to be paid by Kiehn. This was more than 30 percent higher than the normal industry rate.[84]

All the same, a look at the accounts of the Eislingen firm makes it clear that Kiehn had landed himself a "bargain" — even with the loss of the English factory, the commercial balance sheet from 31 December 1939 shows paper factory assets of RM 2,579,086; the tax balance sheet indicated a whopping RM 3,115,830.[85] These figures did not reflect intangible assets, such as market position, product range, customer base, distribution channels, company reputation, and last but not least its entitlement to raw materials quotas. Having paid nary a mark for this sort of goodwill, which is an essential asset of a company and normally paid for in sales transactions, Kiehn became the "owner" of the company, now trading under the name "Papierfabrik Fritz Kiehn." Kiehn's own calculations put the pretax profits of the paper factory during his five years of ownership (1940–1945) at approximately RM 2.5 million.[86] Hardly any other company enjoyed such a fantastic rate of return — some 50 percent per annum — during the war. It was incomparable to the profit opportunities in "normal" times.

We can only make plausible speculations about how Kiehn ultimately succeeded in putting his competitor and experienced "Aryanizer" Schickedanz out of contention for the factory — especially since Schickedanz's denazification records contain no information whatsoever on his failed Aryanization attempt in Eislingen. In a 1945 police interrogation, Kiehn made contradictory statements about Schickedanz's departure from the sale negotiations. When in custody in 1947, he mentioned that Schickedanz might have withdrawn because of the high purchase price demanded by the Reich financial administration. Two years later, however, he claimed that "Schickedanz was very interested in acquiring the Fleischer paper factory" and stated that the Franconia Gauleiter, Julius Streicher, had a share in the Schickedanz firm that, according to Kiehn, "was made up of approximately 35 corporations."[87] Kiehn said that Streicher had also been the one to bias Gauleiter Murr and the Gau economic adviser in favor of having Schickedanz as the buyer. "How much the two Württemberg party representatives might have earned in the process, if anything," he added, "escapes my knowledge."[88]

There is reason to believe Kiehn's first "explanation" because, when the Nazi Gauleitung in Stuttgart offered Gustav Schickedanz the Fleischer paper factory for Aryanization, his finances were strained from previous Aryanization ventures. The increase in the purchase price, along with the loss of the company's sought-after English subsidiary as a consequence of the war, could have given the coolly calculating Schickedanz reason to pass on the deal.[89] But a different course of events is possible that would fit Kiehn's second reading: several witnesses support the version that Schickedanz, who, like Kiehn, was a reputed "old fighter,"[90] missed his chance, even with the favoritism of two Gauleiter.[91] The account gains plausibility in the context of Julius Streicher's political career. In 1939, the Gauleiter, known for "his blatant corruption," had initiated an "orgy of Aryanization" in Nuremberg and Fürth, where the Jewish economic presence had traditionally been strong. This made Streicher the target of fierce criticism within the party.[92] The economic persecution of the Jews led "to considerable tensions between the Reich and the region" that culminated in the overthrow of the top leaders of the Franconian NSDAP.[93]

Along with Reichsführer-SS Himmler and others, party chancellery leader Rudolf Heß was a fierce adversary of Streicher's. Heß was on the board of appeals that had taken up Kiehn's complaint against the machinations of "individual creatures of the party" in the conflict over the Fleischer company.[94] Compelled by secret investigations by police president Benno Martin and Nuremberg mayor Willy Liebl, Heß apparently initiated the party court proceedings against Streicher in 1939 that ultimately cost the latter his office. In February 1940, the Party Supreme Court found Streicher "unfit for leadership." He was dismissed from the Gauleiter office and put under house arrest.[95] The legal justification for this spectacular punishment, amid further accusations, was the charge made by an almost three-hundred-page report from the office of the director of the Four-Year Plan, Hermann Göring, "about the Aryanizations undertaken in the Franconia Gau during the period from 9 November 1938 to 9 February 1939."[96] The practices that came to light flagrantly contravened existing law and the disposition interests of the Nazi state. However, these practices in Nuremberg and Fürth varied from those of other regions, where Jews were seldom represented as strongly in the propertied bourgeoisie, only in the degree to which they occurred. The wealth-grabbing campaigns by soldiers of fortune and party barons had to be more shocking in these places than in the surrounding regions, where Jews with their own small businesses were few and far between.[97] The circumstances under which the Aryanization of the Franconian economy was expedited were marked by unbridled corruption, cronyism, and glaring wealth grabs by both individual party functionaries and the Nazi Gauleitung, at the expense of local Jews and the Reich treasury.[98] The Schickedanz name actually surfaced in the most extensive part of the report initiated by Göring, entitled "Illegalities and Abuses in the Franconia Gau." The experts from the Reich Economics and Finance Ministries who drew up the report of the investigation labeled Schickedanz a "Gauleitung favorite"[99] and described him as having been the preferred prospect "in the Aryanization of the Jewish Mailänder brewery … even though another interested buyer, Director Schülein from the Grüner-Bräu company, had been attempting to Aryanize the brewery for much longer." The report contained detailed criticism of the procedures in this "Aryanization example," which were strikingly similar to Kiehn's "efforts" to acquire the Fleischer company. For example, the investigators preparing the report criticized the Franconia Gau economic adviser for simply refusing "to approve Schülein's Aryanization [proposal]" at the local Gauleitung's behest, "even using the bogus reasoning that there was danger of consolidation." The buyer with beer industry experience had thus been "extremely unfairly … squeezed out from his almost completed contract." Even "when prospective buyer Schickedanz lost interest in purchasing the Mailänder brewery," the Gauleitung had continued to put "all conceivable difficulties" in Schülein's way.[100]

Schickedanz had called upon his friendly relationship with the NSDAP Gau organization leader and director of the Städtische Elektrizitätswerke power company in order to have a chance at the Mailänder brewery deal despite the anticipated competition. Many of those who had served "the party" well had no intention of passing up the opportunity to Aryanize this company, which included thirty-six inns. Thus, in addition to the aforementioned prospective buyers, a large number of brokers and one "rights upholder" were also jockeying for potential commissions. The Gauleitung had stipulated that it would take 7.5 or 10 percent of the selling proceeds from the Jewish sellers for its own fund. The city of Fürth was not going to waste the opportunity of this "large-scale Aryanization" either. Mayor Jacob had therefore required that the "Aryan" buyer of the company finance a "hall for 4–5,000 fellow citizens [*Volksgenossen*]." The more than RM 700,000 in estimated construction costs for this hall constituted a considerable increase in the financial outlays beyond the designated purchase price of some RM 1.8 million, especially since additional "donations" were expected to be invested in the Gauleitung. This caused both Gustav Schickedanz, who already owned two small breweries, and Grüner-Bräu brewery director Schülein, Fritz Mailänder's preferred buyer, to lose interest in the sale. In May 1938, Mailänder lodged a complaint with the Reich Economics Ministry, but this courageous step by a Jewish business owner — who apparently remained confident and still trusted in the rule of law, in spite of all the chicanery — was to no avail. There was no sale to the Grüner-Bräu company. Schickedanz, who was, with his Quelle company, mainly in the mail-order business and had rebranded Quelle as a "significant, purely Christian company" with "exclusively German goods," had "since Aryanized the mail-order company of Ignaz Mayer" with the Gauleitung's blessing. This helped the Quelle company to double its client base between 1936 and 1938 and grow to six hundred employees.[101] Gustav Schickedanz had already given proof through his donations of his "good relationships with the local NS power apparatus." Now, however, he exhibited indifference, and blurted to Gau economic adviser Strobl, who suddenly had no prospective buyers once again: "With all due respect, I'm not made of money! How am I supposed to do it?"[102]

What is important in this for the battle with Kiehn over the Eislingen paper company is that, at the end of 1938, the Reich Economics Ministry had been poised to examine the "notarial sale contract between the Fleischer Jew and Herr Schickedanz," which could not turn out favorably for Schickedanz under the circumstances.[103] Ultimately, it appears that Kiehn benefited not only from the protection of the Reichsführer-SS, but also from his tense relationship with the Württemberg Gauleitung: the investigation report on the "secret Reich case" that had been prepared by the Göring Commission must have permanently damaged the regional party offices' reputation with the state administration.[104] As a result, Kiehn — whose "considerable service in establishing the party in Württemberg" had become a known fact in Berlin in the meantime — was able to prevail over Schickedanz after two years of haggling over the Fleischer paper factory, even though Kiehn's "Aryanization methods" were no different from the repudiated practices of his competitor.[105] Four weeks after the Party Supreme Court had derailed Streicher, likely undermining Schickedanz's position in the process as well, Kiehn was awarded the contract for the Fleischer paper factory.[106]

The acquisition of the tissue paper factory in southern Württemberg, not very far from the location of his Trossingen factory, was a sensible economic addition to Kiehn's business portfolio. The products of both — high-quality paper — were similar enough that Kiehn doubtless had the necessary competence to manage the Eislingen operation. The products manufactured in Eislingen included "Efka cigarette papers" until 1948. Despite the fact that the Reich financial authorities had increased the price of the company, the new factory cost Kiehn hardly any money at all — according to later statements of the security department of the French military government (Sûreté) — because the majority of the purchase price was to be paid out of Fleischer company funds.[107] No financial obstacles prevented him from using the boon of war for further expansion — an opportunity that he would exploit to the fullest.

Notes

1. Because new archival material has become available since the German edition of this book first appeared, some of the sources for this chapter have been changed. We have noted where this is the case and where it has provided further information or corrections to previous assumptions.
2. Quoted in Bajohr, *"Aryanisation,"* 185. Numerous studies on the Aryanization of the economy show how much the discrimination against and persecution of the Jews "from the ground up" was impelled by Nazi Gauleitungen and the SS, along with the complicity of state authorities and, of course, ordinary people. The example described here can be considered a paradigmatic case. Kershaw, *Nazi Dictatorship*, 214–217. On everyday anti-Semitism before 1933, see Alheim, *Deutsche*; Ulmer, *Antisemitismus*; Wildt, *Volksgemeinschaft*. Further research is still needed on the practice of Aryanization in important economic regions that were shaped by Jewish industry until 1933, such as Württemberg, as well as on the role of the commercial *Mittelstand*. Only certain regions, mostly cities and industrial sectors, have so far been subjected to thorough empirical studies: Fritzsche, *Ausgeplündert*; Janetzko, *"Arisierung"*; Kreutzmuller, *Ausverkauf*; Selig, *"Arisierung"*; Stiekel, *Arisierung*. Important work has also been done on the role of the financial administration: Bajohr, *"Aryanisation"*; Drecoll, *Fiskus*; Kuller, *Bürokratie*, "Normenstaat." On the role of the NSDAP Gauleitungen, see Janetzko, *"Arisierung,"* 304–309; Kratzsch, *Gauwirtschaftsapparat*, 112–310; on the shoe and leather industry in Württemberg, see Bräutigam, *Unternehmer*, 297–336; on the IHK's involvement, see Janetzko, *"Arisierung,"* 301–12; Selig, *"Arisierung,"* 60–66; Winkel, *Industrie- und Handelskammern*, 103–105; see also Müller, *Stuttgart*, 282–309; Schmidt, *Süssen*, chap. 5; Schnabel, *Württemberg*, 533–68. For an overview, see Barkai, *Boykott*; Barkai, "Unternehmer"; Genschel, *Verdrängung*; Goschler and Ther, *Raub*; for sector or business history studies, see Münzel, *Mitglieder*; Aly and Sontheimer, *Fromms*.
3. This was the stated purpose of the Referral Center, founded through a partnership agreement on 28 Feb. 1936, as described to the Stuttgart board of supervisors by state secretary Karl Waldmüller on 20 Dec. 1935. Quoted in Müller, *Stuttgart*, 298.
4. The Economic Chamber became a partner because of its status as legal successor to the Württemberg Chamber of Industry and Commerce (WIHK).
5. The records of the Referral Center were found after the German edition of this book was published: StAL, FL 300/311, Bü 2511. They partially correct the statements we had relied upon that the center's former managing director, August Dignus, made on 20 March 1952: StAL, EL 902/20, Bü 80828 (denazification records Walter Reihle). See StAL, EL902/20, Bü 90205 (denazification records Otto Lachenmaier).
6. StAL, EL 902/20, Bü 80828. Witness statement by managing director August Dignus of 5 Oct. 1950.
7. RGBl 1938 I, 404; Schitag, *Siebzig Jahre*. This source makes absolutely no mention of Schitag's involvement in Aryanization policy, containing the bland, ambiguous statement that "in the years 1937 and 1938, Schitag once again was able to expand business in all divisions." Ibid., 38. In the 1980s Schitag became part of Ernst & Young, the global management consulting firm.
8. StAL, EL 902/20, Bü 80828, witness statement from Referral Center managing director and IHK case officer Otto Lachenmaier of 12 Oct. 1950; RGBl 1938 I, 414–415; Bajohr, *"Arisierung,"* 223–224.
9. StAL, EL 902/20, Bü 80828, witness statement from Referral Center managing director and IHK case officer Otto Lachenmaier of 12 Oct. 1950. Aryanization offices meant to provide the Gauleiter with access to Jewish property were not created in other regions until quite a bit later, with varying institutional foundations. Württemberg was clearly a pioneer in this regard and possibly a model. See Drecoll, *Fiskus*, chaps. 2–4.

10. Scattered records from the Wirtschaftsdank foundation surfaced after 1945 as part of the examination of National Socialist property. From these it emerged that the Gauleitung had maintained two foundations that together supplied two-thirds of the share capital in 1947 for the Portland cement factory K.G. Rudolf Rohrbach in Dotternhausen, which the Gauamtsleiter for technology had founded. Rohrbach, whose capital infusion of RM 30,000 had made up exactly 2.5 percent of the total contributed by the Gauleitung, remained the personally responsible chief executive, enjoying a distinguished reputation in Württemberg as director of the Portland cement factory after 1945. A credit agreement from 11 June 1943 shows that the Wirtschaftsdank foundation had contributed RM 800,000 at that time. Only RM 450,000 could be attributed to it in 1947, however, whereas the Foundation for Promoting the Technological Sciences (Stiftung zur Förderung der technischen Wissenschaften) invested RM 800,000 in the aforementioned firm. The two foundations also had two properties in Stuttgart with once stately villas that had been partially destroyed in the war. No details are known about the origins of these properties and what became of the money that went into them. StAL, EL 402/25, Bü 724 and Bü 1410; StAS, Wü 13, Bü 2994.
11. Bajohr, *"Aryanisation,"* 251 (cit.); Genschel, *Verdrängung,* 240–248; Drecoll, *Fiskus,* chap. 2.
12. National Socialists adopting this slogan included the new president of the Gau Economic Chamber and Wirtschaftsdank foundation profiteer Rudolf Rohrbach, who used it in his speech at the opening of the Gau Economic Chamber in 1943. This institution replaced the Württemberg-Hohenzollern Economic Chamber. BA DC, Akte Otto Hill, letter from the Reich treasury minister of the NSDAP of 1 May 1944.
13. After 1945 this attitude was reported by the former Reutlingen NSDAP district economic adviser. StAS, Wü 13, T2 no. 1659/038 (denazification records Wilhelm Vetter). Gottlob Berger also circulated information indicating that Murr's "environs" were known for their "positive Aryanizations": letter of 8 Sept. 1941 to RF-SS, in Heiber, *Reichsführer!,* doc. no. 86, p. 96.
14. Reihle declared in his denazification trial that he had suggested the founding of the Referral Center. StAL, EL 902/20, Bü 80828, examination of Reihle on 15 Aug. 1949.
15. Bajohr, *"Aryanisation,"* 199; Genschel, *Verdrängung,* 160–166; on the practice of Aryanization in Vienna, see Witek, "'Arisierungen'"; Friedländer, *Nazi Germany,* 211–268.
16. MAE Colmar, WH C 3541 d 11, Affaire Kiehn; interview of 25 May 1993 with a craftsman who had been employed under Büttner in the Berlin firm. His words contradict the military government's findings: "Büttner had already been dispossessed toward the end of the 1930s." According to him, a company employee belonging to the NSDAP had already become the factory manager before Kristallnacht on 9 Nov. 1938. "Fritz Kiehn then managed to snap up the paper company in Berlin in spring 1940." He relocated the company to Trossingen, the craftsman maintained, because he did not have a sufficient workforce in Berlin.
17. This political testimony about Reihle was given by a board member of Handels- und Gewerbebank Heilbronn on 2 May 1950 as part of his denazification proceedings. StAL, EL 902/20, Bü 80828. These records also contain further personal information on Reihle.
18. Similar descriptions of the three Gau economic advisers (GWB) in Hamburg are in Bajohr, *"Arisierung,"* 179–180. Information about their professions and the multitude of academic titles held by the GWB make it probable that most of them were university educated. See Kratzsch, *Gauwirtschaftsapparat,* 531–533, 535–536.
19. Bräutigam describes comparable methods in *Unternehmer,* 322.
20. The GWB apparently followed nationally uniform criteria in their authorizations, which nonetheless left room for capriciousness and nepotism in their application. Along with the lowest possible purchase price, the GWB ensured the political "reliability" of prospective buyers above all. Bajohr, *"Arisierung,"* 183; Kratzsch, *Gauwirtschaftsapparat,* 179–180, 269–270.

21. StAL, EL 902/20, Bü 80828 (denazification records Walter Reihle, affidavit from Willy and Max Elsas of 30 Mar. 1951). Stuttgart lawyer Dr. Ostertag, demoted by the Nazi state to a Jewish "law officer,"(jüdischer Rechtskonsulent) declared to the denazification court that the forced Aryanizations that took place under Reihle's authority beginning in November 1938 "represented nothing but predatory extortion." According to Ostertag, who after 1945 specialized in reparations issues and was the chair of the bar association (Anwaltskammer) and lawyers' association (Anwaltsverein), there were "hundreds of cases" of the Aryanization of firms for which the Gauwirtschaftsleiter had set the guidelines; these had often turned out to be tougher than in other places. Letter to the Central Denazification Court of 19 Aug. 1949. See the entry for "Benno Ostertag" in Sauer, *Religionsgemeinschaft*, 176; Küster, *In Memoriam*. The reference files for Ostertag, who was chair of the Israeli Cultural Affairs Community in Württemberg in the postwar era and belonged to the Central Council of Jews in Germany from 1950 to 1956, are located in the Stuttgart city archives yet remain untapped for research. We would like to express our gratitude to the city archives director, Dr. Roland Müller, for this information.
22. Statement by Willy O., Reihle's coworker in the GWB office and advocate before the denazification courts, before the Central Denazification Court of North Württemberg. StAL, EL 902/20, Bü 80828.
23. Fichte's works are characterized by a more or less admitted hostility toward Jews, which could be accompanied by both religious motives and resistance to the competitive capitalism emerging in his day. See Jersch-Wenzel, "Rechtslage," 29. Fichte's works were of great importance to the racially and nationalistically oriented youth movements of the 1920s, from which numerous representatives of the Nazi elite hailed. See Herbert, *Best,* 416–418.
24. StAL, EL 902/20, Bü 80828, defense plea by Reihle's lawyers.
25. See chap. 5 for the circumstances under which it became known that Kiehn — in 1932 as an NSDAP member of the Reichstag — had contacted a Jewish wartime comrade to help an acquaintance who had taken out a loan with the Jew. Kiehn asked him kindly to be patient with his debtor.
26. StAL, EL 902/20, Bü 80828, statement from Lachenmaier. An employee in Reihle's Gau office, the chief clerk of Savings Bank O., went on record to say that it had been Reihle who had uncovered Kiehn's Magirus episode and ultimately had him removed from the top ranks of the Gau Economic Chamber.
27. Unless otherwise noted, all additional information on the Fleischer company and the family who owned it, as well as on the Aryanization of the company, is from StAL, EL 905/2II, Bü 199.
28. Letter from Kiehn to RWM, state secretary Dr. Brinkmann, of 12 Nov. 1938, IfZ, MA 288, 9174–9176 (RF-SS Pers. Stab III).
29. The source for the following, unless otherwise noted, is StAS, Wü 29/2B, Bü 1019, criminal proceedings against Otto Stäbler before the Rottweil Regional Court on charges of extortion in the Fleischer "Aryanization matter."
30. Schnabel, *Württemberg,* 546.
31. StAS, Wü 29/2B, Bü 1019, affidavit from Eberhard Mayer, trustee of the Fleischer paper factory, of 3 Jan. 1947.
32. In the 1920s, "nearly 50 percent" of the Fleischer company's turnover came from exports. Sporhan-Krempel, *Papier,* 64.
33. Herbst, *Deutschland,* 200–202; Banken, "Devisenrecht."
34. The Foreign Exchange Control Offices (Reichsstellen für Devisenbewirtschaftung) were placed under the head tax offices of the states in 1934. Bajohr, *"Aryanisation,"* 154. There was disagreement, however, over whether the heads of the Foreign Exchange Control Offices were to be appointed by the senior presidents of finance or by the Reichsbank. A decision was finally made in favor of the Reichsbank. Ernst Niemann, the head of the Stuttgart Foreign Exchange Control Office, justified this in retrospect by arguing that no one could keep abreast of the

multitude of legal requirements around foreign exchange anymore. "The Reichsbank therefore insisted that Reichsbank officials be sent there because it was assumed that they would act in accordance with certain economic ideas." StAL, EL 905/2II, Bü 199. Statement by Niemann's predecessor in the Stuttgart Foreign Exchange Control Office, senior civil servant Jäger, to the Finance Ministry in Tübingen on 27 August 1947, and minutes of examination of Niemann, Public Session of the Central Denazification Court of North Württemberg of 8–9 Dec. 1948, 15. See Kuller, *Bürokratie*, 227.
35. Bajohr, *"Aryanisation,"* 154.
36. Kershaw, *Nazi Dictatorship*, 104. See Drecoll, *Fiskus*; Kuller, *Finanzverwaltung*.
37. The influential distinction between a "normative state" and a "prerogative state" under Nazi rule derives from contemporary witness and political scientist Ernst Fraenkel in *Dual State* (1941). The National Socialist *Unrechtsstaat*, according to him, is based on continuous suppression by the authoritarian state — which is characterized by random acts — of the normative state, which is constituted by laws, court rulings, and administrative acts. Recent empirical studies have shown how the German finance offices helped institutions of the normative state radicalize the Nazi race project. See Bajohr, *"Aryanisation,"* 154.
38. Kulka and Jäckel, *Juden*, doc. no. 298, "Lagebericht des SD-Oberabschnitts Süd-West II 112 von 1937," 255–256.
39. In November 1933, the Württemberg Interior Ministry was already discussing "the state of the Jewish question" and airing possible "solutions" to the "Jewish question in Germany." "Physical extermination — programs [sic]" was rejected at the time but was still explicitly cited as one of four conceivable solutions, along with accelerated assimilation, which was scorned, "transplanting the entire Jewish population into other countries," which would be hindered by other countries, and the "pragmatic solution," allocating the German Jews a special form of citizenship, similar to that of a national minority. Kulka and Jäckel, *Juden*, doc. no. 25, 59–63.
40. Maier was "interrelated" to Jews, having married a Jewish woman who emigrated in 1939. During the Third Reich, he practiced as a lawyer for Jews. In his memoirs, he referred in passing to the zeal for persecution exhibited by the dutiful customs officials who attempted to challenge his right even to his family's last remaining possessions (children's handkerchiefs) as they set off into exile. Maier, *Familie*, 49 (cit.), 46, 51, 53. See also Matz, *Reinhold Maier*; regarding the Württemberg administration, see Ruck, *Korpsgeist*.
41. RGBl 1935 I, 105–118; RGBl 1936 I, 1000–1001, Gesetz zur Änderung des Gesetzes über die Devisenbewirtschaftung vom 1 Dec. 1936. See Bajohr, *"Aryanisation,"* 156.
42. StAS Wü 29/2B Bü 1019, letter from minister-president Reinhold Maier to Waldeck denazification court, 23 May 1947. Niemann (1900–1983) was the son of a bookseller who was killed in November 1914. Niemann's mother died in 1918. He fought in the war in 1918, after which he pursued academic study and worked his way up to being the director of the Reichsbank. Minutes of oral negotiation of 8–9 Dec. 1948. Niemann, who maintained in denazification proceedings that he had "always acted impeccably in my post" and communicated as much in complaints to state bishop Wurm and Federal Republic chancellor Adenauer, was among the few defendants to go through the denazification court proceedings as "Major Offender" (*Hauptschuldige*). The Stuttgart Regional Court, however, rejected a charge of predatory extortion as inadmissible. The extensive records for Niemann impressively demonstrate the bureaucratic practice of calculatingly persecuting and harassing Jews, as well as the postwar attempt to shed light on these practices and prosecute those responsible. StAL, EL 905/2II, Bü 199.
43. StAL, EL 905/2II, Bü 199 (Niemann denazification records).
44. Niemann would dress down the Jews who met with him seeking to emigrate, as well as the lawyers who represented their interests, using mean, disparaging insults such as "Jew slaves," "accursed dogs," "Jew pigs," "criminals," and "black marketeers." Ostertag later stated the fol-

lowing before the denazification court: "We [legal] consultants would tremble when we went into the room to see Niemann." See further statements by RA (attorney) Ludwig Ottenheimer, United States, Stuttgart Regional Court president Robert Perlen, and the emigrants Herbert Schatzki (Conn.) and Carl Levi (Ill.), in StAL, EL 905/2II, Bü 199 (denazification records Ernst Niemann).
45. Bajohr, *"Aryanisation,"* 157–158.
46. Walter Fleischer was on a routine trip to England when his brother Hermann received his first unsolicited visit from Otto Stäbler and banker Heinrich Glaub in May 1938. They identified themselves as Kiehn's intermediaries and urged Hermann Fleischer to sell the company. At this point there were already various other purchase negotiations underway, so he refused. About a week later, he was arrested on orders from the Foreign Exchange Control Office on suspicion of "economic espionage for England's benefit." The Gestapo search of the factory and the Fleischer home did not turn up any incriminating material, but the company accounts were blocked nevertheless. Fleischer, who had initially been released, immediately received a new summons to see Niemann. Instead of going, Hermann crossed the Swiss border illegally, on his way to England to escape further such harassment. The father, uncle, and wives in the Fleischer family, however, were still within the authorities' reach and exposed to those who would Aryanize the company. Affidavit from Hermann Fleischer of 14 Aug. 1947 and letter from attorney Walter Molt of 15 June 1947, StAL, EL 905/2II, Bü 199, Bl. 107–111 (Niemann denazification records).
47. Throughout the Reich, Jewish big business first became a target of Aryanization policy in 1938. The party created a pogrom-like atmosphere in waves; these increased in intensity beginning in the fall of 1937, and the expulsion of all Jews began to look like the clear goal. Barkai, *Boykott,* 140; Kershaw, *Nazi Dictatorship,* 109; Friedländer, *Nazi Germany,* 241–305. In the Fleischer case, the Gau economic adviser had already asked the Economic Ministry and the customs investigation office in Stuttgart "in the utmost confidence" in September 1935 to let him know if there were signs that the firm "whose owners are Jews" was to be moved to England. However, the surveillance measures taken in response yielded no results.
48. StAS, Wü 29/2B, Bü 1019, witness statement by director Albert Roth in the Rottweil Regional Court on 14 Oct. 1948 in the criminal proceedings against Otto Stäbler on charges of extortion against Fleischer.
49. StAS, Wü 29/2B, Bü 1019, Director Albert Roth in the Rottweil Regional Court on 14 Oct. 1948.
50. StAL, EL 905/2II, Bü 199 (Niemann denazification records). Kuno Fleischer's statement to the Israeli Cultural Affairs Association in Stuttgart of 28 Apr. 1947. Lachenmaier's appointment as trustee by the head of the Foreign Exchange Control Office provoked speculation after 1945 about the extent to which Niemann had worked on Kiehn's behalf. No conclusive evidence exists either way.
51. Lachenmaier's responses to police interrogation of 12 Oct. 1950. StAL, EL 902/20, Bü 80828 (denazification records Walter Reihle). The interrogation of Reihle for his own case confirmed this. He testified: "At that time I turned to the Gauleiter and said to him … K.[iehn] made an uncanny profit." Thereafter, Reihle had located an appropriate buyer in Bavaria, the "owner of the Camelia factory, and I kept telling him that he could indeed pay for it and that he should take the firm." See also StAL, EL 902/20, Bü 80828 (denazification records Walter Reihle), minutes of interrogation of 15 Aug. 1949.
52. StAS, Wü 13, Bü 2250, details from Stäbler about his relationship to Kiehn. On Stäbler's role in the Magirus affair, see chaps. 4 and 5.
53. See Blum, *Trick*; on Hermann Dietrich's relationship to this business family, see Mechler, "Hermann Dietrich," 11.

54. StAS, Wü 29/2B, Bü 1019, statement by Heinrich Glaub of 2 July 1949. A witness statement by the managing director of the Referral Center, Lachenmaier, who testified in the denazification proceedings of GWB Reihle, supports other lines of communication besides those mentioned by Kiehn. Lachenmeier stated that in the summer of 1938, Kiehn had told him on the phone that "he was very interested in the Fleischer paper factory. ... The older Fleischer was interested in selling the operation to Zellstoff Kehl AG [another paper company]." Supposedly, Lachenmaier wished to refer Kiehn to the Jewish owners of the Fleischer company as a result.
55. StAS, Wü 29/2B, Bü 1019, matching statements by Dr. Hermann Fleischer, former Fleischer auditor Eberhard Mayer, attorney Ostertag, and retired Reich minister Hermann Dietrich.
56. StAS, Wü 29/2B, Bü 1019, judgment of the Grand Criminal Division of the Rottweil Regional Court of 22 Dec. 1949, based on statements by attorney Ostertag and Hermann Dietrich; StAS, Wü 29/2B, Bü 1019, contract on the sale of the Fleischer company of 21 July 1938; StAL, EL 905/2II, Bü 199 (Niemann denazification records), affidavit from Hermann Carl Fleischer of 14 Aug. 1947 consistent with all substantial elements of 1938 contract, as well as affidavit from his uncle, Kuno Fleischer, of 28 Apr. 1947.
57. Helmut Walter's account of his former superior and persecutor, Niemann and Kuno Fleischer's statement to the Israeli Cultural Affairs Association in Stuttgart of 28 Apr. 1947; both documents: StAL, EL 905/2II, Bü 199 (Niemann denazification records).
58. The October report of the SD Head Office attested to this, claiming that "in the Franconia Gau and in Württemberg ... some of the Jews in individual villages were forced to leave their homes immediately, taking only the bare necessities." The report names Ortsgruppenleiter and Kreisleiter as initiators and mentions "various suborganizations of the party" as the perpetrators of the campaigns, which most of the Catholic population purportedly deplored. Kulka and Jäckel, *Juden,* doc. no. 353, 297–298; see Longerich, *"Davon haben wir nichts gewusst!,"* 119–121.
59. StAS, Wü 29/2B, Bü 1019, affidavit from Eberhard Mayer of 3 Jan. 1947. Fearing that the house would be searched, Mayer's wife disposed of all records "for which it seemed at all prudent," so that Mayer ultimately possessed only documents that recorded "the result of the negotiations that had taken place, but not the methods of the negotiations."
60. StAS, Wü 29/2B, Bü 1019, letter of 5 July 1948 from Stäbler to the restitution authorities of the Ulm local district court and Glaub's statement of 2 June 1949.
61. StAS, Wü 29/2B, Bü 1019, judgment of the Grand Criminal Division of the Rottweil Regional Court of 22 Dec. 1949; StAS, Wü 29/2B, Bü 1019, affidavit from Eberhard Mayer of 3 Jan. 1947 and Colonel Hermann Fleischer of 29 Nov. 1946; affidavit from Hermann Fleischer of 14 Aug. 1947 and report by Kuno Fleischer of 28 Apr. 1947.
62. This partisanship, which had led to a clash between Lachenmaier and prospective buyer Gustav Schickedanz, caused Lachenmaier to be relieved of his post as managing director of the Referral Center at the GWB's behest. In 1950, Lachenmaier still precisely recalled this meeting with the Fürth merchant; he had reproached Schickedanz for how little he would be conforming to party principles if he affiliated his firm with another company in Württemberg: "It may be true that I abetted Herr Kiehn somewhat with my actions. But I dispute that I did so deliberately." StAL, EL 902/20, Bü 90205 (Lachenmaier denazification records).
63. The substantial denazification records of Gustav Schickedanz do not provide proof of business links to Julius Streicher. The records, however, are obviously incomplete: the "race for Aryanization" with Kiehn referred to here is not even documented. StAN, Spk Fürth I Sch-472, vols. 1–10. These records were still under lock and key in 2000, as were the extensive records on the restitution of the numerous Franconian companies "Aryanized" by Schickedanz. Both have since become accessible; the former have been the subject of highly controversial interpretations. See Schöllgen, *Gustav Schickedanz*; Zinke, "'Gauleitung.'" On the difficulties in ascertaining Schickedanz's motives based on the above records, see Drecoll, *Fiskus,* 281, in

which the author reports that the merchant's "dejudaization gains" amounted to "well over RM 7 million," according to calculations by the Nuremberg tax office in June 1942. On the history of the Schickedanz empire, its modest beginnings in the 1920s, and the biography of founder Gustav Schickedanz (1895–1977), see Böhmer, *Grete Schickedanz*. Like other pseudoacademic biographies of the founder of the Quelle mail-order company, Böhmer's account tends toward apologia. See Schneider, "Gustav Schickedanz," 311–312; Schöllgen, *Gustav Schickedanz*; on Schöllgen's biased way of writing the history of corporations in the Nazi period in general, see Rauh, "'Angewandte Geschichte.'"

64. StAS, Wü 29/2B, Bü 1019, judgment of the Grand Criminal Division of the Rottweil Regional Court of 22 Dec. 1949; StAS, Wü 29/2B, Bü 1019 affidavit from Eberhard Mayer of 3 Jan. 1947 and Colonel Hermann Fleischer of 29 Nov. 1946; affidavit from Hermann Fleischer of 14 Aug. 1947 and report by Kuno Fleischer of 28 Apr. 1947. The two vary in their estimations of the purchase price in the contract with Kiehn of 2 Nov. 1938. Presumably one cites the gross amount and the other the net — RM 1,080,000 — given when subtracting company liabilities. StAL, EL 905/2II, Bü 199 (Niemann denazification records).

65. IfZ, MA 288, 9174–9176 (RF-SS Pers. Stab III), Kiehn to RWM of 12 Nov. 1938; StAS, Wü 29/2B, Bü 1019, excerpt from minutes of Tuttlingen KRUA of 11 Apr. 1949, with an account of an otherwise unknown letter from Kiehn to the party chancellery.

66. *Trial of the Major War Criminals before the International Military Tribunal*, 31:517, cited in Friedländer, *Nazi Germany,* 274.

67. The report dates back to April–July 1939, but certainly also illustrates the intentions of the party authorities immediately after the Night of Broken Glass. Kulka and Jäckel, *Juden,* doc. no. 443, 400.

68. StAL, EL 905/2II, Bü 199 (Niemann denazification records), Kuno Fleischer's statement to the Israeli Cultural Affairs Association in Stuttgart of 28 Apr. 1947 and additions from Hermann Fleischer's statutory declaration of 14 Aug. 1947. The spelling of Schickedanz's name was incorrect. There is no record of a "Mr. Schikedanz." The fact that Kuno Fleischer listed not only Gustav Schickedanz but also the latter's attorney and Schickedanz's brother-in-law Kissling, the factory manager of the United Paper Works of Nuremberg, proves that Schickedanz's biographer Schöllgen was wrong to insinuate that Schickedanz and Fleischer never had this meeting and that the contract was never signed. This document from the Niemann denazification records eliminates any doubt as to the validity of the contractual circumstances (which were also attested to by Eberhard Mayer, Fleischer's business manager). StAL, EL 905/2II, Bü 199 (Niemann denazification records). Mayer described how on 22 Nov., the Gau economic adviser had demanded over the phone that he arrive "early tomorrow at Hildenbrandstraße in Berlin for the purpose of concluding a purchase agreement for the Fleischer paper factory." According to this account, Kuno Fleischer had already "been given his marching orders to leave Dachau." Witness testimony from Eberhard Mayer indicates that the contract was concluded under "blatant pressure." StAS, Wü 29/2B, Bü 1019, affidavit of 3 Jan. 1947.

69. IfZ, MA 288, 9174–9176 (RF-SS Pers. Stab III), Kiehn to RF-SS. Kiehn's account is underlined by a letter of 2 Dec. 1938 from the Trade Association for Printing and Paper Processing to Schickedanz's brother-in-law and managing director of the United Paper Works in Nuremberg, Kissling, concerning "a sales commission for the Swan Mill firm in London, i.e., for Messrs. Fleischer." Like the second purchase agreement of the Fleischer family with Kiehn, then, the contract with Schickedanz also provided for the sale of the Fleischers' English subsidiary and meager compensation for the Jewish owners. The value of the English factory — according to Kuno Fleischer's statement of 22 Sept. 1949 — was put at £6,000, equivalent to RM 80,000. Deputy Gau economic adviser Fritz Bernlöhr drew up the purchase agreement and also notarized it. Niemann then inspected it and forwarded it to the Reich Economics Ministry. Even

though the contract seems to be lost, there is a solid chain of evidence documenting its generation. StAL, EL 905/2II, Bü 199 (Niemann denazification records); StAL, EL 902/3, Bü 4030 (denazification records Fritz Bernlöhr); StAL, EL 902/20, Bü 90205 (Lachenmaier denazification records); StAL, EL 902/20, Bü 80828 (Reihle denazification records).
70. BA NS, 19/790, SS-Gruf. Wolff to RWM of 23 Nov. 1938; BA NS, 19/790, RWM to Chef d. Pers. Stabs RF-SS of 7 Dec. 1938.
71. LAB, A Rep. 093-03, letter from Moabit-West tax office of 19 Jan. 1940 to Berlin senior president of finance. This indicates that an auditor brought in by the Reich economics minister fixed the sale price (based on an "expert opinion"). As with the sale price from 1940, this amount would again be revised.
72. RGBl 1938 I, 1709.
73. StAL, EL 905/2II, Bü 199 (denazification record Niemann), Kuno Fleischer's report of 28 Apr. 1947 and statement from Ostertag's oral denazification hearing of 8–9 Dec. 1948; on the Reich Flight Tax, see Longerich, *Politik*, 125–127; on the Jewish Property Levy, see Aly, *Volksstaat*, 61–63.
74. StAL, EL 905/2II, Bü 199, minutes of Kuno Fleischer's interrogation of 22 Sept. 1949 on the Ernst Niemann case; see StAS, Wü 29/2B, Bü 1019, judgment of the Grand Criminal Division of the Rottweil Regional Court of 22 Dec. 1949.
75. StAL, EL 905/2II, Bü 199 (Niemann denazification records), affidavit from Hermann Fleischer of 14 Aug. 1947.
76. *Der Hohenstaufen/Göppinger Zeitung*, 23 Oct. 1939, cited in Voß, *Steuern*, 146–149; Mundorf, "Industrialisierung." To more easily discriminate against and stigmatize Jews, Jewish persons whose first names were not typically Jewish were forced to adopt additional Jewish names, such as Israel for men and Sarah for women.
77. DRA 1939, no. 157 (11 July) and no. 177 (3 Aug.), as well as no. 234 (6 Oct.). The detailed property lists of those mentioned, as well as of their wives, are from the Moabit-West tax office records, LAB, A Rep. 093-03: no. 53187 (David M. Fleischer); no. 53193 (Hermann Karl Fleischer and Grete Babett Fleischer, née Katzauer); and no. 53194 (Walter Fleischer and Ruth Magdalena, née Lorsch). Kuno Fleischer and his wife, who did not choose to emigrate illegally, were not stripped of their citizenship.
78. LAB, A Rep. 358-02, no. 96458, "judgment in absentia" of 27 May 1940, Public Prosecutor's Office of the Regional Court. We can assume that Hermann and Walter Fleischer were also sentenced, although no such records could be found.
79. The companies found to have been Aryanized during the course of Gustav Schickedanz's denazification proceedings are listed in StAN, Spk Fürth I Sch-472, vol. 2. The denazification court found that Schickedanz had "acquired the greatest part of his assets through the 'Aryanization' of Jewish property." Of his total assets in 1949 of DM 9,331,735, over DM 7 million had come from Jewish property. See also Zinke, "*Gauleitung*." Tendentious references to Schickedanz as an "Aryanizer" are in Böhmer, *Grete Schickedanz*, 39–51; Eglau, *Kasse*, 91–93.
80. On 17 Nov. 1939 — after the beginning of the war had eliminated the inclusion of the English Swan firm from the sale of the since confiscated German part of the Fleischer plants — one of the auditors hired by the senior finance office of Württemberg determined the market value of the Fleischer company at between RM 1.34, 1.78, and 1.26 million, depending on the mode of calculation. LAB, A Rep. 093-03, no. 53187, letter from the Moabit-West tax office to the senior president of finance for Berlin, 19 Jan. 1940.
81. By Lachenmaier's own account, in addition to his salary as an employee of the IHK he had received an honorarium of approx. RM 50,000 for his nearly two-year trusteeship, the amount of which had been set by the Foreign Exchange Control Office. He commented on this in the postwar era by observing "that I had no intention of becoming wealthy in this context; rather,

I was made wealthy." He claimed to have increased the paper factory's nominal capital by RM 1,000,000 under his leadership. StAL, EL 902/20, Bü 80828.
82. StAL, 402/9, Bü 235a, purchase agreement of 16 Apr. 1940.
83. StAL, EL 905/2II, Bü 199 (Niemann denazification records), statutory declaration from Hermann Fleischer of 14 Aug. 1947.
84. Ibid. "Industry standard" brokers' commissions for Aryanized businesses were 3 percent. See the investigations of the Göring Commission into Aryanization practices in the Franconia Gau, *Trial of the Major War Criminals before the International Military Tribunal*, vol. 28, Document 1757-PS, p. 99, http://www.loc.gov/rr/frd/Military_Law/pdf/NT_Vol-XXVIII.pdf (accessed 20 Aug. 2012). All the limited partners of the Glaub & Cie bank got a portion of this commission, including Stäbler and Glaub. StAS, Wü 29/2B, Bü 1019, Glaub's hearing of 2 June 1949.
85. StAS, Wü 29/2B, Bü 1019. The aforementioned condition of contributing to a "social fund" is very likely to have benefited the DAF.
86. On the common practice of not compensating in Aryanization deals for goodwill, see Bajohr, *"Arisierung,"* 184. Goodwill sometimes amounted to several times the net asset value of a company. The restitution law of the US military government explicitly stated that Aryanizing firms without giving credit for goodwill violated moral principles. See Law No. 59 in Office of Military Government for Germany (U.S.), *Amtsblatt der Militärregierung Deutschland: Amerikanisches Kontrollgebiet*, http://www.his-data.de/objekt/5/1/0/6/amtsbl,milreg,us.htm (accessed 6 Nov. 2014), issue G (Nov. 1947), part 2, art. 3, no. 3, on p. 1. For Kiehn's statements on his paper factory's profits, see StAS, Wü 29/2B, Bü 1019, questioning of Kiehn of 7 July 1947 in the Reutlingen war criminal camp.
87. StAS, Wü 29/2B, Bü 1019, questioning of Kiehn of 7 July 1947 in the Reutlingen war criminal camp; StAS, Wü 29/2B, Bü 1019, interrogation of Kiehn by the Rottweil Regional Court on 24 June 1949.
88. StAS, Wü 29/2B, Bü 1019, interrogation of Kiehn by the Rottweil Regional Court on 24 June 1949.
89. Schöllgen, *Gustav Schickedanz*, 141.
90. Schickedanz joined the NSDAP on 1 Nov. 1932 and became a member of the NSDAP faction in the Fürth town council in 1935. Böhmer, *Grete Schickedanz*, 42; Schöllgen, *Gustav Schickedanz*, 69–71. He seems to have exploited the economic advantages that the Third Reich offered him, bringing him into partial conflict with the Franconia Gauleitung. His political activities, however, were far more reserved than Kiehn's. This may explain why Schickedanz — despite his Aryanization practices — was ultimately found a mere "supporter" in his denazification proceedings.
91. Not only did Kiehn, Stäbler, and Glaub claim that Streicher had been involved, but Lachenmaier, the trustee, and Kuno and Hermann Fleischer did too, as well as the managing director of the Fleischer company, Eberhard Mayer. Mayer spoke in his sworn declaration about a "Schickedanz purchasing group in Nuremberg," and Glaub mentioned a "Schickedanz Group (Camelia)." "Camelia" was a well-known brand of sanitary napkins, produced by the Vereinigte Papierwerke Heroldsberg AG in Nuremberg, a company that had belonged to Gustav Schickedanz since he had "Aryanized" it in 1934. There is no doubt that the Württemberg Gauleitung favored this group, as the quoted correspondence of the RWM with the head of the RF-SS personal staff shows.
92. Speer, *Tagebücher*, 22 (cit.); on the following, see ibid., 172–173, as well as Müller, *Juden*, 256–257; see also Bytwerk, *Julius Streicher*.
93. Drecoll, *Fiskus*, 81.
94. StAS, Wü 29/2B, Bü 1019, excerpt from Fritz Kiehn's denazification trial of 11 Apr. 1949; on the relationship between Streicher and Heß, see Speer, *Tagebücher*, 172–173; on Streicher's tense relationship with Himmler, see Grieser, *Himmlers Mann*, 38–43.

95. Grieser, *Himmlers Mann*, 196.
96. The Göring Commission report is reproduced in *Trial of the Major War Criminals before the International Military Tribunal*, vol. 28, Document 1757-PS, 55–234, http://www.loc.gov/rr/frd/Military_Law/pdf/NT_Vol-XXVIII.pdf (accessed 20 Aug. 2012). For background on how it came about and the results and consequences of the investigations, see Kuller, *Bürokratie*, 287–93; Drecoll, *Fiskus*, 81–84; Grieser, *Himmlers Mann*. In the polycratic power struggle among the regional authorities, Nuremberg police president Martin acted as the Gauleitung's adversary, keeping the RF-SS's personal staff informed of the corrupt conditions in Middle Franconia.
97. See Volkov, *Juden*, 5; for Nuremberg, see Müller, *Juden*, 202–203.
98. On the following, see *Trial of the Major War Criminals before the International Military Tribunal*, vol. 28, Document 1757-PS, 166–167, http://www.loc.gov/rr/frd/Military_Law/pdf/NT_Vol-XXVIII.pdf (accessed 20 Aug. 2012).
99. Genschel, *Verdrängung*, 240; Grieser, *Himmlers Mann*, 158–159.
100. *Trial of the Major War Criminals before the International Military Tribunal*, vol. 28, Document 1757-PS, 166–167, http://www.loc.gov/rr/frd/Military_Law/pdf/NT_Vol-XXVIII.pdf (accessed 20 Aug. 2012). This applies to the following as well.
101. Böhmer, *Grete Schickedanz*, 40.
102. StAN, Staatspolizeistelle Nürnberg-Fürth Arisierungsakten, police interrogation of GWB and Chamber of Commerce president Otto Strobl on 24 Feb. 1939, 14.
103. BA NS, 19/790, letter from RWM to head of RF-SS personal staff of 7 Dec. 1938.
104. See Rebentisch, *Führerstaat*.
105. LAB, A Rep. 093-03, no. 53187, letter from Moabit-West tax office to Berlin senior presidents of finance, 19 Jan. 1940.
106. The party court proceedings against Streicher took place on 13 Feb. 1940. On 13 Mar. 1940, Kiehn reported to an auditor in Berlin that the Reich Ministry of Finance "had already declared by telephone its agreement with a purchase price of [RM] 1,070,000" and all that remained was to draw up the purchase agreement. StAS Wü 13, T2 no. 2775/001, http://www.landesarchiv-bw.de/plink/?f=6-1039573 (accessed 4 Sept. 2012).
107. StAS, Wü 120, Bü 362, letter from Fritz Kiehn of 26 Nov. 1948 on the previous production program of the Eislingen factory; MAE Colmar, WH C 2220, Kiehn-Trippel. By Kiehn's own account, his Trossingen operation handled sixty to eighty tons of paper a month. StAS, Wü 29/2B, Bü 1019, Kiehn on 24 June 1949.

Chapter 7

WARTIME DEALS AND "MARRIAGE POLITICS"

Kiehn knew from World War I that there were few better sales propositions in wartime than the manufacture of smoking accessories. With this in mind, he set up a branch in Strasbourg (Alsace) in 1941 and one in Posen (Warthegau) a year later.[1] Tobacco and cigarette factories are mentioned in the records of the French military government. They support the idea, though it cannot be determined with any certainty, that Kiehn later had to face accusations that Efka had still been able to place large machine orders with individual special machine suppliers in 1940, whereas Kiehn's competitors could barely keep up their own plants as a result of the dramatic iron shortages. Thus, even during the war, Efka could act as a sort of "court purveyor" to the army and the Reich Labor Service, which led to a substantial increase in sales.[2] Efka cigarette paper became part of German troops' standard supplies. In 1943, the British psychological warfare unit distributed imitation Efka packets to distribute propaganda and urge German soldiers to malinger, feign illness, or avoid reporting for duty. They reproduced the package sleeve and, instead of cigarette papers, inserted thin papers on which soldiers would find messages. Due to the popularity of the brand, the small packets could be distributed without arousing suspicion.[3]

The sales and profits in Efka's accounts make it clear how much the war boosted the company's profits. Annual pretax profits in the first half of the war — not including income from the Aryanized companies — increased nearly tenfold (1943 vs. 1938) and almost doubled again in 1944 (table 4).

Kiehn also continued to expand in his original industry by partnering with a paper processing company in occupied Poland: he acquired 11 percent of the nominal capital of Papierfabrik Solali AG, Saybusch for RM 700,000 in 1942.

Notes from this chapter begin on page 141.

Table 4: Efka's profits and sales, 1928–1948

Year	Profit (in RM 1,000)	Sales (in RM 1,000)[a]	Sales (1938 = 100)	Return on sales (in %)[b]
1928	26	n/s	?	?
1932	31	n/s	?	?
1935	31	n/s	?	?
1938	266	2,477	100	10.7
1943[c]	2,789	9,193	371	30.3
1944[c]	4,866	7,988	322	60.9
1945	864	1,699	69	50.9
1946	705	2,095	85	33.7
1947	692	3,266	132	21.2
1948 (until 20 June)	864	1,794	?	?

a) Excise tax not included. b) Pretax profit as a percentage of sales. c) Profit and turnover figures including the branches in Strasbourg and Posen.
Source: StAS, Wü 120, Bü 362/2, audit of accounts of 20 June 1948 by the Württembergische Verwaltungs- und Treuhandgesellschaft (WVT) in Tübingen, contracted by the Allied Control Council for control of Efka factory assets as provided in Law No. 52.

This investment would earn him a net profit of RM 300,000 in just the first year of business.

At any rate, in 1943 Kiehn's name surfaced on the list of staff under the general commissioner for ball bearing construction, industrialist Philipp Kessler,[4] who had been appointed by armaments minister Albert Speer. Kessler was responsible for reorganizing ball bearing manufacturing, which had been concentrated in Schweinfurt, after American bombings there in summer 1943 had severely damaged this essential part of weapons production. Kiehn apparently had worked in Schweinfurt under Kessler, with whom he was friendly, for a considerable period of time. This suggests that Kiehn was involved in this accelerated decentralization of production to various locations, and that his own factories were filling orders and providing workers.[5] What qualified the paper manufacturer for this task is difficult to say — according to later statements by Schweinfurt police, he always appeared in SS uniform and was addressed as "President."[6]

Kiehn had been on the lookout for new duties in organizing the economy ever since he had been forced to resign as president of the Economic Chamber and the IHK "with a heavy heart" but in consideration of "Herr Gauleiter" and especially the Gau economic adviser.[7] The local Chambers of Industry and Commerce and the Economic Chambers had been dissolved in late 1942, and their former tasks were consolidated into the Gau Economic Chambers. These new agencies, whose territorial jurisdiction extended to the entire Gau, were much more closely linked to the political leadership of the Gauleitungen than the Chambers of Commerce had been.[8] Kiehn could not have remained in office under these conditions; his reputation with the Gauleiter, and especially the Gau economic adviser, had not been improved by the latter's defeat in the Fleischer "Aryanization matter." Moreover, it was precisely Kiehn's other adversary in the Gauleitung, Rudolf Rohrbach, who became the head of the newly created Württemberg Gau Economic Chamber. The Gauamtsleiter for technology had become an independent entrepreneur in 1939, thanks to Aryanization money from the Gauleitung, and thus fulfilled the requirements set out in the Gau Economic Chamber's bylaws for the office of the presidency. In his speech at the inauguration of the Gau Economic Chamber, he harked back once again to the party principle of "common interest before self-interest."[9]

Kiehn too had no intention of missing out on the increases in this "common interest" that was held in such high regard. In late 1942, he sent a letter to the Reich Economics Ministry, writing that since he had taken up his honorary posts, he had been "completely absorbed in the Württemberg economy and in the overall organization of same." As for the fortunes of his company "during these many years (just as during the last years of struggle before the seizure of power)," he had heard reports "only from his managers." Now, he said, the "Gau economic adviser's sour grapes … his stolid, blind hate" compelled him to renounce his office. Alluding to the corruption in the Württemberg Gauleitung, Kiehn remarked that in his "selfless actions" he had "not always met with the approval of all full-time party comrades" because he might not have "been capable of bringing [his] sense of duty as an honorary official into accord" with the "sometimes purely *personal* [emphasis in the original] wishes and demands of individuals." His withdrawal from office, Kiehn wrote, would be lamented by "the gentlemen of the Württemberg economy" and by "party comrades whose decency could not be challenged." By Kiehn's own evaluation, he had exercised his office "in loyalty, selflessness, and discipline for almost a decade." After the Reich Economics Ministry offered him the prospect of "an honorable farewell to Stuttgart," Kiehn wrote he had one burning desire: "During the war and, if necessary, for some time after," he wanted to "to be used for economic leadership in some office with great responsibility." He enclosed a resume with his request, pitching himself "as a soldier of the movement" and explaining that "I … know only the fulfillment of duty; I am responsible, eager to work, and unafraid of any battle if it is fought sensibly and in the interest of the movement and thus for *Volk* and Führer."[10]

Whether this was the application that ultimately led Kiehn to Kessler's staff is unclear. Despite the great shortage of qualified leadership in the wartime economy, Kiehn's advances to the Reich Economics Ministry were treated as a delicate matter and without any special urgency. The ministry official in charge, himself a "decorated" man, initially turned to the head of the "Circle of Friends of the Reichsführer SS," Fritz Kranefuß, to inform him of "what kind of interest the SS … had in Kiehn." Kranefuß, for his part, endeavored to get an opinion from the head of Himmler's personal staff, senior group leader Wolff, using the opportunity to repeatedly impart his "not very positive judgment of Kiehn." Kranefuß added that "Reich Economics Ministry circles" regarded Kiehn "similarly unfavorably." Nonetheless, they wanted "more or less" to let the SS vote on whether and how to use Kiehn.[11] But Wolff, who had grown to like Kiehn in his frequent interactions with him as a generous donor and host of shooting parties and had previously taken an interest in his widowed daughter-in-law, waited months to reply. Instead, he tried to extract a decision from the Reich Economics Ministry about its "further plans for him [Kiehn]." Himmler's aide-de-camp Brandt finally spread the news in late April that the Reichsführer-SS had meanwhile "ordered that K. be put to use in our economic operations" and that the preparations were "already underway."[12] We do not know what, exactly, Kiehn's "honorary" function in the last two years of the war consisted of — nor whether he was working for the SS as planned, and whether his contacts with the general commissioner for ball bearing construction were connected to this. What is certain, however, is that in the very last months of the Third Reich, Kiehn was part of the small circle of people with whom the Reichsführer-SS maintained personal contact.

The strong SS support for Kiehn was also based on kinship ties. Since the marriage of his only daughter in 1941, he had enjoyed an additional direct line to the SS apparatus through his son-in-law. The Kiehns had brought up their daughter Gretl to believe that only an SS member would make a suitable husband. Ernst Fähndrich, an SS storm battalion leader from Ravensburg eight years her senior, seemed the proper candidate for the 23-year-old. Fähndrich was a senior civil servant in Berlin. He had belonged to the Hitler Youth since 1929 and joined both the SS and the NSDAP in 1931. With a doctorate in economics, he also had the professional qualifications to marry a businessman's daughter.[13] Fähndrich had begun his career as a clerk for the Reich Trustee of Labor and the Reich Group for Commerce. But in 1935, this ambitious and high-achieving young man entered the SS full-time. He rose rapidly, becoming the main departmental manager for the Four-Year Plan Division in the Reichsführer-SS's personal staff. In 1939, he was transferred to the office of the Reich Commissioner for the Consolidation of the Ethnic German Nation (Reichskommissars für die Festigung des deutschen Volkstums, or RKF), where he acted as the main department head of the Human Deployment Division (Abteilung Menscheneinsatz) and, beginning in 1940, served at the same time as the RKF's liaison officer to the SD and the Security Police.

With this position, Fähndrich had valuable social capital, an advantage that made him — in Kiehn's eyes — especially well qualified as a son-in-law. Connections were exactly what the embattled "leader of the Württemberg economy" urgently needed in 1941, when a union between his daughter and Fähndrich was in the offing. But the new family bonds, which reactivated Kiehn's old contact to his hunting buddy Kurt Daluege and strengthened his ties to

Heydrich and Himmler as well, also brought the Württemberg manufacturing family into contact with the war crimes committed in the occupied eastern territories. As an RKF functionary and director of health at the Central Office for Resettlement (Umwandererzentrale, or UWZ) at the same time, Fähndrich was part of the elite three-hundred-person Reich Security Main Office (RSHA) cohort that, according to Ulrich Herbert, made up the "core group [responsible for] the National Socialist policy of persecution and genocide."[14]

The RKF was a special agency typical of the regime. It was expected to concentrate all competencies on the ethnic cleansing of Europe under Himmler's authority. Along with regular civil administration, RKF staff were also expected to forcibly expel "alien population elements ... that signify a danger to ... the German *Volksgemeinschaft*" in advance of the "Germanization" of the annexed areas of Poland by resettled native Germans.[15] But above the UWZ, the RSHA also dealt with expulsion policy. There is much supporting evidence that the dynamics of resettlement policy played an important role in how the "Final Solution" to "the Jewish question" was decided.[16]

Fähndrich's job description alone supports such an interpretation: as a departmental manager at the RKF, he chaired a conference in October 1940 on how to "treat" Jewish "Reich members" who lived in the "protectorate" or in the Soviet Union, since "the Reich has an interest in not abandoning Jewish-held assets to the Soviet Russians." Participants in this meeting included Adolf Eichmann, who was later entrusted with implementing the "Final Solution."[17]

To put it bluntly: Fritz Kiehn's son-in-law worked in one of the administrative switch points that transformed the racial fanaticism of the regime into genocidal reality. Fähndrich made the following statements about the significance of the "struggle for a national character" (*Volkstumkampf*), a euphemism for ethnic cleansing, which were indicative of both the scope of his duties and his own identity, during a speaker training course in 1941: "the struggle really begins when the guns go silent. ... The Pole is to be gradually removed from the eastern region and replaced by Germans. These necessary measures must be supplemented by positive ones. Foremost among these is the extraction of all German blood from the Polish race. ... Therefore we must recover the children of these Polonized Germans." In addition to organized kidnapping, Fähndrich suggested that racial criteria be used to select adults: "With the evacuation of the Poles from the eastern areas, the new tasks have already been set in motion. Those identified as Germanic have been sorted from among the deported and deployed to the Altreich [Germany] to be slowly reintegrated into the ethnic German nation. ... This is a delicate problem, naturally, but so far we have had very good experiences."[18]

Fähndrich was speaking as a practitioner of genocide: since 1940, he had directed the health office of the UWZ in Litzmannstadt (Łódź), the first large ghetto in the east (located in the Warthegau of annexed Poland) and collaborated on so-called *Durchschleusungen* (sluicing). This euphemism was code for dividing up the native western Polish population that had been driven into collection camps into "Polonized Germans" and "Slavic subhumans" (*Untermenschen*). Fähndrich the economist had the last word over the doctors in the decisions on individual cases — decisions that often meant life or death for the people affected — and he acted, as complaints to his superiors show, with great highhandedness. One complaint read that all members of the office had "perceived his arrogance ... which he is even less entitled to because his official position does not correspond to his professional experience in any way."[19]

Fähndrich's self-assuredness probably impressed both his bride and his future father-in-law greatly. The couple were quickly engaged, a few weeks after the start of the "Russian campaign." As SS regulations demanded, Fähndrich had sent an "urgent application for engagement and marriage" to the Race and Settlement Main Office (Rasse- und Siedlungshauptamt, or RuSHA) of the SS on 1 September 1941. Three days later he received the news that neither the "genealogical nor medical specialist" had any "substantial reservations" about a conjugal union with Gretl Kiehn. On these grounds, he was issued a "temporary" permit, "subject to the additional approval of the Reichsführer-SS," for the engagement, which had already been scheduled for 7 September. Offering their services as "guarantors for the future bride" were two of Kiehn's friends from the old days, SS group leader Gottlob Berger and Kiehn's frequent hunting guest, SS group leader Hans-Adolf Prützmann.

Three weeks later, Fähndrich and Gretl Kiehn were married in a civil ceremony in Trossingen — both professing to being *gottgläubig,* the Nazi code for being unaffiliated with any church. This was, of course, the official party line, though many members had reservations about it. Identifying oneself as *gottgläubig* thus was a sign of being 100 percent in line with party doctrine. The Reichsführer-SS had received Fähndrich a few days earlier for a private meeting and a meal. We can only guess whether his marriage plans came up. At any rate, Himmler had noted the date of the "wedding of Kiehn daughter-Fähndrich" in his official calendar, and, just in time for the wedding, Gretl Kiehn received a telegram from Himmler: "Marriage approved. My hearty congratulations to you and your fiancé."[20]

Gretl Kiehn's marriage secured her father access to the power center of the SS state, with whose aid he was able to rebuild his strained "old boys'" network. The wedding had also been useful for his status in Trossingen, as it once again proved the ongoing influence and reputation of the "leader of the Württemberg economy." For economist Ernst Fähndrich, a marriage to the well-off daughter of a manufacturer from the provinces was, if nothing else, promising from a business perspective.

Apparently, with so much strategizing, love itself was given short shrift. The marriage between Gretl Kiehn and Ernst Fähndrich was not a happy one, in any event, and lasted only briefly. Two years after the couple had moved into their own home in Dahlem, Berlin, and one year after the birth of their daughter, Gretl officially transferred her place of residence back to Trossingen, where she had already spent most of her marriage anyway. In February 1942, Fritz Kiehn reported to his hunting buddy Kurt Daluege that he had put his daughter to work on the hunting grounds to help "our poor roe deer" through the winter. Daluege was occupied with coordinating the wave of killings by the *Einsatzgruppen,* or mobile death squads. Gretl Kiehn's husband appears to have spent some time on the front as an officer of the Waffen-SS and to have been sick or injured for a lengthy period. After he had received medical treatment from Himmler's trusted confidant, Professor Karl Gebhardt, in Hohenlychen, a military hospital of the Waffen-SS, the Kiehn family felt confident "that he will soon be cured for good and be able to take up his post again."[21] Fähndrich died three years later, on 12 April 1945, obviously after returning to a combat troop. He probably was in one of the German partisan units created on Himmler's orders in occupied south Germany, behind allied lines, using mostly SS members, Hitler Youth, and party functionaries. These combat formations were led by an old Kiehn family acquaintance, SS general Prützmann, who had since been appointed general inspector of special defense. It is not known whether Fähndrich was killed participating in these senseless "defense efforts" or whether he, like Prützmann, committed suicide.[22] Kiehn's family presumed that Fähndrich had taken his own life in light of his involvement in war crimes.

Throughout his efforts at relationship management and marriage politics, and despite time-consuming (if not exactly reconstructible) new duties in the service of "*Volk* and Führer," Fritz Kiehn never lost sight of his personal economic success, even in the midst of "total war." The manufacturer continued to apply himself to new, ambitious business projects in the second half of the war. In 1943, Efka added an extra division — armaments — that took up an entire floor. Small, high-precision parts were manufactured in this area, including detonator pins for bomb fuses. Gretl Fähndrich also got personally involved, training her then six- or seven-year-old nephew, Herbert, in the important task: he was allowed to check the finished detonator pins using a measuring device. Herbert E. Kiehn later recalled feeling "full of importance" during his school vacations, and of working "through the morning," as well as the hopes his aunt raised of him receiving a "War Merit Cross."[23]

A deal with a Berlin merchant in July 1943 marked the end of Fritz Kiehn's wartime acquisitions; Kiehn paid him some RM 6 million for a cellulose and paper factory in Okriftel am Main. The factory employed around five hundred staff and had generated RM 8 million in sales and some RM 1.5 million in profit in the last prewar year.[24] Founded in 1886 by a Jewish manufacturer, Frankfurt commerce council member Philipp Offenheimer, the company was significant in the paper industry, producing almost twenty thousand tons of cellulose annually, with a subsidiary manufacturing specialty papers and a small alcohol factory.

In summer 1938, the Jewish owners had been compelled to sell their company to a Berlin merchant for RM 3,650,000; its net value (not including goodwill) had been assessed in the same year at RM 9,400,000 by a licensed auditor.

The circumstances of this transaction exhibit clear parallels to the Aryanization practices described above. Bullying by the Chamber of Commerce in Höchst, Frankfurt; the inspection agency; various National Socialists in the company; and increasingly even the Gau economic advisor had begun in 1936 and had successively impeded management of the business until the owners finally succumbed to the pressure and sold the enterprise in summer 1938. Determined to emigrate, they sold their company for far below its value to a buyer who was forced on them by a confidant of the Reichsstatthalter and Gauleiter of Hesse-Nassau, Gau economic adviser Prof. Carl Lüer.[25] RM 1 million of the purchase price was to go directly to the German treasury as Reich Flight Tax. But the sellers did not see a pfennig of the rest of the purchase price either, which had been paid into a blocked account. They emigrated to the United States, utterly destitute, with their families in late 1938. Lüer, who presumably received a cut of the deal as a commission, was a useful participant, since he was also president of the Frankfurt IHK and the Hesse Economic Chamber, head of the Reich Group for Commerce, and a member of the Dresdner Bank executive board, giving him excellent connections both in the party and in the business world.[26]

All the same, the buyer that Lüer had selected for the Okriftel company had no liquid capital of his own. Such a shortcoming may not have constituted any sort of setback from the banker's point of view, however, as this enabled his institute to participate in the Aryanization of the company as well. Either way, Dresdner Bank facilitated the change in ownership with a mortgage-backed loan for RM 3 million, secured with the fixed capital in Okriftel. The new owner, Friedrich Minoux, was a coal wholesaler from Wannsee, Berlin. A look at his past would have readily shown that there was little else to recommend him in addition to his lack of funds. Minoux was not exactly known for his good name in the business world. He had risen to prominence as the managing director of the Stinnes empire and was a close political confidant of Hugo Stinnes, Sr. Political differences between the two had ultimately led Minoux to go his own way to build a new life as a coal wholesaler and part owner of a Berlin bank. In 1924, Minoux also became one of the founders and supervisory board members of the Berlin Municipal Electric Company (Bewag). Minoux also enjoyed decisive influence at the Berlin Municipal Water Utility and the Berlin Gas Company (Gasag), as well as the Berlin-Anhalt Mechanical Engineering Company (BAMAG).[27] Lüer's decision to bring in the coal wholesaler was clearly a mistake, as we shall soon see. Three years after Minoux's takeover of Okriftel, the formerly unencumbered factory was heavily in debt, and its owner's white-collar fraud and disloyalty had landed him in prison, far from the upper-class ambience of his villa in Wannsee.[28] Back on the lookout for a new buyer for Okriftel, Lüer, the Frankfurt Gau economic adviser and banker who was well acquainted with Fritz Kiehn, must have remembered that his friend in Trossingen, with all his bright and shining businesses, would be able to raise several million Reichsmarks for

```
FRITZ KIEHN                              TROSSINGEN/WÜRTT., 24. März 1944.
  MITGLIED DES REICHSTAGS               FERNSPRECHER 444
  WEHRWIRTSCHAFTSFÜHRER
  ℋ-OBERSTURMBANNFÜHRER
IM PERSÖNL. STAB REICHSFÜHRER-ℋ
     INHABER DER FIRMEN:
    EFKA-WERK FRITZ KIEHN
  TROSSINGEN—STRASSBURG—POSEN
    PAPIERFABRIK FRITZ KIEHN
         EISLINGEN/FILS


     An die
     Stadtverwaltung
     T r o s s i n g e n .


     Betr.: Bau eines grösseren Wasserbehälters in der Nähe des Fabrik-
            anwesens meiner Firma.
```

Fig. 19: **Pride of title and ownership in Kiehn's letterhead.** (Stadtarchiv Trossingen)

him easily. Kiehn did not let such a chance escape. Even if Kiehn was not the one who Aryanized Okriftel, and although the cellulose factory was now on the brink of ruin, Kiehn made what seemed to him a bargain buy at the time (fig. 19). The coming war events, however, destroyed the basis of this speculation. On 3 July 1943, a notarized purchase contract was concluded in the Brandenburg/Havelzur prison between the jailed Minoux and the "former president of the Stuttgart Chamber of Industry and Commerce, Fritz Kiehn, Trossingen/Wttbg. M.d.R." The Okriftel cellulose factory was to be transferred into Kiehn's ownership effective 1 July 1943 for RM 6 million. The seller reserved the right to withdraw from the contract until the end of 1943, however, in the event that his creditors were not satisfied with the RM 6 million.[29]

The creditors included two Berlin gas businesses, Gas AG and Gaskoks-Vertriebs GmbH, that were in the process of liquidation and whose claims against Minoux were at first difficult to put into numbers. The debts were ultimately found to exceed, by 50 percent, the sum available to discharge them, which should have nullified the contract right then. But Kiehn had no desire to pass up what was probably a once-in-a-lifetime opportunity for vertical integration: to link his paper processing and manufacturing company to a cellulose factory, especially one that was "practically a steal," as a look at the prewar books of the company made clear. So he entered into protracted negotiations with Minoux's creditors to talk them down, finally reaching an agreement with them in early 1945. They reduced their claims to around RM 3.4 million, which Kiehn promptly paid. This brought the purchase price up by another half million or so, making it RM 6.5 million, a third of which Kiehn financed using Efka funds. The rest came from loans from Dresdner Bank (RM 2 million), the Deutsche Effekten- und Wechselbank in Frankfurt (RM 1.7 million), and once again from Glaub & Cie in Stuttgart (RM 300,000).[30]

In the meantime, the profitability of the Okriftel cellulose factory had plunged because of perpetual mismanagement and supply difficulties occasioned by the war, even as the debts from operating losses and especially interest on the loans had grown. When the conveyance deed was finally signed on 24 January 1945, completing the transfer of ownership from Minoux to Kiehn, the Kiehn family believed that it had added a "pearl" to its business portfolio.[31] A poster-sized pencil sketch of the cellulose factory hung in Kiehn's study, and the new acquisition was immortalized in his family photo album alongside illustrations of the

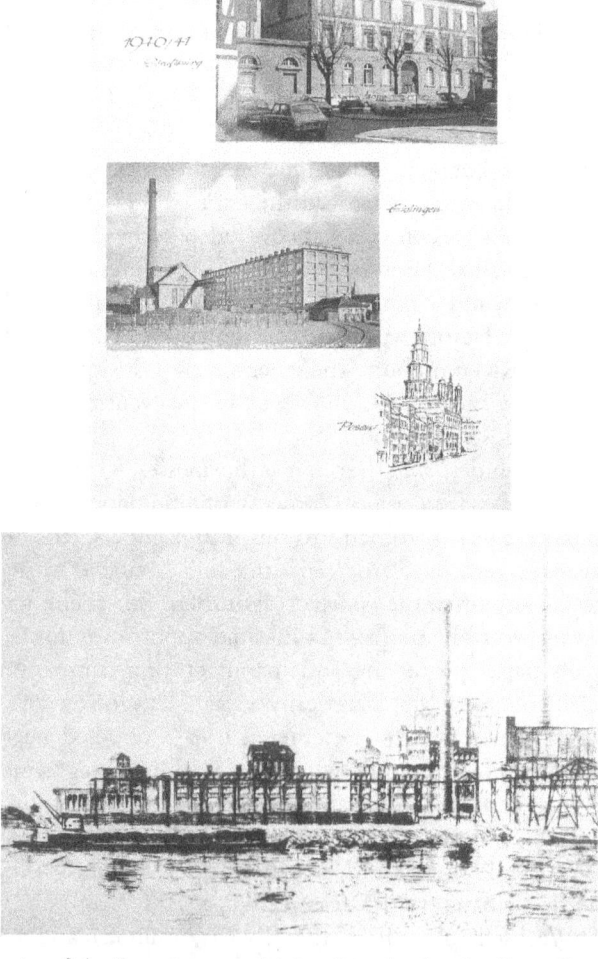

Fig. 20: Souvenirs of the "wartime acquisitions" in the family album from the 1970s. Okriftel is on the bottom. (Private collection of the Kiehn family)

Aryanized "Papierfabrik Eislingen, Fritz Kiehn" and the Efka subsidiaries in Strasbourg and Posen (fig. 20).

At this point in time, factory operations had been shut down for four weeks because of a coal shortage. It was impossible to tell when production might resume. The Allied troops were already nearing the Rhine, whose right bank was less than thirteen miles from Okriftel. Their swift advance into the Reich's interior ultimately also prevented the change in ownership in the cellulose factory from being entered into the Okriftel land register. With no evidence of the purchase, the RM 6.5 million price had been dangerously high. And Kiehn's willingness to make such a daring investment in these circumstances shows that he was incapable of thinking strategically. This also holds true for his naïveté in early 1945, when he evidently believed that the war could turn in the Wehrmacht's favor. His transactions could only generate a profit under the premise that, as a renowned National Socialist, Kiehn would continue to have control of companies that had been extorted from their Jewish owners under the threat of violence. But this inability to plan ahead was apparent on the business side of his large-scale investment as well. The purchase of a cellulose factory the size of the Okriftel plant might have made sense in a planned economy, but it was of doubtful utility for a middle-class businessman of Kiehn's caliber under market economy conditions. The cellulose manufacturing capacity in Okriftel exceeded the amount of paper Kiehn's other businesses required, which under competitive conditions could bring considerable hazards. Added to this was the fact that an individual business owner would not have nearly enough capital to cover the ongoing modernization the paper industry demanded. As with his purchase of the majority of Magirus shares in 1934–1935, Kiehn's wartime acquisitions were driven solely by his urge to pull many times his own weight. This quest was one of the most unhealthy aspirations that a *Mittelstand* businessman could have. It appears to have been a common thread in Kiehn's life and would leave its mark on his economic rebirth in the Federal Republic of Germany, although reparations obligations arising after 1945 diminished his wealth significantly. The political context may have changed, but his business ambitions remained the same.[32]

Notes

1. StAS, Wü 120, Bü 362/2, report of accounts audit of 20 June 1948, conducted by Württembergische Verwaltungs- und Treuhandgesellschaft (WVT).
2. ASD, NL Erler, Box 85, letters from paper goods companies to Erler of 21 Sept. and 25 Oct. 1950.

3. United States Holocaust Memorial Museum, Washington, DC, Robert L. White Collection, http://collections.ushmm.org/search/catalog/irn516736 (accessed Jan. 12, 2015).
4. In the civilian world, Kessler was chairman of the board at the Bergmann-Electricitäts-Werke power company controlled by the Siemens corporation.
5. MAE Colmar, WH C 3541 d 11, Affaire Kiehn. Kessler was head of the Main Munitions Committee, chair of Fritz Todt's Armaments Advisory Board, and a close confidant of Albert Speer after Todt's death. For more on Kessler's activities, see Eichholtz, *Kriegswirtschaft,* 2:559. On Kessler's work as general commissioner for ball bearing construction beginning in October 1943, see ibid., 2:141n137; Janssen, *Ministerium Speer,* 145, 382.
6. MAE Colmar, WH C 3541 d 11, Affaire Kiehn, note of 8 April 1946 from Schweinfurt state police to Tuttlingen police.
7. IfZ, MA 288, 9174–9176 (RF-SS Pers. Stab III), Kiehn to RWM, Ministerialrat Dr. Hassmann, 9 Nov. 1942.
8. Winkel, *Industrie- und Handelskammern,* 125–126.
9. Schnabel, *Württemberg,* 400–401; Winkel, *Industrie- und Handelskammern,* 139.
10. IfZ, MA 288, 9174–9176 (RF-SS Pers. Stab III), Kiehn to RWM, Ministerialrat Dr. Hassmann, 9 Nov. 1942.
11. IfZ, MA 288, 9174–9176 (RF-SS Pers. Stab III), Kranefuß to Ostuf. Heckenstaller, 2 Dec. 1942.
12. IfZ, MA 288, 9174–9176 (RF-SS Pers. Stab III), (author illegible) to Kranefuß, 6 Jan. 1943; IfZ, MA 288, 9174–9176 (RF-SS Pers. Stab III), Ostuf. Brandt to Kranefuß, 27 April 1943.
13. On Fähndrich, see Aly and Heim, *Vordenker,* 152, 159; Himmler, *Dienstkalender,* 678; BA DC, Akte Fähndrich.
14. See Herbert, *Best,* 13. For more on the RKF's mission, including a detailed evaluation of Fähndrich's importance, see Aly, *"Endlösung,"* 75–85; Aly and Heim, *Vordenker,* 148–150, 152. On the practice of "ethnic cleansing" carried out by the UWZ, see Heim, *Verfolgung,* 32–39; Heinemann, *"Rasse,"* 197–198; Koeh, *RKFDV*; Widmann, "Reichskommissar."
15. Quoted in Broszat, *Staat Hitlers,* 395. Resettling Lothringen (Lorraine) with "ethnic Germans" from Dobruja, Bukovina, and Bessarabia was apparently briefly considered. See the entry of 3 March 1941 on the discussion between Himmler and Fähndrich in Himmler, *Dienstkalender,* 125; Jachomowski, *Umsiedlung,* 180.
16. See Widmann, "Reichskommissar."
17. BA DC, Akte Fähndrich; see Aly and Heim, *Vordenker,* 152.
18. BA DC, Akte Fähndrich, Fähndrich's manuscript for courses for "ethnic German orators" in September 1941.
19. BA DC, Akte Fähndrich/SS O, SS-Sturmbannführer Künzel to head of Litzmannstadt Central Office for Resettlement, 3 July 1940.
20. Himmler, *Dienstkalender,* 16 and 24 Sept. 1941, 211 and 216; BA DC, Akte Fähndrich/RS, Sippenakte Fähndrich, Ernst/Kiehn, Gretl. On the racial politics of the SS as an elite "clan community" (*Sippengemeinschaft*), see Schwarz, *Frau,* 17–61.
21. BA DC, Akte Richard Blankenhorn, letter from Kiehn of 16 Feb. 1942. We would like to thank Christine Arbogast for this evidence; on Hohenlychen and Prof. Gebhardt, who conducted experiments on human subjects in this clinic using prisoners from the nearby Ravensbrück concentration camp, see Himmler, *Dienstkalender,* 106; Hahn, *Grawitz.*
22. Henke, *Besetzung,* 945–946.
23. Letter from Herbert E. Kiehn of 22 Feb. 1999.
24. HHStA, Abt. 518/A, no. Ffm 369 (Rückerstattungsakte) and Abt. 519/V, no. 2152-114, vol. 1. The number of employees in wartime varied between 607 (1940) and 355 (1944). Sales fluctuated from 7,597,000 (1941) to 4,438,000 (1944).

25. Lüer (b. 1897) was a prominent National Socialist. He joined the party in 1927, the SS in November 1933, and the Reichstag in 1934. He was the labor trustee for the Hesse Economic Area, the NSDAP Gau inspector for Hesse, a military industrial leader, and a member of the close circle of advisors of the Reich Economic Chamber. He served on the supervisory board of Adam Opel beginning in 1935, and in 1941 became the chair of the same board and plant manager (Betriebsführer). See Rebentisch, *Zeiten*; Kugler, "Behandlung," 57–59; Lilla, Döring, and Schulz, *Statisten*, 391–392; Bähr, *Dresdner Bank*, chap. 3 and 607.
26. HHStA, Abt. 518/A, no. Ffm 369.
27. A capsule biography of Minoux is available at http://www.dhm.de/lemo/html/biografien/MinouxFriedrich/index.htmli (accessed 20 Aug. 2012). On the political role Minoux played in the early Weimar Republic, see Weisbrod, *Schwerindustrie*, 149–150; Hallgarten and Radkau, *Industrie*, 170–179. The latter sources show Minoux, who rejected democracy, as having already been appointed to negotiate with Hitler on Stinnes's behalf in 1923. Geyer, *"Verkehrte Welt,"* 347. For general information, see Feldman, *Hugo Stinnes*, 512–840.
28. HHStA, Abt. 519/A, no. Ffm 369. On 15 Aug. 1941, the Seventh Regional Criminal Court of Berlin sentenced Minoux to five years in jail and imposed a fine of RM 600,000 or an additional six months' imprisonment. Minoux's coal wholesaling business was then sold, as was his imposing villa in Wannsee, which was acquired by the SS and used for the Wannsee Conference in January 1942. Haupt, *Haus*; Tuchel, *Wannsee*.
29. HHStA, Abt. 519/A, no. Ffm 369, sale contract of 3 July 1943.
30. HHStA, Abt. 519/A, no. Ffm 369; StAL, EL 402/9, Bü 235 (restitution records of Fleischer company with experts' reports on the financial situation of Okriftel). According to a settlement reached with the Berlin Gas Company on 15 Feb. 1945, Kiehn paid out RM 3,391,947 in claims against Minoux. What's more, the following claims remained unpaid: RM 2,250,000 of secured bank loans; RM 600,000 fine from Minoux's sentence of 21 Aug. 1941; RM 12,000 in notary costs; RM 40,858 in legal fees; and RM 100,000 in "severance" for Minoux.
31. Supplementary agreement in HHStA, Abt. Z 460, no. 365, letter of 31 May 1949 from attorney Ranft to reparations court; interview with Herbert E. Kiehn of 19–20 May 1998.
32. Memorandum from Herbert E. Kiehn of 24 May 1998.

Chapter 8

"THE KING OF TROSSINGEN"
Fritz Kiehn as a Local Grandee in the Third Reich

The Nazi seizure of power allowed Kiehn, as the "highest party functionary" in the area, to flout the Trossingen social hierarchy and overshadow the local dignitaries who until then had been foremost in the town. After the humiliations of his younger days, Kiehn enjoyed this process to the fullest, "conquering" the streets and squares of his adopted hometown in the spring of 1933. To the people of Trossingen, it seemed as though a new monarch had superseded "harmonica king" Ernst Hohner. The Trossingen NSDAP celebrated after the March elections with gun salutes and a parade, even though the party had clearly fallen short of the results in the rest of Württemberg and across the Reich. On 9 March, SA and NSDAP members marched to the Trossingen town hall "with music" and hoisted the Nazi flag, with its characteristic swastika. Kiehn then spoke from the balcony of the town hall and the black, red, and gold flag of the republic was burned.[1]

Despite the long-standing rivalry and mutual contempt of the Hohner and Kiehn families, no open conflicts broke out between them in 1933. On the contrary, the year was characterized by the search for a new modus vivendi as the two families accustomed themselves to the new hierarchy. Kiehn did not want to risk antagonizing the largest employer in the region, turning him and his workforce against the new state. Hohner, for his part, knew that the rules of the game had changed and that Kiehn now had the upper hand. Head-on collisions could jeopardize Hohner's company and his personal safety. The two thus developed an ambivalent relationship in which they cooperated out of necessity and maintained an outward appearance of harmony amid their mutual distrust.

An early opportunity to protect local interests arrived in the form of attacks motivated by cultural policy on the accordion associations that the Hohner company had only just founded. The clubs, the focus of a new and successful marketing

---

Notes from this chapter begin on page 182.

strategy for the firm, were organized into a German Accordion Association (Deutscher Handharmonika Verband, DHHV) led by the Hohner advertising department. In the midst of the Great Depression, this was an attempt to complement the company's harmonica production that had so far been Hohner's dominant line of production by strengthening the second line, namely, accordions. When NSDAP party members in the DHHV tried to take over the association in spring 1933 and oust Hohner, Kiehn abruptly stepped in and had himself appointed *Gleischschaltung* commissioner, in charge of bringing the organization in line with Nazi politics. Tellingly, on the first day of his "appointment," the board released him from his obligation to attend all meetings. This gave Hohner substantial carte blanche, at least until the accordion association's office was forcibly transferred to Berlin in 1938. The DHHV fell under the formal control of the Reich Chamber of Music (Reichsmusikkammer, or RMK) from fall 1933.[2]

In May, the Hohner factory orchestra paid a visit to Reichsstatthalter Murr that Kiehn facilitated and spearheaded. Murr and Kiehn appear together in various photographs with the accordion players. Not only did this performance provide the Hohner company with free advertising; it also helped guard against ideological attacks from Old Germanic culture warriors from the Rosenberg camp, who

Das Hohner Handharmonika-Orchester   v.l.n.r.: DHHV-Päsident Bleyer, Hohner-

Fig. 21: The Hohner accordion orchestra with *Reichsstatthalter* Wilhelm Murr (1933). (Stadtarchiv Trossingen)

regarded the mass-produced harmonicas and accordions as "intrinsically foreign" instruments to be excluded from the cultural life of the Nazi state. Once again, Kiehn was able to stage-manage his proximity to power; he was celebrated in the local press accordingly. This time he had opened the door to great politics for everyday citizens of Trossingen. The orchestra members were Hohner company employees who still rhapsodized decades later about the visit to Stuttgart. Fig. 21 shows Murr, as the new head at Villa Reitzenstein, the official residence of the Württemberg state presidents in the Weimar Republic, sitting smugly in front of the reverential accordion players. Kiehn stands in the background, along with Hohner's head of advertising and musical director.[3]

The transformation of the Hohner works committee offered another occasion for the new and old "kings" of Trossingen to cooperate. Given the intensely paternalistic management style of the company, the works council had been obliged to "dance to Hohner's tune," as one worker put it, prior to 1933.[4] The Third Reich, however, threatened to overturn this well-oiled system. The new workers' representatives were obviously less servile in their behavior than their predecessors because their position had been created by the Nazi state, which gave them some political clout. As early as fall 1933, Ernst Hohner, as he told Karl Hohner, felt compelled to rein in their "overeagerness" with Kiehn's help: "We are experiencing an uncomfortable thing at the moment. ... I've already discussed the matter with Kiehn. I am definitely counting on Kiehn to intervene so that things will calm down."[5] The intervention had its desired effect. After several similar conflicts, Hohner managed to divest himself of the recalcitrant representative of the factory cell in 1936. Even though Kiehn had helped the harmonica manufacturer to quiet the "troublemakers" inside the factory, in 1933–1934 Hohner still categorically rejected Kiehn's desire that he give preference to "old fighters" in hiring. Insisting on his rights as owner of the company, and steeped in the most profound paternalistic traditions, Hohner balked at any attempt by outsiders to interfere with his firm. He consistently favored experienced skilled workers over "party comrades" who were new to harmonica manufacturing.

A political arrangement was found as well, even if Hohner regarded it as less advantageous. In April 1933, like everywhere else in the Reich, the bringing in line (*Gleichschaltung*) of the town council was due to take place. Kiehn was cracking down ruthlessly on almost all elected representatives who were not members of the NSDAP. Ernst Hohner (who had since changed from the local civic union [Bürgerliche Vereinigung] to the right-wing DNVP) kept his council seat after the seizure of power by the Nazis, without even tentatively protesting the removal of elected council members, but now all of his fellow council members were National Socialists. Kiehn, in his function as district inspector, filled the vacant seats as he saw fit. In the space of a few months, Hohner had gone from being an influential party whip to a marginal figure who was merely tolerated, whereas Kiehn had gone from being an outsider to the man at the top. As if he needed yet another safeguard of his position, in May Kiehn pressed for an SS training facility to be built in Trossingen. From that point on, his status was reinforced by the hundred-member SS troop, which contained almost no citizens from the town.[6]

But that was not all: Kiehn had also begun to stage highly symbolic acts that were to reflect the political regime change and his position as the new "lord" of the realm. For example, the Kiehns presented themselves as the model Nazi family, the antithesis of the "decadent" bourgeoisie of the "system [Weimar] era."[7] Berta Kiehn, who only a few years before had grudgingly been admitted into the Trossingen women's circle, distanced herself in writing from such exclusive pastimes. The "German woman," she wrote, had more important tasks in the Third Reich, which in her case meant becoming the district leader of the National Socialist Women's League. To set an example, she established the NSF office in her own villa in Deibhalde, holding her office hours there as well.

Berta Kiehn orchestrated her daughter Gretl's confirmation on 2 April 1933 as a minor act of state: topping the guest list were Reichsstatthalter Murr and Economics Minister Lehnich, alongside members of the Württemberg Nazi elite.[8] Gretl figured prominently in the local parade on National Workers' Day (fig. 22). Family, professional, and political matters were constantly intermingled. Countless invitations to the Kiehn residence in Deibhalde, their vacation home

Fig. 22: "May Queen" Gretl Kiehn on National Workers' Day. (Martin Häffner et al. *Trossingen. Vom Alemannendorf zur Musikstadt.* Trossingen, 1997)

on Lake Constance, and the family hunting grounds served to establish useful networks. Even before the Nazis seized power, Kiehn had put the entire family into the service of the movement. Not only did his son, Herbert, enter the Hitler Youth early on, but he also campaigned for his father in the 1933 elections. In addition, he took over the leadership of an SS troop and led propaganda efforts for three districts. By Herbert's own account, these activities gave him "sincere satisfaction." "I recognized I had much to correct in my previous worldview."[9] There is also evidence that Herbert appeared at a party assembly in Trossingen in 1934. Standing next to his father, "party comrade Kiehn, Jr." gave a speech full of pride in which, with "spirited words," he recalled the NSDAP party convention in Weimar of 1926. He allegedly took part "as the first Trossingen party comrade in a Hitler Youth uniform."[10] No further evidence exists of any Trossingen political involvement by Herbert Kiehn, who attended university in Cologne. This can probably be attributed to the young man's party euphoria subsiding and his growing liking of elegant clothing and fast cars. Although he occupied the SS rank of master sergeant (Hauptscharführer), his relatives remember him as not being very ideologically reliable.

Like her children, Berta Kiehn joined the local NSDAP early, becoming more fanatical than her husband. Her grandson recalls her as having been one of those who "always" gave "150 percent ... who, whatever her motives, be they ideological conviction, care for the family, prosperity, or even her life, would 'keep her husband on the straight and narrow.'"[11] She was able to back her husband even when he seemed to be rushing headlong from one gaffe to the next. What she too was usually incapable of doing, however, was developing political and economic strategies that promised success.

The intertwining of the personal/familial and political spheres can also be seen in the portraits of the couple taken in honor of their silver (twenty-fifth) wedding anniversary (figs. 23 and 24). The Kiehns posed in front of a bust of Hitler that — like a family altar — adorned a wall in the entrance hall of the Deibhalde villa. In honor of the celebration, a laurel wreath had been hung over the "Führer bust"; well-wishers had sent flower arrangements festooned with swastika ribbons. Berta wore valuable jewelry, including a necklace with a diamond-studded crucifix. The symbolic syncretism that permeated the couple's self-dramatization did not make any sort of bad impression among this cohort — or so it seemed; indeed, it was typical of the culture of "beautiful appearances" that had been a semiofficial aspect of the Third Reich since 1933.[12]

At the same time, a civic habitus shaped these festivities in the circles of friends and relatives in attendance — including Kreisleiter Huber and his wife. They sat together in a convivial and solidly middle-class atmosphere, dressed in civilian clothing; they danced, ate, and drank. Nothing brought to mind a political celebration. There were enough occasions outside Deibhalde for ostentatious, exaggerated political posturing, as shown by their preference for

Fig. 23: Silver wedding anniversary (1936): the private element. (Private collection of the Kiehn family)

Fig. 24: Silver wedding anniversary (1936): the National Socialist element—portrait of a trio. (Private collection of the Kiehn family)

official celebrations, which they would create themselves when push came to shove.

The crucifix alongside the swastika throws significant light on the couple's ideological syncretism. They had been married in a church, and their children had not only been baptized and confirmed but also recited evening prayers. On special occasions, such as when the pastor was a guest at family celebrations, they even said grace. But the Prussian newcomer and the town innkeeper's daughter were not completely integrated into the "bigoted" world of prayer meetings and regular churchgoers. On the contrary, they were outsiders to the culture of Swabian Pietism that still predominated in the region. Fritz Kiehn was more partial to the German national variations of Protestantism. A portrait of Martin Luther, whom he revered as a national hero, hung in his bedroom. Kiehn's grandson explained how important Luther was to his grandfather with a concise cliché: "[A] German man who stood tall."[13]

If Luther watched over the couple as they slept, the Führer kept tabs on them all day. There were a few other sculptures in the manufacturer's villa in addition to the stone-hewn Hitler, namely, the busts of Fritz Kiehn and his beloved daughter, Gretl (fig. 25). The urge for self-presentation also led to a passion for being filmed and photographed. Kiehn's favorite photos were those that showed him alongside prominent figures. He employed personal photographers for this purpose: they would visit him on special occasions or accompany him on his travels. For example, the Kiehns attended the Bayreuth Festival somewhat regularly.

Fig. 25: **The trappings of self-aggrandizement (1936).** (Private collection of the Kiehn family)

Family acquaintances included some members of the Wagner family, who, like the Kiehns, owned a vacation home on Lake Constance. When attending the festival, the Kiehns took advantage of an unexpected run-in with economics minister and Reichsbank president Hjalmar Schacht to have their photo taken with him.

The Bayreuth Opera Festival, which since the 1920s had been characterized by the increasing "classing down" of its audience, giving it more the character of a "national [*völkisch*] festival venue,"[14] offered the ambitious couple from Swabia the chance to take part in a social event, perhaps get a look at the Führer, and, above all, establish and enlarge their network of contacts. The Kiehns' attitude to Wagner's music approached naïveté, as their grandson described it: "Neither of my grandparents was musical, Fritz Kiehn especially so. He liked a particular kind of melodramatic-sounding aesthetic, the source of his weakness for brass bands." Kiehn was not capable of making musical distinctions: "He was interested in Wagner and in being present (before 1945) at the festival [in Bayreuth], as well as the specific atmosphere of the festival and the Upper Franconian landscape around Bayreuth, the splendor of the performances, with their set designs by Emil Praetorius, the pageantry that he interpreted as being national. He loved the *Meistersinger*. … He found Wagner's works merely 'nice,' but he couldn't explain why or even discuss it."[15] Fritz and Berta Kiehn's love of music was as amateurish and bourgeois as that Heinrich Mann described in his novel *Der Untertan* (published in English as *The Patrioteer*). Mann wrote of operas where one "felt immediately at home. Shields and swords, much rattling tin, loyalty to the Emperor, much shouting and raised banners, and the German oak: one was tempted to play along."[16] Hermann Glaser asserted that in the Wagner performances in Bayreuth, "primitive emotions were concealed by a veneer: … nebulous groping for the 'sublime' appears as the search for the Holy Grail."[17]

On two occasions, Kiehn even managed to get a picture with Hitler. The photo taken at the Berlin car show in 1936 (fig. 18, in chap. 4) occupies a place of honor in the family album not far from the picture (fig. 12, in chap. 2) with Gregor Straßer, Kiehn's friend killed on Hitler's orders in 1934. Fig. 26 shows Kiehn encountering his idol on an unknown occasion.

Along with Kiehn's styling of himself as a "historical figure" on familiar terms with the world's greats, the dynastic dimensions of his thinking are another benchmark of his conception of the world. This character trait, typical of the owners of family businesses, was all the more pronounced because he still aspired to the bourgeoisie and was confronted with the successful example of the Hohner clan every single day. He began systematically to develop a family tradition, to commission genealogical research, proudly adopting a family crest in 1936. His hiring of his brothers — and later his sons-in-law — for management positions in the company, as well as the provisions he made for his in-laws in the Neipp family, were a natural part of his patriarchal leadership style. Kiehn differed little from the Hohners and other more established business owners on this particular

Fig. 26: Kiehn and Hitler. (Archiv der sozialen Demokratie der Friedrich-Ebert-Stiftung, Bonn, Erler Papers)

point: his reception of the "blood and soil" (*Blut und Boden*) mystique of Nazi ideology exaggerated this motivation to the point of a narcissistic self-love. The idea of passing on his "valuable" genetic material to the next generations, who would then complete his life's work, seems to have strongly shaped Kiehn's thinking.[18] But his desire to be the progenitor of a dynasty that would continue branching out was not to be fulfilled. Berta and Fritz Kiehn lost two children, each of them a few days after birth. Only Herbert and Gretl survived.

The primary purpose of Kiehn's private and official celebrations was to reinforce the townspeople's awareness of their proximity to the new rulers and safeguard his own position in the party. In the formative stage of the Third Reich, such events were characterized above all by the presence of prominent party functionaries and Gau dignitaries, as well as by their extravagance and coincidence with the official festival calendar of the regime. In 1933, Gretl's confirmation followed the Führer's birthday on 20 April, at which SA special commissioner Hermann Mattheiß and Kiehn spoke after a torchlight procession. One week later, Mattheiß was heading up another procession, for National Workers' Day. Hitler's speech at Tempelhof airfield was broadcast at the Gasthof Rose, the Neipp family inn. On 7 July, Murr paid an official visit to Trossingen, accompanied by Stuttgart economics minister Lehnich and SA special commissioner Mattheiß, during which the Reichsstatthalter was declared an honorary citizen and patron of a street. If prior to 1933 the Hohners had hosted the receptions for comparable occasions, these now took place at the Kiehns'. Hohner's role was limited to a brief tour through his factory and performances by two factory orchestras. On 9 August, when Lehnich visited in his capacity as economics minister, he was briefed by Kiehn, not Hohner, about the situation in the harmonica industry — a clear snub. In mid-October, three events coincided, namely, Kiehn's birthday, the annual meeting of the local NSDAP, and the Reich Craftsmen's Week. All of the factories in Trossingen took part in an impressive torchlight procession right before the NSDAP Gau inspector's eyes, with Efka at its head. Hohner AG, which had more than ten times the number of employees, found itself in fourth place in the parade order. Karlstraße was renamed Fritz-Kiehn-Straße in Kiehn's honor. The expense of such festivities drowned out Hohner's events of 1933. The one hundredth birthday of the company's founder was not celebrated at all, and Will Hohner's memorial service was done on a small scale.[19]

Behind the façade of the new "king of Trossingen," however, people began grumbling as early as 1933. As previously mentioned, Kiehn was forced to give up his post as an NSDAP local group leader (Ortsgruppenleiter) in early 1933 after his own local NSDAP branch had denounced him and the Committee for Investigation and Settlement (Uschla), an internal NSDAP tribunal, had commenced proceedings against him. Obviously, some National Socialists in Trossingen did not like Kiehn's political line and grandiose manner. A climate of personal animosities, envy, and business competition seems to have dominated the small town.

The annual cycle of seasonal Nazi festivities continued in Trossingen with undiminished intensity in 1934, but there was a drop-off in attendance by prominent politicians. Kiehn proved to be a master of raising Trossingen's symbolic value while presenting himself as a link between the new rulers and the denizens of the small town.

Kiehn also used the memory of the "Day of Potsdam." On 21 March 1933, Chancellor Hitler and President von Hindenburg, in a remarkable propaganda ploy, celebrated the alliance between Nazism and Prussian military and monarchical traditions by shaking hands in the Potsdam garrison church, where Prussian kings Friedrich Wilhelm I and Friedrich II were buried. The Day of Potsdam laid the groundwork for the Enabling Act of 1933, which gave the Nazis full legislative powers. One year after the Day of Potsdam, which Kiehn — in his own words — had been "privileged to witness in close proximity to the Führer," he used the beginning of the "labor battle of 1934" to recall the significance of the anniversary. When Hindenburg and Hitler shook hands, he said, the "era of disunity, of dishonor, of ... fawning submissiveness ... an era of groveling, but also of political profiteering, ended forevermore. ... We who know the Führer personally, we who stood up for him and ... his deeds, we knew what we were doing."[20]

A local mourning rally was held during Hindenburg's funeral in August of 1934. Once Ortsgruppenleiter Messner had spoken, there was a radio broadcast from Tannenberg, where Kiehn and the mayor represented Trossingen. It was rumored in town that Kiehn had frequent meetings with Hitler, and it was alleged that Kiehn had sent a check directly to the Führer after the Night of the

Long Knives — almost as atonement for his cooperation with Straßer — whereupon the Führer supposedly "pardoned" him. When Berta Kiehn marched at the head of a contingent of fifty Trossingen citizens in traditional dress for the Reich party convention, the local newspaper reported that she had been "received by our Führer in the hotel 'Deutscher Hof.'" In truth, Kiehn had no access to the dictator and could not even get him to read his letters. Consequently, he was unable to present Hitler with a certificate honoring him as a citizen of Trossingen on 20 April 1934. Instead, the town received a form letter requesting that the overburdened Führer be spared the trouble.[21]

To many Trossingen citizens, however, Kiehn seemed to be a close confidant of the new head of state. When the minister-president of Württemberg, Mergenthaler, came to visit on 27 May 1934, Kiehn closed the event with the request that Mergenthaler "notify the Führer that all of Trossingen, excepting a few know-it-alls, supports him." As early as spring 1933, Kiehn had celebrated Hitler in front of a Trossingen audience "as the liberator of the German people sent by God" and said that he would be "the guiding star for us Germans in the twentieth century for all that will come and go." At an assembly one year later, Kiehn directly addressed Hitler wholly in the style of a prayer: "My Führer! Our special trust in you goes without saying. We will follow you wherever your path leads us. ... We will always stand by you, and because we know that you will always lead our march, we all declare once again: You are our great Führer!"[22] At the harvest festival in 1934, Kiehn first invoked the success of the regime, the vanquishing of the fragmented "38 party state" by the "*Volksgemeinschaft*, the reconciliation of town and country, and the moral renewal." The Führer, Kiehn said, had "converted" the divided German people, who had become estranged from themselves, and made them back into "people of an earlier era ... of objectivity and character. ... But the mysticism of the Führer can only be measured by someone who has once been permitted to see the Führer." Everyone becomes "fulfilled by his presence. ... One ought not only say that it is a gift from God, nay, one must indeed say that the Lord has personally given us this man." In this way Kiehn stoked the pseudoreligious myth of the Führer and made it seem like Hitler stood above everything yet took an interest in the life of this small town. Such quasi-religious rhetoric became more and more important. The illusion of the Führer's omnipresence extended to the loudspeaker broadcasts of his speeches, which often immediately followed Kiehn's remarks. According to the local newspaper, "the nicest moment of the day" of the 1934 harvest festival occurred after the speeches by the important National Socialist local figures, when "the beloved voice of the Führer" rang out over the rooftops of the small town. Following Hitler's address, the celebration ended with "a throng of bared heads ... joining in singing the Horst Wessel song and the national anthem with grateful hearts."[23]

This magic spell bewitched many, but by no means all. Eyewitnesses have confirmed that the effect of Kiehn's appearances was large, but not uniform. One

Trossingen resident favorably disposed toward Kiehn praised his combination of charisma and "acting ability." If needed, he said, Kiehn could "cry on command." He "appealed to people" because he often managed to meet their expectations to a tee.[24] A more critical observer commented that Kiehn had been an "extremely clever, modern man" with charismatic traits whose theatrical abilities had to be recognized no matter the reservations one had about his character. He had a gift for orchestrating everything and leaving nothing to chance: "Anything he did was a show from A to Z." The speeches in front of the town hall, in particular, were consistently the sort of "spectacle" that otherwise was rare in town. Many townspeople were very impressed by this; others found it absolutely ridiculous.[25]

Minister-President Mergenthaler referred to the latter (those who found it ridiculous) when in 1934 he turned against the "whiners" and "know-it-alls" in Trossingen that the regime had had problems with throughout the Reich and who were the intended targets of one of Goebbels's centrally led campaigns. In both of the pseudoreferendums of 12 November 1933, the results in Trossingen fell significantly short of the Reich average, despite Kiehn's nomination as a Reichstag candidate and his personal dedication to campaigning for the regime. Fourteen percent of voters (563) had invalidated their ballots for the sham Reichstag elections. In the "people's survey" regarding Germany's withdrawal from the League of Nations, 7.7 percent of voters used this method to express their disagreement, and 5.6 percent voted no. As far as the NSDAP was concerned, these could not have been "true citizens of Trossingen." Although Kiehn impressed many at the local level, and the events put on by the new state initially offered a spectacular change to everyday small-town tristesse, Trossingen had little in common with the "stronghold of National Socialism" invoked by Kiehn. In order to prevent a repeat of his disgrace, especially after the Night of the Long Knives, Kiehn prepared for the referendum of 19 August 1934 with military precision. It was to decide on Hitler's usurping of the presidency of the Reich, but in fact it also sought to determine people's opinions of the SA purge. Despite the fact that most targets marked for removal were accessible on foot, the NSDAP organized a car service to pick up political "unreliables." Each car had an SS man as a "passenger" and was "richly decorated" with flowers and pictures of Hitler. Loudspeakers targeted specific houses until their occupants went out to vote. Even so, participation and approval ratings were slightly under the previous year's. A total of 509 Trossingen residents had voted no this time; 82 had invalidated their ballots. The rate of dissent had risen to 14.7 percent altogether, clearly surpassing the Württemberg average of 10.5 percent, but slightly under the Reich average of 15.7 percent. Three days later, in the ghostly atmosphere produced by hundreds of torches in front of the town hall, Kiehn harshly confronted the "egoists" who "in all their puny numbers" had considered it necessary to "hurl their no votes at the Führer." He had urgently needed a better result in order to make an impression on higher places. But the resistance from the Social Democrats, some old liberals, and the small Catholic milieu of the factory town had gone against him.[26]

What did all of this mean for the relationship between Kiehn and the Hohners, and how did the harmonica manufacturers came to terms with the political regime change? Ernst Hohner, whose loss of influence had also left him personally aggrieved, largely retreated from the public eye in 1933, although he likewise made it clear that he was not fundamentally opposed to the regime. At the end of the year, he praised the merits of "our great people's chancellor" for the first time. These declarations increased in volume in 1934. Before the national referendum of 19 August 1934, Hohner AG called upon its employees in a newspaper ad to carry out a "unified expression of [their] will." The company provided two of its vehicles to the NSDAP voter transport service (*Schlepperdienst*) free of charge.[27] While in public Hohner went from indignantly distancing himself from the regime to cautiously approaching and finally explicitly supporting it. Behind the scenes, however, things came to a showdown when the established mayor, Walter Bärlin, was transferred to Friedrichshafen in February. First Kiehn made himself and his brother-in-law, the Ortsgruppenleiter, into provisional administrators, even though an earlier council resolution had designated Hohner as second deputy. Kiehn then arranged to have the mayoral vacancy filled by a teacher who was loyal to him. But the Reichsstatthalter, the interior minister, the district administrator, and the Kreisleiter forced through a technocrat, the young "party comrade" Emil Kienzle. During the process of filling the vacancy, Hohner resigned from the town council "as a result of overwork and because of certain incidents." Kiehn then forced Hohner to disclose his reasons. Hohner insisted that his economic importance entitled him to political privileges: "I represent the largest commercial enterprise in Trossingen by far ... and therefore must refuse to be a second-class councilor."[28]

The headwind from Stuttgart taught Kiehn that snubbing Hohner in such a fashion had been a mistake. He let the harmonica manufacturer know that the whole issue had been due to an oversight: no one had been able to reach Hohner before arrangements were made. But Hohner dug in his heels and insisted on resigning his seat. The council refused to allow this, so Hohner's absence from all meetings was deemed "unexcused." Neither could Bärlin, Kienzle, or Kreisleiter Huber convince him to change his mind over the course of the year. They repeatedly confirmed to him in writing, to his satisfaction, that the largest employer "must" have a seat on the council, since this was the only way to "guarantee objective cooperation between the town and the company."[29] Hohner finally wrote to Kienzle on 23 April 1935 to offer his return "on two conditions." Not only did he want a formal apology, but it would also "be nice if a second representative of my firm ... were also to be appointed to the council." Both conditions were met in May. In June 1935, the Kreisleiter appointed Kiehn and Hohner as first and second deputy mayor, respectively.[30] Both posts had been introduced by the Nazi German Municipal Code. Even though the deputy mayors also belonged to the council (which had been demoted to a "consultative" body), they simultaneously constituted a new authority between the council and the mayor, who had been given near-dictatorial powers. The "deputy mayors" could stand in for the mayor and had to be heard on important issues. The Kreisleiter rationalized his choice on the grounds that Kiehn was the "political representative at the local level" and Hohner's company the most important taxpayer. Hohner's company "therefore has a right to be represented in municipal governance." This concluded the formative stage of National Socialism in Trossingen local politics.[31]

Even though Hohner had had to put up with a dramatic loss of power, he was able to keep from being cut out completely and to use the conflict over the new mayoralty to reclaim some of his territory. Considering the circumstances, being second deputy mayor was the most he could hope for: in this position, he could not be completely ignored. Nevertheless, the Third Reich visibly reduced the municipality's room for maneuver so that large companies became less influential in configuring local interests anyway.

Kiehn had come up against the limits of his political influence yet again in 1933 when he actively but ultimately fruitlessly worked to have the acting Tuttlingen district administrator, in office since 1926, replaced by one of his minions. At the same time, this process once again demonstrates machinations by Kiehn that not only became his personal trademark, but also the prevailing style of the entire Nazi regime. In May of that year, he was authorized by the Interior Ministry in his capacity as Kreisinspektor to meet with the ostensibly alcoholic district administrator and exercise his influence on him, so that — in Kiehn's words — he could "be moved to turn away from his depraved lifestyle." In June, Kiehn informed the ministry that he had not been able to meet with him, but that "SA and SS people" had seen the official "only a few days ago ... in a completely drunken condition." He also knew, he wrote, that the district administrator was "already talking about his retirement some time ago. ... I therefore request that [he] be retired immediately. What's more, as far as I know, the district administrator is ... well-to-do, such that he would be able to live very well and make room for a younger official with a sense of duty." Kiehn stepped in again in July and presented his chosen candidate. "But I most kindly and urgently request ... you not be bothered by [his] comparatively young age." Kiehn signed the letter as a member of the Reichstag and explained his intervention tersely: "You will understand ... that I am naturally very interested in the post being filled." After all, he had "extraordinarily much to manage with the Oberamt [his administrative unit]."[32] The Interior Ministry did not follow this line of argument, and — as remained its general approach in Württemberg — chose to go with a different, more professionally qualified candidate instead of with political careerists thrusting themselves forward.

As Kreisinspektor for the "restoration of the professional civil service," i.e., in charge of purging it, Kiehn was responsible for replacing politically undesirable or Jewish officials, as his rush to restaff the district administrator post shows. In this capacity, he placed great pressure on officeholders to save their posts by quickly joining the NSDAP. On 30 April 1933, for example, the Oberamt in Spaichingen summoned all of the municipal administrators, teachers, clergy, and civil servants to a meeting at which Kiehn instructed them in the "guidelines of the government." He had precise knowledge of public servants' attitudes, for example, seeing to it in May 1933 that the "present treasurer ... who is without a doubt a Marxist" be denied further employment.[33] In other cases, and particularly in Trossingen, he sometimes turned a blind eye, which gave him a reputation for being a "humane Nazi."

In his administrative district and beyond, Kiehn distinguished himself as an aggressive orator, yet one who had no topics of his own and was instead reeling off an agenda that came from the top: from *Volksgemeinschaft* to anti-Bolshevism, from the National Socialist "jobs miracle" to foreign policy revisionism, from the Hitler myth to anti-Semitism. Strikingly seldom did he air his opinions — as a businessman and economic functionary — about his very own field of work, economic policy. And when he did, he kept his comments exceptionally generic. Neither was he capable of putting his own particular accent on topics in this area. He cheered the demand-oriented employment policy of the regime and the departure of the "alien, Jewish-influenced, international red leaders." He called for an autarkic military economy and "the activation of our German trade balance," "the creation of more publicly funded state enterprises," and the complete subordination of the economy to the will of the Führer. Kiehn repeatedly seized on Hitler's empty economic platitude of "common interest before self-interest." If we can speak at all of an individual accent in his views on economic policy, it would be his warning against capitalists from the "system era," whom he counterposed against the National Socialist "model industrialist," a role that he supposedly embodied. "Nothing was more difficult than convincing the capitalist and liberalist-minded employer that a company has to serve the people and no one else. It was difficult to convince the employer that he is worth no more and no less ... than the least of his employees." This anecdotal entrepreneur "knew only his own 'I'; he no longer knew of the people ... of his workers; he did not understand their hardships and their concerns or did not want to. Contemptible gold had put the entrepreneur entirely under the spell of profit-seeking greed." "Flagrant materialism," Kiehn argued, had propped up the "November men"[34] and their "international system." "Today everything has taken a turn for the better, and everyone is making an effort ... even if it sometimes is difficult." He juxtaposed this guarded, almost disarming criticism of the economy in the Nazi state with significantly fiercer words for those members of the traditional elites who would try to challenge the position of "old fighters" such as himself: "The Third Reich was not built by intellectuals; these contemporaries did not come calling until after the seizure of power.

The Third Reich was not won through capital or materialism, but" through those "working classes that were always the pillars of the nation."[35]

The fact that Kiehn often sought to draw attention to himself in his remarks by going above and beyond the stipulated party line is impressively established in his speech about the forced sterilizations introduced by the regime, which were a prelude to "euthanizations" and the mass murder of the Jews. At the same time, it provides an example of how Nazism had its own particular dynamic wherein individuals tended to become more radical on their own. "Working toward the Führer" was Kiehn's motto too.[36] On the basis of the 1933 Law for the Prevention of Hereditarily Diseased Offspring, or sterilization law, some 360,000 people who had been defined as diseased, "antisocial," or "racially inferior" were sterilized against their will between 1933 and 1945. Kiehn, however, went so far as to support an implementation that surpassed the actual number of cases of forcible contraception and even the most radical plans of the regime. For example, at a district training conference in 1934 he already declared himself in favor of a "hereditary health policy" of gigantic proportions: "When we are perhaps no longer around … only then will the Führer be thanked for the great feat he has achieved with the sterilization law. … Fifty million useful people are worth more than sixty million when ten million of them must be dragged through life."[37]

But this ideological agitator who had a perfect command of the regime's phraseology and occasionally outdid it was but one side of the "king of Trossingen." The other, less aggressive Fritz Kiehn, who strove to come to terms with his enemies, was studiedly affable and possessed the common touch. His speech on 1 May 1934 began with extensive remarks about the "gardens and fields … in fresh green" and the "Hitler weather, shall we call it, created by our Lord especially for the German labor holiday." In his speeches, Trossingen usually became at least a symbol, and often even the hub of the new Germany. He conveyed pride in his adopted hometown and its accomplishments to his audience. He also invoked the "deterrent of the Swabian racial corpus" that Württemberg had used to defy economic crises and Marxism. Even when he spoke of the hated "system era," his words softened as soon as he approached the microcosm of his small town. "By and large," he said, most "local businessmen" had a "softer spot for their fellows" before 1933 than the entrepreneurs in large centers of industry did. Such a statement, made in the presence of Ernst Hohner and hundreds of Hohner employees, signaled that old paternalistic loyalties continued to endure, and that anyone — in Kiehn's view — could adjust to the Third Reich. On another occasion, he praised the ingenuity and appreciation for quality among Swabian workers and industrialists, mentioning the name of his local archrival in the same breath as those of the Württemberg industrial nobility, "Bosch, Daimler, Mauser, … Bleyle, and Voith."[38] Because the majority of the population distinctly identified with the instrument manufacturer, such paeans of praise garnered Kiehn more points in his local environment than exacerbating old conflicts.

In order to demonstrate his and the Führer's generosity, Kiehn took care of former SPD and KPD functionaries who had been delivered to the nearby Heuberg concentration camp, some of whom held him personally responsible for their detention,[39] even though all seven had returned to Trossingen by 1934. There was usually an inquiry sent to Kiehn before their release; later, he would monitor their compliance and their professional reintegration. As a result, even the former chair of the KPD was able to return to his position with the municipal administration in 1934. This way of dealing with "reformed" NSDAP adversaries gave Kiehn his reputation as a "humane Nazi" that has endured to this day. At the same time, however, it was typical of the regime's policy toward workers who were willing to conform, which aimed to integrate all "racial comrades."[40] A key motivation for this practice can be seen in the shoring up of local respect. If Kiehn had taken a hard line, it would have been construed as violating the precept of local solidarity, something taken very seriously in the small town. This is exactly the sort of accusation Kiehn did not want leveled against him, since he considered the local arena to be of central significance. "Kiehn was humane. All those arrested did come back," was how an apolitical worker summed it up.[41] Kiehn's monetary donations to practically all of the associations and institutions in the town also show how important local recognition was to him. He even helped the Catholic parish obtain a construction site for a new house of worship and promised them bells for the tower. Even if internal party criticism of Kiehn's behavior kept him from fulfilling this promise until after 1945, the parish repaid his goodwill by hanging large swastika banners from its church tower (fig. 27).[42]

Kiehn's actions within municipal politics, however, can also be characterized as openly taking advantage in a way that went far beyond the favors that local businessmen had previously exacted. This behavior stood in striking contrast to the glorious intentions Kiehn had declared in the town council in May 1933. On that occasion, he had begun by denouncing the "unsurpassable mismanagement" of democracy. The "party economy" was being replaced by the "national economy," he said: "We want foremost … a clean administration … we will not allow any cliqueish economy to take root."[43] The reality looked completely different and included an exchange of property between Kiehn and the town, which the council had repeatedly refused to allow prior to 1933. In 1935, the car enthusiast ordered a Mercedes for himself but decided before it had even been delivered that he no longer wanted it. As a result, he "made it possible" for the town to take over his contract. Repairing the streets that led to his house was a priority, since he "always received many visits from leading figures."[44] "Old fighters" received preference in hiring for municipal jobs. Instead of the job and wage cuts he had so vehemently demanded in 1933, he now campaigned for increased employment and higher pay scales for workers. The NSDAP also dipped into Trossingen's coffers with gusto and nailed down subsidies for uniforms and festivals, as well as contributions to travel and "campaign costs." The SA needed a

Fig. 27: Trossingen in a sea of swastikas. (Stadtarchiv Trossingen)

tool shed, and the Kreisleiter wanted RM 5,000 for new offices. Of course, such practices were common in many communities after 1933.[45]

The cronyism Kiehn established was unheard of in its scope, as the following examples demonstrate. "Councilor Kiehn requests that the master plasterer … be removed from consideration for municipal work contracts because he left the NSDAP in the so-called time of crisis." A carpenter who "frequently made no donations for winter relief" received a warning.[46] Before municipal job contracts were given out, the local NSDAP group would give the mayor a list with the names of local craftsmen followed by opinions that mixed political judgments with personal caprice: one tradesman had "seriously transgressed on 1 May and is one of the whiners." Another was "in the D.A.F. and N.S.V.," but "sometimes unbearable otherwise." The "malicious enemy of the third [sic] Reich" was critical of the "impeccable S.A. man." All in all, the new rulers regarded the craftsmen as troublesome: "[S]ometimes he acts as if he were the best National Socialist, holding his nose! ... You can offer him a 'Heil Hitler' a thousand times, then out comes a 'good day' or 'good night.'"[47] This system, one that many Trossingen residents characterized as a "good ol' boys' club," took on such vast dimensions that in 1935, National Socialist craftsmen expressly asked not to be given preference in the future because otherwise they would be "completely avoided [because of their status as party comrades] and incur great financial damage as a result."[48]

When Kiehn's local and personal interests contradicted basic Nazi ideological principles, the latter had to give way. This became apparent in his oft-criticized "lack of consistency on the Jewish question."[49] Of all people, Toni Hunger, Kiehn's long-standing employee who had risen to become Efka's authorized signatory, had a Jewish grandmother. She nevertheless boasted about her status as the first female National Socialist in Trossingen ("Member Number 2"). The NSDAP Gau court expelled her from the party in 1934 for infringement of Section 3 of the party bylaws; in other words, for her Jewish family connection. The "quarter Jewess" — as she was referred to in cynical Nazi jargon — had brought the proceedings on herself in 1933 when, with utter naïveté, she had protested to her idol Adolf Hitler and his half-sister, Angela Raubal, about Hunger's sister's dismissal from the civil service. The simple matter of having a Jewish grandmother who later converted should not be enough, she wrote, to burn a "mark of Cain" into the "forehead" of staunch National Socialists. The stigma of her Jewish descent, she believed, ought to have been erased by her inner convictions and personal sacrifices for the party. For Toni Hunger, "the race of National Socialism" was "a matter of the heart." Kiehn and others objected mightily to her expulsion from the party. Even Gauleiter Murr suggested "the mercy of the Führer" for "the soul of women's work in Trossingen." Both the League of German Girls (Bund Deutscher Mädel, or BdM) troop directed by Hunger and the Trossingen Nazi Women's League NSF threatened to collectively resign from the party. The Ortsgruppenleiter enumerated the rebuked Hunger's merits, beginning with a head wound she sustained at a brawl during a political meeting in the "time of struggle" and extending to her tireless typing work and the indefatigable procurement of new members. Others recalled how she "waited on" SA men with the "coffee or tea" after their night tours of duty. It is striking how staunch National Socialists struggled with the Nazi race concept and pointed out the psychological strain on their deserving party comrade. Bärlin, the former mayor, rendered the Nazi ideology of race absurd in maintaining that even if "Fräulein Hunger" was not a "full Aryan," he had never noticed anything "un-German or even Jewish in any of her behavior, actions and allowances, or character." This "truly German woman," he argued, had to be allowed to be "retained" unconditionally for the "movement." Last, Kiehn let the Kreisleiter know of the consequences her exclusion from the party would have for the Efka factory. It made her, Kiehn wrote, "basically unusable" in her post as authorized signatory. In any case, the hoped-for "merciful Aryan declaration from the Führer" was not forthcoming. In 1935, however, the protest letters moved Hitler to revise the Gau court verdict from 1934, and Hunger was allowed to remain a simple party member.[50]

Kiehn presented himself locally as a high-level Nazi functionary that people could speak with and who also would occasionally turn a blind eye, as long as he noticed at least a minimal readiness to assimilate. Many of his contemporaries that we interviewed agreed on this assessment. In fact, Kiehn protected Social Democrats and even Communists. There is a case of Kiehn protecting a left-wing Efka employee — who had come into the firm with the Aryanization of the Büttner company in Berlin — from attacks by a fanatical foreman. Even though the Efka staffer in question became a KPD candidate after 1945 and must have known what Kiehn had done to his former employer, he would not say a single word against him in the interview but rather praised his Trossingen boss's humane, caring attitude.[51] Berta Kiehn was also ceaselessly committed, and not just to the party. She seems to have helped many people through her husband's social position and his political contacts, whether by releasing them from work obligations, fending off the threat of reprisals, or engaging in pure charity, such as distributing food to the needy. Berta Kiehn offered such practical aid without consideration for the political or religious convictions of those receiving it. Former forced laborers also attested to the Kiehns treating them decently and feeding them.

But sufficient evidence exists that the couple could also play a different tune. In 1938, a worker set a fire that destroyed paper in the Efka factory worth RM 6,000. The local newspaper reported on the background to his act of revenge under the headline, "Dangerous Public Enemy [*Volksschädling*] in Court!" The perpetrator had previously already been forced to while away two days in jail at Kiehn's behest, "for churlish mischief." This time he was sentenced to two years' imprisonment.[52] In 1948, a Trossingen resident made serious accusations against Berta Kiehn, claiming that she had directly assisted the Gestapo, spied on her fellow citizens, and intimidated them with threats. She had also allegedly passed on the defeatist declarations of an acquaintance's daughter to the Gestapo, driving the desperate mother to take her own life.[53]

In addition to this occasional harshness, the Kiehn "royal family" relied time and again on providing evidence of their "generosity" and smoothing over repeated failings beyond the region through ostentatious posturing. For example, Kiehn regularly had the local newspaper refer to him as "President Fritz Kiehn M.d.R." In addition to his SS uniform, from 1935 to 1937 Kiehn also sometimes wore the uniform of a Gauamtsleiter, a privilege Gauleiter Murr granted him by virtue of his position as deputy Gau economic adviser.[54] He also purchased various luxury sedans. These always had a pennant over the passenger-side wheel well, usually bearing the symbol of the SS but occasionally the hunting association's logo as well. Drivers from his firm in SS uniform would act as his

Fig. 28: Kiehn's Mercedes, with SS pennant. (Stadtarchiv Trossingen)

chauffeurs as though he were a prominent member of the regime. This conveyed the impression that Kiehn was always engaged in official business. One of the three two-seater Mercedes convertibles he bought in 1936, with its special black-and-ivory paintwork, was chosen by a Trossingen resident as the background for a private photograph (fig. 28).

Kiehn's love of sports cars was also reflected in his friendship with Bernd Rosemeyer, a racecar driver famous during the Third Reich. After Rosemeyer died in an accident in 1938 while trying to break the speed record of 272 miles per hour, the Kiehn family maintained close contact with his widow, Elly Beinhorn, a legendary aviator. Beinhorn even moved to Trossingen in 1943 to escape the bombs and was Gretl Kiehn's maid of honor in 1949, when she remarried.

As district commissioner of the NSF, Berta Kiehn counted herself among the "Führer's decision makers." Distinguished, like her husband, by her tendency to overestimate herself, she put out a call "to German women!" to vote in the sham referendum of 1936, even though her party positions were limited to the local sphere. She turned her afternoon coffee with "Frau Walter Funk" into the object of a press release that presented Kiehn's pipe dreams as reality: "This visit is renewed proof for us that the actions … of our party comrade Kiehn in the developmental work of the Führer are meeting with the greatest … approval in even the highest circles of government."[55]

Her dealings with the heads of the Nazi regime also had an awkwardness that was similar to her husband's attempts to get close to them. In October 1935, she approached Frick directly, allegedly without her husband's knowledge, about Kiehn's upcoming fiftieth birthday. She first reminded the Reich interior minister of an earlier stay in Trossingen. She then "devotedly" confessed:

> I know that no greater good fortune could befall my husband ... on his birthday than to receive congratulations from his Führer — whatever the form! My most fervent request and question to you, honored Herr Interior Minister, is now (please take this as it is meant, coming from me openly and honestly as a woman and old fighter) would it be at all possible for you to mention my train of thought to our Führer? ... You know my husband, and you certainly also know how he has promoted the cause of our Führer with life and limb, with goods and blood, and campaigns anew everyday. I have chosen to come to you because my husband prizes you so dearly and is so enthralled by your actions.

Frick, who evidently was anything but pleased, acquitted himself of the irksome task with a one-line telegram he dispatched himself to the "old nat. soc. pioneer."[56]

The town made Kiehn an honorary citizen for his fiftieth birthday. Mayor Emil Kienzle had to dispel the district leader's misgivings beforehand. The certificate extolled Kiehn as a "tireless fighter for Adolf Hitler ... who has successfully contributed to the shape of the Third Reich ... leader of the southern German economy ... [and] a hometown patron prepared to make sacrifices." At least in Trossingen, Kiehn now ranked alongside Hindenburg, Hitler, and Murr. The encomiums filled three full pages of the newspaper. In a melodramatic gesture, Kiehn thanked "Providence" and "the Almighty" for "steering his path ... to Trossingen" and, following a Hohner tradition, gave gifts to the town, though significantly fewer than those from the harmonica manufacturers.[57]

Efka celebrated its "twenty-fifth anniversary" in 1937, even though Kiehn had only started doing business under this name in 1920, which was also when production began. Kiehn had merely acquired the paper goods store in 1912. Even though many townspeople still remembered his modest local beginnings, "company director Präsident Fritz Kiehn, M.d.R." now claimed to have founded his "own business" in 1912, "after many years working as a salesman in management positions at home and abroad."[58] He commissioned a company coat of arms (fig. 29) for the anniversary that could not have turned out any more overblown: the Reich eagle sat enthroned on a number twenty-five that was encircled with a laurel wreath. "Efka" was spelled out over the state symbol. Below the coat of arms was a battle cry that put the National Socialist entrepreneurial spirit he propagated front and center.

The motto for the two-day celebration was, "With God for Führer and *Volk*." Throughout the town, "hundreds of lit swastika banners" proclaimed to "even the simplest racial comrades that a celebration was happening here that went far beyond the scope of an ordinary company party." The town considered it an "internal need" to pay for the rental of the banners and the manufacturing of the

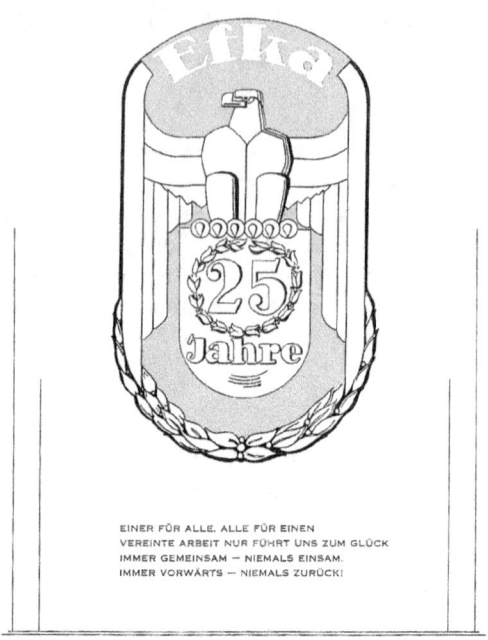

Fig. 29: Invitation to Efka factory anniversary, bearing the new company coat of arms, 1937. (Stadtarchiv Trossingen)

flagpoles (fig. 27). The 270 Trossingen workers and 80 sales representatives of the Efka company took part in the ceremony, along with a few honored guests who had no importance outside the region. They had chosen the slogan, "Our honor means loyalty," transferring the SS motto to the company in slightly modified form. In his official speech, the speaker for the sales representatives emphasized his wish that "more such company directors may yet be won for our Führer." The "social evening" had the typical elements of a National Socialist celebration, including a "commemoration of the dead." A one-pot stew — the "sacrificial meal" of the Third Reich that was to demonstrate the *Volksgemeinschaft*, in which everyone shared the same modest food — was served and convictions demonstrated.[59] The "factory band" played numbers from the national songbook. The "factory throng, in their dapper uniforms" put on a play, "Your Nation [*Volk*] Is Everything." Toni Hunger delighted the "followers" with not only a congratulatory speech but performances of various songs as well, including "Ueber die Heide geht mein Gedenken," with lyrics by the Nazi's favorite poet, Hermann Löns, whom Kiehn revered. Kreisleiter Huber recalled Kiehn's "thorn-filled path" and the "heart's blood" he had spilled for the NSDAP. He called him one of "the very few industrial leaders who [had] already found the path to the Führer during the time of struggle." As a surprise, the first "Efka factory film" premiered, depicting "pictures from [Kiehn's] silver anniversary," the staff outing, and the company's most recent midsummer festival. "The social evening concluded with a dance."[60]

One year after his company's "twenty-fifth anniversary," Kiehn instituted a new holiday tradition that combined his cumulative insecurity about status with the hubris that resulted from it. One could also say that it reproduced the Nazi regime's megalomania in miniature. The local newspaper described it in momentous terms in July 1938: "It corresponds ... to a natural obligation ... to thank and acknowledge on such occasions the men who have rendered invaluable and unforgettable service to the rebuilding of our Reich. Among these men is our own party comrade President Fritz Kiehn, revered in the widest circles of our people. ... It was 16 July 1908 when Herr Fritz Kiehn first set foot on Trossingen soil." The description of Kiehn took on hagiographic tones: he was purported to have come from an "old military family" and described himself as a "royal" merchant. Again he showed off his now-proverbial "human kindness and generosity" and donated RM 20,000 to the town. A large photo of Kiehn in his SS uniform ran alongside the text. No longer was the path to Trossingen a decision made by a traveling salesman seeking work, but an indication from God and "Providence." Kiehn's methods and rhetoric increasingly approximated those of Hitler and Goebbels. Both were fond of invoking the higher powers of destiny and engaging in systematic self-mythologizing and self-sacralization.[61]

In December 1938, Kiehn dedicated the "town's new landmark," his firm's new building (fig. 30). "The most modern and most beautiful, lightest and airiest factory building is finished. ... When dusk falls, a great illuminated tree shines in the factory courtyard, and on the tower high above, the 'Efka' factory name and a tremendous swastika are lit up: two symbols that in this firm have combined into one unique and inseparable concept." The celebration hosted in 1938 was not least intended to enhance the public image of the model Nazi industrialist. Kiehn had been accepted onto Himmler's personal staff that summer and hence had invited his "SS comrades ... from the Reich leadership," including SS senior leader Walter Stein and SS senior group leader Kurt Daluege, to attend. In view of these guests, Kiehn worked even harder than usual, and he announced that "based on the National Socialist principle whereby the purpose of work is for the common good," he would be increasing his voluntary contributions to employee benefits. The measure was primarily a response to the rising labor shortages, of course, taken as it was in the year that the Siegfried Line was constructed. Kiehn reveled in nostalgia, recalling the era before 1933 when "all of his followers [*Gefolgschaft*] made themselves available to the Führer in the battle against the [Weimar] system," and had gone with him "from brawl to brawl ... laughed at, hated, persecuted, ostracized, and boycotted." Today, said Kiehn, Efka was not just "the most modern cigarette paper factory in the world," with its "abundant light, air, and sun," but, more importantly, his *Arbeiter der Stirn und Faust* (blue- and white-collar workers) would "no longer be defrauded of their wages

Fig. 30: **Efka factory with political propaganda.** (Martin Häffner et al. *Trossingen. Vom Alemannendorf zur Musikstadt.* Trossingen, 1997)

by Jews." This was an allusion to the "dejudaization of the German economy," which had reached its final stages a few weeks before with the Night of Broken Glass, on 9 November, and which Kiehn expertly exploited. The Kristallnacht had not extended to Trossingen, since by 1938 there were no more Jews living in the small town. To conclude, Kiehn thanked "our Führer and Providence" for making 1938 "a shining year in every sense of the term." The informal part of the evening followed, with Kiehn, the official district huntsman, presenting home movies of a deer-stalking expedition or of his grandson, born in 1937, "little Herbertle," taking his first steps.[62]

Efka was its own sort of "model Nazi plant," even though the DAF never awarded it this honorary title. For a relatively small company with two hundred to four hundred workers, employee benefits were considerable. Kiehn invoked them at every opportunity as proof of the fulfillment of the National Socialist ideal. He had to offer something special for pragmatic reasons too, however, since Efka was competing with Hohner in a tight local labor market. Like many other company owners, he tried to generate perks by providing social benefits to workers, since direct wage raises were prohibited and labor shortages were everywhere. His employees received an additional 5 percent of their already relatively high normal salaries paid directly into their savings accounts. Factory employees were allowed to spend two weeks' paid vacation per year at a vacation home on

Lake Constance that had already been dedicated in 1935 with great pomp in the presence of Murr and Wilhelm Dreher. The company took care of all expenses. Efka staff received RM 50 extra for weddings, births, and "calamities." On top of this they received subscriptions, paid for by Kiehn, to the DAF/SS magazines *Arbeitertum* and *Schwarzes Korps,* as well as reduced-price tickets for events put on by the Nazi cultural association and regular "social evenings." The factory library boasted two thousand titles. In 1937, every Efka employee received a copy of *Mein Kampf* for Hitler's birthday. Other years, they were given Nazi propaganda texts with Kiehn's picture pasted on them. "Letters to honored staff members, with noteworthy sums of money" were distributed on company anniversaries.[63] Kiehn ended company roll calls with the "Dutch Prayer," in direct allusion to Reich party conferences. "Social evenings," with out-of-town functionaries in attendance at Kiehn's invitation, followed at the Gasthof Rose inn auditorium. Meetings of the company's council of trust, something that many other firms regarded as an unpleasant obligation, were written up in the local press.[64]

At Christmas time, the "Efka family" celebrated a "social evening" true to Kiehn's motto: "Shared work in the factory and shared joyous celebration cement an inseparable heart." Kiehn would hand out "those popular letters" with money inside, the amount of which was graded according to workers' length of employment, marital status, and number of children. Small presents were also given to the "children of the factory community," in the presence of "President Kiehn and his wife … it may have been the eighty children whose voices loudly affirmed to the Solstice Man [a Nazi modification of the German Christmas tradition] that they had been good. … Herr Kiehn gave a speech to the children present and their mothers, describing the meaning of Christmas in our time … at the end, the children were treated to a screening of two of their very favorite films." Next, "the entire staff," together with the "company director's family" and "party guests," were invited to an evening meal at the "Rose [inn]." The usual praise and propaganda speeches, performances by the factory band and women's choir, presentation of hunting films, and reports from the factory crowd about "badge sales" and "one-pot Sunday" filled out the evening, which closed with everyone singing together.[65] The appearance of the "Solstice Man," an ideologically correct substitution for Father Christmas, seems to have been a bizarre exception at the company Christmas party, which was traditional in all other ways. Without a doubt, however, Kiehn continued trying to "brownwash" the paternalism of his midsized business and smuggle the principles of National Socialist celebrations into the company. For example, there are reports of company festivals to celebrate the summer solstice being made into a new tradition.[66]

All things considered, the Efka factories were unusually strongly Nazified in comparison to other companies of similar size. Ernst Hohner had taken part in almost all of the larger Efka celebrations since 1935. In the meantime, he had given up on displaying any reluctance toward the regime, at least in public. At times he developed a considerable mixture of routine and confidence when dealing with Kiehn. His speech lauding Kiehn at Kiehn's fiftieth birthday did not lack for irony: calling out to the Westphalian in front of the assembled guests, Hohner declared, "We've known you a long time. We know that you, as a true citizen of Trossingen, are deeply rooted in it, with hearth and home." It was especially "reassuring to us," he said, to know that the "leadership of the southern German economy" was in such responsible hands. Increasingly, Hohner no longer expressed his competition with Kiehn by exhibiting a polite distance, instead presenting evidence of political equality and symbolically reestablishing his firm's dominance through events whose splendor surpassed that of the Efka factory festivals. At any rate, Hohner was capable of assembling a much larger crowd of people from his staff and immersing his company in a considerably larger sea of swastika banners. Their donations to the city and various associations also reflected their sheer competitiveness, though Hohner easily won in this field thanks to his wealth.[67]

Whereas most Hohner family members kept their distance from National Socialism both internally and largely externally, Ernst Hohner was tactically motivated to adopt a demonstrative orientation toward the regime. External pressure and self-protection, social responsibility and profit interests, partial approval and deception, the concentration on his business as his sole concern, and psychological distance combined in him to create a peculiar alliance typical of many businessmen in the Nazi regime. As the leading figure on the board of directors, Hohner was in the spotlight, representing his company and family. Like all Trossingen notables, Ernst Hohner had been encouraged by Kiehn to join the NSDAP, in 1933 at the latest. But despite his readiness, he was not accepted into the party until 1937, when a general block that had been imposed on memberships was lifted. From the outside, his willingness to engage with the regime appeared limitless, yet he was primarily driven by his desire to protect his firm and his family. After all, he and his family were living practically under the nose of the most prominent Nazi economic functionary in Württemberg, a man they believed capable of anything. Personal resentments on both sides made the situation even more explosive. The NSDAP had absolutely no qualms about dealing with businessmen they deemed disagreeable. Reprisals ranged from smear campaigns to nighttime demonstrations in front of private homes, from operational restrictions on companies to outright closures.[68]

Considering what had happened to the Magirus company, Hohner's concern was not unfounded by any means. Indeed, Kiehn sought to acquire Hohner stock and muscle his way onto its supervisory board. Success eluded him, however, because the family owned over 90 percent of the shares or had mortgaged them in Switzerland. Threatening scenarios of a lesser order than a hostile takeover, however, were also possible, such as having a trustee take control or imposing limits on production. Hohner was also guided by marketing considerations. The closing and/or drastic reduction of important export markets forced Hohner to shift sales to the ideologically fraught German musical instrument market. Yet harmonica playing had already been decried as "un-German," resulting in repeated demands that it be restricted; certain cultural policy makers even called for the Hohner company to be closed. The executive board therefore wished to prevent any and all political conflict. It must be said, however, that Kiehn never tried to play the cultural ideology card: that kind of frontal attack on the largest employer in the region would probably have done great damage to him personally.[69] Despite the great pressure to conform to the regime that Kiehn, in particular, generated in Trossingen, there were tight limits on the extent to which the townspeople could be mobilized. Kiehn's wishful dream of a Nazi stronghold was not to be realized. In 1934, the local Nazi group had no more than 240 members. As we have already seen, the number of dissidents in the first referendum, when elections were not yet systematically fraudulent, was almost twice as high as the local party membership. Few dared to engage in more dangerous expressions of disapproval, such as chopping down a Hitler oak in the night or setting fires in the Efka factory. The wide majority of Trossingen residents fell somewhere between the small groups of active party members on one side and the resolute opponents of the regime on the other. Their conduct swung between the poles of partial approval and half-hearted conformity, internal indifference and structural resistance. Excepting the small local newspapers, the National Socialist press was hardly read in Trossingen, and negligent flag flying on houses regularly occasioned criticism. The local clubs also reflected the town's lackluster support for the regime in their superficial adaptation. As the town administration reported to the Political Police: "Upon closer inspection, [local clubs] had not grasped by a long shot ... what was really going on." It was "not enough ... for a club director ... to give a lively speech at the beginning of the event and then roll out a program that has no relationship ... to the ... speech."[70]

The limits of Nazification were apparent not only in light of the surfeit of ubiquitous propaganda and holidays by decree;[71] the Pietistic milieu proved to be difficult territory for the NSDAP as well, although many practicing Christians had outwardly conformed. As soon as National Socialism tried to penetrate the interior life of the church, it ran up against a massive line of defense. For example, for a long time no one was disturbed by the fact that both National Socialist publications and the church's Sunday newsletter were distributed by the same deliveryman. When the NSDAP made him choose one or the other, however, he decided in favor of the Sunday newsletter.[72] Kiehn, who was fond of invoking the "Lord" in his propaganda speeches, had similarly disagreeable experiences with the Pietistic resistance when he resigned from the church in 1937 and called on Trossingen residents to follow his example. The response was shatteringly small: just twenty-two townspeople, including the Kiehn family, left the Protestant Church in 1937.[73]

The unsuccessful movement for en masse resignations from the church marks a first turning point in Kiehn's local standing. To many townspeople, he had now exceeded the limit of what he could reasonably expect from them and put himself squarely outside the town's long-established sociocultural milieu. There were tensions within the Kiehn family as well. Whereas the Kiehns had celebrated their daughter's confirmation in a semipublic way, with prominent Nazi dignitaries, in later years Kiehn refused to take part in religiously oriented family celebrations. He now considered it incompatible with his position as a "senior SS leader" to encounter pastors on such occasions. This break with old traditions bewildered the Neipp side of the family, such that Kiehn felt obliged to explain his absence through multipage letters.[74]

The juxtaposition of external conformity and internal distancing was a thorn in the side of the NSDAP. In his Christmas speech of 1937, Kiehn lashed out at "the ingratitude of so many racial comrades ... their carping and predilection for criticism." The initial enthusiasm over the new national holidays soon turned to weariness. Voluntary events like the Kraft durch Freude (Strength through Joy, or KdF) theater evening were "usually a fiasco" in relation to the number of visitors they drew and their cost. However, this local reluctance only marginally disturbed the functioning of the regime. A report from 1938 noted that the isolated town led an "independent sort of existence" and had "come to National Socialism only with difficulty." "Otherwise the population is very good to work with."[75]

Kiehn documented his rise in the 1930s through the education of his children and the expansion of his property. He and his wife made sure their son and heir Herbert, born in 1933, had significantly better schooling than they themselves had. After attending boarding school at Schloss Ettersburg in Weimar and upper secondary school (*Oberrealschule*) in Würzburg, Herbert Kiehn studied economics in Cologne and Munich. To smooth his path to higher society, Herbert was expected to marry into an established industrialist family if at all possible. Berta had made the necessary preparations — invitations to appropriate candidates and their parents, for example — but these did not have the desired effect. In fact, Herbert had already fallen in love while he was at school, with the daughter of one of his teachers in Würzburg. This match, less than ideal to his parents, survived their fierce opposition and even a one-year communication ban.

The grounds around Kiehn's villa were rounded off with the purchase of additional adjacent properties, and the house was renovated from the ground up in 1934. By 1939, the total area of the property in Deibhalde had grown to over one million square feet. Once the grounds were fenced in, Kiehn felt he had fulfilled a longtime dream. Added to this were three artificial ponds. The family now lived in a self-contained parkland; in their own words, they could call "the largest contiguous piece of private property in the Trossingen district" their own. The national construction ban imposed in 1938 because of the building of the Siegfried Line along the French border did not deter Kiehn from constructing an annex that added a large terrace to the first floor.[76] Visitors would encounter Kiehn's passion for hunting at every turn, closely linked as it was to his social ambitions. Hunting trophies took up a large part of the property's interior decoration. Countless antlers and taxidermied animals directly referred to the class-appropriate hobby of the "leader of the Württemberg economy," who had received the title of Württemberg's official hunting commissioner.

Kiehn's only son, Herbert, died in a car accident in 1936. His stricken father had a stone columbarium constructed for his mortal remains. On the one hand, the site was an expression of profound grief: Kiehn had lost his beloved son and his only male heir. Then again, the architecture of the columbarium and mourning rituals once again reflected Kiehn's mixing of social ambitions and the political/ideological and private/familial spheres.[77] After young Herbert's demise, the local newspaper stylized him as one of "the pioneers of National Socialism. ... Even in his tender boyhood years, he intuited the greatness of our worldview and comprehended it, for at fourteen years of age he had already become an active member of the HJ [Hitler Youth]." This would have been in 1927 — three years before his parents joined the party.[78] SS senior leader Walter Stein, a family friend, wrote an appreciation in the SS weekly *Das Schwarze Korps* of "SS Oberscharführer [technical sergeant] Herbert Kiehn ... one of our oldest and most loyal SS comrades."[79]

The structural design of the columbarium, which Kiehn had built on the spacious grounds of Deibhalde, not far from an ornamental pond, alludes to received set pieces from upper-class sepulchral culture, SS mysticism, and Nazi veneration of the dead. A rounded swastika was affixed to to the apex of the vaulted ceiling beams. The urn was set into a niche in the wall. In the middle of the hall was a pedestal on which a bronze sword had been mounted, along with an adage taken from a Wagner libretto: "live joyously in light / die fiercely heroically / laughing love / shining death." Kiehn had consulted knowledgeable SS comrades on the architectural details. Only the fundamental decision to memorialize his son in an explicitly Nazi manner was his own idea. The funeral service was limited to the family, however, and was not a public or party affair. This let them maintain a vestige of middle-class intimacy, just as they had done with their silver wedding anniversary.

Kiehn did not associate with SS mysticism circles, nor did he read the corresponding literature. His grandson described his attitude as follows:

> Fritz Kiehn "took part" ... in numerous rituals. ... *Pathos* was always involved, to a greater or lesser degree, never irony, self-mockery or jokes. ... Fritz Kiehn had a strong symbolic bent. But there was one thing he was not: mythological. ... What's more, he had far too much Prussian stiffness instilled in him from very early on ... the honorary dagger was of foremost importance to him in the SS; if Quedlinburg and other phenomena interested him at all, it was in accordance with his "duty." ... He was no SS mysticist. He was a realist, albeit not always a successful one. But in his opinion,

the SS was — if not *the* elite, then above all a *future* elite, and I think that it must have seemed very, very advantageous to him to belong to it.⁸⁰

The strategic thinking Kiehn demonstrated in this, along with his enthusiasm for pathos and rituals of any kind, may explain why he took up cultish forms of SS expression to a certain degree. The distinctions he was awarded, such as the Yule lantern and his appointment as "SS honor chevron carrier," an honor bestowed on "old fighters," filled him with great pride. But it was unmistakable that he primarily utilized SS mysticism for functional purposes. For strategic reasons, simply anything the SS did was of interest. SS symbolism especially fascinated Kiehn since it brought him power and prestige. Impatient to receive the SS honorary dagger, he relentlessly badgered the Reichsführer-SS. He was able to show off this status symbol beginning in 1939: fig. 16 (chap. 3) shows him with the coveted power accessory.

When it comes to SS mysticism, it almost seems as if Kiehn merely tried out individual set pieces only to abandon them again. They may have remained foreign to him, and certainly were alien to his Trossingen surroundings, including his own family. Fritz Kiehn had indeed harked back to Old German Yuletide customs once already at Christmastime, and had arranged for the "Solstice Man" to make an appearance instead of the traditional German Father Christmas. But these rather cautious attempts to de-Christianize the rituals of Christmas never dominated. These elements played a demonstratively large role at company parties in 1937 — probably in close connection with the church resignation movement initiated that year — one not matched in either earlier or later years.

In private, the Kiehns differed from hardened SS families;[81] unperturbed by SS mythology and holiday customs, they held fast to civic family traditions shaped by German inwardness. Herbert E. Kiehn recalled that the Yule lantern played no role, whereas the Christmas tree had a large one, displaying "every kind of traditional Christmas tree decoration, including many tinsel angels." The reading of the story of Christmas did not happen for ideological reasons; carols were not sung out of consideration for the family's lack of musical gifts. The family Christmas rituals also had patriarchal, authoritarian features: "Decorating the Christmas tree ... took almost a day and was personally supervised by my grandfather. ... He would sit in an armchair, with family and staff taking care of the work according to my grandfather's overbearingly precise instructions."[82]

Herbert's death in 1936 destabilized the patriarchal organization of the family. As they mourned the loss of their beloved son, they knew that Kiehn now lacked a direct heir to succeed him. Who would carry on his life's work, which was decidedly geared toward his own family? How would he pass on the managerial functions that were such a central part of his identity as paterfamilias? These questions would haunt Fritz Kiehn for the rest of his life. He never did find what he considered a satisfying answer; instead, he became a repeated victim of his own naïve gullibility, which various sons-in-law knew how to exploit. His son's death broke off a cornerstone of the life he had designed for himself, a loss that he never completely recovered from.

To the family's great joy, however, it turned out that the male line would not die out after all: Herbert's fiancée gave birth to his son in 1937. The proud grandfather immediately obtained special authorization for the mother to be referred to as "Mrs." and be allowed to use Kiehn as her married name. The love child was given not only his father's first name, but also his last. His mother enjoyed Fritz Kiehn's generous support from then on. Until 1941, when the mother remarried, she and her son, Herbert E. Kiehn, lived in Deibhalde or in Nußdorf on Lake Constance. Even afterward, Kiehn gave them use of a high-class home in Stuttgart that he had previously maintained as his residence when he was president of the Economic Chamber. Like his father, Herbert received an excellent education that took him to the exclusive Salem boarding school in 1947. In 1952, Kiehn's grandchild officially became his son when Kiehn adopted him.

The Kiehns' daughter became the focus of their family life in the late 1930s. Known as Gretl, Margarete had been born in 1918. According to her father's resume, she joined the BdM "at age fourteen" and after completing secondary school studied sculpture at the wood-carving school in Oberammergau and with a Munich sculptor.[83] Kiehn gave her a Mercedes convertible for her eighteenth birthday. In 1937, she went to England for six months for language studies. In this too the family's conscious imitation of the upper-middle class education model is unmistakable. Like a "higher-born" daughter, Gretl was expected to have an education in aesthetics and languages to prepare her for her role as the perfect mate for a male successor who would head the company and had yet to be found. At her husband's side (but without direct access to his world of work), she would fulfill her duties of competent and decorative representation.

Submission to "duty," whatever that may have meant in concrete terms, was the top educational priority in the Kiehn household. As late as 1960, Kiehn announced in a Festschrift that the "principles by which children … should be brought up" were to "be strong and bravely carry out [their] duty."[84]

Fritz and Gretl Kiehn enjoyed an especially strong bond; father and daughter adored each other. Since the age of sixteen, Gretl had shared her father's passion for hunting and often accompanied him on excursions to hunting grounds or on trips. It is likely that she aligned herself with her father's political views more out of filial love than real conviction. Her father became even more fond of her after her brother's death, since Gretl was now his only direct physical descendant. From then on, she was not to expose herself to any avoidable risks and was no longer allowed to fly on an airplane, for example. She worked as an intern at the Efka factory to gain insight into the firm and to be at least roughly equipped should there be a succession crisis.

Kiehn continued to lose backing from the Gauleitung and even within the SS, and after the war began, this had an effect within Trossingen as well. Starting with the defeat at Stalingrad, if not before, the general loss of confidence in the regime also accelerated Kiehn's declining status at the local level. While the churches in Trossingen started filling up again in 1943, Berta and Fritz Kiehn increasingly lost prestige, especially since Fritz's work in Schweinfurt kept him away from the town more and more. In 1944, it appears that Berta Kiehn lost her post as head of the district NSF on orders from the Gauleitung.[85] As a result, the locals increasingly felt that the Kiehns no longer had time on their side. The Hohner family returned to the fore within the town, not least because of their impressive support of residents and their families. The sheer size and financial might of the company proved to be an unbeatable advantage. What's more, Hohner had succeeded in taking over public responsibilities in the area of food rationing.[86]

By the same token, the town assisted the Hohner company in its efforts in 1943 to construct a music academy in Trossingen for strategic marketing reasons, in the middle of "total war." Kiehn, putting on airs again and referencing his connections to the country's powers that be, claimed that a state construction subsidy Hohner had applied for directly contravened "an order from the Führer." The project was accomplished even without this money, however, under a dubious interpretation of the law that defined the town as the sponsor and Hohner as the actual operator of the institution.[87]

But Efka had priority when it came to the allocation of foreign workers, probably because of Kiehn's connections to Speer's ministry. In 1945, the factory received 113 workers, the largest contingent in Trossingen relative to its size. Hohner had likewise begun producing armaments, and by the end of the war employed eighty-three foreign civilian workers, along with seventy-two French and twenty-one Russian prisoners of war. Both companies treated these workers apparently tolerably. In 1945, foreign workers rallied to the aid of company leaders and defended them against the invading Allied troops.[88]

In the town council, Kiehn also took a less prominent role during wartime, seldom speaking up. There were no longer any reasons for grandiose celebrations. Kiehn's obsession with prestige flared up only occasionally, and he would satisfy his desire by stylizing even the most trivial local happenings into national concerns. For example, he once campaigned for a side street to be repaired by invoking the tight rubber supply in the Reich. A smoother surface, he argued, would reduce the wear on Trossingen bicycle tires, benefiting the German war economy. In November 1942, under the headline "Great Hunting Success," the local newspaper reported: "Now that we are at war … the art of hunting has been completely committed to the war economy. Good fur today … is being put entirely at the disposal of the German army. … In this sense, every hunter taking part in the great hunts last Saturday and Sunday on the grounds of President Fritz Kiehn was performing a service for our army."[89]

But Kiehn could no longer halt the erosion of his local position that had begun with his exit from the Württemberg political stage. The town's more established locals now had time on their side. The Hohners' commitment to the *Volksgemeinschaft* enabled them to symbolically possess part of the public space once again and rename a street, despite all regulations to the contrary. The newly lengthened Hohner Street now stretched from the entrance of the town to the factory and was longer than both Fritz Kiehn Street and Adolf Hitler Street.[90] The throne of the new "king of Trossingen" was wobbling, even as Kiehn continued to reaffirm his reputation as a "humane Nazi" in the local context. When anti-Fascists in Trossingen and across the country were taken into custody after the assassination attempt on Hitler of 20 July 1944, Kiehn did not hesitate to assert his influence in their favor. Those detained included Social Democrat Hans Neipp, who was not a close relative of Kiehn's in-laws and would later become the first postwar mayor of Trossingen. After his son went to Kiehn seeking help, Neipp was freed within twenty-four hours, along with several other Trossingen citizens. Other party functionaries would also attribute this to their own moderating influence later on, of course.[91] But it was undoubtedly Kiehn who freed a Deisslingen couple from the clutches of the Gestapo; they had harbored a French Air Force officer who had parachuted out of his crashing aircraft.[92]

There were renewed controversies in the local NSDAP group during 1944 and 1945 that once again shed light on the characteristic internal condition of the regime. The conflict ignited around what had become a matter of life and death for some Trossingen residents: which of them, in view of the ever more hopeless war situation, would be sent out of town to serve in the war effort or even fight in the army. Each person was most concerned with saving their own skin and preventing their own labor force or other protégés from being drafted or redeployed to work elsewhere. In this context, Kiehn's brother-in-law, Christian Messner, the acting mayor, got into an argument with the Tuttlingen district party office over whether the director of the Trossingen electricity company and local railway should be drafted. By then Gottlieb Huber was no longer in charge, but rather district leader Immanuel Baptist, who distinguished himself by his especially radical nature in the last days of the regime.[93] Messner had fallen out with Wilhelm Schlüter, who as the director of the District Office for Technology was part of the district leadership, because the latter had supposedly called him a "straw man" while drunk.[94] Another reason was that Messner, the owner of the sawmill, held Schlüter responsible for *his* office and *his* household losing workers, "both of which were already under heavy strain at the beginning of the war."[95] When shortly thereafter the acting mayor announced to the town council that he intended to incorporate the local electric company into the interconnected Swabian electricity system (which would have made Schlüter's position redundant and resulted in him being transferred after almost thirty years of civil service in Trossingen), many presumed that the wartime economy was not solely to blame. But the forthcoming Ardennes Offensive was actually widely considered to be the only remaining possibility for the German army to avert the looming military collapse, so the last remaining forces were expected to be mobilized.[96]

Since Schlüter was among the most fervent "old fighters" in Trossingen and was a known Hohner adversary to boot, Kiehn went to bat for him, filling in the Kreisleiter on the personal dimensions of Messner's decision. Bringing the Kreisleiter into the loop, however, now got Kiehn's son-in-law, the acting mayor, mired in a party court proceeding because of alleged "defeatist statements," which earned Messner a strong reprimand.[97] Messner and Kiehn, who lived next door to each other, began writing each other long, reproachful letters. Whereas Messner denied that he had any personal interest in the Schlüter matter and claimed to have only been complying with his official obligations, Kiehn invoked party discipline and comradely duty: "Loyalty for loyalty. This is the Führer's watchword for the old fighters; it therefore must be ours as well." Kiehn excused Schlüter's alleged faux pas by arguing that the words of "an old party comrade" could not and should not "be weighed too carefully, especially not those that have been said while drinking alcohol. ... His condition [under the influence] at the time must be taken into account."[98] Probably without being aware of it, Kiehn was confessing how local party notables regarded the mission of "total war," with collapse looming: he felt that the deployment of a deserving "old fighter" was unreasonable.

In February 1945, Kiehn reminded his brother-in-law that Schlüter had "pledged himself to the Führer" back in the "time of struggle" and had "always supported" the local NSDAP group "in deed," which Kiehn would "*never forget.*"[99] Among the ways Kiehn expressed his gratitude was to offer Schlüter a position at his newly acquired factory in Okriftel. Schlüter, however, declined. The argument over his future use then intensified. Messner and Schlüter insulted each other and invoked various local grievances that had nothing to do with the issue, such as the debts that Messner's sawmill owed to the municipal utilities and irregularities in how Schlüter had discharged his office. Dealings among the local Nazi notables were defined by mutual denunciations and petty animosities. They increasingly got caught up in the polycratic chaos and used their respective connections to adjacent officials to gain advantages over one another.

The main argument Kiehn used to culminate his protection of Schlüter in February 1945 was that "the Führer himself" would not send Schlüter to the front.[100] Messner, on the other hand, believed that Hitler would judge the matter very differently. He was "firmly convinced ... that the Führer ... without being narrow-minded" would "1. not only cut Dir. Schlüter's post, but also a number of the [work]force ... not all of whom you would like, perhaps, and 2. if he were to see the interminable letters that have been written to prevent the drafting of an old comrade, he would immediately verify whether the writers were expendable." The acting mayor garnished this threat with some advice: Kiehn's impassioned motto, "Stand tall or crumble," was not compatible with relieving an "old party comrade" of his "obligation" to "the Reich and the Führer."[101]

The reference to the Führer was typical of the mental state of many Nazis. Kiehn believed himself to be completely in accordance with Hitler's will; just as in the "time of struggle," he still purported to be "working toward the Führer."[102] He had largely lost touch with the reality of the sixth year of war.

The already reprimanded Messner indicated this to his brother-in-law in his reply: "Dear Fritz, I too know what I owe to an old party comrade; but the dictate of the moment and the obligation of all party comrades to the Reich *and the Führer* stands above that. ... You say that old party comrades should live in harmony. Yes, Fritz, they should ... but neither should they lose the courage to always put the cause [of the Führer] above the person."[103] Messner, whose family had already suffered heavy losses in the war, was evidently judging the war situation more realistically, even if, in the Schlüter case, he had utilized the regime's drive to mobilize the last reserves for personal reasons. This private correspondence glaringly illuminates the structural causes that led the Nazi state to become more and more incapable, as battle conditions intensified, of efficiently implementing the "total war" it had proclaimed. As local authorities gained successively more influence over the labor deployment, housing distribution, food rationing, and, in the end, even military defense, the abuses within the party during the war almost inevitably paralyzed local life as well.

When Christian Messner sent his last letter about the Schlüter matter to Deibhalde in February 1945, he saw his fears confirmed. Even as negotiations continued — this time in the Gauleitung — over whether Schlüter would stay or go, the Ardennes Offensive ended in German defeat; Soviet troops were standing along the Oder, the Western Allies on the Rhine. The day before, bombs had fallen on Trossingen for the first time. In a likely allusion to the accusation of defeatism made against him, Messner sent his brother-in-law a question: "Is it not the case that even we will soon have to take up our guns?"[104] They did not get past considering this move, since neither man was enough of a fanatic to join an actual battle.

In 1944–1945, Kiehn once again briefly managed to enjoy close contact to the regime's highest level of command. But it was due to the looming military defeat alone: Hitler had declared Himmler commander of the line of defense at the Rhine. Himmler's headquarters were located in Triberg, not far from Trossingen. Looking for accommodation that was safe and relatively close by, the Reichsführer-SS had chosen Kiehn's villa. Whether this amounted to a requisition by the SS, carried out against the family's will — as they claimed after 1945 — seems improbable.[105] Much evidence suggests that the family was proud to be allowed to accommodate the Reichsführer-SS. Kiehn's seven-year-old grandson had already spent weeks preparing for the great day when he would be permitted to see Himmler. He had been brought specially to Trossingen from Nußdorf, where he lived with his mother. When asked about his grandfather's relationship with Himmler, his grandson recalled "that the 'Reichsführer' shimmered like some kind of higher being just by being mentioned."[106]

In 1948, a Trossingen resident testified that Berta Kiehn had been involved in the construction of a "liaison office for the Gestapo to Himmler's staff," procuring the local premises and materials. "In whatever fashion, they [the Gestapo staff] were likely in touch with where Himmler was staying at the time; indeed, he spent many nights at the Kiehn villa as well. They also seem to have had something to do with preparing the escape of those who at that time were the highest authorities."[107] Even if the latter statement could not be verified, at the end of 1944 and beginning of 1945 Deibhalde became a conspiratorial safe haven for Himmler and his entourage. Considering the hardship nationwide, their drinking sprees and luxurious provisions outraged some Trossingen residents.

Klaus von Bismarck, who at that time was an officer in the army and later would become director general of the West German Broadcasting Service, reported in his memoirs on a meeting he had with Himmler over Christmas in 1944 that took place "in the villa of some industrialist friend of his" in Trossingen. The reason for the meeting was to award medals to officers, some of whom had been ordered there from the eastern front just for that purpose; Himmler was acting "on behalf of the Führer" that day. Bismarck described the mood in Deibhalde as "spooky." The Reichsführer-SS so distrusted the officers he was honoring that he would only receive them unarmed. After they protested, however, they were allowed to keep their weapons. The ambience of the villa suited the character of the Reichsführer-SS to a tee; Bismarck wrote that he reminded him of a "teacher collecting herbs," but did not correspond to the image of a "dark, sinister figure" he had anticipated. Himmler had given "pearls of friendly, petty bourgeois wisdom in a middle-class atmosphere. ... Today I know that this mixture of philistine banality and brutal consistency, used to put an arrogant ideology into practice, reflected much more of the nature of National Socialism than I was aware of in Trossingen."[108]

Himmler's appointment calendar shows a meeting with Hungarian interior minister Gábor Vajna in Triberg on 10 December 1944. Kiehn participated in Himmler's lunch with the guests of state, together with Gottlob Berger and four other SS leaders.[109] On 6 January 1945, Himmler spent the entire afternoon and evening in Deibhalde. At four p.m., the "Kiehn family" invited him to tea in the presence of Reinhard Heydrich's wife, SS senior group leader Karl Hermann Frank, and Frank's aide-de-camp, Major Hoffmann. Himmler then interrupted their shared dinner to speak with Heydrich's wife and Frank individually.[110] The Kiehns had finally managed to get one of the most powerful men in the Third Reich to sit at their table. It seems not to have dawned on them that by this point in time the Reich was already sinking, and they were receiving their guests in a "spooky" atmosphere. Their joy at this high-ranking house call, and the rise in social capital that accompanied it, was just too great to give reality a chance.

These contacts certainly were no help to Kiehn in restoring his local supremacy within the small-town society; indeed, with the Allies fast approaching, they made him into more of an outsider and source of danger. Some Trossingen residents attributed aerial attacks on the town solely to Himmler's temporary presence there. All in all, the breakdown in Kiehn's power and the reconsolidation of Hohner paternalism accelerated during the last months of Nazi rule. Whereas Ernst Hohner did everything he could to prevent pointless defense efforts or the execution of Hitler's Nero Decree, which would have destroyed his immediate hometown, especially his factory (a process that was entirely typical of important local figures toward the end of the war),[111] Kiehn cleared out early, in March 1945. Baptist, the district leader, did not flee until 21 April. Camouflaged in the uniform of a Luftwaffe senior lieutenant, the "political leader" abandoned his "kingdom," but not before throwing the population into turmoil with a "rabble-rousing speech" and threatening to have the newly dovish Trossingen Ortsgruppenleiter shot, along with anyone else who wished to wave a white flag.[112] Kiehn did not transmit the misanthropic calls to persevere that were implemented in many towns with brutal consistency. He decided to take refuge just in time to be able to hide valuable assets. The "harmonica king," on the other hand, prevented home guard (*Volkssturm*) units from being established, negotiated with German and French officers, and, together with other Trossingen residents and the French foreign workers, was able to secure the peaceful handover of the town. Meanwhile, Kiehn had taken his entire family and fled toward his hunting grounds in Leutasch, Tyrol, ahead of the advancing French troops. On 12 May, four days after Germany surrendered, US soldiers acting on orders from the Supreme Headquarters, Allied Expeditionary Force (SHAEF) put Berta and Fritz Kiehn under "automatic arrest" in Innsbruck.

Little is known about what then happened to his wife and daughter in those days; they must also have ended up in temporary American custody. Not long afterward, both women went to stay at their residence in the American-occupied zone in Ermingen, near Ulm. To this day, legends persist about the details of the family's escape. We can exclude the one about Trossingen becoming an assembly point for Nazi functionaries in 1945, who from there retreated with Kiehn to the "Alpine fortress" in Tyrol, which was nothing but a propaganda chimera. There was no safe haven for Nazis anywhere toward the end of the war. There is also practically no evidence of the "large long-haul truck" the family was said to have used to save their worldly goods. But circumstantial evidence supports the story that some of the family briefly returned to Trossingen after the town had been occupied by French troops so that they could remove some of their assets to a safe place. They had little success, however, because someone betrayed the Kiehns' hiding place, and its contents were looted or seized.[113] The part of the family silver that had been buried in Nußdorf was later recovered.

Not only were both escaping and securing assets typical actions taken by many important Nazi figures,[114] they also contrasted sharply with what most Trossingen residents perceived as the "selfless and heroic" behavior of Ernst Hohner. But the judgments formed about the Kiehns in the last days of the war — "cowardly desertion" of their hometown and "selfish greed" — would be revised all too soon in Trossingen public opinion.[115]

Notes

1. See StAT, A 1238, report from Mayor Bärlin to Tuttlingen Oberamt of 10 Mar. 1933; StAT, Häffner interview collection. See WABW, B 35 II, Bü 822, letter from E. Schittenhelm to Will Hohner of 6 Mar. 1933.
2. See WABW, B 35 I, Bü 732, DHHV board minutes from 20 May and 16 June 1933.
3. In other photos, Kiehn also appears in uniform with the players. See AVT, 31 May 1933.
4. Interview by Hartmut Berghoff of 26 May 1993.
5. WABW, B 35 II, Bü 415, letter from Ernst Hohner to Karl Hohner of 7 Nov. 1933. See StAT, A 1222, letter from the mayor to the Political Police of 26 Sept. 1933, which allowed a detained Hohner representative and KPD member to exercise his profession; StAT, A 1070, written correspondence of 24 Mar. and 6 Apr. 1934 concerning an SA man Hohner refused to hire.
6. See StAT, A 501, records relating to the reshuffling of the town council membership in 1933; StAT, B 79, GRP of 22 May and 6 and 21 July 1933; Schnabel, *Württemberg*, 281–290.
7. "System era" (*Systemzeit*) was a derogatory term used by the Nazis to denounce the years of the Weimar Republic.
8. AVT, 3 Apr. 1933.
9. Letter from Herbert Kiehn of 15 Dec. 1933, private collection.
10. AVT, 2 Jan. 1934. Transcript in MAE Colmar, WH C 3541 d 11, Affaire Kiehn.
11. Letter from Herbert E. Kiehn to the authors of 12 Dec. 1998.
12. See Reichel, *Schein*; Vondung, *Magie*; Behrenbeck, *Kult*.
13. Letter from Herbert E. Kiehn to the authors of 21 Apr. 1999.
14. Gebhard and Zingerle, *Pilgerfahrt*, 61–62.
15. Herbert E. Kiehn, in letter of 15 June 1998.
16. Mann, *Der Untertan*, 361–62; English translation in Glaser, *Roots*.
17. Glaser, *Roots*, 90. See also Bloch, *Erbschaft*, 380.
18. See letter from Herbert E. Kiehn of 30 Aug. 1998; StAT, A 938, Festschrift 1955, in which Fritz Kiehn invoked the "healthy genetic constitution" of his ancestors.
19. See AVT, 16 Oct. and 12 and 28 Dec. 1933; Freitag, "Führermythos."
20. AVT, 21 Mar. 1934.
21. StAT, A 423, records of Hitler's honorary Trossingen citizenship; AVT, 28 May 1934.
22. AVT, 21 Apr. 1933 and 21 Mar. 1934.
23. AVT, 1 Oct. 1934. See Kershaw, *Myth*, 53–64; Vondung, *Magie*, 83; Behrenbeck, *Kult*; Freitag, "Führermythos"; interview by Hartmut Berghoff of 10 May 1993; StAT, A 423, records of Hitler's honorary Trossingen citizenship.

24. Interview by Hartmut Berghoff of 24 Feb. 1993.
25. Interview by Hartmut Berghoff of 7 July 1993.
26. All quotes from AVT, 28 May 1934 and 13 Nov. 1933; StAT, A 422, NSDAP Ortsgruppe decree on voter transport services of 18 Aug. 1934; AVT, 21 Aug. 1934. See also AVT, 20 Aug. 1934; Bracher, "Stufen"; Schnabel, *Württemberg*, 522.
27. AVT, 28 Dec. 1933 and 18 Dec. 1934; StAT, A 422, NSDAP Ortsgruppe decree on voter transport services of 18 Aug. 1934.
28. StAT, A 483, letters from Hohner to mayor's office of 11 and 18 Apr. 1934. See also StAT, B 80, GRP of 27 Feb., 19 Apr., and 11 June 1934.
29. StAT, A 483, letter from Bärlin to Kienzle of 22 Mar. 1935.
30. Ibid. See also StAT, B 81, GRP of 20 June 1935.
31. StAT, A 483, letter from Hohner to Kienzle of 23 Apr. 1935. See also StAT, B 81, GRP of 20 June 1935.
32. HStAS, E 151/21, Bü 129, letter from Kiehn to Interior Ministry of 6 June 1933; StAS, Wü 40, vol. 2, no. 13, letter from Kiehn to Interior Ministry of 31 July 1933. The ministry accused the old district administrator of having "embarrassed the NSDAP" by providing the Kreisleiter with a job "because this position was seen as an office for a card-carrying party member." HStAS, E 151/21, Bü 129, note from the Interior Ministry, 16 June 1933. The authors are grateful to Michael Ruck for pointing out this instance. The rejection of a young candidate qualified solely for his party membership corresponded to the pronounced efforts of the Württemberg administration at "corporate self-assertion." Rauh-Kühne and Ruck, *Eliten*, 46–58; Ruck, *Korpsgeist*.
33. MAE Colmar, WH C 3541 d 11, Affaire Kiehn, invitation from Spaichingen Oberamt of 24 Apr. 1933 and duplicate transcript of a GRP of 22 May 1933.
34. This term refers to the November Revolution of 1918. Those who were responsible for it were seen as perpetrators in conservative circles and presented as such in Nazi propaganda, which most often referred to them as "November criminals."
35. AVT, 2 May 1934, Kiehn's speech for National Workers' Day; AVT, 29 Jan. 1936, Kiehn's speech on "public and private business."
36. Quoted in Kershaw, *Hitler, 1889–1936*, 527.
37. ASD, NL Erler, Box 85, duplicate of a meeting report from Tuttlingen *Gränzbote* newspaper of 3 Jan. 1934. On forced sterilizations and the Holocaust, see Bock, *Zwangssterilisation*, 353–368, 452–456.
38. AVT, 2 May 1934 and 29 Jan. 1936.
39. StAS, Wü 13, T2 no. 2775/001, http://www.landesarchiv-bw.de/plink/?f=6-1039573 (accessed 4 Sept. 2012), attorney Sieger to SK Maier of 8 Oct. 1948.
40. See Peukert, *"Volksgenossen,"* 217–219; Berghoff, "Hitler."
41. Interview by Hartmut Berghoff of 2 June 1993.
42. See interview by Hartmut Berghoff of 4 Sept. 1992. According to the church architects, it was owing to Kiehn's "personal intervention with the municipal administration ... that the church received the worthy space desired by the bishop's ordinariate and the Catholic parish." See Darlegungen des Diözesan-Angestellten MdL Schneider, Verhandlungen des Landtags, 107th session, 25 July 1951, p. 2100.
43. Kiehn called for the mayor's "strictest and most conscientious fulfillment of duty" in the "spirit and sense of our incomparable Führer." StAT, B 79, GRP of 23 May 1933.
44. StAT, A 1349, memorandum on settlement. See also StAT, B 79, GRP of 24 Jan. 1933; StAT, B 87, GRP of 18 Feb. 1939; StAT, B 80, GRP of 2 Feb. 1934; StAT, B 81, GRP of 25 Mar. and 7 Oct. 1935.
45. See StAT, B 79, GRP of 25 July 1933; StAT, B 80, GRP of 2 and 27 Feb. and 16 Aug. 1934; StAT, B 81, GRP of 17 Apr., 11 July, and 6 June 1935; StAT, B 84, GRP of 27 July 1936;

StAT, B 85, GRP of 25 Feb. and 25 June 1937; StAT, B 87, GRP of 4 Feb. and 23 July 1939; Schnabel, *Württemberg,* 306–308; Rauh-Kühne, *Milieu,* 329–330.
46. StAT, B 79, GRP of 21 Dec. 1933.
47. StAT, A 1344, justification for development of settlement works, no date (1935).
48. On the following, see StAT, B 81, GRP of 21 Nov. and 19 Sept. 1935.
49. BA DC, Akte Kiehn, Kiehn's assessment of 14 Dec. 1938 relating to the Gau court proceedings.
50. BA DC, Akte Hunger, letter from Hunger to Hitler of 4 Nov. 1933; BA DC, Akte Hunger, letter from Hunger to Raubal of 19 Mar. 1934; BA DC, Akte Hunger, letter from Huber to the *Gau* court of 1 Oct. 1934; BA DC, Akte Hunger, letter from Bärlin to Trossingen Ortsgruppe of 5 Sept. 1933; BA DC, Akte Hunger, letter from principal Kommer to Trossingen Ortsgruppe of 15 Sept. 1934; BA DC, Akte Hunger, letter from Spaichingen Ortsgruppe to Trossingen Ortsgruppe of 14 Sept. 1934; BA DC, Akte Hunger, letter from Trossingen Ortsgruppe to Murr, no date; BA DC, Akte Hunger, letter from Murr to the Gau court of 5 Apr. 1935. On the "Aryan declarations," see Rigg, "Riggs Liste."
51. See StAT, Häffner interview collection.
52. AVT, 9 Sept. 1938.
53. It is unclear whether this allegation is true. StAT, Ordner Kiehn, unsigned report, no recipient, of 12 Feb. 1948.
54. MAE Colmar, WH C 3541 d 11, Affaire Kiehn.
55. AVT, 28 Mar. 1936 and 1 Aug. 1935.
56. BA NS, 46/7, letter from Berta Kiehn to Frick of 10 Oct. 1935 and telegram from Frick to F. Kiehn of 15 Oct. 1935.
57. StAT, A 481, letter from Kienzle to Huber of 25 Sept. 1935; AVT, 15 Oct. 1935; StAT, A 481, letter from Kiehn to Kienzle of 14 Oct. 1935.
58. AVT, 7 July 1937.
59. Michael and Doerr, *Nazi-Deutsch,* 142.
60. AVT, 12 July 1937; StAT, B 85, GRP of 1 July 1937.
61. AVT, 19 July 1938; StAT, A 481, letter from Kiehn to Kienzle of 14 Oct. 1935. For general information, see Vondung, *Magie*; Kershaw, *Hitler-Mythos,* 67–71.
62. All citations in the paragraph are from AVT, 20 Dec. 1938.
63. AVT, 23 Feb. and 12 July 1937. See also AVT, 9 July 1935.
64. AVT, 12 July and 23 Feb. 1937.
65. AVT, 16 Dec. 1937.
66. See AVT, 12 July 1937.
67. See AVT, 15 Oct. 1935 (cit.) and 4 May 1938; WABW, B 35 II, Bü 640; HMT.
68. See Bräutigam, *Unternehmer,* 338–349; Burth et al., "Wirtschaftslenkung," 206–208; Bluhm, "'Wirtschaft,'" 247–262; Rauh-Kühne, "Unternehmer."
69. See Berghoff, *Kleinstadt,* 353–355, 368–390; Berghoff, "Konsumgüterindustrie."
70. See AVT, 20 Jan. 1934 (cit.); BA DC, Akte Hunger; AVT, 9 Sept. 1938; StAT, A 563, report from town administration for Political Police of 2 Feb. 1935. Similar documents can be found for the small Catholic town of Ettlingen in Rauh-Kühne, *Milieu,* and for the Saarland area in Mallmann and Paul, *Herrschaft.* On the concept of resistance, see Broszat and Fröhlich, *Alltag,* 49–73; Mallmann and Paul, "Resistenz." See Rauh-Kühne, "Katholikinnen," 36, for an opposing view.
71. On the decreasing response to Nazi holiday culture, see Freitag, "Führermythos," 37–39.
72. Interview by Hartmut Berghoff of 10 May 1993.
73. The German Christians, a Nazi-oriented movement within the Protestant Church, had only twenty to thirty followers. See LKAS, Altreg. Tuttlingen.
74. But Kiehn did not want to part with his portrait of Luther; letter from Herbert E. Kiehn to the authors of 21 Apr. 1999.

75. AVT, 16 Dec. 1937; StAT, B 87, GRP of 25 Sept. 1939; StAT, A 1539, report for Defense Recruiting Office in Tuttlingen of 22 Nov. 1938.
76. Kiehn, *Unsere Deibhalde*, 8 (cit.).
77. See Behrenbeck, *Kult,* 374–388.
78. AVT, 3 Dec. 1936, Herbert Kiehn's obituary. Herbert Kiehn reported elsewhere on his involvement as a uniformed Hitler Youth member in the NSDAP party convention in Weimar in 1926. See AVT, 2 Jan. 1934.
79. *Das Schwarze Korps,* no. 51 (17 Dec. 1936): 18.
80. Herbert E. Kiehn in letter to the authors of 15 June 1998.
81. See Schäfer and Klockmann, *"Mutter,"* 123–125.
82. Letter from Herbert E. Kiehn to the authors of 22 Feb. 1999.
83. StAT, A 938, Fritz Kiehn's resume, dated 1935.
84. Sinz, *Fritz Kiehn.*
85. StAL, EL 902/22, Bü 1502 (Berta Kiehn denazification records), reporting form and defense plea of 22 Jan. 1948 by attorney Wizigmann.
86. On the following, see StAT, B 87, GRP of 27 Oct. 1939; StAT, B 88, GRP of 27 Mar. 1940; StAT, B 90, GRP of 20 Sept. 1944.
87. WABW, B 35 I, Bü 776, manuscript "Trossinger Handharmonika-Schule," 31; StAT, B 89, GRP of 2 Apr. 1943.
88. See StAS, Wü 13, Bü 2289 (K. Krämer denazification records); Berghoff, *Kleinstadt,* 504–509; 514–515.
89. AVT, 30 Nov. 1942; emphasis in the original.
90. There was also a plan to rename Hindenburg Square Jacob Hohner Square, but this did not happen because of the war and the massive resistance from authorities. See StAT, A 481, records from Jacob Hohner's eightieth birthday, 1941; WABW, B 35 II Bü 641, list of Jacob Hohner's donations in 1941.
91. See StAS, Wü 13, Bü 2224 (Ortsgruppenleiter Ernst Deiss denazification records).
92. See MAE Colmar, WH C 3541 d 11, Affaire Kiehn.
93. See Arbogast, *Herrschaftsinstanzen,* 66, 135, 241.
94. HMT, NL Ernst Hohner, letter from Kiehn to Messner, 3 Feb. 1945.
95. HMT, NL Ernst Hohner, letter from Messner to Kiehn of 10 Feb. 1945; HMT, NL Ernst Hohner, letter from Schlüter to Kiehn of 17 Jan. 1945.
96. Henke, *Besetzung,* 340–341.
97. StAS, Wü 13, Bü 2663 (Messner denazification records); HMT, NL Ernst Hohner, letter from Messner to Kiehn of 22 Jan. 1945.
98. HMT, NL Ernst Hohner, letter from Kiehn to Messner, 3 Feb. 1945.
99. Ibid.
100. Ibid.
101. HMT, NL Ernst Hohner, letter from Messner to Kiehn, 10 Feb. 1945. See also HMT, NL Ernst Hohner, letter from Schlüter to Kiehn of 17 Jan. 1945; HMT, NL Ernst Hohner, letter from Messner to Kiehn of 22 Jan. 1945; StAS, Wü 13, Bü 2287 (Messner denazification records), copy of a letter from Kreisleiter Baptist to district administrator (Landrat), 28 Dec. 1944.
102. There are numerous examples of businessmen whose trust in the Führer remained unbroken to the end. See Henke, *Besetzung,* 341, 426–427.
103. HMT, NL Ernst Hohner, letter from Messner to Kiehn of 10 Feb. 1945 (authors' emphasis).
104. Ibid.
105. StAL, EL 902/22, Bü 1502 (Berta Kiehn denazification records), letter from Kiehn's attorney Wizigmann to Ulm regional denazification court of 16 Dec. 1947.
106. Letter from Herbert E. Kiehn to the authors of 31 Aug. 1998.

107. StAT, Ordner Kiehn, unsigned report, no recipient, 12 Feb. 1948.
108. Bismarck, "Weihnachten," 21–22.
109. See BA NS, 19/1793, Himmler's appointments from 10 Dec. 1944 to 6 Jan. 1945, p. 103.
110. Ibid. See also Heydrich, *Leben*.
111. See Gehrig, *Rüstungspolitik*, 295–296; Henke, *Besetzung*, 451–453; Boelcke, "Befehle."
112. These accusations were brought against Baptist in his denazification proceedings. Arbogast, *Herrschaftsinstanzen*, 241; information given by former Ortsgruppenleiter Ernst Deiss in his denazification proceedings, StAS, Wü 13, Bü 2224.
113. Letter from Herbert E. Kiehn to the authors of 16 May 1999.
114. See Arbogast, *Herrschaftsinstanzen*, 241–242; Henke, *Besetzung*, 779, 789. On the people's war weariness, see Henke, *Besetzung*, 821–823, and on the cowardly escape of the "district kings," see Henke, *Besetzung*, 830–835.
115. See StAL, EL 902/22, Bü 1502 (Berta Kiehn denazification records) (cit.); StAT, Häffner interview collection; interview with Herbert E. Kiehn of 19–20 May 1998.

Chapter 9

From "War Criminal No. 1" to Sought-After Employer

Once the French had taken Trossingen, Kiehn's reputation hit its absolute nadir. To his fellow citizens he personified the regime that had ruined Germany and put them at the mercy of the violent French occupying authority. This version of events held that Kiehn and others like him were the only ones to blame for the escalating poverty, the hunger and disease, and the billeting and requisitioning; they were responsible for the humiliations wrought by the French occupiers and the fates of the soldiers who were missing, killed, or imprisoned.

All adults were required to attend film presentations documenting the concentration camps. Anyone who was still unclear about the character of Nazi rule at the time of surrender would not have been able to turn a blind eye to the regime's apocalyptic crimes against humanity after viewing these. Himmler, who visited the Kiehns several times in 1944 and 1945, held the greatest responsibility for the Holocaust after Hitler. For a long time, the proximity to those in power that Kiehn had always emphasized had worked to the region's advantage and filled many Trossingen residents with pride. The facts were now completely reversed, especially after Kiehn had fled. An important reason for the shift in morale was that the small town was bombed for the first time on 9 February 1945; Trossingen had previously been spared air bombardment because it was neither strategically nor economically important to the war economy. Even decades later, many residents felt that the attack only happened because of Kiehn's villa and the important SS figures frequenting it. Eleven people were killed, and there was considerable property damage. Kiehn was accused of having carelessly put innocent townspeople's lives at risk. His insistence on wearing his SS uniform to the memorial ceremony for the bombing victims, coupled with the general prohibition on any Christian rites at such services to honor "the fallen," provoked

---

Notes from this chapter begin on page 200.

widespread indignation, given that the collapse of the regime was in sight.¹ The "banquetry" in Deibhalde was another strike against Kiehn, since supplies to the town's population were growing worse and worse. So when Deibhalde was looted, requisitioned, and turned into a relief hospital, many talked about what had happened with schadenfreude.

Many townspeople were very keen to settle accounts with Kiehn in those first months after the occupation. This sentiment was all the stronger because, being imprisoned, Kiehn was absent and powerless. It was easy and safe for people to vent their wrath and attribute responsibility to one individual. With their belated revolt, it was as if they had turned to the side of the victors. On 1 May, before the German Reich had even surrendered, the former names of Kiehn Street, Hitler Street, and Murr Street were already restored, whereas a main artery was renamed in Ernst Hohner's honor. After this early signal that the "old king" of Trossingen would once again rule, the people wanted to send a clearer sign of the radical political shift that summer. The exposure of Kiehn's role, his inglorious escape from the town, and the rumors circulating about his supposed death had made the SS lieutenant colonel (Obersturmbannführer) into the target of many residents' fury. He offered a psychological outlet for their own feelings of culpability; some of the townspeople hatched a plan to humiliate Kiehn by driving him through town trapped in a boar cage. But since Kiehn was not available, they found a stand-in for him in another of Hohner's local adversaries, building commissioner Wilhelm Schlüter, the same person Kiehn had so vehemently defended a few months before. The rumors circulating about Schlüter ranged from collaboration with the Gestapo to attempted compliance with Hitler's Nero Decree. He was specifically accused of intending to blow up the public utilities or poison the drinking water. On 1 June 1945, the Trossingen police (a temporary workforce assembled from those who were not "politically incriminated") made Schlüter run the gauntlet. They dragged him through the town in oversized shoes wearing a sign that read, "I am Trossingen's war criminal no. 2." Summoned by a bell, the townspeople followed the procession, some in shock and others threatening and heaping abuse on Schlüter. The humiliated man killed himself with a potassium cyanide capsule the same day, in a detention cell at the town hall. Even though Schlüter had joined the NSDAP back in 1931 and had exploited his posts for his own personal advantage, he was not one of the especially fanatical National Socialists in town. But the "Prussian newcomer," who had not even erased the "stigma of his origins" by marrying a Trossingen woman, as Kiehn had, made a more suitable scapegoat than anyone else.²

In many respects, the sacrifice by proxy of an unimportant Nazi functionary who was not integrated into the local solidarity network of more established local residents is characteristic of how communities dealt with the legacy of the Third Reich locally. The town's perception of Kiehn as "war criminal no. 1" points to the unclear evaluation criteria and narrowing of perspective typical of postwar

German society. People could accuse Kiehn of many things, from his energetic support of the NSDAP before and after 1933 to his membership in Himmler's personal staff and his unrestrained attempts to enrich himself, but war crimes were not one of them. Moreover, we must interpret Kiehn's escape, and his complete indifference to a military defense of Trossingen or complying with the Nero Decree, as a lucky break for the town. The alternative would have been senseless destruction and death, as well as the brutal crimes against civilians that occurred elsewhere in the final stages of the war.[3]

Schlüter's death had not been anyone's intention, and to many it soon seemed a glaring injustice. The humiliating treatment he had received thus contributed substantially to the discrediting of the "anti-Fascist forces" concentrated in the auxiliary police, who increasingly rubbed townspeople the wrong way with other arrests and the endless, divisive requisitioning and billeting. More than half of the police quit the force by September 1945 as a result. Finally, what happened with Schlüter made it patently obvious just how difficult it was to bring supporters of Nazi rule to justice. The experience under French rule of seeing new injustices constantly being added on top of old ones began to shape people's political awareness in the summer of 1945. The transition from the regimented everyday life of wartime to the chaos of the early occupation era was associated with traumatic humiliations and experiences of powerlessness. Public order collapsed after the French took over. The victors gave free rein to their desire for revenge, looting, and triumph. Women were raped; businesses and factories were looted, deserted, and sometimes smeared with feces; private households were robbed. A number of days passed before the local commander and auxiliary police managed to put an end to these excesses. Even then, order remained precarious, as a police report from September 1945 shows:[4]

> Every day women and men would come ... and complain that their chickens, rabbits, pigs, and calves had been stolen by the Moroccans. The Moroccans also broke into their homes and pilfered food, watches and jewelry, and many other things. ... Russians, Poles, Armenians etc. also participated in the raids ... and the saddest chapter in the history of the town of Trossingen was — is — that part of the civilian population carried out the same thefts, together with or under the protection of these elements.

Extensive requisitioning and billeting, as well as organizing the population into a labor force for the French, created a steadily growing group of residents who felt like victims of arbitrary measures. When in June 1945 the French military detained Trossingen soldiers a second time and took them away, the same persons whom British and American armed forces had already released to their hometown, the small-town society reacted with great indignation. Most difficult were the punitive political actions organized by the occupiers. "Hateful National Socialists" had to be named and then either give up their residences to French officers or hand over their furniture. In May and June 1945, thirty-one especially incriminated persons were arrested. There was no consensus in the town about the selection or number of those accused, nor about the legitimacy of their detention. What some experienced as an act of political justice, others perceived as an indefensible infringement on the town's solidarity. This solidarity was especially needed because numerous evacuees and, beginning in 1947, refugees were competing with the locals for scarce food and shelter. It was not long before the order of the day was to close local ranks and fend off external attempts to intervene.

The rapid discrediting of the occupying power and the concentration on an increasingly difficult struggle for survival explain why the townspeople soon departed from taking a hard line toward coming to terms with the past. The new mayor, Social Democrat Hans Neipp, was appointed by the French on 23 April 1945 at the suggestion of French prisoners of war. In November, Neipp was still both demanding a "cleansing campaign" of "public offices" and offering a "list of Nazis who have come into question" in his monthly report to the district administrator.[5] A few days earlier, the town had stripped Kiehn, Murr, and Hitler of their honorary citizen status.[6] One month later, however, Neipp was summing up the changed mood in the region: "The population is calm and wants ... nothing to do with politics. The political arrests have contributed a lot to this."[7]

The beginning of the denazification mandated by the Allies in the French zone is also likely to have led most people to abandon their desire for a reckoning. Once the district committees for political cleansing had been formed, the realization grew that it was not only exposed officeholders of the Nazi regime who would have to take responsibility. In April 1946, Neipp's report "on a year of occupation" called for unity among the people (after lengthy descriptions of the problems of everyday life) and posited that local solidarity should take precedence over individual recriminations: "We are all of us, some more and some less, to blame for this misery, for which we have the Hitler regime to thank, and we are therefore obligated to bear its resulting burdens together."[8] In the space of a few months, the "hated Nazis" had once again become fellow citizens who, it was believed, were needed in the work of rebuilding. The plan to ostracize them quickly turned into a desire for their integration.

The resurgence of local political life also reflects this about-face. On 28 August 1945, a provisional committee (Arbeitsausschuss) was appointed as a sort of ersatz town council. Neipp was in charge of selecting new representatives for the citizens. With the exception of Ernst Hohner — who, as the largest employer in town, was immunized, as it were, against the effects of the systemic political changes of 1933 and 1945 — none of the committee members had belonged to the NSDAP or, after 1933, the town council. At any rate, after 1945 Hohner was beyond all criticism to most Trossingen residents, who regarded him as the town's "savior." At the committee's inaugural meeting in late August, chairman Georg Bäuerle, a Social Democrat, described the "elimination of any Nazi and militaristic spirit from the life of our town and the removal of all incriminated representatives of this system" as a committee task that remained urgent. What's more, the committee needed to "lay the foundation stone for a ... democratic Germany" and "get the life of the town back on an orderly path." In addition, all of the work of the council and the municipal administration from the last twelve years needed to be critically reviewed.[9]

This would never happen, however. As has already been stated, by late 1945 the zest for a new political order had cracked against the conditions everyone had to live under. The first town council election after the war fell on 15 September 1946. The liberal, Hohner-led Deutsche Volkspartei (German People's Party, or DVP, refounded in January 1946 in Stuttgart) won five of the ten seats. The rest were divided up between the new Christliche Demokratische Union (Christian Democratic Union, or CDU, with three) and the SPD (with two). The Social Democrats, who had previously dominated the ersatz council (Arbeitsausschuss) of the immediate postwar phase, now found themselves once again in the minority. Apart from Hohner, none of the council members from the Nazi era reentered the town council, preserving the sting of the sea change in its membership. Neipp stayed on as mayor, swearing the new councilors to a new, modern course of action as part of their induction into office. They were in a difficult "time of need," he said; the issue was "to be or not to be." Consequently, nonpolitical objectivity and unconditional cooperation were needed — a formula that truly tied in with the slogan of the middle-class parties during the Great Depression. "The town council is no place for politically charged discussions." In the "interest of peace ... and for the good of our town," Neipp said, as mayor he was not inclined to "devote much time to high politics. ... After all, great things will not be decided in Trossingen."[10]

Like most of the population, Neipp now wanted to let bygones be bygones and concentrate on the urgent problems of the present. These included ensuring physical survival in the face of food shortages and high morbidity rates, as well as combating class-based fears of downward mobility. There were also concerns about missing and imprisoned family members. This accumulation of problems led to extensive political desensitization and a pronounced consensus to repress the past, each of which in turn resulted in the local tendency to wrap up denazification quickly and the establishment of an exoneration cartel that transcended party lines.

Thus, neighbors helping neighbors became a signal element of the town's denazification proceedings. Surprising as it may be that Communists and Social Democrats attested to the personal integrity of their National Socialist neighbors, their behavior fit the logic of local solidarity. They were often returning the favor of protection that they themselves had been given since 1933. Many of them had known each other since early childhood and had attended school together or worked at the same company; they maintained the pronounced Württemberg sociability of clubs and the age cohorts for people born in a certain year. This class and year system extended across various milieus and created a strong sense of local community. As a long-established innkeeper, Mayor Neipp was well integrated into the local network. The Social Democrat probably had Kiehn to thank for his release from a Gestapo prison, and may even have owed him his life. How could Neipp, when the power differential between the two men was reproduced in reverse after 1945, choose a lasting and unforgiving course against less exposed Nazis while he was lenient with Kiehn? It was also clear to all those involved that they would have to live alongside one another in the future, and that they would not be able to avoid each other. Finally, we cannot underestimate the dense network of family connections in the small town. All these factors favored an atmosphere of forgiving and forgetting.

The repeated changes in institutional and legal foundations and the shift in the general political climate brought on by the approaching Cold War were not the only barriers to the denazification proceedings.[11] They also faced great practical problems, including local circumstances that were inscrutable to outsiders. This was all the more true because the proceedings were taking place amid collapsing societal conditions and thereby substantially increasing solidarity among the townspeople, who were very vulnerable to economic pressures.[12] Incriminating evidence went unmentioned, and every small disagreement with National Socialist authorities was exaggeratedly portrayed as heroic resistance. This was also an opportunity for the town's more established dignitaries to wield their social clout; they were able to reconsolidate their positions through their function as contact points for "embattled" residents. In Trossingen, it was obvious that no one issued as many "exoneration certificates" (popularly dubbed *Persilscheine*) as Ernst Hohner and the clergy. The manufacturer continued to relieve material suffering in town using the connections and resources of his company, including international ones. From 1946 on, the largest employer, honored citizen, and first deputy mayor held all the cards.

The mayor too put in a good word for the "embattled citizens." Though it was not carried out, he suggested that Ernst Hohner be appointed to the district review committee for the denazification of the economy, believing him to be the "most suitable" candidate, despite his many years of membership in the NSDAP and the variety of positions he had held in the Nazi economic system.[13] At times, the actions taken to benefit incriminated townspeople were coordinated quite publicly. For example, in 1947 Hohner announced in the town council that he would have one of his company's authorized officers "support" the cinema owner in his denazification proceedings and asked those present to provide further exonerating statements.

The case of Christian Messner clearly illuminates the workings of the denazification cartel. In 1945, Kiehn's brother-in-law, as a former Ortsgruppenleiter and acting mayor, was detained within the framework of the "automatic arrests" program imposed by the Allies. The first to testify for his exoneration was his former shop steward, a DAF functionary who now revealed himself to be an old Social Democrat. One of Messner's employees at the sawmill testified that she was the daughter of one of the cofounders of the Trossingen SPD. Moreover, several witnesses (including a lodger of Messner's), both Catholic and Protestant clergy, various former foreign workers, numerous other company employees, and even Ernst Hohner had nothing but good things to say about Messner. Kiehn and Huber, the former Tuttlingen party district leader, said of their fellow prisoner that they had only managed to persuade Messner to take over leadership of the local NSDAP group in 1934 after he had resisted for a long time. It was a matter of protecting the region, they said, since after Kiehn's resignation this post would otherwise have gone to "an undesired, dictatorial tyrant."[14] Kiehn was very obviously endeavoring to make amends for what he had done to his brother-in-law in early 1945, when Kiehn's efforts had gotten Messner caught up in party court proceedings.

The head of the district committee was unimpressed, even though he had no concrete evidence incriminating Messner, apart from his formal position. Nevertheless — and this demonstrates the initial harshness and inflexibility of the proceedings — the sanctions he suggested in 1947 would have destroyed Messner's professional life. "Revocation of his capacity as company chief operating officer for a period of ten years, confiscation of operations for a period of five years. Garnishment of 50 percent of profits for another five years."[15] Faced with this draconian punishment, Messner pinned all his hopes on the denazification court system that was also introduced in the French-occupied zones in the summer of 1947. Almost as soon as he learned the details of this court system, he and Kiehn's former chauffeur requested that the town council support classifying the two of them as "Priority Level I," which would guarantee that their cases be reopened preferentially and that they would be quickly released from the detention camp. The small SPD faction alone was responsible for this request being denied. Although they did not wish "to further burden the prisoners," they also "had no cause to intervene especially on their behalf. ... Besides, the parties concerned have sufficient testimonials from private individuals." The other party factions took the position that, considering the "urgent situation ... the council ... had nothing to lose" by supporting the application. A scant four weeks later, the town council had to consider another application from Messner; he was writing from the labor camp in Balingen to request that the construction of an addition to his sawmill be classified as "urgent." In the pragmatic, reconstruction-focused climate of the council, no one considered that Messner's unfinished denazification trial could be a hindrance to his continued corporate leadership or that they should await the outcome: the "urgency" of the building application was acknowledged without debate. Messner's release was nevertheless delayed until the summer of 1948, when the special denazification court for the Balingen camp ordered Messner to be classified as a "Lesser Offender" and sentenced him to a fine of DM 2,000, legal costs of DM 970, and four years' disenfranchisement.[16] The former Ortsgruppenleiter had been classified in the same offender category as Kiehn, and had remained in prison almost as long as his once-so-influential brother-in-law.

One key motivation that united broad swaths of the local society was bringing the detained sons of the town back home. Neipp and Hohner visited the French authorities repeatedly. In some cases, they managed to lessen conditions of detainment or even prevent arrest; in others, the prisoners were able to work in Trossingen during the week as day laborers from the Balingen camp; this allowed them to stay with their families during the week so that they resided at the camp only on weekends.[17] Amid these efforts, the line between prisoners of war, war criminals, and political offenders became blurred. The dominant view was that each man should return as quickly as possible to his place in society, regardless of what he had done. The town administration repeatedly certified that one Waffen-SS member who had been charged in France with taking part in massacres had come from a "very honorable, peace-loving family." The accused was the real victim, the council asserted, because he had enrolled in the Waffen-SS voluntarily under the impression that he would otherwise suffer the "merciless criticism … of his fellows" who would have derided him as a "shirker" for his deferrals from military service. "Finding him not guilty," therefore, the council averred, should "no longer be a problem."[18]

When Fritz Kiehn began to benefit from the local denazification cartel is unclear. Because of his special position, there were more reservations about him than anyone else. In addition, the proceedings against him were not opened until 1949. Finally, for a long time Kiehn had been used by practically all of the local NSDAP members as a scapegoat to exonerate themselves. It was rare for a denazification proceeding to pass without the defendant asserting that Kiehn had persuaded or compelled him to join the party. Even the pastors, who otherwise exercised leniency toward almost everyone, began with severe accusations against Kiehn. In the later proceedings against Kiehn, however, the clergy and most other Trossingen citizens did not uphold these statements, even though the accusations had been entered into the record multiple times in their own and other proceedings. This throws significant light on denazification practices: evidently, each case was heard separately and records were not shared across cases. This means that a defendant could scapegoat a particular person in order to exonerate him- or herself without incriminating that person in his or her own, later proceedings, even if the case was heard in the same court. CDU politician Thaddäus Mayer, the Staatskommissar für die politische Säuberung (state commissioner for political cleansing, or SK), issued a blistering statement in 1949 that "even the witnesses for the prosecution … were extraordinarily reticent … in front of the denazification court."[19]

It is true that the Trossingen trade unions and the SPD lodged a complaint with the state commissioner for political cleansing against the denazification verdict of "Lesser Offender" for Kiehn. But in the hearing itself, an SPD representative from the Trossingen town council limited himself to statements that would exonerate the defendant, even though in the opinion of the Interior Ministry he must quite obviously have known "something incriminating." The same note also criticized Ernst Hohner for his behavior, saying that he surely could have "made important statements" about Kiehn's actions, but "knew how to keep a low profile so he would not have to testify."[20] Kiehn thus benefited from the silence or evasion of most of the Trossingen witnesses; not even his old adversary Ernst Hohner took advantage of this opportunity to exact vengeance for his humiliations. The workers' movement was divided, to say the least, and evidently did not muster the strength to take a stand against Kiehn. The proceedings against Berta Kiehn, which took place in Ulm, included only two statements for the prosecution, whereas thirty-seven letters were admitted in support of the defendant. Only one of the two negative testimonials was from Trossingen. Despite his appeal early on for leniency in general, this time Mayor Neipp elected to make a clear statement. All other members of his party kept silent.[21]

Decisive in Kiehn's creeping rehabilitation was his importance as an employer and taxpayer, an aspect that was momentous in view of the economic hardship. The Efka factory had experienced growth during the war, up until 1943–1944. During these years the company produced some 8.8 billion cigarette papers each year. The German army was one of Efka's major buyers; cigarette paper was considered a basic need for the troops. Sales in 1944 remained at largely the same level as their peak in 1943. The end of the war in 1945 brought on a collapse, but Efka was the only cigarette paper manufacturer in the three Western zones to come through undamaged. Although production capacity had been lost in Posen and Strasbourg and factories had suffered from the removal of individual machines and general supply problems, company figures show that sales in 1945 still reached 1937 levels — even with only the limited capacity of the Trossingen factory. Average industrial production in the bizone did not return to even 50 percent of 1936 levels until late 1947, and in the French zone at the time, this value stood at 48 percent.[22]

The "changeover necessary because of the occupation" only required the factory to be closed for a week. The number of employees at the Trossingen works dropped from some 200 in the last years of the war to 125 in June 1946. The demand for cigarette paper remained high since demand for this consumer good was anticyclical, rising precisely during difficult times. In this respect business was remarkably good: Efka claimed it held about 70 percent of the German market in 1946.[23]

That this business carried on essentially as usual throughout the tremendous shift in the political system had to do with the fact that Kiehn's absence from the company did not require any great changes, since his political offices had already spurred him to withdraw from day-to-day business much earlier. Immediately after the occupation, the Efka factory was sequestered by the occupying power. Law No. 52 of the Allied Control Council, which the military governments adopted for each of their respective zones, created the legal foundation for the control of assets belonging to the NSDAP, the Reich, its states, and politically incriminated individuals, as well as property of formerly Jewish ownership. On 15 August, general management was handed over to French custodian Paul Schlageter. The Alsatian was from the French cigarette paper sector, so Efka had found its way into qualified hands. Schlageter used his position to benefit the French competition, however, allowing French manufacturer JOB to distribute Efka cigarette papers.[24] This procedure was right in line with French occupation policy, which generally worked to weaken German firms for the benefit of their French competitors. On 28 April 1948, the French forced administration ended when Tübingen's Württembergische Verwaltungs- und Treuhandgesellschaft (WVT) of the Finance Ministry of the state of Württemberg-Hohenzollern assumed control of the Efka factory. Nonetheless, Schlageter's guardianship had long-lasting, deleterious effects: he made use of the insider knowledge he had acquired in Trossingen to engage in the systematic smuggling of French products into Germany that imitated Efka cigarette papers when he worked for the French competitor JOB in 1949–1950. This did great damage to both the German Treasury and the Trossingen firm.[25]

As everywhere else, the shortages in electricity and raw materials hampered the development of the company. According to Efka records, one-third of the machines had also been lost in a frenzy of dismantling, in addition to the regular withdrawals that started later.[26] Nonetheless, the Efka plants recovered quickly. Between 1945 and 1947, sales rose from RM 1.7 to RM 3.3 million. By 1949, the number of Trossingen employees had doubled to 260, significantly exceeding the highest number reached during the war. Return on sales was 34 percent in 1946 and 21 percent in 1947. But the company was struggling at the end of the 1940s as a result of numerous investments, high replacement costs, ongoing restitution payments, irregular capital removals (including those made for Kiehn's benefit), French contraband and an expansionist company policy amid cash flow shortages.

Despite his imprisonment, Kiehn seems to have taken a more active role in his company than he did before 1945. Stays at hospitals and health resorts, passes to leave camp for the day, and people visiting him in the camp gave him a variety of opportunities to do so starting in mid-1948 at the latest. He also used the mail to intervene in details of company management directly from the camp. For example, he instructed the Efka custodian "in strict confidence, not to be disclosed to *anyone*" to disregard the denazification court's verdict when rehiring a former Trossingen employee who had been the leader of the Trossingen SS Motorsturm.

Fig. 31: **No industrialist mansion: the Ermingen homestead.** (Private collection of the Kiehn family)

When the professionally qualified foreman was released from detention, Kiehn wrote, he could not be expected to put up with a three-year exclusion from leadership positions, which would also have an adverse effect on the company. Not least, it threatened to do damage to "job satisfaction," since the foreman was both a "comrade and authority."[27]

After Kiehn's release on 4 January 1949, he was initially prevented from returning to Trossingen because the military government had banned him from the district. Like his family, he therefore went to live in Ermingen first, in the district of Ulm, where his daughter had commissioned the construction of a small cottage using the proceeds from her late husband's life insurance policy (fig. 31). Once the French military vacated the Kiehn vacation home they had occupied in Nußdorf, on Lake Constance, Berta and Fritz Kiehn moved in there. Kiehn opened an office in the American zone in Stuttgart, where he gathered some of his former prison companions around him, including former district leader Huber and former Stuttgart police president Heinrich Wicke.[28] From that point on, Kiehn had his employees and even the official custodian of his Trossingen factory come to Stuttgart for meetings. He also visited the Efka factory in Trossingen, despite the district ban. As Kiehn candidly acknowledged to the state parliamentary review committee in 1951: "After I was released from the camp, I was working for my firm from morning to night."[29] It does not seem to have bothered anyone that he continued to be legally prohibited from taking an active part in the management of said firm.

Furthermore, there is no doubt that at the time when Kiehn's denazification proceedings entered the crucial stage, Efka generated the second-highest business taxes in town, accounting for 31 percent of the total in Trossingen.[30] Indeed, the very lucrative excise tax on cigarettes made Efka the most significant revenue source in the state of Württemberg-Hohenzollern. This is why various other German states attempted to induce Kiehn to relocate his profitable company before consumption taxes were redirected to the German Federal Treasury in April 1950.

In 1949, when Kiehn's rehabilitation came to a standstill, he spread rumors that a transfer of the firm's headquarters was imminent. This threat had a real background, and both state and town politicians took it very seriously.[31] In contrast to the 1920s, when a similar push from Kiehn had failed miserably with the town, this time he knew how to make the most of his talents. In 1949 many in Trossingen feared that an Efka relocation would bring a damaging collapse in tax revenues, an even stronger dependency on the large Hohner corporation, and the loss of 260 jobs. Some thousand residents would be affected by this loss, in a town of around seven thousand five hundred people. The town council and municipal administration, therefore, worked ever harder to justify their inaction in Kiehn's denazification case. They issued the following declaration in August 1949, after the verdict in Kiehn's denazification trial had been quashed for the second time, delaying the conclusion of his denazification process yet again: "We have always had the utmost interest in … retaining the Efka factory, with its capacity to generate revenue and employment opportunities, and still do today. But we have thus far been neutral in the proceedings against Herr Kiehn, and will remain so in the future."[32]

Kiehn mobilized his workforce for the purposes of his rehabilitation and systematically exploited other dependencies. Anyone who did not take part was in for serious disadvantages. A CDU town council and Efka employee of many years was put "on the list" of those to be "extracted" because he had refused "to sign a declaration drafted by Kiehn that was to say that Kiehn had not hounded anyone into the party. … The others signed so that they could keep their jobs. I still remember," a witness testified before the state commissioner for political cleansing, "these events, when … employees went door to door with this declaration." This witness also mentioned a press release in which Efka claimed to have dismissed forty employees for political reasons and indicated that he himself had experienced damage pertaining to his "health and financial life" for pulling out of the local denazification cartel.[33]

Kiehn wanted to achieve three goals in the fall of 1949: to put an end to the custodianship of his company, repeal the district ban affecting him, and accelerate the conclusion of his denazification process. The chair of the Efka works committee, a Social Democrat, managed to get the attention of the highest authorities in the state: he was able to present the matter personally to state commissioner

Mayer, economic minister Mosthaf, a representative of the finance ministry, and even state president Müller. In consequence, Mayer and Müller actually petitioned the military government to lift the district ban, since the relocation of Efka "could have an extraordinarily detrimental effect on the Trossingen economy."[34] When in early December Mayor Neipp went to speak about this delicate matter with the French military governor Jean Lucien Estrade in Tuttlingen, accompanied by the Efka works committee chair and representatives from all political factions in the town council and trade unions, the military governor made the welcome announcement that the district ban on Kiehn had just been lifted. Moreover, Estrade indicated that German authorities would be in charge of political cleansing, effective immediately.

A few days later, the town council addressed a petition the Efka works committee had submitted on 1 December, "with the consent of the entire staff," in light of Kiehn's imminent final denazification hearing. The petition requested that the council renounce its previous neutrality and throw its full support behind "the return of Herr Kiehn as the head of the company." It also invoked "the threatening specter of poverty" and considered the prospect of a mass demonstration in Kiehn's favor that would put pressure on all parties. The key phrase of the petition was the assertion that, "all political reasons aside," the council only needed to recognize "Herr Kiehn's great services to his company and the town of Trossingen."[35]

In the debate in the town council, the SPD and KPD voiced their concerns about losing the Efka factory and their outrage at Kiehn's actions. The rumor that Kiehn had demanded Neipp's dismissal as a condition of his return aroused particular outrage — the mayor had been the only Trossingen citizen to incriminate Berta Kiehn in her denazification proceedings. KPD councilor Kunz, who as a political and social outsider was on the margins of the small-town society, not only believed there was a capitalist conspiracy at the factory, but also complained about the inconsistency of his fellow citizens: he pointed out that "everyone was grousing in 1945" and had fingered Kiehn as the chief culprit. "Hanging seemed to them an insufficient punishment. The same people are back at it again today, calling for him. It is deeply regrettable that the very people who were known detractors of National Socialism have publicly taken Fritz Kiehn's side today." In fact, even council members whom Kiehn had stripped of their offices in 1933 but who had now been reelected were advocating his return. The dominant party in the town council, the DVP, scarcely participated in the debate. Ernst Hohner, the local top dog, politically, remained silent. Kunz was therefore the only person to take up Estrade's suggestion at the end of the meeting; the military governor had been critical of "the public's" short memory and had encouraged a public meeting to discuss Kiehn's role during the Third Reich and the town's dealings with him. This request met with overall disapproval from the town council. The mayor even expressed the fear that doing so would bring out "the shouters," and that those with "respectable" views would "stay home."[36]

In the end, the mayor's proposal to accelerate Kiehn's proceeding was accepted unanimously, which at this point was tantamount to a vote for Kiehn's rehabilitation. No one wanted to be responsible for unemployment and declining tax revenues and thus making enemies of the Efka employees and their families.[37] While not all the concerns about Kiehn had disappeared from Trossingen by late 1949, it is not difficult to discern the sources of the townspeople's uncertainty and disquiet. The council decisions quoted above were anything but votes of confidence. With the exception of Kiehn's own family and friends, as well as the Efka workforce, most residents did not intend to welcome him with open arms, but they were also wary of rejecting him outright. Rather, they agreed to tacitly accept Kiehn as an employer and taxpayer and let bygones be bygones. Like everywhere else in the young Federal Republic of Germany, this developed into a stable consensus to repress the past.[38] It is unsurprising that even in Trossingen, the long road from the townspeople's condemnation of Kiehn to their capitulation out of what appeared to be necessity was traveled relatively quickly.

Notes

1. See interview by Hartmut Berghoff of 10 May 1993; StAT, Häffner interview collection; LKAS, Allg. Registratur Trossingen, Pfarrbericht 1949; Häffner, Ruff, and Schrumpf, *Trossingen*, 244–245, 527.
2. See StAT, Häffner interview collection; StAT, B 91, Beilage 6, activity report of police guards; Häffner, Ruff, and Schrumpf, *Trossingen*, 249, 528.
3. In northern Württemberg and Baden, some two hundred villages were destroyed and more than two thousand civilians killed in the first three weeks of April 1945. See Henke, *Besetzung*, 777–795.
4. StAT, B 91, Beilage 6, activity report of police guards, p. 2. See Berghoff, *Kleinstadt*, 515–522; Wolfrum, *Französische Besatzungspolitik*. In contrast, see Henke, *Besetzung*, 364–366, 695, on the comparatively orderly actions of the American occupiers in southern Germany.
5. StAT, A 1221, report on morale from the mayor of 7 Nov. 1945.
6. StAT, B 90, mayoral decree of 2 Nov. 1945.
7. StAT, A 1221, mayor's report on activities and morale of 6 Dec. 1945.
8. StAT, B 91, labor committee proceedings of 26 Apr. 1946.
9. StAT, B 91, labor committee hearings of 28 Aug. 1945.
10. StAT, B 91, GRP of 22 Sept. 1946.
11. For general information, see Henke, *Politische Säuberung*, 168–175; Rauh-Kühne, "Die Unternehmer," 330–331; Rauh-Kühne, "Entnazifizierung."
12. See Henke, "Grenzen," 130; Woller, *Gesellschaft und Politik*, 126–137.
13. He would then have been able to have an impact on his own denazification proceedings. See StAT, A 1633, letter from Neipp to district administrator of 15 Jan. 1946. On Hohner's strong position, see Berghoff, *Kleinstadt*, 515–522, 527–532, 593–600.
14. StAS, Wü 13, Bü 2287 (Messner denazification records), Kiehn's affidavit of 5 Feb. 1948, featuring Huber's signature.

15. Ibid. On this course of events, which was characteristic of early denazification efforts of the economy in southern Württemberg, see Rauh-Kühne, "Unternehmer."
16. StAT, B 92, GRP of 24 Oct. and 18 Nov. 1947. See also StAS, Wü 13, Bü 2287 (Messner denazification records).
17. The standard wording used by Hohner: "Our factory has large export delivery obligations, so that we urgently require each and every specialized worker." WABW, B 35 II, Bü 826, letter from Hohner to the Balingen labor camp director of 12 June 1946. See also MAE Colmar, AEF C 547/35, various reports from the French economic administration.
18. StAT, A 1632, "official certification" of the Trossingen municipal administration of 28 July 1950.
19. StAS, Wü 13, T2 no. 2775/001, http://www.landesarchiv-bw.de/plink/?f=6-1039573 (accessed 4 Sept. 2012), letter to local SPD branch in Trossingen of 24 June 1949.
20. StAS, Wü 13, T2 no. 2775/001, http://www.landesarchiv-bw.de/plink/?f=6-1039573 (accessed 4 Sept. 2012), confidential note from the interior minister of 5 May 1949. See chap. 10.
21. StAL, EL 902/22, Bü 1502 (Berta Kiehn denazification records), letter from Neipp to Ulm regional denazification tribunal of 14 Mar. 1947 and 5 Feb. 1948.
22. Abelshauser, *Wirtschaftsgeschichte*, 34; see Manz, *Stagnation*, 17–19.
23. StAT, A 932, short report from the French sequestrator of 12 June 1946.
24. See ibid.; MAE Colmar, AEF C 517/76, contract of the custodian for Efka and the Eislingen paper factory of 21 Apr. 1947; StAS, Wü 1, Bü 100, note from the Finance Ministry regarding Efka of 2 June 1950; letter from Herbert E. Kiehn to the authors of 12 Dec. 1998; Häffner, Ruff, and Schrumpf, *Trossingen*, 261.
25. MAE Colmar, WH C 3541 d 11, Affaire Kiehn.
26. See Anon., *Fritz Kiehn*, 27. On the dismantling practices in the French zones, see Henke, "Widersprüche."
27. StAS, Wü 120/362, letter from Kiehn to judge, date illegible.
28. A witness testified before the PUA in 1950 that "a purely National Socialist tone" prevailed in Kiehn's office; "Heil Hitler" was a common greeting. StAS, Wü 1, Bü 100a, PUA, 6th public meeting, p. 24. On Wicke, see Müller, *Stuttgart*, 501; Wilhelm, "Württembergische Polizei," 313–315.
29. StAS, Wü 1, Bü 100a, PUA, 8th public meeting, p. 53.
30. Hohner paid 50 percent. Commercial taxes were the main source of local revenue. StAT, B 94, GRP of 11 Mar. 1949.
31. StAS, Wü 1, Bü 100a, PUA, 8th public meeting, pp. 34–36, statement from Sieger, Kiehn's attorney.
32. StAT, B 94, GRP of 15 Aug. 1949.
33. StAS, Wü 13, T2 no. 2775/001, http://www.landesarchiv-bw.de/plink/?f=6-1039573 (accessed 4 Sept. 2012), letter to the SK of 4 Jan. 1951.
34. Ibid., SK Mayer to Commissaire de la Rep. Française of 25 Nov. 1949.
35. StAT, B 94, GRP of 12 Dec. 1949.
36. Ibid. A published version of Estrade's notes is available; see Estrade, *Tuttlingen*.
37. Ibid. The council's decision did not further accelerate the proceedings. On the waning enthusiasm for political cleansing, see Rauh-Kühne, "Life."
38. See Frei, *Vergangenheitspolitik*; Berghoff, "Verdrängung."

Chapter 10

"Scot-Free, by the Skin of Their Teeth"
Denazification and Compensation

In hindsight, the integration of former proponents of the Nazi regime into postwar German society seems to have happened all too quickly and smoothly. This is all the more true in view of the human suffering that the regime inflicted on its victims, for whom compensation attempts, in most cases, came far too late. Finally, we must also consider the material and moral burdens that the German state and German society are still struggling with generations after the end of the war.

Nonetheless, we should not overlook the complications that arose when perpetrators returned to "normal everyday life": it was frequently not as straightforward and untroubled as it may have appeared in retrospect.[1] The example of Fritz Kiehn can illustrate the magnitude of this watershed moment in the biographies of Nazi elites in the postwar era and their temporary ostracism from mainstream society. In Württemberg, Kiehn was one of those who spent the longest in prison. Not until January 1949, after three years and eight months of internment, was the almost 65-year-old once again a free man. The military government and German authorities alike rightly feared that releasing the "Nazi industrialist" back into the public would awaken resentments and be interpreted as confirmation of the accusation that denazification was only for the smaller fish while worse offenders were let off the hook. Kiehn had gone through fourteen camps, in either American or French custody; he had been interrogated on multiple occasions and for a time had been seriously ill. When Kiehn was temporarily put into a Tuttlingen police prison in March 1946 and questioned by the Sécurité of the French military government after doing time in American custody, he noted in his diary the "very comfortable" conditions and praised the "humane treatment" he received during his interrogation, "a pleasant contrast" to his experiences up to

---

Notes from this chapter begin on page 221.

that point. Shortly thereafter, without discernible reason, the war criminal investigation (Brigade de recherches des criminels de guerre) called for Kiehn to be transferred to the so-called war criminals' camp in Reutlingen. He was regarded as a "presumptive war criminal"; his assets were expected to be confiscated.[2]

The German institutions responsible for "cleansing" proceeded with the denazification of the southern Württemberg economy with great seriousness until the summer of 1947, and the military government — in haphazard fashion — further intensified these efforts. Those who had distinguished themselves as activists were subject to harsh penalties, as were those in exposed social positions who had become "followers" and thus set a bad example. At the time, this led to businessmen whose political offenses were only minor compared to Kiehn's being sentenced to lengthy, sometimes lifelong bans on doing business, at the suggestion of the denazification committees at the district level.[3] Many received heavy fines of hundreds of thousands of Reichsmarks or through the confiscation of all of their assets.[4] Beginning in the spring of 1947, however, the anti-Fascist consensus that had often been invoked in the first months after the collapse of the Nazi regime began to disappear. The Cold War altered the political priorities of the occupying powers. The military government's often arbitrary interventions in the cleansing proceedings, and the hardships for some affected individuals, brought denazification into discredit. The denazification proceedings targeted at establishing individual guilt were adopted from the American zone and introduced in French-occupied Württemberg-Hohenzollern from 1 July 1947. The rigorous verdicts from previous cleansing proceedings could now be challenged. This generated the prospect of a lenient outcome for Kiehn as well, whose denazification proceedings still had not even begun. The saying that "life punishes latecomers" was reversed for him and for the bulk of Nazi offenders.[5]

In September 1947, Kiehn arrived at the Balingen labor camp, the internment center in the Swabian Alps where two to three thousand people had once been interned as part of the "automatic arrests" by the French military government of southern Württemburg. The dismantling of Efka equipment that had been feared was not carried out. At the time Kiehn was taken to Balingen, the French military government had just transferred oversight of the camp to the Württemberg state government. There were still some seven hundred internees, whose political positions during the Nazi era had varied enormously. Most of them had been Nazi functionaries at the Kreis (135) or local group level (445), as well as some of middling rank in the SA and SS (174). Civil servants, most of them teachers, were especially numerous. The few remaining had belonged to the NSDAP at the Reich or Gau level. In spring 1947, there were still sixty-one internees from the Tuttlingen Kreis alone.[6] Kiehn was one of the oldest. Just as he had experienced at the American camp in Ludwigsburg, Kiehn encountered many political companions in Balingen from years before: relatives like his brother-in-law Messner, the former Trossingen Ortsgruppenleiter; close confidants like former Tuttlingen Kreisleiter Gottlieb Huber; once sought-after acquaintances like Württemberg minister-president and cultural affairs minister Mergenthaler and economic minister Oswald Lehnich; and adversaries from within the party, such as former Gauamtsleiter for technology and current cement manufacturer Rudolf Rohrbach.[7]

For those at the camp who were fit for work, everyday life was shaped by their deployment to nearby factories. Monotony marked the days of those who were not. There appear to have been no measures at the camp for either political reeducation or diversion.[8] It was an open secret at Efka that one of the workers regularly supplied food to the boss interned in Balingen. What's more, Kiehn — and presumably other camp internees — frequently attended the Paradies café in Balingen, where he received family members, his attorney, and Efka managers, including the official custodian.[9] Presumably, such lax conditions only became the rule in Balingen when the camp came under German supervision. Even in early summer 1947, the prisoners had been prohibited from receiving care packages with food, and a strict military routine was expected so as to maintain order. At the beginning of 1948, however, it was declared in the state parliament that "the most radical National Socialists in the Balingen internment camp occupy the leading positions … [they] terrorize the reasonable elements, exclude them from the community as traitors to National Socialism, and assign them tough, dirty jobs."[10] Kiehn remained completely inconspicuous, staying out of any sort of office at the camp; in later years he said little about his internment experience. Comments by his wife testify that despite his unbroken talent for organization and the use of bribes to make prison life easier, the internment years left deep scars. She repeatedly complained to her grandsons of her husband's "camp psychosis" in the years that followed and indicated that Fritz Kiehn never fully returned to his old self after coming back from the internment camp (fig. 32).[11]

But Kiehn undoubtedly developed noteworthy activities from within the camp that not only benefited his company but also, by all appearances, served his interests in obtaining a lenient denazification verdict for his wife. Unlike her husband, and indeed unlike most former district heads of the National Socialist Women's League of Württemberg, Berta Kiehn escaped a prison sentence.[12] She lived with her daughter and grandchild in the American occupied zone for almost two years, undisturbed by the authorities, and passed herself off in her new place of residence in the Ulm district as an evacuee from Berlin. Berta and her daughter were able to settle into a home of their own in 1948 that local villagers in Ermingen had helped them to build (see fig. 31, in chap. 9). The fraud was discovered when a municipal employee denounced them. As a "new resident" from the east, the Ermingen villagers had welcomed him less wholeheartedly than the Swabians who had claimed to come from Berlin. It may be that he had therefore made some inquiries into Berta Kiehn. As a consequence, the political assessment

Fig. 32: Kiehn, "not fully his old self," with his wife and daughter after his release from internment. (Private collection of the Kiehn family)

on Berta Kiehn found its way to the denazification court, that, per curiam, Mayor Neipp had made a month before, as discussed in the previous chapter. Neipp's judgment of "the wife of well-known Nazi delegate to the Reichstag Fritz Kiehn" asserted that she had often appeared publicly as the district commissioner of the NSF and had been "very ruthless" in her "hate campaign against dissenters." The industrialist's wife, he wrote, had made use of every opportunity to induce others to join the Nazi organization. He also made negative comments about her departure from the church, the feasting at Deibhalde with "SS-Himmler" and "other important Nazi figures," and her escape from town, which allegedly had been carried out using a "large long-haul truck."[13] As a result of Neipp's judgments, the public prosecutor of the Ulm denazification court classified Berta Kiehn as an activist.[14] The Law for Liberation from National Socialism and Militarism[15] stipulated four categories of incrimination: these ranged from "Major Offenders" to "Offenders" and "Lesser Offenders," and finally "Followers." Anyone acquitted of sharing any responsibility for National Socialism went into the group of "Persons Exonerated." Berta Kiehn's classification as an activist put her at risk of being declared an "Offender" by the court, which could involve sentencing her to time at a labor camp.[16]

Her Ulm attorney, therefore, endeavored to prove "that Frau K., as a 56-year-old woman" had been harshly affected by the Law for Liberation[17] simply by virtue of being formally incriminated. Fritz Kiehn's attempts to produce material that would exonerate him in his own denazification proceedings, for which he needed a lot of money and people to help him, were very likely also undertaken to benefit his wife. A new family friend well versed in the law, Dr. Werner Kaufmann, proved to be both committed and imaginative in his work for this cause. Kaufmann, a former assistant to Ferdinand Porsche, had supervised the establishment of the Volkswagen factory and later worked as an "industrial lawyer" at AEG. Soon rumors were circulating that this young man with industrial experience, a friend of Gretl Kiehn's deceased husband Ernst Fähndrich, would become Kiehn's son-in-law.[18] Whether such talk was founded on reality is unknown. What is certain, however, is that Kaufmann soon had a reputation for miles around as Kiehn's "denazification manager." Bearing a writ of power of attorney that Fritz Kiehn had signed over from within the internment camp, Kaufmann — officially declared a "substitute" — went back and forth among the denazification offices, traveling around the region and amassing an impressive raft of exoneration certificates (*Persilscheine*). He was skilled at pushing his requests through using financial donations and promises of all kinds. There are many signs that he ordered the disposal of a variety of incriminating material: the state parliamentary review committee later dubbed him "Manager of Making Records Disappear." Kaufmann himself, who denied any manipulations, admitted that in 1950 he had procured new positions at Efka for the secretary of the state commissioner for political cleansing, as well as her jobless husband. With denazification winding down, the woman had been on the lookout for new employment prospects.[19] Kaufmann's headhunting work for Kiehn cannot have come cheap, because the new employee was anything but undemanding. The one-time secretary knew how to take advantage of her formerly key position, helping a long line of incriminated business owners whitewash their Nazi involvement. When large-scale denazification abuses were discovered in early 1950 in the neighboring federal state of Württemberg-Baden, the trail led to Württemberg-Hohenzollern as well, right up to the state commissioner's secretary. Visitors who came seeking advice on experienced attorneys were referred by Frau H. directly to a "denazification broker" who was at the center of the "denazification scandal" in Württemberg-Baden for actively bribing the chief prosecutor of Stuttgart's central denazification court.[20]

Kaufmann's methods were thus neither unique nor limited to the French zone. On the contrary, they characterized the late stages of denazification, in which the enthusiasm for "cleansing" had generally subsided as corruption flourished and new, albeit short-lived job titles, such as "denazification assistant," sprang up. Moneyed professionals were not the smallest group to benefit from this development, many of whom were still waiting to be rehabilitated in appellate proceedings. According to some information that cannot be verified, Kaufmann drove over thirty thousand miles to "assemble denazification materials" and paid out DM 100,000 toward "preliminary work on Herr Kiehn's denazification."

This friend of the family, documented in the Efka books as a "sales representative," lined up the necessary money by invoicing excessive commissions and expenses and giving the company custodian no reason to intervene.[21]

As a result of Kaufmann's efforts, there were thirty-six exoneration certificates available for Berta Kiehn's defense plea, lodged by her lawyer in spring 1948. With very few exceptions, these were *Persilscheine*, or whitewashing certificates, which those familiar with Kiehn's social circle had little trouble recognizing as the favors they were. Their issuers included several Efka employees; a girlfriend of Berta's, Ragnhild Bärlin, the wife of the former mayor of Trossingen; and Elly Beinhorn, Gretl Kiehn's aviatrix friend and the widow of renowned racecar driver Bernd Rosemeyer. But they also came from "Displaced Persons," former foreign workers, and evacuees. They had been employed in Kiehn's private household or at Efka or for the wife of their former employer (or sometimes accommodation provider), attesting that they had been treated with "kindheartedness and deeply felt humanity" by "married couple Fritz and Berta Kiehn."[22] The affidavits signed by Estonians and Latvians were formulated in impeccable German, though some had no signature, only the "X" customary among illiterates. A number of exoneration certificates featured the addresses of various internment camps, which did not improve the appearance of political integrity among their authors.

On the other hand, the Ulm denazification court must have been mollified that a recognized "victim of fascism," Lolo Mattheiß, the widow of police president Hermann Mattheiß, who had been executed by firing squad in 1934, also became an advocate for Berta Kiehn and declared that the Kiehns, just like her husband, had supported Gregor Straßer's direction for the party. According to her, they had "adamantly opposed the dictatorship and Himmler's system of violence." She had known "Herr and Frau Kiehn since 1930" and knew them to be "most decent, noble, and readily obliging people." In the summer of 1934, they had provided her and her husband (murdered shortly thereafter) with access to their vacation house in Nußdorf at "great personal risk" as a means of escaping "Himmler's pursuit."[23]

Hers was a very idiosyncratic representation of the roles Hermann Mattheiß and Kiehn had played. The denazification court was impressed, nonetheless, especially in view of the sheer abundance of exoneration materials. This is why, scarcely a year after its initial requests for information, the court sent another message to Trossingen to verify whether the negative assessment submitted from there was accurate. Mayor Neipp did not waver, declaring that the information about Berta Kiehn's political past had been "kept extremely modest." This was an accurate assessment; Neipp had even suppressed details that he had ascertained through renewed questioning of those who had faced political persecution in Trossingen. These details included Berta Kiehn being the "only woman" in 1933 to have taken a tour of the Heuberg and Kuhberg concentration camps in southern Württemberg, in the company of camp commanders who had since been sentenced to death. She was also said to have denounced others — with dire consequences for the targets of her accusations.

The denazification court heard nothing about this. Instead, it was confronted with a defense plea from Berta Kiehn's attorney, according to which the former NSF leader had "in reality" been "only caring, charitable, and helpful, but in no way politically active." The defense rested on an affidavit from former Kreisleiter Gottlieb Huber, which devoted not a single word to his friendly relationship with the Kiehns but certified that Frau Kiehn had dedicated herself to the tasks "that particularly suited her as a housewife and mother and are carried out in similar fashion in religious women's associations as well." For example, she had given "courses in home economics, nutrition, nursing, infant care, [and] treatment of the sick and wounded" and had rendered outstanding service in the district "helping neighbors" and in "general social welfare work." This was the classic exoneration discourse, the same one that by the summer of 1948 had already proved successful in the denazification proceedings of numerous female National Socialist activists. If men facing the denazification courts invoked the chaotic political conditions of the Weimar Republic, economic hardship, their social efforts, and above all their love for the fatherland as motives for their political commitment to the NSDAP, the basic tenor of female defendants was wholly apolitical: "As women, they had had nothing to do with politics during National Socialism, because women ... were not interested in such things and understood none of it."[24] The position or political actions of their husbands, on the other hand, always played a certain role in the proceedings.

Berta Kiehn's defense counsel applied a similar argument when he stated, "in 1930, when she became a member of the newly created local Nazi group in Trossingen at her husband's encouragement, she completely lacked any form of political orientation." At that time, no one had been able to believe "in Hitler's possible despotism ... least of all a hitherto apolitical woman. ... Added to this was the fact that her husband Kiehn was a friend of Gregor Straßer, and they remained unwavering in this friendship through Gregor Straßer's fall ... up until his execution in 1934, regardless of the grave danger to themselves." Apolitical, yet somehow oppositional was the concise formula used in the paradoxical defense strategy of Berta Kiehn's attorney, who in a stereotypical manner also tried to make a plausible case that his client had only taken up the position of director of the NSF at the repeated urging of the Kreisleiter. He stated that the Gauleitung had been extremely dissatisfied with how she executed her office: "She was considered to be not politically active enough, too middle-class, too fond of the church, too candid in her criticism of National Socialist measures." According to her attorney, Berta Kiehn had never ascribed to Nazi racial theory. Her husband had maintained "friendly relations with Jews to the end" and had Jewish sales representatives. Once again, Gottlieb Huber provided substantiation for the claim. The former Kreisleiter, who at the time in question was no longer even in office, claimed to have heard that Berta Kiehn had incurred the "bitter antagonism of the Gauleitung" and as a result had been monitored by the SD. His successor as Kreisleiter had ultimately relieved her of her office in 1944.[25] Finally, a former staff officer at Himmler's field command office testified that the visits the Reichsführer-SS paid to Deibhalde in winter 1944–1945 had been seen in entirely the wrong light in Trossingen. Fritz Kiehn's residence, he said, had been "seized" by the field command office and "used as accommodation for certain of Himmler's guests." Himmler had stayed in Trossingen on purely official business and had never boozed it up at the Kiehn family's expense; on the contrary, "food and drink … were delivered by the special field command train, as was the waitstaff."[26]

Impressed by the multitude of exoneration certificates and above all by the testimony of the widow Mattheiß, the court ruled in favor of the defense plea:[27] in consideration of her poor health, Berta Kiehn was denazified in writing; she learned by mail of her declaration as a "Lesser Offender." Despite being an industrialist's wife, she qualified as indigent, because the Kiehns' business and personal property was still sequestered; consequently, her penalty amounted to only RM 1,000. She also had to pay RM 400 in legal costs. Berta Kiehn settled these debts a few days before the currency reform, that is, with money that had lost most of its former value. However, she made no move to perform the twenty days of community service she had been sentenced to. Instead, she submitted an application in summer 1948 to be reclassified "as a Follower [*Mitläufer*] in subsequent proceedings," invoking the second amendment to the Law for Liberation that had taken effect in the American zone on 25 March 1948. It worked "like an amnesty for the heavily incriminated" and ensured that at the end of the denazification procedure, both "equal and unequal" groups ended up in the same "innocuous category of mere followers." This was because, in the American zone, "Offenders" and "Minor Offenders" could be recategorized as "Followers" by means of rapid proceedings whose verdict was not subject to review by the military government.[28] This is how Berta Kiehn was ultimately downgraded to a mere "Follower."

Whereas Fritz Kiehn's wife had thus made it through denazification unscathed, there was still no end in sight to his imprisonment. Although practically no one believed at that point that he would have to permanently relinquish his company, which had been placed under custodianship, worrisome things were going on at Efka. The image of his Efka trademark was at risk of being diluted under the influence of a French sequestrator. The French competition was pushing into the German market with goods produced in Trossingen. The German Treasury had put forward horrendous tax claims. The rightful owners of the factory, which Kiehn had obtained through its Aryanization, were suing for compensation. What's more, some of his staff had not hesitated to line their own pockets. By the time of the currency reform at the latest, when Kiehn needed to position his own company in the new market, he must have realized that this situation could threaten his livelihood.

As a result, when the currency reform caused custodianship of his company to be transferred to the Württembergische Verwaltungs- und Treuhand (WVT) in May 1948, Kiehn immediately used the opportunity to win over the new sequestrator through generous payments and promises. Before losing all of his assets in the war, Albrecht Richter had owned his own business in Silesia. He now earned just DM 850 per month working for the WVT. This was too little to keep him from looking out for lucrative sidelines. Fritz Kiehn seems to have recognized the opportunity right away: from the beginning of Richter's role as custodian in May 1948, Kiehn gradually took back control over his firm's operations, even though his denazification proceedings at first caused renewed vexation in March 1949. This time, trade union representatives from the ranks of the Tuttlingen district review committee attempted to persuade Kiehn to transform his company into a cooperative by dangling the prospect of a beneficial outcome to his denazification proceedings. But these local attempts at turning individual into collective property lacked political backing from either the state or the military government.[29] On the other hand, it soon became apparent that the ambitions and demands of his company's new custodian went further than Kiehn had bargained for.

Richter's trusteeship for Kiehn started out on a comfortable footing. When the Fleischer family filed a claim for restitution, Richter helped Kiehn obtain a ten-day leave from the camp. The intervention of the French officer in charge of monitoring the camp put an abrupt end to this leave, however.[30] Richter had requested that the Efka owner come to the WVT for work because he considered it desirable to talk through the details of "what had led to the purchase in 1940 of the factory in Eislingen belonging to Herr Fleischer ... with Herr Fritz Kiehn personally."[31]

Businessmen Hermann and Walter Fleischer (who had emigrated to England) had already contacted the Eislingen factory's trustee in February 1946 and asserted their claims to ownership. Their uncle, Kuno Fleischer, who lived in the United States, had now also submitted a restitution claim. His two children had emigrated before their parents had. The son, Kurt Fleischer, had been killed fighting for the Americans in the Pacific; the daughter had participated in the invasion of Europe as a nurse.[32] David M. Fleischer, the oldest family member involved in the partnership, had died on 12 February 1945 in England. The rest of the family, except for the daughter, had survived the war, but "with great difficulty." German bombs had completely destroyed the Fleischer sons' paper factory, located in a London suburb. Walter Fleischer told a loyal Eislingen employee of the tragedies the family had endured: "The parents of our wives — harmless people who lived a secluded life — were massacred and gassed by executioners, some in France, some in Poland. They disappeared without a trace; practically our wives' entire families were eradicated."[33]

In summer 1947, Hermann Fleischer suddenly surfaced as an officer of the British army in the war criminals' camp in Reutlingen. There he interrogated Kiehn about the events leading to the Aryanization of the Eislingen factory. According to Kiehn's statements, "Colonel Fleischer" also appeared before the municipal administration in Trossingen and allegedly demanded a sum of RM 1.3 million in addition to the return of the paper factory in Eislingen, as well as the Efka factory itself, in order to compensate his family for their loss of assets and income.[34] During his interrogation of Kiehn, Hermann Fleischer obviously left no doubt that he held the person sitting opposite him chiefly responsible for robbing his family. He accused the buyer of his father's company, along with his "advisor" Stäbler and Glaub, the Stuttgart banker involved in Aryanizations, of concerted blackmail. "He badgered me for two hours in the most dreadful manner," wrote an outraged Kiehn years later, complaining of the "tremendously impertinent, overbearing way" Fleischer had behaved toward him and of how he had "fed" on Kiehn's misfortune.[35] Fleischer had also denounced Stäbler in plain words to the Tuttlingen police, describing his role as an "instigator and accomplice of Kiehn's," and Stäbler himself as a "profiteer and blackmailer, economic highwayman and vulture."[36]

But before a denazification or ordinary court could address the allegations against Kiehn and his intermediaries, a mediator from the restitution court in Ulm mandated the immediate return of the Eislingen factory in summer 1948 in a partial settlement reached with the Jewish former owners.[37] Extrajudicial agreements appear to have been reached about additional financial claims in the amount of approximately DM 750,000.[38]

The degrading circumstances of the change in ownership played no role before the reparations court, where the civil legal framework established by the restitution law defined the limits of how National Socialist injustice could be dealt with.[39] The fact that Kiehn had knowingly acquired the factory from Jews was enough to formally justify a restitution claim, so the question of the buyer's personal responsibility for the damages and suffering of the Aryanization victims went unaddressed in the proceedings. Whereas Stäbler had represented Kiehn's interests during Aryanization, as his authorized representative, during the restitution phase the custodian of Kiehn's company, Richter, and Kiehn's attorney handled the details. From Kiehn's perspective, the return of the Eislingen factory unfolded as an anonymous bureaucratic act, just like its acquisition. It only left traces in the company accounts, as tax-deductible operational expenses.[40] Kiehn later stated that he personally had "never seen a member of the Fleischer family and thus [had] never negotiated with any of them," apart from the encounter with Hermann Fleischer that he had found so unpleasant. The utmost discretion was used in the restitution of the Eislingen factory — the same factory that ten years prior had been so disgracefully taken from its rightful owners. There was neither a moral reckoning with the "perpetrators" and beneficiaries nor any form of *symbolic* atonement for the victims before the mediators of the restitution chamber. Public opinion did not generally favor the victims at that time:[41] the very discretion with which most restitution proceedings were handled courted the misunderstanding that monetary damages were the only matter at hand. The suffering of Jews affected by Aryanization measures remained largely hidden in the postwar era, as did the coarse and immoral methods many buyers of Aryanized property employed. In addition, the decision makers within the restitution courts often revealed themselves to be biased; frequently these were people who had loyally served the Nazi regime and who were not free of anti-Semitism.[42] As late as the 1960s, there was intense agitation by so-called victims of restitution, who articulated their interests as loudly as the "denazification victims" had done before them.[43] Even in 1969, representatives of the governing coalition relabeled the reparations payments of those required to pay them a "special sacrifice for the Federal Republic" before the German Bundestag.[44] This long sustained an image of Germany's Nazi past in which the "National Socialist state" alone "was responsible for the private 'Aryanizations,' and not the profiteers themselves."[45]

The Jewish victims of Kiehn's Aryanizations did not gain any satisfaction from Kiehn's denazification proceedings either, which we will cover in more detail below. When the Tuttlingen district review committee (Kreisuntersuchungsausschuss, or KRUA) took up the case in April 1948, all of the locals involved were eager for Kiehn to be rehabilitated — because of the employment issue — and for the ban on his residing in the district to be lifted. This is why they did not wish to see Kiehn emerge from his denazification court proceedings as an "Offender" in any way, shape, or form, regardless of the good reasons for such a verdict.[46] Even though the committee could not refrain from establishing "that the elements of an Aryanization were formally fulfilled in the Eislingen case," they agreed that "the special circumstances of this case" forbade them from "classifying [Kiehn] as an Offender, with the far-reaching consequences the law attaches to this classification." The committee had access to a wealth of incriminating material on Kiehn's Aryanization deals, including the letter in which Kiehn had appealed to his SS legal adviser for "comradely help" in the proceedings before the Party Supreme Court. In it, he had stated: "If I emerge 'reformed' from these proceedings, it is the Herr Reichsführer-SS's point of view that there should be nothing to stand in the way of the Fleischer paper factory being transferred to me."[47] The KRUA, which only a year before had advocated a rigorous cleansing process to the state commissioner and the denazification courts,[48] now sympathetically declared in Kiehn's case:

> The defendant's interest ... in the Eislingen factory cannot be held against him as a political transgression, since purely economic interests were decisive here: the committee has just as little ability to especially incriminate the defendant on account of this;

he later tried by every means to obtain the permit for his intended purchases, because his efforts in this respect were not directed against the Fleischer family but against the attempts by Gauleiter Murr and Streicher to stand in his way. Naturally he could only defend himself against these by harnessing political authorities for his own cause, in this case probably the Reichsführung-SS.[49]

Witness Hermann Fleischer's allegations that Kiehn and his intermediaries had put political pressure on the Fleischer company owners were tersely dismissed as "inherently untenable." Obviously completely uninformed about the Gauleitung's Aryanization practices, the committee failed to see why it might have made a lot of sense for Kiehn's faction to threaten the sellers even *after* they had already signed their company over to Kiehn. Yet at the time Kiehn decided to buy the Fleischer paper factory, legal transactions with Jews had no coercive validity unless they had been sanctioned by the Gauleitung, even if these had been notarized. One can easily imagine, then, that until the Kiehn-Fleischer contract had cleared all bureaucratic hurdles, Kiehn and his representatives would have done their utmost to prevent the sellers from engaging in other negotiations with purchasers more to the Gau economic adviser's liking. "Well-meant" warnings of ostensibly imminent attacks could therefore be an expedient in inducing the Fleischer family to abandon their home address for the foreseeable future.[50]

The cleansing committee did not put the pieces together and ascribed no importance to the impressive accounts from Fleischer's main witness, the auditor Mayer. Nor did the committee make any effort to find out how another purchase contract between the Fleischers and Schickedanz could have sprung up so quickly after the contract with Kiehn. Instead, they wrote off Hermann Fleischer as an unreliable witness and subsequently characterized this victim of the Nazis as a liar. The committee preferred to rely on the statement from Kiehn's lackey, Tuttlingen merchant Otto Stäbler, who had been accused by various witnesses of exerting pressure during the sale negotiations. Stäbler, who along with Kiehn and Glaub, the banker, was being sued in the Rottweil Regional Court for blackmail, not only denied having pressured the Fleischers but also disputed that he had been Kiehn's plenipotentiary at all. David M. Fleischer had commissioned Glaub's bank to do the sale negotiations, Stäbler claimed, and he himself "had made every attempt to save what could be saved for the Fleischer family."[51] This was untrue, but it could not be disproven by the committee. A few months later Stäbler was acquitted of the blackmail charge because of insufficient evidence, while the proceedings against Kiehn and Glaub were abandoned.[52] A close reading of the grounds for the verdict, however, makes it clear that none of the three defendants could disprove the numerous witness allegations that they had repeatedly and severely threatened the Jewish owners of the Eislingen factory. The court merely came to the conclusion that instrumentalizing the latent and constant danger — which increased dramatically in 1938 — that all Jews faced in the

National Socialist state in order to benefit one's own business did not satisfy the definition of blackmail. The penal code, as this case also documents, was very limited in its scope for punishing individuals involved in persecution practices legitimized by the state.[53]

At any rate, Stäbler was considered a "personnage plus que douteux" (a very suspicious individual) in the French military government as well, where it had been disclosed that even though he was a Freemason and not a Nazi party comrade, he had been close to Kiehn and to Gottlob Berger, the director of the SS Head Office, and had given Berger expensive gifts. In return, his Chiron factories — already expanded through Reich subsidies for large-scale weapons manufacturing — received production commissions from the SS.[54]

Stäbler and Kiehn, both provincial industrialists, had been interconnected since the early 1920s in a series of business deals as dubious as they were lucrative. Stäbler's sideline in Stuttgart as a banker and financial adviser of sorts always played an important role in these ventures. When the the Klöckner-Humboldt-Deutz AG corporation resold the Magirus shares in 1936, for example, Stäbler collected a commission to the tune of RM 106,000.[55] The Aryanization of the Fleischer paper factory brought in another RM 45,000 for him and his fellow partners at Glaub & Cie.[56] And the contract concluded between Kiehn, the Trick company, and the Fleischer owners in July 1938 bears Stäbler's signature — he had signed as Kiehn's plenipotentiary. Finally, statements from several witnesses cite Stäbler's handling of the negotiations as the reason why the Jewish sellers concluded a purchase price with Trick and Kiehn in 1938 that was at least 50 percent less than the established value of the company.[57] Nevertheless, in Kiehn's denazification proceedings the Tuttlingen committee considered it opportune to give more credence to Stäbler's statement than to the victim of the Aryanization, Hermann Fleischer. The societal contempt for victims of Aryanization, expulsion, and destruction could hardly have been more obvious.[58] Stäbler himself, as a nonparty member, was classified by the Tübingen denazification court on 8 June 1949 as an "Exonerated Person" — a group that very few people were put into. The court recognized Stäbler as a "cosmopolitan-minded, influential Freemason, friend to Jews, and adversary of the Nat. Soc. regime." It also worked in his favor that he had spent the last months of National Socialist rule in jail — for attempted foreign currency fraud. To the denazification court this became an "arrest ... for purely political reasons." Such reasons became even more plausible and significant in light of Stäbler's choice of Reinhold Maier as his attorney, who was suspected of having "Jewish kin." Maier had supposedly helped Jews and others facing persecution on repeated occasions.[59]

A witness who had worked closely with Stäbler did state that "when he was pursuing a deal, he had no concern for anyone."[60] But the court relied on the statement from Reinhold Maier, who had since become the minister-president of Württemberg-Baden and had "testified with total certainty" that Stäbler "had always decisively rejected and fiercely condemned the disenfranchising measures of Nazi tyranny." Thus, the court arrived at an opinion that was tantamount to mocking the victim: "If the conduct of the defendant was seen as a threat by members of the Fleischer family, there was doubtless a misunderstanding."[61]

Kiehn's restitution of the Okriftel cellulose factory was similarly discreet and completely unremarkable. Kiehn sent his attorney in this case to the reparation court hearing before the Frankfurt Regional Court on 26 July 1949; the previous factory owners attended in person, having traveled from the United States specifically for this purpose.[62] Kiehn's legal representative acknowledged that Minoux's acquisition of the cellulose factory in 1938, which had been valued at at least RM 9.4 million, for the ridiculously low price of RM 3.6 million marked a gross violation of moral standards.[63] At the same time, however, his attorney claimed that his client had not been aware that it was a formerly Jewish-owned company when he took it over some years later for approximately RM 6 million. The aim of this line of argument was to construct a legal situation of coercively acquired property, rather than aggravated confiscation, in order to limit Kiehn's liability. As the attorney for the other side stated, this was admittedly a version that presented "all too great a challenge … to people's credibility. … Does Herr Kiehn believe," he asked, "he can fool anyone into thinking that he would lay 6 million on the table for a company without acquainting himself with every single detail about the origins and history of such a factory?"[64]

But Minoux's side had its own brazen claims to make. Friedrich Minoux had died after being released from jail in 1945, leaving his wife and two adult daughters to face the restitution demands of the Offenheimer and Bloch families. The families' attorneys argued, on the one hand, that none of the women had any insight into Minoux's business dealings. On the other hand, they forcefully claimed that it was irrelevant whether Minoux, "who at the time was himself extremely wealthy," had "made a profit from Okriftel." He had "placed the utmost value … on helping" the Bloch and Offenheimer owners and had therefore agreed to send part of the purchase price he paid for the cellulose factory (which the attorneys argued had in reality been much higher) abroad in an illegal money transfer.[65] No witnesses could be procured for this version of events, which accused the victimized Jews of making unwarranted demands for restitution. Quite the contrary: a banker made known by the Minoux family who had dealt with the sale declared to the court that he knew nothing about any efforts to make an illegal transfer. Besides, he knew of "no case in which one could characterize the behavior of Herr Minoux toward the Offenheimer family as particularly respectable."[66] Despite this, the rumor that Bloch and Offenheimer were seeking to get rich from spurious restitution claims had soon spread to the company in Okriftel as well. Based on mere hearsay to this effect, the outgoing custodian of the company denounced the owners to the Hesse State Chancellery, ostensibly in order "to fend off damages from the state of Hesse," but actually because of his exasperation at having been fired by the Blochs and Offenheimers. With completely transparent motives, he called for "the firm's assets" to remain locked and for the Bloch and Offenheimer families' reparations claims to be reviewed.[67]

The restitution proceedings forced the victims of Aryanization to learn that everyone had "meant well" toward them in the past. But when they demanded the return of property that had been taken from them, people did not shy away from denouncing them anew and peppering them with unfounded accusations.

The settlement in the Okriftel case concluded before the restitution court in Frankfurt turned out surprisingly well for Fritz Kiehn, whereas the banks that had financed the purchase of the cellulose factory in 1945 had to pay substantial fines. Those entitled to restitution, by contrast, were completely unable to be indemnified for the decrease in their company's value and the profits that had been lost. Efka had braced itself for "losses of at least [DM] 2,000,000" from Okriftel and had obtained a preventive deferral from the German tax office in the amount of DM 700,000. The deferral was granted because "if the restitution claims were not satisfied," it could lead to "foreclosure on the most important taxpayer in the region." In the end, Kiehn only had to pay DM 700,000 over and above the restitution of the cellulose factory. With the tax deferral, the state had prefinanced Okriftel's restitution costs in their entirety. While there were other pending claims for restitution and damages, it quickly became clear that despite temporary liquidity shortages, Efka would still be able to swiftly absorb these burdens, now estimated at over DM 1 million.[68]

Nevertheless, Fritz Kiehn appeared to have been completely unmoved by the unfortunate lot of the Fleischers and the Offenheimers and Blochs, who remained strangers to him. On the contrary, whenever he spoke of "his Aryanizations," his words revealed only contempt and self-righteousness. His grandson could not remember ever hearing any remarks indicating a sense of wrongdoing: "not about Eislingen and not about Okriftel."[69] Thus, even from prison Kiehn had no qualms about threatening legal action against the Fleischers (who had now regained possession of their company) because they were still "unlawfully" signing documents in the name of Kiehn's old firm (Papierfabrik Fritz Kiehn).[70]

In the early postwar years — and true to National Socialist tradition — he hardly ever spoke about those he had harmed without expressly labeling them as "Jews." For example, the minutes of Kiehn's interrogation by Colonel Hermann Fleischer, which took place at the Reutlingen prison camp, contains the following telling passage: asked about how the purchase price came about, Kiehn declared, "Occasionally I would hear only that all negotiations were futile, since all the *Jews* of this establishment had run away. One of these *Jews* supposedly stayed behind. I don't know which *Jew* of this firm it was ... I saw this man so little and knew as little of him as of any of the other *Jews* belonging to the firm." Two years later, when he was interrogated again on the same matter because of the suspicion that he had collaborated with Stäbler and Glaub to commit blackmail, Kiehn not only disputed Hermann Fleischer's accusations but made his allegations in language that was more suited to the time: "It is my strong conviction that ... *Herr* Fleischer himself is absolutely convinced that his recrimination against me ... is false."[71]

In 1949, the two Fleischer sons lost their lives in quick succession.[72] Kiehn is said to have remarked upon this news with great schadenfreude and cynicism: "[S]ix were already burnt [*verheizt*], and I'm buying the seventh one for myself."[73] When he was finally confronted with these comments before the state parliamentary review committee in 1951, Kiehn did not dispute them. Because he had "managed the factories in Eislingen as a trustee in the best sense," he said, the committee had to understand that he would wish ill on the colonel who had so badgered him on that day in Reutlingen. Kiehn's intransigent attempt to justify his actions provoked a remark from only one KPD delegate, who reprimanded the industrialist. This caused Kiehn to toot his own horn yet again: "I can only say that I managed the firm ... completely selflessly. I had to take care of everything. My position on the Jewish question, how many Jews I helped, should be evident from my [Nazi] Party court proceedings."[74] This falsehood was enough to get him off the hook, and in the end, like many others who had profited from the National Socialist persecution of Jews, he probably believed it himself. As Herbert E. Kiehn recalls, "I can still hear my grandmother talking about this, gifted booster for my grandfather that she was: it had been confirmed ... to my grandfather that the Jewish previous owners of the factory got it back in better condition than they had left it in."[75]

It was now a short jump for Kiehn to go from being a supposed friend and benefactor of the Jews to an alleged victim of Nazi persecution, or even an opponent of National Socialism. His former proximity to SS murder victim Gregor Straßer and his later opposition to the Württemberg Gauleitung were just the thing to turn this former SS lieutenant colonel and Himmler protegé into a would-be martyr and the Gau economic adviser's archenemy into an opponent of Nazi tyranny. It was not Kiehn's "unbridled business acumen" but honorable political motives that had been the cause of his tensions with the Gauleitung. "So the Gauleitung rejected me, simply because I was a Straßer supporter," Kiehn declared at his blackmail trial at the Rottweil Regional Court in 1949.[76]

Kiehn also invoked his dead friend Straßer in a wholly questionable historical context when the Ellwangen Regional Court tried him for murder, along with missing former SS Southwest Regional Headquarters director Prützmann and two of the SS leaders involved in the arrest of Hermann Mattheiß. In the meantime, a third party had attested to Kiehn's credibility as a near victim in the Night of the Long Knives: a former SS man purported to have witnessed Mattheiß being transported to the SS battalion in Ellwangen in the early hours of 1 July 1934. The witness gave his occupation as "Trossingen merchant": he was an Efka sales representative after the war.[77] His sworn statement about the arrest or even the shooting of Mattheiß was extremely vague; everyone he incriminated was already dead. The "Trossingen merchant" spoke about only one thing with any specificity: he purported to have heard that immediately after Mattheiß had been transported, the battalion leader in Ellwangen[78] was said to have remarked to another SS leader in passing, "Kiehn — Trossingen — might be coming tonight or early tomorrow; he's exactly the same *Schwein*."[79] It is unclear whether the court recognized that this statement had no inherent credibility — the case records were destroyed. Nor can we establish whether Kiehn bribed the witness. In December 1950, the Ellwangen Regional Court abandoned the proceedings against Kiehn on the charge of accessory to the murder of Hermann Mattheiß. The resolution to abandon the trial includes this statement: "Kiehn was very good friends with Dr. Mattheiß and Gregor Straßer. Kiehn too would have been arrested, and probably shot, on 30 June 1934, had he not managed to avoid arrest by going on the run."[80]

In the end, when the restitutions had been dealt with, all criminal trials had been abandoned, and Kiehn had been declared a "Lesser Offender" by the denazification court, he evidently thought of himself as an opponent of the Nazis and a victim of National Socialist persecution — one who had simply been unlucky enough to have ended up with a few brown stains on his record. He declared at a company meeting in the summer of 1950: "In 1933 I was an ardent National Socialist. But when I got to know the tyranny of the system, I spent all twelve years trying to combat the party … my denazification is proof of this. People argued about whether to classify me as a Follower or a Lesser Offender." Anyone who did not believe this version would have had a tough time in Kiehn's adopted hometown, since, as he continued in his speech to his employees, "While a note against me by the current mayor was being read aloud, one of the committee members shouted, 'and such a man is mayor of Trossingen.' The committee member from the Social Democratic Party said these very words out loud: 'I am ashamed to belong to the same party as Herr Neipp.'"[81] A scant year later, in a personal conversation with Tuttlingen district governor Estrade, Kiehn finally "ceremonially" expressed "his anti-National Socialist views." Again alluding to his trial before the denazification court, he declared to the Frenchman: "You know my record, so you know that I have always fought against National Socialism."[82]

Indeed, Estrade knew Kiehn's denazification record — which has since been lost — backward and forward.[83] He had studied it thoroughly on many occasions and was therefore convinced that Kiehn's "denazification" should not have been left to the Germans alone. Kiehn's classification as a "Lesser Offender," with its fine of DM 15,000 and five-year disenfranchisement, as the lower court judgment in Kiehn's denazification case had read, was proof enough for the governor that the court was only concerned with whitewashing (*blanchir*) a heavily incriminated

Nazi as quickly as possible. After the state commissioner for political cleansing had already quashed the judgment once, causing the court to reconfirm its prior verdict, the only remaining legal option was for the military government to dismiss the verdict again in order to obtain harsher sanctions against Kiehn.[84] What was needed, Estrade therefore wrote to his superiors in Tübingen in June 1949, was for the military government to rise to this challenge so that Kiehn, who was doubtless "un des plus grands nazis de l'Allemagne" (one of the most prominent Nazis of Germany), would get the punishment he deserved. The district governor argued for Kiehn to be classified as a "Major Offender," or at least as an "Offender," and suggested sanctioning him by confiscating his business and banning him from any management position for fifteen years.[85]

He based this not only on the formally incriminating characteristics that Kiehn had exhibited on numerous occasions because of his offices and posts. Indeed, the Sûreté had made meticulous observations about his political past, used local and regional newspapers to document Kiehn's public appearances in 1930–1934, reconstructed his donations to the SS and the Nazi Party based on the Efka account books, and found fault with his behavior toward NSDAP opponents during the seizure of power stage. Kiehn's failed attempts to publish a Nazi newspaper and acquire confiscated printing presses were well known; there was as much proof of his involvement in the events of the Night of the Long Knives as of the Aryanization of the paper factory in Eislingen that he had pulled off with the aid of his SS connections. What's more, it was clear to the Sûreté that Colonel Hermann Fleischer and his main witness, the auditor Eberhard Mayer, had more credibility than Kiehn or Stäbler.

The French intelligence service discovered other incriminating evidence as well. For example, it found that prominent party members such as Gregor Straßer, Wilhelm Frick, Martin Bormann,[86] Wilhelm Kube,[87] Gottfried Feder, and Gertrud Scholtz-Klink had been frequent guests of Kiehn's. Moreover, as a member of the Reichsführer-SS's personal staff, Kiehn had enjoyed the trust of all the high-ranking "éminences SS," such as Reinhard Heydrich, the head of the SD; Karl Wolff, the head of the Reichsführer-SS's personal staff; Gottlob Berger, the head of the SS Head Office; Hermann Fegelein, Himmler's liaison officer in the Führer's headquarters; and Professor Karl Diebitsch, director of the SS office in Munich in charge of art. This is how the image of Kiehn as "propagandist no. 1" of the Nazi regime in southern Germany came about. Very little of the information was false — such as the allegation that Kiehn had been the official Gau hunter — or imprecise, for example, particular statements about investments and earnings performance in Kiehn's various companies.[88]

Once the second denazification court verdict had been quashed by the Germans (the state commission also had reservations about such obvious whitewashing of one of the most prominent National Socialists in the region), the military government tried to stall for time.[89] Kiehn's file was forwarded to Godesberg to be decided by French High Commissioner François-Ponçet. To Kiehn's great annoyance, he still had not been fully denazified, and both the district ban and control of his assets continued. The latter consequence, above all, had a major financial impact on the industrialist, because it delayed Efka becoming incorporated, an act that was imperative for tax reasons, and threatened to sink it altogether.[90] In view of his company's acute liquidity shortages, this might have threatened the existence of the company. Consequently, during these months Kiehn considered relocating the firm's headquarters from Württemberg to Hesse, where his past was less of a concern and he was welcomed as a taxpayer.[91] At any rate, an insider indicated that every month Efka continued in its given legal form was costing the company around DM 60,000. The German tax office had allowed Efka to defer payment of this money since early 1949, but it would fall due immediately if the company could not be incorporated by the end of 1949.[92] Had this happened, we can assume that the firm would have gone bankrupt.

If the delay in his denazification doubtless implied considerable problems, at least he did not have to worry about a fundamentally harsher verdict, and not only, as the Trossingen SPD suspected, because he had deployed "unlimited monetary means" and supplied "a multitude of mendacious exoneration letters" produced under pressure or for pay.[93] In addition, the denazification courts had long since become mere agents of rehabilitation. As the saying went, "They go out to Tübingen as big Nazis and come home as little ones."[94] Those at the state commissioner's office were also aware that rehearing the case was unlikely to bring any sweeping change. In October 1949, information leaked out that the French high commissioner had ordered the Tübingen military government to bring Kiehn's still-pending denazification proceedings to a close.[95] Following this, after local representatives of all political stripes had protested against the district ban to German and French authorities, it was lifted on 7 December. Efka had already been incorporated by 1 December; the authorities evidently considered lifting the controls on Kiehn's assets to be nothing more than a formality. On 9 December 1949, company custodian Richter made a note in the record that the military government had put Kiehn's denazification into German hands. Once Kiehn's files arrived from Godesberg, Richter noted, the state commissioner in charge of it would ensure "that a new denazification proceeding will be opened and will issue a new verdict as soon as possible, likely within eight days." Hints that this verdict would hardly bring any unpleasant surprises also came from the commissioner: "he [state commisioner Mayer] expects that they will leave in the content of the old verdict, but the fine could be increased somewhat if need be."[96] Indeed, this is what happened. On 14 December 1949, Kiehn's case was tried a third time before the Tübingen denazification court. The final verdict deemed Kiehn a "Lesser Offender," "with a period of probation of two years, until 9 April 1951" (actually only eighteen months). It also revoked his right to vote and to engage in political activity until the same date and, purposely skirting Kiehn's profession, it prohibited him from working as "a teacher, educator, preacher, publisher, author, or radio commentator." Whereas the probation period had been reduced by two-thirds from the first verdict, the fine of DM 30,000 was double the previous amount.[97] As state president Gebhard Müller would declare to the state parliament two years later, this was the "highest fine not only in Württemberg-Hohenzollern, but perhaps in Württemberg-Baden as well. ... Of course," he added, "that won't cause him any difficulty."[98]

Notes

1. For more about the political cleansing of former Nazi elites, see Henke, "Trennung"; Herbert, "Rückkehr," 162–163; Niethammer, *Mitläuferfabrik,* 577.
2. StAL, EL 402/9, Bü 235, note from Property Control Office (PCO) to Finance Ministry of 28 May 1947.
3. On the structure of the cleansing apparatus in southern Württemberg, see Henke, *Politische Säuberung,* 53–56, 72–79; Rauh-Kühne, "Die Unternehmer," 308–311.
4. For further detail, see Rauh-Kühne, "Die Unternehmer"; for the quotation and its sources, see ibid., 327. For examples of the drastic punishment of business owners whose formal incrimination was only minor, see ibid., 323–328.
5. See Rauh-Kühne, "Life."
6. Verhandlungen des Landtags, 16th session, parliamentary inquiry of 4 Feb. 1948 regarding the conditions in Balingen internment camp; StAS, Wü 2, Bü 1435, report on transfer of camp to German authority as of 2 May 1947; Henke, *Politische Säuberung,* 40–41.
7. StAS, Wü 13, Bü 246, list of detainees as of 15 Sept. 1948. At that time, ninety people were still being held in Balingen.
8. StAS, Wü 2, Bü 1435.
9. StAS, Wü 1, Bü 100a, PUA, 6th public meeting, pp. 30, 72.
10. Verhandlungen des Landtags, 16th session, parliamentary question of 4 Feb. 1948 regarding the conditions in Balingen detention camp; StAS, Wü 2, Bü 1435, report on transfer of camp to German authority as of 2 May 1947.
11. Interview with Herbert E. Kiehn of 19–20 May 1998.
12. See Arbogast, *Herrschaftsinstanzen,* 214–217, 234–238.
13. StAL, EL 902/22, Bü 1502 (Berta Kiehn denazification records), letter from Trossingen mayor's office to Ulm regional denazification court of 14 Mar. 1947.
14. StAL, EL 902/22, Bü 1502 (Berta Kiehn denazification records), complaint of 11 Apr. 1947.
15. See Office of Military Government for Germany, *Denazification (Cumulative Review). Report of the Military Governor (1 April 1947–30 April 1948),* no. 34. http://archive.org/stream/Denazification/OfficeOfTheMilitaryGovernmentForGermany-Denazificationen1948174P.Scan_djvu.txt. (accessed 4 Sept. 2012).
16. Schullze, *Gesetz zur Befreiung.*
17. On denazification in the American zone, see Niethammer, *Mitläuferfabrik*; for other literature, see Rauh-Kühne, "Entnazifizierung."
18. StAS, Wü 1, Bü 100a, PUA, 6th public meeting, p. 18; StAS, Wü 1, Bü 100a, PUA, 7th public meeting, p. 15; written information from Herbert E. Kiehn of 6 Dec. 1998.

19. StAS, Wü 1, Bü 100a, PUA, 6th public meeting, p. 64. On the difficulties that members of the denazification bureaucracy had in finding work after "cleansing" had ended, see Rauh-Kühne, "Entnazifizierung," 57.
20. For more on the receptionist's "indecent connection" to Nürtingen broker Meyer's office and to Kiehn, see StAS, Wü 2, Bü 885, letter from Ravensburg district court of 20 Jan. 1950 and state commissioner's file memo of 16 Mar. 1950. See also StAS, Wü 1, Bü 100a, PUA, 6th public meeting, p. 64. For general information, see Bräutigam, *Unternehmer*, 385–387; Matz, *Reinhold Maier*, 301–302.
21. StAS, Wü 1, Bü 100a, PUA, 6th public meeting, pp. 38, 61–62.
22. StAL, EL 902/22, Bü 1502 (Berta Kiehn denazification records), declaration by Latvian evacuee of 17 Sept. 1947 (cit.), Memmingen displaced persons camp, and by displaced persons of unknown nationality in Bad Cannstatt camp of 17 July 1947.
23. StAL, EL 902/22, Bü 1502 (Berta Kiehn denazification records), sworn statement by Lolo Mattheis [*sic*] of 2 Dec. 1947.
24. Arbogast, *Herrschaftsinstanzen*, 234, 236; see also Grote and Rosenthal, "Frausein." On the integration of women into the Nazi *Volksgemeinschaft*, see Harvey, *Women*; Saldern, "Victims"; Steinbacher, "Frauen"; Steinbacher, *Volksgenossinnen*; for the most pointed account, see Kühne, *Belonging*, chap. 5.
25. StAL, EL 902/22, 47/29/83 (Berta Kiehn denazification records), affidavit of Gottlieb Huber of 19 Oct. 1947.
26. StAL, EL 902/22, 47/29/83 (Berta Kiehn denazification records), affidavit from Dr. Wilhelm Führer of 21 Nov. 1947.
27. StAL, EL 902/22, 47/29/83 (Berta Kiehn denazification records), letter from Trossingen mayor's office to Ulm regional denazification court of 5 Feb. 1948; report of 12 Feb. 1948 from a victim of political persecution from Trossingen, StAT, without classmarks.
28. Vollnhals, *Entnazifizierung*, 23; Henke, "Trennung," 51; Niethammer, *Mitläuferfabrik*, 603.
29. StAS, Wü 13, T2 no. 2775/001, http://www.landesarchiv-bw.de/plink/?f=6-1039573 (accessed 4 Sept. 2012), affidavit from Werner Kaufmann of 23 Mar. 1949; State Commissioner Mayer to Kiehn's attorney of 28 Mar. 1949.
30. StAS, Wü 1, Bü 100a, PUA, 8th public meeting, p. 42.
31. StAS, Wü 120, Bü 362, contract of 3 May 1948 between Balingen detention camp and the WVT to provide workers; StAS, Wü 120, Bü 362, WVT to compensation office of 18 May 1948.
32. StAL, EL 905/2 II, Bü 199 (Niemann denazification records), Kuno Fleischer's letter to the Israelite Cultural Association (Israelitische Kulturvereinigung).
33. StAL, 402/9, Bü 235c, letter from Fleischer to the Eislingen paper factory trustee of 27 Feb. 1946. Notice of D.M. Fleischer's death in *Aufbau*, 9 March 1945.
34. StAS, Wü 1, Bü 100a, PUA, 8th public meeting, pp. 45–48. Kiehn described Colonel Fleischer's interrogation as having taken place in summer 1948. But records from the public prosecutor for the preliminary inquiry against Kiehn, Stäbler, and Glaub charging them with conspiring to blackmail the Jewish owners of the paper factory in Eislingen show that it took place on 7 July 1947 at the Reutlingen camp. StAS, Wü 29/2B, Bü 1019, minutes of interrogation.
35. StAS, Wü 1, Bü 100a, PUA, 8th public meeting, pp. 45–46.
36. MAE Colmar, WH C 3541 d 11, Affaire Kiehn, minutes of examination of 7 July 1947; MAE Colmar, WH C 3541 d 11, Affaire Kiehn, undated report from Fleischer to the Tuttlingen police; ASD, NL Erler, Box 85.
37. The legal foundation was Law No. 59 of the American military government of 10 Nov. 1947. On reparations policy, see Goschler and Ther, eds., *Raub*; Lillteicher, *Raub*.
38. The precise amount of compensation Kiehn had to pay the owners of the Fleischer company could not be determined. His tax consultant informed the Tuttlingen tax office on 12 Sept.

39. Lillteicher, *Raub,* 198–199.
40. StAS, Wü 120, Bü 362, letter of 2 July 1949 to the Tuttlingen tax office from Efka's tax advisory firm Binder-Dachs-Streit. This letter discusses the issue of whether the accounting allowances for restitution payments from Efka company assets were "deductible as business losses," a question that at the time was still being disputed under the law. Gustav Schickedanz's biographer mentions that he was able to deduct all of his restitution obligations from his taxes in 1951–1952, totaling DM 5.3 million. Schöllgen, *Schickedanz,* 231. We were not able to ascertain the speed with which or amounts by which Kiehn was able to deduct funds used for restitution from his own taxes and thus saddle German taxpayers with the burden of his individual compensation obligations for his morally offensive business dealings. Tax records remain confidential for eighty years, a period that was not reduced for this study. Letter from Staatsarchiv Sigmaringen of 21 Oct. 1997.
41. The restitution law could be traced to the military laws of the Allies, generating doubt among the German public about the legitimacy of reparations claims. By this reading, the Allied laws made "private persons ... unjustly responsible for their conduct during National Socialism." Lillteicher, *Raub,* 199, 488.
42. Lillteicher, *Raub,* 198.
43. SPD delegate Martin Hirsch declared to the Bundestag in 1964: "In recent months and years, we have all been flooded with letters from restitution victims, reparation victims, etc." Cited in Lillteicher, *Raub,* 484.
44. Quote from CDU delegate Franz-Josef Würmeling, cited in ibid., 488.
45. Beginning in the late 1960s, the demands from many who had paid restitutions were partially reimbursed through voluntary state subsidies under the Equalization of Burdens Law (Lastensausgleichsgesetz) of 1952. Since then, the Equalization of Burdens offices have classified some forty-three thousand people and four thousand legal entities as "loyal restitution claimants" entitled to reimbursement. The total amount of restitution paid out by the offices in the postwar era "corresponded to circa 56 percent of all restitution payments produced by private beneficiaries." "Based on the quantity of payments, the Federal Government thus considered half of the restitution decrees to have been unjustly enacted against 'Aryanizers.' Accordingly, the state, as the actual liable party, now had to pay for it." Lillteicher, *Raub,* 480–500 (cit. 488–489).
46. The KRUAs in the French occupation zone were simply investigative authorities. With their knowledge of local conditions, they were tasked with providing the central denazification courts with recommendations on how to classify implicated individuals and which sanctions to take. See Henke, *Politische Säuberung,* 190–91.
47. BA DC, Akte Kiehn, letter from Kiehn to SS colonel Tondock of 16 Jan. 1939. Kiehn's SS records and documentation relating to his Aryanizations were also available to the committee. StAS, Wü 1, Bü 100a, PUA, 6th public meeting, pp. 29, 40, 62–63; StAS, Wü 1, Bü 100a, PUA, 7th public meeting, pp. 21–22.
48. The Tuttlingen committee had threatened to collectively resign unless the denazification courts stopped watering down its suggested sanctions. Henke, *Politische Säuberung,* 190.
49. StAS, Wü 29/2B, Bü 1019, transcript of Tuttlingen KRUA meeting of 11 Apr. 1949.
50. See chap. 6.
51. StAS, Wü 13, Bü 2250, verdict of the third denazification court of 8 June 1949. Stäbler's allegation is refuted by the Reich finance minister's commitment to buy, dating from 19 Apr. 1939. According to the Moabit tax office, it was directed to Stäbler, "as President Kiehn's plenipotentiary." LAB, A Rep. 093-03, no. 53187, letter of 15 Sept. 1940.

An astonishing number of those who benefited from the Aryanization of Jewish property claimed after 1945 to have leaped to the assistance of the Jews who had been robbed. For example, the notary who testified as a witness in Stäbler and Glaub's defense alleged that in a cloak-and-dagger operation in 1938, he had induced Glaub & Cie to provide a record of the purchase contract with Kiehn and Trick that had been wrested from David M. and Kuno Fleischer. He claimed to have been "close" to the Fleischers for a long time: "Because of my diametrically opposed political views, I always made sure that the interests of the Jewish sellers were not compromised any more than was unavoidable." StAS, Wü 29/2B, Bü 1019, letter from notary H. to state commissioner of 6 July 1949; StAS, Wü 29/2B, Bü 1019, letter from notary H. for banker Heinrich Glaub of 8 Feb. 1949. In contrast, on 29 Nov. 1946, Colonel Hermann Fleischer had dressed down the notary before the Tuttlingen police for "stooping to [such] shady activities."

The managing director of the Referral Center at the Stuttgart IHK, appointed as the trustee of the Fleischer paper factory in 1938, also claimed to have helped the Fleischers where he could, increasing nominal capital during his trusteeship by more than RM 1 million. StAL, EL 902/20, Bü 80828. In 1952, after having disappeared for several years in order to avoid criminal prosecution, GWB Reihle declared, "I did no more or less than the authorities demanded at that time." Ibid.

52. StAS, Wü 29/2B, Bü 1019, resolution of 14 Sept. 1949 to abandon proceedings against Kiehn in public prosecutor's indictment of Stäbler.
53. See Diewald-Kerkmann, *Politische Denunziation,* 155–158. In the case of Kiehn and his intermediaries, it would only have been possible to condemn them for blackmail if it could have been proven that they had intentionally threatened the Fleischers with something unpleasant (arrest) and that they were in the position to bring about such an outcome. Yet they were not in such a position, precisely because of Kiehn's tense relations with the Gauleitung.
54. MAE Colmar, WH C 2970, Stäbler, Chiron-Werke Tuttlingen.
55. StAS, Wü 13, Bü 2250, letter from KHD management to Tuttlingen police commission of 10 June 1948.
56. StAS, Wü 13, Bü 2250, report of investigation in the Heinrich Glaub case of 7 Jan. 1947.
57. StAS, Wü 29/2B, Bü 1090, Rottweil Regional Court verdict of 22 Dec. 1949 in criminal blackmail case against Otto Stäbler.
58. Victims of political persecution under Nazism were also held in contempt. See Lillteicher, *Raub,* 202.
59. StAS, Wü 13, Bü 2679. After Stäbler's acquittal by the Rottweil Regional Court, the verdict against Kiehn was once again reviewed in the appeal proceedings and ultimately confirmed. For Stäbler's dubious role, see chapters 3 and 6.
60. One of Glaub's fellow Freemasons issued a similar judgment of the banker, claiming that Glaub was "a ruthless businessman who did not shy away from any means of earning money." The same witness stated that "like many of his lodge brothers, he doubted whether Glaub had not worn a party badge off and on; in any case, he had strongly sympathized." StAS, Wü 13, Bü 2250, report of investigation in Heinrich Glaub case of 7 Jan. 1947.
61. MAE Colmar, WH C 2970, Stäbler, statement of former Chiron authorized officer to the Sûreté; StAS, Wü 13, Bü 2679, grounds for Tübingen denazification court verdict in Stäbler case of 8 June 1949.
62. HHStA, Abt. 519/A, no. Ffm 365.
63. StAS, Wü 120, Bü 362, letter from Binder-Dachs-Streit accounting firm to Tuttlingen tax office of 2 July 1949.
64. HHStA, Abt. 519/A, no. Ffm 369, written pleading of 21 Apr. 1949 by American attorney for the Offenheimer/Bloch party.
65. HHStA, Abt. Z 460, no. 365, letter from attorney Hans Correll.
66. HHStA, Abt. Z 460, no. 365, witness examination of banker, 26 July 1949.

67. HHStA, Abt. 519/V, no. 2152-114, Bd. 1, letter from receiver's attorney to Hesse minister-president's office of 5 Aug. 1949.
68. StAS, Wü 120, Bü 362, letters from Binder-Dachs-Streit accounting firm to Tuttlingen tax office of 2 July and 12 Sept. 1949. Open restitution claims at this point were still some RM 1 million. Some of these were still allocated to the Fleischer company, others to the Stuttgart press (Druckerei AG) and the Schwäbische Tagwacht company in Stuttgart. Both publishing houses were suing for damages for the printing machines Kiehn had purchased, which had been purloined from them by the Nazi state.
69. Letter from Herbert E. Kiehn of 22 Feb. 1999.
70. StAS, Wü 120, Bü 362, letter from Kiehn of 26 Nov. 1948 to custodian Richter.
71. StAS, Wü 29/2B, Bü 1019, Rottweil public prosecutor's examination of Kiehn on 24 June 1949. Authors' emphasis; notice the change from "Jew" to "Herr."
72. In 1954, long-standing chief executive Eberhard Mayer bought the factory, which he resold in 1957 to the Waldhof cellulose operation. After a string of changes in ownership, the factory was shut down in 1991. In 2008, a commemorative plaque honoring the Fleischers was dedicated on the former grounds of the company in Eislingen. In 2011, the children of the industrialists who had been expelled in 1938 visited their parents' home. See Sporhan-Krempel, *Papier,* 61–67; Mundorff, "Eislingen," 60–62; *Südwestpresse,* 27 July 2011.
73. StAS, Wü 2, Bü 476. The correct statement is presumably, "Three were already burnt, and I'm buying the fourth one for myself." This alleged remark by Kiehn was circulated by the editor in chief of the *Schwäbische Zeitung,* Albert Komma, in a letter to state president Müller of 11 Dec. 1950. See also StAS, Wü 1, Bü 100a, PUA, 6th public meeting, p. 40 (accusation); StAS, Wü 1, Bü 100a, PUA, 8th public meeting, pp. 46f. (statement by Kiehn).
74. Kiehn was referring to the trial against him within the party in 1938–1939. StAS, Wü 1, Bü 100a, PUA, 8th public meeting, p. 48. See Ch. 5.
75. Letter from Herbert E. Kiehn to the authors of 22 Feb. 1999.
76. StAS, Wü 29/2B, Bü 1019, interrogation of Kiehn by the Rottweil Regional Court.
77. This could be reconstructed because the same witness also testified on internal business matters at Efka at PUA investigations in 1950. Questioning of his contemporaries revealed without a doubt that the SS man in Ellwangen and the Efka sales representative of the postwar era were identical.
78. This is a reference to Curt von Gottberg, who took a leading role in the SS crimes committed in the Soviet Union and committed suicide at the end of the war. See Wilhelm, *Einsatzgruppe A,* 458.
79. StAL, EL 902/2, Bü 7588 (denazification records of Beck, a participant in Mattheiß's arrest).
80. StAL, EL 902/2, Bü 7589, resolution of 30 Dec. 1950. See Ch. 5.
81. ASD, NL Erler, Box 85, meeting of Chiron works committee of 30 June 1950.
82. MAE Colmar, WH C 2963, Trippelwerke Molsheim, note d'information confidentiel of 26 June 1951.
83. The record with call no. 16/T/O/1086, which was missing when the research for the German edition of this book was underway, remained unaccounted for after the inventories of denazification in Baden-Württemberg had been digitized. A letter of 1 Sept. 1950 by the state commissioner for political cleansing indicates that the record contains one volume of main files 1–490 as well as two decisions, nine ancillary files, and one volume of photocopies. The files were still circulating among the authorities in the mid-1950s, since the final legal proceedings in which Kiehn's political history played a role were not abandoned until December 1954. A substantial amount of material incriminating Kiehn, including the record of his proceedings before the Württemberg Gau court in 1938–1939, can be found in the digitized brief of state commissioner Thaddäus Mayer, StAS, Wü 13, T2 no. 2775/001, http://www.landesarchiv-bw. de/plink/?f=6-1039573 (accessed 4 Sept. 2012). The Sûreté conducted its own investigations

on behalf of the military government, independently of the "cleansing record" drawn up by the German side. The French "Dossier Fritz Kiehn" is preserved at the MAE Colmar under the call no. WH C 3541 d 11.
84. StAS, Wü 13, T2 no. 2775/001, http://www.landesarchiv-bw.de/plink/?f=6-1039573 (accessed 4 Sept. 2012), state commissioner's press release of 6 May 1949 announcing the rejection of the lower court's verdict.
85. MAE Colmar, WH C 3541 d 11, Affaire Kiehn, letter from Estrade to the délégué supérieur of 15 June 1949; letter from Estrade's aide-de-camp, Lt. Hoffmann, to the délégué supérieur of 27 July 1949.
86. Kiehn's social circle seems to have been recruited primarily from Nazi delegates in the Reichstag. See Lilla, Döring, and Schulz, *Statisten,* 33–35 (on Berger), 55–56 (on Bormann), 151–152 (on Daluege), 133–134 (on Feder), 160–161 (on Frick), 412–414 (on Heß), 237–238 (on Heydrich), 348–350 (on Kube), 237f. (on Heydrich), 481f. (on Prützmann), 652 (on Straßer), and 735–737 (on Wolff). We were not able to verify visits by Bormann.
87. Kube (1887–1943) was an NSDAP party whip in the Prussian state parliament from 1930 to 1933 and a Reichstag member from November 1933. Presumably because he had Himmler's protection, Kube became an SS group leader in 1934; after the Russian campaign began, he was promoted to general commissioner of Byelorussia. He was assassinated in Minsk on 23 Sept. 1943. See Weiß, *Biographisches Lexikon,* 285–287; on Diebitsch, see Klee, *Kulturlexikon,* 100.
88. MAE Colmar, WH C 3541 d 11, Affaire Kiehn.
89. From the beginning, the judgments of the Tübingen denazification court drew the ire of the state commissioner for political cleansing. Thaddäus Mayer's predecessor had already established that the decisions were "in many cases considerably too lenient" and did not correspond to what should justifiably have been expected. Henke, *Politische Säuberung,* 190.
90. In 1949, the highest tax rate on business partnerships was 90 percent. Corporations were taxed substantially less.
91. StAS, Wü 1, Bü 100a, attorney Sieger before the PUA, 8th public meeting, pp. 34–37.
92. StAS, Wü 1, Bü 100a, Werner Kaufmann to PUA, 6th public meeting, p. 17; StAS, Wü 120, Bü 362, letter of 15 Sept. 1949 from custodian Richter to Kiehn.
93. StAS, Wü 13, T2 no. 2775/001, http://www.landesarchiv-bw.de/plink/?f=6-1039573 (accessed 4 Sept. 2012), local Trossingen SPD branch to state commissioner of 17 June 1949. Kiehn himself claimed before the Trossingen town council in 1954 that he had furnished 140 exoneration certificates for his denazification proceedings. StAT, B 99, GRP of 8 Feb. 1954.
94. Letter of 12 May 1948 from state commissioner Traber to denazification court chairs, cited in Henke, *Politische Säuberung,* 191.
95. StAS, Wü 13, Bü 2775, attorney Sieger to state commissioner of 6 Oct. 1949.
96. StAS, Wü 120, Bü 362.
97. StAS, Wü 13, T2 no. 2775/001, http://www.landesarchiv-bw.de/plink/?f=6-1039573 (accessed 4 Sept. 2012), memo from state commissioner to WVT of 19 Dec. 1949.
98. Verhandlungen des Landtags, 87th session, 1 Aug. 1950, p. 1704. Kiehn's legal costs went far beyond any penalties he had to pay. The sum in dispute was set at DM 4 million, meaning that approximately DM 200,000 would be incurred. Because Kiehn's denazification records could not be located, neither the exact amount nor the exact time of the payout could be determined, nor were we able to discover whether the amount to be paid was ever reduced out of clemency. StAS, Wü 13, Bd. 2, no. 3192 (N-Register). As a basis of comparison for the amounts given, the denazification in Württemberg-Baden of Backnang leather manufacturer Carl Kaess caused a similar sensation. Kaess, who was less exposed politically, had profited tremendously from Aryanizations. But the denazification court classified him as a mere "Follower" in April 1948 and imposed a penalty of RM 2,000. The sum in dispute was set at RM 9,464,400, resulting

in legal costs of 5 percent or RM 473,220. The currency reform devalued these to a mere 10 percent, so that Kaess had to pay around DM 47,000. By petitioning for clemency, however, he succeeded in having these reduced by more than DM 34,000. A state parliamentary review committee discovered that Kaess had paid DM 21,000 for the services of a dubious "denazification broker," whose bribing practices had caused the "denazification scandal" mentioned above. See Bräutigam, *Unternehmer,* 382–385.

Chapter 11

"Ripe for Satire"
Entering the Social Market Economy with Public Loans

When Kiehn's denazification proceedings finally came to a close, the verdict caused at best "a certain commotion" in and around Trossingen. The head of the Tuttlingen administration reported that in the run-up to the proceedings, there were misgivings "in anti-National Socialist circles" that Kiehn would come off "too well" because of his "far-reaching connections."[1] But most people were convinced that this would finally give them a "clean break" with their prominent fellow citizen's past. The denazification court had at least declared him a "Lesser Offender," whereas many former prominent Nazis, together with millions of simple "party comrades," had been heaped into the innocuous category of "Followers."[2] Because of the late date of his proceedings, Kiehn also had to pay his fines and extremely high procedural costs after the currency reform of 1948, that is, in the hard currency of the new Deutschmark (DM).

His denazification case ended up as a topic of conversation in southwest Germany for years afterward and became a bone of contention among political parties. This had less to do with the court's verdict, however, than with Kiehn's business comeback and the politically insensitive actions of the government of the small German federal state of Württemberg-Hohenzollern: before the denazification court's verdict had even come into force, and with the Efka factory still under trusteeship, the government of state president Gebhard Müller gave Kiehn a loan of DM 3 million. The purpose was to allow the Trossingen manufacturer to acquire the Chiron company in Tuttlingen, which was facing bankruptcy, and return it to profitability — the same company that Kiehn's fellow businessman Stäbler had used Reich loans and SS connections to build into an important supplier in the aviation industry during the war. As former weapons manufacturers, Chiron and its subsidiary in the American zone had since become subject to

---

Notes from this chapter begin on page 251.

assets controls and were being managed by a custodian appointed by the Finance Ministry. Eighty percent of the machines had been dismantled; most of the factory space was empty. Like other companies in the surgical instrument and mechanical engineering industries, the Chiron factories had been under great financial strain since the currency reform. Export orders had fallen short, sales were stagnating, stocks of finished goods were rising alarmingly, and the factory space was much too big for existing production. The company was heavily indebted and faced the threat of additional payment obligations with the looming Equalization of Burdens Law. In the fall of 1949, Chiron finally entered insolvency. Between 250 and 300 employees had to work without pay and feared for their jobs. When the custodian wanted to start bankruptcy proceedings, company owner Stäbler announced that his longtime business partner Kiehn could be a potential buyer.[3]

Even though the regulations of Allied Control Council Law No. 52 stipulated that Kiehn had as little power over his assets as Stäbler, was not allowed to enter the Tuttlingen district, and had his own company in Trossingen that was in "very dire financial straits," Kiehn promised Stäbler DM 1.5 million.[4] Kiehn assured his friend that taking over the Chiron factory was "a matter of honor" for him; it would "signify his rehabilitation."[5] As in 1934–1935, when he had gotten mixed up in the Magirus venture with Stäbler's assistance, Kiehn was once again animated by the hope that his plan to rescue the company would earn him a reputation as a benefactor of workers, indeed, as a "pillar of city and state."[6] After that, who would care about his ban from the district or his denazification?

In purchasing the Chiron factory, Kiehn also saw a chance to expand his Trossingen operation and achieve what he considered a long-overdue diversification; he feared that the end of the product life cycle for cigarette papers was nigh. Demand for tobacco products had risen enormously following the currency reform and the repeal of ration cards for tobacco products. Now he had to quickly expand production capacity, since this, along with paper sources, would initially create the crucial competitive advantage. Efka had to grow, and there was no time to lose; Kiehn, his custodian, and the company management were agreed on that.[7] Numerous orders for new machines had gone in during Richter's custodianship, despite scarce space and liquidity. The takeover of three smaller Efka competitors may have further expanded the Trossingen plant's stock of machinery in 1949. The conditions at Efka were so cramped that Kiehn needed a new DM 1.5 million building. He complained to a Tuttlingen city councilor in late November 1949 that it was not expected to be finished before 1952. Since he did not want to waste these three years, he hoped to be able to use the "empty space [in the Chiron factory] for his manufacturing." The councilor (a city administrative official who was also a member of the state parliament) promised to give Kiehn "every support" and spread rumors in the state government that Kiehn was planning to move to Hesse. At the same time, he saw to it that meaningful progress was made on lifting Kiehn's district ban.

There was another reason for Kiehn's interest in Chiron, which may have been the deciding factor: his daughter Gretl had remarried in September 1949, and his new son-in-law was dying to direct a company. The widow's new husband was not former Porsche clerk Dr. Werner Kaufmann, as some had expected, who had proved his worth as Kiehn's "denazification manager." Instead, it was Hans Trippel, whom Kiehn reportedly met at the French military prison in Rastatt. Born in 1908, Trippel was exactly the same age as his "predecessor" Fähndrich. Like Fähndrich, he loved to hunt and had previously rendered outstanding service to the NSDAP as an "old fighter" — albeit in the SA. He crossed over to the SS during the war after a dispute with his SA chief of staff, Viktor Lutze. As a staff leader at the SS Head Office, for a time Trippel enjoyed the personal support of the Reichsführer-SS.[8] He had drawn attention to himself by designing an amphibious vehicle (*Schwimmwagen*) that Gottlob Berger, director of the SS Head Office, had recommended to Himmler as "especially suited ... to fighting partisans."[9]

The son of a colonial goods dealer, Trippel became a skilled retail salesman and a self-taught technician. During the Great Depression, he scraped along for a time as a traveling cigarette salesman. This may have been what biased Kiehn in the "inventor's" favor. Although he had been tinkering with building a racecar until 1933, Trippel redirected his energies afterward into developing the aforementioned amphibious vehicle. Around two hundred "Trippel-Schwimmwagen" were produced during the war, but serial production was never achieved. Trippel was a creative tinkerer, but experts were skeptical of the industrial feasibility of his inventions. Even so, his political ties during the war got him a job as chief operating officer at the erstwhile Bugatti factory in Molsheim, Alsace, an important armaments producer with more than two thousand employees. Having brought in his numerous patents, he was personally invested in the factory to the tune of RM 900,000.[10] But Trippel ultimately lost his SS and party backing, in part because he was suspected of embezzling Reich funds.[11]

In the last months of the war, Trippel and some of his workforce — including prisoners from SS forced labor camps — were "transferred" to a temporary operation at Sulz am Neckar in Württemberg. With the Allied troops advancing, Trippel scarpered back to Bavaria, taking all of the firm's records with him and leaving behind liabilities of RM 8.5 million. He planned to open a temporary production facility in Allgäu, but the end of the war forestalled the project, and Trippel then spent a long time in jail.[12] He was sentenced by a French military court in 1947 to five years in detention, presumably on charges of mistreating forced laborers, but was free again after twenty-five months.[13]

In June 1949, when the Kiehn family took a trip to Hamburg, they visited Trippel in Hanover. He was newly engaged, and had been freed from prison only a few months before. He was taking a crack at developing a hydraulic prosthetic leg, but dreamed of continuing his career as an automobile designer and industrialist by creating a reasonably priced small car.

Fritz and Berta Kiehn seem to have spontaneously gained confidence in Trippel's talent and — despite the presence of his fiancée — in his suitability as a potential son-in-law shortly thereafter. As far as the business side of things was concerned, the Kiehns doubtless had their expectations confirmed by a confidant of Trippels, Dr. W., whom Otto Stäbler also knew.[14] An attorney, Dr. W. had an office in an upscale part of Hanover. Until 1945, he had been the senior civil servant (Regierungsrat) at the Economics and Budget Office of the Reich Aviation Ministry (Reichsluftfahrtministerium, RLM), where he had witnessed the intense conflicts over Trippel between the individual military units and the Reichsführung-SS.[15] No technological expert himself, Dr. W. evidently considered Trippel a great inventor and design engineer who could make good money if only he were given the necessary start-up capital to do it.[16] It was probably not least because of this speculation that Dr. W. became Trippel's constant companion in the months that followed. He also testified as an exoneration witness in Trippel's denazification proceedings, and advised Fritz Kiehn on the Chiron matter.[17]

About six weeks after the meeting in Hanover, then thirteen-year-old Herbert E. Kiehn was flabbergasted when his grandmother notified him of his aunt's imminent marriage to the "automobile designer," who still seemed to be happily engaged to someone else. The wedding took place on 25 August 1949 in Überlingen, on Lake Constance. Just as she had eight years before with Fähndrich, Kiehn's daughter had married in a flash; business demanded it.

By September, Trippel had already moved his automobile endeavors from Hanover to Bad Cannstatt in Stuttgart. There he once again took up his development work, at a company called Protek. Gretl Trippel became the chief executive officer: her husband was still missing the denazification certificate indispensable to setting up a business in the American zone.[18] The couple moved into a house in Bad Cannstatt. The father of the bride took care of the costs, as well as the necessary investments in Protek and the lavish wedding reception. Kiehn also paid for the wedding gift, a two-seater Volkswagen convertible, and the honeymoon the couple took in it. The industrialist, whose company was still under forced administration, evidently had no trouble dipping into Efka's coffers.[19]

As Herbert E. Kiehn remembers it, Trippel possessed "sufficient targeted ambition to seem credible to Fritz Kiehn, who fell for him hook, line, and sinker."[20] Scarcely had Trippel been promoted to son-in-law when Kiehn began hatching plans to take over Chiron, despite warnings not to. As Kiehn's plenipotentiary Werner Kauffmann described it, "outside of Herr Kiehn and Herr Trippel," no one at Efka supported the purchase of the Chiron factory. Kaufmann did not think much of Trippel, and he had "expressly warned" the less technically competent Fritz Kiehn, also pointing "to the Magirus and Fleischer affairs." When he saw the empty factory floors in Tuttlingen for the first time, he purportedly said to Kiehn, "I would not wish to be in charge of this dump even if you gave me the thing."²¹ Kiehn, however, a car buff himself, embarked on an adventure in the automotive sector without any knowledge of the industry, qualified staff, or sufficient capital. He thirsted for action, just as in 1935, and once again was blind to the immense weaknesses of his latest project.

Officials at the Tübingen Finance Ministry probably first discussed the troubles at Chiron in late October 1949, and Fritz Kiehn was brought up right away as a possible savior for the company. The Chiron custodian, Wilhelm Burmeister — Kiehn had dangled before him the prospect of a "comfortable position" after his custodianship ended — declared to his state-level superiors that Efka was "the only company that could close up Chiron's liquidity gaps organically and thus restore it to profitability."²² They raised the idea of allowing Efka to defer payment of its excise taxes so that Kiehn could provide "additional" funds to rehabilitate the Chiron factory; they had no idea that liquidity at Efka was in short supply. With no regard for the controls on Kiehn's and Städler's assets, the ministries asked them along with their advisers to enter into negotiations; the paper goods manufacturer was given the opportunity to present his "rehabilitation plan." No active role was envisioned for Trippel, however.

On 2 November 1949, the "design engineer" living in Bad Cannstatt approached the central denazification court of North Württemberg, in Ludwigsburg, with a request to accelerate "my denazification ... so I can fulfill the purely external prerequisites for my return to work in the commercial and technical field."²³ The court did not hesitate, and on 27 December 1949 released Trippel from his presumed "Major Offender" status — as expressed in the charges from 15 November 1949 — and reclassified him as a "Follower." The proceedings were a farce, leading to the suspicion that Trippel benefited from the bribery scandal in which the chief prosecutor of this particular denazification court was embroiled at about that time.²⁴ The evidence hearing was manifestly tendentious. The decision to declare Trippel a "Follower" flew in the face of his well-documented political past as an SA tough from the "time of struggle," SS protegé during the war, and dubious "chief operating officer" afterward. Officials in the denazification court not only failed to notice his three-year sentence from the French military court, but they were ignorant of his embezzlement charge as well. Instead, the public prosecutor at the court parroted Trippel's own portrayal of himself as an apolitical victim of enforced National Socialist conformity, an inspired inventor, and a benefactor of the Alsatian workforce. "The people came to me," Trippel claimed, "and since I had been a party comrade since 1930, I didn't have to put up with anything, and I helped out where I could." He produced a handful of witnesses to confirm this version, but their professional and business links to Trippel should have sown doubt about their credibility from the start. The witnesses included Dr. W., the former senior civil servant in the RLM, who was handling the Chiron matter for Kiehn at the same time. Dr. W. characterized Trippel as a person "who was completely ... devoted to technological progress" and told of the "harsh battles" the inventor had fought with the SS and various party authorities. Dr. W. left unmentioned that Trippel's reputation had ultimately hit rock bottom with the German Air Force as well. In his version, chief of aircraft procurement and supply Erhard Milch never asked Himmler in the summer of 1944 to have Trippel replaced with someone "better suited," singling out his performance as the reason. With his request Milch enclosed complaints from the Gauleiter in charge of Alsace, Robert Wagner, and German Labor Front (DAF) head Robert Ley. The accusations culminated in the verdict of the Gaulamtsleiter for the DAF in Baden, Reinhold Roth, who maintained that Trippel was incapable of becoming the chief executive officer of a large factory. "He lacks the character required," was the statement used in his verdict, which should of course be read with a critical eye: "He is untrue, unclear, and a schemer." Under Trippel's leadership, Roth said, it would be "quite impossible to gain employees' confidence in the running of the operation or in the German cause." Trippel's inventions had been "very controversial" among experts. More and more, this "gifted wheeler-dealer and opportunist" was becoming an imposition. The DAF Gauamtsleiter was manifestly convinced that it would also be "in the interests of armament" if Molsheim could finally get some "good leadership" and Trippel could be "replaced by an appropriate person."[25] The Ludwigsburg denazification court did not dispute Trippel's political past, nor did it intrude upon Kiehn's plans to take over the Chiron factories.

While Kiehn's son-in-law was not unknown to the Tübingen government, no one there seems to have wondered what role he was intended to play in the plan to return Chiron to profitability, which had its own problems in any case. The highest official in the Württemberg-Hohenzollern Finance Ministry, undersecretary Paul Vowinkel, had a key role in granting Kiehn the loan. Vowinkel headed the ministry on behalf of state president Gebhard Müller and was also in charge of controlling assets; during the war in the office of the German civil administration in Alsace he had had to control the weapons industry.[26] Vowinkel had met Trippel and his advocate, Dr. W., while working in this capacity. It was even claimed that Kiehn had Trippel's links with Vowinkel especially to thank for getting the loan for Chiron. Rumors that Vowinkel was bribed cannot be proved or disproved. At any rate, Vowinkel cannot have been unaware that Trippel owed his position to his political connections and that his professional competence had been repeatedly called into question. No matter: in 1949 the undersecretary emerged as a crucial advocate of the Chiron rescue campaign Kiehn initiated. Vowinkel paid a visit to the industrialist at his home in Nußdorf on a questionable pretext — at that time Kiehn was still banned from the district and subject to control of his assets — and met with Trippel there as well. A few months later, Vowinkel made sure that the state cabinet's approval of the loan went smoothly.

On 16 December, two days after Kiehn had been declared a "Lesser Offender," the State Ministry unanimously agreed "after extensive consultation" to grant "the Trossingen Efka factories, whose owner Fritz Kiehn intends to acquire the Chiron factories incorporated in Tuttlingen," a secured loan against his tobacco tax "in the amount of DM 3 mio. [million]" with a repayment term of a year and a half and interest of 7.5 percent. As the memorandum read, "these measures should allow the shutdown of the Chiron factories to be avoided."[27] The Chiron works committee and the trade unions had agreed to the sale of the company, as had the SPD representative in Müller's cabinet, interior minister Viktor Renner.[28]

A few days later, ownership of the Chiron corporation was transferred to Kiehn. Instead of paying Stäbler the DM 1.5 million they had agreed on, however, he gave him only DM 450,000, bringing their friendship of almost three decades to an end. The amount was barely a third of the price the industrialist had promised Stäbler verbally, and less than what Kiehn would receive four months later for reselling the branch plant in the American zone.[29] These were not the only things to turn out differently than Kiehn, his family, creditors, and proponents had expected.

In early June 1950, disturbing news made the rounds in Tuttlingen: Trippel, who an SS observer had already attested was "so impulsive that he scandalizes everyone,"[30] had made his debut at Chiron. The "airs" he put on caused complaints right away. The district head of the Deutscher Gewerkschaftsbund (Confederation of German Trade Unions, or DGB), Fleck, who had previously agreed to let Kiehn buy Chiron, now demanded an explanation of "the groups around Kiehn and behind the management of the property." The organized workers were wondering, he informed the government, at whose mercy they would be "for the consequences." He declared of Trippel that "one could overlook the fact that this man was once an active fighter for the 3rd Reich [sic]," but it was all the worse "that in our view, he still is."[31]

In the meantime, the *Gränzbote* newspaper had reported that Protek was being transferred from Stuttgart to the Chiron factories, under the headline "Important Engineering Firm in Tuttlingen." Trippel beat the propaganda drum himself and announced on 16 January 1950, to general surprise, his plans to design a small car in Tuttlingen that was to be "especially favorable aerodynamically." He also unabashedly declared that this constituted the "continued development" of his "amphibious vehicle experiences," and that the "pilot series" of this car was to be built in Tuttlingen. There was also talk in Tuttlingen of Kiehn's plans to produce a portable Swiss typewriter under license. His intentions came to naught. Amid these seemingly bizarre projects, for which the paper goods manufacturer lacked experience in launching, doubts arose as to whether Kiehn's intent to rehabilitate the company was serious, and whether the millions had been appropriately invested, adding economic reservations to the existing political ones.

Those around Kiehn were uneasy about Trippel's rush to proceed. Kaufmann, the Efka CEO, and Burmeister, Chiron's custodian until March 1950, had to register their concerns that Trippel — incompetent in commercial enterprise as he was — had usurped the management of Kiehn's company. When his in-laws moved back into the Deibhalde villa in 1950, Trippel and his wife went with them, demonstrating his claim to succession in the "family empire." It was purportedly Berta Kiehn's doing to hand over the reins to their dominant son-in-law.[32]

Kaufmann and Burmeister, who distrusted Trippel's plans, undertook investigations into his shady past, which meant the end of their employment. Kiehn's dear friend Kaufmann, who had worked so hard to have both of the Kiehns rehabilitated, was dismissed without notice, albeit with a considerable severance payment, whereas Burmeister's hopes of ending up in a "comfortable position" were smashed.[33] Two authorized officers of Efka were also dismissed around the beginning of 1950. One had testified at his own denazification proceedings that his boss had compelled workers and employees to join the party before 1933. The other confirmed that this practice was "common at the Efka factory." When their denazification files were leaked to Kiehn, he fired both of them on the spot.[34] The crowd of disappointed aspirants and embittered enemies grew alarmingly.

In Tuttlingen, Kiehn quickly succeeded in calming the waves that Trippel's confusing propaganda had made. He countered articles alleging that Chiron was giving up on surgical instrument manufacturing, and he arranged a meeting with Trippel and two trade union representatives. Fleck, the DGB district chair, announced once again that "political reservations" should take a backseat to "economic and social considerations." The works committee even agreed to come to terms with Trippel becoming a second managing director. However, the union representatives made a point of stressing that Trippel should not become "the workers' and employees' boss" but that Fritz Kiehn, "described by his former employees as extremely generous with benefits," should take over management of the company. Fleck reported to the Finance Ministry on 4 February 1950 that with these measures, the unions considered "the matter of the takeover of the Chiron works by the Efka works ... settled."[35]

At first, no one outside the Tuttlingen district paid any heed to the fact that the business expansion of former Nazi economic leader Kiehn was being financed with money from the state. The loan to Kiehn had been nothing special, as far as the Tübingen government was concerned. The German federal state of Württemberg-Hohenzollern had already ensured the survival of a series of companies in the postwar era by granting them loans or acting as a guarantor, ignoring the political past of the owners of those companies. In all cases, the aid from the state had been granted exclusively for reasons of economic and social welfare. For example, former president of the Gau Economic Chamber Rudolf Rohrbach repeatedly received money from the public purse for his cement factory in Dotternhausen before he was even released from internment. No one had taken exception to this, including the military government.[36] Why, they may have said to themselves in Tübingen, should the Chiron case be any different?

But this time there was an uncommonly high amount in play and a loan made in hard currency. "Many trusted entrepreneurs who ended up in financial distress because of the war and its consequences," as well as those "whose operations were shut down for political reasons by the National Socialists in power," had gone after such subsidies in vain.[37]

One man's intransigent attitude kept the townspeople from simply going back to business as usual after the change in ownership of the Chiron company in Württemberg: because of him, they were again confronted with the difficulties of how to come to terms with the past appropriately. This was SPD politician Fritz Erler, who had been head of the Tuttlingen district administration before his election to the first German Bundestag and was well versed in the local goings-on. Erler (1913–1967) had been a member of Berlin's Socialist Workers Youth and had been a leader of the Neu Beginnen (New Beginning) resistance group during the Third Reich. In 1939, the People's Court had sentenced him to ten years in jail for "high treason," and he had spent "dreadful years" in various concentration camps and jails. He composed a manifesto in 1946 entitled "Socialism as a Duty of the Present," where he sketched out a model of a new economic order. Socialization of the economy, exclusion of Nazi elites, integration of the youth who had been led astray by National Socialism, and restitution for National Socialist injustice were Erler's chief issues. He retained substantial influence with the SPD in Württemberg, even if he had only belonged to the state council for a few weeks.[38]

For reasons relating to the politics of the past and economic regulation, Erler opposed making a loan of millions to a prominent former National Socialist and the undisputed market leader of the cigarette paper sector. He was convinced that "any fool would have been able to make Chiron profitable again with 3 million," remarking to a party colleague indignantly that "a cry of outrage ought to have gone up from the Württemberg business community when the Finance Ministry … announced that they needed an old Nazi to hold on to 250 jobs. The businessmen took this ignominy lying down."[39]

Erler not only had an aversion to Kiehn's history as an "old Nazi" and National Socialist economic functionary, one who had used his position as head of the "cigarette filter tubes" division — according to complaints from his competitors — to add to his own personal wealth until 1945. Erler also fought the "monopolist" in Kiehn, whose industry peers lamented his "liberalist" methods to Erler. In this, Erler's socialist convictions joined together with traditional *Mittelstand* resentments. Summing up the situation, one of Kiehn's industry colleagues remarked, "No one would fear an honorable competitor who is true to his word. … The effect in the end, however, is that it is not the capable one who emerges victorious, but the one with more capital who simply defeats his opponents with the aid of advertising and the mass psychosis [it produces]. … Liberalization therefore only benefits big capital. … It furthers the contrasts between poor and rich, small and large, and annihilates smaller and midlevel livelihoods merely by putting out capital and advertising. ... In any case," the letter writer announced, "I will use any legal means possible to put a stop to Kiehn's thoughts of monopoly." He even suggested that "the corporation of other manufacturers could at any time carry on the business as a private, limited company," and that concerns about employees were therefore misplaced.[40]

Erler did his best to "neutralize" the Trossingen industrialist.[41] He committed a year and a half to the "Kiehn case": questioning witnesses, collecting incriminating material, informing his party comrades in the state parliament, writing articles in the press, and criticizing the Wholesale Purchasing Company of German Consumer Cooperatives (Großeinkaufs-Gesellschaft Deutscher Konsumgenossenschaften, GEG), an organization close to the SPD, for working "with the Fritz Kiehn firm in Trossingen." The GEG responded that the business relationship with Efka had been in place since 1925. Of course, the directors were aware, Erler was told, "that Herr Kiehn was one of the high officials during the 3rd Reich [sic]." But their efforts to switch their orders to products from a different manufacturer had been futile, "since the buying cooperatives we supplied demanded Efka cigarette papers almost exclusively. ... Our sales with the KIEHN firm are not insignificant. We cannot see clearly," the party comrade wrote to the SPD delegate, "why we as the GEG should do without these sales."[42]

Erler initiated an inquiry among the SPD faction in the Bundestag to determine whether the German federal minister of finance or the state of Württemberg-Hohenzollern had promised Kiehn a tax deferral.[43] A parliamentary inquiry of the SPD faction in the state parliament followed, and finally SPD delegate Kalbfell brought forward a motion in the name of his party to appoint a parliamentary review committee. The Tübingen parliament's council of elders spoke out against establishing such a committee. Most of the people's representatives favored rebuilding, not engaging in a public reckoning with the past. They called for a commission of the finance committee — shielded from the public — to look into the circumstances of the loan being granted and used. The SPD withdrew its motion as a result.

In early May 1950, the SPD faction turned to the state commissioner for political cleansing and requested that Kiehn's denazification proceedings be reopened. It was believed that new incriminating material had been located, including the Gau court verdict from 1939, as well as additional witnesses. But it came to light that all of the ostensibly new material that had supposedly been so shocking to those who saw the files had already been known to the denazification court when it declared Kiehn a "Lesser Offender," so there was no chance of reopening the case after all.[44]

The finance committee's investigations threatened to fizzle out. Contradicting Kiehn's promises to the Finance Ministry, Trippel pushed for the Tuttlingen plant to stop producing surgical instruments. The ministry, which meanwhile had come under fire from the public, did not allow it.⁴⁵ On 13 June, an article by Erler plainly criticizing the Tübingen government appeared in the *Neue Zeitung* newspaper published by the American military government: "The Taxpayer and the Loan for Millions: Württemberg-Hohenzollern Draws an Unlucky Hand." The Bundestag delegate concentrated primarily on the implications of the state loan for the national economy, dropping only discreet hints about Kiehn's political past. Erler, who was able to draw on information from the numerous disgruntled former managers of Efka and Chiron, had discovered that even as Kiehn was applying for a state loan — ostensibly to return Chiron to profitability — he had been putting substantial sums into other projects. Smaller firms competing with Efka had been bought up, new companies such as Trevit had emerged, and DM 1.2 million had been put toward a "building materials company in North Rhine-Westphalia."⁴⁶ Erler first informed the public of the ominous small car project, writing critically of the shortfalls in "all technical requirements of production." In the meantime, the surgical instrument manufacturing at Chiron that was vital to the export economy was going to be sold off in an irresponsible fashion. Valuable equipment and tools would be "sold for scrap," and established skilled workers would be laid off in order to employ new staff and increase the numbers of those working for "the fanciful amphibious vehicle engineer."⁴⁷

Kiehn ordered all the copies of the *Neue Zeitung* destined for southern Württemberg to be bought up.⁴⁸ As a result, a continuation of Erler's article was published on 15 June, shedding extensive light on Kiehn's past and asking the question: "Is there really no other possibility for rebuilding German industry than using perpetual opportunists in the mold of Herr Kiehn?"⁴⁹ Up to this point, the papers in Württemberg had skipped over the topic without comment. They evidently needed a "suggestion" from the military government's chief of cabinet in order to finally address the subject on their front pages.⁵⁰ After that, no newspaper in the state failed to report on the matter in detail. Colonel Corbin de Mangoux considered it "pleasing proof of the views against renazification,"⁵¹ whereas the CDU in southern Württemberg denounced Erler's "treason" and criticized the press for supposedly acting as the military government's lackeys.⁵² Interest in the Tübingen events also began to emerge in neighboring Württemberg-Baden: "State Loan of Three Million DM for SS Chief Storm Leader [Captain] Kiehn," read the main headline in the *Stuttgarter Zeitung*, whose title page featured a photograph of a resplendent Kiehn in his SS uniform.⁵³ An article from the *Bote vom Heuberg* registered the political explosiveness that had been tamped down for so long: "For the state of Württemberg-Hohenzollern to give such a man a loan for such an astounding amount. ... Poor the state, and even poorer the democracy, that the people must come to the aid of once again ... [the very] people ... they [the state and democracy] had held in camps for years!" The paper vividly described the disastrous effect that subsidizing "one of the most unscrupulous and yet ... most successful beneficiaries of the Third Reich" had to have on the political culture of the state, accusing the government of having double standards: "It will not do for you [the government] to deny an official his former place just because he had Nazi convictions, when at the same time you grant Kiehn, who had no convictions but is 'well-heeled,' a loan so that he can spread himself even further." The article culminated in the remark, "Senior SS leader and Reichstag member Fritz Kiehn as a savior — the subject is ripe for satire."[54] Others could not resist taking the bait, composing malicious rhymes about Kiehn's dealings and thus delivering forceful proof of the politically disastrous signals coming from the loan issue.[55]

Even as the newspapers tossed barbs his way, Kiehn likely took pleasure in the solidarity of his workforce and the support of the trade unions. Some of his employees, out of protest against the "newspaper campaign," collected enough signatures to force an extraordinary all-company meeting in the "Chiron-Protek works" on 30 June 1950. Even the union members present distanced themselves from critical articles and praised their employer Kiehn, who on 1 May (International Workers' Day) had made a good impression on his workers by paying them each five Deutschmarks extra. Besides this, twelve employees had already been sent "to the [company] vacation home in Ludwigshafen." The representative from the IG-Metall union welcomed the fact "that a company with such social welfare facilities has finally come to Tuttlingen; this should, by all means, serve as an example to the rest of the business owners in Tuttlingen."

The "works elder" at the Efka factory declared it "a profoundly sad sign that Erler and his crowd would sling mud at Herr Kiehn, whom I have always known to be exemplary in any situation. Such filthy articles occasion our disgust. ... Herr Kiehn was a National Socialist and had to atone for that long enough, and every prisoner and criminal is left alone after he has served his sentence — but in Herr Kiehn's case the grumbling is constant." Even Heinrich Wicke, a former SS colonel and president of the Stuttgart police who had been hired by Kiehn in the meantime, considered it necessary, "as a friend of Herr Kiehn's, to stand up for him."

Finally, Kiehn himself appealed to his "dear work comrades" with a resentment-laden philippic against Erler that was bursting with self-righteousness: "I do not know Herr Erler," he admitted, but said he was sure that "never in his entire life has he accomplished what I have." Kiehn rejected Erler's attacks on the grounds that "he understands nothing ... of economics and economic governance, or of rebuilding a company." He dismissed the reporting on his political past as "horse puckey," inventing stories of a grueling twelve-year battle against his party, but he avoided discussing Erler's role as a resistance fighter. He dispensed a slogan — "Today what matters is the man, and nothing else" — and complained that "I must endure criticism from incompetents and ne'er-do-wells."[56]

Another company assembly, attended by Fritz Erler at the invitation of Chiron management, ended in an uproar when the SPD politician and victim of

Nazi persecution was methodically shouted down by the employees. Two Chiron employees spoke in his place, again singing Kiehn's praises and this time even threatening to boycott the local newspaper "if the press carries on in this way."[57] The State News Agency of Württemberg-Hohenzollern spread the news of Erler's flop to all the newspapers and radio stations, while the *Schwäbisches Tagblatt*, under the headline, "Have We Come This Far Again Already?," remarked that "they have managed here to rope in the workers for the personal interests of the company management in a way that is embarrassingly similar to the methods of the Third Reich. ... Democracy was grossly offended in the [actions against the] person of Bundestag delegate Erler."[58]

As Fritz Erler would later acknowledge, "loneliness among his own people" had shaped his life in the Third Reich. According to his biographer, Hartmut Soell, his sadness about it was "perceptible even decades later," in part because this loneliness "could only be broken through in places" after 1945. His experiences at the Chiron factory in 1950 must have been formative in this regard. Soell claimed that "the conduct by the Tuttlingen trade unions on the Kiehn matter also undeniably caused Erler to lose his interest in the Rottweil/Tuttlingen electoral district" and to choose a different district in which to run for office in the Bundestag elections of 1953.[59]

Fig. 33: The Chiron factory celebrates: "The President's 65th Birthday" (1950). (Private collection of the Kiehn family)

The state parliament, noting the lively response in the media, finally addressed the matter of the DM 3 million loan on 1 August 1950, focusing on the loan recipient. FDP/DVP delegate Haux, the respected owner of a long-established company in Ebingen, pronounced the verdict: "Herr Fritz Kiehn is well known in Württemberg and beyond for his smarmy wheeling and dealing — which even some of his former party comrades have objected to. The coldly calculating industrialist Kiehn is certainly not the typical Swabian entrepreneur." With the SPD and the Freie Demokratische Partei (Free Democratic Party, or FDP/DVP) voting in favor, the state parliament ultimately resolved to establish a parliamentary review committee "to clear up the Kiehn-Trossingen matter." In keeping with their majority in the state parliament, the committee was dominated by the CDU, which also held the chair.[60] From the beginning, the work of the committee suffered from its imprecise investigative mandate. To the end, its members continued to argue about whether their chief task was to illuminate Kiehn's and Trippel's past or to check the necessity and appropriate use of the loan, or whether the primary matter at hand was how far the state government had acted in the legally correct manner and in the interests of the state. One consequence of the vague aim of the review was that evidence hearings got out of hand. Twenty-four witnesses were heard in eight public and three closed meetings, among them the entire squad of former authorized officers, custodians, and chief executives at

Fig. 34: Trippel and the Kiehns at a social evening at Chiron (ca. 1950). (Private collection of the Kiehn family)

Chiron and Efka who had been given the ax by Kiehn and Trippel, as well as officials from the Finance and Economics Ministries and the Assets Control Office, not to mention Stäbler, Trippel, and Kiehn. What was discussed, as the *Deutsche Zeitung* in Stuttgart accurately put it in March 1951, was "often dirty laundry": tax evasion, infringement of assets controls, the failure of forced administration, taking advantage, bribery, blackmail, and false accounting.[61]

Albrecht Richter, the Efka custodian, had committed the worst transgressions. Indescribable mismanagement had arrived in Trossingen under his trusteeship. Anyone could dip into Efka's coffers, provided they gave Richter "his share." Profiteers of his time in office included the management staff and not least Fritz Kiehn, who had to scrape deep into his purse to satisfy Richter's insatiable desires but could then have carte blanche to do as he liked, almost as if the controls on his assets did not exist. Richter collected DM 1,000 monthly, in addition to his custodian's salary, for "advising in restitution matters" and drawing up an incorporation contract. He also pocketed another DM 16,000 that was listed in the account books as a loan. In return, he authorized commissions for Efka representatives that were "higher than the salaries of minister-presidents."[62] Some Deutschmarks were also diverted to Fritz Kiehn in this fashion, so he kept quiet about them, even as Richter's desires took on "ever larger forms."

All of this took place without the Finance Ministry noticing that Richter had appointed himself chief executive officer of the WVT,[63] making him both the executive and controlling authority. The repeated complaints about his custodianship fell on deaf ears. Kiehn's attempt to rid himself of Richter by paying him off failed too; in response, Richter threatened to go public with the fact that incriminating documents had gone missing in Kiehn's denazification proceedings, and things remained the same. In the meantime, Richter acquired copies from Kiehn's denazification records, passed them off as originals, and attempted to use these as blackmail to obtain a five-year contract in a highly remunerative position.[64]

Nevertheless, the business connections between the two lasted even after the assets controls were lifted. Richter switched to a sales representative position at Homogen, the Stuttgart company run by Dr. W., while he continued receiving a salary from Kiehn.[65] To the review committee this looked like some kind of hush money, but like many suspicious facts it had uncovered, this could not be proven. Kiehn had also generously "compensated" those who might have known the real circumstances; they were not exactly bursting with information for the review committee.

Nor was the committee able to bring any clarity to the central issues. When the committee ended its review, newspapers ran the headline, "Only Incomplete Work in Bebenhausen."[66] The committee chair himself, a delegate named Schneider, declared to the state parliament that "finding the truth was an unresolvable task for the parliamentary review committee." This confession contradicted his own concluding report, which had described the loan "to Fritz Kiehn's

Efka factory in Trossingen" as being correct "in the interest of the state." No proof had been found of "any improprieties."[67]

It remained unclear whether the DM 3 million had really been necessary in order to save the 250 jobs at Chiron, or how much of the money Kiehn had put into his Trossingen company or some other one. It could not be established where the manufacturer, who had serious liquidity issues of his own in the fall of 1949, had found the funds to invest in firms like Protek, Trevit, and Homogen, in addition to fulfilling his own restitution obligations. The subscription to a bond issuance from a construction company in North Rhine-Westphalia for DM 1.2 million, occurring at almost the same time as the opening of the loan in Württemberg, posed another conundrum.[68] The confidentiality of tax records stood in the way of a detailed investigation of Kiehn's transactions. Although the tax investigation against Kiehn began in the summer of 1950, this confidentiality law continues to prevent us from clarifying this aspect of the "Kiehn matter" even today.[69]

The circumstances of the loan also remained unclear, above all the role played by the head of the Finance Ministry, undersecretary Vowinkel. There is proof that Vowinkel had known Kiehn's son-in-law since the war, as well as his attorney Dr. W. The representations of the nature and intensity of this relationship, however, varied widely. Both of the Efka authorized officers that Kiehn had fired after becoming infuriated at their accusations to a denazification court testified under oath before the review committee that Trippel had nearly gone into raptures upon learning that the authority at the Tübingen Finance Ministry was his acquaintance from back in the Molsheim days. "We have no need for any more worry. ... My dear father. ... You'll get your three million DM, I guarantee you," they quoted Trippel as saying to Fritz Kiehn during a crisis meeting of the company management, apparently gesturing at the same time to indicate that Vowinkel could be bribed.[70]

These "very substantiated statements" made under oath against a leading government official were simply dismissed by the CDU majority on the committee without closer examination as "unfounded gossip."[71] Instead, they believed the denials from Kiehn and Trippel, both of whom invested great effort into portraying Vowinkel as an irreproachable official with whom neither of them, they wished to convey, had any closer connection.[72] The committee failed on this issue because of the traditionally pronounced esprit de corps among the senior Württemberg officials, the intraparty solidarity among the CDU faction, and a reverential reluctance to find fault with the government, or even the state president, that extended to the ranks of the opposition.[73]

How little the parliament saw itself as a controlling body of the government is clear from a remark by liberal delegate Haux (FDP/DVP), who had advocated the creation of a review committee to clarify the "Kiehn matter" before the parliament but then immediately added that "the conduct of our state government, especially the state president and our Finance Ministry, is beyond reproach." A parliamentary review committee would come to the same conclusion, he said.[74] Vowinkel himself held the government responsible for defending him "against such unjust attacks" as those expressed before the committee. If it did not, he said, it might occasionally give the "impression that it is not Kiehn under accusation, but myself."[75]

At the first public meeting of the committee, member Otto Künzel (SPD) submitted a request to present evidence. When his series of open questions touched on Vowinkel's role, the state president, who was there as an observer, interrupted him, ostensibly because his questions were "a severe defamation to the state government." The committee chair immediately revoked the floor from Künzel and afforded Vowinkel the opportunity to defend himself.[76] According to Schneider, the committee chair, Künzel had severely transgressed the right every delegate had to rebuke people for abuses before the state parliament: "The harsh formulations were repeatedly and fundamentally directed at our state president."[77] When weeks later Vowinkel appeared before the committee for the second time as a sole witness — this time under official subpoena — he was the only witness who was not sworn in. SPD members rebelled, refusing to accept the undersecretary's seemingly "off-limits" status, but their efforts were in vain.[78]

The SPD spokesperson rightly accused Schneider's concluding report of an "extraordinarily one-sided assessment of the evidence." Schneider had dedicated a mere two sentences of his remarks to pointing out that criminal investigations were underway against a series of people — including Kiehn — on suspicion of blackmail, favoritism, disloyalty, and tax offenses. In only one case (authorized officer B., the chief prosecution witness against Vowinkel) had the committee chair submitted a criminal complaint for suspicion of perjury. The accusation was thrown out by the public prosecutor's office of the Tübingen Regional Court after extensive investigation, which had taken the contrary view that "the true facts of the matter follow mainly from B.'s statements."[79]

The committee's report failed to mention that the bills of exchange Kiehn had issued "to date have not been redeemable and that the initially short-term secured loan ... wholly contrary to the optimistic remarks made by Herr Undersecretary Vowinkel to the review committee — had to be changed into an investment loan with an approximately five-year term."[80] No bank had been willing to step in as creditor in the state's place. In response, the question of whether, in comparable conditions, the state could have found less politically dubious saviors for the Chiron factories was raised with new vehemence. But even in the ranks of the SPD, almost no one wanted to deal with the "Kiehn matter" anymore. Delegate Metzger had written to Fritz Erler that she "had no intention of doing anything else about this case" either: when she called out state parliament member Fritz Fleck, DGB president for the Tuttlingen district, for his "conduct when converting the loan," she had to "listen to the usual impertinences from Gen. Fleck once again." None of her party comrades had supported her, she complained; "on the contrary, it was once again stated that no one cared about the Kiehn matter outside the state [of Württemberg]."[81] Under these conditions, it was no wonder that a request raised in the state parliament by the FDP/DVP faction to postpone closing the investigations until the criminal proceedings had been decided found no majority support. Instead, the majority agreed with state president Gebhard Müller, who had pleaded that they should "let the Kiehn case go" and content themselves with "not being responsible for Herr Kiehn's denazification proceedings leaving him as company manager."[82]

While the tax authorities and public prosecutor's office continued their investigations, and Otto Stäbler filed a civil suit against Kiehn because he felt he had been cheated, the first item of business for the Efka boss was to put his company and family back in order — his daughter's marriage to Trippel, the supposedly brilliant automotive engineer, had fallen apart. By the fall of 1950, a few weeks after their child was born, Trippel had already moved out of Deibhalde. Kiehn's daughter and grandchild both took Kiehn's name, and Trippel became a taboo topic in the Kiehn household.[83] His business collaboration with Trippel's attorney, Dr. W., likewise came to an abrupt end. The lawyer left his position as managing director even before the Homogen works burned down in 1952.[84]

On 25 April 1951, Fritz Kiehn paid a visit to the French Tuttlingen district governor Jean Lucien Estrade in order to inform him that the Protek company headquarters was being moved again, and that Trippel would no longer be his son-in-law. After that, Trippel moved back to Stuttgart. The "pilot series" of his small car had never come into being, but the "amphibious vehicle" design engineer did not give up his automotive dreams, even after his sudden departure from Tuttlingen. He never achieved economic success, however, and by 1953 was said to have accumulated many liabilities "as a result of his incompetent bookkeeping," as an informant to the judicial authorities put it. In September 1954, the Baden-Württemberg Ministry of Justice ordered the unrecoverable procedural costs of Trippel's denazification expunged; they had been reduced in stages from their original amount of DM 45,250 to an ultimate cost of DM 300. "The debtor has nothing that can be seized and is highly indebted," established the authorities.[85]

After the disastrous end of his daughter's marriage, Kiehn finally recognized Trippel's weaknesses as a businessman and technical expert. He declared to Estrade that Trippel had been arrogant to employees, had understood little about business, and had lacked the necessary steadiness in his engineering work. The Efka boss wanted to head Chiron himself for the time being, stating to the district governor that he considered its rehabilitation finished.[86] Despite the economic recovery of the surgical instrument market, his estimation bore little semblance to reality. After shifting about a fourth of Efka's monthly cigarette paper production from Trossingen to Tuttlingen, as well as about half of the cardboard box production, Chiron was still deeply in the red in 1952, causing even more production to be transferred. The government's loan missed the target in terms of both business management and labor market policy. Chiron had no new revenues to offset its additional costs for cigarette paper and cardboard box manufacturing. What first looked like an impressive increase in employee numbers at the Chiron factory actually derived from more experienced workers commuting in from Trossingen. As a graduate student in business management in 1957, Kiehn's grandson, Herbert, had tried to estimate the damage that Chiron had done to the family business and came out with an amount of "around DM 14 million." It cannot be verified whether these figures stand up to critical inspection. It must therefore remain a mystery whether, under the specific conditions of the developing market of 1949–1950, rapidly increasing production facilities and diversifying production may have given Efka a crucial strategic advantage. We also cannot determine how much of the losses were absorbed through tax-deductible depreciation and thereby partly imposed on the state and the municipality.[87] This much was clear to Herbert E. Kiehn, however: "Idiocy and helplessness, combined with clueless advisers and poor insight into human nature, occasioned an inglorious entrepreneurial adventure, over which the still-shining profits from the core cigarette paper business soon drew a merciful veil."[88]

Fritz Kiehn's intention to gain recognition among the Tuttlingen townspeople by rescuing the Chiron factories failed resoundingly too. Kiehn announced to district governor Estrade that he wanted to silence the industrialists in the district, none of whom — as he knew — liked him, because in their opinion his employee benefits were too generous. It was therefore a matter of honor for him, he said, to help the Chiron works achieve a veritable boom.[89] Nothing came of this either. The investment loan from the state had just been paid off and preparations for the expansion of the Efka factory in Trossingen were underway when in early 1957 (according to Herbert E. Kiehn), after continuous high losses, Kiehn sold Chiron to Düsseldorf pipe wholesalers Hoberg & Driesch "for a song."[90]

His failed takeover of Chiron had legal repercussions for Kiehn and two codefendants. Various statements before the review committee had brought evidence of criminal acts to light. The resulting investigations undertaken by the public prosecutor's office confirmed that Efka management had violated the law on numerous occasions while the company was under forced administration. Kiehn, who had bought the good behavior of "his" custodian, had been involved as well, which contradicted his statements to the review committee. He was therefore charged with perjury and active bribery. Kiehn's political past, on the other hand, played no role before the court, nor did the case deal with the loan from the state. As the indictment soberly put it, no "prosecutable actions" had been established "regarding the attainment and use of the loan or the purchase of shares in the Chiron business." The main defendant was not Kiehn, in any case, but Richter, the former Efka custodian, who had to answer for charges of attempted blackmail, taking bribes in office, embezzlement, and perjury.[91]

Nevertheless, Kiehn was already portraying himself as a victim of supposedly politically motivated justice in the run-up to the trial, which did not conclude until late 1954. His snub by the Trossingen town council reinforced his desire to play this role: council members from the SPD, CDU, and FDP/DVP, informed of Kiehn's past and the pending legal proceedings, had demonstratively refused to cooperate with the industrialist after his reelection to the council in 1953.[92]

Kiehn's choice of defense counsel corresponded to his self-image as a victim of political persecution, bringing the manufacturer into contact with important former members of the Nazi elite. These people had been removed from power in 1945 but had escaped practically any legal consequences and were already rising back up through the ranks of society. Kiehn had engaged the services of "general amnesty lobbyist and international law expert" Professor Friedrich Grimm, a top lawyer who had been highly esteemed in international law circles since the Weimar Republic for representing the German heavy industrialists during the occupation of the Ruhr (1923–1925). At that time, Grimm had defended captains of industry such as Fritz Thyssen, Robert and Hermann Röchling, and Gustav Krupp von Bohlen und Halbach in French military tribunals. In the late 1920s, he was defense counsel to members of the Black Reichswehr paramilitary group in the trials prosecuting so-called *Fememorde,* or secret political murders. Even before the Nazi era, he had been the spokesperson for the campaign to grant amnesty to Rhineland fighters and Free Corps (Freikorps) killers. A law professor, Grimm had advised Hitler on questions of international law during the Third Reich. He prosecuted the charge against the Jewish assassin of Wilhelm Gustloff in a court in Grisons, Switzerland; Gustloff was the founder of the Swiss Nazi organization for German party members abroad. Grimm also prosecuted Herschel Grynszpan, who assassinated the low-ranking German diplomat Ernst vom Rath in Paris.[93] However, he also defended Cologne mayor Konrad Adenauer and Center Party politician Mönning against accusations of corruption in the Görres-Haus case in Cologne.[94]

Grimm settled in Freiburg in the postwar era after several years in prison, but became a lively presence in Bonn circles. Together with the Essen law office of North Rhine-Westphalia FDP politician Ernst Achenbach, where Werner Best, the former "SS crown jurist," and Professor Franz Alfred Six, a former SS senior group leader, also found an institutional home,[95] Grimm professionally pursued the rehabilitation of Nazi perpetrators. The efforts by Grimm and his allies, most of whom were committed to the cause for their own benefit, were aimed at "liquidating" the prosecution of all Nazi crimes as rapidly as possible.[96] When in 1951 the Munich public prosecutor's office filed murder charges against Werner Best, who was among those chiefly responsible for the killings on the Night of the Long Knives, Grimm used his legal expertise to argue that the

Führer's decree exempting those responsible for the acts on 30 June 1934 from punishment had to be respected as a "legal amnesty" in the Federal Republic of Germany as well, "lest justice again be misused for political aims."[97] Werner Naumann could count on legal support from Grimm too. Imprisoned in January 1953, he had been state undersecretary in the Reich Propaganda Ministry, and Hitler had named him Goebbels's successor in his will. Naumann was taken into custody, together with six other "ringleaders," in a spectacular operation by the British military government in 1953. Both the British and German intelligence services then received information that the group they had apprehended, including high-ranking former members of the NSDAP, had specifically infiltrated the North Rhine-Westphalia FDP and was making preparations to "take back power in West Germany." Grimm's partner, Achenbach, had played a crucial role in this subversive process; his office had seen a diverse array of interconnections between the propagandists for amnesty and the proponents of a nationalist, anti-Western course for the FDP.[98]

Kiehn would have met Grimm by 1933 at the latest, when the professor entered the Reichstag.[99] Three years after the review committee had ceased its work on the "Kiehn matter," the case was tried before the Tübingen Regional Court.[100] Kiehn and Richter were the only ones still facing charges. The third accused, authorized officer B., had committed his alleged offenses in the period before 15 September 1949, and because these were considered to be minor, they met the requirements for amnesty under the first German federal law granting immunity from prosecution of 13 December 1949. With this law, Adenauer's administration had wanted to make a clean break with "the past, with its poverty, its complexity, and its primitiveness born of war and the postwar era."[101] Richter was also able to take partial advantage of this amnesty. In addition, he benefited from the fact that he had not been a civic official in any legal sense as the head of WVT or as Efka's custodian. Because of this, regardless of his level of corruption, he could not technically be guilty of being bribed. This is how he ended up receiving a three-month prison sentence for perjury and given credit for time served from his pretrial imprisonment.[102]

Just as Richter's charge for accepting bribes was dropped, the charge brought against Fritz Kiehn for actively making them was automatically canceled as well. Consequently, when the case was finally tried before the Criminal High Court of the Tübingen Regional Court, the only charge Kiehn still faced, with the help of two prestigious attorneys, was that of perjury. The charge was based on a "statement of little importance," without any political implication. It must have seemed downright ridiculous, then, when Kiehn's top attorney used the trial to make a closing argument lasting several hours that depicted the case as one of utmost significance: "Your Honor, a case of very special importance has been tried before you in these days, a case that in its way represents a piece of contemporary history ... a case with a political background!"[103] Grimm invoked the confirmation by Karl Gengler, a CDU delegate in the Reichstag and former state parliament president, not to mention a personal friend of the Kiehns, who, as requested, had confirmed that the "committee to clear up the Kiehn-Trossingen matter" had been appointed "only for political reasons."[104] This indisputable fact, however, in no way permitted the conclusion that the same applied to the public prosecutor's charge. Kiehn's statement — "If I hadn't been a National Socialist, I wouldn't be standing here"[105] — was only correct insofar as the loan granted to him had only become a political issue because of his brown-shirted past.

Grimm used the "Kiehn case" as propaganda to campaign once again for a general amnesty, claiming that a general sense had spread "that criminal prosecution on account of the anomalous events connected to the war [is] no longer permissible." The "international law principle of *tabula rasa*" had gained legal force, he argued, because of "the normative strength of the facts." He alleged that a general amnesty was "already law — unwritten law, but law," and that, consequently, the suspension of Kiehn's proceedings was the only option.[106] With a mix of pathos, intransigence, and impertinence, he vividly described in his summation the dangers of "our legal culture." Acting as though he — of all people — had been appointed to demand the rule of law, he concluded, "At first we may not have really noticed that the totalitarian system took the legal ground out from under us. ... The path back to law is difficult! We must find it!" He believed that regaining complete national sovereignty was the key to doing so. Oddly enough, Grimm left his audience in suspense as to how justice had been misused for political ends, and by whom; he drew parallels between conditions in the Weimar Republic and under National Socialism, as well as in the present day. "Trials with political intent! This has become a very serious problem that has taken on ever more terrifying forms in all the countries of our [German] culture since World War I. ... 'Justice has become the prostitute of politics!'" It was time to put an end to it, he said, and appealed to the court to "dispense justice!" His suggested model, of all things, was Old Germanic law, which had been overused by the Nazi "justice" system as well: "When someone was accused, the people who knew him took the stand as compurgators and swore: 'This man is not capable of any perjurious act.'" Grimm recalled Kiehn's success in the recent town council elections and declared, "All of them were compurgators. You can consider me one too. ... Acquit Kiehn of the charge!"[107]

The court did not intend to go that far, but it did imply that Kiehn had not deliberately spoken an untruth, and therefore convicted him of mere "negligent false testimony" and fined him DM 1,500. Kiehn knew how to turn this into a great success. One day after the trial had concluded, Professor Grimm explained the outcome of the trial to the Efka employees to loud cheers: "Really, this sentence of a fine is so trivial that it should be regarded as a de facto acquittal."[108] Kiehn sent the minutes of the company assembly to friends and acquaintances, while nearly four hundred copies of Grimm's closing argument were printed and distributed to public figures, business partners, acquaintances, employees, sales representatives, and relatives. Recipients included the many radical nationalists around Ernst Achenbach, who had himself received thirty copies of the text. Among those who got the text through Achenbach were his loyal assistant, Werner Best, the chair of the North Rhine-Westphalia association of the FDP; Achenbach's personal aide, Friedrich Middelhauve; Wolfgang Diewerge, who headed the radio division of the Propaganda Ministry until 1945 and had revealed himself to be a fanatical anti-Semite; former prisoner Werner Naumann; and Siegfried Zoglmann, a former member of the Hitler Youth leadership who now published an FDP-affiliated journal called *Die Zukunft* (The Future). "Nazi poet prince" Hans Grimm, still an active and successful writer, was given a copy as well, as was Princess Helene Elisabeth von Isenburg, the head of an "extremely nationalistic 'aid agency.'" Other recipients were Bundestag member Adolf Thadden,[109] a standout in the German Reich Party outlawed in 1953, and finally some true has-beens, such as journalist and dissident Ernst Hanfstängel; the politically passive former Baden minister-president Walter Köhler, who had become a successful businessman; his colleague, retired interior minister D. Karl Pflaumer; as well as the widows of Gregor Straßer and Joachim von Ribbentrop, the former Nazi Foreign Minister whom the Nuremberg Military Tribunal had sentenced to death in 1946. That large-scale industrialists like Springorum and Tengelmann were also among the recipients leads to speculation that industry stood behind Grimm's general amnesty campaign. The Institute for Occupation Matters in Tübingen seems to have been a communications hub, as does far-right publisher Grabert, also in Tübingen.[110]

None of those who answered Kiehn's mail and sent him multiple congratulations came from this right-wing scene. Efka sales representatives were overwhelmingly the ones thanking him for the "informational material" and reporting that they had used it to "respond appropriately to the range of questions from customers."[111] Kiehn also heard from some of his fellow industrialists, including Tuttlingen shoe manufacturer Roland Rieker, who sent him an encouraging letter. A paper producer from Baienfurt expressed his happiness that Kiehn had emerged victorious from his tough struggles, assuring him, "I know what this means; I myself had nasty altercations following the collapse with the former 'rulers' — most of them Communists." Another letter writer felt the need to congratulate Kiehn "on the victory over your muckrakers," and a third, anonymous correspondent suggested: "The most apt response you could give to the far-fetched verdict would be to order construction to begin immediately on the new Efka factory. You couldn't give your enemies a more fitting slap in the face."[112]

Kiehn, who had appealed the Tübingen verdict, was ultimately able to enjoy the second law on immunity from punishment, passed on 17 July 1954. Grimm had played a substantial part in its realization.[113] Following the advice of his attorneys, the industrialist had dispensed with initiating another trial in hopes that he might be acquitted before the German Federal Court. Now he was finally able to wipe the slate of his brown-shirted past very clean.[114] The Tübingen Regional Court decided to abandon proceedings on 20 October, and once again the news was sent to numerous newspaper editorial offices, acquaintances, and business partners. On the other hand, Kiehn made no effort to maintain closer contact with the stalwarts in Grimm's orbit. He evidently was more concerned with ingratiating himself with CDU politicians in Württemberg, so that he might be accepted into the Trossingen town council's good graces after all. He sent Grimm's closing argument to Josef Schneider, the chair of the state parliamentary review committee, and used the opportunity to "sincerely and very warmly" thank the former delegate "for all of your kindnesses." At the same time, he let the CDU member know that he was interested in meeting face-to-face.[115] He wrote to former state secretary Paul Binder to ascertain the mood in the CDU. However, Kiehn found out that two businessmen who had been asked about him viewed him in an "absolutely negative" light. Binder remarked of Kiehn's ill-starred entry into the Trossingen town council: "It would perhaps have been more correct if you had checked out the territory a bit before putting your name forward as an independent candidate." He gave Kiehn, who was now almost seventy, the dubious consolation "that only with the passage of time will things gradually loosen up," and let him know that attempts by Bundestag delegate Gengler to get Trossingen CDU members to regard Kiehn more positively on their ballots had produced exactly the opposite effect. In consequence, even after his rehabilitation before the law, Kiehn had to bide his time quite a while before being accepted back into the elite.

Notes

1. StAS, Wü 13, T2 no. 2775/001, http://www.landesarchiv-bw.de/plink/?f=6-1039573 (accessed 4 Sept. 2012), confidential message from interior minister [Renner] to state commissioner of 5 May 1949.
2. Henke, "Trennung," 52 (cit.), 40; Rauh-Kühne, "Die Unternehmer," 306.
3. StAS, Wü 1, Bü 100, note from the Finance Ministry of 2 June 1950.
4. StAS, Wü 120, Bü 362, letter of 15 Sept. 1949 from Efka custodian Richter to Kiehn in Nußdorf. Richter asked Kiehn "to make sure that no larger immediate payments are agreed upon" and pointed to pending tax claims and restitution payments of more than DM 1 million.
5. StAS, Wü 1, Bü 100a, Stäbler before the PUA, 6th public meeting, p. 49.
6. ASD, NL Erler, Box 85, minutes of a speech by Fritz Kiehn during a company assembly at Chiron on 30 June 1950.
7. StAS, Wü 120, Bü 362, application for excise tax deferral of 12 Sept. 1949; StAS, Wü 1, Bü 100a, PUA, 8th public meeting, p. 39.

8. BA DC, Akte Trippel; BA NS, 19/2683, battalion (Sturmbann) leader Dr. Brandt, personal staff RF-SS to SS group leader Berger of 30 Apr. 1942 (reproduced in Heiber, *Reichsführer!*, doc. no. 108, pp. 117–118.)
9. IfZ, MA 326, 9613–9615 (RF-SS Pers. Stab II), letter from Berger to Himmler of 26 Mar. 1942.
10. The French region of Alsace was occupied by the Germans in 1940. The previous factory owner, Ettore Bugatti, was Italian. He escaped to Bordeaux, in unoccupied France, with most of the factory equipment that could be moved. On 15 January 1942, he sold the Molsheim plant and everything remaining inside to the Reich Aviation Ministry for RM 7.5 million. MAE Colmar, WH C 2963, Molsheim Trippel factories, report on state of assets; Hau, "Les entreprises," 240–242; Vogler and Hau, *Histoire économique*, 292–303.
11. IfZ, MA 326, 9613–9615 (RF-SS Pers. Stab II), telegram from SS group leader Müller, RSHA, to RF-SS of 20 Jan. 1943.
12. MAE Colmar, WH C 2963, Molsheim Trippel factories, report on state of assets of 8 May 1945 and 30 April 1947. The debts listed did *not* include the approximately RM 6.3 million in liabilities to the Reich. Open claims against the RLM, the Society for Aviation, and the Reichsführung-SS put another approximately RM 1.7 million against these additional debts.
13. MdL Haux, Verhandlungen des Landtags, 87th session, 1 Aug. 1950, p. 1698.
14. Dr. W. had taken the stand as an exoneration witness in Stäbler's denazification proceedings. StAS, Wü 13, Bü 2250, affidavit by Dr. W. of 25 Nov. 1948.
15. In March 1942, Dr. W. advocated for Trippel to the RF-SS at the behest of General Field Marshal Milch. IfZ, MA 326, 9613–9615 (RF-SS Pers. Stab II), letter from Berger to Himmler of 23 Mar. 1942.
16. StAL, EL 902/20, Bü 80957 (Trippel denazification records), affidavit from Dr. W.
17. StAS, Wü 1, Bü 100, minutes of a 19 Apr. 1950 meeting between Kiehn and his attorney W. in the Finance Ministry.
18. StAS, Wü 1, Bü 100a, PUA, 8th public meeting, p. 30.
19. Interview with Herbert E. Kiehn of 19–20 May 1998 and letter from Herbert E. Kiehn of 15 May 1999.
20. Letter from Herbert E. Kiehn of 14 Apr. 1999.
21. StAS, Wü 1, Bü 100a, PUA, 6th public meeting, p. 18; StAS, Wü 1, Bü 100a, PUA, 7th public meeting, pp. 12, 15.
22. StAS, Wü 1, Bü 100a, PUA, 5th public meeting, pp. 17, 19 (cit.); StAS, Wü 1, Bü 100a, PUA, 6th public meeting, p. 17.
23. StAS, Wü 1, Bü 100, note from the Finance Ministry of 30 June 1950 concerning a meeting with Kiehn on 22 Nov. 1949.
24. See chap. 10. A few weeks after Trippel's proceedings, the bribery scandal was revealed, the focus of which included Heinz May, chief prosecutor of the central denazification court, who was also the prosecutor in Trippel's trial. May was sentenced to a one-year prison term on 11 May 1950 for aggravated corruptibility. Bräutigam, *Unternehmer*, 386.
25. IfZ, MA 302, 7405–7462 (RF-SS Pers. Stab II).
26. StAS, Wü 1, Bü 100a, PUA, 7th public meeting, p. 14. Information from Werner Kaufmann indicates that Vowinkel was a "removal officer." Vowinkel himself stated his functions during the war with less specificity: he had been "employed under the chief of civil administration and dealt with matters of wages." Ibid.
27. StAS, Wü 1, Bü 100, transcript of 140th session of the State Ministry on 30 Jan. 1950.
28. StAS, Wü 1, Bü 100, minutes of a meeting 3 Feb. 1950 between DGB president for southern Württemberg Fritz Fleck, Kiehn, and Trippel regarding the Efka and Chiron plants.

29. StAS, Wü 1, Bü 100, note from the Finance Ministry of 30 June 1950; StAS, Wü 1, Bü 100a, PUA, 5th public meeting, pp. 3–5. Stäbler lost a civil suit he had brought against Kiehn for breaking his word on 18 Sept. 1953 in the Stuttgart Regional Court.
30. IfZ, MA 302, 7405–7462 (RF-SS Pers. Stab II), letter from Obersturmbannführer Hoffmann to RF-SS personal staff of 22 July 1941.
31. StAS, Wü 1, Bü 100, Fleck to Economics, Finance, and Interior Ministries of the State of Württemberg-Hohenzollern, 13 Jan. 1950 (copy).
32. StAS, Wü 13, T2 no. 2775/001, http://www.landesarchiv-bw.de/plink/?f=6-1039573 (accessed 4 Sept. 2012), statement from Kiehn's attorney Sieger before the state commissioner for political cleansing on 17 July 1950.
33. ASD, NL Erler, Box Nr. 85, letter from Burmeister to MdL Schneider of February 1952. Kaufmann was said to have received DM 107,000 but to have continued making claims against Kiehn. StAS, Wü 1, Bü 100a, PUA, 6th public meeting, p. 18; Verhandlungen des Landtages, 107th session, 25 July 1951, pp. 2106–2109.
34. StAS, Wü 13, T2 no. 2775/001, http://www.landesarchiv-bw.de/plink/?f=6-1039573 (accessed 4 Sept. 2012), letter from Kiehn dismissing authorized officers B. and V. from employment.
35. StAS, Wü 1, Bü 100, ministerial department head Vowinkel to DGB of 1 Feb. 1950; StAS, Wü 1, Bü 100, letter from district office for southern Württemberg-Hohenzollern to Finance Ministry.
36. Verhandlungen des Landtags, 107th session, 25 July 1951, p. 2109; StAS, Wü 2, Bü 774, 42nd meeting of 26 Mar. 1946 of state directorate, RM 500,000 in backing for Portland cement works of Rudolf Rohrbach KG, Dotternhausen, and 92nd meeting of 26 Nov. 1946, RM 100,000 for Rohrbach KG "because the factory has developed good building materials."
37. Speech by state parliament delegate Dr. Friedrich Haux, (Demokratische Volkspartei, DVP), Verhandlungen des Landtags, 87th session, 1 Aug. 1950, p. 1698. Himself an industrialist harmed by National Socialism, Ebingen textile manufacturer Haux spoke from his own experience. See Rauh-Kühne, "Mittelständische Unternehmer," 110–111.
38. Soell, *Fritz Erler*, chaps. 2, 3, 4, 6, and 7.
39. ASD, NL Erler, Box 85, letter from Erler to MdL Otto Künzel of 22 Sept. 1950.
40. ASD, NL Erler, Box 85, letters from cigarette filter tube manufacturer B. of 21 Sept. 1950 and 25 Oct. 1950. On the spread of attitudes hostile to competition and advertising in the economy, see Gries, "Selbstbild."
41. All quotes can be found in StAS, Wü 2, Bü 783, minutes of State Ministry meeting of 28 Nov. 1950. Erler's activity in the "Kiehn case" is documented in ASD, NL Erler, Box 85; see Soell, *Fritz Erler*, 106–107, 132–133.
42. ASD, NL Erler, Box 85, letter from chair of GEG board of directors to Erler of 4 Jan. 1951.
43. The suspicion that federal money had gone to the excise tax credit was not confirmed.
44. StAS, Wü 13, Bü 2775, SPD faction to state commissioner of 12 May 1950; StAS, Wü 13, Bü 2775, state commissioner Mayer to PUA of 29 Jan. 1951.
45. StAS, Wü 1, Bü 100a. On 11 Feb. 1950, Kiehn had assured the Finance Ministry that he would maintain the surgical instrument manufacturing in Tuttlingen. On 10 Mar. 1950, however, his attorney Dr. W. informed the ministry that profit considerations had forced him to abandon this production.
46. This information proved not to be entirely true. Kiehn had invested the DM 1.2 million in fall 1949 as a "tax-saving model" to subscribe to a loan made to a residential construction company in North Rhine-Westphalia. There was also a building materials company with an address in Werfmershalde, Stuttgart, however, called "Homogen." It too belonged to "Kiehn's concern" in 1950, according to information Kiehn's attorney gave to the state commissioner. StAS, Wü 13, Bü 2775.
47. *Neue Zeitung*, 13 June 1950.

48. Kraushaar, *Protest-Chronik,* 1:242. It is unclear whether Kiehn also bought up all the editions from 15 June containing the second part of Erler's article. It drew on broad excerpts from the NSDAP Gau court verdict and had a much fiercer tone than the more moderate first article.
49. *Neue Zeitung,* 15 June 1950.
50. StAS, Wü 2, Bü 476; *Schwäbische Zeitung* (Leutkirch), 2 Dec. 1950.
51. StAS, Wü 2, Bü 476, note of 5 June 1950 from State News Agency to "Herr State President," with handwritten memo.
52. See "Prügelknabe Presse" commentary from the *Schwäbische Zeitung* (Leutkirch), 2 Dec. 1950.
53. *Stuttgarter Zeitung,* 29 June 1950.
54. *Bote vom Heuberg,* 28 June 1950.
55. ASD, NL Erler, Box 85.
56. ASD, NL Erler, Box 85, minutes of company meeting on 30 June 1950 in Chiron-Protek works.
57. *Schwäbische Zeitung* (Leutkirch), 19 July 1950.
58. *Schwäbisches Tagblatt* (Tübingen), 19 July 1950.
59. Soell, *Fritz Erler,* 63, 132–133.
60. Verhandlungen des Landtags, 87th session, 1 Aug. 1950, p. 1698; Verhandlungen des Landtags, 107th session, 25 July 1951, p. 2100.
61. *Deutsche Zeitung* (Stuttgart), 10 March 1951, 5th public meeting, p. 7.
62. StAS, Wü 1, Bü 100a, PUA, 5th public meeting; and 6th public meeting, statement from former manager with statutory authority Karl B., pp. 29–30.
63. StAS, Wü 1, Bü 100a, PUA, 5th public meeting, pp. 1–14.
64. HStAS, EA 4/403, Bü 121, judgment of 8 Mar. 1954 from Tübingen criminal court in the criminal proceedings against Richter and Kiehn.
65. StAS, Wü 1, Bü 100a, PUA, 6th public meeting, p. 38.
66. *Deutsche Zeitung* (Stuttgart), 10 Mar. 1951.
67. Verhandlungen des Landtags, 107th session, 25 July 1951, p. 2106. Report from the PUA to clear up the Kiehn matter, Trossingen.
68. This "tax-saving model," again arranged by Dr. W. in favor of the Westfälische Wohnstätten company in Dortmund, had already infuriated some Swabians because it involved an entrepreneur who had profited from state funds investing his money "into northern Germany." See *Deutsche Zeitung* (Stuttgart), 10 Mar. 1951.
69. *Schwäbische Zeitung* (Leutkirch), 4 July 1950, states that Kiehn's tax offenses were already the object of a serious investigation that had been going on for over five months and had extended to several German federal states.
70. StAS, Wü 1, Bü 100a, PUA, 6th public meeting, pp. 26–27, statement from authorized officer Karl B. Former authorized officer V. also confirmed this comment made by Trippel, allegedly made in his presence, almost word-for-word. He claimed not to have been aware of any accusation of bribery, however. Ibid., 58.
71. StAS, Wü 1, Bü 100a, PUA, 6th public meeting, p. 55.
72. StAS, Wü 1, Bü 100a, PUA, 8th public meeting, pp. 24–25, 44.
73. ASD, NL Erler, Box 85, see the eight-page report, "Der Untersuchungsausschuß Kiehn in seiner bisherigen Tätigkeit," of which Otto Künzel (SPD) was the likely author.
74. Verhandlungen des Landtags, 87th session, 1 Aug. 1950, p. 1700.
75. StAS, Wü 2, Bü 783, minutes of the 187th meeting of the State Ministry of Württemberg-Hohenzollern of 28 Nov. 1950.
76. StAS, Wü 2, Bü 783, minutes of the 142nd meeting of the State Ministry of 28 Nov. 1950.
77. Verhandlungen des Landtags, 107th session, 25 July 1951, report from the PUA for clarification of the Kiehn matter, Trossingen, 2108.

78. Delegate Gertrud Metzger (SPD) wrote this in her concluding report to the state parliament (authorized only by the SPD minority) on the PUA's activity. Verhandlungen des Landtags, 107th session, 25 July 1951, p. 2114.
79. HStAS, E 4/403, Bü 121, indictment of Richter, B., and Kiehn of 22 Nov. 1952.
80. MdL Metzger (SPD), Verhandlungen des Landtags, 107th session, 25 July 1951, p. 2110. Gebhard Müller had to concede: "It is correct that we had to prolong the loan and allowed Kiehn other conditions. ... [F]rom the outset, experts believed it was impossible to expect the loan to be paid back in two years. ... But we were of the opinion that the Efka factories would succeed in getting another bank to refund the state's collateral-based loan of an initial one-to-two-year term within this time."
81. ASD, NL Erler, Box 85, letter from Metzger to Erler of 2 July 1951.
82. Verhandlungen des Landtags, 107th session, 25 July 1951, pp. 2118 (cit.), 2119.
83. Letters from Herbert E. Kiehn of 14 Apr. 1999 and 15 May 1999.
84. StAS, Wü 1, Bü 100a, PUA, 6th public meeting, p. 71.
85. StAL, EL 902/20, Bü 80957 (Trippel denazification records), letter of 14 Mar. 1953 from Trippel's plenipotentiary; StAL, EL 902/20, Bü 80957 (Trippel denazification records), and order by the Justice Ministry of 9 Sept. 1954.
86. MAE Colmar, WH C 2963, Trippelwerke Molsheim, Estrade, note d'information confidentiel of 26 Apr. 1951.
87. In January 1951, SPD delegate Künzel calculated the alleged losses in local business taxes to the municipality of Trossingen at DM 145,000 for 1949 and DM 250,000 for 1950. StAS, Wü 1, Bü 100a, PUA, 7th public meeting, p. 41. Delegate Haux, an expert in business taxation, estimated that in 1950, the state of Württemberg-Hohenzollern lost approximately DM 500,000 in corporate taxes because the losses at Chiron were used to offset the gains at Efka. Verhandlungen des Landtags, 87th session, 1 Aug. 1950, pp. 1699–1700.
88. Letter from Herbert E. Kiehn of 14 Apr. 1999.
89. ASD, NL Erler, Box 85, minutes of a speech by Fritz Kiehn at a company assembly of the Chiron-Protek works on 30 June 1950; MAE Colmar, WH C 2963, Trippelwerke Molsheim, Estrade, note d'information confidentiel of 26 Apr. 1951.
90. Letter from Herbert E. Kiehn of 11 May 1998.
91. HStAS, EA 4/403, Bü 121, public prosecutor's indictment in Tübingen Regional Court of 22 Nov. 1952.
92. See chap. 12.
93. Grimm, who had copublished the *Deutsche Juristenzeitung* since 1923, held an honorary professorship in Münster, and was an honorary governor of the Universität Marburg, represented the private joint plaintiffs in both trials. Gustloff's assassin, David Frankfurter, was sentenced to eighteen years in prison. The start of the war prevented Grynszpan's trial from ever being concluded. Grimm, *Visier,* 129; on Grimm's importance as political commentator in the Third Reich, see Stockhorst, *Fünftausend Köpfe*; for the period after 1945, see Tauber, *Eagle,* 1:478, 1:481, 1:524–525, 2:1233; Frei, *Vergangenheitspolitik,* 127; Herbert, *Best,* 449–450.
94. Grimm, *Visier,* 132–133.
95. During the war Achenbach headed the political division of the German Embassy in Paris and was one of those in charge of deporting Jews in France. He established himself as an attorney in Essen in 1946, and was a lawyer for the defense in both the IG Farben and Wilhelmstraße trials of the International Military Tribunal at Nuremberg. He was an FDP delegate to the state parliament of North Rhine-Westphalia and chaired the FDP foreign policy committee, a function in which he, together with like-minded colleagues, endeavored to prevent the Federal Republic of Germany's integration into the West and to stir up nationalist emotions by exploiting the "war criminal question." He presented the public with his Preparatory Committee to Bring about a General Amnesty in 1952. This committee, which had industry money behind it and

Werner Best as its intellectual spokesperson, developed into a political powerhouse. Buchna, *Sammlung*; Frei, *Vergangenheitspolitik*, 106–110, 281, 365. On Werner Best, see Herbert, *Best*; on Achenbach, see ibid., 444–472; on Six, see Hachtmeister, *Gegnerforscher*.
96. Frei, *Vergangenheitspolitik*, 106, 165.
97. Herbert, *Best*, 449–450. On Best's responsibility for the murder of Kiehn's alleged friend Hermann Mattheiß, see chap. 3.
98. Buchna, *Sammlung*, 53–62, 193–203; Frei, *Vergangenheitspolitik*, 361–396.
99. Their acquaintance may have gone further back, although Grimm was not involved with the NSDAP before 1933, having instead been close to the DVP. At any rate, Grimm claimed in his 1954 defense speech that "I have known this man for twenty-five years." The speech survives in KAT, Bestand II, no. 100, Friedrich Grimm, "Der Fall Kiehn: Ein politischer Prozeß," defense speech in the Criminal High Court, Tübingen, 6 Mar. 1954.
100. HStAS, EA 4/403, Bü 121, judgment by the criminal court of the Tübingen Regional Court of 8 Mar. 1954.
101. Frei, *Vergangenheitspolitik*, 29–53, quote from letter of justice minister Dehler to state justice minister of 3 Oct. 1949, 32.
102. Richter took his own life following the verdict. Reference files for Fritz Kiehn perjury trial, private collection.
103. KAT, Bestand II, no. 100, Grimm, "Der Fall Kiehn," 2.
104. Ibid., 21–22.
105. *Trossinger Zeitung*, 5 Mar. 1954.
106. Defense plea from Kiehn's lawyers Grimm and Sieger of 28 Sept. 1953, private collection.
107. KAT, Bestand II, no. 100, Grimm, "Der Fall Kiehn," 38–40.
108. Minutes of the Efka company assembly of 9 Mar. 1954, private collection.
109. For details on Thadden's political activities, see Tauber, *Eagle*.
110. List of addresses in the records of the perjury trial, private collection. For more on this circle, see Buchna, *Sammlung*; Herbert, *Best*; Frei, *Vergangenheitspolitik*; Tauber, *Eagle*. On their importance in Kiehn's social circle in the 1950s, see chap. 12.
111. Letter from Heinz Wicke to Efka of 27 Mar. 1954, private collection. At the time, Wicke was Efka's general distributor and ran a warehouse in Freiburg.
112. Various letters to Kiehn, private collection.
113. HStAS, EA 4/403, Bü 121, decision by the criminal court of the Tübingen Regional Court of 20 Oct. 1954; Frei, *Vergangenheitspolitik*, 100.
114. Letter from attorney Sieger to Kiehn of 29 Oct. 1954, private collection.
115. Letter from Kiehn to director Josef Schneider of 15 Apr. 1954, private collection.

Chapter 12

"KIEHN LEFT NO ONE BEHIND"?[1]
The "Factory Community" as a Network of "Old Comrades"

The integration of hundreds of thousands of Third Reich functionaries into the society of the Federal Republic of Germany is one of the key factors, along with the "economic miracle," in explaining the surprisingly slight importance of organized right-wing extremism and the consequent stability of the young democracy. All the same, the social history of former Nazi functionaries in the Federal Republic is still largely unwritten.[2] The long-term continuity of their careers should not conceal that, at first, the political upheaval occasioned severe fissures in their careers. Those who were forced to flee, dismissed from office, subject to detention and exclusion, or underwent denazification and criminal persecution experienced traumatic phases of downward social mobility and existential uncertainty. "Mercy fever" (*Gnadenfieber*) and the desire for a clean break with the past did not take hold immediately; instead, little by little, these tendencies, which emerged in the early 1950s, led to a pervasive leniency in dealing with supporters of the Nazi regime. The chances of professional reentry also varied widely, depending on the occupational group.

Those with senior or quasi-official positions in the NSDAP and its organizations found it particularly hard to reintegrate. This group of people used the numerous networks of former party comrades, as we have already seen in the exhaustively researched examples of two members of higher SS offices. Werner Best, the highest-ranked surviving representative of the Gestapo, SD, and Reich Security Main Office (RSHA), was shut out of returning to the civil service because he had later been Reichsstatthalter in Denmark. His "redeployment" would have provoked international complications, so Achenbach's law office and his Preparatory Committee to Bring about a General Amnesty for Nazi perpetrators helped Best to return to an elevated professional career outside the civil

---

Notes from this chapter begin on page 271.

service in which he eventually became general counsel for the Stinnes corporation. SS brigade leader Franz Alfred Six, the card-carrying Nazi professor, former head of the SD press office, and an undersecretary in the Foreign Office, was not allowed to return to the Foreign Office because of his lack of formal qualifications and his unsuitable background. Yet with the help of Achenbach and Friedrich Flick, whom he had met in the war criminals' camp in Landsberg, Six nevertheless succeeded in rejoining the professional world. After seven years in prison, he made a name for himself as the director of a publishing company and a corporate consultant. In the 1950s Achenbach, who had worked at the German Embassy in Paris with Best and Six during the war, became a "spider in the network of younger members of the Nazi civil service elite looking for a new political and professional direction."[3]

The Federal Republic of Germany did not tolerate an overt union of former top Nazi functionaries or declared commitments to far-right positions. Anyone who did not grasp this — like Naumann, who had switched from the FDP to the neo-Nazi camp — ultimately ended up on the sidelines. Those who learned their lesson and renounced all nationalist fringe groups could pursue their careers unhindered. Achenbach, for example, became a long-term FDP delegate to the Bundestag and its foreign policy spokesperson in the Brandt/Scheel era, as well as a delegate to the European Parliament, and he nearly rose to the position of Commissioner of the European Community in Brussels.[4]

Unlike Achenbach, Naumann, and their ilk, Fritz Kiehn spared himself the risky experiment of being actively involved in organized right-wing nationalism; he seems to have been aware of the danger this sort of Russian roulette could present to his personal ambitions. At any rate, he stayed away from all of the neo-Nazi splinter parties. Any contact Kiehn had with the lobby aggressively agitating for an amnesty for convicted Nazi perpetrators only lasted as long as they served his personal rehabilitation. Both before and after he was released from the camp, Kiehn was "realist" enough to put his company and family ahead of politics and ideology. He was urged on anew by his old dream of a patriarchal thousand-man operation where company leadership would be passed on within the family.

But there was no lack of attempts to involve Kiehn in the conspiratorial activities of the groups surrounding Achenbach. Naumann, for example, who knew Kiehn from the Freundeskreis of the Reichsführer-SS, visited Kiehn at Deibhalde in 1952 or 1953, but by all appearances returned to Düsseldorf without tangible evidence of success. Other former Nazi functionaries paid repeated calls to Trossingen as well. Friedrich Christian Prinz zu Schaumburg-Lippe, former Reich speaker for the NSDAP and personal aide to Joseph Goebbels, spent two days there. Known as the "prince," he had invested his assets in promoting the NSDAP before 1933 and now had a leading role in the Bund der Heimatvertriebenen und Entrechteten (BHE, Alliance of the Expellees and Rights-Deprived), a right-wing party that essentially gathered together refugees, exiles, and former National

Socialists. In 1953 the BHE even made it all the way to the Bundestag and sent two ministers to Konrad Adenauer's second cabinet.[5] It is unknown what occasioned or came out of these meetings with Kiehn, although it is clear that he kept his distance from the organized radical right.

Former Nazi elites were much more likely to deny their past political positions than to openly profess them, as politicians such as Adolf von Thadden (Deutsche Reichspartei), Naumann, and Schaumburg-Lippe did. The Allies had already noticed a "contest of opportunism, disavowal, and denial"[6] in the internment camps. The circumstances, largely shaped by the debacle of Germany's defeat, exerted a strong pressure to conform, one that a social striver like Kiehn was least able to defy. As early as November 1945, he impressed his interrogators at the US Army internment camp in Ludwigsburg as a notorious opportunist who had taken leave of his earlier ideological convictions with the collapse of the Third Reich. The transcript of his questioning reports of Kiehn, "The accused claims to be politically disillusioned. He is the typical case of a large-scale industrialist who now sees that he bet on the wrong horse and appears to regret it. He also tells the usual fairy tale of conflicts with the party, even though he profited from Nazism and supported it almost to the end."[7] The *Mittelstand* entrepreneur was neither prepared to ruin his life out of loyalty to his convictions nor open to political experimentation. The American official, at least, had believed he was the "large-scale industrialist" he made himself out to be. Kiehn's main concern was a swift return to an upper-middle-class lifestyle; his time in prison had obviously not cured him of his need for recognition.[8] But this did not by any means preclude him from actively supporting his besieged comrades. Kiehn established a small, informal network for some of his comrades in arms who had met with difficulty when trying to reenter the job market and whom he could easily help as head of his firm. He was guided primarily by social considerations, which were linked inseparably with his feeling of belonging to a community of fate betrayed by history. The biographies of Best and Six are not the only ones that impressively demonstrate how long the pronounced esprit de corps under the Nazi state retained its effect, and how much it bound together followers in almost all of the occupational categories of West German society.[9]

Following his release from prison, Kiehn not only rallied around him all the party comrades who had been present at his company in large numbers before 1945,[10] but also assembled a considerable number of former Nazi functionaries who had no prior history with his firm. Huber, the former Kreisleiter for Tuttlingen, was probably the first to benefit from Kiehn's aid to his comrades; he began working for Kiehn immediately after being released from prison. Summer 1950 marked the beginning of Otto Kappeler's time at Efka. Kappeler had been deputy district group leader for Schramberg and rose to become technical director of Kiehn's company. Otto Sponer, Kreisleiter for Reutlingen and one of Kiehn's fellow prisoners at Balingen, was made managing director in 1950 of a subsidiary

Kiehn founded in Stuttgart. Before 1945, he was considered a fanatical National Socialist, especially among Reutlingen manufacturers. He had picked fights with some of the industrialists in his territory out of his resentment against "VIPs"; for example, he had Fritz Fallscheer, the chairman of important industrial firm Emil Adolff, sent to a punishment battalion directly after Fallscheer completed an unjustly imposed prison sentence for his alleged foreign exchange crimes.[11] Kiehn may have hired Sponer for more reasons than to help an "old fighter," since the former Kreisleiter also possessed the advantage of commercial training.

The now politically inconspicuous former Kreisleiter had little in common with the "incorrigible" and "aggressively nationalistic"[12] Hermann Schäfer, a former SA member who had been at the Reich Propaganda Ministry and started at Efka in 1950. We can presume that he and Kiehn knew each other from Kiehn's time at Magirus. Kiehn appointed Schäfer as his sales and public relations director. Schäfer directed the company celebrations and proved to be very skilled at it. Like many of those Kiehn hired out of consideration for old loyalties, however, Schäfer was a terrible fit. He left the company in 1955 or 1956, after differences arose with Kiehn's new son-in-law.

Dr. Helmuth Gesler, an attorney with a brown-shirted past whom Kiehn had first met during his internment and who did not manage to return to the civil service, still needed tending to, in any case. After first working as "travel director," a position that had been created specifically for him, he filled Efka's general counsel post that became vacant in 1950. Kiehn dismissed Gesler about two years later, just as he had dismissed Gesler's predecessor, for providing incriminating information in the denazification proceedings of an Efka employee.[13]

Another employee, likewise hired at Efka after spending some time at Kiehn's Contra company in Stuttgart, was Heinrich Wicke. Wicke had been appointed SS senior leader and colonel of the Schutzpolizei in 1944, and in April 1945 had organized the transfer of inmates from the Stuttgart jails and satellite concentration camps to Dachau. He was denazified as a "Lesser Offender" in 1949. By the early 1950s he was working in a leading position at Kiehn's company and even had power of attorney.[14] In Trossingen he managed to camouflage himself perfectly as a polite man of "integrity" who was apolitical through and through. Herbert E. Kiehn found it unthinkable to associate Wicke even remotely with Nazi war criminals; Wicke never spoke about politics in Kiehn's grandson's presence.[15] However, he was able to remove the mask that fit him so perfectly on occasion and — at least outside his new place of residence — give free rein to his otherwise carefully hidden resentments toward his ideological enemies, such as Fritz Erler. At a Chiron company assembly in 1950 that was meant to mobilize employees to fend off the accusations against Kiehn detailed in chapter 11, Wicke vouched for the industrialist as an "old friend." "I too am a National Socialist — or was one, you could say. ... Today, five years after the end of the war, it's time they stopped slinging mud at us. We have atoned and been restored to favor in human society and … have … the right to live and to do our duty, and we have the courage to do so. Judge by your common sense — then you shall judge correctly."[16]

Viktor Brack, one of the main organizers of the murderous human experiments in Auschwitz and the T4 Euthanasia Program that killed some fifty thousand children and adults, both sick and well, was sentenced to death in the Doctors Trial at Nuremberg and executed in Landsberg in 1948. He may have met Kiehn face-to-face before 1945, since Brack was on friendly terms with Himmler and had been his liaison with Hitler's chancellery.[17] Whatever the case, in 1949 Brack's wife and six children popped up in Trossingen. One of her sons was later hired by Efka. Material support was also given to the family that SS senior colonel (Oberführer) Walter Stein left behind; he had been executed in East Germany after 1945. His sister-in-law worked at the Efka vacation home in Ludwigshafen for a time during the postwar era. Frau Stein and her sister continued to give Herbert E. Kiehn the impression of being "staunch National Socialists" and joyfully attested to Herbert E.'s "proper Nazi blood" by virtue of his descent.[18]

Gretl Kiehn's third marriage proved to have serious repercussions for the expansion of her father's network of old comrades, which also included a large number of low-ranking former party members. After her first marriage with Heinrich Himmler's personal staffer Ernst Fähndrich, who perished in April 1945, and her second in 1949 with unsuccessful design engineer Hans Trippel, who enjoyed Himmler's protection nonetheless and was divorced from Gretl in 1951, she married Fritz Wieshofer in 1955, the former adjutant of the Vienna Gauleiter, Reichsstatthalter, and Hitler Youth leader Baldur von Schirach. Wieshofer was described as extremely charming and entertaining (fig. 35). Born in Vienna in 1914, he was struggling along in the 1950s as a freelancer for the DuMont Schauberg publishing house following his internment and denazification. He had joined the SA in 1932, at the age of seventeen, and the NSDAP in 1933. Without any formal professional training, he was given a job in the Vienna NSDAP Gauleitung in 1933. After Germany's annexation of Austria, Wieshofer rose rapidly to become a propaganda expert for various NSDAP Gauleitung offices in Carinthia. He switched from the SA to the SS in 1939. During the war, he held the rank of Obersturmführer, equivalent to first lieutenant. In 1940, Wieshofer was working as an adjutant to Carinthia Gauleiter Pachneck, as the officer in charge of the resettlement of South Tyroleans into the Reich, and as deputy liaison to the Foreign Office for the Gauleitung. That same year, he was appointed to the protocol division of the Foreign Office, where he met Baldur von Schirach. Wieshofer's experience in the diplomatic service, even if he was there for only a short time, apparently qualified this Viennese man for the position of Schirach's chief of protocol. To enhance Wieshofer's standing, Schirach intervened with Robert Ley, the head of the German Labor Front, and managed to get Wieshofer formally promoted to the rank of Reichshauptstellenleiter, Reich Central Office Manager, in the NSDAP on the basis of his official party work in the Vienna Gauleitung. Because the Gauleitung and Reichstatthalter offices were organizationally linked, all threads came together in the Central Bureau that Wieshofer headed. We can assume from this that Wieshofer was also directly involved in the deportation of sixty thousand Viennese Jews, which was carried out under Schirach's direction after 1940. A close relationship of mutual trust developed between Wieshofer and Schirach beginning in 1940. For example, the adjutant did not leave his boss's side until the last minute, and joined him on the run until the two were arrested. Before the Nuremberg trial against the main war criminals, Schirach's defense attorneys got hold of Wieshofer in an internment camp and called on him to act as an exoneration witness for Schirach, exactly as Wieshofer's fellow adjutant, Gustav Dietrich Höpken, had done.[19]

Wieshofer's refined manners made him appealing, and when he met Kiehn's divorced daughter in 1954, he recognized the opportunity that marrying into the manufacturing family would afford him. Wieshofer joined the management ranks at Efka even before his marriage in 1955, though he had no commercial experience whatsoever. This jack-of-all-trades, who, like both of his predecessors, shared his wife and father-in-law's passion for hunting, knew how to adroitly gloss over this deficit. Fritz Kiehn's fondness for Wieshofer — to his grandson's knowledge — had nothing to do with Wieshofer's past on Schirach's staff. "What [Kiehn] valued were [Wieshofer's] connections, his charm, his imposing manner." Herbert E. Kiehn, on the other hand, saw the extroverted Wieshofer as a rival in the battle for leadership of the family business and as a "clever con man who outdid F. K. [Fritz Kiehn] when it came to overstatement."[20]

The now seventy-year-old patriarch saw a ready successor in his smart son-in-law. Grandson Herbert E., adopted in 1952, did not finish high school until 1956, making him much too young to lead the company at the time. Crafty Wieshofer understood how to win over both Kiehn and his daughter and to gain a large influence both inside and outside Efka. In 1959, he began representing the interests of Efka and his father-in-law on the Trossingen town council. Busy Wieshofer also used his diverse contacts to give new momentum to the Kiehns' social life, becoming a founding member of the Tuttlingen Rotary Club. His father-in-law became involved with the Lions Club in the district capital. Wieshofer enjoyed good connections to the FDP as well and introduced Kiehn to Siegfried Zoglmann, a former SS Obersturmführer and member of the Hitler Youth leadership who had found a job with the FDP of North Rhine-Westphalia as a press secretary and edited the right-wing journal of Friedrich Middelhauve, the party's chair in that state. Zoglmann also belonged to the FDP executive committee for the state of Württemberg. Zoglmann became a frequent guest of Kiehn's, leasing hunting grounds together with him in Tyrol. FDP federal economics minister Dahlgrün joined the lease. Wieshofer also introduced his father-in-law to the Austrian Order of Hubertus and may have had a hand in

Fig. 35: Portrait with the new star of the family, from the left: Fritz and Gretl Wieshofer, as well as Herbert E., Berta, and Fritz Kiehn. (Private collection of the Kiehn family)

creating connections to the University of Innsbruck, which named Kiehn an "honorary citizen" in 1962. Wieshofer did these things because he knew exactly how much such contacts and trophies flattered his father-in-law, and how well he could improve his own position at Efka by playing the role of intermediary with the elegance of a con artist. At the height of his favor, there were even efforts to give him the Kiehn name so that there could be a second "Fritz Kiehn." The plan was never put through, however.

Wieshofer's cosmopolitan manner gave him a great deal of room to maneuver at the company too, for example, when choosing second-level management personnel. Wieshofer doggedly used this opportunity to accommodate his old comrades from his Vienna days. The first of these was Höpken, whom he brought to Trossingen less than a year after marrying Gretl Kiehn. Höpken had accompanied Schirach on his escape as well but had absconded before his arrest. At Efka, Höpken was promoted to manager of the staff office that reported directly to the company executives and was known as the Central Bureau, likely in homage to Wieshofer's work in Vienna. A skilled physical education teacher who had worked for the Hitler Youth since 1939 and a loyal aide to the Hitler Youth director, as well as director of Schirach's Central Bureau in Vienna in the end, Höpken was not the least bit prepared for the business world.

Shortly thereafter, three more of Schirach's former colleagues ended up coming to Trossingen thanks to Wieshofer's intervention. Heinz Diesing was named sales manager for plastics, while Herbert Gasser took on a management position in Efka's subsidiaries. Richard Heil was made "sales manager for smoking accessories" and head of organization during Wieshofer's tenure. In 1972 he was appointed managing director of the company. Heil, who enjoyed wearing his decorations from the Third Reich, got into a brief but fierce conflict with some of Kiehn's family because of the sweeping changes he made to product quality on his own authority, to the detriment of the company. His obsession with bureaucratic perfection soon meant that no business transaction went through at Efka without a form drafted expressly by Heil in unambiguous colors, meaning that the man from Schirach's Reichstatthalter offices introduced the exaggerated organizational mania typical of Nazi bureaucracy into Kiehn's company. It is difficult to imagine a greater contrast to the corporate culture of a *Mittelstand* company, with its informal, patriarchal style of leadership. These services for his comrades mainly led to friction and unnecessary expenses.[21]

Höpken became the link between the Kiehn family and Baldur von Schirach. Specifically, the adjutant felt so beholden to his former superior, even after 1945, that he looked after his son. Schirach's children had ended up in a difficult situation during his time in Spandau Prison. This led to an aid campaign by Schirach's former confidants to administer to his children in need. Höpken had taken on responsibility for Schirach's son Robert, born in 1938, who thus moved with him to Trossingen in 1955. Robert left school and took up an apprenticeship at Efka.

Höpken's protégé developed close relationships with Wieshofer and Kiehn, likely not least because Höpken was bringing him up frugally and the young Schirach was impressed by the spendthrift lifestyle of his employer. This became the background to Robert's 1962 marriage to Kiehn's granddaughter Elke, Gretl's daughter from her first marriage, who was born in 1943. She had been raised by Gretl and her third husband, Fritz Wieshofer. Thus, we have the son of the Hitler Youth leader marrying the stepdaughter of his father's adjutant. At the time they were married, however, Wieshofer had just lost his status as Kiehn's son-in-law and managing director, because Gretl had filed for divorce. As far as the Kiehn family was concerned, this marriage of an underage bride to a 24-year-old manual laborer was not exactly made in heaven. Quite the opposite: the "family was raging."[22] Fritz Kiehn soon calmed the waves, however, and the two came to terms with each other. As a consequence, Robert von Schirach made a career in his grandfather-in-law's company. After Robert had done some work in sales that was characterized by modest successes and high expenses, Kiehn gave him power of attorney and in 1967 entrusted him with leadership of the plastics division. He became managing director in 1968, when he was still under thirty.

Baldur von Schirach was released from Spandau Prison in the fall of 1966. After various stopovers, he found a new home in Trossingen in 1968, first with

Fig. 36: Baldur von Schirach wishes Gretl Wieshofer-Kiehn a happy fiftieth birthday (1968). (Private collection of the Kiehn family)

Robert and then in Deibhalde. In the years that followed, Gretl Wieshofer-Kiehn was the one who looked after the former Hitler Youth leader the most: he called himself a "writer" (fig. 36). Circumstantial evidence points to them having at least a temporary romantic relationship, but it did not last, causing Baldur von Schirach to abandon his Trossingen exile in 1972, a year and a half before his death in Kröv, a town on the Moselle River.

His former adjutant, Fritz Wieshofer, had already been forced into a hurried farewell in 1961, when Fritz Kiehn kicked him out of his house and his company after problems in the marriage surfaced. Wieshofer then resigned his seat on the town council, left Trossingen, and got divorced. Wieshofer's former confidants from the Reichsstatthalter offices remained where he had put them at Efka, however. Robert and Elke von Schirach also divorced, in 1970.

Filling management positions with "old comrades" no doubt had a negative effect on Efka. Kiehn's preference for former Nazi functionaries and other, usually older, acquaintances ran counter to economic rationality. None of these ex-Nazi functionaries had adequate training or appropriate experience to push a paper manufacturing brand. Amateurism and lack of business sense became the hallmark of Efka's management staff. What's more, these were usually "old" comrades, meaning men who were approaching or had already reached retirement age. Herbert E. Kiehn lamented the excessive age of these members of staff and the fact that his grandfather only hired people who were "underperformers" and gave "bad" advice.[23] Insider loyalty and social priorities, patriarchal generosity, and — in the case of Trippel, Wieshofer, and Robert von Schirach's promotions to managing director — an overreliance on family all ran afoul of economic common sense. The failure of Gretl's three marriages also had negative effects on the company; each time, management positions had to be reshuffled on short notice, and the problems of succession escalated.[24]

The Kiehn patriarch's fickleness undermined his family's sense of security as well. Even though Kiehn had his eye on Herbert, his only male grandson, to be his successor, this plan became "considerably distorted with the hope-laden arrival of a son-in-law and his [later] disappointment-ridden departure." Herbert E. Kiehn's recollections were not without bitterness: he used the proverbial "two steps forward, one step back (and sometimes two), promises and denial" to describe "my path through ... childhood and adolescence — torn among my mother, grandmother, aunt, and grandfather, who laid down the law. ... At any rate, I *never* felt sure of succeeding my grandfather," which, in his view, had much to do with Fritz Kiehn's goodwill or lack of it.[25] Despite the patriarchal leadership role that Fritz Kiehn was aware of all his life, the family was always seething with resentment, not least due to the comings and goings of those who aspired to take on a leadership role in his stead. But the mood in the family improved when they were forced out of the company in 1972. "Once the company was gone, the family began to get along."[26]

Fritz Kiehn remained active in business until 1972, when he turned eighty-seven. He never gave up on his life's goal of a "thousand-man operation," even though he never achieved it after 1945. He pursued it ceaselessly from the first day of his release from internment. He was intent on making permanent, as fast as possible, what he had so quickly achieved under the conditions of the Nazi regime. All the same, in 1950 he was already sixty-five years old. His motto reflected his impetuous desire to expand at any price: "We're expanding. And companies that expand are doing well."[27] The springboard for his considerations was his profitable core industry, that is, the manufacturing of rolling papers for cigarettes. Demand for these, however, was nowhere near enough to justify large-scale expansion. The market for cigarette papers was also subject to constant fluctuations and contracted to the same extent that prosperity improved during the "economic miracle" of the 1950s and 1960s. By the 1960s, more and more smokers could afford to purchase machine-manufactured cigarettes. The trend did not reverse until 1972, when hand-rolling cigarettes suddenly became fashionable among young people and increased taxes on cigarettes boosted the sale of ready-made cigarette tubes.

With the drop in tobacco leaf sales, Efka looked to the future and accelerated the manufacture of paper cigarette tubes that had been going on at a smaller scale since 1932. These had the advantage over papers of not requiring rolling, and the tobacco could be easily inserted with a stuffing device. What's more, the end product looked enough like a proper cigarette to be taken for one. Crucial for the success of tube production was Efka's close collaboration with Bremen tobacco company Martin Brinkmann, which started in 1967. This joint venture used the Privileg brand and the division of labor meant that Efka supplied the market with tubes and tube-filling devices, while Brinkmann sold the fine-cut tobacco to be used with them.

But Fritz Kiehn the businessman had no other lucky breaks apart from this successful progression in his core product. His business activities were characterized by their rampant and aimless diversification. The aquisition of Chiron, as scandalous as it was financially devastating, corresponded to Kiehn's muddled expansion strategy. When Kiehn notified the Tuttlingen administration and town council of his plans to buy Chiron in 1950, he announced that he would be initiating manufacture of nine to ten different product groups in order to insulate the factory from crises.[28] The disaster at Protek has already been detailed in chapter 11; things hardly went better at Contra. The founding of this new company was a reaction to Kiehn's being banned from the district, but the name was a protest against all the other restrictions on Kiehn's entrepreneurial spirit: internment, denazification, and control of his assets. Werner Kaufmann and Kiehn's daughter, Gretl — who, unlike her father, had already been denazified — functioned as the official chief executives of Contra, with DM 5,000 in capital.[29] The business purpose of the Contra company remains unclear. Above all, it was meant to restore an entrepreneurial foot in the door and prepare for new investments. The same goes for Kiehn's flirtation with the cosmetics industry in 1949–1950, an adventurous step for a paper goods manufacturer. The Trevit company, located in Bad Cannstadt, pretentiously advertised its company headquarters as being in "Geneva-Paris-New York" and sold hair creams, men's cosmetics, and insecticides. Trevit had some success in the early 1950s, when the consumer hunger for goods was still largely undifferentiated. The gradual transition to a buyer's market with greater selection and competition, however, revealed the amateurishness of Trevit's management (run by former district leaders Sponer and Huber), and the company could no longer keep pace with the large cosmetic producers. Production was therefore incorporated into the Efka factories and abandoned in 1968 as a result of ongoing deficits. Kiehn also acquired a cigar holder operation in Neunburg/Oberpfalz around 1952. But since cigar use declined sharply in the 1950s and manufacturers touting holders were quitting the market in droves, Efka had banked on a product whose life cycle was nearing its end. What's more, a separate sales system had to be established for this gift item. Without a reliable accounting system, the management regularly clashed over whether this product line was making them any profit at all. Neither this uncertainty nor the shrinking market stopped Efka from buying the last remaining competing cigar holder manufacturers in 1960, located in Alsenborn. A few years later, production of this item was discontinued in Trossingen as well.

Previously, Kiehn had gone into plastics injection molding in order to save money on producing the mouthpieces of the cigar holders. Because production of this small item taken up in 1953 did not occupy a full division, however, the company had no choice but to look for more injection-molding products. Soon Efka had added heat sealing and thermoforming to the injection-molding section, even though there was no one in the company with the necessary technical competence or existing sales leads. The company ended up adding capacities haphazardly and developing the products afterward, resulting in a motley and multicolored product range that was difficult to sell. Ultimately, the division placed a certain focus on mail-order household goods, but it remained a problem child, directed by Heinz Diesing beginning in 1958 and Robert von Schirach beginning in 1967. It was sold off in 1971.

In 1955–1956, Efka took up production of a tire pressure gauge for cars that never caught on in the market. Manufacturing of the item was abandoned in the mid-1960s. In 1960, the company began selling disposable lighters produced by the French firm Dupont. Even though these items, relatively novel at the time, fit well into Efka's core product range and initially sold well, the level of sales the company needed would have required disproportionately high advertising costs. The collaboration ended in 1967, when Dupont was acquired by Gillette.

In 1961, Efka began manufacturing water-saturated cigarette filters advertised as having supposedly anticarcinogenic properties. This branch of the business "neither lived nor died" and generated insignificant, marginal returns. In 1968, by now high-living Robert von Schirach finally convinced Kiehn to start producing water meters without undertaking prior analysis of the market. When the marketing channels for these proved to be inaccessible, production on this item — completely inappropriate for a paper manufacturing operation — was abandoned with substantial losses. The fantastical peak of Kiehn's failed investments, comprehensible only against the backdrop of his obsession with prestige and his passion for hunting, came in the mid-1950s, when he got involved in buying into an East African farm called Momella on the border of Kenya and Tanganyika, now known as Tanzania. This move toward a safari, taken at Wieshofer's instigation, proved to be a fiasco: they chose the wrong cattle breeds to raise; the coffee plantations were ruined by wild animals; and the cheese-making business failed to deliver the desired results. Kiehn was only able to sell the place for a half-decent price in 1963, after several large failed investments, because of an initiative by Bernhard Grzimek, a renowned animal conservationist, to establish a national park on the land. Kiehn's grandiloquent dream of having a large estate in East Africa, and the sources of wealth that would spring from it, had burst like a soap bubble.

The main losses at the parent factory in Trossingen were coming from the printing section, which had been set up during the Great Depression in anticipation of potentially large orders from the NSDAP; Kiehn had advertised it on a letterhead as a "large graphics firm." He maintained an oddly irrational attachment to his printing shop for the rest of his life. He clutched at this division as if driven by an idée fixe, even personally managing sales of printed matter until 1966. If company management questioned the point of the print shop, the boss felt personally attacked. The problems of the notoriously deficit-laden division were its constant underutilization, insufficient specialization and job preparation, the acquisition of machines on too small a scale, technical problems with the migration to offset printing, and an outdated sales division partly populated by musicians. The company patriarch had promised them local jobs in his position as a patron of the Trossingen town band, providing another characteristic example of his unprofessional employment policy.

By the time Kiehn's grandson, Herbert E. Kiehn, joined the company's management team in 1966, Efka was badly in need of restructuring. Herbert E. Kiehn had studied business administration at the Universities of Frankfurt and Munich, spent several years assisting Efka executives, and attended the Business School Lausanne for a year. Efka's only profitable division was the core industry of cigarette paper manufacturing, including the future-oriented production of cigarette tubes, and had allowed the company to absorb the costs of the numerous failed investments up to that point, as well as to support the lavish lifestyle of Fritz Kiehn and his family (table 5). Against this backdrop, it made sense to

Table 5: Staff and sales at Efka, 1957–1973

Year	Staff (as of 31 Dec.)	Net sales proceeds (DM 1,000)
1957	598	n/s
1958	n/s	n/s
1959	654	n/s
1960	n/s	n/s
1961	861	n/s
1962	811	n/s
1963	866	n/s
1964	818	21,491
1965	803	21,287
1966	768	21,281
1967	835	23,086
1968	757	22,893
1969	781	27,580
1970	432	18,501
1971	287	15,995
1972	208	16,497
1973	217	20,481

Divisions spun off and not included in figures: printing (after 1969) and polymer processing (after 1970).
Source: Annual audit reports 1964–1973 according to Herbert E. Kiehn's letter of 15 Sept. 1998.

restructure the unprofitable business sectors where possible — those that had not already been abandoned — and to sell them off in order to concentrate on the company's core competencies. Efka's printing arm was spun off as part of this strategy in 1969 and sold to the Papierwerke Waldhof Aschaffenburg paper company in 1970. The plastics division was jettisoned by merging it with the Continua firm in Mengen. All that was left was the sound core of Efka, which to this day remains a top national producer of cigarette papers and tubes.

Even so, when tobacco leaf sales took a surprising dive in 1971, the company ended up in a crisis that threatened its existence. In addition, the mania for haphazard diversification that defined the previous two decades had eroded any savings. It was also unfavorable that the new cash cow of tube production was not fully up and running yet. Finally, there were still two construction projects straining the company's finances. A new modern factory was being built on the outskirts of the city, for one thing. In addition, Kiehn's grandson-in-law Robert von Schirach was having a house built for what at that time was the exorbitant cost of DM 800,000; he insisted, with "neurotic vehemence,"[30] on living at the same standard as the rest of the family. Construction had not even been finished when he left the family.

The company was facing the threat of insolvency by 1972. Restructuring was carried out jointly by the large tobacco producer Martin Brinkmann and Dresdner Bank. With the chaotic developments that had occurred during the preceding decades, it is no surprise that both investors demanded that the Kiehn family retire from leading the company and called for an independent advisory board. Before 1972 was over, two new chief executives had been appointed who had no relations with the family. One of these was Richard Heil, who came from Wieshofer's sphere of influence and had won the trust of Brinkmann and Dresdner Bank. Before the restructuring had even finished, demand for cigarette papers suddenly shot up because hand-rolling cigarettes had become fashionable among young people and taxes on tobacco had changed. It turned out very favorably that the threat to the company's existence and internal resistance to necessary restructuring measures crashed together, and the new management acted professionally and uniformly for the first time. This is how an impressive restructuring could take place in a short period of time. By 1973, Efka was already distributing profits of half a million Deutschmarks and could almost completely erase its liabilities to banks. Despite the considerable number of business errors that had been made, Efka's long-term survival as a cigarette paper and tube manufacturer was assured. The Kiehn family, on the other hand, lost its influence over the direction of its company, though it still retained 100 percent ownership.

In conclusion, the failure of Kiehn's lofty plans can be traced back to a clearly identifiable cluster of causes. A misguided employment policy that was primarily shaped by personal and familial loyalties was paired with a chaotic product policy that, as in the case of the printing shop, was determined by the sometimes irrational preferences of the aging patriarch. The problem of succession that had been acute since the mid-1950s was never solved; instead, it was aggravated by intrafamilial upheavals and dragged on in a way fairly typical of *Mittelstand* family businesses. Not until the crisis of 1972, and the external pressure that arrived with it, was a remedy finally achieved. Added to this was the aimless expansion at any price that led Efka into completely unfamiliar industries. With no consideration of profit, Kiehn preferred to increase sales and employee numbers. Success did not come until Efka "was led according to the points of view" that Fritz Kiehn "would have rejected."[31] Many of Kiehn's investments unmistakably reflected his high tolerance for risk and trust in his own intuition. Finally, he was becoming increasingly susceptible to influence with age. Consequently, he repeatedly placed his trust in advisers who knew little about the issue but much about his own psychology and therefore were able to spark his interest in adventurous projects again and again. Meanwhile, he turned a deaf ear to professional, independent business advisers. This is why the breakdown of his business plans followed on the heels of his failed political ambitions.

Notes

1. StAT, Häffner interview collection.
2. Much work is available on certain groups, however, especially on officials and members of the judiciary: Ruck, *Korpsgeist*; Garner, "Öffentliche Dienst"; Döscher, *Verschworene Gemeinschaft*. Rauh-Kühne, "Entnazifizierung," includes literature on the judiciary. On district leaders (Kreisleiter) and district NSF leaders, see Fait, "Kreisleiter"; Arbogast, *Herrschaftsinstanzen*, 241–253. For general information, see Herbert, "Rückkehr."
3. Hachmeister, *Gegnerforscher*, 306.
4. See Herbert, *Best*, 461–472. On the FDP's infiltration by former Nazi Party members, see Langewiesche, *Liberalismus*, 293–294.
5. Stöss, "Block"; Schaumburg-Lippe, *Welt*, preface, 14.
6. Herbert, "Rückkehr," 162–163.
7. MAE Colmar, WH C 3541 d 11, Affaire Kiehn.
8. Herbert, "Rückkehr," 163 (cit.).
9. For officials, see Ruck, *Korpsgeist*; for business owners, see Rauh-Kühne, "Entnazifizierung"; Rauh-Kühne, "Sozialpartnerschaft"; Hachmeister, *Schleyer*.
10. StAS, Wü 1, Bü 100a, PUA, 6th public meeting, p. 73, statement from authorized manager Messner.
11. Sponer was released from his denazification proceedings by the court in December 1948 as an "Offender," indicating an unusually severe political offense. StAS, Wü 13, Bü. 3147. See Arbogast, *Herrschaftsinstanzen*, 144, 212; Rauh-Kühne, "Die Unternehmer," 315.
12. This is Herbert E. Kiehn's judgment, from the interview of 19–20 May 1998.
13. StAS, Wü 120, Bü 362, Gesler to custodian Richter of 21 Aug. 1948; interview with Herbert E. Kiehn of 15–16 June 1999.
14. Born in 1886, Wicke had trained as a merchant. He joined the NSDAP in 1930 and the SS in 1931. Before becoming director of police in Heilbronn in 1938, he worked as a sales

agent and managing director of the German Automobile Club in the Württemberg Gau. He was interned until 1948. Müller, *Stuttgart,* 501, 529; Wilhelm, "Württembergische Polizei," 313–314.
15. Herbert E. Kiehn in letter to the authors of 22 Oct. 1998 and interview with the authors of 19–20 May 1998.
16. ASD, NL Erler, Box 85, minutes of company meeting of 30 June 1950, in which Wicke is spelled "Wittke."
17. See Lifton, *Nazi Doctors,* 280; Klee, *Euthanasie*; Klee, *Was sie taten.*
18. Interviews with Herbert E. Kiehn of 19–20 May 1998 and 15–16 June 1999.
19. BA DC, Akte Wieshofer/SS 0; Lang, *Hitler-Junge,* 291–293, 392–430; Wortmann, *Baldur von Schirach.*
20. Interview with Herbert E. Kiehn of 19–20 May 1998; letter from Herbert E. Kiehn to the authors of 15 June 1998.
21. See memo from Herbert E. Kiehn of 24 May 1998. Wieshofer also placed his brother Anton at Efka. Interview with Herbert E. Kiehn of 15–16 June 1999.
22. Interview with Herbert E. Kiehn of 19–20 May 1998.
23. Ibid.
24. Most of the following paragraphs, except where otherwise indicated, are based on an interview with Herbert E. Kiehn of 19–20 May 1998 and his memos and letters to the authors.
25. Herbert E. Kiehn in letter to the authors of 31 Aug. 1998.
26. Interview with Herbert E. Kiehn of 19–20 May 1998.
27. Letter from Herbert E. Kiehn to the authors of 15 June 1998. Efka employed 685 regular workers and 130 outworkers in 1962. See Anon., *Mit dem Herzen dabei.*
28. MAE Colmar, WH C 3541 d 11, Affaire Kiehn.
29. StAS, Wü 1, Bü 100a, PUA, 7th public meeting, 26 Jan. 1951.
30. Interview with Herbert E. Kiehn of 19–20 May 1998.
31. Letter from Herbert E. Kiehn to the authors of 25 May 1998.

Chapter 13

HONORED CITIZEN AGAIN
Kiehn and the "Economic Miracle"

After Kiehn's release from internment, he not only put great effort into expanding his company but also attempted to overcome the downward social mobility foisted on him by the postwar political upheaval. The combination of internment, denazification, sequestering of his assets, his ban from the district, the loan scandal, and penal trials had nullified the partial successes Kiehn had had on the arduous path to the upper middle class through 1945, even putting him on the margins of society for a time. It was not apparent in the late 1940s that the damage to his life's work could yet be repaired. Later on, Fritz Kiehn would benefit from the fact that West German society in the 1950s and 1960s was forward-looking and avoided retrospective self-criticism.

Between 1933 and 1945, Kiehn had spurred his social advancement with political offices and titles. Not only were these means of distinction lost to him with the demise of the Nazi regime; they were also an obstacle to restoring his social reputation. Added to this was his advanced age, which disqualified him for many posts and reduced his chance of a new career start in the Bonn Republic. Kiehn nevertheless remained true to his obsession with titles and renown, and so tried emphatically to make gains in these areas beginning in 1950. The absurd embarrassments that resulted did not take long to appear. He had grown so attached to the "Herr Präsident" honorific since his time at the top of the Stuttgart IHK that he founded a joint advisory council for Efka and Chiron in 1950 so that he could be its president, even though it served no actual function. Whether the committee ever met is unclear; there are no traces of it in the register of companies. At any rate, it allowed Kiehn to rescue his beloved title. According to his grandson, he always remained "a highly narcissistic child — easily corruptible."[1]

Notes from this chapter begin on page 288.

Kiehn's passion for hunting constituted another key feature of his social self-assertion. Soon after his release from internment, he dedicated himself anew to his old hobby, at great expense. He maintained as many as seven different hunting grounds, including an alpine area in Styria, Austria. In 1956, he was appointed the official district hunter as chair of the district hunting association in Tuttlingen. This post, prestigious in hunting circles, gave Kiehn contacts to the regional elite. Hunting also served to get him closer to more prominent contemporaries, just as it had before 1945. By the late 1950s, Kiehn's hunting friendships included the heads of the political parties in Bonn and even extended into Adenauer's cabinet, but the industrialist also met with former Nazi hunting officials: in 1955 he invited Walter Frevert, the former head of the Forestry Office for Rominten, Hermann Göring's East Prussian hunting reserve for guests, to come to Trossingen. Frevert, who visited Trossingen in the company of Ulrich Scherping — the "Official Hunter General" of the Third Reich — is still regarded by hunters today as one of the highest authorities on the custom and practice of the sport. He composed various reference works on these topics that remained part of every hunter's toolbox even after 1945, albeit with the Nazi contents hastily removed. Beginning in the 1950s, Frevert headed a public forestry office in the Black Forest.[2] His Trossingen visit resulted in a long-term friendship with the Kiehns, which only added to Kiehn's sterling reputation in hunting circles. They traveled to East Africa together to go big-game hunting. The safaris Kiehn started to undertake regularly in 1956 were the inducement for his bad investment in Momella. Not only did they allow him to decorate his residence with exotic hunting trophies, they also allowed him to meet prestigious people such as Momella's owner, big-game hunter Margarete Trappe,[3] famous at the time, and Herbert von Stackelberg, the German general consul in Nairobi. Stackelberg became Bonn's envoy to Washington DC in 1963 and the ambassador to Addis Ababa in 1970. Even though the Kiehn and Stackelberg families came from extremely different social milieus, they developed a long-term friendship based on their common enthusiasm for hunting.

Despite these foreign contacts in high places, during the 1950s Kiehn devoted his primary attention to winning back the local reputation he had lost in Trossingen. His return to the ranks of the local notability started in early 1950, when the family returned to the old villa in Deibhalde, even though it had become almost unrecognizable. Deibhalde had been requisitioned by the French occupying forces from May to November 1945 and had then stood empty until 1947. It was looted and damaged during both phases. The villa served as a branch of the Trossingen hospital from 1947. Its conversion back into a stately home and the continuation of the upgrades halted in 1938–1939 started right away. The renovations to the villa had scarcely finished when a smaller extension with its own gardens was constructed, to which Kiehn added a greenhouse in 1959. The leveling of the surrounding land, begun in 1939, was completed in 1952. The tennis court was finished in 1953, and the garden was transformed into a picture-perfect guesthouse that became an imposing home in 1967. A factory building was constructed in 1954 that Efka used commercially until 1959, when it was left to the local horseback riding association to be used as a riding arena. In 1955, Berta and Fritz Kiehn moved into a newly constructed, modern home located on a rise in Deibhalde with views of the grounds. In addition, more lots were acquired, forest parcels were laid out, and a bridge to the island in the larger artificial pond was constructed. Deibhalde — grown to over twenty-eight acres of parkland, with its own road of nearly a mile, three prestigious houses, imposing entrance, and well-tended atmosphere — would have been a tribute to any large-scale industrialist (fig. 37). At least as far as his home life was concerned, Kiehn had achieved his life's goal.

Fig. 37: The park behind the new house in Deibhalde. (1) House occupied in 1924; (2) Guesthouse; (3) House Fritz and Berta Kiehn retired to in 1955; (4) Greenhouse; (5) Apiary; (6) Tennis court; (7) Efka production site later used as stables and riding arena; (8) Messner sawmill; (9) Settlement built in 1930s. (Private collection of the Kiehn family)

Berta and Fritz Kiehn considered the estate their life's work. For the 1968 Christmas holidays, they documented the "development of our Deibhalde" in detail in a booklet for their descendants and the "coming generations." The company founder's identity was reflected in the narrative, which began like the divine revelations in the legends of saints by describing what had led Fritz Kiehn to settle down in Trossingen: on a sunny Sunday morning in 1923, he had been so captivated by the "dazzling landscape" that he had decided on the spot to settle right there. The couple's legacy ("our wish … to Providence") was this: "May Deibhalde always remain in our family's possession."[4]

The luster of the well-maintained parkland spread to its owners, since visitors could scarcely fail to notice the impressive atmosphere. The restoration and expansion of Deibhalde required considerable financial means, a problem Kiehn managed to solve. Other obstacles were not so easily removed from his path back to respectability. Foremost among these was the altered social and political constellation in his adopted hometown.[5] For one thing, the Hohner harmonica dynasty once again held all the trump cards: the company of Kiehn's archrival was many times bigger than Efka and employed the majority of Trossingen workers. In addition, the Hohner family made tremendous donations to the city and to needy townspeople. If until 1949 their focus had been on overcoming the postwar poverty and misery, in the early 1950s the Hohners developed an ambitious construction program with "their" municipal administration. It included an outdoor swimming pool, a hospital, public parks, hundreds of new homes, and even the Ernst Hohner Concert House, which opened in 1961 with over a thousand seats. The instrument manufacturer also saw to it that Trossingen became the site of a music academy. These projects, remarkable for a small town in the 1950s, could not have been realized without Hohner's donations and tax payments. The harmonica company always had several delegates on the town council. Ernst Hohner "transferred" his seat in 1959 to his cousin Walter, who occupied it until 1974. The party of the Hohner family was the DVP/FDP. In southwest Germany, this party hewed to the dominant and traditional left-liberal line and had no affinities with the far-right trends that have already been described in connection with Naumann and Achenbach in chapter 11. In Trossingen, the Hohners' party was the strongest faction in the town parliament until 1959. Ernst Hohner also benefited from the city councilor position he occupied until 1959 (which was then "taken over" by his cousin), his almost impeccable political record, and his excellent relationship with the municipal administration. Neipp, who held the office of mayor until 1952, and Maschke, his successor, were intimate confidants of the Hohner company management.

Trossingen native Rudolf Maschke was particularly indebted to Hohner. He had worked at the town hall since 1922 and had occupied the important office of town clerk from 1927 to 1943. He found his way to the NSDAP through the SPD. Despite the fact that Maschke did not join the party until 1936 (although

Fig. 38: Mayor Maschke congratulates the old and new honorary citizen of Trossingen on his seventieth birthday. (Martin Häffner et al. *Trossingen. Vom Alemannendorf zur Musikstadt*. Trossingen, 1997)

Kiehn provided him with a party ID card dated 1 May 1933), he became one of the staunchest-seeming National Socialists in town, rising to become the head of education for the local wing of the party and openly preaching racist hatred.[6] Released from American captivity as a prisoner of war in 1946, the administrative expert knew how to make himself indispensable to the inexperienced Neipp right away. When the military government instructed him to vacate his post, the town retained him to draw up account statements at his private home. Ernst Hohner made himself available to Maschke as an exoneration witness during his denazification proceedings. After the KRUA's suggestion on 14 January 1948 that Maschke be categorized as a "Follower," Hohner and the town immediately went to work expediting his reemployment. When it was time to decide how to fill a newly created position in the municipal administration as Stadtamtmann, only the SPD opposed nominating their renegade former party colleague, calling him one "of the most aggressive Nazis in Trossingen." But Maschke's experience and expert knowledge counted in his favor, as did the fact that all the other candidates were from out of town and, as Mayor Neipp flatly put it, "similarly politically incriminated." Ernst Hohner's clear vote in Maschke's favor was crucial, as it had been in his rehiring and the covert work he had done at home. Moreover, Maschke was a recent convert to Hohner's party, the DVP/FDP.[7]

His official installation in office was delayed pending the State Commissioner for Political Cleansing's revision of his denazification proceedings. Nevertheless, the town council decided on 9 July 1948, amid protests from the SPD, to allocate Maschke an office in the town hall on a provisional basis. His certificate of appointment was delivered on 1 October 1948, even though the denazification court had not even met yet. When the court classified Maschke as a "Follower" late that year, after another formal statement from Hohner, and additionally imposed a fine of DM 50 and a two-year disenfranchisement, the military government ordered a review of the verdict. The French government considered Maschke an "uncompromising [Nazi] party member and … the biggest fanatic in the party." The repeated hearing did not prompt the council to furlough Maschke; on the contrary, the group again mobilized all its forces to exonerate him. Mayor Neipp informed the denazification court "that the outstanding expert" enjoyed the undiminished confidence of the entire population and that "the municipal administration considers the penalty assessed to be perfectly sufficient." The proceedings ended in 1949 with the confirmation of the prior verdict. The "Follower" was allowed to remain a municipal civil servant but could not occupy any political office until 31 January 1950. Fifteen months after this period had ended, Maschke did not hesitate to run for office as Neipp's successor. Once again, he owed a great part of his success to Hohner's tremendous support: Maschke was elected mayor with 96 percent of the vote. He retained this office until 1970. The Trossingen market square was named after him in 1978.[8]

Maschke largely had Hohner to thank for his political rehabilitation and professional advancement. This relationship laid the groundwork for the mostly seamless cooperation in the 1950s and 1960s between the Trossingen administration and the largest employer in town. Hohner could always count on Maschke. For example, the mayor prevented new industries from taking hold in the town in order to reduce competition in the narrow labor market. For the same reason, Efka's plans for expansion met with great resistance, just as they had in the 1920s. Basic municipal policy was hammered out at the offices of Hohner's board, where the harmonica manufacturer regularly summoned the mayor using his "red telephone," a dedicated phone line to the town hall. Kiehn harbored a grudge against Maschke, and not just because the mayor favored the harmonica company and had disparaged Kiehn personally: the Efka leader despised the servile technocrat for having switched parties two times. Whereas "old fighters" facing hardship could rely on Kiehn's support, Maschke, in Kiehn's derisive view, was the eternal follower.

With circumstances as they were, Kiehn's return to respectability and recovery of his influence in local politics required active campaigning at various levels. For one thing, he continuously deployed donations to associations, social facilities, and churches; these had already proven highly effective in his small-town milieu. Kiehn made a name for himself in particular as a grand patron of sports and became a generous honorary member of a number of different associations. He paid special attention to soccer and horseback riding. The riding club made him an honorary board member after he gave them access to his stables and the large riding arena in Deibhalde mentioned above. In 1957, he played a substantial part in the reestablishment of the music association, which made Kiehn its first chairperson. Along with his direct financial contributions, he offered musicians jobs at his own company. The Alliance of Southern German Folk Musicians awarded him its merit pin in 1958 for this involvement.

His donations, while remaining far below those of Hohner, were always welcomed by the city and its residents regardless of their donor's brown-shirted past. In 1957, Kiehn tried to counter the lavish centennial celebrations of the Hohner company by putting DM 200,000 toward financing a large community sports center. The town council unanimously agreed to name the center after Kiehn, a name it bears to this day.[9] The Protestant Church also took its "wayward son" back into its bosom when Kiehn threw considerable donations its way for expenses such as a new organ.

He staged this event so effectively that it was as if he had never headed a movement to sway people to resign from the churches. He arrived at the church with a carriage drawn by a team of horses for all the town to see. An intense friendship between Kiehn and Trossingen pastor Nill developed in the years that followed. Nill even accompanied Berta and Fritz Kiehn on one of their longer vacation trips and administered Holy Communion to them at their villa. A donation campaign from 1959 manifestly reflected the local hierarchy. After Matthias Hohner, who had been part of the local Protestant Church council for decades, had donated a new main church bell, Kiehn paid for another smaller one. In 1960, the Efka owner celebrated his seventy-fifth birthday with great ceremony, as usual. "The night before," he had "once again" displayed "his social sensitivity, his humanity" in donating DM 75,000 to the town for the local museum and DM 500 to DM 1,000 each to all of the sports clubs, kindergartens, and elementary schools.[10] In other words, there was almost no one in the small town who did not benefit from Kiehn's bonanza.

To top off his path back to the local elite, Kiehn even regained his local political office. He found a new political home in the Freie Wählervereinigung (Free Voters' Association, or FWV), the staff of which had much in common with the former local NSDAP office — but otherwise did not engage in any extremist activities. The old rivalry between Fritz Kiehn and Ernst Hohner was directly reproduced in local politics: just as the DVP/FDP was universally recognizable as the party of the harmonica dynasty, the FWV primarily represented Efka's interests and also appealed to a few other smaller manufacturers and trade professionals. Kiehn, however, did not take a prominent stand himself until 1953. The local election of 1951 more or less reflected the economic hierarchy in town. The FWV won its first seat on the council, only to face six other seats occupied by Hohner's DVP/FDP. Four Social Democrats and three Christian Democrats rounded out the group. The head of the CDU faction was an employee and distant cousin of Hohner's. Two "Hohnerites" belonged to the SPD faction. Ernst Hohner, Neipp, and Maschke represented Trossingen on the county council. Hohner further expanded his supremacy in the 1952 election, when his loyal confidant Maschke became mayor.

Some of the townspeople had long since been turned off by Hohner's omnipotence and high-handed style. Even the employees at his own factory had doubts about the advisability of this one-sided relationship. The industrialist's disdain for the town council was primarily expressed in his absences from its meetings, his briefings with the mayor undertaken in advance of these meetings, and his influence over many of the councilors. In 1953, Ernst Hohner attended only three of twenty-five meetings. Two of these were budget consultations. This behavior, which verged on disenfranchising the council, was viewed by many townspeople with growing disquiet. Only one person could put this uneasiness to use: the second-largest employer in town, Fritz Kiehn. In some ways, this repeated the situation from 1931, when Kiehn had benefited from the public discomfort at being governed by a small number of local dignitaries. Unable to count on the support of nationally known politicians, which had been so important for him then, Kiehn now relied on the effect of other VIPs. With an unmistakable knack for the effects of populism, in the summer of 1953 Kiehn engaged Fritz Walter, the quintessential sports hero of the 1950s and player for the top-ranked Kaiserslautern soccer team, to play a friendly game in Trossingen. Hohner, however, was able to prevent Kiehn's coup by using his representatives on the board of the local soccer association: the match ended up being held in Schwenningen in front of fifteen thousand spectators. A team reception followed in Trossingen, where gift bags from Efka were distributed. This sensational event earned Kiehn a lot of good feeling, and it launched his political comeback. What's more, he benefited from his self-possessed and affable manner, his good relationship with his workers, and his generous support of the sports association. His economic success and his shrewdness in dealing with municipal and judicial authorities even brought him some unconcealed admiration. Neither his Nazi past nor his internment seem to have done damage to this versatile member of the *Mittelstand,* much less the French occupying power or the justice system of the Federal Republic of Germany. "Kiehn is clever" was the frequent observation.[11]

These reasons make it clear how Kiehn, now running for the FWV, was able to achieve a completely unexpected triumph in the council election of 1953. In an astonishing parallel to the 1931 election, he won the highest number of votes and knocked Ernst Hohner into second place. Three of the seven empty seats went to the FWV. The FDP lost one delegate, but with five seats remained the strongest faction. The SPD and CDU each lost one delegate and now had only three and two seats, respectively. This result was "sensational" and shocking at the same time. Many townspeople who were not Efka employees or staunch party-line voters had chosen Kiehn as a counterweight to Hohner but had no desire to see him win. The dismay of some "Hohnerites" at having let down their boss in 1953 lasted a long time. One contemporary said that Ernst Hohner "just about lost it." But he soon converted his outrage into political action and took on his old rival's declaration of war.[12]

When the new council set its constitutive meeting unusually late, three months after the elections, Hohner sprang a surprise coup: he managed to get all of the councilors from the FDP, CDU, and SPD to close ranks against Kiehn. They expressed their distrust of the industrialist in a joint declaration and refused to work with him on committees. The declaration had been kept secret before the meeting and had obviously been prepared by Ernst Hohner (the first signature was his). It gave five reasons for their rejection of Kiehn: First, he had expelled the democratic parties from the council in 1933; two of the delegates affected were now back on the council and could not be expected to work with him. Second, he had shamefully forsaken the town in March 1945. Third, he had attempted to blackmail the town on multiple occasions by threatening to move his factory out of Trossingen. Fourth, Kiehn was damaging the "social peace" and was bringing "seeds of division into Trossingen associations."[13] There actually was a strong polarization in the small town between Hohner and Efka employees, which even caused disagreements within individual families. Fifth, in 1953 the criminal proceedings against Kiehn for the perjury charge described in chapter 11 were still pending.

After the declaration had been read aloud, Kiehn was fuming with rage. He bemoaned the "old political, economic, and social hatred" confronting him once again, claiming it was not enough for the "political parties represented here in the rest of the town councilors" that he spent

> almost four years in a concentration camp. ... Any decent man of reason should also be able to forget [Kiehn's past]. If I erred in my former party membership, then I believe that I have paid the penalty in abundance. This was the view of the denazification court in any case. ... I was ... already always in the way politically; today I am ... economically. I have ... become aware, to my satisfaction, that I do not have your confidence. You think I care about your confidence? The important thing is that my employees have given me their confidence and the people of Trossingen ... gave me convincing proof of their confidence with their votes. I had this confidence twenty-three years ago. ... I never harmed anyone during the Third Reich; back then I only helped, time and time again, just as I do today and always will. One hundred and forty testimonials gave proof of this in my denazification proceedings. Your lack of confidence is an honor for me. ... You have challenged me today, but I promise you, you haven't seen anything yet.[14]

Kiehn, who had been interned for his energetic championing of the criminal Nazi regime and had experienced very favorable prison conditions as punishment, presented himself as a concentration camp survivor and democratically legitimized benefactor. The perpetrator thus became the victim, a pattern of thought that captured the popular imagination in the early 1950s and, in the bureaucratic language of the time, transformed war criminals into "war convicts."[15] Kiehn threatened the mayor with legal action, had his lawyers draw up a disciplinary complaint and a demand for prosecution, and announced once again that he would be relocating his company. During this stage, Kiehn suffered great damage when the national press suddenly published stories of his spectacular altercation in the council and his role during the Third Reich, which evidently had been planted by his local enemies. A few weeks later, the *Trossinger Zeitung* spent a week reporting on his perjury trial. That summer, the council refused to answer an open letter from Kiehn. Despite the unambiguous election result, Kiehn lost the power struggle playing out behind the scenes. Not until early 1955 — almost a year after his first attempt, and after he had been granted amnesty — did he venture into another council meeting. He seldom made an appearance after that.

After his political comeback failed, so did his plans for local economic expansion. Kiehn had been negotiating with the town since 1953 for Efka to be allowed to acquire another piece of property for a large new building. The precise course of events can no longer be reconstructed. What we know for certain, however, is that Maschke drew out the process, both sides were uncompromising in their confrontation, Kiehn threatened to relocate his firm, and several private landowners were obstructionist. The efforts failed conclusively in 1956, in what Kiehn considered a conspiracy by Hohner and the municipal administration. Things came to a head at a town hall meeting a short time later, when Kiehn and Maschke berated each other in front of 350 attendees. Kiehn complained of "known excesses in the town council" and the boycott of his firm. The quarrel, in which the Efka owner repeatedly referred to the mayor as a "Hohner mayor" and the council as "Hohner-dependent," continued in open letters and council meetings. Ernst Hohner, who had both personal and labor market reasons for preventing Efka's expansion, exercised elegant restraint in public and urged discretion. The feud ended for the time being when Kiehn resigned his council seat in 1956 and expanded the company into Deißlingen, Rottweil, although he did not relocate Efka's headquarters. Obviously Kiehn never seriously considered making his Tuttlingen factory the base of his operations. Efka made do with considerably expanding the Trossingen factory in 1958, tripling the usable floor space (fig. 39). The six-story building was anything but optimal for manufacturing; the only advantage was its relatively small footprint. The paper goods manufacturer had drawn the short straw in this conflict with the town as well.[16]

By 1956 at the latest, Kiehn had lost a conflict that dealt primarily with the local pecking order and economic opportunities. The declaration by the councilmen

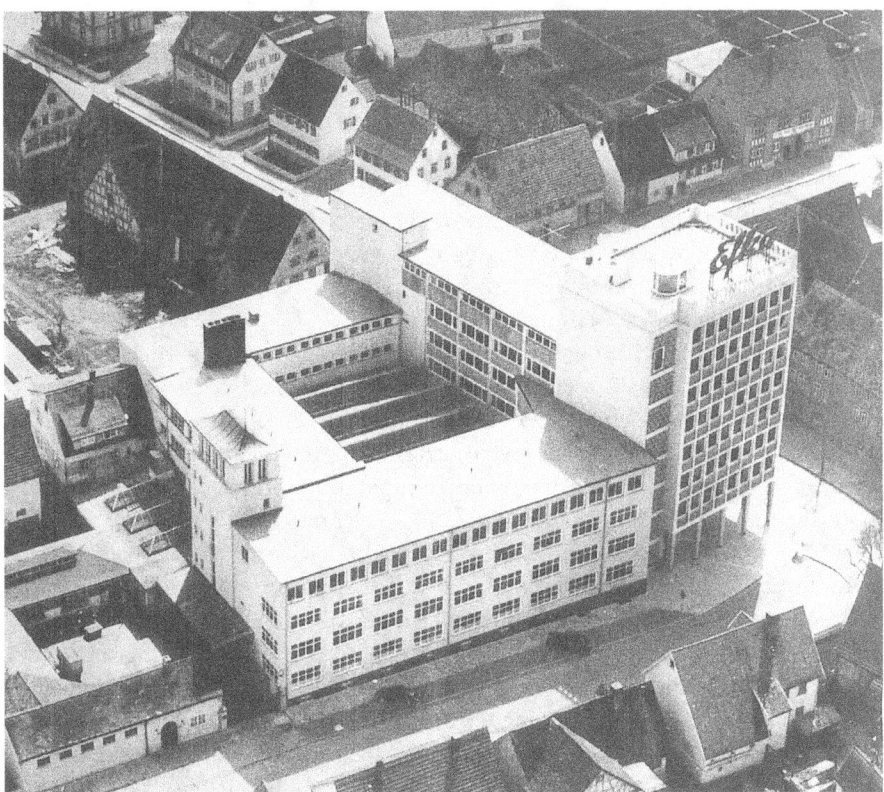

Fig. 39: New Efka building (1958). (Martin Häffner et al. *Trossingen. Vom Alemannendorf zur Musikstadt.* Trossingen, 1997)

had alluded to his brown-shirted past for purely instrumental reasons: as long as Kiehn did not disturb the balance of power and did not offend the mayor and the council, he would be accepted without his past playing a role. It was symbolic compensation of a sort for Kiehn's harsh treatment in local political matters when in 1955, in honor of his seventieth birthday, the council quietly returned the honorary citizen status revoked in 1945 (fig. 38). The procedure was extremely odd: his title was restored without any sort of committee officially resolving to do so, and without any written documentation. Nevertheless, the city suddenly returned to addressing Kiehn as an honorary citizen and recognized him with appropriate gifts on milestone birthdays until the end of his life.[17]

A critical examination of the Nazi past did not occur; indeed, during these years people made assiduous efforts to keep this past under wraps as much as possible. "Communicative silence,"[18] as Hermann Lübbe so aptly dubbed the oppressive atmosphere of the 1950s, found its clearest expression in the personnel decisions of the town and in local historical documentation. For the thirty-year jubilee of the town's incorporation and the centenary of Hohner's harmonica firm in 1957, the council commissioned a chronicle that focused on praising the Hohner family's services to Trossingen. The history explicitly stated that there was "little cause" to dwell on "the course of the years from 1933 to spring 1945." "For the larger and better part of the Trossingen citizenry — regardless of the loyalty and good faith with which they had carried out their service," this "misguided period" had become "a piece of the past that, though bitter, had been overcome."[19] A few statements ranging from general to cryptic were all that preceded an effortless leap into the postwar era. Kiehn's name went unmentioned, as did those of other, local National Socialists.

Kiehn, by contrast, explicitly dealt with his past during this time, in order to stand up to it being instrumentalized in the local trenches. He also seems never to have fully put the years from 1933 to 1945 behind himself psychologically; in his view, these were the years of his greatest triumphs. At a company Christmas party thrown by Efka, Kiehn made the Freudian slip of not only recalling the Christmas holiday, but also the old German "Yuletide" celebrated "by our ancestors" every year at the same time.[20] The beloved National Socialist terminology of "factory community" (*Betriebsgemeinschaft*) and "social evening" (*Kameradschaftsabend*) was still in use in the early 1950s, but such verbal relapses remained the exception. In his own domain, however, Kiehn could never stop referring proudly to his earlier offices and titles, unless they had obviously been discredited politically. He often spoke of his IHK presidency or his Reichstag seat, for example, but not of his career in the SS. Occasion for this nostalgia was provided by the expensive celebrations he held in quick succession in the 1950s and 1960s, most of which featured speeches by Kiehn. In 1954, when his amnesty and the end of the perjury scandal were imminent, the Kiehn family hosted a summer party at Deibhalde. This was Kiehn's way of symbolically reannouncing his claim to a top spot in the local social hierarchy, as well as his response to the snub from the town council.

The annual company party provided an external setting to be repurposed into a lavish display of showmanship by Hermann Schäfer, who had learned his trade in Goebbels's ministry. Kiehn had the driveway to his villa submerged in a sea of national and state flags. Even if the colors had changed, these inevitably harked back to the company party from 1937. Various radio, theater, and ballet celebrities had been hired for entertainment. Marching bands, hunting delegations, and sports associations were also deployed. All of the commercial units at Efka were represented by standard bearers. What was now a sea of black, red, and gold flags — parades of representatives in dark double-breasted suits carrying banners for their districts — had a few years before been filled with columns of uniformed SS and Nazi Party members on the march amid banners displaying swastikas.

"The undisputed high point ... however, was the entrance of the top-ranked Kaiserslautern soccer club. The stars of the soccer World Cup in Bern marched at the forefront. ... Indescribable cheering broke out when the soccer team paraded past the guests, led by the marching band, and was greeted by the Kiehn family on the stage." Sepp Herberger, the coach of the national team, also graced the party with his presence for a few hours. Even the Hohners had not yet succeeded in creating such a sensation, and autographs from the world champions were toted home like precious trophies. Kiehn had managed to bask in the light of the soccer World Cup title, which in itself was extremely important for West German pride and international recognition.[21]

Kiehn's seventieth birthday followed in 1955, in a smaller setting. The high point of this celebration was the restoration of his status as an honorary citizen. A small Festschrift contains an outline of the history of his life and firm; the years from 1933 to 1945 are practically omitted. Since the war left "all soldiers clamoring for Efka paper," Kiehn had to build "subsidiaries near the front." "After the collapse," it is noted, Kiehn was "interned like so many other entrepreneurs," but returned to work "unbroken" in 1950 despite this "great misfortune." The Festschrift offered an explanation for Kiehn's successes that bordered on Nazi jargon and was conspicuously out of touch with contemporary political correctness in the Federal Republic: "The secret of his strength lies in the healthy genetic constitution of his parents."[22]

Once Kiehn had inaugurated the sports center named after him in 1957, his next big celebration honored the fiftieth anniversary of his first encounter with

Fig. 40: A symbolic handshake: Ernst Hohner and Fritz Kiehn (1957). (Private collection of the Kiehn family)

Trossingen (fig. 40). This event essentially restaged the absurd party of 1938 that had also recalled this "moment of glory." Kiehn commissioned the writing of a brief biography for this purpose that openly praised some of the posts he had occupied between 1933 and 1945 and acquitted him of any wrongdoing. "His actions ... were reviewed and dissected in detail after 1945. ... Once there was some distance from the era in which rumors and machinations had inflamed people's passions, the citizens of Trossingen issued their verdict on Fritz Kiehn: In 1954, he received the most votes ... in the town council election. He resigned his seat in 1956 because it was better for his health."[23]

Kiehn celebrated his seventy-fifth birthday in 1960 and commissioned a brief new biography. This one outdid its predecessor in narcissistic pathos, stylizing Kiehn into a "proven helmsman" who had maneuvered the "little Efka boat" through the "storms of the war and the postwar era." His political career was addressed merely with a terse description of the "hardships and misery" he suffered from 1945 to 1950, which were attributed only to his tragic entanglements, "because nothing is more difficult 'than doing right by the powers that be.' Yet to the end, Fritz Kiehn had preserved his center and his strength. ... With the wisdom of age, it becomes apparent that it is not important what we burn for, but that we burn for something, and ever more purely." Plentiful discussion of "mountains of accomplishments," "seriousness of will," "love of the gods," and "social common sense" then followed. The portrait was rounded out with a contemplation of his kind-hearted features and his soul, "suffused with beauty and difficulty alike."[24] Sculptor Countess Barbara von Kalckreuth created busts of Fritz and Berta Kiehn for the same occasion, and the Kiehns also had their portrait done by Conrad Hommel. Both the painter and the sculptor, who was his wife, had been part of Magda and Josef Goebbels's entourage before 1945. It is believed that Robert von Schirach introduced this artistic couple to the Kiehns.[25]

The large and grandiose celebrations were once again attended by numerous VIPs from the political and economic circles of the region, as well as by Efka employees. In honor of his commitment as a patron of sports, the industrialist received a plaque from the Track and Field Association, a pin from the Württemberg Sports Association, and a "gamekeeper's badge" from the German Hunters' Association, one of that group's highest awards. For the first time, a representative from one of the federal ministries sent his congratulations from Bonn, in this case an official of the Ministry of Economics. After the Efka works committee chair had honored Kiehn's "foresight," "acumen," and "nobleness of heart ... from the employee's perspective," and the Efka boss's motto ("Without striving, there is no life") had been announced, "the man took the microphone ... with the waves of gratitude nearly crashing together above him." Deeply moved by the "bright and dark sides of existence," Kiehn volunteered his version of his own biography. As he had in 1954 before the town council, he tearfully complained anew that he had been forced "to become acquainted with seventeen prisons and concentration camps in four years." The Nazi accomplice had fashioned himself into a victim — impulsively in 1954, but now with careful consideration. This was a monstrous provocation to the next of kin of those who had been tortured and murdered by the National Socialist regime. The "transition from falsehood to self-deception" described by Primo Levi seemed in Kiehn's case to have finally succeeded.[26] Such melancholy, however, did not occur to anyone there that night, as all were occupied with the entertainment that followed: a sensational tightrope act and "gaiety" lasting for hours. Once again, the supporting program was carried by "selected players from radio, stage, and vaudeville." Kiehn also announced at the end of his speech that he would be giving DM 100 to every adult Efka employee.[27] Furthermore, he repeated his donations to the city and all of the kindergartens, schools, and clubs in Trossingen. The council conveyed its gratitude in a unanimous resolution to name the square between the Efka factory and the Rose Inn (the erstwhile favorite Nazi Party destination) after Kiehn. Even the SPD acknowledged his "merits ... over the past ten years."[28]

Within ten years of the founding of the Federal Republic of Germany, Kiehn had succeeded in returning to the ranks of the bourgeois elite of his hometown. He had to accept clear boundaries in his local environment, but these boundaries merely reflected the socioeconomic balance of power in his adopted hometown. In other words, they had nothing to do with a critical reckoning with Nazi history. Kiehn withdrew from active politics in 1956 and transferred representation of his factory's interests on the town council first to his son-in-law Fritz Wieshofer (from 1959 to 1961) and then to his daughter, Gretl (from 1965 to 1974). The primary reason that his plans for economic expansion failed was not the local opposition but rather his previously described entrepreneurial missteps. But the tremendous resistance in political and economic spheres in no way prevented Kiehn from restoring himself to the status of a universally honored person. As long as he accepted the local hierarchy, practically no one was bothered by his political past or his multiyear internment, the dubious circumstances of his denazification and the various scandals in which he had been implicated, his perjury trial, or the influx of Kiehn's "old comrades" from near and far. Not even his embarrassing attacks on the council and the mayor were enough to make him a persona non grata for any length of time.

These dark stains — to the extent they were ever even seen as such — were pitted against an imposing list of merits that all could see: as the second-largest taxpayer and employer in the town, Kiehn put food on the table for more than five hundred townspeople, paid above-market wages, and provided numerous benefits; he was beloved by his employees, their families, and clubs, was a shining and committed patron, and knew how to win people over. As long as he did not tangle with the powerful duo of Hohner and Maschke, the social fabric of Trossingen would always make room for the former "leader of the Württemberg economy" to take second place.

Notes

1. Letter from Herbert E. Kiehn to the authors of 15 Sept. 1998 and interview of 15–16 June 1999.
2. See Frevert, *Brauchtum*; Frevert, *Rominten*. On Frevert's role as a war criminal, see Gautschi, *Walter Frevert*; Bode and Emmert, *Jagdwende,* 150, 154.
3. See Lettow-Vorbeck, *Fuße*.
4. Kiehn, *Unsere Deibhalde,* 1, title page. All details ibid., 6–28.
5. On the following explanations, see Berghoff, *Kleinstadt,* 515–532, 572–600.
6. See AVT, 25 Feb. 1942.
7. StAT, B 93, GRP of 18 Mar. 1948.
8. StAS, Wü 13, Bü 2238 (Maschke denazification records). See StAT, B 93, GRP of 18 Mar., 1 Oct., and 26 Nov. 1948.
9. StAT, B 102, GRP of 27 Jan. 1956; TZ, 14 Oct. 1957.
10. TZ, 17 Oct. 1960; letter from Herbert E. Kiehn to the authors of 21 Apr. 1999.
11. Interview by Hartmut Berghoff of 7 July 1993.
12. Interview by Hartmut Berghoff of 4 Sept. 1992. See also TZ, 5–9 Mar. 1954 and 14 Oct. 1955; StAT, Häffner interview collection; TZ, 16 Nov. 1953. A rolling local elections system continued to be the rule, where only half of the council seats were up for election in each election cycle.
13. ASD, NL Erler, Box 85, letter from Trossingen town councilors to mayor of 8 Feb. 1954.
14. StAT, B 99, GRP of 8 Feb. 1954.
15. See Herbert, "Rückkehr," 166; Herbert, *Best,* 437–444; Frei, *Vergangenheitspolitik,* 266–268.
16. StAT, A 939, undated newspaper clippings. See also the following in StAT: B 99, GRP of 20 July, 17 Sept., and 3 Dec. 1954; B 101, GRP of 25 Sept. 1956; B 102, GRP of 27 Jan., 28 Feb., and 13 June 1956; B 104, GRP of 26 Feb. and 11 Mar. 1957. See also TZ, 25 Jan. and 9 Feb. 1955; TZ, 27, 28, 30 Apr., 12, 16, 19 May, 28 Nov. 1956; TZ, 15 Jan. 1957; Häffner, Ruff, and Schrumpf, *Trossingen,* 303–306.
17. Häffner, Ruff, and Schrumpf, *Trossingen,* 501.
18. Lübbe, "Nationalsozialismus," 594.
19. Lenz, *Hand,* 102–103.
20. Letter from Herbert E. Kiehn to the authors of 22 Feb. 1999.
21. TZ, 26 July 1954. See Frei, *Finale Grande*; Leinemann, *Sepp Herberger*.
22. StAT, A 938, Festschrift from 1955.
23. Anon., *Fritz Kiehn,* 28. The election took place in 1953.
24. Sinz, *Fritz Kiehn,* no page number.
25. Schaumburg-Lippe, *Dr. Goebbels,* 173; letter from Herbert E. Kiehn to the authors of 28 Sept. 1998.
26. See Levi, *Die Untergegangenen,* 27.
27. TZ, 17 Oct. 1960. See also TZ, 15 Oct. 1960.
28. StAT, B 109, GRP of 11 Oct. 1960.

Chapter 14

THE TWILIGHT YEARS OF AN HONORED WEST GERMAN

Even into advanced age, Kiehn's hunger for titles did not subside.[1] Wieshofer's contacts in Austria proved advantageous in this regard. In 1960, Kiehn was made a knight of the International Order of St. Hubertus, a hunting society in Vienna. Kiehn had the local newspaper refer to him as a "Knight Commander" (Großoffizier).[2] The obscure order, which seems to have been revived after 1945, was tailor-made for people like Fritz Kiehn who adored titles and rituals and were prepared to pay a high price for them in the form of substantial donations. His membership allowed Kiehn to wear a green robe and the traditional brick-red buckskin shoes, as well as decorate himself with other insignia. Being ranked according to a highly differentiated hierarchy, with a nuanced variety of titles that ranged from Grand Master to Knight, was as fascinating to him as the group's solemn ceremonies. His ability, as official district huntsman, to organize a Hubertus mass at the Beuron monastery filled him with satisfaction and offered a replacement for the disenchantment with the world that devout supporters of the Nazis had been left with after the collapse of the regime. The robe of the order stood in for the SS uniform, and the society's insignia — a green Maltese cross with a stag's head — replaced the Yule lantern and honorary dagger, identifying membership in what they considered a privileged community. Kiehn did abstain from a public "knighthood investiture" in Trossingen that Weishofer had initially planned for him, in which he was to have been escorted by two "squires," namely, Robert von Schirach and Herbert E. Kiehn. Wieshofer's divorce sidelined him as director of the extravaganza, and Kiehn's grandson refused to take over because of his experiences at the elitist boarding school of Salem Castle on Lake Constance, where he had been exposed to more upper-class tastes. Kiehn had to content

---

Notes from this chapter begin on page 309.

himself with being awarded his title in a lesser context, but he did not fail to commission a portrait of himself in his St. Hubertus finery by Conrad Hommel.[3]

Having only completed a Realschule diploma (with which students leave school around age sixteen to enter vocational training), Kiehn, the perennial social climber, now found himself remarkably drawn to academia. Universities, in his view, embodied sacred institutions whose recognition and prestige he wished to obtain, and whose abundant rituals excited him. As academic distinctions were present among the bourgeoisie, they were somewhat pertinent to the lifestyle that Kiehn aspired to. His old rival, Ernst Hohner, was an honorary senator of the University of Tübingen and the Stuttgart Technical College (Technische Hochschule), as was Kiehn's close friend Wilhelm Kraut of the Bizerba scale manufacturing company in Balingen. Kiehn, on the other hand, had no connections of any kind to actual academic life: he was too far removed from educational traditions. He had no affinity for any particular field or research topic that he could have chosen to promote.

There were various reasons that Kiehn chose to seek academic distinction from the University of Innsbruck in Austria. He made an obvious point of steering clear of the Württemberg colleges; whether he wished to distinguish himself from his rival Hohner or expected him to raise objections is unclear. Perhaps he wanted to make sure there would be no complications, which could not be ruled out given his sufficiently well-known political past. Austria was a good prospect because of the contacts Kiehn had cultivated through his son-in-law Fritz Wieshofer, his membership in the Order of St. Hubertus, and his hunting preserves in Styria and Tyrol. What's more, there had been a German Circle of Friends of the University of Innsbruck since 1954, whose goal was to support the exchange of financial and symbolic capital, that is, donations and titles. Circle of Friends members included many businessmen, and the connection to its Innsbruck alma mater had arisen from the geographical proximity of Tyrol's capital to the Federal Republic of Germany and the high percentage of German students at the university. Added to this was the University of Innsbruck's great receptiveness to "commercial honors." In the 1950s, the Austrian minister of education criticized it for this reason, but the institution reacted indignantly and carried on with the same policy.[4]

So it was that Kiehn joined another elite "circle of friends" in approximately 1960, once again calling attention to himself with exorbitant donations. Neither he nor his new friends had any doubt that there was a correlation between their financial contributions and receipt of an honorary academic title. Both sides immediately began pressing emphatically and with unusual directness to redeem their respective prizes quickly. The chair of the Circle of Friends, Munich attorney Max Kessler, had already approached the university rector twice about the matter before the end of 1962. As a result of his visits, and because the university insisted on "a careful selection process," the rector sought to obtain references for Kiehn so as to judge his "reputation, ... achievement, and ... civic conduct."[5] The various letters of reference replying to this delicate inquiry spotlight the differing ways that West German government officials dealt with the legacies of individuals' involvement in the Nazi regime, from whitewashing to remaining silent, and occasionally speaking the truth. Kurt Georg Kiesinger, minister-president of Baden-Württemberg and later federal chancellor, and Kurt Geiger, Tuttlingen district administrator, avoided making any comment about Kiehn. Kiesinger, who himself had been a member of the Nazi Party, did not even answer. Geiger did not respond to the letter from Innsbruck until Kiehn's honorary title had been granted. The Tübingen deputy district president mostly kept a low profile but made a dark reference to Kiehn's "National Socialist activity" as the reason he had not yet received any special honors from the state: "I was not able to learn the details of this activity."[6] This was probably true, since Kiehn's denazification records inexplicably disappeared, along with various judicial records. Tübingen mayor Hans Gmelin and Trossingen mayor Maschke were full of praise for Kiehn and avoided any reference to the Third Reich. Gmelin had headed the SA student group in his university town and was interned in Balingen after 1945 along with Kiehn. He had become close friends with Kiehn after 1950, describing him as one "of the most successful industrialists in central Swabia" and a "generous patron." Maschke indicated that Kiehn had been an "honored citizen of our town for many years" and that a square and a sports center bore his name. "I believe these facts prove the importance of this figure in an impressive fashion ... such that I can endorse your project without further explanation."[7]

One particularly detailed and equally whitewashing reply came from the managing director of the Rottweil IHK, who discussed the period before 1945 in detail without mentioning Kiehn's enrichment through acquisition of Jewish property:

> Kiehn was an old and devoted follower of the NSDAP who held high party offices. However, this did not detract him from accommodating dissidents. ... I have only the highest recommendation for Fritz Kiehn as a president and as a person. He made ... no distinction between comrades from inside or outside the party. He helped out wherever he could in an unselfish and gracious manner. Partisanship, despotism, arrogance, and presumption were alien to him. ... His civic conduct is that of a man with ... the wisdom of experience.[8]

Only Gebhard Müller, who had meanwhile become president of the Federal Constitutional Court, spoke clearly of Kiehn's political activities. Before and after 1933, he wrote, Kiehn had been "one of the most active members of the NSDAP. ... In this, he may absolutely have been one of those who joined the party for idealistic reasons, but this did not prevent his measures ... from causing many to suffer greatly." Müller then made reference to Kiehn's detention, as well as his achievements in society and in business, and predicted that "the intended honor would doubtless be as welcomed [by some citizens] as they would be criticized by those in the know."[9]

Thus armed with full knowledge of Kiehn's political offenses, the academic senate of the University of Innsbruck nonetheless decided to award the former Nazi functionary the title of honorary citizen and its "Excellenti in Meritis" distinction. Yet approval had to be obtained from the Austrian Federal Ministry of Education first. In his application to the Viennese authorities, the rector summarized solely the positive statements about Kiehn and withheld all references to the Nazi era. Political or moral reservations — when there were any at all — took a backseat to the lucrative prospect of tying a generous donor to the university. This calculation proved to be successful, and brought the expected heavy windfall for the Innsbruck alma mater. When the Circle of Friends pressed to have Kiehn promoted from an honorary citizen of the University of Innsbruck to an honorary senator, the rector approvingly acknowledged the 532,000 Austrian schillings Kiehn had already donated. "To my knowledge, this is the largest financial sum that an honorary senator has ever rendered to the university. ... A further DM 60,000 would be made available."[10] In fact, the amount had already been deposited in the Circle of Friends' account, with instructions to forward it to the university as soon as the academic senate and the Ministry of Education agreed to grant Kiehn the title of senator.

The otherwise glacial-paced university acted quickly in view of this temptation; the senate voted unanimously to approve the application within just two weeks of submission. This process generated uneasiness within the university community. The arts faculty pointed out that another German businessman was going through the process at the same time, and in that case, the usual procedures as well as the dignity of the university were being maintained. Specifically, this businessman, Ernst Willi Piepenstock, who was also from Baden-Württemberg, had provided a donation without an allocation clause. Piepenstock's entire manner — according to the dean of the arts faculty — had been "pleasantly" different from the "Kiehn case."[11] Likely because of these irritations, it took months before the Ministry of Education in Vienna deigned to grant permission for Kiehn's honorary senator status. Once the permit was finally issued, Kiehn considered himself "felicitously honored and distinguished." When the Innsbruck rector inquired whether he would accept the title offered, he "respectfully" answered with "a sincere and delighted 'yes.'"[12] The ceremony to award Kiehn the senator title finally took place on 9 July 1966 with his entire family present (fig. 41). It had cost Kiehn a tidy sum for the splendid solemnities, held at the university's Kaiser Leopold Hall. The event included the entrance by the academic senate and honorary senators in their gowns, headgear, and chains of office; the reserved seats of honor; the lofty encomiums; the musical accompaniment; and the banquet with the rector. But for him, it was worth it. As an honorary senator of the University

Fig. 41: Academic honors at the University of Innsbruck in the 1960s. (Private collection of the Kiehn family)

of Innsbruck, Fritz Kiehn ranked among the governors of Tyrol and South Tyrol, the president of the Tyrol state parliament, several well-known university dons, Daimler-Benz executive Hans-Martin Schleyer, and a host of other business luminaries. Schleyer, who would later serve as president of both the Federation of German Industries and the Confederation of German Employers' Associations simultaneously, was kidnapped and murdered in 1977 by the terrorist Red Army Faction because of his Nazi past. Like Kiehn, Schleyer had belonged to the SS. He had held the rank of second lieutenant (Untersturmführer) and had shared responsibility for the economic exploitation of Bohemia and Moravia during the time that Czechoslovakia had been a German protectorate.[13]

Kiehn's political past did not play a role in either 1962 or 1965–1966. But the Innsbruck rector would have to deal with it in 1972, when he received a letter of protest listing Kiehn's offices in the Nazi regime and containing a picture of Kiehn in his SS uniform. The rector did not consider notifying the university committees of the case and appeased the outraged letter writer with a barefaced lie: "Regrettably ... the facts you cited were not known to the University of Innsbruck at the time the title was solicited."[14] Kiehn, therefore, had no need to fear losing the senator title he had purchased; he enjoyed flaunting it on official occasions. It had given him a string of new contacts to top-ranking figures in public life.

Kiehn spent his entire postwar life hoping to receive equally prestigious accolades from the Federal Republic of Germany. On his milestone birthdays, he would speculate that perhaps the highest national representative present would pull a medal out of his bag at the end of his speech, bestowing upon Kiehn the Order of Merit of the Federal Republic of Germany. His hopes were in vain — which is surprising, since Kiehn had had influential friends in the governing parties since the 1950s. These included Bundestag representative Karl Gengler (CDU); the two men and their wives had been on friendly terms since at least the mid-1950s. They were already celebrating New Year's Eve together by 1954. Nonetheless, Gengler, who was almost the same age as Kiehn and lived in Rottweil, had a very different political past. He had come from the Christian trade union movement and had represented the Center Party in the Württemberg state parliament during the Weimar Republic. After 1934, he had struggled along in Cologne as the legal adviser for the Federal Social Insurance Board but had been forced to vacate this position in 1935. To escape unemployment, he then founded a harmonica school in Cologne with help from the Hohner company. To escape the damage from aerial bombardments and the increasing intensity of persecution, Gengler moved to Trossingen in 1944, his wife's hometown, where Ernst Hohner accommodated him at his factory. He may have encountered Kiehn during this time. Gengler cofounded the regional branch of the CDU after 1945 and became a member and president of the state parliament of Württemberg-Hohenzollern. He was a member of the Bundestag from 1949 until 1957. Gengler had declared during Fritz Kiehn's perjury trial that the state parliamentary review committee had been appointed "solely for political reasons. ... The loan issue ... certainly would not have been cause for complaint if it had not been associated with the Kiehn name."[15]

Another friendship Kiehn struck up in the mid-1950s was with Dr. Bruno Heck. A Catholic born in Swabia in 1917, Heck had a PhD in classics and was one of the most influential southern German politicians of the Adenauer era. He represented the Rottweil-Tuttlingen district in the Bundestag from 1957 to 1976, was federal whip for the CDU from 1952 to 1957, and finally was the party's general secretary until 1971. Heck organized the election campaign of 1957, in which Adenauer rode to victory with a triumphant absolute majority under the slogan, "No experiments." From 1962 to 1968, Heck served as federal family minister under Adenauer, Erhard, and Kiesinger. He then switched to the CDU party foundation, which he led until 1989.[16] Heck and his wife were regular visitors at Deibhalde and participated in family celebrations. Through Heck, the Kiehns made more contacts to prominent CDU representatives in the Bundestag, such as Heinrich Krone, who served as chair of the conservative CDU/CSU faction in the Bundestag from 1955 to 1961, deputy party chair from 1958 to 1964, and federal minister of various departments from 1961 to 1965.

There were various reasons Kiehn chose to associate with high-ranking CDU representatives rather than those of other parties. For one thing, Kiehn did not have a great selection to choose from among the established parties. The SPD, still anticapitalist, was out of the question for him as a businessperson, and the FDP was too closely linked to his local archrival, Hohner. For another, proximity to power was what mattered most to Kiehn; it made those friendships as prestigious as they were useful. With the help of such friendships, he could reap a substantial economic advantage from time to time. For example, in the early 1950s Kiehn successfully solicited Karl Gengler to intervene in tax policy matters that were of crucial importance to his business, resulting in a retail price reduction for a pack of cigarettes from forty-five to twenty-five pfennigs, which naturally boosted sales tremendously. Last, Kiehn's affinity for the CDU was also politically motivated. Specifically, Kiehn did not hold himself at a distance from the Bonn Republic, but wholeheartedly identified with Adenauer's politics and admired the chancellor. Kiehn agreed unreservedly with Adenauer's strategy, which was grounded in authoritarian leadership and focused on the integration of the West, remilitarization, a tough course of action against Communists, and lenient treatment of former Nazis.

Unfortunately, it has not been possible to reconstruct in detail how this implacable opponent of Weimar democracy and Nazi functionary was transformed into a West German "republican by reason" (*Vernunftrepublikaner*). Three primary aspects can be observed, however. First of all, few exposed Nazi functionaries were ostracized from the early Bonn Republic for any great length of time. Most of them were allowed to return to a bourgeois existence, and indeed it was made markedly easy for them to do so. This is not the place to judge the striking injustice of this treatment against what was suffered by the victims of the Nazi regime. When it comes to the republic's knack for political integration and stability, however, Adenauer's methods of dealing with the past appear to have worked. Second, the convincing economic performance of the new state lent overwhelming legitimacy to its political system. The prosperity achieved in the Federal Republic soon surpassed most of its citizens' early expectations. This experience was true for Fritz Kiehn as well, who went from an internment camp back to the executive floor of his company, which initially was growing by leaps and bounds. Third, we must not underestimate the extent of continuity at the political level, as well as in people's attitudes. Painting communism as the enemy served both the Nazi state and the Federal Republic as an ideology for integration. In the case of Kiehn and many others who were attracted by the *Volksgemeinschaft* ideology, defusing social antagonisms also played a key role. For all of their clear differences, there were definitely points of contact and continuities between the *Volksgemeinschaft* and business ideology of National Socialism and the enlightened entrepreneurial class now part of the social market economy.[17] Kiehn was able to cultivate the same leadership style within his company after 1950 as he had before 1945.

One could pass from the Nazi regime to the Bonn Republic without having to distance oneself from one's own past. After 1950, Kiehn seldom spoke about the Third Reich, even with his former party comrades. This was also true of his contact with Baldur von Schirach. The two men were now related to each other by marriage and saw each other regularly between 1966 and 1972, but according to Herbert E. Kiehn they never talked about the Third Reich. During visits by former political allies or their survivors, like the widow of the executed Kurt Daluege, National Socialism was never discussed, nor were the causes of its collapse or the roles they themselves played in it: "The past was a taboo subject." Walter Funk, by contrast, could not remain silent. When Kiehn's grandson, Herbert E. Kiehn, went to meet him with Robert von Schirach after Funk's release from Spandau Prison, the former economics minister had constructed an explanation for his past that testified to an apocalyptic worldview and a confused helplessness. According to Funk, Hitler had been destined by Providence "to destroy this world order so that it could be built anew."[18]

Some of the common arguments to justify those years were heard within the Kiehn family. As Berta Kiehn explained to her grandson: "But the Führer did us a lot of good too!" She voiced her suspicions that photos of mountains of corpses of concentration camp prisoners actually depicted victims of the Allied bombing of Dresden. She doggedly placed the number of murdered Jews at four million, as if this fundamentally changed the way it should be judged. According to Herbert E. Kiehn, at some point the "repression ... had become perfect, and it was difficult to get my grandmother to talk about political issues."[19] When the paper factory in Eislingen so brutally Aryanized by Kiehn came up, the "Jewish previous owners" would continually resurface in the conversation. Herbert E. Kiehn noted that "I never heard any comments about awareness of injustice, not about Eislingen and not about Okriftel. But I can still hear my grandmother talking about this: it had been confirmed ... to my grandfather that the Jewish previous owners of the factory got it back in better condition than they had left it in."[20] Concerning Fritz Kiehn's perjury trial, Herbert E. Kiehn attested that his grandfather had shirked any blame: he remained convinced that he had been a victim of political justice and a plot by Ernst Hohner.[21]

Like other Nazi perpetrators, Kiehn never spoke openly about his own past to his offspring. For these perpetrators, recollections revolved around excuses and self-serving declarations, "communicative shutdown"[22] and half truths. Key chapters of one's own biography were hermetically sealed, so to speak. For example, in the 1960s and 1970s Werner Best's SS comrades asked for any letters referring to their collaboration with the Third Reich to be sent to their post office boxes rather than their homes, "because the children knew nothing of their father's past" and things should stay that way.[23] Fritz Kiehn knew how to abridge central elements of his political biography and misrepresent the facts to respond to the critical inquiries of his curious grandson. The aid he provided to his "fellow comrades" after 1948 was so perfectly camouflaged that what today looks like an obvious network evident in the Efka leader's staffing policy looked to his relatives like a series of coincidences, if they were even aware anymore of his old connections. His old comrades had been perfectly disguised.

The first years after the war were the nadir of Berta and Fritz Kiehn's lives. Their arrests and enforced separation, the "desecration" of Deibhalde, the forced administration of the company, and the loss of the firms acquired after 1933 had been hard on the family. They wrote in 1968 of what they considered the barbaric destruction of Deibhalde by occupying soldiers: "In May 1945, the French soldiers ... lived here like vandals: nothing was sacred to them. They broke both of the barred, leaded windows in the columbarium, they threw the hand-forged bars and the sword ... in the big pond." The Kiehns made themselves into victims in retrospect: they complained that the "occupiers" had so little regard for the beauty of the well-kept Deibhalde that the French soldiers had actually drained the ornamental pools in order to search for weapons. They lamented how thoughtlessly the Americans had acted when they arrested the family in Tyrol, "disrespectfully" opening "the urn with our Herbert's ashes" they had brought with them on their escape.[24] They bemoaned the lack of respect for their personal space exhibited by the Allies when they detained the remaining Nazi high officials who had scattered in the Alps even as the full extent of the apocalyptic crimes against humanity became visible as the concentration camps were liberated. It appears to have been lost on them that Heinrich Himmler had been a guest in their home just a few weeks before and that they had spent fifteen years actively campaigning for National Socialism.

As far as Kiehn was concerned, the Nazi regime had ultimately failed because of "Hitler's insanity," which had ostensibly set in during the second half of the war. Like Gottlob Berger, Kiehn's companion in struggle from the early years who was himself a former leader of the SS Main Office and still marveled at the fact "that the higher and highest leaders played fast and loose [with us],"[25] Kiehn never arrived at the idea that he could have been personally complicit in the "German catastrophe."[26] Rather than a "mistake," Kiehn considered the mass murder of the Jews to have been a tactical blunder by a government with a long track record of success — he would have opted for the uniform expulsion of German Jews. Certain anti-Semitic ideas used to explain the crises of the Weimar years, such as an international Jewish conspiracy, retained their power after 1945 for Kiehn and many ex-Nazis. One of the contradictions of Kiehn's life was his ability to reconcile this kind of attitude with his wholly unabashed view of his own actions before 1945, as well as with his admiration of Adenauer and acceptance of the Bonn Republic. This post-1945 dichotomy was one he shared with thousands upon thousands of former Nazi activists and adherents of the idea of a German *Volksgemeinschaft*.[27] What today seems like an astounding lack of self-reflection is particularly apparent in Kiehn's family photo albums. Among the snapshots of an unspoiled family idyll are unexpected pictures of Kiehn standing next to Straßer, Hitler, or Adenauer. Kiehn's heart's desire had been fulfilled in the 1960s when

Fig. 42: Bruno Heck arranges a meeting between the Kiehns and Chancellor Adenauer. (Martin Häffner et al. *Trossingen. Vom Alemannendorf zur Musikstadt.* Trossingen, 1997)

he met the first chancellor of the Federal Republic of Germany, an event that naturally was captured on celluloid (fig. 42). Kiehn's friend Bruno Heck, federal whip for the CDU from 1952 to 1957, had arranged for the two old men to meet.

It is difficult to comprehend why CDU politicians who had been persecuted under Hitler, such as Heinrich Krone and Karl Gengler, disregarded Kiehn's past and took up with him as friends. Dr. Heinrich Krone, a close confidant of Konrad Adenauer's, had been involved in an association to counter anti-Semitism during the Weimar Republic and had also helped victims of persecution after 1933 through the Aid Committee for Catholic Non-Aryans. Together with Erich Ollenhauer (SPD) and Ernst Lemmer (DDP), he had organized an all-party demonstration of youth clubs against Hitler's attempted coup in 1923 and had been a member of the Reichstag from 1932 to 1933. In this capacity, Krone personally witnessed the campaigns that Kiehn and his faction had used to single-mindedly destroy the country's first parliamentary democracy. In 1933, he lost his Reichstag seat and was fired as deputy general secretary of the Catholic Center Party, which was soon dissolved. The politician, who had trained as a teacher, had to struggle along after that as a sales representative. As Krone had contact with the Jakob Kaiser resistance group, he was arrested after the attempted assassination of Adolf Hitler in 1944 and detained at the Sachsenhausen concentration camp for several weeks.[28]

Karl Gengler, for his part, was well aware of Kiehn's brown-shirted actions because he came from Rottweil, where Kiehn had been president of the IHK. He had also been in Trossingen at the end of the war and must have known of the industrialist's proximity to Himmler. Gengler's statement in Ernst Hohner's denazification proceedings had heavily incriminated Kiehn before the KRUA. Gengler had actually been on the committee when Hohner's case was being tried, and he played a remarkable dual role as both judge and defender of his former protector. Kiehn's role was repeatedly discussed during these proceedings. Furthermore, Kiehn's scandalous past had become public, at the latest when the parliamentary committee was investigating the Chiron affair. Gengler nevertheless testified in a way that clearly favored the defendant in the perjury proceedings against Kiehn, which subsequently discredited the denazification committee.[29]

That Gengler and Heck were the very people who maintained close friendships with Kiehn after 1950 was an expression of the pervasive desire for a clean break with the past that characterized German society in the 1950s. Perhaps they, like so many others, surrendered to Kiehn's charisma and the allure of his luxurious villa. It may simply have been opportune for them, as party politicians, to maintain good relations with a generous business owner. After all, Kiehn also donated to the CDU; the requests the manufacturer put forward, including a suggestion that he join the party, were diplomatically but firmly rejected by the federal whip. The gist of things, according to Heck, was that his support need not go that far. He must have found Kiehn interesting not only for his financial means, but also because of his influence on Efka employees and their families. In small towns like Trossingen, workers and employees were still somewhat influenced by the political preferences of their bosses in political elections into the 1960s. Hence, Hohner's town was a pronounced stronghold of the small liberal FDP, while the Efka employees tended to opt for Adenauer's party instead, the Christian conservative people's party of the CDU.

Kiehn also had good contacts to the FDP through its Bundestag delegates Siegfried Zoglmann and Rolf Dahlgrün, both of whom were joint leaseholders on his alpine hunting grounds in Styria. Dahlgrün had joined the NSDAP in 1933 and served as minister of finance in the federal cabinet from 1961 to 1966. Zoglmann was a former SS lieutenant colonel (Obersturmbannführer) who was promoted to parliamentary whip in 1961 and advanced to become the deputy chair of his party's faction in 1963. He also belonged to the FDP's federal executive board for a time.[30]

Kiehn's entrance into the Tuttlingen Lions Club founded in late 1960 connected the *Mittelstand* entrepreneur to an international network. This step may seem surprising, since Kiehn had regarded "international" as a dirty word: an insult for unreliable people and tied to anti-Semitic prejudices. Once again, however, Kiehn was likely motivated by the contacts and the prestige. Kiehn had no quarrel with the objectives of the organization, which was founded in the

United States in 1917 and had been present in the Federal Republic of Germany from 1952: "Its fundamental principles, Western and international as they were, seemed quite self-evident to him."[31] It escaped his and other members' notice that his behavior from 1933 to 1945 had been in diametric opposition to the service club's ethical guidelines. Their acceptance of the manufacturer, which apparently occurred without resistance or any discussion of Kiehn's past, made a mockery of the organization's values. The Lions Club charges its members to preserve dignity, industry, and personal integrity in their careers: "To seek success and to demand all fair remuneration or profit as my just due, but to accept no profit or success at the price of my own self-respect. ... To remember that in building up my business it is not necessary to tear down another's. ... To hold friendship as an end and not a means. ... To aid others by giving sympathy to those in distress, aid to the weak ... and to preserve world peace."[32]

According to its own literature, the Tuttlingen Lions Club was committed to "healing wounds from the wholly incomprehensible wars between the peoples of France and Germany." The link to a French Lions Club was understood as a "beacon for the desire of general international understanding," a goal that accommodated Kiehn's old weakness for France.[33] Kiehn participated with particular joy in numerous meetings with French Lions Clubs, as his grandson reported: "You had to be amazed at how 'international' he had become. Naturally he was limited by his complete lack of foreign language ability. But often he was even able to ignore this. ... He felt at ease there [with the French Lions Clubs]; he dreamt of Europe and just thought everything was grand."[34] The decisive factor in his joining the club was the acceptance by the elites of his home region, and he was able to participate in the club's "modern" activities such as international understanding.

Analysis of Kiehn's social circle confirms that the former Nazi functionary had become fully integrated into West German society. His connections covered a wide spectrum that ranged from noble-born career diplomats in Bonn ranking at the level of a Herbert von Stackelberg or various federal ministers to the lower-middle-class members of social clubs in Trossingen, as well as his "old comrades" from the NSDAP and SS; from the Lions Club to the German Circle of Friends of the University of Innsbruck; and from hunting companions from all walks of life to sports stars. For example, soccer player Fritz Walter frequently stayed at Deibhalde with his wife, Italia (fig. 43). Walter, who played for the Kaiserslautern soccer club in Rhineland-Pfalz, was one of five players known as the "Heroes of Berne." He had captained the German national team to its triumph at the World Cup in Switzerland in 1954, sending the entire country into paroxysms of joy. In the mid-1950s there was almost no one who came close to the popularity of this soccer hero; having Walter as his guest must have reflected well on Kiehn.[35]

Kiehn also maintained a close relationship with Swabian luminaries such as beloved Tübingen mayor Hans Gmelin (1954–1974) or the widely known

Fig. 43: The Kiehns and the Walters in Deibhalde. (Private collection of the Kiehn family)

manufacturer Wilhelm Kraut, whose Bizerba company had an international reputation as a manufacturer of technologically advanced scales. Both figures were also former NSDAP party comrades and had actively campaigned during the war for the victory of National Socialism. Gmelin had been an adviser at the German embassy in Bratislava (then known as Pressburg) and shared responsibility for crimes against the Jewish population of Slovenia.[36] In the 1960s Kiehn also associated with Dresdner Bank's CEO, Erich Vierhub, whose daughter was engaged to Kiehn's grandson, Herbert E. Kiehn, for many years and was married to him from 1965 to 1966. Kiehn and Vierhub broke off contact after the rapid divorce of their offspring.

Fritz Kiehn also had weaker ties to the once high-ranking Nazi economic functionary and Nazi Reichstag delegate Carl Lüer in Frankfurt. These ties extended to "occasional agreeable contact" with grandson Herbert as well, who was studying in Frankfurt. Although Lüer had held party offices, chamber presidencies, and board positions under the Nazi regime, he too ultimately managed to return to the middle class after internment by the British and the Americans. The "diverse relationships" that one-time Nazi economic leader Lüer appears to have enjoyed afterward, however — at least according to Herbert E. Kiehn — drew on the more conventional institutions for selecting elites, such as student fraternities. The economic basis of Lüer's prosperity was his work as the representative of a Turkish bank in Frankfurt.[37]

Another class of Fritz Kiehn's contacts both in Germany and abroad took the form of business friends. Noteworthy among these were the close relationships that Kiehn, a former SS lieutenant colonel and member of Heinrich Himmler's personal staff, was able to maintain with Jewish emigrants. The Lerners were a Viennese family active in special purpose machine manufacturing. Kiehn had bought machines from the family before 1933, but in 1938 they were forced to flee Germany and reestablish their company in England. Efka returned to working closely with the Lerner family firm after 1950, and an intense personal relationship developed despite all the historical handicaps. This friendship included reciprocal visits. The Lerner family also put up an Efka intern in their home for several months. Kiehn was also close to Arnold Kastner, a Jewish émigré from Mannheim who owned a Canadian cigarette tube factory and rented tube machines from Efka. Kastner had emigrated as a child, and affectionately called Kiehn *Opa* (grandpa), even after the Third Reich.[38]

Despite numerous honors and excellent political and private connections that extended to the federal cabinet, Kiehn was denied his secret wish to be awarded the Order of Merit of the Federal Republic of Germany, unlike some of his other politically incriminated business colleagues. There were various reasons for this. One was that Kiehn had not held any offices with more than local significance after 1945. He had as little chance of acquiring important or even merely decorative political posts as he had of becoming a functionary in any associations or chambers of commerce. As we can see from the letter from the Tübingen regional council (Regierungspräsidium) to the University of Innsbruck from 1962 quoted above, the authorities responsible for granting such honors were abundantly aware of Kiehn's role in the Third Reich and considered this an obstacle to singling him out for distinction. As conspicuous as Kiehn was, no award could be made without triggering a scandal. His somewhat insensitive declaration of his important past, coupled with his uninterrupted loyalties to old friends, did not fit well with the predominant culture of silence. Last, we should not forget that since 1968, Kiehn had been providing accommodation to Baldur von Schirach, one of the top representatives of the Nazi state, which may have pitted Kiehn's local adversaries against him.

Consequently, Kiehn had no choice but to leverage his lavish lifestyle to obtain the symbolic capital that the new republic denied him. As he had already done through his patronage of sports and culture, he laid out considerable sums to cultivate his reputation. The most money went into hunting, and more than just in his various preserves; he had fallen especially hard for East African safaris. "I've bagged all the big game in Africa,"[39] Kiehn bragged in an interview he had set up to cultivate his own image and whose audio recording he bequeathed to his family. Kiehn took other hunting trips to Hungary, Poland, the former Yugoslavia, and Alaska. The hunting trophies that decorated his home reminded Kiehn and his visitors of these excursions. A professional photographer, Siegfried

Fig. 44: **Kiehn, the big-game hunter, in Africa.** (Personal collection of the Kiehn family)

Lauterwasser, the official photographer of Bayreuth, also accompanied Kiehn to produce pictures and films to document the safaris, which likewise served as reminders (fig. 44).[40] Lauterwasser had been friends with Kiehn's son, Herbert, before his untimely death, as well as with Siegfried Wagner's children. In order to comply with his professional obligations to the Kiehns, Lauterwasser also went along on a long hunting trip to Momella. In 1970, Kiehn's "East Africa film" was publicly screened in Schwenningen; he had previously shown it to his clients and employees. Kiehn also had some of his "zoological and ethnological collection" exhibited.[41]

Along with his support of sports and music associations, Kiehn also began donating to the plastic arts in 1960. Like many large-scale industrialists, Fritz Kiehn had always had a special affinity for sculptures, among them busts of "the Führer" and of his daughter.[42] Sculptors make works that are to last forever, giving permanence to transience, a fact that appears to have won many industrialist art fans over to this genre. The expense of the materials used and the space required to present the art are further reasons that sculptures appeal particularly to prosperous industrialists, who can thus declare their taste in art and satisfy their need for conspicuous consumption at the same time. For his seventy-fifth birthday, in 1960, Kiehn's company honored him with an animal sculpture, a cast-metal gerenuk, also known as Waller's gazelle. He became enthralled with the creator of the work, Fritz Behn, a sculptor born in 1878, as well as with his naturalistic animal sculptures, probably largely because of Behn's predilection for African fauna. Behn, who had served the German colonial movement both before and after World War I, was an important animal sculptor and had been appointed as a professor in Munich in 1911. His large body of work, distinguished by its perfect craftsmanship, included the award-winning colonial memorial in Bremen (1932), originally intended for the Reich capital, and portraits of internationally renowned personalities: historical figures such as Louis XIV, imperial chancellor Otto von Bismarck, dictators Benito Mussolini and Adolf Hitler, and federal chancellor Konrad Adenauer. Behn produced busts of famous artists such as poets Rainer Maria Rilke, Gerhard Hauptmann, and Ricarda Huch; doctor Albert Schweitzer; singer Maria Callas; and Pope Pius XII. His political and aesthetic proximity to National Socialism under Gauleiter Baldur von Schirach in 1938 helped him to obtain a professorship at the Academy of Fine Arts in Vienna in 1939, but they also caused him to be removed from his post in 1946 and provoked critical debates in the 1970s.[43]

Robert von Schirach was behind both the gift to Fritz Kiehn and Kiehn's contact with Behn. Once Kiehn and Behn discovered their common passion for hunting and for Africa, the manufacturer resolved to become a patron of art. Kiehn must have appreciated that Behn, who belonged to Kiehn's generation and, like him, had been a soldier in World War I, was, in Kiehn's view, a victim of the regime change of 1945, since he was not able to continue his career as a university lecturer after that year. Kiehn's contact with Behn revived another of his maxims: "Don't do anything halfway." Rather than buying select individual works, Kiehn put the sculptor on retainer and promised to find a home for his oeuvre. As thanks Kiehn received all rights to the estate of Fritz Behn after the artist died in 1970, including various sketches, drawings, and paintings. In 1973, Kiehn established a Behn museum within the cultural center at the spa resort of Bad Dürrheim in collaboration with the local municipal administration after plans to do so in Trossingen had failed.[44]

Kiehn's art patronage left traces that have persisted into the present, since even today Behn sculptures can be seen in both the Deibhalde park and in various public squares in Trossingen. Even though Kiehn had never previously dealt with plastic arts in any particular detail, he laid out substantial sums for the sculptor's work. His personal liking for Behn and his admiration for Behn's naturalistic forms may have also played a role, as well as his determination to distinguish himself as part of the upper middle class in yet another field.

At the opening reception of the museum in Bad Dürrheim in 1973, Kiehn presented himself as a connoisseur and paid tribute to Behn as one of the most important German sculptors of the twentieth century, embittered by "tough blows of fate" after 1945. "In our frequent extensive conversations, we established that we had much in common and had experienced many of the same things. Fritz Behn was a nature lover, and art was his calling! I am a nature lover and an art admirer! Fritz Behn was an expert hunter! I too am a follower of St. Hubertus and St. Petri. ... We also both believed in Germany!" This is why, Kiehn said, he had offered "to share our bread with him" after the artist had become a godparent to Kiehn's great-grandchild. Not until thirty-five years later, in 2007, was the collection of Behn's works that Kiehn had gathered "broken up and auctioned off in Munich with great success."[45] Back when the museum was established, Kiehn had wished not only to distinguish himself as a patron of art but once again to be the center of attention himself. When the Behn museum opened, the town of Bad Dürrheim installed a collection of Kiehn's hunting trophies in the same building, so that a Kiehn museum stood right next to the Behn museum.[46]

Kiehn's compulsion to orchestrate his successful social advancement only — all too often — to lose his sense of proportion also had a deep impact on his private assets, as he sank progressively deeper into debt. The role he had chosen for himself as an art patron, sports donor, party financier, and international big-game hunter was in flagrant contradiction to the culture of the Efka family business. One of Kiehn's basic principles was that the firm's profits not be distributed to stockholders as dividends, but rather plowed back into the company to be available for further investments. The family members were to obtain what they needed to live from their salaries as managing directors. But these salaries could not exceed a certain amount according to the laws of the time without being subjected to extremely high taxes as hidden profit distribution. This created an increasingly large gulf between the costs of Kiehn's extravagant lifestyle and his liquid assets. The liabilities piling up worried the family as well as the banks, so in 1974 Kiehn sold the rest of his shares in the company (2 percent of the total share capital) to Martin Brinkmann. Because these shares granted veto power, Kiehn obtained a high price that allowed him to pay off his debts.[47] After the crisis of 1972, the investors doing the restructuring managed to apply enough pressure to get plural voting rights transferred to an auditor who acted as a trustee. In other words, in 1972 Fritz Kiehn lost the authority to make decisions about his own company and in 1974 he lost the last capital shares in his life's work.

Even at an advanced age, Kiehn could not overcome the contrast — which had shaped his whole life — between his de facto *Mittelstand* existence and his upper-class ambitions. Indeed, his private debt crisis once again revealed the essential amateurism of his all-consuming desire for advancement. As with his political career, the decisions he made on behalf of his company were far more strongly shaped by his social origins than by instrumental rationality. These events were concealed from the public in order to protect the family's reputation and the legend of Kiehn-as-high-achiever that had been so carefully cultivated.

Kiehn's continuing dedication to self-aggrandizement was reflected not only in his extreme need for admiration but also in his disingenuous dealings with the past and present, as well as the lenience the former Nazi functionary encountered at the local level. In 1962, for example, a thick, high-gloss commemorative volume was published in honor of the firm's fiftieth anniversary and Berta Kiehn's seventieth birthday. It was a relatively detailed summary of the history of the company and the family and continued the trend of the Kiehns commissioning homages to themselves that had already started in the 1950s. Not only was the evolution of the business described as a flawless success story, and Efka as a hypermodern factory with a human face, but Fritz Kiehn himself was glorified as a titanic figure, watching over the fortunes of his business empire from a "a sun-filled study" with the "keen gaze of the hunter." In this, he was portrayed as being interested in other things besides profit: "He wants to do more than manufacture. He wants to make a difference and improve something in this world." Concerning the Third Reich, the detailed historical retrospective contained only a terse justification: The "scandalous ... special-interests economy" of the Weimar Republic had induced Kiehn "to become more and more political," although his political activities had always been "selfless" and "for the greater good."[48]

Participating in the public ceremony celebrating the firm's anniversary and Berta's birthday, which was held at the Ernst Hohner Concert House, were the regional political elites who had long since stopped keeping their distance from Kiehn: the mayor, regional council delegates, chamber presidents, and parliamentary delegates. Minister of the Treasury Hans Lenz (FDP) was there as well, making him the first federal government representative to appear alongside the former Nazi functionary in an official capacity. Lenz was from Trossingen and had close family, professional, and political party ties to the Hohners. In his speech, he referred to the high esteem the federal government had for industrialists like Kiehn. Almost all of the other speeches exemplified "communicative shutdown": rather than completely passing over the delicate past of which the attendees were largely aware, they reframed, distorted, abridged, and downplayed it. Bärlin, the former mayor who, after his successful denazification, was now a municipal leader in Freudenstadt, indulged in "cheerful recollections of his time ... in Trossingen (1928 to 1933)." It appears to have slipped the speaker's mind that these were years involving the destruction of the Weimar Republic, escalating hardship, and brutal political conflicts in Trossingen as well, and that Kiehn had been a key player in these. Mayor Maschke's speech on this occasion also exemplified the "communicative shutdown" that carried the day. He invoked 16 July 1908 — in line with Kiehn's own self-portrayal — as the happy day Kiehn had first set foot in Trossingen. Even after "the total collapse of all values" in 1945, he noted, Kiehn "had been allowed to put his nose back to the grindstone at precisely the right time." The townspeople had "repeatedly expressed their staunch confidence" in Kiehn "by electing him to the town council." His status as an honorary citizen, Maschke continued, had for many years been an acknowledgment of "the ... love and loyalty with which Fritz Kiehn has fought for Trossingen for five decades." Maschke did not say a word about this distinction having been revoked for ten years, nor about the dramatic consequences Kiehn's electoral success had wrought. The nadir of German history appeared to be 1945 rather than 1933. Maschke concluded his recollections with the impassioned comment that "for five decades," the Kiehns had "struggled, suffered, and finally also prevailed in Trossingen." Berta Kiehn donated a fountain for Fritz Kiehn Square to the city as thanks. The man of the hour also received an honorary membership in the association of tobacco product retailers. The celebration was followed by a communal one-pot meal for guests and employees, as at the anniversary celebration in 1937.[49]

Kiehn's eightieth birthday in 1965 was also observed with a large celebration, this time at the packed Fritz Kiehn Sports Center. The staff received a collective gift of DM 100,000; Trossingen associations got almost DM 7,000 each, and the city was given a small bandstand. The chair of the works committee declared Kiehn's modern, benefits-focused stewardship of the company to be a model for the entire German economy, even a historic alternative model. "If all employers held such views ... we would have been spared a hundred years of social struggle." The keynote address was given by federal family minister Bruno Heck, a friend of Kiehn's and another high political representative of the Bonn Republic. Following Heck's address, Kiehn once again insisted on reciting his heroic career.[50] His ninetieth birthday was celebrated at the concert house in a similar but more modest fashion in 1975.[51]

The company crises and the radical measures of the early 1970s were concealed from outsiders as much as possible. The same message was repeated in various forms: "Everything is absolutely fine." The local newspaper ran a photo of Kiehn contentedly lighting a cigar alongside its report on the dedication of a new Efka factory on the outskirts of the city. The chief administrator of the Tuttlingen district "congratulated" the manufacturer and his wife, who had seen "'their life's work blossom anew.'"[52] No one had a clue that Kiehn had recently been forced to sell almost all of his shares because of his private debts. The transformation of the German culture of remembrance that began with the large media response to the Eichmann trial in Jerusalem and the Frankfurt Auschwitz proceedings in the late 1950s and was continued by the German student movement and finally the American "Holocaust" television series in the late 1970s did not bring any change to Trossingen's relationship with its brown-shirted honorary citizen.[53]

If the perjury trial and the conflicts with Ernst Hohner (which were not settled until around 1960) kept Kiehn from resting in the 1950s, his grandson, Herbert E. Kiehn, reported that after 1960, he led "a peaceful life unaffected by political or historical hostility. He enjoyed it for what it was and remembered as little [of his Nazi years] as possible." Fritz Kiehn himself had become "a remarkably 'correct' Democrat — who, by the way, was not a real 'witness' to '1968' and its consequences at all." For the sake of effect, the Kiehns had an encounter with the hippie scene during a visit to Brussels that was arranged by a business friend of his as a kind of tourist attraction. It shocked them to their core: they probably could not have imagined a clearer rejection of their lifelong motto, "Stand tall or crumble." "But in Trossingen the world had stayed largely intact. ... Nothing disturbed ... the peace. ... Looking back, to me the whole thing looks like a peculiar 'grace period.' ... The Conditio Germaniae had fundamentally altered for him, and in the last decades of his life it was good to him," Kiehn's grandson wrote in 1999.[54]

When the Efka founder died on 1 September 1980, a few weeks prior to his ninety-fifth birthday, the local newspaper had this to say: "With Fritz Kiehn, the Hohner town has lost a distinguished business figure and a committed citizen who rendered outstanding service to this town in a way that few others have." His offices in the Third Reich and his aid to former Nazi Party friends were openly addressed but qualified with a reference to the "voice of the people": "Kiehn's role in this fascist era, however, is respectfully observed by Trossingen residents today; the word today is that back then ... there were some he rescued from the concentration camp."[55] By the end of the long, reframing discourse, the "old fighter" and beneficiary of the Nazi regime had been made into a savior of the persecuted, if not a resistance fighter.

This interpretation went uncontested for almost two years, until Efka's seventieth anniversary in 1982 occasioned a new historical retrospective. This time, the local newspaper published a signed article, next to its customary congratulatory text, entitled "Fritz Kiehn's Past: A Trossingen Taboo." It listed Kiehn's important functions during the Nazi regime and also his scandals in the postwar era. The writing was dead-on: "Every Trossingen resident knows it; no one talks about it."[56] Afterward, the paper received two letters to the editor from approving readers from outside the region. The silence then continued until the firm's seventy-fifth anniversary in 1987, when the announcement in the paper again included a reference to the "shadows of the past,"[57] albeit a very brief one.

Even the history of the town that was published as part of the 1997 celebrations of the seventieth anniversary of Trossingen's town charter qualified Kiehn's role by praising his "humane behavior in contrast to other important Nazi figures." This popular stereotype is used all over Germany, even today, in an attempt to exonerate one's own environment and its people of the painful memories of their former enthusiasm and collective responsibility for a criminal system.[58] Of the total of 544 pages of Trossingen's history, three deal with the subject of "The Victims and Beneficiaries of the Third Reich in Trossingen." Kiehn's name is not mentioned. The offices he held are listed elsewhere in the book, but there is no critical overall evaluation of this "honorary citizen" of the town.[59] Through the end of the twentieth century, there was no open discussion in Trossingen of the correct way to remember National Socialism and how to deal with the problematic legacy of the "honorary citizen" title, as well as the naming of streets and public buildings after a functionary and collaborator in the Nazi state who was a popular figure among the townspeople.

Notes

1. Unless otherwise noted, this chapter is based on the authors' interview with Herbert E. Kiehn of 19–20 May 1998, and on memoranda and letters he sent to the authors of 24 May, 15 June, 30 Aug., and 15 and 29 Sept. 1998.
2. TZ, 15 Oct. 1960.
3. Letter from Herbert E. Kiehn to the authors of 28 Sept. 1998.
4. See Oberkofler and Goller, "Universitätsideologie."
5. Universitätsarchiv Innsbruck, Akte Fritz Kiehn, letter to the rector of 9 Apr. 1962.
6. Ibid., letter from the deputy district president to the rector of 30 May 1962.
7. Ibid., letters from Gmelin and Maschke to the rector of 11 and 17 Apr. 1962; StAS, Dep. 40, no. 21 (Balingen camp list of internees).
8. Ibid., letter from managing director, quoted in letter from Tübingen deputy district president to the rector of 30 May 1962.
9. Ibid., letter from Müller to the rector of 12 Apr. 1962.
10. Ibid., letter from rector to the senator of the arts faculty of 22 Sept. 1965. Actually, another senator donated many times over the amount of 532,000 schillings. See reply to the rector of 23 Sept. 1965.
11. Ibid., letter from senator of the arts faculty to the rector of 24 Sept. 1965.
12. Ibid., letter from Kiehn to the rector of 27 Dec. 1965.
13. See Hachmeister, *Schleyer*. On the protectorate see 165–224.
14. Universitätsarchiv Innsbruck, Akte Fritz Kiehn, letter from the rector of 22 June 1972.
15. Gengler's declaration of 1 Mar. 1954, private documentation of perjury trial.
16. Aretz, "Bruno Heck," 213–232.
17. See Rauh-Kühne, "Sozialpartnerschaft."
18. Interview with Herbert E. Kiehn of 19–20 May 1998.
19. Herbert E. Kiehn, in letter of 27 Aug. 1998; interview with Herbert E. Kiehn of 15–16 June 1999.
20. Letter from Herbert E. Kiehn of 22 Feb. 1999. In the 1950s Kiehn again became interested in the paper factory in Eislingen, which was then absorbed into the Waldhof cellulose factory.
21. Interview with Herbert E. Kiehn of 19–20 May 1998.
22. Lübbe, "Nationalsozialismus."
23. Herbert, *Best*, 506.
24. All quotes are from Kiehn, *Unsere Deibhalde*, 19.
25. Quoted in Scholtyseck, "Berger," 105.
26. Meinecke, *Catastrophe*.
27. See Thießen, "Erinnerungen."
28. See Kleinmann, *Heinrich Krone*.
29. On the continued discrediting of denazification authorities, see Rauh-Kühne, "Unternehmer."
30. See Klee, *Personenlexikon*, 698. Kiehn had no direct line to the traditionally strongly left-liberal FDP of Baden-Württemberg.
31. Letter from Herbert E. Kiehn to the authors of 25 May 1999.
32. On the history of the Lions Club in Germany, which began in 1951 with a club in Düsseldorf, see Thomas, *Löwe*. Purpose and ethics quotes translated from various German-language brochures of the Lions Club.
33. *Schwarzwälder Bote*, 27 Feb. 1986.
34. Letter from Herbert E. Kiehn to the authors of 25 May 1999.
35. See Brüggemeier, *Platz*; Raithel, *Fußballweltmeisterschaft*; Michel, *Fritz Walter*. Walter wrote some of his memoirs of the 1954 World Cup at the Kiehn home. These were published by

Co-Press/Hoffmann-Hess-Verlag, which belonged to Heinrich Hoffmann, the uncle of Robert von Schirach and the son of Hitler's former personal photographer.
36. Tönsmeyer, *Reich*; Senfft, *Schweigen*; Sting, "Fuchs."
37. Rebentisch, *Zeiten*, 205; letter of Herbert E. Kiehn of 28 Sept. 1998.
38. Interview with Herbert E. Kiehn of 15–16 June 1999.
39. Interview recording of 11 Dec. 1959, family's collection.
40. Interview with Herbert E. Kiehn of 19–20 May 1998.
41. TZ, 5 Feb. 1970.
42. August Thyssen revered the French sculptor Auguste Rodin, seven of whose marble statues he installed in the conservatory of his Landsberg castle. Paul Reusch also outfitted the garden of his Katharinenhof palace with sculptures. See Rasch and Feldman, *August Thyssen*, 105–106; Rauh-Kühne, "'Wirkungskreis,'" 244. The sculptor Arno Breker was appropriated by National Socialism and remained in demand as an artist even after 1945, portraying industrialists Gustav Schickedanz, Hermann Josef Abbs, Günter and Herbert Quandt, and August Oetker.
43. Munzinger-Archiv, Lieferung 17/70 - K - 3455 a, entry on Fritz Behn; http://de.wikipedia.org/wiki/Fritz_Behn#cite_ref-0 (accessed 10 Aug. 2012); Zeller, "Kolonialkunst," http://muc.postkolonial.net/files/2011/07/BehnMUC2010-1.pdf (accessed 15 Aug. 2012); Zeller, "Tierplastiker."
44. Interview with Herbert E. Kiehn of 19–20 May 1998.
45. http://de.wikipedia.org/wiki/Fritz_Behn#cite_ref-0 (accessed 10 Aug. 2012); see also "Herbst-Bilanz bei Neumeister," *FAZ-Feuilleton*, 12 Jan. 2008.
46. Kiehn family archives, manuscript of Kiehn's opening address on 30 Oct. 1973. See also Kiehn family archives, Kiehn's file memo of 26 Aug. 1970; Kiehn family archives, "Meine Gedanken" [My thoughts] on the establishment of the museum of 25 Apr. 1972; letter from Herbert E. Kiehn to the authors of 28 Sept. 1998.
47. To avoid potentially calamitous inheritance taxes, in 1963 Kiehn gifted the majority of his shares to his daughter and adopted son (his grandson, Herbert E. Kiehn), while retaining beneficial use of these for himself and his wife for the rest of his life; this left him with only 2 percent of shares. At the same time, he ensured he would have control over his company through plural voting rights. In 1972 he transferred 1 percent of his shares to an auditor, who then became a special partner with veto power. Kiehn kept only 1 percent of shares. In 1974, both his remaining shares and those of the special partner were sold to Brinkmann. Letter from Herbert E. Kiehn to the authors of 30 Aug. 1998; interview with Herbert E. Kiehn of 15–16 June 1999.
48. Anon., *Mit dem Herzen dabei*, 90, 92–93. See ibid., 32.
49. StAT, A 938, various newspaper articles from July 1962.
50. Hamburger Weltwirtschaftsarchiv, Pressesammlung, newspaper article of unknown origin from 18 Oct. 1965.
51. See TZ, 16 Oct. 1975.
52. TZ, 1 Dec. 1973.
53. Classen, *Bilder*; Horn, *Erinnerungsbilder*; Krause, *Eichmann-Prozess*; Vollnhals and Osterloh, *NS-Prozesse*.
54. Letter from Herbert E. Kiehn to the authors of 25 May 1999.
55. TZ, 3 Sept. 1980.
56. TZ, 15 July 1982.
57. TZ, 12 Sept. 1987. See also TZ, 21 July 1982. In 1988, Trossingen awarded Gretl Wieshofer-Kiehn its Ring of Merit; she had been an FWV delegate to the town council from 1965 to 1974.

58. Such conduct was accurately characterized as an "escape from memory" and "defense against a painful confrontation with one's 'own' share of Hitlerism." Werner, *Adolf-Hitler-Platz,* 35, 181. On the construction of family remembrances, see Welzer, Moller, and Tschuggnall, *"Opa."*
59. Häffner, Ruff, and Schrumpf, *Trossingen,* 222–224.

Chapter 15

COMING TO TERMS WITH THE PAST IN THE TWENTY-FIRST CENTURY

The publication of the German edition of this book in spring 2000 touched off vigorous debates. National newspapers took advantage of the new release to report on "Fritz Kiehn and Trossingen's failure to grapple with its Nazi past." We gave newspaper, radio, and television interviews. The book was launched in a packed room at the city hall in Stuttgart, the state capital. Well-known Bielefeld historian Hans-Ulrich Wehler acknowledged the results of the study and attested that Kiehn had possessed an "absolutely breathtaking ruthlessness" in his Aryanization of Jewish property. Wehler concluded his lecture with a bold and simple challenge: to get rid of anything memorializing Kiehn in any way.[1] The thirty Trossingen residents who had traveled to the event took note of his exhortation, as did readers of the Trossingen local press.

These events exerted increasing pressure on Trossingen to issue a response. Four weeks after the Stuttgart event, the small town had its own public discussion, at which we presented the results of our research and answered questions. The mayor and members of the town council also participated in the event, which was held at another fully packed venue, the Trossingen concert hall. Even if individual attempts were made to hamper the event, including posters advertising it being removed from school corridors, the past had become a widely discussed subject by this point, with the most spirited debate pertaining to the issue of honorary citizenship. The response by the nearly two hundred attendees was deeply divided and sometimes fraught with emotion. In this town hall meeting, the silence was broken, and sensitivities were made explicit. It was as if the town had abandoned its reticence.

Awkward consternation and demands for a clear dissociation from Kiehn were aired alongside statements that made reference to Kiehn's service to the region.

Notes from this chapter begin on page 321.

Older residents denied that the younger generation had any capacity to judge the brown-shirted past: some older residents called us hacks and questioned our understanding of that era, particularly as we had not even been born then. "What do they even know about hard times. ... How can they be so full of hate?"[2] Others professed unease at having to cross through Kiehn Square on a daily basis, or having to explain to foreign visitors — possibly Israelis — who the town was honoring with the name. One woman put down the book as one-sided "malice" with "degrading content." Others called it a "stroke of luck" for the town, recalling that "innocent people were denounced by Fritz Kiehn" and had wound up in concentration camps. After 1945, they said, "reality had been warped, with good reason" in order "to move forward again." Kiehn had not been a "humane person" by any means.[3]

Mayor Lothar Wölfle declared that not everyone was "born to be a hero" or could muster the strength to resist, as if Kiehn had merely been some fellow traveler. The mayor argued that because the town council had never passed a formal resolution to restore Kiehn's "honorary citizen" title, the current town parliament did not have to act, even though Kiehn had been described as an honorary citizen in municipal documents. With the exception of the Greens, all the parties sitting on the town council objected to renaming the square and the sports center. In July 2000, however, at the SPD's urging, the town council did, after all, take up the question of Kiehn's honorary citizen status and confirmed that it had been revoked in 1945 and had never been reissued or restored. This was not exactly false, but it ignored the many years of de facto treatment of Kiehn as an honorary citizen, and thus left this practice unmentioned. Since then, municipal publications have refrained from referring to Fritz Kiehn as an honorary citizen of Trossingen. One consequence of this maneuvering was that graffiti appeared on the Fritz Kiehn Sports Center that September, featuring slogans such as "Down with Fritz Kiehn."[4]

The debate went on behind closed doors, in families, associations, and political circles, and occasioned a number of letters to the editor. The Free Voters' Association (FWV) did not consider our book proper historiography. To them, Kiehn was just "one of millions"; there was no need for us to "make such a big deal out of it." Germans on the whole, they argued, should not make themselves susceptible to "blackmail" by reevaluating the past in this way.[5]

The storm triggered by the publication of our biography of Kiehn had scarcely abated when *Stern,* an important magazine with a high national circulation, spread more embarrassing details in November 2000 about Trossingen and Efka: the firm had not contributed to Remembrance, Responsibility and Future, the German foundation sponsored by industry whose purpose was to support Eastern European survivors of forced labor during the period of National Socialism. Started in 1999, it had been operating since 2000. Efka had no plans to join the foundation in the future. Many of the survivors suffered from long-term medical woes caused by their treatment in Germany and lived poverty-stricken, often miserable, existences in their native countries. The German Industry Foundation Initiative and the German federal government were each expected to raise half of the total of €5.2 billion needed. The foundation had been established after victims of forced labor under the Nazis had filed class action lawsuits in the United States against German corporations. The goal of the foundation, which had come into being with the active participation of the German government, was not least to avert such suits, a strong symbolic gesture to provide practical aid to victims and to spare companies doing business internationally legal battles in the future. But there was criticism of this type of de facto, government-financed foundation, especially from the industrial *Mittelstand*. Many of these companies were not directly exposed to the risk of a class action suit. They doubted in any case that they were within the jurisdiction of the American legal system, and remained unconvinced that international law allowed legal claims for individual compensation to be made against injustice caused by the war. In addition, they recalled that more than sixty years had passed since the war had ended, and the Federal Republic of Germany had already paid out billions in taxpayer money as compensation for Nazi injustices.[6] There had been fierce public debates in the run-up to the foundation's establishment in August 2000. The politics of the Clinton administration dealt more directly with the historical repercussions of the Holocaust than any previous US administration, lending weight to plaintiffs' claims. Bill Clinton declared that "progress" had been made "towards setting history straight" and mentioned "an especially sacred obligation to elderly survivors." He mobilized political and diplomatic resources toward "providing compensation for lost or stolen assets and forced or slave labor" in conjunction with the Holocaust.[7] The class action suits were a "political instrument" in that they provided an occasion to make the public aware of the fates of elderly victims of the Nazis who had "the right of history and the power of emotion on their side."[8] The repercussions that the lawsuits had in the international media contributed to globalizing the remembrance of forced labor and the Holocaust during the 1990s. Clinton's new approach to dealing with the Nazi past and its repercussions in the media also altered the culture of remembrance in Germany, in which forced labor had previously played almost no role. It now became an omnipresent topic in the German-language media and added moral pressure to the calls for a fund financed by German industry.[9]

By November 2000, some 4,600 corporations had joined the foundation. Many of these companies had not even existed prior to 1945 or had not employed forced laborers. Their voluntary contributions to the organization, half of which were tax deductible, constituted a symbolic gesture of recognition for the more than twelve million surviving forced laborers and a practical measure to give them access to medical care and dignity in their old age. By 2007, 1.7 million survivors had been given payouts from the fund.[10]

Despite appeals from the German president and the chancellor, from trade associations, and trade unions, many companies were reluctant to join, especially those from the *Mittelstand*. As a result, by the fall of 2000, German industry had raised only a little more than half of the targeted amount. A journalist from the German magazine *Stern* drummed this up into a scandal with reference to Efka, the very company whose brown-shirted past our book had made public across Germany. Efka had employed more than a hundred workers from Eastern Europe during the war, yet its managing director, Heinrich W. Ruppert, saw no reason to take part in the foundation. He did let it be known, however, that "the subject of forced labor is so unimportant to us; we have so many other things to do. ... You know, my people are only upset when Efka's good name is besmirched."[11] In the *Schwarzwälder Boten* newspaper, he stated that "nothing" was known "about the existence of such people."[12] He upped the ante in November, repudiating any "moral responsibility" for compensation issues: "Those who worked at Efka should seek their own compensation personally. We're not paying anything into the foundation's fund." In order to prevent Efka from being implicated, he did not wish to get "involved ... in an ideological discussion."[13]

Herbert E. Kiehn also issued a statement to *Stern* on behalf of the family: "We have deliberately stayed out of the discussion. I don't think much of the idea."[14] Kiehn's grandson referred to his high tax burden. He added that the Kiehn family was no longer responsible, given that Efka had just been transferred to the ownership of British Imperial Tobacco. The sale negotiations, concluded in October 2000, had actually been taking place in the early fall of 2000 — at the same time the debates about the past were going on. The fate of Efka was a lively topic of conversation in Trossingen, a town that had been weakened by the decline of its formerly strong industrial base, and it pushed the debate over Fritz Kiehn into the background. Mayor Wölfle was visibly overjoyed that the more than two hundred jobs at Efka would be safe, but he dodged the compensation issue. There was hardly any public criticism in Trossingen of the company's hostile stance toward the foundation's fund. Although documentation is lacking, there is much evidence that the British corporate leadership demanded that Efka contribute to the fund before the final closure of the sale. At any rate, Efka issued the surprising statement in December 2000 that the Kiehn family would be paying into the fund and that the company would be adding to this contribution. A chastened Ruppert, along with the Kiehn family, now made it "expressly clear that they had always been aware of their ... responsibility."[15]

The *Stern* article, which had used Efka to skewer the aversion to the Remembrance, Responsibility and Future foundation among many *Mittelstand* businesses and, referring to our book, linked this attitude to the unresolved local Nazi history, became the biggest scandal in Trossingen that autumn. The article ran a photo of Kiehn proudly standing next to Adolf Hitler and practically made him a representative of the entire town, about which readers learned only the most contemptuous details. "Here is where the dog is buried," the journalist reported about her journey through Trossingen, which she perceived as nothing more than "a splotch in the rearview mirror." Stick a finger in the earth of the cemetery, she said, and it would "turn brown."[16] This disparaging snap judgment aggrieved many townspeople, engendered angry outbursts of local patriotism, and completely supplanted the debate on whether the foundation made sense. Those who had always rejected any argument from outsiders were reassured. Townspeople realized to their horror that *Stern* was on display on magazine racks in New York, Paris, and Johannesburg.

Attacks on town archivist Martin Häffner followed; he was accused of being the "driving force" behind our book and of assisting the *Stern* journalist. He had indeed supported our research and assisted the journalist, both exercises of his official duties. He had also pointed the journalist toward other pieces of internal information she then mentioned in the article, specifically that the town council had blocked general access to the archival holdings on the Third Reich back in the 1980s. The council summoned Häffner and questioned his loyalty to the town. But the mayor and the majority of the council stood behind him in this tense situation. Once again, hardly a word was said about Efka's position on the foundation. A CDU council member criticized the demand that Efka join the foundation; a Green member spoke out in favor of it. The council finally decided to lodge a complaint with the German Press Office about the "indescribably shoddy effort" in *Stern*.[17]

Nevertheless, the municipal administration behaved admirably in documenting the debates of the year 2000 in detail in its yearbook published in 2001 and in providing an opportunity for this book's authors, various contemporary witnesses, and townspeople to air their respective views. This generated an open forum for debate where various opinions and conceptions of history could be contrasted with one another.

On the other hand, few saw any cause to reflect on the injustice to forced laborers, let alone contribute to their symbolic compensation. In this the culture of remembrance in the small town was only seemingly different from the media portrayal of a mainstream that was so highly attentive to former forced laborers. Whenever findings about Nazi injustice concern people's daily experience, historical reality turns out to be far more complex. This makes it incompatible with the often trivial black-and-white depictions of demonized perpetrators and their victims, as are all too common in film and television.[18] Even after Efka had given up its obstructive approach to the foundation fund, there were no local initiatives in Trossingen to commemorate the fate of the town's forced laborers, for example, with a museum exhibit or by inviting survivors to come back and visit. "After more than fifty years," one should "let sleeping dogs lie," a former neighbor of Kiehn's declared in a written statement that recalled Kiehn with gratitude.[19]

Most Trossingen residents walled themselves off or played down the issue, or simply felt they had been mistreated. To outside observers, the efforts by townspeople to face up to their history made an interesting subject. For example, a television journalist named Sebastian Drost began to document, with considerable effort and expense, how the town was dealing with its past. He ultimately had to abandon this project because the wall of silence remained insurmountable. His requests for interviews were declined, or initial acceptances were retracted when the interviewees found themselves threatened or after they had consulted with friends. One person told him he would only speak on camera if he intended to move out of town the next day: "You understand that I would like to live out the rest of my years here in Trossingen in peace."[20]

Our source, Herbert E. Kiehn, had invited us to talk about the book in Cologne with his family and friends. But after some family members were obviously anything but pleased with our work, this meeting never came to pass. Kiehn's grandson, who had supported the development of the book through interviews and had given us access to private documents, now partially distanced himself from our book, which he had discussed with us in the proof stage, some of it critically, but largely approvingly. Whereas before we had found him an intellectually stimulating man who was sincerely interested in the truth, he now voiced an ambiguous judgment. Calling the book "persuasive" and "a solid scientific work" based on its factual contents, Kiehn also publicly criticized it as too "polemical" and "emotional." "The honest purpose of the book cannot be fulfilled when it has harmed many fellow citizens and awakened the Jacobin in others, when public appearances have turned into tribunals where victims' wounds have been reopened." We had no opportunity to respond to this criticism; we lost contact with Herbert E. Kiehn in 2001. Fritz Kiehn's grandson and adoptive son passed away in 2007.

Over the course of 2001, things calmed down in Trossingen and remained that way for a long time. Our biography received positive reviews from the academic community, and the lack of comparable studies about other *Mittelstand* entrepreneurs and their local surroundings was repeatedly lamented.[21] The Haus der Geschichte in Stuttgart, the historical museum for the state of Baden-Württemberg, opened a permanent exhibition in 2002 that presents the political upheaval of 1945 from a biographical perspective. Here visitors encounter Fritz Kiehn as a model representative of the erstwhile regional Nazi elite, who passed through internment camps and denazification and embarked on a new life in democratic southwest Germany with these formative experiences. Depicted next to him, as examples of opposing groups, are a concentration camp survivor and a destitute woman refugee who was lucky to have escaped with her life. The stories of perpetrators and victims are juxtaposed, to the occasional irritation of museumgoers.[22] Most Trossingen residents are apparently unaware that the official exhibition of the history of their state, located in the prestigious Stuttgart museum, is dedicated to this aspect of their local history.

Local debates were reignited in 2008, when a new generation appeared on the scene. Members of the local Jusos group in Trossingen, the SPD's youth organization, had been too young to intervene in the debates of the year 2000. Now they took advantage of the seventieth anniversary of the Night of Broken Glass in 1938 to send an open letter to the mayor calling for Fritz Kiehn Square and Fritz Kiehn Sports Center to be renamed. An emotional debate followed that lasted several weeks, although this time it remained limited to the local and regional level. Again the traditionalists prevailed, with the SPD faction failing to champion the youth organization's proposal in any way. The *Gränzbote* newspaper, published in neighboring Tuttlingen, summarized the discussion two days before 9 November 2008 as follows: "That Fritz Kiehn assumed a different face after the war and became very committed to the people and the town … is reason enough for many townspeople and council members not to take his name off the square and the hall." As the CDU faction chair put it, Kiehn had "lived two lives: one in the era of National Socialism and one afterward." After the war, Kiehn had been "an exemplary businessman and had been sorry for his conduct during the Nazi era." The Free Voters (FWV) argued that changing the name after so many years "would also smack of suppression." What's more, the young people were admonished that there was a limit to how much they were entitled "to point fingers at those who actually lived through the Nazi era." After the earlier debates, the SPD did not want "to start any further attempt now." New mayor Dr. Clemens Maier likewise saw "no reason" for a change of name: "The state of affairs has not changed since 2000."[23]

Seventeen months later, however, an unexpected reversal occurred when on 19 April 2010, the town council decided (with six dissenting votes) to change the name of Fritz Kiehn Square to Theresien Square. A regional newspaper referred to it as a "hushed-up dumping"[24] because the resolution had been taken in a meeting that was closed to the public and the measure had not been presented as a measure to disassociate the town from Kiehn. Mayor Maier, eager to avoid the conflict flaring up again, justified the step in terms of the new name: "In honor of the 75th anniversary of the Theresien Church, we wish in this way to acknowledge the Catholic parishioners of Trossingen."[25] It is precisely because of this avoidance of conflict that — as this updated book goes to print — the local sports hall continues to bear Kiehn's name, as does a street in the neighboring town of Deißlingen. Many Trossingen residents hope that the renaming of the square has brought the debate over Kiehn's difficult legacy to a close. Fifteen years after the controversy over the German edition of our book, it seems that the discourse around the memory of the local Nazi past in Trossingen has been exhausted.

Also indicative of this is the unspectacular passage of Efka's one hundredth anniversary in 2012. No debates took place. Much was said about Kiehn's performance as an employer, less about his involvement in the crimes of the Nazi regime. The brown-shirted past of the company's founder was addressed only occasionally; it was obviously difficult to find the right words to classify his "first life." The mayor praised Kiehn, emphasizing "that the entrepreneur had also managed to provide economic advantages to Trossingen through his party membership during the Third Reich."[26] Newspaper articles hewed uncritically to Kiehn's self-portrayal in the audio recording made in 1960, referencing his support for local churches and his ostensibly unselfish dealings with the Magirus shares. According to the local media, the regional Nazi Party leaders' anger over Magirus and Gauleiter Murr's hostility toward Kiehn had been the only factors inducing him to "rise higher in the hierarchy, in order to make himself unassailable." His pursuit of profit became charity, his career in the party self-protection. Local media reported with pride that Kiehn had been "a highly influential figure throughout Württemberg" and had often shown foresight. His calculated investments in the SS Main Riding School — a pet project of Hitler and Himmler's — became altruistic "donations." All the same, the local paper made it clear that the "local hero" was a "fervent Nazi" and profited from Aryanizations.[27]

Meanwhile, Efka has become a "center of excellence" within a multinational corporation, Imperial Tobacco. Imperial also took over the second-largest supplier in the German tobacco market, Reemtsma, in 2002, which itself had benefited tremendously between 1933 and 1945 from its ties to the party and Aryanizations. Efka management appears to be nurturing the hope that interest in the company founder's Nazi past has blown over. In peculiar contradiction to the guiding principles on the company's web page, which call for "open communication,"[28] National Socialism is unceremoniously skipped over in the synopsis of Efka's history published on the same site: "Production of the first cigarette tubes began in 1924. After the Second World War, the factory was rebuilt and substantially expanded."[29] The web summary describes an unbroken line of tradition characterized by economic success and social responsibility. "For a hundred years, EFKA has been firmly anchored in the tradition of a business community with clearly defined values and social responsibility in Trossingen and the surrounding region."[30] Despite Reemtsma's history during the Nazi regime, which has since been well researched, Imperial Tobacco does not mention the cigarette manufacturer's active Aryanizations and uses the headline "ein rauer Wind" (A Harsh Wind) to transform it into a politically besieged company: The "pragmatic" Reemtsma brothers understood how to find "a way out" and to rescue the company by making "concessions to the new rulers."[31] A new brochure on the remodeled web site, entitled "Reemtsma 100 Years," mainly depicts happy employees worried about European Union restrictions on the marketing of cigarettes for reasons of health policy and briefly reminds the reader that in 1940–1945 the company also suffered from "restrictions of the sales, advertising and production of cigarettes."[32]

The difficulties in dealing with local history are by no means unique to Trossingen. Indeed, the town's problems with the politics of history make it very typical in many respects, as a few highlights from other communities show. In Celle, a town in northern Germany, the recommendations from a street-naming commission first convened in 2010 led to tumultuous controversies and various name changes, including a street originally named after Helmuth Hörstmann, the town's mayor from 1973 to 1986. Hörstmann had joined the NSDAP and the SS in 1933 and had later reached the rank of first lieutenant (Obersturmführer). Münster rededicated a street in 2012 that had been named after eugenicist Karl Wilhelm Jötten, who before 1945 had advocated forcibly sterilizing children who attended remedial schools.[33] In Tübingen, a Green stronghold and university town, there were fierce debates in 2012 over the posthumous revocation of the honorary citizen title from a politically incriminated local bigwig. Hans Gmelin, the town's beloved mayor from 1954 to 1976, had joined the SA in 1933 and had led a Freikorps battalion in 1938 that provoked border incidents in the run-up to Germany's annexation of the Sudetenland. Gmelin was involved in the deportation of some fifty-nine thousand Slovakian Jews in 1942, most of whom were murdered in extermination camps. He was made an honorary citizen of Tübingen's French partner city, Aix-en-Provence, in 1966, and in 1975 he was awarded the title of honorary citizen of Tübingen.[34] A parallel discussion was taking place in Konstanz at the time of this book's publication: Bruno Helmle, who was mayor from 1959 until 1980, may be stripped of the honorary citizen title awarded to him in 1980 because of his collaboration as a financial adviser in the Aryanization of Jewish household effects and the subsequent falsification of his resume.[35]

The list of similar cases could almost be endless. Not until after the turn of the twenty-first century did countless cities identify both victims of persecution and Nazi perpetrators within their own ranks. To their surprise and unease, they realized that more than a few of them had led lives after 1945 as highly regarded and honored citizens.[36] One prerequisite for these delayed revelations was the opening of the archives in Eastern Europe after the fall of the Berlin Wall in 1989; another was the digitization of archival holdings and the improved research opportunities of the Internet.

Two problems are reflected in these examples. First, it is difficult to grasp National Socialism as part of one's own local history. It is simpler to see it as a kind of foreign rule imposed on the town from outside. There is something deeply unsettling about acknowledging the proximity of the Third Reich to one's own day-to-day life, when one's own family, neighbors, and colleagues were involved. It is equally unsettling to realize that one lived in harmony alongside perpetrators. Historical investigation has made it clear that the overwhelming majority of Germans have "negative associations" with National Socialism and share its consequences as a "legacy of guilt." The willingness to engage with and actively remember the crimes and injustice of the Nazi era, however, is usually dampened when local or family identities are at stake.[37] Many people obviously find it difficult to stomach the idea that their personal milieu — their place of employment, their home, to which their identity is connected — bears a relationship to the history whose moral inscrutability they believed they understood, primarily from television and film. This is no different in Trossingen than anywhere else.[38]

Furthermore, many former National Socialists were largely integrated into the democratic Federal Republic of Germany after 1945 and rendered service to the public interest. It is difficult to weigh these actions against past guilt, and many would also consider it inappropriate. Should we judge the whole of a biography, or can we divide it into separate parts along the interfaces between changes in the political system? What does the likable neighbor and family man have to do with his former self, the man involved in the apocalyptic crimes against humanity of National Socialism? Truly, it is no simple task to find answers to these questions and draw conclusions, going forward, on how to deal with this fractured history.

Notes

1. Quoted in TZ, 2 July 2000.
2. This is a paraphrase of the feelings expressed at the time; they were not put down in writing and published until 2001 in *Trossinger Jahrbuch 2000*, 108.
3. All quotes from TZ, 28 June 2000.
4. A chronology of the year's events, as well as various position statements, can be found in *Trossinger Jahrbuch 2000*, 87–116.
5. TZ, 29 June 2000.
6. On the Federal Republic of Germany's efforts to redress Nazi injustice, see Brodesser et. al., *Wiedergutmachung*; Goschler, *Schuld*; Spoerer, "Zwangsarbeit"; Hockerts, Moisel, and Winstel, *Grenzen*.
7. Bill Clinton, "Remarks at the Partners in History Dinner in New York City," 11 September 2000, http://www.gpo.gov/fdsys/pkg/PPP-2000-book2/html/PPP-2000-book2-doc-pg1793.htm (accessed 24 January 2014). See Surmann, *Shoah-Erinnerung*; for a global perspective, see Berg and Schäfer, *Justice*.
8. Spiliotis, *Verantwortung*, 32, 47.
9. Ibid., 47. On the change in the culture of remembrance in Europe, see also Maissen, *Erinnerung*, 57–106.
10. See Jansen and Saathoff, *Responsibility*.
11. Quoted in *Stern* 46 (2000).
12. Quoted in press release of 17 Dec. 2000 from DRUCK+PAPIER trade union, http://fm1.apm.ag/verdi_fachbereiche_wcms/dup/fmpro?-db=verdi_fb_dup.fp5&-lay=eingabe&-format=text.html&-error=fehler.html&-recid=33200&-find (accessed 12 May 2013).
13. Paraphrased from TZ, 10 Nov. 2000.
14. Quoted in *Stern* 46 (2000).
15. Letter from Efka management to TZ of 7 Dec. 2000.

16. Quoted in *Stern* 46 (2000).
17. See TZ, 6 Dec. 2000; *Trossinger Nachrichten*, 6 Dec. 2000.
18. See Zimmermann, "Holocaust-Erinnerung"; Levy and Sznaider, *Holocaust*.
19. Quoted in *Trossinger Jahrbuch 2000*, 98–99.
20. Quoted in ibid.
21. See Jacobs, *Rauch*; Lindner, *Reemtsmas*; Köster, *Hugo Boss*.
22. Information from curator Dr. Paula Lutum-Lenger, 30 June 2012.
23. *Gränzbote*, 7 Nov. 2008.
24. *Neckarquelle*, quoted in *Trossinger Jahrbuch 2010*, 13.
25. *Trossinger Nachrichten*, 27 Apr. 2010.
26. TZ, 22 July 2012.
27. TZ, 5 and 7 Aug. 2012.
28. Reemtsma Company Homepage, http://www.reemtsma.com/images/stories/unternehmen/Unternehmensleitlinien_2012-01.pdf (accessed 6 Aug. 2012).
29. Reemtsma Company Homepage, http://www.reemtsma.com/index.php/unternehmen/standorte/trossingen.html (accessed 6 Aug. 2012).
30. Reemtsma Company Homepage, http://www.reemtsma.com/index.php?option=com_content&view=article&id=492:efka-werk-in-trossingen-feiert-100-jaehriges-firmenjubilaeum&catid=83:pressemitteilungen&Itemid=289 (accessed 27 Dec. 2013).
31. Reemtsma Company Homepage, http://www.reemtsma.com/index.php/presse/presseinformationen/meilensteine.html (accessed 15 Aug. 2012). On Reemtsma, see also Jacobs, *Rauch*.
32. Reemtsma Company Homepage, http://www.reemtsma.com/images/home/Reemtsma_100-Jahre-Broschuere.pdf (accessed 27 Dec. 2013). The links given in this and previous notes to the Reemtsma website were nonworking at the end of 2013. The spirit of hushing up and denying the company's involvement seems to have remained intact.
33. See Dicke, *Eugenik*.
34. See http://de.wikipedia.org/wiki/Hans_Gmelin. (accessed 12 Dec. 2012)
35. http://www.konstanz.de/rathaus/medienportal/mitteilungen/03619/index.html?lang=de (accessed 27 Nov. 2013); http://de.wikipedia.org/wiki/Bruno_Helmle.
36. See Abmayr, *Stuttgarter NS-Täter*, containing an erroneous entry on Ernst Niemann (chap. 6).
37. Werner, *Adolf-Hitler-Platz*, 35, 181; Welzer, Moller, and Tschuggnall, *"Opa."*
38. Pieper, *Musealisierung*, 10.

Conclusion
The (A)Typical Life of an Industrialist?

Fritz Kiehn was a social climber. The former traveling salesman and shopkeeper was able to take the crucial career leap into manufacturing during the hyperinflation of the Weimar Republic because he had support from his mother-in-law, a feel for economic opportunities, and a readiness to take on risks. In addition, Kiehn's recipe for success was simply to get there first. He acted more quickly to purchase materials and machines than his competitors during the hyperinflation, and he beat currency devaluation by moving his money into tangible assets. The construction of his Deibhalde villa likewise showed that his ability to act promptly, take risks, and think big yielded rapid progress. This experience inspired Kiehn to buy up an entire year's production from a manufacturer of special-purpose machines during the Great Depression. His considerable investment into Magirus shares, his immediate resale of them to the Klöckner-Humboldt-Deutz corporation, and his participation in the race to Aryanize Jewish companies also demonstrate Kiehn's resolve for fast, daring deals. His political conduct was of a piece with his business principles, as shown by his meteoric rise from local Nazi group leader to NSDAP delegate in the Reichstag, his switch from the SA to the SS, and his sudden move away from National Socialism in the spring of 1945. His propensity for speed, however, also proved to have its hazards; it repeatedly put him on thin ice, for example, in his rush to purchase confiscated printing presses from the labor union printing plant and his overeagerness in the Magirus affair, as well as his buyouts of Okriftel and Chiron.

All in all, Fritz Kiehn was a successful industrialist, which he owed to his lucky choice of cigarette paper, or more specifically the products used in hand-rolling or hand-stuffing cigarettes. All other business activities turned out to be failures that threatened the existence of Efka. Yet the core product was so robust that the firm survived even the most egregious missteps. Even when the real meat of Efka was noticeably harmed by the takeover of Chiron or the notoriously deficit-laden printing division that Kiehn was so passionate about

---

Notes from this chapter begin on page 336.

maintaining, the losses balanced out, at least in the long run. It was of the utmost importance for the firm's success (and hence for Kiehn's political career, which substantially depended on his capacity for donations) that its chief product was most in demand during economic crises, guaranteeing the company an anticyclical trade cycle. The hyperinflation of the Great Depression, the years of an economy of scarcity after 1945, and the fragile, extremely modest start to the West German economic miracle all proved to be strong growth phases for Efka. This "crisis bonus" is behind most of the big shifts in Kiehn's life: his rise from the lower middle class in 1923, his swift political career beginning in 1930, his lenient denazification, and his successful rehabilitation and reintegration into society after 1950.

All the same, Kiehn had no long-term strategy. Quite the contrary: his successful moves were the product of improvised trial and error and personal preferences. The dilemma for this *Mittelstand* industrialist was that his core product line offered only limited opportunities for growth, yet he had no other line of business anywhere near as profitable. He therefore made every conceivable effort to realize his lifelong dream of a thousand-man operation, from risky buyouts of other companies to wild attempts at diversification that were as lacking in forethought as they were in success, all of which peaked in his bizarre acquisition of a large farm in East Africa. Kiehn's herculean efforts to reach the next rung of the social ladder form an unbroken line with his economic actions during the Third Reich, which began with his futile attempt to make Efka into the largest printing shop for the Württemberg NSDAP. It continued with his plan — ambitious and precipitous in equal measure — to use Magirus to become a large-scale industrialist with the help of his political offices, and ended with his ruthless acquisition of Jewish property.

If we look at the start of his entrepreneurial career alone, that is, at his core business that generally flourished, we can recognize a diverse array of strategic alternatives in retrospect. Had Efka developed solid diversification strategies with the help of intelligent advisers and prudently reinvested its occasionally tremendous profits, Kiehn probably would have become a large-scale industrialist on his own steam; he could have skipped the whole political strongman act and the loss-heavy Russian roulette. That this is not what happened can be attributed to the influence Kiehn's lower-middle-class origins had in shaping his identity and the *Mittelstand* business culture they fit into.[1] At no point in his life was Kiehn ever able to resolve the contradiction between his invariably limited means and his upper-class aspirations.

His biography has both exceptional and exemplary features that derive from his generational and social background and must be distinguished in these terms. Members of his generation experienced both their primary and secondary socialization completely under German imperial rule; it was typical for him and his cohorts in all levels of society to be drawn to the attractive bourgeois model of life, to hold the military in high esteem and treat civilians with contempt, to reject liberalism and parliamentarianism, and to yearn for national greatness; likewise, they all had experienced the state's all-encompassing ability to intervene. The ideas of order that underlay the authoritarian German Empire dominated in the household of Kiehn's father, a Prussian police officer. World War I, and Germany's defeat even more, destroyed what in retrospect was the comparatively tidy world of the Wilhelmine era. The discrepancy between the value system internalized during the imperial era and that of the comparatively lackluster and aimless Weimar Republic became a formative experience for Kiehn's generation. Their guiding theme in politics was "revision" in practically all fields, from foreign to cultural policy, which made them susceptible to political radicalization.[2]

Not all aspects of Kiehn's biography can be neatly placed into this catalog. On the contrary, his life path contradicted the general tendencies of his generation in some respects. The anticyclical shift in his economic situation, the spectacular social advancement he achieved during the Weimar Republic, his economic liberalism, his fondness for France, and his admiration of the United States do not conform to the familiar picture.[3] Many contradictions in Kiehn's personality are confusing because they do not fit into a consistent profile. This aficionado of fast cars and modern technology was only reactionary about cultural and political issues. His ideas of organic integration and corporate social responsibility stood in direct opposition to his single-mindedness in business affairs. The idea of the *Volksgemeinschaft* appealed to him, even if he loved nothing more than status symbols that created distinctions and clear hierarchies. He was so fascinated by law and order that when the police mercilessly apprehended thieves right in front of him, he almost danced for joy — even in the postwar era — to see the criminals lying there tied up on the ground.[4] Nonetheless, he himself flouted the law on numerous occasions and did not always maintain order. Rather, he felt markedly at ease in the "prerogative state" (*Maßnahmenstaat*) of the Third Reich. The chaotic muddle of a polycratic state, where personal relationships counted more than rules and structures, gave him considerable room to maneuver. The disadvantages of his origins had a disproportionately stronger effect in the more orderly but also more rigid structures of a "normative state" governed by the rule of law.

The hope that political upheaval would lead to personal progress was especially common in the social milieu Kiehn came from, as evident in the particularly strong appeal the NSDAP enjoyed among those between the blocs of capital and labor. This is not to say, however, that ideological considerations were not also significant. The social promise that many members of the middle class had seen in Hitler's seizure of power was at least partially fulfilled. The Third Reich may have initially counted on coming to an arrangement with the old elites, but party members from the lower middle classes, such as Kiehn, saw an opportunity to obtain prestige, material advantages, and not least power by holding a party office or working in a Nazi organization. Like Kiehn, a large number of "provincial leaders" derived from the lower middle classes and sought to attain social status by their activism.

Because the administration of the Nazi system was so inefficient, most such leaders were able to remain in office for long periods despite their usually scant professional qualifications, tactical blunders, and, in many cases, scandals. This system opened up new opportunities for advancement, but also provided the latitude for burgeoning despotism and corruption, sheer greed, and astonishing incompetence, as well as preening vanity, to emerge. Kiehn developed a remarkable feel for the rules of the game in the Nazi state; they fit well with his own disposition. Above all, he comprehended that in this political system, far more than in any other, personal relationships were invaluable assets and represented priceless capital. He was unscrupulous about using any available means to establish contact with the key power centers, from private invitations to targeted political donations, from hunting party hospitality to strategically marrying off his own daughter.

As much as Kiehn fit the typical social profile of regional Nazi functionaries in terms of his origins and education (or lack of it), he stood out for both his relatively advanced age (almost fifty in 1933), his position as a businessman, and his upscale lifestyle.[5] His education and his age also distinguished him from card-carrying industrialists like Hans Kehrl and Paul Pleiger. Unlike Kiehn, Nazi careerists such as erstwhile sales clerk Adolf Eichmann and factory employee Wilhelm Murr did not acquire the trappings of an upper-class existence until National Socialism came around. But Kiehn's economic position was not really consolidated; indeed, it was always under threat. What's more, we can see an odd discrepancy between the material status he achieved and the somewhat backward attitudes that continued to be influenced by his lower-class upbringing.

Combining business with the private sphere was characteristic of the lower middle class Kiehn came from, as was high regard for the family as one's most important retreat and sanctuary. The lower middle classes also frequently harbored pronounced resentment toward the establishment. In Kiehn's case, this concept of the enemy manifested itself in two ways: first, he cultivated common, vague ideas of an international Jewish conspiracy and of anonymous financial capital, which by its very nature allowed for irresponsible as well as unaccountable behavior. Second, he had specific life experience with the long-established Swabian industrial nobility, which he loathed and envied in equal measure. In the small-town microcosm of Trossingen, the Hohners represented the dignitaries who made no secret of their contempt for the "little newcomers" and their "small shops."

Neither was Kiehn ever able to let go of the status insecurity so characteristic of his middle position between the upper class and the proletariat. This explains some of the fundamental contradictions in his life, such as the juxtaposition of public, often exorbitant, consumption with private, occasionally petty, thrift. Kiehn strived to be recognized by the upper classes but felt most at ease when dealing with ordinary people, especially "his" workers and employees. His efforts to take part in "high culture" often ended up bogged down in a pretension most obviously manifested in his extensive library of unread books. The primary purpose of his visits to Bayreuth was to put himself on display and cultivate contacts; cultural edification was less important. He preferred to listen to music at concerts by "his" Trossingen marching band. He felt far more at home in his small-town surroundings of clubs and associations than in the slippery world of official receptions. In Trossingen, he very convincingly played the role of jovial manufacturer, "important" politician, and "humane" Nazi functionary. He was a brilliant actor in many ways, impressing those around him, but in Stuttgart and Berlin he seldom had the chance to display what passed for charisma in the provinces. Many there considered him a somewhat clumsy and backward character of dubious breeding, an opportunist and a schemer, or a notoriously corrupt parvenu.

His contact with traditional elites was defined by uncertainty, as were his business activities once these exceeded the limits of *Mittelstand* enterprise. We need only think of his imprudent strategy and unprofessional approach to buying shares in Magirus, or his gullible reliance on dubious advisers. He seldom managed to find the right balance, as is evident from his awkward preparations to have honorary doctorates awarded to the Bosch leaders and, decades later, the run-up to his own distinction from the University of Innsbruck, as well as his transgression of the consumption standards befitting his status. This made him a repeated source of irritation to the upper classes, and he often incurred criticism from the NSDAP for the same reason.

These conflicts point to Kiehn's shortcomings in dealing with the "refined distinctions" that play a key role in the coherence of social groups. The intricate nature of these distinctions explains the persistently high rate of self-recruitment among social elites. We cannot overestimate the value of an upper-class education in imparting crucial cultural capital. Kiehn's haphazard path through life exemplifies this connection *ex negativo* exceptionally sharply. In later life, it took enormous effort to compensate for the deficits of his childhood and adolescence, the education he did not receive, his lack of intimate knowledge of linguistic and behavioral codes, and his inadequate social sensitivity, when he was able to do so at all.

His insecurity about status, and the habitual inconsistency that resulted from it, were compounded by his lifelong thirst for upward mobility mixed with a fear of downward mobility. His biography became an unresolved roller-coaster ride. His unstable childhood and the loss of his father were followed by a precarious existence as a traveling salesman. His felicitous marriage in 1912 to a wealthy innkeeper's daughter — one of the few truly stable factors in Kiehn's life — gave him access to independence and laid the groundwork for the expansion of his business. The promising beginning of his work as a retailer was interrupted two years later with the advent of World War I. In peacetime, Kiehn managed to advance to manufacturing in a spectacularly short time, only to see this called into question once again in 1923. In the space of a few years, however, the tide turned once again, and the Great Depression gave Efka's core product another crisis boost. At the same time, Kiehn's early commitment to the NSDAP — also determined by economic calculations — seemed like a guarantee of social recognition and business success. The seat in the Reichstag that he won on the basis of that status affirmed this assessment.

Kiehn believed that the National Socialist seizure of power had thrown the door wide open to an even more splendid career for himself. He was quickly disabused of this notion. We can recognize two reasons why his ambitious plans failed: one is that in 1933, the NSDAP had chosen to cooperate with traditional leadership classes for the purpose of economic recovery and was reluctant to completely swap out the functional elite of German society. This put traditional structural elements into a constant tug-of-war with the social dynamics of the political upheaval after 1933.[6] The other reason is that unlike his "card-carrying industrialist" peers from the *Mittelstand* such as Pleiger, Kehrl, and Rohrbach, Kiehn lacked technological or economic knowhow, intellectual agility, and political fanaticism. Above all, he was missing the patronage of Göring, Todt, or Speer, who could have used Nazi economic controls or the NSDAP's Gau system to make him the head of a large corporation. Even under the special, hubris-tempting conditions of the Third Reich, Kiehn remained a provincial businessman at heart, whose prospects focused on his company and his adopted home in Trossingen. This did not exclude occasional excursions into great politics, but these remained only excursions. Switching to a desk in Berlin or one of the occupied territories, entering a different sector closer to armaments but unfamiliar to him, or building up a state or SS-driven company were not his cup of tea.

Both the preservation of the system of property ownership in existence before 1933 and the limited personal possibilities and prospects for the *Mittelstand* paper goods manufacturer explain why Kiehn had to settle for comparably modest successes in the unstable forcefield of the Nazi state. Nevertheless, as president of the Chamber of Industry and Commerce, a member of the supervisory boards of various companies, and the chair of Magirus, as well as a major supplier to the German army and the buyer of important companies in the paper and cellulose industry, he managed to have a career that would have been unthinkable without regime change. But these achievements were never really secure at any point. The opposition was not long in coming; Kiehn's performance in his official posts provoked one scandal after another, and his commercial efforts clashed with the covetousness of other Nazi officeholders. In this respect, he had good cause for his omnipresent fear of a sudden fall from grace.

The end of the Third Reich brought Kiehn to his knees. His multiyear internment and the sequestration of his company, the confiscation of his home and assets, and the dispersal of his family made him long doubt that he would be able to return to the level he had reached before 1933. The tide turned in Kiehn's favor once again, however. His position as an important taxpayer and employer became useful at this point because economic uncertainty was still prevalent and unemployment high. Added to this was the new global political climate, which under the banner of the approaching Cold War made leniency seem appropriate in handling Germany's Nazi past. Consequently, Fritz Kiehn quickly regained a foothold in business in the 1950s, even if he put this success at risk again right away with his large-scale industrial ambitions. Purchasing Chiron, not least in order to provide for his new son-in-law, quickly turned out to be a rash and poor investment. At the same time, the commercially promising marriage of his daughter ended in a divorce debacle. Errors in strategy prevented Efka from growing in a sustainable way, and the family's exorbitant lifestyle generated high private debts. A restructuring forced by outsiders in 1972 helped to quickly dispel both the business and private crises but deprived Kiehn of his power as owner. From then until his death in 1980, he led the carefree life of a universally respected retiree, which was a new kind of experience after the constant seesaws of his long life.

Kiehn's desire for social harmony can be observed at every turn, and is characteristic of both the class he came from and the wartime generation and *Mittelstand* business class he belonged to. His need to reconcile class tensions fed on the universal experiences of the riven class-based society of the German Empire and the Weimar Republic, as well as on Kiehn's personal background of poverty and precarious employment as a traveling sales representative. With his company, he believed that he embodied the "healthy middle" between the threatening monoliths of capital and labor. This worldview was as typical of the *Mittelstand* as his leadership style, which transferred the paternalism played out in his family directly to the workplace.

The employers who moved into decision-making positions in the first half of the twentieth century generally ascribed great importance to solving the social question by diminishing the gulfs between the classes. Indeed, labor relations in this era were marked by a level of conflict unmatched in intensity before or since. Defusing the explosive social tensions was of primary importance to all employers, although the favored approaches varied greatly depending on their type and sector of business. Numerous variations on the "factory community" concept emerged in the 1920s. Common to all of them was an antiunion stance and a technocratic emphasis aimed at rationalization through "social engineering." In 1925, these efforts found their institutional expression with the support of the German Institute for Technical Labor Training (DINTA) founded by Ruhr industrialists, whose preliminary work the DAF was able to build on after 1933.[7]

Employers from the *Mittelstand* were not at the head of these efforts. Instead, they overwhelmingly relied on their traditional paternalism and gradually incorporated bits and pieces of more modern reform concepts. Even though the NSDAP had no specific plans before 1933 for how to shape future labor relations and instead relied on vague slogans, the party found a sympathetic ear among at least some employers. The prospect of "overcoming the class struggle," of an "organic *Volksgemeinschaft*" with social components alongside the complete shutdown of the unions and the banishment of the communist menace once and for all were welcome promises. The "factory leader" (*Betriebsführer*), the Nazi ideal of a socially minded boss — the exact opposite of a soulless, profit-seeking capitalist — made an attractive model in the 1930s and 1940s, particularly for self-made businessmen who wanted to demonstrate their status by doing good for their "followers" (*Gefolgschaft*). Otto Stäbler, Kiehn's shady business colleague in Tuttlingen, was fully equal to his longtime friend in this regard. When the wartime economic boom finally spread to his Chiron factories, after decades of meager returns in the surgical instrument market, the profits had hardly appeared on his balance sheet before Stäbler was outdoing Kiehn in demonstrating the benefits he provided to workers. Numerous *Mittelstand* industrialists in Württemberg seem to have espoused similar ideas in the 1930s and 1940s. In any event, they boasted in their denazification proceedings that what they understood as the "socialism" of the NSDAP had especially appealed to them. Their workers also attested to their employers' truly caring nature, and there is no evidence that any of these were empty statements extracted as favors.[8]

Kiehn introduced his own pioneering elements of employee benefit policy, from profit sharing to subsidized vacation homes. Through the benefits he provided and his partial politicization of company celebrations, he attempted to make a name for himself as a genuinely National Socialist employer. But his leadership style was conspicuous for its overwhelmingly traditional and paternalistic traits, which he clothed with political correctness by adopting National Socialist phrases and symbols. Efka workers appreciated their boss's benefits efforts nonetheless, and even employees close to the labor movement remained loyal to Fritz Kiehn.

Kiehn's pronounced tendency to include external aspects when making business decisions was also typical of family-led *Mittelstand* firms in general. This orientation can be conducive to business success but at the same time economically counterproductive. Efka's establishment and expansion would have been unthinkable without the support of the entire Kiehn family. By the 1950s at the latest, however, Kiehn's paternalistic leadership style became a liability for the company. The problem of succession was exacerbated by his inability to delegate or relinquish his hold, let alone listen to younger or more competent advisors. The way he recruited workers and made strategic decisions on the basis of personal preferences goes a long way toward explaining many of the company's problems. Kiehn's penchant for self-aggrandizement and his virtually obsessive fixation on the number of workers as a measure of personal success undermined operational efficiency.

Anyone who, like many *Mittelstand* employers, believes in the necessity of going it alone in all things has less time and opportunity to cultivate close friendships. This is all the more true for those who make a beeline for the limelight — like Kiehn. His networks may have been widespread, but they were largely defined by superficial, utilitarian calculations. His few close friendships had been founded on professional concerns. Neither political dissent, as was the case with the Freemason Stäbler, nor racial prejudices, as in the case of Kiehn's Jewish friend Lerner, could hamper these relationships, and they outlasted caesuras occasioned by regime changes. If the economic link disappeared, however, the friendship would be severed too; indeed, Kiehn's friendly relationships with figures such as Chiron seller Stäbler or "denazification broker" and close confidant of the family Werner Kaufmann seem to have been sacrificed for business reasons.

As for the features of political behavior typical of the *Mittelstand* economic class, Kiehn shared the distrust that this group continues to voice toward the complex regulatory mechanisms of the modern state even today. This unease with bureaucracy and the judiciary need not end in contempt for democracy, but this was undoubtedly the case with Kiehn. He expected the authoritarian decree, the "order from the Führer," to replace the "inefficient wrangling" of the pluralist Weimar Republic. Kiehn was impressed by the Nazi "prerogative state"(*Maßnahmenstaat*): such a system could uphold the law with stringency when useful or make short work of things when this was perceived as the more effective tactic. This corresponded to the attitudes of many small independent businesspeople who tended to turn a blind eye when formalities stood in their way. This explains, for example, the unscrupulousness with which Fritz Kiehn ignored both party norms and legal requirements before and after 1945. Kiehn's love of the law and an aversion to anarchy went hand in hand with circumventing formalized regulations and bureaucratic procedures on his own authority.

In Württemberg, where self-employment was especially prevalent, few of the important industrialists were actively committed to the NSDAP before or after 1933. Like Fritz Kiehn, these activists predominantly came from a group of up-and-coming small business owners whose companies were new or fairly new. The more established business community usually stayed in the background, almost never sided with the NSDAP before 1933, and only seldom offered the Nazis financial support. Most of the "old fighters" came from the class of craftsmen, retailers, and other small tradespeople with companies of fewer than twenty employees. Even after 1933, most industrialists kept their distance from the NSDAP, their lesser representatives, and the "time-wasting and culturally unrefined Nazi organizations."[9] The predominant model of behavior before 1933 was maintaining distance coupled with a wait-and-see attitude. The period after 1933 was not dominated by political careerism, in the narrower sense of the term, but by opportunistic conformity, defending one's own company turf, and exploiting the new opportunities created by the regime. For the most part, established entrepreneurs derived their self-confidence from a solid economic foundation or long-standing family tradition. Kiehn had neither of these. His activist political conduct, which the more established economic leaders obviously regarded as unbecoming of their social position and middle-class habitus, made this striver into an exception among his professional peers.[10]

The line differentiating the more established employers from those still on the rise also clearly explains the divergent patterns of behavior toward Jewish competitors. It seems to have been no coincidence that Kiehn and Schickedanz — two textbook strivers — sought to outdo each other in their unscrupulous race to Aryanize the Eislingen factory even as no other competitors emerged. This divergence could also be observed in the leather industry, where the established members of the sector behaved in a reserved to overtly upright manner, while up-and-comers behaved aggressively and ruthlessly and soldiers of fortune swooped in from other industries.[11] In the private mining industry, the "younger" Flick and Otto Wolff corporations were particularly shaped by their individual owners and differed from the more reserved, "older" companies, although the decisive factor was not "a more 'moralistic' mindset" but the "differing expansion demand" alone.[12] In the Aryanizations in Hamburg, those who were "first-time owners or making sidewards moves from other companies" were overrepresented compared to "established businesspeople."[13] More case studies are needed before we can make generalizations about these findings, which contradict Avraham Barkai's thesis of a *Mittelstand* economy generally characterized by "rapacity."[14]

Kiehn's case is a vivid lesson in how German society dealt with its Nazi past after 1945 as well, first for the relative harshness of denazification, and then for the corrupt practices and escalating leniency of the same. Kiehn, out of the game for a comparatively long time because of his internment for over three and a half years, was classified as a "Lesser Offender" in 1949. It is very likely that he had previously eliminated important incriminating evidence. He then managed to make a quick and successful entrance into West German society, albeit a slightly bumpy one, riding on the almost obsessive desire of West Germans to swiftly return to "normality" and concentrate on rebuilding the economy and their private lives. The collective leniency toward former Nazi functionaries was at its clearest in this case when an employer whose denazification was not even legally binding yet was given a loan worth millions of Deutschmarks. With this money, even while his company was still under forced administration, Kiehn was able to reembark on his long-cherished expansion plans that he had so recently pursued by means of Aryanizations and wartime acquisitions. Minister-president Gebhard Müller laconically described the prevailing mood in the founding years of the Federal Republic of Germany by remarking that one now had to "accept even the nasty stuff"[15] for the purposes of improving employment.

Kiehn himself pursued a strategy of self-victimization that was typical of many former Nazi activists after 1945. Delusion and seduction rather than economic calculations and ideological affinities were now said to have paved his way to the NSDAP. The party court proceedings that had been directed against his tendency to "hunt down" connections and engage in corrupt business practices were offered as proof of his persecution by the Nazi regime. As an ostensible Straßerite, Kiehn claimed to have been in constant latent danger since 1933. He had only assumed his many offices, he said, to prevent worse things from happening. He had restructured the Aryanized companies so that they would gain in value until they were returned; in Kiehn's estimation, the lawful owners actually owed him a debt of gratitude. In contrast, he passed off his long but comparatively comfortable postwar internment as time in a "concentration camp." The parliamentary and legal proceedings that were meant to clarify how Kiehn had been awarded a loan for millions were nothing more than "rabble-rousing," in the opinion of Kiehn and his attorneys, an irresponsible "political witch hunt," machinations by his "competition and … groups that stood to gain some sort of advantage" from his defamation.[16]

Since Kiehn's brown-shirted past was too widely known to simply be hushed up or denied, he chose to outrun it. When in 1954 he had to stand trial on charges of perjuring himself before the state parliamentary review committee, he hired the same celebrity attorney who had finagled the release of FDP politician Werner Naumann the year before from his imprisonment for National Socialist subversion. Friedrich Grimm, a former legal adviser to Hitler, had been one of the most enthusiastic proponents of a general amnesty for National Socialist crimes since the founding of the Federal Republic. By hiring this man, Kiehn once again demonstratively presented himself as an erstwhile Nazi VIP. The politically explosive "Kiehn affair," which occupied the courts until the mid-1950s because of a petty juridical matter, offered Grimm the opportunity to popularize his amnesty campaign in southwest Germany. On the other hand, Grimm likely first brought Kiehn into contact with the circle of younger FDP politicians from North Rhine-Westphalia who openly pledged themselves to the politics of a "right-wing obligation."[17] If it was briefly conceivable that preventing Kiehn from reintegrating into Trossingen's local political elite in 1954 could have induced him to go back to sponsoring a radical nationalist group, it soon became apparent that the industrialist would remain averse to any sort of party-affiliated activity in the future "for reasons of prior experience." Though Kiehn went hunting with Siegfried Zoglmann, a man closely associated with Naumann, he kept his distance politically.[18]

Reframing and victimization remained Kiehn's leitmotifs when dealing with his past. This persistent lie ultimately became unconscious self-delusion. What is certain is that the repression and reframing dominated his private life as well. His frequent wholehearted and public references to his popularity in the Third

Reich after the conclusion of his denazification must be regarded as slips, once again demonstrating his lack of tact. Nonetheless, his years in the Nazi regime still seemed to him an integral and valuable part of his biography after 1950; after all, he had achieved far more titles, offices, and important relationships between 1933 and 1945 than ever before or since. His pride at having personally met the most important men in the Third Reich lasted the rest of his life, as indicated by the pictures he lovingly pasted into the Kiehn family albums of his meetings with Straßer, Schacht, and Hitler.

His brown-shirted past was temporarily used as a weapon in the local political battles of his adopted hometown, and he had to accept the reestablishment of the old hierarchy of local dignitaries with gritted teeth, but Kiehn was still allowed to spend the twilight of his life as a respected "man of honor." He managed to return to the *Bürgerlichkeit*[19] — the coziness and security of the middle classes — even though he always jeopardized this with the heedless way he led his business during these years. His social circles extended to the corridors of power of the Germany economy and even into Adenauer's cabinet. At the same time, he supported his former fellow party members and "old comrades" who had fallen on hard times, some of whom he did not meet until his internment or afterward, out of "comradely" solidarity. This employment policy disadvantaged his company and turned Efka into a collecting tank for over-the-hill party functionaries.

Kiehn's material resources proved to be immensely helpful in rehabilitating his image. Jobs, tax payments, and donations were important currencies, winning him election to the town council in 1953 with the largest number of votes of any candidate and causing even the SPD to support awarding him public honors, beginning in 1957. But Kiehn's acceptance at the local level and the long silence of his fellow townspeople cannot be attributed to his economic prowess alone. Adding to the general consensus supporting repression were people's contradictory experiences and the lack of criteria for making judgments. In individual cases, Kiehn absolutely had helped people — the SPD member from Trossingen and certain Jewish business colleagues — and this counted more for the locals than the forgivable circumstance (from their point of view) that Kiehn had actively collaborated in establishing the Third Reich prior to 1933. He also did not fit the profile of a violent Nazi perpetrator: in Adenauer's words, the "fully fledged criminal"[20] that West German society had constructed as a scapegoat. Many Trossingen citizens had cheered Kiehn on during the Third Reich, at least for a time. He was not a violent man who had personally tortured and murdered people, but rather was conciliatory toward his fellow townspeople in his adopted hometown in ways that went beyond the limits of political expediency. As time went on, the fact that he had nevertheless supported those chiefly responsible for the Nazi killing machine, and had sought to get close to them in order to safeguard his own ambitions, seemed of secondary importance compared to his local, "decent" way of life.[21]

While it may trigger justified moral outrage that Kiehn was able to return to prosperity, given the large number of victims of the Nazi regime forced to live in poverty at the same time, we must ask if there were any more prudent alternatives in dealing with the legacies of the Third Reich's personnel. It is doubtful that marginalizing these figures permanently, especially the larger number of small and midlevel functionaries, would really have been the better political path. After all, it was easy for "old fighter" Fritz Kiehn to become an admirer of Adenauer after his social rehabilitation of the mid-1950s and to reconcile himself to parliamentary democracy. The first federal chancellor's choice to integrate former National Socialists was often (and rightly) lamented with respect to political justice, but, as Kiehn's case shows, it yielded results, whose contribution to the internal stability of the young republic cannot be overestimated. It therefore remains a purely hypothetical question: what would have happened if Fritz Kiehn and the hundreds of thousands of other former Nazi functionaries had put all of their energy and far-reaching connections into opposing the Bonn Republic instead of investing their financial resources, as Kiehn did, in expensive hobbies, charitable causes, and even donations to the CDU?

Business owners with ample material resources and access to the media had every opportunity to redefine the roles they had played in the past. In this regard Kiehn was no different from the man he had competed against to Aryanize the Fleischer paper factory, Gustav Schickedanz, who became an icon of the German economic miracle. Although the two businessmen differed from each other in many ways, they had a very similar understanding of how to present themselves to the public with a clean slate. For his part, Kiehn claimed to have helped "many Jews"[22] when he went before the state parliamentary review committee in 1951 — a claim that went unchallenged — and managed to increase his reputation as a brown-shirted Samaritan in the decades that followed; in Schickedanz's case, the Quelle mail order company distributed a publication in the 1980s stating that he "and his relatives ... never repudiated their Jewish friends." The ceremony to celebrate Schickedanz's one hundredth birthday featured an encomium by Henry Kissinger. The former US secretary of state and winner of the Nobel Peace Prize had been forced because of his Jewish ancestry to leave Fürth, his hometown, in 1938 at the age of fifteen. He told the assembled guests that his mother, who had lived in Fürth when it was still a small town, had always said "that the Schickedanz family was one of the most decent families."[23] Schickedanz's daughter arranged for a biography of her father to be published in 2010. Without historical evidence, the author stylized his subject into a weapons deal refusenik, a benefactor to foreign workers, and a friend of persecuted Jews — in short, a "serious and decent person."[24]

Very similar messages could be heard in Trossingen: what could be so bad about Fritz Kiehn, the "humane Nazi," who had so generously supported local organizations and even the Catholic Church, who treated his employees fairly and gave Christmas presents to their children? Kiehn garnered the support of many people with his jovial manner and radiant charisma, even those whose politics differed widely from his. In the climate of leniency and amnesia that prevailed after the war, it seemed unimaginable to associate devoted fathers and upstanding officials, liberal college teachers and charitable manufacturers with the Nazi regime, which was usually demonized. Could such law-abiding fellow citizens have brought such political and moral guilt upon themselves? These prevailing attitudes, which, along with strategies for covering up and reframing past events, tremendously complicated the identification of the "has-beens" in the early days of the Bonn Republic, were encapsulated by Ralf Dahrendorf in his statement "that the same people are not the same at different times."[25] Not until the Eichmann trial in 1963 did people become more aware of the polymorphism of Nazi perpetrators. Kiehn's past, however, had no tangible ramifications for his image until and beyond his death. Even after the publication of our biography of Fritz Kiehn, the local culture of remembrance has proved to be largely resistant to findings that have identified the successful and hard-working businessman, generous patron, and jovial service club member as a collaborator in National Socialist injustice.

Notes

1. For general information, see Berghoff, "End."
2. See Sontheimer, *Denken*.
3. On the ambivalent image of the United States, see Lüdtke, Marßolek, and Saldern, *Amerikanisierung*. The attitude toward France was, in part, similarly conflicted. See Herbert, *Best*.
4. Interview with Herbert E. Kiehn of 19–20 May 1998.
5. However, there are clear correlations to the biography of Metzingen textile manufacturer Hugo Boss. Like Kiehn, Boss was born in 1885, came from the Swabian lower middle class, and joined the NSDAP in 1931, though he never became an important Nazi functionary. See Köster, *Hugo Boss*.
6. See Berghoff, "Hitler."
7. See Frese, *Betriebspolitik*, 10–27.
8. This was true of Ebingen manufacturers Christian Ludwig Maag and Max and Oskar Gühring, whose family businesses were known as "Nazi companies," even as their employees attested to having the best labor and wage conditions. StAS, Wü 13, 1/SO/KW 219/48 (Maag); StAS, Wü 13, 1/So/KW 332/48 (Oskar Gühring); StAS, Wü 15, Bü 316 (Max Gühring). Kiehn's friend Stäbler was also fascinated by the idea that factory life could be shaped into a harmonious community, and he shared capital and profits with his workers. "The Chiron community is no ordinary business," he declared to his employees, "but a … fellowship of comrades who stand up for one another." StAS, Wü 13, Bü 2679, verdict of Tübingen denazification court of 8 June 1949; StAS, Wü 13, Bü 2679, declaration of Chiron works committee of 8 Oct. 1948.

9. Rauh-Kühne, " Unternehmer," 318–320; Niethammer, *Mitläuferfabrik,* 557 (cit.); Kater, *Nazi Party.*
10. See Rauh-Kühne, "Unternehmer," 321.
11. See Bräutigam, *Unternehmer,* 332–336.
12. Mollin, "Eisen- und Stahlindustrie," 476.
13. Bajohr, *"Aryanisation,"* 201. See also Jacobs, *Rauch,* 137–163.
14. Barkai, "Unternehmer," 233.
15. StAS, Wü 1, Bü 100a, Verhandlungen des Landtags, 107th session, 25 July 1950, p. 2117.
16. Defense plea in perjury trial, private collection; KAT, Bestand II, no. 100, defense speech by attorney Grimm.
17. Frei, *Vergangenheitspolitik,* 365, 380.
18. StAS, Wü 1, Bü 100a, PUA, 8th public session, p. 51.
19. Herbert, *Best, 475.*
20. Quoted in Brochhagen, *Nürnberg,* 74.
21. On the topos of ex-Nazis supposedly retaining their "decency," see Herbert, *Best,* 471.
22. StAS, Wü 1, Bü 100a, PUA, 8th public meeting, p. 49.
23. Böhmer, *Grete Schickedanz,* 40, 52.
24. Schöllgen, *Gustav Schickedanz,* 157, 161, 204. Reviews of the book were uniformly scathing. See Rauh, "'Angewandte Geschichte.'"
25. Dahrendorf, *Society,* 240.

BIBLIOGRAPHY

Archives

Archiv der sozialen Demokratie der Friedrich-Ebert-Stiftung, Bonn
Archives de l'Occupation française en Allemagne et en Autriche, Colmar
Bundesarchiv Berlin
Bundesarchiv Koblenz
Bundesarchiv-Militärarchiv Freiburg
Harmonikamuseum Trossingen
Hauptstaatsarchiv Stuttgart
Hauptstaatsarchiv Stuttgart-Militärarchiv
Hessisches Hauptstaatsarchiv Wiesbaden
Hessisches Wirtschaftsarchiv Darmstadt
Institut für Zeitgeschichte, Munich
Kreisarchiv Tuttlingen
Landesarchiv Berlin
Landeskirchliches Archiv Stuttgart
Materials possessed by the Kiehn family
Rheinisch Westfälisches Wirtschaftsarchiv zu Köln
Staatsarchiv Ludwigsburg
Staatsarchiv Nürnberg
Staatsarchiv Sigmaringen
Stadtarchiv Trossingen
Universitätsarchiv der Leopold-Franzens-Universität Innsbruck
Wirtschaftsarchiv Baden-Württemberg, Stuttgart-Hohenheim
Zentrale Stelle der Landesjustizverwaltungen, Ludwigsburg

Printed and Online Literature

Abelshauser, Werner. *Wirtschaftsgeschichte der Bundesrepublik Deutschland 1945–1980.* Frankfurt, 1983.
Abmayr, Hermann G., ed. *Stuttgarter NS-Täter: vom Mitläufer bis zum Massenmörder.* 2nd ed. Stuttgart, 2009.
Alheim, Hannah. *Deutsche, kauft nicht bei Juden! Antisemitismus und politischer Boykott in Deutschland 1924 bis 1935.* Göttingen, 2011.
Aly, Götz. *"Endlösung": Völkerverschiebung und Mord an den Europäischen Juden.* Frankfurt, 1995.

———. *Hitlers Volksstaat: Raub, Rassenkrieg und nationaler Sozialismus*. Frankfurt, 2005.
Aly, Götz, and Susanne Heim. *Vordenker der Vernichtung: Auschwitz und die deutschen Pläne für eine neue europäische Ordnung*. Hamburg, 1991.
Aly, Götz, and Michael Sontheimer. *Fromms: Wie der jüdische Kondomfabrikant Julius F. unter die deutschen Räuber fiel*. 2nd ed. Frankfurt, 2007.
Angermund, Ralph. "Korruption im Nationalsozialismus: Eine Skizze." In *Von der Aufgabe der Freiheit: Politische Verantwortung und bürgerliche Gesellschaft im 19. und 20. Jahrhundert—Festschrift für Hans Mommsen zum 5. November 1995*, ed. Christian Janssen, Lutz Niethammer and Bernd Weisbrod, 371–383. Berlin, 1995.
Anon. *Fritz Kiehn: Fünfzig Jahre in Trossingen*. Trossingen, 1958.
———. *Mit dem Herzen dabei: Ein Bericht aus den Efka-Werken*. Trossingen, 1962.
Arbogast, Christine. *Herrschaftsinstanzen der württembergischen NSDAP: Funktion, Sozialprofil und Lebenswege einer regionalen NS-Elite 1920–1960*. Munich, 1998.
Arbogast, Christine, and Bettina Gall. "Aufgaben und Funktionen des Gauinspekteurs, der Kreisleitung und der Kreisgerichtsbarkeit der NSDAP in Württemberg." In Rauh-Kühne and Ruck, *Regionale Eliten*, 151–170.
Arendt, Hannah. *Eichmann in Jerusalem. A Report on the Banality of Evil*. New York, 1963.
———. *Eichmann in Jerusalem: Ein Bericht von der Banalität des Bösen*. Expanded paperback ed. Munich, 1986.
———. *Elemente und Ursprünge totaler Herrschaft. Antisemitismus, Imperialismus, totale Herrschaft*. Piper, München-Zürich, 1986.
———. *Totalitarian Rule: Its Nature and Characteristics*. Wesleyan University Press, 1968. Reprint, 1986.
Aretz, Jürgen. "Bruno Heck." In *Zeitgeschichte in Lebensbildern*, vol. 8., ed. Jürgen Aretz, Rudolf Morsey, and Anton Rauscher, 213–232. Mainz, 1997.
Bähr, Johannes, with Ralf Ahrens, Michael C. Schneider, Harald Wixforth, and Dieter Ziegler. *Die Dresdner Bank in der Wirtschaft des Dritten Reiches*. Munich, 2006.
Bähr, Johannes, and Ralf Banken, eds. *Wirtschaftssteuerung durch Recht im Nationalsozialismus: Studien zur Entwicklung des Wirtschaftsrechts im Interventionsstaat des "Dritten Reiches."* Frankfurt, 2006.
Bajohr, Frank. *"Arisierung" in Hamburg: Die Verdrängung der jüdischen Unternehmer 1933–1945*. Hamburg, 1997.
———. *"Aryanisation" in Hamburg. The Economic Exclusion of Jews and the Confiscation of their Property in Nazi Germany*. London and New York, 2002.
———. "Interessenkartell, personale Netzwerke und Kompetenzausweitung: Die Beteiligten bei der 'Arisierung' und Konfiszierung jüdischen Vermögens." In *Karrieren im Nationalsozialismus: Funktionseliten zwischen Mitwirkung und Distanz*, ed. Gerhard Hirschfeld and Tobias Jersak, 45–55. Frankfurt, 2004.
———. *Parvenüs und Profiteure: Korruption in der NS-Zeit*. Frankfurt, 2001.
Bajohr, Frank, and Michael Wildt, ed. *Volksgemeinschaft: Neue Forschungen zur Gesellschaft des Nationalsozialismus*. Frankfurt, 2009.
Banken, Ralf. "Das nationalsozialistische Devisenrecht als Steuerungs- und Diskriminierungsinstrument." In Bähr and Banken, *Wirtschaftssteuerung durch Recht im Nationalsozialismus*, 121–236.
Barkai, Avraham. "Die deutschen Unternehmer und die Judenpolitik im 'Dritten Reich.'" *Geschichte und Gesellschaft* 15 (1989): 227–247.
———. *Vom Boykott zur "Entjudung": Der wirtschaftliche Existenzkampf der Juden im Dritten Reich 1933–1943*. Frankfurt, 1988.

Behrenbeck, Sabine. *Der Kult um die toten Helden: Nationalsozialistische Mythen, Riten und Symbole, 1923–1945.* Vierow bei Greifswald, 1996.
Benjamin, Walter. *Das Kunstwerk im Zeitalter seiner technischen Reproduzierbarkeit.* Frankfurt, 1963.
Bennecke, Heinrich. *Die Reichswehr und der "Röhm-Putsch."* Munich, 1964.
Berg, Manfred, and Bernd Schäfer. *Historical Justice in International Perspective: How Societies Are Trying to Right the Wrongs of the Past.* New York, 2009.
Berghahn, Volker R., and Paul J. Friedrich, *Otto A. Friedrich. Ein politischer Unternehmer. Sein Leben und seine Zeit 1902–1975.* Frankfurt, 1993.
Berghahn, Volker, Stefan Unger, and Dieter Ziegler, eds. *Die deutsche Wirtschaftselite im 20. Jahrhundert: Kontinuität und Mentalität.* Essen, 2003.
Berghoff, Hartmut. "Did Hitler Create a New German Society? Continuities and Changes in German Social History before and after 1933." In *Weimar and Nazi Germany: Continuities and Discontinuities,* ed. Panikos Panayi, 74–104. London, 2001.
———. "Konsumgüterindustrie im Nationalsozialismus: Marketing im Spannungsfeld von Profit- und Regimeinteressen." *Archiv für Sozialgeschichte* 36 (1996): 300–320.
———. "Marketing Diversity: The Making of a Global Consumer Product—Hohner's Harmonicas, 1857–1930." *Enterprise and Society* 2, no. 2 (2001): 338–372.
———. "The End of Family Business? The Mittelstand and German Capitalism in Transition, 1949–2000." *Business History Review* 80, no. 2 (2006): 263–295.
———. "Unternehmenskultur und Herrschaftstechnik—Industrieller Paternalismus: Hohner von 1857 bis 1918." *Geschichte und Gesellschaft* 23 (1997): 167–204.
———. *Zwischen Kleinstadt und Weltmarkt: Hohner und die Harmonika, 1857–1961—Unternehmensgeschichte als Gesellschaftsgeschichte.* Paderborn, 1997.
———. "Zwischen Verdrängung und Aufarbeitung: Die bundesdeutsche Gesellschaft und ihre nationalsozialistische Vergangenheit in den Fünfziger Jahren." *Geschichte in Wissenschaft und Unterricht* 49 (1998): 96–114.
Berghoff, Hartmut, Jürgen Kocka, and Dieter Ziegler, eds. *Business in the Age of Extremes: Essays in Modern German and Austrian Economic History.* Cambridge, 2012.
Berghoff, Hartmut, and Cornelia Rauh-Kühne. *Fritz K. Ein deutsches Leben im zwanzigsten Jahrhundert.* Stuttgart, Muniche, 2000.
———. "From Himmler's Circle of Friends to the Lions Club: The Career of a Provincial Nazi-Leader." In *Biography between Structure and Agency: Central European Lives in International Historiography,* ed. Simone Lässig and Volker Berghahn, 182–200. New York, 2008.
Biedermann, Edwin A. *Logen, Clubs und Bruderschaften.* 2nd ed. Düsseldorf, 2007.
Bismarck, Klaus von. "Von Weihnachten bis Weihnachten." In *Weihnachten 1945,* ed. Claus Heinrich Casdorff, 20–36. Frankfurt, 1989.
Bloch, Ernst. *Erbschaft dieser Zeit.* Frankfurt, 1962.
Block, Niels. *Die Parteigerichtsbarkeit der NSDAP.* Frankfurt, 2002.
Bluhm, Gabriele. "'Wirtschaft am Pranger': Die Berichterstattung des württembergischen 'Kampfblatts' 'Flammenzeichen' über unangepaßtes Verhalten von Gewerbetreibenden." In Rauh-Kühne and Ruck, *Regionale Eliten,* 247–262.
Blum, Franz. *Ludwig Trick: Sein Leben und Wirken 1885–1900—mit einer Geschichte seiner Vorfahren. Ein Gedenkblatt zur hundertsten Wiederkehr seines Geburtstages 17. Dez. 1935.* Heilbronn, 1935.
Bock, Gisela. *Zwangssterilisation im Nationalsozialismus: Studien zur Rassenpolitik und Frauenpolitik.* Opladen, 1986.

Bode, Wilhelm, and Elisabeth Emmert. *Jagdwende: Vom Edelhobby zum ökologischen Handwerk.* 3rd ed. Munich, 2000.
Boelcke, Willi A. "Hitlers Befehle zur Zerstörung oder Lähmung des deutschen Industriepotentials 1944/45." *Tradition* 13 (1968): 301–316.
Böhmer, Christian. *Grete Schickedanz. Vom Lehrmädchen zur Versandhauskönigin.* Berlin, 1996.
Bracher, Karl Dietrich. "Stufen der Machtergreifung." In *Die nationalsozialistische Machtergreifung: Studien zur Errichtung des totalitären Herrschaftssystems in Deutschland 1933/34,* ed. Karl Dietrich Bracher, Wolfgang Sauer, and Gerhard Schulz, 348–368. Cologne, 1962.
Bracher, Karl Dietrich, Wolfgang Sauer, and Gerhard Schulz, eds. *Die nationalsozialistische Machtergreifung: Studien zur Errichtung des totalitären Herrschaftssystems in Deutschland 1933/34.* Cologne, 1962.
Bräutigam, Petra. *Mittelständische Unternehmer im Nationalsozialismus: Wirtschaftliche Entwicklungen und soziale Verhaltensweisen in der Schuh- und Lederindustrie Badens und Württembergs.* Munich, 1997.
Brochhagen, Ulrich. *Nach Nürnberg: Vergangenheitsbewältigung und Westintegration in der Ära Adenauer.* Hamburg, 1994.
Brodesser, Hermann-Josef, Bernd Josef Fehn, Tilo Franosch, and Wilfried Wirth. *Wiedergutmachung und Kriegsfolgenliquidation: Geschichte—Regelungen—Zahlungen.* Munich, 2000.
Broszat, Martin. *Der Staat Hitlers: Grundlegung und Entwicklung seiner inneren Verfassung.* Munich, 1969.
———. "Soziale Motivation und Führer-Bindung des Nationalsozialismus." *Vierteljahrshefte für Zeitgeschichte* 18 (1970): 392–409.
———. "Zur Struktur der NS-Massenbewegung." *Vierteljahrshefte für Zeitgeschichte* 31 (1983): 52–76.
Broszat, Martin, and Elke Fröhlich, *Alltag und Widerstand. Bayern im Nationalsozialismus.* Munich, 1987.
Brüggemeier, Franz-Josef. *Zurück auf dem Platz: Deutschland und die Fußball-Weltmeisterschaft 1954.* Munich, 2004.
Brustein, William. *The Logic of Evil: The Social Origins of the Nazi Party 1923–1933.* New Haven, CT, 1996.
Buchheim, Christoph, and Jonas Scherner. "Corporate Freedom of Action in Nazi Germany: A Response to Peter Hayes." *Bulletin of the German Historical Institute* 45 (2009): 43–50.
Buchheim, Hans. "Befehl und Gehorsam." In *Anatomie des SS-Staates,* vol. 1, 1–323. 2nd ed. Munich, 1979. Originally published 1967.
———. "Command and Compliance." In *Anatomy of the SS State,* 303–396. New York, 1968.
———. *Totalitarian Rule: Its Nature and Characteristics.* Wesleyan University Press, 1968. Reprint 1986.
Buchna, Kristian. *Nationale Sammlung an Rhein und Ruhr: Friedrich Middelhauve und die nordrhein-westfälische FDP 1945–1953.* Munich, 2010.
Burth, Wolfgang, Stephan Link, Birgit Rettich, Andreas Ritthaler, Thomas Schäfer, and Michael Thrautig. "Nationalsozialistische Wirtschaftslenkung und württembergische Wirtschaft." In Rauh-Kühne and Ruck, *Regionale Eliten,* 195–219.
Bütow, Tobias, and Franka Bindernagel. *Ein KZ in der Nachbarschaft: Das Magdeburger Außenlager der Brabag und der "Freundeskreis Himmler."* Cologne, 2003.

Bytwerk, Randall L. *Julius Streicher: The Man Who Persuaded a Nation to Hate Jews.* New York, 1983.
Classen, Christoph. *Bilder der Vergangenheit: Die Zeit des Nationalsozialismus im Fernsehen der Bundesrepublik Deutschland 1955–1965.* Essen, 1999.
Clay, Catrine, and Michael Leapman. *Master Race. The Lebensborn Experiment in Nazi Germany.* London, 1995.
Conradt-Mach, Annemarie. *"Arbeit und Brot": Die Geschichte der Industriearbeiter in Villingen und Schwenningen von 1918 bis 1933.* Villingen-Schwenningen, 1990.
Crossick, Geoffrey, and Heinz-Gerhard Haupt. *The Petite Bourgeoisie in Europe, 1780–1914.* London, 1995.
Dahrendorf, Ralf. *Gesellschaft und Demokratie in Deutschland.* Munich, 1965.
———. *Society and Democracy in Germany.* New York, 1967.
Dean, Martin. *Robbing the Jews: The Confiscation of Jewish Property in the Holocaust, 1933–1945.* Cambridge, 2008.
Dederke, Karlheinz. *Reich und Republik. Deutschland 1917–1933.* 2nd ed. Stuttgart, 1973.
Dicke, Jan Nikolas. *Eugenik und Rassenhygiene in Münster zwischen 1918 und 1939.* Berlin, 2004.
Diewald-Kerkmann, Gisela. *Politische Denunziation im NS-Regime oder die kleine Macht der "Volksgenossen."* Bonn, 1995.
Döscher, Hans-Jürgen. *Verschworene Gemeinschaft: Das Auswärtige Amt unter Adenauer—zwischen Neubeginn und Kontinuität.* Berlin, 1995.
Drecoll, Axel. *Der Fiskus als Verfolger: Die steuerliche Diskriminierung der Juden in Bayern 1933–1941/42.* Munich, 2009.
Edelmann, Heidrun. *Vom Luxusgut zum Gebrauchsgegenstand: Die Geschichte der Verbreitung von Personenkraftwagen in Deutschland.* Frankfurt, 1989.
Eglau, Hans Otto. *Die Kasse muß stimmen: So hatten sie Erfolg im Handel.* Düsseldorf, 1972.
Eichholtz, Dietrich. *Geschichte der Deutschen Kriegswirtschaft.* 2 vols. Berlin, 1971–1985.
Ericsson, Kjersti, and Eva Simonsen, eds. *Children of World War II. The Hidden Enemy Legacy.* Oxford, 2005.
Erker, Paul. *Industrie-Eliten in der NS-Zeit: Anpassungsbereitschaft und Eigeninteresse von Unternehmern in der Rüstungs- und Kriegswirtschaft 1936–1945.* Passau, 1993.
Erker, Paul, and Toni Pierenkemper, eds. *Deutsche Unternehmer zwischen Kriegswirtschaft und Wiederaufbau.* Munich, 1999.
Estrade, Jean Lucien. *Tuttlingen April 1945–September 1949.* Tuttlingen, 1990.
Evans, Richard J. *The Third Reich in Power.* New York, 2005.
Fait, Barbara. "Die Kreisleiter der NSDAP: Nach 1945." In *Von Stalingrad zur Währungsreform: Zur Sozialgeschichte des Umbruchs in Deutschland,* ed. Martin Broszat, Klaus-Dietmar Henke, and Hans Woller, 3rd ed., 213–299. Munich, 1990.
Falkenhausen, Freiherr von. "Das Anleihestockgesetz und seine Durchführung." *Bank-Archiv* 34 (1935): 283–290.
Fallada, Hans. *Kleiner Mann was nun?* Hamburg, 1998.
Falter, Jürgen W. *Hitlers Wähler.* Munich, 1991.
Feldman, Gerald D. *Hugo Stinnes: Biographie eines Industriellen 1870–1924.* Munich, 1998.
Figge, Reinhard. "Die Opposition der NSDAP im Reichstag." PhD diss., University of Cologne, 1963.
Fraenkel, Ernst. *The Dual State.* New York, 1941.
Frei, Alfred Georg. *Finale Grande: Die Rückkehr der Fußballweltmeister.* Berlin, 1994.

Frei, Norbert. *Vergangenheitspolitik: Die Anfänge der Bundesrepublik und die NS-Vergangenheit.* Munich, 1996.

———. "German *Zeitgeschichte* and Generation, or How to Explain the Belated Career of the Nazi *Volksgemeinschaft.*" *Social Research* 81 (2014): 569–582.

———. *Hitlers Eliten nach 1945.* Munich, 2003.

Freitag, Werner. "Der Führermythos im Fest. Festfeuerwerk, NS-Liturgie, Dissens und '100% KdF-Stimmung.'" In *Das Dritte Reich im Fest: Führermythos, Feierlaune und Verweigerung in Westfalen 1933–1945,* ed. Werner Freitag, 11–69. Bielefeld, 1997.

Frese, Matthias. *Betriebspolitik im "Dritten Reich": Deutsche Arbeitsfront, Unternehmer und Staatsbürokratie in der westdeutschen Großindustrie 1933–1939.* Paderborn, 1991.

Frevert, Walter. *Jagdliches Brauchtum.* Berlin, 1936.

———. *Von Rominten nach Kaltenbronn.* Munich, 1993.

Friedländer, Saul. *Nazi Germany and the Jews.* Vol. 1, *The Years of Persecution, 1933–1939.* New York, 1997.

———. *The Years of Extermination: Nazi Germany and the Jews, 1939–1945.* New York, 2006.

Fritsche, Christiane. *Ausgeplündert, zurückerstattet und entschädigt: Arisierung und Wiedergutmachung in Mannheim.* Ubstadt-Weiher, 2013.

Fritz, Eberhard. "Das Haus Württemberg und der Nationalsozialismus: Motive des Widerstands gegen Hitler und seine Bewegung." In *Adel und Nationalsozialismus im deutschen Südwesten,* ed. Christopher Dowe, 132–162. Stuttgart, 2007.

Garner, Curt. "Der öffentliche Dienst in den 50er Jahren: Politische Weichenstellung und ihre sozialgeschichtliche Folgen." In *Modernisierung im Wiederaufbau: Die westdeutsche Gesellschaft der 50er Jahre,* ed. Axel Schildt and Arnold Sywottek, 759–790. Bonn, 1993.

Gautschi, Andreas. *Walter Frevert: Eines Waidmanns Wechsel und Wege.* Hanstedt, 2004.

Gebhardt, Winfried, and Arnold Zingerle. *Pilgerfahrt ins Ich: Die Bayreuther Richard Wagner-Festspiele und ihr Publikum—eine kultursoziologische Studie.* Konstanz, 1998.

Gehrig, Astrid. *Nationalsozialistische Rüstungspolitik und unternehmerischer Entscheidungsspielraum: Vergleichende Fallstudien zur württembergischen Maschinenbauindustrie.* Munich, 1996.

Gelatelly, Robert. *Hingeschaut und weggesehen: Hitler und sein Volk.* Bonn, 2003.

Genschel, Helmut. *Die Verdrängung der Juden aus der Wirtschaft im Dritten Reich.* Göttingen, 1966.

Geyer, Martin H. *"Verkehrte Welt": Revolution, Inflation und Moderne—München 1914–1924.* Göttingen, 1998.

Goebbels, Joseph. *Die Tagebücher von Joseph Goebbels.* Vol. 1, *Aufzeichnungen 1923–1941.* Ed. Elke Fröhlich on behalf of the Institut für Zeitgeschichte with the support of the Staatlicher Archivdienst of Russia. Munich, 1998–2006.

Goschler, Constantin. *Schuld und Schulden: Die Politik der Wiedergutmachung für NS-Verfolgte seit 1945.* Göttingen, 2005.

———. *Wiedergutmachung: Westdeutschland und die Verfolgten des Nationalsozialismus 1945–1954.* Munich, 1992.

Goschler, Constantin, and Philipp Ther, eds. *Raub und Restitution: "Arisierung" und Rückerstattung des jüdischen Eigentums in Europa.* Frankfurt M., 2003.

Gradinger, Sebastian. *Service Clubs zur Institutionalisierung von Solidarität und Sozialkapital.* Saarbrücken, 2007.

Gregor, Neil. *Stern und Hakenkreuz: Daimler Benz im Dritten Reich.* Berlin, 1997.

Gries, Rainer. "Zum Selbstbild westdeutscher Werbeunternehmer der Nachkriegszeit: Eine ideologiegeschichtliche Bestandsaufnahme." In *Geschäft mit Wort und Meinung:*

Medienunternehmer seit dem 18. Jahrhundert, ed. Günther Schulz, 251–274. Munich, 1999.
Grieser, Utho. *Himmlers Mann in Nürnberg: Der Fall Benno Martin—eine Studie zur Struktur des Dritten Reiches in der "Stadt der Reichsparteitage."* Nuremberg, 1974.
Grimm, Friedrich. *Mit offenem Visier: Aus den Lebenserinnerungen eines deutschen Rechtsanwalts*. Revised by Hermann Schild. Leoni am Starnberger See, 1961.
Grote, Christiane, and Gabriele Rosenthal. "Frausein als Entlastungsargument für die biographische Verstrickung in den Nationalsozialismus?" *Tel Aviver Jahrbuch für deutsche Geschichte* 21 (1992): 289–318.
Gruchmann, Lothar. "Korruption im Dritten Reich." *Vierteljahrshefte für Zeitgeschichte* 42 (1994): 571–593.
Gruner, Wolf, ed. *Die Verfolgung der europäischen Juden durch das nationalsozialistische Deutschland*. Vol. 1, *Deutsches Reich 1933–1937*. Munich, 2008.
Hachmeister, Lutz. *Der Gegnerforscher: Die Karriere des SS-Führers Franz Albrecht Six*. Munich, 1998.
———. *Schleyer: Eine Deutsche Geschichte*. Munich, 2004.
Häffner, Martin, Karl Martin Ruff, and Ina Schrumpf. *Trossingen: Vom Alemannendorf zur Musikstadt*. Trossingen, 1997.
Hahn, Judith. *Grawitz / Genzken / Gebhardt. Drei Karrieren im Sanitätsdienst der SS*. Münster, 2008.
Hallgarten, George W. F., and Joachim Radkau. *Deutsche Industrie und Politik: Von Bismarck bis in die Gegenwart*. Rev. ed. Frankfurt, 1986.
Hamburger Stiftung für Sozialgeschichte des 20. Jahrhunderts and Angelika Ebbinghaus, eds. *Das Daimler-Benz-Buch: ein Rüstungskonzern im "Tausendjährigen Reich."* Hamburg, 1987.
Hartmann, Heinrich, ed. *Mit dem Herzen dabei: Ein Bericht aus den Efka-Werken*. Trossingen, 1962.
Harvey, Elizabeth. *Women and the Nazi East: Agents and Witnesses of Germanization*. New Haven, CT, 2003.
Hau, Michel. "Les entreprises Alsaciennes." In *La vie des entreprises sous l'occupation: Une enquête à l'échelle locale*, ed. Alain Beltran, Robert Frank and Henry Rousso, 237–249. Paris, 1994.
Haupt, Heinz-Gerhard, and Geoffrey Crossick. *Die Kleinbürger: Eine europäische Sozialgeschichte des 19. Jahrhunderts*. Munich, 1998.
Haupt, Michael. *Das Haus der Wannsee-Konferenz: Von der Industriellenvilla zur Gedenkstätte*. Paderborn, 2009.
Hayes, Peter. "Corporate Freedom of Action in Nazi Germany." *Bulletin of the German Historical Institute* 45 (2009): 29–41.
———. *Die Degussa im Dritten Reich: Von der Zusammenarbeit zur Mittäterschaft*. Munich, 2004.
Heiden, Konrad. *Geschichte des Nationalsozialismus: Die Karriere einer Idee*. Berlin, 1932.
Heim, Susanne, ed. *Die Verfolgung der europäischen Juden durch das nationalsozialistische Deutschland, 1933–1945*. Vol. 2, *Deutsches Reich 1938–August 1939*. Munich, 2009.
Hein, Bastian. *Elite für Volk und Führer? Die Allgemeine SS und ihre Mitglieder 1925–1945*. Munich, 2012.
Heinemann, Isabel. *"Rasse, Siedlung, deutsches Blut": Das Rasse- und Siedlungshauptamt der SS und die rassenpolitische Neuordnung Europas*. Göttingen, 2003.
Henke, Klaus-Dietmar. *Die amerikanische Besetzung Deutschlands*. Munich, 1995.

———. "Die Grenzen der politischen Säuberung in Deutschland nach 1945." In *Westdeutschland 1945–1955*, ed. Ludolf Herbst, 127–133. Munich, 1986.

———. "Die Trennung vom Nationalsozialismus: Selbstzerstörung, politische Säuberung, 'Entnazifizierung,' Strafverfolgung." In *Politische Säuberung in Europa: Die Abrechnung mit Faschismus und Kollaboration nach dem Zweiten Weltkrieg*, ed. Klaus-Dietmar Henke and Hans Woller, 84–106. Munich, 1991.

———. "Politik der Widersprüche: Zur Charakteristik der französischen Militärregierung in Deutschland nach dem Zweiten Weltkrieg." In *Die Deutschlandpolitik Frankreichs und die Französische Zone 1945–1949*, ed. Claus Scharfe and Hans-Jürgen Schröder, 49–89. Wiesbaden, 1979.

———. *Politische Säuberung unter französischer Besatzung: Die Entnazifizierung in Württemberg-Hohenzollern*. Stuttgart, 1981.

Herbert, Ulrich. *Best: Biographische Studien über Radikalismus, Weltanschauung und Vernunft, 1903–1989*. Bonn, 1996.

———. "Rückkehr in die Bürgerlichkeit? NS-Eliten in der Bundesrepublik." In *Rechtsradikalismus in der politischen Kultur der Nachkriegszeit: Die verzögerte Normalisierung in Niedersachsen*, ed. Bernd Weisbrod, 157–173. Hanover, 1995.

Herbst, Ludolf. *Das nationalsozialistische Deutschland 1933–1945*. Frankfurt, 1996.

Heydrich, Lina. *Leben mit einem Kriegsverbrecher*. With comments by Werner Maser. Pfaffenhofen, 1976.

Himmler, Heinrich. *Der Dienstkalender Heinrich Himmlers 1941/42*. Ed. Peter Witte, Andreij Angrick, Christoph Dieckmann, Christian Gerlach, Peter Klein, Dieter Pohl, Martina Voigt, Michael Wildt and Peter Witte. Hamburg, 1999.

———. *Reichsführer! ... Briefe an und von Himmler*. Ed. Helmut Heiber. Stuttgart, 1968.

Hockerts, Hans Günter, Claudia Moisel, and Tobias Winstel. *Grenzen der Wiedergutmachung: Die Entschädigung für NS-Verfolgte in West- und Osteuropa 1945–2000*. Göttingen, 2006.

Hoffmann, Alfred. "Der 'maßlose Drang, eine Rolle zu spielen': Gottlob Berger." In *Täter—Helfer—Mitläufer: NS-Belastete von der Ostalb*, ed. Wolfgang Proske, 21–51. Münster, 2010.

Horn, Sabine. *Erinnerungsbilder: Auschwitz-Prozess und Majdanek-Prozess im westdeutschen Fernsehen*. Essen, 2009.

Horn, Wolfgang. *Führerideologie und Parteiorganisation in der NSDAP (1919–1933)*. Düsseldorf, 1972.

Hüttenberger, Peter. *Die Gauleiter: Studie zum Wandel des Machtgefüges in der NSDAP*. Stuttgart, 1969.

Jachomowski, Dirk. *Die Umsiedlung der Bessarabien-, Bukowina- und Dobrudschadeutschen: Von der Volksgruppe in Rumänien zur "Siedlungsbrücke" an der Reichsgrenze*. Munich, 1984.

Jacobs, Tino. *Rauch und Macht: Das Unternehmen Reemtsma 1920 bis 1961*. Göttingen, 2008.

Janetzko, Maren. *Die "Arisierung" mittelständischer jüdischer Unternehmen in Bayern 1933–1939. Ein interregionaler Vergleich*. Ansbach, 2012.

Jansen, Michael, and Günter Saathoff, eds. *A Mutual Responsibility and a Moral Obligation: Final Report on Compensations Programs of the Remembrance, Responsibility and Future Foundation*. New York, 2009.

Janssen, Gregor. *Das Ministerium Speer: Deutschlands Rüstung im Krieg*. Berlin, 1968.

Jersch-Wenzel, Stefi. "Rechtslage und Emanzipation." In *Deutsch-jüdische Geschichte in der Neuzeit*. Vol. 2, *Emanzipation und Akkulturation 1780–1871*, ed. Michael Meyer and Michael Brenner, 15–56. Munich, 1996.

John, Jürgen, Horst Möller, and Thomas Schaarschmidt. *Die NS-Gaue: Regionale Mittelinstanzen im zentralisierten "Führerstaat"?* Munich, 2007.
Jünger, Ernst. "Der Kampf als inneres Erlebnis" (1st edition 1922). In *Sämtliche Werke. Vol. 7. Essays I*, S. 9–103. Stuttgart, 1980.
Kater, Michael H. *The Nazi Party: A Social Profile of Members and Leaders, 1919–1945.* Cambridge, MA, 1983.
Kershaw, Ian. *The "Hitler Myth."* Oxford, 1987.
———. *Der Hitler-Mythos. Volksmeinung und Propaganda im Dritten Reich.* Stuttgart, 1980.
———. *Popular Opinion and Political Dissent in the Third Reich: Bavaria 1933–1945.* London, 1983.
———. *Hitler, 1889–1936: Hubris.* New York, 1999.
———. *Hitler, 1936–1945: Nemesis.* New York, 2000.
———. *Nazi Dictatorship: Problems and Perspectives of Interpretation.* London, 2009.
Kettenacker, Lothar. "Sozialpsychologische Aspekte der Führer-Herrschaft." In *Der "Führerstaat": Mythos und Realität. Studien zur Struktur und Politik des Dritten Reiches,* ed. Gerhard Hirschfeld and Lothar Kettenacker, 98–130. Stuttgart, 1981.
Kiehn, Fritz. *Unsere Deibhalde.* Privately printed. Trossingen, without year.
Kißener, Michael, and Joachim Scholtyseck, eds. *Die Führer der Provinz: NS-Biographien aus Baden und Württemberg.* Konstanz, 1997.
Kissenkoetter, Udo. *Gregor Straßer und die NSDAP.* Stuttgart, 1978.
Klee, Ernst. *Das Kulturlexikon zum Dritten Reich: Wer war was vor und nach 1945.* Frankfurt, 2007.
———. *Das Personenlexikon zum Dritten Reich: Wer war was vor und nach 1945.* Frankfurt, 2003.
———. *Euthanasie im NS-Staat: Die Vernichtung lebensunwerten Lebens.* Frankfurt, 1983.
———. *Was sie taten—Was sie wurden: Ärzte, Juristen und andere Beteiligte am Kranken- oder Judenmord.* Frankfurt, 1990.
Kleinmann, Hans-Otto, ed. *Heinrich Krone: Tagebücher 1945–1961.* Düsseldorf, 1995.
Koeh, Robert L. *RKFDV: German Resettlement and Population Policy 1939–1945—a History of the Reichskommission for the Strengthening of Germandom.* New Haven, CT, 1957.
Köster, Roman. *Hugo Boss, 1924–1945: Die Geschichte einer Kleiderfabrik zwischen Weimarer Republik und "Drittem Reich."* Munich, 2011.
Kratzsch, Gerhard. "Das wirtschaftspolitische Gauamt: Der Gauwirtschaftsberater." In *Die NS-Gaue: Regionale Mittelinstanzen im zentralistischen "Führerstaat,"* ed. Jürgen John, Horst Möller, and Thomas Schaarschmidt, 218–233. Munich, 2007.
———. *Der Gauwirtschaftsapparat der NSDAP: Menschenführung—"Arisierung"—Wehrwirtschaft im Gau Westfalen-Süd. Eine Studie zur Herrschaftspraxis im totalitären Staat.* Münster, 1989.
Krause, Peter. *Der Eichmann-Prozess in der deutschen Presse.* Frankfurt, 2002.
Kraushaar, Wolfgang. *Die Protest-Chronik 1949–1959: Eine illustrierte Geschichte von Bewegung, Widerstand und Utopie.* 4 vols. Hamburg, 1996.
Krausnick, Helmut, and Hans-Heinrich Wilhelm. *Die Truppe des Weltanschauungskrieges. Die Einsatzgruppen der Sicherheitspolizei und des SD 1938–1942.* Stuttgart, 1981.
Kreutzmüller, Christoph. *Ausverkauf. Die Vernichtung der jüdischen Gewerbetätigkeit in Berlin 1930–1945.* Berlin, 2012.
Kugler, Anita. "Die Behandlung des feindlichen Vermögens in Deutschland und die 'Selbstverantwortung' der Rüstungsindustrie: Dargestellt am Beispiel der Adam Opel

AG von 1941 bis Anfang 1943." *1999: Zeitschrift für Sozialgeschichte des 20. und 21. Jahrhunderts* 3, no. 2 (1988): 46–78.

Kühne, Thomas. *Belonging and Genocide: Hitler's Community, 1918–1945.* New Haven, CT, 2010.

———. *Kameradschaft: Die Soldaten des nationalsozialistischen Krieges und das 20. Jahrhundert.* Göttingen, 2006.

Kulka, Otto Dov, and Eberhard Jäckel, eds. *Die Juden in den geheimen NS-Stimmungsberichten 1933–1945.* Düsseldorf, 2004.

Kuller, Christiane. "Der arrangierte Normenstaat: Die staatliche Finanzverwaltung und die wirtschaftliche Ausplünderung der deportierten Juden." In *Der prekäre Staat: Herrschen und Verwalten im Nationalsozialismus,* ed. Sven Reichardt and Wolfgang Seibel, 213–239. Frankfurt, 2011.

———. *Bürokratie und Verbrechen: Antisemitische Finanzpolitik und Verwaltungspraxis im nationalsozialistischen Deutschland.* Munich, 2013.

———. *Finanzverwaltung und Judenverfolgung: Die Entziehung jüdischen Vermögens in Bayern während der NS-Zeit.* Munich, 2008.

Küster, Otto. "In Memoriam Dr. Benno Ostertag." *Freiburger Rundbrief,* nos. 33–36 (1956): 71–72. http://www.freidok.uni-freiburg.de/volltexte/7032/pdf/Freiburger_Rundbrief_1956_33_36.pdf (accessed 23 October 2013).

Lang, Jochen von. *Der Hitler-Junge: Baldur von Schirach—der Mann, der Deutschlands Jugend erzog.* Hamburg, 1988.

Lang, Jochen von, and Claus Sibyll. *Der Adjutant: Karl Wolff—der Mann zwischen Hitler und Himmler.* Munich, 1985.

Langewiesche, Dieter. *Liberalismus in Deutschland.* Frankfurt, 1988.

Leinemann, Jürgen. *Sepp Herberger: Ein Leben, eine Legende.* Berlin, 1997.

Lenz, Hanna. *Die offene Hand.* Trossingen, 1957.

Lettow-Vorbeck, Gerd. *Am Fuße des Meru Das Leben von Margarete Trappe, Afrikas großer Jägerin.* Hamburg, 1956.

Levi, Primo. *Die Untergegangenen und die Geretteten.* Munich, 1990.

Levy, Daniel, and Natan Sznaider. *Holocaust and Memory in the Global Age.* Trans. Assenka Oksiloff. Philadelphia, 2006.

Lifton, Robert Jay. *The Nazi Doctors: Medical Killing and the Psychology of Genocide.* New York, 1986.

Lilla, Joachim, Martin Döring, and Andreas Schulz. *Statisten in Uniform: Die Mitglieder des Reichstags 1933–1945—ein biographisches Handbuch. Unter Einbeziehung der völkischen und nationalsozialistischen Reichstagsabgeordneten ab Mai 1924.* Düsseldorf, 2004.

Lillteicher, Jürgen. *Profiteure des NS-Systems? Deutsche Unternehmen und das "Dritte Reich."* Berlin, 2006.

———. *Raub, Recht und Restitution: Die Rückerstattung jüdischen Eigentums in der frühen Bundesrepublik.* Göttingen, 2007.

Lindner, Erik. *Die Reemtsmas: Geschichte einer deutschen Unternehmerfamilie.* Hamburg, 2007.

Lingen, Kerstin von. *SS und Secret Service: "Verschwörung des Schweigens"—die Akte Karl Wolff.* Paderborn, 2010.

Linz, Juan, J. "Typen politischer Regime und die Achtung der Menschenrechte: Historische und länderübergreifende Perspektiven." In *Totalitarismus im 20. Jahrhundert: Eine Bilanz der internationalen Forschung,* ed. Eckhard Jesse, 2nd ed., 519–571. Bonn, 1999.

Longerich, Peter. *"Davon haben wir nichts gewusst!" Die Deutschen und die Judenverfolgung 1933–1945*. Munich 2006.
———. *Goebbels: Biographie*. Munich, 2010.
———. *Heinrich Himmler: A Life*. Oxford, 2011.
———. *Politik der Vernichtung. Eine Gesamtdarstellung der nationalsozialistischen Judenverfolgung*. Munich, 1998.
Lübbe, Hermann. "Der Nationalsozialismus im deutschen Nachkriegsbewußtsein." *Historische Zeitschrift* 236 (1983): 579–599.
———. *Vom Parteigenossen zum Bundesbürger: Über beschwiegene und historisierte Vergangenheiten*. Munich, 2007.
Lüdtke, Alf, Inge Marßolek, and Adelheid von Saldern, eds. *Amerikanisierung: Traum und Alptraum im Deutschland des 20. Jahrhunderts*. Stuttgart, 1996.
Lurie, Samuel. *Private Investment in a Controlled Economy: Germany 1933–1939*. New York, 1947.
Maier, Reinhold. *Bedrängte Familie*. Tübingen, 1962.
Maissen, Thomas. *Verweigerte Erinnerung: Nachrichtenlose Vermögen und Schweizer Weltkriegsdebatte 1989–2004*. 2nd ed. Zürich, 2005.
Mallmann, Klaus-Michael, and Gerhard Paul. *Herrschaft und Alltag: Ein Industrierevier im Dritten Reich*. Bonn, 1991.
Mann, Heinrich. *The Patrioteer*. New York, 1922.
Manz, Mathias. *Stagnation und Aufschwung in der französischen Besatzungszone 1945–1948*. Ostfildern, 1985.
Matz, Klaus-Jürgen. *Reinhold Maier (1889–1971): Eine politische Biographie*. Düsseldorf, 1989.
McKale, Donald M. *The Nazi Party Courts: Hitler's Management of Conflict in His Movement 1921–1945*. Lawrence, KS, 1974.
McNab, Chris. *World War II Data Book: The SS, 1923–1945*. London, 2009.
Mechler, Wilhelm. "Hermann Dietrich: Kehler Bürgermeister 1908–1914, Badischer Minister—Reichsminister—Vizekanzler." *Die Ortenau: Zeitschrift des Historischen Vereins für Mittelbaden* 60 (1980): 51–64.
Meinecke, Friedrich. *The German Catastrophe: Reflections and Recollections*. Cambridge, Mass., 1950.
Meinl, Susanne, and Jutta Zwilling. *Legalisierter Raub: Die Ausplünderung der Juden im Nationalsozialismus durch die Reichsfinanzverwaltung in Hessen*. Wissenschaftliche Reihe des Fritz-Bauer-Instituts 10. Frankfurt, 2004.
Meyer, Sibylle. *Das Theater mit der Hausarbeit*. Frankfurt, 1982.
Michael, Robert, and Karin Doerr. *Nazi-Deutsch/Nazi-German: An English Lexicon of the Language of the Third Reich*. Westport, Conn., 2002.
Michel, Rudi, ed. *Fritz Walter: Die Legende des deutschen Fußballs*. Stuttgart, 1995.
Müller, Arnd. *Geschichte der Juden in Nürnberg 1146–1945*. Nuremberg, 1968.
Müller, Roland. *Stuttgart zur Zeit des Nationalsozialismus*. Stuttgart, 1988.
Müller, Rolf-Dieter. *Der Manager der Kriegswirtschaft: Hans Kehrl—ein Unternehmer in der Politik des Dritten Reiches*. Essen, 1999.
———. "Hans Kehrl: Ein Parteibuch-Industrieller im 'Dritten Reich'?" *Jahrbuch für Wirtschaftsgeschichte*, no. 2 (1999): 195–213.
Mundorff, Martin. *Eislingen und seine Fabriken*. Eislingen, 2001.
———. "Industrialisierung in Eislingen: Soziale Veränderungen und die Entwicklung der Arbeiterbewegung." *Hohenstaufen* 10 (2000): 175–216.

Münzel, Martin. *Die jüdischen Mitglieder der deutschen Wirtschaftselite 1927–1955: Verdrängung—Emigration—Rückkehr.* Paderborn, 2006.
Neliba, Günter. *Wilhelm Frick: Der Legalist des Unrechtsstaates.* Paderborn, 1992.
Nichol, John, and Tony Rennell. *The Untold Story of Allied Prisoners of War in Germany 1944–1945.* London, 2003.
Niethammer, Lutz. *Die Mitläuferfabrik: Die Entnazifizierung am Beispiel Bayerns.* Bonn, 1982. Originally published 1972.
Oberkofler, Gerhard, and Peter Goller. "Betrachtungen zur bürgerlich-restaurativen Universitätsideologie: Am Beispiel des Innbrucker Universitätslebens nach 1945." In *Repraesentatio Mundi: Festschrift zum 70. Geburtstag von Hans Heinz Holz,* ed. Hermann Klenner and Hans Heinz Holz, 394–398. Cologne, 1997.
Office of Military Government for Germany (US). *Denazification (Cumulative Review). Report of the Military Governor (1 April 1947–30 April 1948).* No. 34. http://archive.org/stream/Denazification/OfficeOfTheMilitaryGovernmentForGermany-Denazificationen1948174P.Scan_djvu.txt (accessed 4 September 2012).
Orlow, Dietrich. *The History of The Nazi Party.* Vol. 1, *1919–1933.* Pittsburgh, 1969.
Padfield, Peter. *Himmler Reichsführer-SS.* London, 1990.
Peukert, Detlev. *"Volksgenossen" und "Gemeinschaftsfremde": Anpassung, Ausmerze und Aufbegehren unter dem Nationalsozialismus.* Cologne, 1982.
Pieper, Kathrin. *Musealisierung des Holocaust: Das Jüdische Museum Berlin und das U.S. Holocaust Memorial Museum in Washington D.C. Ein Vergleich.* Cologne, 2006.
Plato, von Alexander. "'Wirtschaftskapitäne': Biographische Selbstkonstruktionen von Unternehmern der Nachkriegszeit." In *Modernisierung im Wiederaufbau: Die Westdeutsche Gesellschaft der 50er Jahre,* ed. Axel Schildt and Arnold Sywottek, 377–391. Bonn, 1993.
Pommerin, Rainer. *Geschichte der TU Dresden, 1828–2003.* Cologne, 2003.
Priemel, Kim Christian. *Flick: Eine Konzerngeschichte vom Kaiserreich bis zur Bundesrepublik.* Göttingen, 2007.
Raithel, Thomas. *Fußballweltmeisterschaft 1954: Sport—Geschichte—Mythos.* Munich, 2004.
Rasch, Manfred, and Gerald D. Feldman, eds. *August Thyssen und Hugo Stinnes: Ein Briefwechsel, 1898–1922.* Munich, 2003.
Rauh, Cornelia. "'Angewandte Geschichte' als Apologetik-Agentur? Wie Erlanger Forscher Unternehmensgeschichte 'kapitalisieren.'" *Zeitschrift für Unternehmensgeschichte/Journal of Business History* 56 (2011): 102–115.
———. "Wirtschaftsbürger im 'Doppelstaat': Zur Kritik der neueren Forschung." In *Unternehmen im Nationalsozialismus: Zur Historisierung einer Forschungskonjunktur,* ed. Norbert Frei and Tim Schanetzky, 100–115. Göttingen, 2010.
Rauh-Kühne, Cornelia. "Die Entnazifizierung und die deutsche Gesellschaft." *Archiv für Sozialgeschichte* 35 (1995): 35–70.
———. "Die Unternehmer und die Entnazifizierung der Wirtschaft in Württemberg-Hohenzollern." In Rauh-Kühne and Ruck, *Regionale Eliten,* 305–332.
———. *Katholisches Milieu und Kleinstadtgesellschaft: Ettlingen, 1918–1939.* Sigmaringen, 1991.
———. "Life Rewarded the Latecomers: Denazification during the Cold War." Trans. Edward G. Fichtner and Sally Robertson. In *Germany and the United States in the Era of the Cold War 1945–1990,* vol. 1, ed. Detlef Junker, 65–72. Cambridge, 2004.
———. "Mittelständische Unternehmer in Konflikt mit Partei und Staat." In *Formen des Widerstandes im Südwesten 1933–1945,* ed. Thomas Schnabel, 105–114. Ulm, 1994.

———. „Katholikinnen zwischen Vereinnahmung und Resistenz". In *Frauen gegen die Diktatur – Widerstand und Verfolgung im nationalsozialistischen Deutschland*, ed. Christl Wickert, 34–51. Berlin 1995.

———. "Sozialpartnerschaft aus dem Geiste der Kriegskameradschaft: Hans-Constantin Paulssen (1892–1984)." In *Deutsche Unternehmer zwischen Kriegswirtschaft und Wiederaufbau*, ed. Paul Erker and Toni Pierenkemper, 109–192. Munich, 1999.

———. "Zwischen 'Verantwortlichem Wirkungskreis' und 'häuslichem Glanz': Innenansichten wirtschaftsbürgerlicher Familien." In *Die wirtschaftsbürgerliche Elite in Deutschland im 20. Jahrhundert*, ed. Dieter Ziegler, 215–249. Göttingen, 2000.

Rauh-Kühne, Cornelia, and Michael Ruck, eds. *Regionale Eliten zwischen Diktatur und Demokratie: Baden und Württemberg 1930–1952*. Munich, 1993.

Rebentisch, Dieter. *Führerstaat und Verwaltung im Zweiten Weltkrieg: Verfassungsentwicklung und Verwaltungspolitik 1939–1945*. Stuttgart, 1989.

———. *Schwere Zeiten. Die Frankfurter Wirtschaft zwischen Republik, Diktatur und Krieg 1914 – 1945*. In *"Dem Flor der hiesigen Handlung" 200 Jahre Industrie- und Handelskammer Frankfurt am Main*, ed. Werner Plumpe and Dieter Rebentisch, 178–217. Frankfurt, 2008.

Reibel, Carl-Wilhelm. *Das Fundament der Diktatur: Die NSDAP-Ortsgruppen 1932–1945*. Paderborn, 2002.

Reichardt, Sven. *Faschistische Kampfbünde: Gewalt und Gemeinschaft im italienischen Squadrismus und in der deutschen SA*. Cologne, 2002.

Reichel, Peter. *Der schöne Schein des Dritten Reiches: Faszination und Gewalt des Faschismus*. Munich, 1991.

Rempel, Gerhard. "Gottlob Berger: 'Ein Schwabengeneral der Tat.'" In *Die SS: Elite unter dem Totenkopf—30 Lebensläufe*, ed. Ronald Smelser and Enrico Syring, 45–59. Paderborn, 2000.

Riedel, Matthias. *Eisen und Kohle für das Dritte Reich: Paul Pleigers Stellung in der NS-Wirtschaft*. Göttingen, 1973.

Rigg, Brian Mark. "Riggs Liste," http://www.zeit.de/1997/15/Riggs_Liste (accessed 23 September 2013).

Roth, Claudia. *Parteikreis und Kreisleiter der NSDAP unter besonderer Berücksichtigung Bayerns*. Munich, 1997.

Ruck, Michael. *Korpsgeist und Staatsbewußtsein: Beamte im deutschen Südwesten 1928 bis 1972*. Munich, 1996.

Rüther, Martin. "Zur Sozialpolitik bei Klöckner-Humboldt-Deutz während des Nationalsozialismus: 'Die Masse der Arbeiterschaft muß aufgespalten werden.'" *Zeitschrift für Unternehmensgeschichte* 33 (1988): 81–117.

Saldern, Adelheid von, "Victims or Perpetrators? Controversies about the Role of Women in the Nazi State." In *Nazism and German Society 1933–1945*, ed. David Crew, 141–166. London, 1994.

Sauer, Paul. *Wilhelm Murr: Hitlers Statthalter in Württemberg*. Tübingen, 1998.

———. "Württemberg im Nationalsozialismus." In *Handbuch der baden-württembergischen Geschichte*, vol. 4, *Die Länder seit 1918*, ed. Hansmartin Schwarzmaier and Gerhard Taddey, 231–319. Stuttgart, 2004.

Sauer, Paul, and Israelitische Religionsgemeinschaft Württembergs. *Jüdisches Leben im Wandel der Zeit: 170 Jahre Israelitische Religionsgemeinschaft Württembergs*. Berlingen, 2002.

Schäfer, Ingeburg, and Susanne Klockmann. *"Mutter mochte Himmler nie": Die Geschichte einer SS-Familie*. Hamburg, 1999.

Schaumburg-Lippe, Friedrich Christian Prinz zu. *Dr. Goebbels: Ein Porträt des Propagandaministers.* Berlin, 1963.

———. *Gegen eine Welt von Vorurteilen.* Breslau, 1937.

Scherer, Peter, and Peter Schaaf, eds. *Dokumente zur Geschichte der Arbeiterbewegung in Württemberg und Baden 1848–1949.* Stuttgart, 1984.

Schilling, Heinz. *Kleinbürger. Mentalität und Lebensstil.* Frankfurt, 2003.

Schitag. *Siebzig Jahre im Dienste der Wirtschaft 1919–1989: Schitag Schwäbische Treuhand-Aktiengesellschaft.* Stuttgart, 1989.

Schmidt, Gilya Gerda. *Süssen Is Now Free of Jews: World War II, the Holocaust, and Rural Judaism.* New York, 2012.

Schmidt, Sabine. "Vom Hilfsarbeiter zum Kreisleiter. Eugen Maier, NSDAP-Kreisleiter von Ulm." In Kißener and Scholtyseck, *Führer der Provinz,* 361–404.

Schmidt-Bachem, Heinz. *Aus Papier: Eine Kultur- und Wirtschaftsgeschichte der Papierverarbeitenden Industrie in Deutschland.* Berlin, 2011.

Schmiechen-Ackermann, Detlef. "Einführung." In Schmiechen-Ackermann, *"Volksgemeinschaft,"* 13–54.

———, ed. *"Volksgemeinschaft": Mythos der NS-Propaganda, wirkungsmächtige soziale Verheißung oder soziale Realität im "Dritten Reich"?* Paderborn, 2012.

Schnabel, Thomas, ed. *Die Machtergreifung in Südwestdeutschland: Das Ende der Weimarer Republik in Baden und Württemberg 1928–1933.* Stuttgart, 1982.

———. "Die NSDAP in Württemberg 1928–1933: Die Schwächen einer regionalen Parteiorganisation." In *Die Machtergreifung in Südwestdeutschland: Das Ende der Weimarer Republik in Baden und Württemberg 1928–1933,* ed. Thomas Schnabel, 49–82. Stuttgart, 1982.

———. *Württemberg zwischen Weimar und Bonn: 1928 bis 1945/46.* Stuttgart, 1986.

Schneider, Jürgen, with Peter Moser. "Gustav Schickedanz (1895–1977)." *Fränkische Lebensbilder,* n.s., 12 (1986): 307–327.

Schoenbaum, David. *Hitler's Social Revolution: Class and Status in Nazi Germany 1933–1939.* New York, 1966.

Schöllgen, Gregor. *Gustav Schickedanz: Biographie eines Revolutionärs.* Berlin, 2010.

Scholtyseck, Joachim. *Der Aufstieg der Quandts: Eine deutsche Unternehmerdynastie.* Munich, 2011.

———. "'Der Mann aus dem Volk,' Wilhelm Murr, Gauleiter und Reichsstatthalter in Württemberg-Hohenzollern." In Kißener and Scholtyseck, *Führer der Provinz,* 447–502.

———. *Robert Bosch und der liberale Widerstand gegen Hitler 1933–1945.* Munich, 1999.

———. "Der 'Schwabenherzog': Gottlob Berger, SS-Obergruppenführer." In Kißener and Scholtyseck, *Führer der Provinz,* 77–110.

Schuhladen-Krämer, Jürgen. "Die Exekutoren des Terrors: Hermann Mattheiß, Walter Stahlecker, Friedrich Mußgay, Leiter der Geheimen Staatspolizeileitstelle Stuttgart." In Kißener and Scholtyseck, *Führer der Provinz,* 405–444.

Schullze, Erich, ed. *Gesetz zur Befreiung von Nationalsozialismus und Militarismus.* 3rd ed. Munich, 1948.

Schulz, Gerhard. "Wilhelm Frick." In *Neue Deutsche Biographie,* 5: 432–433. Berlin, 1961. http://daten.digitale-sammlungen.de/0001/bsb00016321/images/index.html?seite=448 (accessed 25 October 2013).

Schumacher, Martin, ed. *M.d.R. Die Reichstagsabgeordneten der Weimarer Republik in der Zeit des Nationalsozialismus.* 3rd ed. Düsseldorf, 1994.

Schwarz, Birgit. *Geniewahn: Hitler und die Kunst*. Vienna, 2009.
———. *Hitlers Museum: Die Fotoalben "Gemäldegalerie Linz"—Dokumente zum "Führermuseum."* Vienna, 2004.
Schwarz, Gudrun. *Eine Frau an seiner Seite: Ehefrauen in der "SS-Sippengemeinschaft."* Hamburg, 1997.
Selig, Wolfram. *"Arisierung" in München: Die Vernichtung jüdischer Existenz 1937–1939*. Berlin, 2004.
Selle, Gert. "Die Sinnlichkeit der Gewalt: Oder—das Kleinbürgertum als Produzent und Adressat faschistischer Sozialisationsstrategien." In *"Neue Erziehung," "Neue Menschen": Ansätze zur Erziehungs- und Bildungsreform in Deutschland zwischen Kaiserreich und Diktatur*, ed. Ulrich Hermann, 91–103. Weinheim, 1987.
Senfft, Alexandra. *Schweigen tut weh: Eine deutsche Familiengeschichte*. Berlin, 2007.
Simms, Brendan. "Karl Wolff: Der Schlichter." In *Die SS: Elite unter dem Totenkopf*, ed. Ronald Smelser and Enrico Syring, 441–456. Paderborn, 2000.
Sinz, Fritz. *Fritz Kiehn: Portrait eines Unternehmers*. Trossingen, 1960.
Soell, Hartmut. *Fritz Erler: Eine politische Biographie*. 2 vols. Berlin, 1976.
Sontheimer, Kurt. *Antidemokratisches Denken in der Weimarer Republik*. Munich, 1968.
Speer, Albert. *Spandauer Tagebücher*. Berlin, 1975.
Spiliotis, Susanne-Sophia. *Verantwortung und Rechtsfrieden: Die Stiftungsinitiative der deutschen Wirtschaft*. Frankfurt, 2003.
Spoerer, Marc. "Die Automobilindustrie im Dritten Reich: Wachstum um jeden Preis?" In *Unternehmen im Nationalsozialismus*, ed. Lothar Gall and Manfred Pohl, 61–68. Munich, 1998.
Spoerer, Mark. "Zwangsarbeit im Dritten Reich und Entschädigung: Ein Überblick." In *Zwangsarbeit in der Kirche: Entschädigung, Versöhnung und historische Aufarbeitung*, ed. Klaus Barwig, Dieter R. Bauer, and Karl-Joseph Hummel, 15–46. Stuttgart, 2001.
Sporhan-Krempel, Lore. *Papier aus dem Filstal einst und heute*. Stuttgart, 1955.
Stachura, Peter D. "Der Fall Strasser. Strasser, Hitler and National Socialism, 1930–1932." In *The Shaping of the Nazi State*, 88–130. London, 1978.
———. *Gregor Strasser and the Rise of Nazism*. London, 1983.
Steinbacher, Sybille. "Frauen im 'Führerstaat.'" In *Das "Dritte Reich": Eine Einführung*, ed. Dietmar Süß and Winfried Süß, 103–120. Munich, 2008.
———, ed. *"Volksgenossinnen": Frauen in der NS-Volksgemeinschaft*. Göttingen, 2007.
Stiekel, Sebastian. *Arisierung und Wiedergutmachung in Celle*. Bielefeld, 2008.
Sting, Paul. "Allzeit Fuchs und Has': Hans Gmelin prägte 20 Jahre Tübinger Kommunalgeschichte." *Tübinger Blätter* 62 (1975): 51–53.
Stockhorst, Erich. *Fünftausend Köpfe: Wer war was im Dritten Reich*. Velbert, 1967.
Stöss, Richard. "Der Gesamtdeutsche Block/BHE." In *Parteien-Handbuch: Die Parteien der Bundesrepublik Deutschland 1945–1980*, vol. 2., ed. Richard Stöss, 1424–1459. Opladen, 1984.
Stöver, Bernd. *Volksgemeinschaft im Dritten Reich: Die Konsensbereitschaft der Deutschen aus der Sicht sozialistischer Exilberichte*. Düsseldorf, 1993.
Surmann, Jan. *Shoah-Erinnerung und Restitution: Die US-Geschichtspolitik am Ende des 20. Jahrhunderts*. Stuttgart, 2012.
Tauber, Kurt A. *Beyond Eagle and Swastika: German Nationalism since 1945*. 2 vols. Middletown, CT, 1967.
Thacker, Toby. *Joseph Goebbels: Life and Death*. Basingstoke, UK, 2009.

Thamer, Hans-Ulrich, and Simone Erpel, eds. *Hitler und die Deutschen: Volksgemeinschaft und Verbrechen.* Dresden, 2010.
Thießen, Malte. "Erinnerungen an die 'Volksgemeinschaft': Integration und Exklusion im kommunalen und kommunikativen Gedächtnis." In Schmiechen-Ackermann, *"Volksgemeinschaft,"* 319–334.
Thomas, Heinrich. *Der menschenfreundliche Löwe aus Chicago: Historische Untersuchung der amerikanischen Wesenszüge des Lionismus.* Wiesbaden, 1996.
Tönsmeyer, Tatjana. *Das Dritte Reich und die Slowakei 1939–1945: Politischer Alltag zwischen Kooperation und Eigensinn.* Paderborn, 2003.
Tooze, Adam. *The Wages of Destruction: The Making and Breaking of the Nazi Economy.* London, 2006.
Trevor-Roper, Hugh R. *Hitlers letzte Tage.* Zurich, 1946.
Tuchel, Johannes. *Am Großen Wannsee 56–58: Von der Villa Minoux zum Haus der Wannsee-Konferenz.* Berlin, 1992.
Turner, Henry Ashby. *German Big Business and the Rise of Hitler.* New York, 1985.
———. *Die Großunternehmer und der Aufstieg Hitlers.* Berlin, 1985.
Turner, Henry Ashby, Jr. "Otto Wagener: Der vergessene Vertraute Hitlers." In *Die braune Elite 2: 21 weitere biographische Skizzen,* ed. Ronald Smelser, Enrico Syring, and Rainer Zitelmann, 441–456. Darmstadt, 1993.
Ulmer, Martin. *Antisemitismus in Stuttgart: Studien zum öffentlichen Diskurs und Alltag.* Berlin, 2011.
Vogelsang, Reinhard. *Der Freundeskreis Himmler.* Göttingen, 1972.
Vogler, Bernard, and Michel Hau. *Histoire économique de l'Alsace.* Strasbourg, 1997.
Volkov, Shulamit. *Die Juden in Deutschland 1780–1918.* Munich, 1994.
Vollnhals, Clemens, ed. *Entnazifizierung: Politische Säuberung und Rehabilitierung in den vier Besatzungszonen 1945–1949.* Munich, 1991.
Vollnhals, Clemens, and Jörg Osterloh, eds. *NS-Prozesse und deutsche Öffentlichkeit: Besatzungszeit, frühe Bundesrepublik und DDR.* Göttingen, 2011.
Vondung, Klaus. *Magie und Manipulation: Ideologischer Kult und politische Religion des Nationalsozialismus.* Göttingen, 1971.
Voß, Reimer. *Steuern im Dritten Reich: Vom Recht zum Unrecht unter der Herrschaft des Nationalsozialismus.* Munich, 1995.
Weale, Adrian. *Army of Evil. A History of the SS.* Berkeley, 2012.
Wehler, Hans-Ulrich. "Die Geburtsstunde des deutschen Kleinbürgertums." In *Bürger in der Gesellschaft der Neuzeit,* ed. Hans-Jürgen Puhle, 199–209. Göttingen, 1991.
Weisbrod, Bernd. *Schwerindustrie in der Weimarer Republik. Interessenpolitik zwischen Stabilisierung und Krise.* Wuppertal, 1978.
Weiß, Hermann, ed. *Biographisches Lexikon zum Dritten Reich.* Frankfurt, 1998.
Welzer, Harald, Sabine Moller, and Karoline Tschuggnall. *"Opa war kein Nazi": Nationalsozialismus und Holocaust im Familiengedächtnis.* Frankfurt, 2002.
Werner, Marion. *Vom Adolf-Hitler-Platz zum Ebertplatz: Eine Kulturgeschichte der Kölner Straßennamen seit 1933.* Cologne, 2008.
Wheeler-Bennett, John. *The Nemesis of Power: The German Army in Politics 1918–1945.* 2nd ed. Basingstoke, UK, 2005.
Widmann, Peter. "Reichskommissar für die Festigung deutschen Volkstums." In *Enzyklopädie des Nationalsozialismus,* ed. Wolfgang Benz, Hermann Graml, and Hermann Weiß, 5th ed., 740. Munich, 2007.

Wildt, Michael. *Generation of the Unbound: The Leadership Corps of the Reich Security Main Office*. Jerusalem, 2002.
———. *Volksgemeinschaft als Selbstermächtigung: Gewalt gegen Juden in der deutschen Provinz 1919 bis 1939*. Hamburg, 2007.
Wilhelm, Friedrich. *Die Polizei im NS-Staat*. Paderborn, 1997.
———. "Die württembergische Polizei im Dritten Reich." PhD diss., University of Stuttgart, 1989.
Wilhelm, Hans-Heinrich. *Die Einsatzgruppe A der Sicherheitspolizei und des SD 1941/42*. Frankfurt, 1996.
Winkel, Harald. *Geschichte der württembergischen Industrie- und Handelskammern Heilbronn, Reutlingen, Stuttgart/Mittlerer Neckar und Ulm 1933–1980: Zum 125-jährigen Bestehen*. Stuttgart, 1980.
Winkler, Heinrich August. *Der Schein der Normalität: Arbeiter und Arbeiterbewegung in der Weimarer Republik 1924 bis 1930*. 2nd rev. ed. Berlin, 1988.
———. *Weimar 1918–1933. Die Geschichte der ersten deutschen Demokratie*. Munich, 1993.
Witek, Hans. "'Arisierungen' in Wien: Aspekte nationalsozialistischer Enteignungspolitik 1938–1940." In *NS-Herrschaft in Österreich 1938–1945*, ed. Emmerich Talos, Ernst Hanisch, and Wolfgang Neugebauer, 199–216. Vienna, 1988.
Wolfrum, Edgar. *Französische Besatzungspolitik und deutsche Sozialdemokratie: Politische Neuansätze in der "vergessenen Zone" bis zur Bildung des Südweststaates 1945–1952*. Düsseldorf, 1991.
Woller, Hans. *Gesellschaft und Politik in der amerikanischen Besatzungszone: Die Region Ansbach und Fürth*. Munich, 1986.
Wortmann, Michael. *Baldur von Schirach*. Cologne, 1982.
Wörtz, Ulrich. "Programmatik und Führerprinzip: Das Problem des Straßer-Kreises in der NSDAP." PhD diss., University of Erlangen-Nürnberg, 1966.
Zeller, Joachim. "Umstritten, vergessen: Der Tierplastiker Fritz Behn." In *Tierplastik deutscher Bildhauer des 20. Jahrhunderts: Sammlung Karl. H. Knauf*, ed. Ursel Berger and Günter Ladwig, 42–51. Berlin, 2009.
Zimmermann, Moshe. "Die transnationale Holocaust-Erinnerung." In *Transnationale Geschichte: Themen, Tendenzen und Theorien*, ed. Gunilla Budde, Sebastian Conrad, and Oliver Janz, 202–216. Göttingen, 2006.
Zinke, Peter. "'Er drohte wieder mit der Gauleitung': Gustav Schickedanz und die Arisierung." *Jahrbuch des Nürnberger Instituts für NS-Forschung und Jüdische Geschichte* (2008): 63–80.

INDEX

Achenbach, Ernst, 247, 248, 250, 255, 257, 258, 276
Adenauer, Konrad 7, 124, 247, 248, 259, 274, 294, 295, 297, 298, 299, 304, 334, 335, 342, 343, 359
Amann, Max 76
Arendt, Hannah 68, 340

Bärlin, Ragnhild 207
Bärlin, Walter 30, 156, 162, 182, 183, 184, 207, 306
Bäuerle, Georg 190
Bajohr, Frank 9, 98, 99, 100, 103, 108, 120, 121, 122, 123, 124, 128, 337, 340
Baptist, Immanuel 177, 181, 185, 186
Barkai, Avraham 121, 125, 332, 337, 340
Beck, Johann 70, 225
Behn, Fritz 303, 304, 305
Beinhorn, Elly 164, 207
Berchtold, Hermann 55, 57, 70
Berger, Gottlieb 63, 68, 72, 82, 99, 122, 136, 180, 214, 219, 226, 230, 251, 252, 285, 297
Bernlöhr, Fritz 114, 127
Best, Werner 55, 247, 250, 257, 258, 259, 296
Binder, Paul 86, 251
Bismarck, Klaus v. 180
Bismarck, Otto v. 304
Bloch, Siegfried 215, 216
Bormann, Martin 219
Brack, Viktor 261
Brandt, Rudolf 134
Brandt, Willy 258
Braun, Eva 61
Brinkmann, Carl 114, 267, 270, 305, 310
Broszat, Martin 4
Brüning, Heinrich 47, 48
Bütefisch, Heinrich 62
Büttner, Hugo 104, 122, 163
Buch, Walter 96

Buchheim, Hans 97, 99
Bugatti, Ettore 230, 252
Burmeister, Wilhelm 232, 234, 235

Clinton, Bill 314

Dahlgrün, Rolf 262, 299
Dahrendorf, Ralf 336
Daluege, Kurt 59, 70, 134, 137, 167, 296
Dehlinger, Alfred 54
Diebitsch, Karl 219
Diesing, Heinz 264, 268
Dietrich, Sepp 72
Diewerge, Wolfgang 250
Dignus, August 121
Dreher, Wilhelm 169
Drost, Sebastian 317

Ebert, Friedrich 24
Eichmann, Adolf 68, 135, 307, 326, 336
Elsas, Max 105
Elsas, Willy 105
Erler, Fritz 46, 152, 236, 237, 238, 239, 240, 244
Estrade, Jean Lucien 199, 201, 218, 219, 245, 246

Fähndrich, Ernst 66, 72, 134–37, 206, 230, 231, 261
Fallscheer, Fritz 260
Feder, Gottfried 41, 219
Fichte, Johann Gottlieb 106, 123
Fleck, Fritz 234, 235, 244, 252
Fleischer, David Moritz 107, 110, 115, 116, 128, 213, 224
Fleischer, Grete 116, 128
Fleischer, Hermann 107, 109, 112, 113, 115, 116, 123, 124, 125, 126, 127, 129, 210, 211, 213, 214, 216, 217, 219
Fleischer, Kuno 107, 110, 112, 114, 115, 125, 126, 127, 128, 129, 210, 224

Fleischer, Walther 107, 116, 124, 210
Flick, Friedrich 62, 258, 332, 350
Fegelein, Hermann 61, 71, 219
Frank, (SS-Obergruppenführer) 180
Frankfurter, David 255
Frevert, Walter 274
Frick, Wilhelm 41, 48, 49, 50, 51, 52, 53, 67, 68, 71, 73, 75, 96, 165, 219
Funk, Walther 68, 92, 164, 296

Gasser, Herbert 264
Gebhardt, Karl 137, 142
Geiger, Kurt 291
Gengler, Karl 248, 251, 294, 295, 298, 299
Gesler, Helmut 260
Glaub, Heinrich 78, 79, 98, 111, 124, 125, 126, 129, 211, 213, 216, 224
Glück, Otto 55
Gmelin, Hans 291, 300, 301, 309, 320
Göring, Hermann 5, 66, 118, 120, 128, 129, 274, 328
Goebbels, Joseph 42, 67, 155, 167, 248, 258, 284, 286
Gottberg, Curt v. 225
Grimm, Friedrich 247, 248, 249, 250, 251, 256, 333, 337
Grimm, Hans 250
Gühring, Max 336
Gühring, Oskar 336
Gustloff, Wilhelm 247, 255

Häffner, Martin x, 22, 35, 69, 70, 182, 277, 316
Hanfstängel, Ernst 250
Haux, Friedrich 241, 243, 255
Hayler, Franz 62, 71
Heck, Bruno 294, 298, 307, 359
Heil, Richard 264, 270
Helfferich, Emil 62
Herberger, Sepp 285
Herbert, Ulrich 135
Heß, Rudolf 37, 52, 75, 118, 129
Heydrich, Reinhard 55, 114, 134, 219
Himmler, Heinrich x, 3, 48, 53, 55, 56, 59–65, 67–69, 71, 72, 93, 96, 98, 107, 114, 118, 129, 134–37, 142, 179–81, 187, 189, 205, 207, 209, 217, 219, 226, 230, 233, 261, 298, 299, 302, 319
Hitler, Adolf 1, 3, 5, 7, 8, 26, 35, 36, 37, 39, 40, 42, 43, 44, 45, 47, 48, 49, 50, 52–54, 56, 59, 61–63, 67, 68, 69, 70–72, 75–76, 85, 98, 99, 107, 108, 113, 143, 148, 150, 151, 152, 153, 154, 155, 158, 159, 162, 163, 165, 167, 169, 171, 163, 177, 178, 181, 182, 187, 188, 190, 201, 208, 247, 248, 250, 261, 262, 263, 264, 265, 296, 297, 298, 304, 310, 315, 319, 325, 333, 334
Höpken, Gustav Dietrich 262, 263, 264
Hörstmann, Helmuth 320
Hoffmann, Heinrich 180
Hohner, Ernst 28, 30, 42, 144, 146, 156, 159, 169, 170, 181, 182, 188, 190, 192, 193, 195, 199, 276, 277, 278, 279, 281, 282, 285, 290, 294, 296, 299, 306, 307
Hohner, Karl 146
Hohner, Matthias 279
Hohner, Will 19, 20, 22, 23, 153
Hommel, Conrad 286, 290
Huber, Gottlieb 148, 156, 166, 177, 193, 197, 200, 204, 208, 259, 262, 267
Hunger, Toni 36, 162, 163, 166

Isenburg, Helene Elisabeth Prinzessin v. 250

Kaess, Carl 226, 227
Kaiser, Jakob 298
Kalckreuth, Barbara Gräfin v. 286
Kalbfell, Oskar 237
Kappeler, Otto 259
Kastner, Arnold 302
Kaufmann, Werner 206, 207, 230, 231, 234, 235, 252, 253, 267, 331
Kaul, Kurt 98, 101
Kehrl, Hans 4, 5, 9, 24, 27, 62, 73, 326, 328
Keppler, Wilhelm 4, 5, 62, 73
Kessler, Max 290
Kessler, Philipp 132–33, 142
Kershaw, Ian 87
Kiehn, Berta 15, 18, 21, 22, 36, 45, 55, 56, 147, 148, 151, 152, 154, 163, 164, 172, 176, 180, 181, 195, 197, 199, 204, 205, 207, 208, 209, 231, 235, 263, 275, 276, 279, 286, 296, 297, 305, 306, 207
Kiehn, Herbert 21, 37, 61, 148, 172–73, 297, 303
Kiehn, Herbert E. 70, 137, 142–43, 152, 168, 174, 175, 217, 231, 246, 260, 261, 262, 263, 265, 266, 269, 289, 301, 307, 310, 315, 317
Kiehn, Margarete (Gretl) 11, 21, 134, 136–37, 147, 150, 152, 164, 175, 206, 207, 230, 231, 261, 263, 264, 265, 266, 267, 287, 310

Kiehn, Otto 57, 58
Kienmayer, Franz 64
Kienzle, Emil 158, 165
Kiesinger, Georg 291, 294
Kilpper, Gustav 46
Kissel, Wilhelm vii, 77
Kissinger, Henry 335
Köhler, Walter 250
Kranefuß, Fritz 62, 63, 71, 133, 142
Kraut, Wilhelm 290, 301
Krone, Heinrich 294, 298
Krupp, Gustav v. Bohlen und Halbach 247
Künzel, Otto 244, 254, 255
Kube, Wilhelm 219
Kunz, Hugo 199

Lachenmaier, Otto 102, 106, 110, 112–13, 117, 121, 123, 125–29
Lauterwasser, Siegfried 303
Lehnich, Oswald 147, 152, 204
Lemmer, Ernst 298
Lenz, Hans 306
Lerner, Jüd. Familie 38, 302, 331
Ley, Robert 45
Lindemann, Karl 62
Löns, Hermann 66, 166
Lohse, Hinrich 96
Lübbe, Hermann 7, 283
Lüer, Carl 138, 301
Luther, Martin 150
Lutze, Viktor 230

Maag, Christian Ludwig 336
Maier, Eugen 79, 95, 96
Maier, Reinhold 55, 71, 72, 108, 109, 214
Maier, Clemens 318
Malsen-Ponickau, Johannes Erasmus Freiherr v. 69
Mangoux, Corbin de 238
Mann, Heinrich 151
Martin, Benno 118
Maschke, Rudolf 276, 277, 278, 280, 282, 287, 291, 306
Mattheiß, Hermann 5, 54, 55, 56, 57, 58, 59, 60, 69–70, 152, 207, 209, 217, 218, 225
Mattheiß, Lolo 56, 207
Mauthe, Fritz 34
Mayer, Eberhard 112, 123, 125–27, 129, 219, 225
Mayer, Ignaz 119
Mayer, Thaddäus 194, 225, 226
Menzel, Adolf 63, 64, 71, 72, 92

Mergenthaler, Christian 49, 68, 85, 154, 155, 204
Messner, Christian 36, 58, 70, 153, 177, 178, 179, 193, 194, 204, 275
Metzger, Gertrud 244, 254
Middelhauve, Friedrich 250, 262
Milch, Erhard 233
Minoux, Friedrich 138, 139, 140, 143, 215
Mönning, Hugo 247
Mosthaf, Walter 199
Müller, Gebhard 1, 199, 221, 228, 233, 234, 245, 254, 291, 332
Müller, Hermann 23
Murr, Wilhelm 1, 46, 48, 49, 55, 68, 74, 75, 80, 82, 84, 85, 92, 94, 96, 97, 103, 104, 106, 117, 122, 145, 146, 147, 152, 162, 163, 165, 169, 188, 190, 213, 319, 326, 351, 352

Naumann, Werner 63, 71, 248, 250, 258, 259, 276, 333
Neipp, Hans 177, 190, 191, 192, 194, 195, 199, 205, 207, 218, 276, 277, 278, 280
Neipp, Berta 11, 205
Niemann, Ernst 109–10, 115, 123–28

Ohlendorf, Otto 62, 71
Offenheimer, Philipp 137, 215, 216
Ollenhauer, Erich 298
Ostertag, Benno (lawyer) 109, 111, 122–24, 126, 128

Pachneck (Gauleiter Kärnten) 261
Pfannenschwarz, Karl 97, 98
Pflaumer, Karl 250
Pick, Edgar 21, 78, 79, 80, 94
Piepenstock, Ernst Willi 292
Pleiger, Paul 4, 5, 73, 326, 329
Pohl, Oswald 62, 71
Porsche, Ferdinand 206
Praetorius, Emil 151
Prützmann, Hans-Adolf 57, 60–61, 65–66, 69, 70, 72, 92, 99, 136, 137, 217

Ranft, Horst 143
Rasche, Karl 62
Rath, Ernst v. 247
Raubal, Angela 162
Reihle, Walter 93, 103–107, 109–10, 113–14, 122–23, 125, 224
Renner, Viktor 234
Reusch, Paul 310

Richter, Albrecht 210, 211, 220, 229, 242, 246, 248, 256
Ribbentrop, Joachim v. 250
Rieker, Roland 250
Röchling, Hermann 247
Rösener, Erwin 71
Rohrbach, Rudolf 83, 89, 90, 91, 92, 98, 103–104, 121–22, 133, 204, 235, 253, 328
Rosemeyer, Bernd 164, 207
Roth, Albert 110
Ruck, Michael 47, 99, 183
Ruppert, Heinrich W. 315

Schäfer, Hermann 71, 260, 284
Schacht, Hjalmar 151, 334
Scharr, Walther 74, 75, 84
Schaumburg-Lippe, Friedrich Christian Prinz v. 258, 259
Scheel, Walter 258
Scherping, Ullrich 274
Schickedanz, Gustav 6, 102, 113–14, 116–20, 126–30, 213, 223, 310, 332, 335
Schieber, Walter 71
Schirach, Baldur v. 7, 261, 262, 263, 264, 265, 268, 270, 286, 296, 302, 304, 310
Schirach, Elke v. 264, 265
Schirach, Robert v. 264, 265, 268, 270, 286, 289, 296, 304
Schlageter, Paul 196
Schleicher, Kurt v. 47
Schleyer, Hans-Martin 293
Schlüter, Wilhelm 177, 178, 179, 195, 188, 189
Schmid, Jonathan 69
Schneider, Josef 242, 244, 251
Scholtz-Klink, Gertrud 219
Schröder, Freiherr Kurt v. 62, 81, 86, 346
Schülein, Wilhelm 119
Six, Franz Alfred 247, 258, 259
Soell, Hartmut 240
Speer, Albert 5, 24, 62, 132, 142, 176, 328
Sponer, Otto 259, 260, 267, 271
Springorum, Friedrich 250
Stäbler, Otto 78, 79, 82, 94, 98, 110–13, 116–17, 123–26, 129, 211, 213, 214, 216, 219, 222, 223, 224, 228, 229, 231, 232, 234, 242, 245, 252, 330, 331, 336
Stackelberg, Herbert v. 274, 300

Stein, Walter 167, 173, 261
Stinnes, Hugo 138, 143, 258
Stortz, Wilhelm 90, 91, 92, 93, 99
Stauß, Emil Georg v. 81, 85
Straßer, Else 39, 53
Straßer, Georg 5, 25, 37, 38, 39, 40, 41, 47, 48, 49, 50, 52, 53, 54, 56, 59, 69, 70, 75, 87, 151, 154, 207, 208, 217, 218, 219, 250, 297, 333, 334
Streicher, Julius 70, 100, 113, 117–18, 120, 126, 129–30, 213
Stresemann, Gustav 24, 27
Strobl, Otto 120, 130

Thadden, Adolf 250, 259
Thyssen, August 310
Thyssen, Fritz 247
Todt, Fritz 92, 99, 142, 328
Tondock, Martin 85, 93, 94, 95, 96, 100
Traber, Anton 226
Trappe, Margarete 274
Trefz, Karl 77, 79, 80, 85, 97
Trippel, Hans 230, 231, 232, 233, 234, 235, 237, 241, 242, 243, 245, 254, 261, 265

Vajna, Gábor 180
Vierhub, Erich 301
Vowinkel, Paul 233, 243, 244, 252

Wagener, Otto 45, 50
Wagner, Richard 151, 173
Wagner, Robert 233
Wagner, Siegfried 303
Waldmüller, Karl 121
Walter, Fritz 280, 300, 301
Walz, Hans 62, 71, 90–91, 98–99, 101
Wehler, Hans-Ulrich 312
Weise, SS-Obersturmbannführer 188
Wicke, Heinrich 197, 239, 260
Wieshofer, Fritz 261, 262, 263, 264, 265, 268, 270, 287, 289, 290, 291
Wittwer, Konrad 89, 99
Wölfle, Lothar 313, 315
Wolff, Karl 64, 93–94, 96, 97, 113, 114, 133, 134, 219
Wolff, Otto 332
Wüst, Walther 62

Zoglmann, Siegfried 250, 262, 299, 333

www.ingramcontent.com/pod-product-compliance
Lightning Source LLC
Chambersburg PA
CBHW072142100526
44589CB00015B/2051